GERMAN-BALKAN
ENTANGLED HISTORIES
—— *IN THE* ——
TWENTIETH CENTURY

RUSSIAN AND EAST EUROPEAN STUDIES

JONATHAN HARRIS, EDITOR

GERMAN-BALKAN
ENTANGLED HISTORIES
— *IN THE* —
TWENTIETH CENTURY

EDITED BY
MIRNA ZAKIĆ
& **CHRISTOPHER A. MOLNAR**

UNIVERSITY OF PITTSBURGH PRESS

Published by the University of Pittsburgh Press, Pittsburgh, Pa., 15260
Copyright © 2020, University of Pittsburgh Press
All rights reserved

Printed on acid-free paper

ISBN 13: 978-0-8229-6675-3
ISBN 10: 0-8229-6675-1

The Library of Congress has Cataloged the hardcover edition as follows:

Names: 1 Molnar, Christopher A., editor, aut | 1 Zakić, Mirna, 1982- editor, aut
Title: German-Balkan entangled histories in the twentieth century / edited by Christopher Molnar and Mirna Zakić

Description: 1 Pittsburgh : University of Pittsburgh Press, [2 | Series: 0 Russian and East European stu | Includes bibliographical references and in
Identifiers: LCCN 2020027882 | ISBN 9780822946458 (cloth) | ISBN 9780822987918 (ebook)
Subjects:
Classification: LCC DR38.3.G3 G467 2020 | DDC 327.49704309/041--dc23
LC record available at https://lccn.loc.gov/2020027882

Jacket image: Soldier in front of a sign about the destruction of Kaldanos as a "retaliation measure,"1943. Translation: *In retaliation to the brutal murder of paratroopers and combat engineers in an ambush by armed men and women, Kandanos was destroyed.* Bundesarchiv, Bild 101I-779-0003-22 / Segers (Seegers). Licensed by CC-BY-SA
Jacket design: Melissa Dias-Mandoly

CONTENTS

Acknowledgments   vii

INTRODUCTION. German-Balkan Entangled Histories in the Twentieth Century   3
CHRISTOPHER A. MOLNAR AND MIRNA ZAKIĆ

PART I. WAR AND EMPIRE IN THE BALKANS

1. "A Colony of the Central Powers": War, Raw Materials, and the Subjection of Romania   29
DAVID HAMLIN

2. A New Light on Yugoslav-German Trade Relations and Economic Anti-Semitism: The Ethnic German Poultry Product Cooperative in the Vojvodina during the 1930s   45
BERND ROBIONEK

3. Racializing the Balkans: The Population of Southeastern Europe in the Mind of German and Austrian Racial Anthropologists, 1914–1945   61
CHRISTIAN PROMITZER

4. "My Life for Prince Eugene": History and Nazi Ideology in Banat German Propaganda in World War II   79
MIRNA ZAKIĆ

5. Nazi Germany and the Holocaust in the Independent State of Croatia, 1941–1945   95
MARK BIONDICH

6. German Collective Guilt in the Narratives of Southeastern European Holocaust Survivors   114
KATEŘINA KRÁLOVÁ AND JIŘÍ KOCIÁN

PART II. AFTERSHOCKS AND MEMORIES OF WAR

7. Multiply Entangled: The Gottschee Germans between Slovenia, Austria, Germany, and North America   137
JANNIS PANAGIOTIDIS

8. We Had to Leave Our Really Good Dog: American Gottscheers and the Memories of World War II in Slovenia   158
GREGOR KRANJC

9. From Model to Warning: Narratives of Resettlement "Home to the Reich" after World War II   180
GAËLLE FISHER

10. Commemorating the Lost *Heimat*: Germans as *Kulturträger* on the Monuments of the Danube Swabians   202
JEFFREY LUPPES

11. Croatian Émigrés, Political Violence, and Coming to Terms with the Past in 1960s West Germany   216
CHRISTOPHER A. MOLNAR

12. Photographic (Re)memory: The Holocaust and Post–World War II Memory in Yugoslavia   231
AMILA BECIRBEGOVIC

13. The Politics of Screen Memory in Nicol Ljubić's *Stillness of the Sea*   250
ANNA E. ZIMMER

Notes   267
Contributors   357
Index   361

ACKNOWLEDGMENTS

The editors would like to thank the entire team at the University of Pittsburgh Press, especially Director Peter Kracht and series editor Jonathan Harris for their interest in the book. This book could not have happened without their encouragement, hard work, and attention to detail. We thank Emily Jerman Schuster for expertly copyediting the text, as well as the two anonymous peer reviewers for their insightful comments and suggestions. This book began with a panel we created for the 2012 Association for the Study of Nationalities Convention in New York titled "Entangled Histories: German-Yugoslav Relations Before, During, and After World War II." Little did we suspect then that the panel would blossom into a multiyear project resulting in this volume. Last but not least, many thanks to all the contributors for agreeing to add their knowledge, wit, and research to this volume, and for their patience and good cheer during the editing and publication process.

GERMAN-BALKAN ENTANGLED HISTORIES
IN THE
TWENTIETH CENTURY

INTRODUCTION

GERMAN-BALKAN ENTANGLED HISTORIES IN THE TWENTIETH CENTURY

CHRISTOPHER A. MOLNAR AND MIRNA ZAKIĆ

The German chancellor Otto von Bismarck famously declared in a speech to the Reichstag in late 1876 that "the entire Orient is not worth the bones of a single Pomeranian grenadier."[1] In July 1875, a crisis had erupted in the Balkans when Christian peasants in Bosnia and Herzegovina rebelled against Muslim landowners and local Ottoman officials. By early 1876, the uprising had spread through much of the Balkans, where passions were inflamed by nationalist sentiments and the brutal suppression of rebels by Ottoman forces. In July 1876, Serbia and Montenegro declared war on the Ottoman Empire. As the crisis escalated, it quickly became apparent that the conflict had the potential to draw in Europe's great powers, leading to a much larger and more dangerous conflagration.[2] It was against this backdrop that Bismarck made his comment about the Orient's supposed worth, which he intended to be a clear signal that he did not view the Balkans, and the Ottoman Empire more generally, as being vital to German interests.[3] Indeed, as the Ottoman Empire grew weak over the course of the nineteenth century, Britain, France, Russia, and Austria-Hungary all developed plans to manage the decline of this empire in a manner most advantageous to themselves. During that century, Prussia, later Germany, was the only great power without a major interest in the Balkans, though this would change shortly.[4]

In 1877, the conflict in the Balkans expanded from a Bosnian peasant uprising into a major war between Russia and the Ottoman Empire. After the conclusion of the Russo-Turkish War in 1878, Germany's seeming indifference toward the region led, paradoxically, to Bismarck playing a key role in the congress that would redraw the borders of the Balkans. It was Germany's relative lack of interest in the Balkans that allowed Bismarck to present himself as an "honest broker" who could help resolve great power disputes in the region at the Congress of Berlin in 1878.[5]

While Bismarck's lack of interest in the Balkans—similar to his early opposition to the establishment of German colonies in Africa—cannot be denied, his views represent only part of the story of German relations with the Balkans in the late nineteenth century. Other German thinkers and politicians cast a decidedly more covetous glance toward the southeast and projected onto it some of the colonialist fantasies with which they regarded Poland as well as Africa. Around the same time that Bismarck was disavowing German ambitions in southeastern Europe, others were pushing for Germany to deepen its ties in the region through both war and trade. Paul Lagarde, a radical Pan-German nationalist, argued that Bismarck's unification of Germany was incomplete, and that all Germans in central Europe should be unified in a conservative, Prussian-dominated "Mitteleuropa" (Central Europe). As part of this vision, he called for Germany to wage a war to push Russia out of the Balkans, which would then become the focus of German colonization efforts in this new eastern empire, which Lagarde called "Germania."[6]

In the early 1880s, the journalist and German nationalist Paul Dehn developed a less martial plan for Germany to gain power in southeastern Europe. He proposed that Germany invest heavily in the construction of railroads in the Balkans, which he imagined would further the construction of a German-led Mitteleuropa. He envisioned the Balkans as a key supplier of raw materials for Mitteleuropa, enthusing over Romania, Serbia, and Bulgaria's "still increasable grain cultivation in the plains and their strong livestock production in the mountains," as well as Bosnia's timber and Thessaly, Macedonia, and Thrace's "abundance of fruit, wine, and commercial crops such as madder, cotton, silk, olives, tobacco, rice, etc."[7] These plans to expand German economic might and influence in the Balkans picked up steam with Kaiser Wilhelm II's enthusiastic support of the Berlin–Baghdad railway at the turn of the century.[8]

Bismarck's contention that Germany had no interest in the Balkans thus already had been challenged during his two decades as chancellor of Germany (1871–1890). But it was not until the twentieth century that Germany's history became much more deeply entangled with the Balkans. During the first half of the twentieth century, Germany greatly expanded its economic influence in the region, established alliances with states in southeastern Europe, and carried out military campaigns in the region during both world wars. During the Third Reich, in particular, what had previously been only a vision of German dominance in the region came to fruition in nightmarish fashion. The Third Reich's policies in the Balkans led to widespread destruction and terrible suffering. World War II wiped out much of the prewar social and political elite in the Balkans; left behind destroyed landscapes, economies, and physical infrastructures; and brought death on a massive scale.[9] Hundreds of thousands of soldiers from southeastern Europe died in the war, but civilians—among them Jews, Roma, Serbs, Greeks, and, ultimately, the ethnic Germans who had long resided in southeastern Europe—paid a much higher toll.[10] The scale of the death and destruction, for Germany and the Balkans, meant that the war would not soon be forgotten and that "mastering" this past would prove to be a difficult and ongoing affair.

The emergence of the Cold War in the late 1940s led to a significant reduction in German-Balkan interactions, as all of the states of southeastern Europe, with the exception of Greece and Yugoslavia,[11] became part of the Soviet-dominated Eastern Bloc and therefore had limited relations with the new West German state.[12] Throughout the postwar era, however, Germans continued to negotiate the meaning of the Third Reich's invasion of the Balkans. This was particularly the case for the ethnic Germans who were uprooted—sometimes voluntarily, sometimes forcibly—from their homelands in southeastern Europe during the war and its immediate aftermath. As the twentieth century came to a close, the bloody dissolution of Yugoslavia led Germany once again to engage much more directly with the Balkans, through both the acceptance of Bosnian war refugees and participation in the NATO bombing campaign against Serbia during the Kosovo War.

GERMANY, "THE EAST," AND SOUTHEASTERN EUROPE

This book brings together scholars from North America and Europe to explore the history, aftershocks, and memory of Germany's fateful push for power in the Balkans during the era of the two world wars. Each chapter focuses on one or more of four interrelated themes: war, empire, (forced) migration, and memory. This volume makes a significant contribution to the historiography of German-Balkan history by bringing together the era of the world wars, for which there is already an extensive literature, and the long postwar period, which is a less well-developed field of inquiry. The first section of the book, "War and Empire in the Balkans," explores Germany's quest for empire in southeastern Europe during the first half of the century, a goal that was pursued by economic and military means. The book's second section, "Aftershocks and Memories of War," focuses on entangled German-Balkan histories that were shaped by, or a direct legacy of, Germany's destructive push for power in southeastern Europe during World War II. Finally, this book seeks to highlight the exciting new research being done on German-Balkan history and to encourage scholars to more fully integrate southeastern Europe into histories of Germany and the east.

Geographically, this volume features eight chapters that focus on German entanglements with different regions of Yugoslavia, two chapters on

Romania, and three chapters that deal with multiple Balkan states or their peoples. The emphasis on Yugoslavia is in part a function of the editors' research expertise, but it also reflects the historical record, for Germany and the Yugoslav lands' histories have been deeply entangled throughout the entire twentieth century. While most states in southeastern Europe had fewer encounters with Germany and Germans during the Cold War, this was distinctly not the case for Yugoslavia, where one can point to the long legacy of the wartime and postwar expulsion of ethnic Germans, generally close economic relations—including labor migration from Yugoslavia to West Germany and West German mass tourism to Yugoslavia—and, of course, when the Cold War ended, German involvement in the Yugoslav Wars of the 1990s. While most contributors are historians, three of the authors (Becirbegovic, Luppes, and Zimmer) come from the field of German studies. This interdisciplinarity enables the volume to highlight how cultural production has been an important means of working through the troubled German-Balkan past. Moreover, it allows for the inclusion of material on German-Balkan entanglements in the 1990s, an era that has for the most part yet to attract historians' attention.

German engagement with eastern Europe has deep roots in history, from the violence of the crusading Teutonic Knights in the Baltics beginning in the early thirteenth century, to the generally more peaceful movement of German settlers into the east beginning in the High Middle Ages.[13] According to Michael Burleigh, Prussia's annexation of part of Poland in the late eighteenth century and subsequent efforts to justify the annexation led, in the nineteenth century, to the widespread belief that "the Germans had an historical mission to bring order, civilization and government to Poland in particular and the East as a whole," which Germans imagined to be a barbaric and backward space.[14] Motivated in part by this notion of a German civilizing mission in the east, Germany launched two world wars during the first half of the twentieth century. Far from bringing "order" or "civilization" to the east, both of these wars had a profoundly destructive impact on the states and peoples of eastern Europe.

Germany's long history with the east, as well as the scale of destruction that Germany wrought in eastern Europe, particularly in World War II, has led to an outpouring of research on the broad theme of "Germany and the east."[15] These studies present strong continuities in German perceptions of the east, from the German Empire through the Third Reich. In general, the east appears as a backward and threatening land open to German expansion and conquest.[16] Many studies of Germany and the east, however, focus on Poland and Russia, largely neglecting southeastern Europe. The focus on Poland and Russia is easy to understand, particularly for the history of the twentieth century. Germany occupied large swathes of Poland and Russia (the Soviet Union after 1922) during the world wars and perpetrated the Holocaust primarily in those two countries, and when World War II ended, more Germans were expelled from Poland than from any other state in eastern Europe.

In recent years, historians have moved beyond this traditional focus on Poland and Russia by producing studies of Germany's fraught relations with places such as Ukraine, the Baltics, Czechoslovakia, and Hungary during the twentieth century.[17] Similarly, as this volume attests, scholars have shown increased interest in Germany's engagement with southeastern Europe.[18] These studies have deepened and broadened our understanding of Germany's engagement with eastern Europe in the twentieth century, particularly during the era of the two world wars. Nonetheless, it remains the case that German-Balkan histories are rarely incorporated into larger studies of "Germany and the east." This relative neglect of southeastern Europe is difficult to comprehend. The German military fought in and occupied territories in southeastern Europe during both world wars, carried out the Holocaust there, and caused a political and demographic reordering of the Balkans during World War II. At the conclusion of the war, ethnic Germans faced expulsions and terrible reprisals. The memory of World War II and the experience of the Cold War, moreover, shaped West German relations with all of eastern and southeastern Europe. This volume hopes to bring attention to common patterns but also divergences in Germany's entanglements with southeastern Europe, such as trade, the movement of peoples, and Germany's reengagement with the region during the violent dissolution of Yugoslavia in the 1990s.

Many of the broad studies on "Germany and the east" explore German perceptions of eastern Europe. These studies focus, for instance, on the "German myth of the east" or on the image of the east as both "enemy and dreamland."[19] Methodologically, these works follow a trail blazed by Larry Wolff, who, inspired by Edward Said's *Orientalism*, argues that during the Enlightenment, "it was Western Europe that invented Eastern Europe as its complementary other half." Western "civilization," Wolff contends, "discovered its complement, within the same continent, in shadowed lands of backwardness, even barbarism."[20] In a similar vein, Maria Todorova claims that in the past two centuries, the Western world developed a discourse on the Balkans that characterized its people as being primitive, barbaric, and, above all, violent.[21] Drawing on the works of travelers, journalists, scholars, diplomats, and politicians, these studies have immeasurably advanced our understanding of how Germans, and

Westerners more generally, have constructed "the east" as a backward and dangerous space, which allowed Germans and Westerners to understand themselves as more cultured or civilized in comparison.

Studies of German and Western perceptions of the east, however, often unwittingly have the effect of making the borders between "the west" and "the east" appear fixed and impermeable, even as they highlight the constructed nature of geographic and cultural knowledge. The present volume adopts a new approach. Rather than focusing primarily on German perceptions of eastern or southeastern Europe, it explores German-Balkan "entangled histories." Growing out of critiques of comparative history as well as the increasing prominence of global and transnational history since the 1990s, entangled history is an approach that emphasizes the interactions and interconnections between societies, states, regions, and peoples. Entangled histories, according to Eliga Gould, "are concerned with 'mutual influencing,' 'reciprocal or asymmetric perceptions,' and the intertwined 'processes of constituting one another.'"[22] This approach is particularly well-suited to German-Balkan history, for Germany and southeastern Europe had profoundly interconnected histories throughout the twentieth century, encompassing war, trade, migration, and memory. These entangled histories, moreover, played out at the level of the region, the state, the group, and the individual.

From the fourteenth century through World War I, the history of the Balkan peninsula was shaped by the Ottoman and Habsburg Empires. The Ottomans began their conquest of the Balkans in the fourteenth century, while the Austrian Habsburgs pushed into the western Balkans beginning in the seventeenth century, as Ottoman military power began to wane.[23] The weight of the Ottoman past, in particular, is so strong that, according to Todorova, "it would not be exaggerated to say that the Balkans are the Ottoman legacy."[24] But as the Ottoman and Habsburg Empires weakened and then were wiped off the map after defeat in World War I, Germany aggressively pushed into southeastern Europe both militarily and economically. This was a fundamentally new development. While many of the chapters that follow touch on aspects of the Ottoman and Habsburg legacies in southeastern Europe, the volume's focus is firmly on the history, aftershocks, and memory of Germany's quest for power and influence in the Balkans during the era of the two world wars.

The following section provides a skeletal history of German-Balkan entanglements, focusing on this volume's themes of war, empire, migration, and memory. It seeks to orient readers to what might be unfamiliar terrain.

A BRIEF HISTORY OF GERMAN-BALKAN ENTANGLEMENTS

With the first lines of his influential book *Mitteleuropa*, the German liberal nationalist Friedrich Naumann made a clear connection between war and empire:

> As I write this fighting is going on in the East and in the West. I write of set purpose in the midst of it all, for it is only in war time that our mood enables us to entertain broadly transforming thoughts of reconstruction. Once the war is over our everyday spirit will quickly take possession of us, and in the everyday spirit Mid-Europe [Mitteleuropa] can never be fashioned. Bismarck founded the German Empire during and not after the war of 1870, and our statesmen must lay the foundations of this new structure during this war, in the midst of bloodshed and the upheaval of the nations. Later it might, and it would, be too late.[25]

Naumann wrote these words in 1915, during World War I, when German forces had already pushed deep into western and eastern Europe. He was calling for the creation of a German-dominated economic, military, and political union—Mitteleuropa—which, ostensibly through democratic means, would extend joint German and Habsburg dominance deep into eastern and southeastern Europe.[26] One of the chief benefits of establishing Mitteleuropa, according to Naumann, was that Germany would finally gain access to the raw materials and resources it needed to satisfy its growing population and the demands of its ever-expanding industry, and to prepare for future wars.[27] This linking of war and empire would be a constant theme in German-Balkan relations during the era of the two world wars.

Germany's military role in the Balkans during World War I was relatively limited, at least when compared to its heavy military commitments in France and Russia throughout the war. After the Serbian military repulsed Austro-Hungarian offensives in 1914, Germany sent ten divisions to join Austro-Hungarian and Bulgarian forces against Serbia, which they soundly defeated in October 1915. The Habsburg military established a brutal occupation regime in Serbia, while German troops remained dug in with their allies at the Salonika front, where they were finally defeated by Entente forces in September 1918. In the summer of 1915, Bulgaria joined the Central powers, because they could promise more territorial gains (Vardar Macedonia and much of Thrace) than the Entente. Romania ended its neutrality and sided with the Entente in August 1916, hoping to acquire Transylvania and Bukovina, which the Entente had promised. German and Austro-Hungarian forces promptly attacked Romania, and occupied much of the country, including Bucharest, by December 1916. The Russian Revolutions in 1917 left Romania isolated and without hope for a breakthrough against the Central powers, and in May 1918, Romania sued for peace.[28]

The war marked a turning point in German strategic thinking about eastern and southeastern Europe. In Germany, the war caused dire shortages of basic consumer goods as well as the capital and resources required to prosecute the war. The combination of Great Britain's control of financial markets and its naval blockade of Germany contributed significantly to these shortages. That reality led many Germans to conclude that Germany, waging a war against global empires which dominated international markets, needed to expand its own sphere of influence—that it needed, in short, to establish its own economic bloc, or informal empire, in eastern Europe. It pursued this policy through occupation regimes in the Baltics and Poland and through the Treaty of Brest-Litovsk with Russia (March 1918), which called for a massive expansion of German power in the east. Less well known, however, is that Germany also sought to carry out similar policies in the Balkans. During its occupation of Romania and especially in the Treaty of Bucharest (May 1918), Germany granted itself extensive control over Romania's oil industry, grain, transportation networks, and more, and imagined that these concessions would continue as part of Germany's economic empire in the postwar era. Germany also squeezed its ally Bulgaria for its stores of meat, grain, and tobacco, while at the same time trying, and generally failing, to convince Bulgarian elites that their state would play a leading role in a German-dominated Mitteleuropa.[29]

During the war, Germany had tried to use both hard and soft power to create an economic empire in eastern Europe, but Germany and Austria-Hungary's defeat in World War I meant that Mitteleuropa was not to be, at least not yet. In the interwar period and especially in the early Nazi era, Germany once again used soft power to create what Stephen Gross calls an "informal economic empire" in southeastern Europe.[30] German business elites, in particular, viewed southeastern Europe as a promising market, as the region was close to Germany and possessed resources that Germany needed, German was used as a language of trade, German minorities in the region could facilitate trade, and the new, small states in the region could hardly resist Germany's economic power. By 1934, Germany and Austria together had become the dominant economic powers in the region, and Germany's position in the Balkans grew continuously through the German annexation of Austria in 1938. The Nazis used economic influence to pressure states in southeastern Europe to push Jews in the Balkans out of trade and industry, and by 1939 Germany's trade dominance translated into significant political leverage over the royal regimes in Romania, Bulgaria, and Yugoslavia. Ultimately,

Germany's construction of an informal empire in southeastern Europe provided Adolf Hitler with the resources he required to launch a war of annihilation in eastern Europe.[31]

Germany's involvement in the Balkans during World War II was both much more extensive and more destructive than had been the case during World War I. Facing immense German pressure, Romania and Bulgaria joined the Tripartite Pact in November 1940 and March 1941, respectively, and both states enjoyed significant autonomy throughout the war. Yugoslavia also joined the Axis, but when a military coup installed a pro-British government in March 1941, Hitler decided to launch an invasion of both Yugoslavia and Greece. With support from Italy, Hungary, and Bulgaria, Germany invaded Yugoslavia and Greece on April 6, 1941. Within weeks, both countries had been defeated and occupied. Greece was divided into Italian, German, and Bulgarian occupation zones, while Yugoslavia was effectively dismembered: Germany established a military occupation in Serbia; Germany and Italy created the Independent State of Croatia (Nezavisna Država Hrvatska, NDH), encompassing Croatia and Bosnia and Herzegovina and ruled by the Ustašas, a Croatian fascist party; and other parts of Yugoslavia were annexed or occupied by Germany, Italy, Bulgaria, and Hungary.[32] By the spring of 1941, every state in the Balkans was either occupied by or allied with the Axis powers.

World War II in the Balkans was characterized by radically redrawn borders, the uprooting and targeting of minority groups, and overlapping civil wars. The period defies all attempts at concise summation. Perhaps the most salient feature of Germany's push into southeastern Europe during World War II was that Germans authorized and committed extraordinary acts of violence against civilians. Germany also inflicted a great deal of suffering through its systematic exploitation of the region's economic resources. Greece was particularly hard hit, with about forty thousand civilians starving to death just in the first year of Germany's occupation.[33] Brutal occupation regimes in Greece and Yugoslavia soon gave rise to massive rural resistance movements, which the German military attempted to put down with exceptional and indiscriminate cruelty.[34] In Greece, for example, between Mussolini's fall in September 1943 and liberation in late 1944, German anti-guerrilla campaigns led to more than a thousand villages being looted, burned down, and destroyed, affecting more than a million Greeks, including twenty-five thousand who were killed.[35] German counter-insurgency operations in Yugoslavia were even more deadly.[36]

Much of the violence that Germany unleashed in southeastern Europe targeted ethnic and religious minorities. In territories under German occupation, such as Serbia and parts of Greece, Germans carried out the majority of the violence themselves. They murdered thousands of Serbian Roma, killed most Serbian Jews by mid-1942, and began deporting Jews from Salonika—where half of Greece's Jewish population resided—to Auschwitz in early 1943.[37] But they also found many willing helpers among their allies and collaborators in southeastern Europe. For example, the Third Reich granted ethnic German inhabitants of the Serbian Banat region effective administration of the territory, but required them to take part in the persecution of Banat Jews. The ethnic Germans carried out this task readily, in part because of the material benefits it brought them.[38]

Motivated by the desire both to please Germany and to ethnically cleanse their own territories, Romania, Bulgaria, and the NDH all perpetrated violence against ethnic and religious minorities. Germany's allies Romania and Bulgaria had long sought to consolidate cohesive national identities, in part defined against minority populations. Both states gained new territories in the early years of the war, and their goals of "nationalizing" these new territories meshed well with Nazi demands to murder Jews or deport them to the death camps in Poland. In April 1943, Bulgaria deported just over 11,000 Jews from Macedonia and Thrace—newly acquired territories—to Treblinka. Under the military dictatorship of Ion Antonescu, Romanian forces targeted Roma and Jews, and turned their newly acquired territories—Bukovina, Bessarabia, and Transnistria—into killing fields. In total, Antonescu's regime killed somewhere between 280,000 and 380,000 Romanian and Ukrainian Jews, sometimes with German assistance, but more often acting on its own. After the tide of the war in the east began to turn in late 1942, with Germany bogged down at the Battle of Stalingrad, both Bulgaria and Romania rejected German demands that they deport Jews from their core territories to death camps in the east. These policy changes saved the lives of hundreds of thousands of Jews, as about 375,000 Jews survived the war in Romania.[39]

The collaborationist Ustaša movement that ruled the NDH needed little prodding from Germany to begin murdering Roma and Jews within its territory, which it did primarily in its own camp system, but also through deportations to Nazi death camps.[40] The Ustašas also carried out an extensive campaign of execution, deportation, and forced conversion to Roman Catholicism against the sizeable Serbian Orthodox Christian minority (about 1.9 million out of a population of 6.3 million). Ante Pavelić, the leader of the NDH, no doubt felt emboldened to carry out this policy when Hitler, during their first meeting, told him that "if the Croatian state was to be really stable a nationally intolerant policy had to be pursued for fifty years, because only damage resulted from too much tolerance in these matters."⁴¹

Germany's domination of southeastern Europe during World War II resulted in the widespread destruction of physical spaces, the rending of the social fabric, and the persecution and murder of numerous individuals from majority and especially minority communities throughout the region. Germany's defeat prepared the way for communist parties, backed by the Soviet Union, to come to power in every country in southeastern Europe by 1947, with the exception of Greece, where the Western-backed government defeated Greek communists in a brutal civil war that ended in 1949.⁴² The rise of communist regimes throughout most of southeastern Europe, together with the emergence of the Cold War in the immediate postwar years, marked a rupture in the history of German-Balkan relations.

During the Cold War, the political influence and unrivalled market power that Germany had enjoyed in the Balkans during the 1930s and World War II vanished. In the realm of politics, the Soviet Union replaced Germany as the regional hegemon. Communist East Germany, moreover, did all it could, until the 1970s, to hinder West German efforts to establish closer relations with the communist states of eastern and southeastern Europe.⁴³ A combination of Eastern Bloc reserve toward West Germany and the Federal Republic's policy—the Hallstein Doctrine—of not establishing diplomatic relations with states that officially recognized Communist East Germany, resulted in West Germany having no diplomatic relations with the communist states of southeastern Europe until the late 1960s or the early 1970s.⁴⁴ West Germany emerged as southeastern Europe's leading trade partner in western Europe, but during the first two decades of the Cold War, the communist regimes in the region conducted the overwhelming majority of their trade with the Soviet Union and other states in eastern Europe (or with China, in the case of Albania).⁴⁵ To take one extreme example, during World War II, about 80 percent of Bulgaria's lucrative tobacco crop went to Germany, but during the Cold War, when Bulgaria was at times the largest cigarette exporter in the world, about 90 percent of Bulgaria's cigarette exports went to the Soviet Union.⁴⁶ As the only noncommunist state in southeastern Europe, Greece constituted a major exception to these political and economic trends. West Germany maintained close diplomatic relations with Greece during the Cold War and already by 1950 had become Greece's largest trade partner within Europe.⁴⁷

Despite the general narrowing of relations between West Germany and the Balkans during the Cold War, their histories remained entangled, if now in a more limited and substantially different manner than before. Until 1945, German-Balkan encounters were centered on trade and war. After 1945, German-Balkan entangled histories frequently played out at the intersection of migration and memory.

During World War II, the immediate postwar years, and the Cold War, numerous groups of people moved forcibly or voluntarily from southeastern Europe to the German lands. As part of the Third Reich's Heim ins Reich (Home to the Reich) program, Germany uprooted about 175,000 ethnic Germans from Romanian territories and settled them in newly conquered Polish territories in 1940–1941, where they were supposed to help "Germanize" Hitler's new eastern empire. A much smaller number of Germans were resettled from Slovenia, Serbia, and Croatia in 1941–1942.[48] Many of these resettlers fled to or were expelled into Germany proper at the end of the war and in the first few years after the end of the war. Another wave of migration began when ethnic Germans in southeastern Europe fled or were evacuated to Germany starting in the fall of 1943, after the tide of the war had turned in the east. This movement of ethnic Germans out of southeastern Europe continued after the communist takeover of most of the Balkans. The new Communist regime in Romania, which came to power in 1945, persecuted ethnic Germans and deported a significant number to the Soviet Union as forced laborers, yet allowed most ethnic Germans to remain in the country. In Yugoslavia, however, Tito's regime all but eliminated the remaining ethnic German population through a combination of executions, mass death in internment camps, and expulsions.[49]

Resettlers and expellees from southeastern Europe made up part of the much larger flight and expulsion of Germans from eastern Europe at the end of World War II. Collectively, resettlers and expellees from eastern Europe shaped the conservative politics and memory culture of the young Federal Republic. By loudly proclaiming themselves innocent victims of communist terror, they played a fundamental role in creating and sustaining the conservative, anti-communist consensus that characterized West German politics through at least the early 1960s. Their widely publicized tales of victimhood helped to create a memory culture in which West Germans came to view themselves as a nation of victims. The Third Reich's crimes and the memory of its victims found little place in this conservative and exculpatory memory culture, a reality that only began to change in the 1960s when a series of prominent trials—most famously the trial of Adolf Eichmann in Jerusalem in 1961—confronted Germans again with their complicity in wartime crimes.[50]

A new wave of migration from the Balkans to West Germany, this time voluntary rather than forced, and prompted by economic opportunity rather than war, began in the early 1960s. This reprised a long history, reaching back to the nineteenth century, of labor migrants from eastern Europe, especially Poland, heading to Germany to find work. Indeed, even the young Josip Broz Tito spent time as a migrant laborer in Germany in the years just prior to World War I.[51] During the Cold War, the Iron Curtain put an end to this traditional pattern of migration for most of eastern and southeastern Europe. But Greek and Yugoslav guest workers began to arrive in West Germany in large numbers in the 1960s, after their governments signed labor recruitment agreements with West Germany.[52] These labor migrants, together with Turks, Italians, and others, helped to propel Germany's postwar economic miracle and transformed the German cityscape.[53] Although not driven to Germany by war, the presence of these labor migrants at times led Germans to recall the Third Reich's occupation of Greece and Yugoslavia during World War II. Greek immigrant activists in Germany who opposed the military junta in their homeland (1967–1974) loudly proclaimed "fascist continuities" between the Third Reich and the military junta, and thereby gained allies among parts of the West German political left.[54] Moreover, from the late 1960s through the 1970s, the Social Democratic chancellor Willy Brandt, West German officials, and the media frequently claimed that positive relations between Germans and Yugoslav guest workers would help overcome not only the Cold War division of Europe, but also the dark shadow of war and occupation.[55]

A new phase in German-Balkan entangled histories began with the collapse of communism in eastern Europe and the end of the Cold War. These developments paved the way for German reunification in 1990 and the dissolution of Yugoslavia through a series of brutal civil wars beginning in 1991. During the 1990s, Germany repeatedly found itself drawn into the conflict in the Yugoslav lands, and memories of World War II loomed large over this new engagement with the Balkans.

In December 1991, Germany broke with the European Economic Community and unilaterally recognized Croatia and Slovenia as independent states. This led to exaggerated fears among some in the United Kingdom, France, and Serbia that the "over-mighty Hun," now reunified, was preparing to once again flex its muscles in Europe, just as it had done in earlier decades.[56] The conflict also brought hundreds of thousands of war refugees to Germany; between 1991 and 1996, Germany accepted more refugees from Bosnia and Herzegovina than the rest of the European Union states combined. But as soon as the Dayton Accords ended the conflict in Bosnia and Herzegovina in 1995, conservative politicians in Germany insisted that Bosnians needed to return home and rebuild their destroyed homeland, just as Germans had done in 1945. In 1996,

Germany became the first state in Europe to forcibly return Bosnians to their devastated and ethnically cleansed homeland.[57]

Finally, in 1999, German politicians committed Germany to its first active military engagement in its post-1945 history, joining the NATO aerial bombardment campaign against Serbia during the Kosovo War. This intervention provides a clear example of how developments in the Balkans could reshape German politics. Since the 1960s youth movement, the Federal Republic's left and center-left parties had frequently proclaimed "never again war" and "never again Auschwitz," thereby using the memory of the Nazi past to call for a pacifist foreign policy. But Foreign Minister Joschka Fischer, a member of the generally pacifist Green Party, signaled a significant shift in German foreign policy and in German memory of the Holocaust when he pushed for Germany's participation in the war in Kosovo by intoning "never again Auschwitz." Fischer and other German politicians repurposed that slogan to argue that in this case, Germany needed to go to war to halt a potential genocide.[58]

Germany and the Balkans remain closely intertwined in the twenty-first century. Indeed, between 2009 and 2016 Germany's relationship with southeastern Europe stood at the very center of European politics. Germany's status as the European Union's economic powerhouse and its insistence, following the economic crash of 2008, that southern European states adopt severe austerity measures, in return for financial assistance, led to a prolonged and politically explosive standoff between Germany and Greece that sent tremors through the rest of the European Union. Greek officials and journalists drew a connection between the debt crisis and the German occupation of Greece during World War II. As Greece's financial situation deteriorated, its government repeatedly demanded that Germany pay reparations for the destruction it wrought in Greece during World War II.[59]

Before that issue was resolved, a new crisis emerged. Between 2014 and 2016, more than a million refugees, especially from Syria, Iraq, Afghanistan, and Balkan states, fled over the so-called Balkan route to Germany, where most sought asylum. Hungary responded to the influx of refugees by erecting a fence along its southern border with Serbia and Croatia, while states in southeastern Europe took severe and in some cases illegal measures to close off the Balkan route. The European Union's attempt to stem the tide of refugees through a March 2016 agreement with Turkey—an agreement that contains disturbing echoes of the Greco-Turkish population exchange of 1923—has established the Balkans as an important frontier in Fortress Europe. Moreover, the flow of refugees through the Balkans in recent years also transformed Germany's domestic politics, most notably with the rise of the far-right, anti-immigrant party Alternative for Germany.[60]

ORGANIZATION AND CHAPTER SUMMARIES

This volume is organized thematically as well as chronologically. The first section, "War and Empire in the Balkans" covers the period of the two world wars. It focuses on Germany's intensive push for power and influence in southeastern Europe, and the ways in which this new, more imposing German presence was navigated by various Balkan states and ethnic groups before and during Nazi Germany's domination over Europe in the late 1930s and early 1940s. Bridging the historical caesuras of World War I, the rise of the Nazis, and the outbreak of World War II, growing German political and economic influence as well as violent intrusion proved to be a salient feature of Balkan states' development between 1914 and 1945. The chapters in this section explore the complex negotiations of group and national identity; the violent exclusion or even elimination of certain individuals and entire groups; and imperial, post-imperial, and Nazi German desires for economic and political hegemony as well as the responses to these overtures and pressures in Romania, Yugoslavia, Bulgaria, and Greece through 1945.

This section opens with David Hamlin's chapter on German-Romanian relations in World War I; the contribution challenges Fritz Fischer's interpretation of German intentions in this war as the pursuit of continent-wide domination—a goal which, according to Fischer, scarcely changed over several decades. Hamlin offers a dynamic view of evolving German attitudes toward and goals in the southeast, with a focus on the economic benefits Germany could derive from access to Romanian oil fields and agricultural surpluses, all of which culminated in the 1918 Treaty of Bucharest between the two countries. Hamlin complicates the monolithic Fischer model by showing how the Imperial German government, the German armed forces, and individual German businesspeople and trade magnates had different agendas with regard to Romania. Lacking an overseas empire and finding its international trade restricted during the war, the German government responded to the challenge posed by British and American successes in global trade and empire building by attempting to secure reliable markets for its goods and sources of raw materials within Europe. This led Germany to view Romanian oil, agriculture, waterways, railways, and state debt as either leverage or resources that Germany wished to secure for its exclusive benefit, essentially removing them from Romanian control. The Romanian government, in turn, responded to these pressures as best it could, but was only saved from becoming a dependency of Germany's imperial ambition by the latter's defeat in late 1918. Hamlin's conclusions urge the reader to reconsider German views of eastern and southeastern Europe in the light of multiple, sometimes competing agendas, as well as the extent to which states like Romania could and did negotiate with Germany for the assertion and preservation of their economic and political independence.

Bernd Robionek too explores the connection between the economic, the ethno-national, and the political by examining the fortunes of "Avis," an economic cooperative meant to facilitate bulk exports of eggs from ethnic German producers in Yugoslavia to Germany. By founding Avis in 1931, the ethnic German community in the Kingdom of Yugoslavia demonstrated its economic ambition as well as its desire for closer relations with the Weimar Republic. Ethnic German political leaders, who also tended to preside over ethnic German banks and economic cooperatives, used Avis as a way to pressure ethnic German poultry farmers into thinking of their profit margin in terms of not just individual economic benefit, but as a means of consolidating the ethnic community and its ties to Germany. After 1933, while the Third Reich used this preexisting economic connection as a means to nazify the Yugoslav ethnic Germans, not all ethnic Germans proved eager to embrace National Socialism. Moreover, ethnic German leaders and rank and file alike had to walk a tightrope between the desires of the Nazis and those of their home state of Yugoslavia. Even the seemingly simple matter of exporting eggs was complicated by changing German norms for import quality, which Yugoslav suppliers could not always meet. Ethnic German producers could not satisfy import quotas on their own, forcing Avis to purchase eggs from Serbian and Jewish producers, thus exposing the sham of ethno-economic self-sufficiency. No matter how much the ethnic Germans may have wanted to symbolically separate themselves from their Balkan surroundings and claim a special relationship with the Third Reich, the complex realities of southeastern Europe kept intruding.

Further developing the theme of continuities and discontinuities between German perceptions and attitudes toward the Balkans both before and during the Nazi period, Christian Promitzer looks at anthropology in the German-speaking world and how it morphed into Nazi racial science (*Rassenkunde*). Starting with anthropological research conducted among Serbian prisoners of war in World War I and continuing through research trips to the southeast in the 1930s, and then the application of this research to SS policy in the east and southeast, this chapter demonstrates the lengths to which science with a racial cast could go in order to sort complex human realities into tiny boxes with simple racial labels. Entire ethnic groups were depicted as objectively superior and to be emulated, or as inferior, pernicious, and to be violently disparaged and destroyed. Promitzer introduces a cast of scholars and researchers, in most of whom professional ambition meshed neatly with ideological prejudices that the Nazis used and exacerbated to their own ends. Promitzer also reminds us that the scientific research the Nazis used to justify their murderous policies was produced by a tightly knit scholarly community, members of which attended the same schools; worked in a handful of institutes, museums, and universities; and published in the same journals. These researchers continued to reinvent themselves, first as scholars in service to the Third Reich, and then as esteemed scholars in the postwar period, when they continued to pass on to their students fundamental assumptions about humanity that the Nazis would have recognized, long after the Nazis themselves were gone.

The intertwining of ideology, scholarship, and stereotype also features in Mirna Zakić's chapter on the manipulation of historical memory among the ethnic Germans of the Serbian (western) Banat. By focusing on the figure of Prince Eugene of Savoy, the Habsburg general and statesman who spearheaded the settlement of German-speakers in the Banat and Bačka regions in the early eighteenth century, Zakić shows how Prince Eugene was (mis)remembered among those German-speakers' descendants in the 1930s and 1940s. Influenced by Nazi ideology but also their desire to assert themselves as both members of the German Volk—as defined by the Nazis—and as members of a unique German minority, the Banat Germans altered Prince Eugene's legacy from that of an imperial loyalist to that of a proto-Nazi, who built up the "German" Balkans in order to preserve Europe from the savage east and southeast. Eugene himself served as a precursor and equivalent to Adolf Hitler, as one of the two men who marked the high points of (ethnic) German historical development: greatness past and greatness reclaimed. This deliberate use of the past to suit the ideological needs of the present served dual, not always compatible needs among the Banat Germans: to assert themselves as equals to the Germans from the Third Reich and to preserve their own communal sense of self rooted in historical pride and exclusivity. Even in the postwar period, ethnic German expellees continued to replicate many of the same Nazified tropes about Prince Eugene, while his erstwhile enemies were depicted as the bogeymen that haunted the Nazi imagination: the Jews, the Slavs, and the Bolsheviks. Zakić points out how Nazi ideology was embraced by ethnic Germans and how it suborned history to a mostly coherent ideological worldview, thus demonstrating the endurance of the worldview the Nazis had engendered.

The last two chapters in this section examine the Holocaust in southeastern Europe as both the end result of Nazi policy and a complex process that unfolded differently over relatively small geographic distances. Mark Biondich analyzes the Holocaust in the Independent State of Croatia (NDH), the nominally sovereign state encompassing both Croatia and Bosnia, which seceded from the Kingdom of Yugoslavia in April 1941 and was propped up (and divided into occupation zones) by Nazi Germany and Fascist Italy. Biondich argues that the persecution of the Jews in Croatia stemmed from domestic policies of the Ustaša (Croatian fascist) government, rather than top-down dictates issued by Berlin. From January 1942, the Europe-wide Holocaust set in motion and executed by the Nazis dovetailed with the Holocaust already unfolding in Croatia. In the eight preceding months, Croatian anti-Jewish policy was spurred on by several overlapping factors. These included native, exclusionary anti-Semitism; the anti-Ustaša insurgency and the bloody cycle of retaliatory violence; and the Ustašas' guiding ideological principle: their desire to achieve and consolidate independent statehood in an ethnically homogeneous state. The brutality the Ustašas unleashed against the ethnic Serbs and the Jews in Croatia and Bosnia nevertheless affected the Jews the worst—no fewer than 75 percent of the Jews in the NDH perished, most of them murdered in their home state. While the Ustašas' eagerness to collaborate with the Nazis—a factor without which an independent Croatia would have been impossible—and the ripple effect of Nazi anti-Semitism influenced the course of events, Biondich argues that it was domestic, grassroots dynamics which drove the speed and scale of the anti-Jewish violence in the NDH. The Holocaust was thus another element in the overlapping cycles of violence wrought by foreign occupation and civil war in the Yugoslav lands.

Complementing Biondich's examination of anti-Jewish policy, Kateřina Králová and Jiří Kocián explore the varieties of anti-Semitic persecution in the Balkans with an emphasis on the victims' experiences told in their own words. Králová and Kocián work with testimonies filmed by the USC Shoah Foundation and present a rich panoply of Jewish memory in Romania, Yugoslavia, Greece, and Bulgaria. The pattern that emerges from the wealth of quoted testimony is the survivors' inability to fully master or overcome the trauma of loss and suffering, more than fifty years after the war. However, within that framework of lingering trauma, the survivors display starkly different attitudes toward the Germans as the ultimate cause of their suffering: those from areas that experienced German occupation (Yugoslavia, Greece) tended to see the Germans as bearing collective guilt or blame for the Holocaust, whereas those from collaborationist states that were not occupied (Romania, Bulgaria) saw the Germans as individuals with free will and individual responsibility for their actions. Whereas the Jewish survivors' own agency comes through as important to their self-perception, their attribution of agency to the Germans tallies with the survivors' perception of the Germans as a destructive and murderous collective, or as a group of people who could act in destructive and murderous ways. This chapter also engages with how survivor testimony is used and excerpted by scholars. Králová and Kocián explore local dynamics of persecution, the varied effects that German policy (and sometimes occupation) had on parts of the southeast, and the attitudes of local inhabitants toward the Germans and Nazism. Finally, the authors introduce issues of how individual and group memory develops over time, and the elisions and lacunae of traumatic memory.

The mass violence and displacement of entire ethnic groups during World War II continued into the postwar period, with the flight and expulsion of ethnic Germans from across the east and southeast. These forced population movements had an unexpected epilogue in the voluntary labor migration from the Balkans to West Germany and North America. Ethnic German, Slovene, and Croatian individual and group identities in the postwar period have hinged on remembered pain and grievances from the war years, but also unwillingness or inability to accept one's own share of responsibility for Nazi crimes. Perpetrators and collaborators reinvented themselves as victims of communist persecution, ensuring that while the Nazi past was history, it was not truly past. The violent breakup of Yugoslavia in the 1990s reinvigorated—but did not resolve—issues of suffering, loss, and identity, and the question of whose memories dominated public discourse and media representation of violence in the Balkans. The chapters in this volume's second section, "Aftershocks and Memories of War," explore the long shadow of the Third Reich in southeastern Europe through the lens of postwar migrations, expellee narratives and monuments, the pro-Nazi legacy of certain immigrant groups in postwar Germany, literature studies, and the study of visual culture and media representation of atrocity.

The first two chapters in this section address the historical fortunes of the same ethno-linguistic group: the German-speakers of the Gottschee (Kočevje) region in Slovenia. In his account of the Gottscheers' political fortunes and migrations in the twentieth century, Jannis Panagiotidis argues that the forced displacement of the Gottscheers after World War II followed earlier emigration patterns driven by poverty and lack of labor opportunities. Unlike many other German minorities after World War II, for whom absorption into the West German or Austrian polity was the best option, the Gottscheers had long-standing familial and business ties to their conationals in North America. These ties both impelled them to see migration in a more global context and provided them with opportunities to frame their arrival in the United States and Canada as a reunion rather than a displacement. Using his own family history as well as documentation on refugees, emigrants, and displaced persons, Panagiotidis shows how the Gottschee Germans navigated multiple political caesuras, including the dissolution of the Austro-Hungarian Empire, the destruction of the Kingdom of Yugoslavia, and the second Yugoslavia's sanguinary birth. The Gottscheers' ambiguous national identity lent itself to some renegotiation, as after the war they strove to prove themselves as candidates for American citizenship, yet they did not shed all of their original ethnic markers. This intertwining of individual identity, family, and ethnicity demonstrates the agency of individuals but also the limits of ethnic hybridity in the turbulent twentieth century.

The Gottscheers' fortunes in the United States are the focus of the next chapter, by Gregor Kranjc. Whereas Panagiotidis focuses on the transformations of Gottscheer identity across 1945, Kranjc examines the preservation of the Gottscheers' group sense of self and how the survivors of war and displacement have remembered and narrated their experiences. Kranjc problematizes the term collective memory by showing how individual memories were shaped and modified in conversation with each other, both in person and through Gotschee expellees' newsletters and commemorative events. Collective memory emerges from this analysis as the end result, rather than a starting point, of memory formation. Furthermore, Kranjc shows how Gottschee expellees formed an exculpatory narrative of their wartime experiences. They claimed that their wartime resettlement to Styria at Nazi behest was imposed upon them, thus absolving themselves of both agency and blame for the displacement of Styrian ethnic Slovenes, into whose homes and businesses the Gottscheers moved. They glossed over Slovene experiences as well as their own use of forced labor, provided by the Nazis, focusing instead on their supposed hardship in their new homes. While postwar suffering, imprisonment, and expulsion loom especially large in the Gottscheers' memories, since the 1980s they also have displayed increased sensitivity to the Slovenes' own suffering during and after the war. This, in turn, allowed Nazi anti-communism to live on among the Gottscheers, under the guise of opposition to Yugoslav postwar communism. Ultimately, the convoluted nature of memory and its evolution over time reveal the indivisibility of the Gottscheers' trauma from their postwar group identity, as well as their inability to truly face up to their place in the Nazi legacy.

Gaëlle Fisher continues the theme of ethnic German identity and memory in her chapter on the ethnic Germans resettled in 1940 from the Bukovina as a part of the Nazi project "Heim ins Reich." Fisher addresses

Nazi perceptions of the resettlers as neither German enough nor Nazified enough to fully count as members of the Volk; the resettlers' disappointment at their treatment by Nazi officials; and the broader implications of Nazi plans to use the resettlers as the human raw material for the colonization of the occupied east, with all the murderous violence against Slavs and Jews this entailed. The Bukovina Germans proved receptive to Nazism as both an ideology and a system of rule. While their home region had been split in two in 1940, one part occupied by the Soviets and the other remaining part of Romania, even the ethnic Germans from the Romanian part chose to be resettled by the Nazis. Upon arrival in Nazi camps for resettlers, the Bukovina Germans' social and ethnic diversity as well as the relatively late date of their resettlement resulted in their mistreatment by Nazi officials, which might have dispelled the appeal of National Socialism in the resettlers' eyes. Yet, as Fisher demonstrates, the experience of resettlement became the key element of the Bukovina Germans' postwar identity as a group within the greater German polity. Unable to defend National Socialism after its defeat, the Bukovina Germans shifted the terms of discussion to defend their resettlement as ultimately justified because it brought them "home" to Germany. Only since the end of the Cold War has this oversimplified memory become complicated by a greater receptivity to discussing the Nazi period in terms of the damage it did to others as well as its supposed benefits to the Bukovina Germans.

The challenges of fitting a complicated and often painful past into a narrative that allows a group to see itself as the suffering yet ultimately vindicated heroes—or at least the fortunate survivors—of historical upheaval are the focus of Jeffrey Luppes's chapter. Luppes studies the monuments erected by expellee organizations of the so-called Danube Swabians (ethnic Germans living along the Danube in southeastern Europe) in West Germany, as examples of the selectivity of ethnic German memory and its negotiation of why the ethnic Germany legacy should be preserved even as the expellees claimed their place within the postwar German nation. Through analyzing the images and inscriptions on a range of monuments, Luppes shows how the expellees perpetuated certain Nazi tropes in emphasizing their role as *Kulturträger* (bearers of culture), who allegedly had civilized the Balkans and made it a part of Europe as well as, implicitly, affirming its connections to the German heartland. Monuments also stressed the loss of their homeland through expulsions at the end of World War II. Danube Swabian expellees did not argue in favor of postwar border revision, nor did they build most of their monuments in the heyday of expellee political activism in West Germany in the 1950s. Rather, the Danube Swabians in the Federal Republic used monuments to affirm their connection to German culture and ethnicity, and to stress their role as builders of Germany even beyond its borders and, since the war, as members of the West German polity. They used the past to their own ends, in order to preserve and affirm their dual identity as both ethnic Germans and expellees, and as newly minted West Germans.

Christopher A. Molnar moves away from the ethnic German memory of Nazism and how it allowed ethnic Germans to create new homes and identities after 1945, to consider how West Germans' own sense of self evolved with relation to the Nazi past, the Cold War, and the Balkans and its peoples. Molnar uses as his starting point an incident that took place in 1962, when Croatian extremists living in West Germany, with ties to the remnants of Croatia's wartime Ustaša regime, attacked the Yugoslav Trade Mission in Bonn in the hope of using their subsequent trial as a platform from which to condemn communist Yugoslavia. They also hoped to drum up sympathy from the German public and government for the supposed suffering of the Croatian people and for their loss of independent statehood more than fifteen years earlier. Molnar shows how the overlapping legacies of the Nazis and the Ustašas continued after 1945, as Croatian émigrés in West Germany presented themselves as victims of communist oppression and initially were accepted as such by a German public unwilling to delve deeply into its own recent past. However, by the early 1960s a new narrative about the Nazi past began to emerge, one more willing to confront the reality of pervasive Nazi influence in Germany—and less likely to tolerate political violence or to let Germany's wartime allies perpetuate a narrative of uncomplicated victimhood. If the West Germans proved ready in the 1960s to confront their own violent legacies by also confronting Ustaša violence, the dominant narrative among the Croatian émigrés failed to keep up with the times. Like many ethnic German expellees, Croatian nationalists in West Germany continued to see their flight from communist Yugoslavia as itself a site of memory and a communal touchstone.

The last two chapters in this volume explore how the intersection of war, violence, and displacement is experienced, remembered, and represented in photojournalism and fiction. Amila Becirbegovic's survey of media representations of the violence and human-rights abuses during the civil war in Bosnia and Herzegovina in the 1990s uncovers how war photography and reporting were imbued with tropes inherited from depictions of Nazi atrocities. For example, photojournalists depicting the emaciated bodies of Bosnian men imprisoned by Serbs arranged their subjects visually in a way that echoed famous photographs of people in Nazi concentration camps. This triggered the viewer's memory of similar images and implicitly drew a parallel between past and present events, but also shaped the public perception of the war in Bosnia. Consciously or not, the visual parallels between the Holocaust and abuses in Bosnia imposed an interpretation of the latter events that owed as much, if not more, to the memory of World War II as it did to the ostensible subject of war reporting in the 1990s. With reference to the phenomenon she terms (re)memory, Becirbegovic argues that representation does not merely reflect perception—representation shapes how we see and understand the world. Texts and images serve as both mnemonic devices and as representations in their own right, which, in turn, become the raw material from which historical narratives are shaped. Becirbegovic's point about how the memory of one atrocity is overlaid onto another later horror serves as a cogent reminder that narrative and representation, while necessary in order to make sense of events, can obscure as much as illuminate. Even in the absence of malicious or exculpatory intent to conceal past or present crimes, memory operates simultaneously on multiple, interpenetrating levels.

Anna E. Zimmer rounds out the volume with her discussion of using historical events as the springboard for fictional narratives, specifically the 2010 novel *Stillness of the Sea* (*Meeresstille*) by the Croatian-German author Nicol Ljubić. The novel addresses how Germany's national identity and its position in Europe and the world have changed since 1945; how the transnationalism of contemporary Europe maps onto the continent's troubled legacies of war and violence; and how Nazi crimes, while seemingly relegated to the past, can seem both current and urgent when compared to the recurring violence in the former Yugoslavia since the early 1990s. Zimmer's analysis addresses the interconnectedness, not just of past and present, but of Germany and the Balkans, German nationalism since 1945 and the multiplicity of "Yugoslav" nationalisms. Through the story of a turbulent romance between a young Croatian-German and a recent Serbian immigrant, *Stillness of the Sea* raises troubling questions about to whom, exactly, responsibility for and memory of World War II and the Holocaust belong; whether German perceptions of Germany and of southeastern Europe can ever be fully compatible with Balkan perceptions of the same; and how shock at and interest in the violence in 1990s Yugoslavia may serve as a way of bypassing the lingering shadow of the Nazi past, by transposing the potential for violent acts from the Nazis' descendants onto the non-German Other. Zimmer argues that, in the novelist's bleak assessment, dialogue—with oneself as well as with another (an Other)—becomes stymied by different and incompatible national and individual identities, despite professed commitment to transnationalism, pluralism, and overcoming the past.

The continued entanglements of Germany and the Balkans reached an interesting and telling moment—a new chapter rather than a culmination or conclusion—in October 2019, when Peter Handke, the Austrian author whose support for the Slobodan Milošević regime and whitewashing of Serbian war crimes in Bosnia in the 1990s has courted enduring controversy, won the Nobel Prize for Literature. A few days later, the Bosnian-German author Saša Stanišić won the German Book Prize for his novel *Herkunft* (*Origin*), an autobiographical tale of family, memory, and history in 1990s Bosnia and among Bosnian refugees in Germany. Stanišić commented: "I had the good fortune to escape what Peter Handke fails to describe in his texts,"[61] thus neatly and acerbically encapsulating the long and complicated history of the perceptions, imaginings, and obfuscations present when German-speakers looked to the southeast and the peoples of the Balkans challenged and navigated that German and Austrian gaze.

I
WAR AND EMPIRE IN THE BALKANS

CHAPTER 1

"A COLONY OF THE CENTRAL POWERS"

War, Raw Materials, and the Subjection of Romania

DAVID HAMLIN

On May 7, 1918, German foreign minister Richard Kühlmann signed the Treaty of Bucharest. Kühlmann remembered it as a remarkable, joyful moment. Crowds thronged the streets as he and the Romanian prime minister Alexandru Marghiloman strolled afterward. The Romanians, he thought, were pleased to have escaped the full consequences of defeat.[1] Kühlmann was also pleased with the gains for Germany. The treaty provided for a sweeping expansion of German influence inside Romania. In particular, Germany was poised to gain considerable control over the Romanian oil industry, the rail and river transportation systems, the finances of the Romanian states, and temporarily over Romanian grain exports. Germany was to become the dominant economic force inside Romania, reorganizing its institutions and trade patterns to suit the needs of Germany.

Classic accounts of German war aims, such as that of Fritz Fischer,[2] argue that the expansive goals revealed in 1918 in the Treaties of Brest-Litovsk and Bucharest were the reflection of enduring German ambitions. For Fischerites, these treaties were not emergency responses to desperate food shortages at home, examples of a so-called "bread peace." Nor were they simply the response to the improved geopolitical position of the Reich as a result of the collapse of Russian power.[3] Rather, Fischerites argue, those treaties reflected a lengthy current of German thought that placed the expansion of German capital and exports with the assistance of German state power at the center of German state policy. Fischer saw these treaties as the fruit of the German decision to go to war; the terms were reflections of prewar ideas about the relationship between exports, capital, and state power.

The implicit assumption in Fischer's argument that the First World War could change everything about the world except the reasons for which it was fought seems open to challenge. A careful consideration of German ambitions for the Treaty of Bucharest demonstrates that

29

German policy evolved over time, and, moreover, that the German state's ambitions were not always aligned with those of German capital. German perceptions of Romania were always plural, and always sensitive to the transnational networks within which Germany and Romania were embedded. The German state perceived Romania differently than did German bankers and merchants, such that German diplomatic relations with Romania could fray even as German capital investment boomed.

These perceptions also changed over the course of the First World War. As Christopher A. Molnar and Mirna Zakić argue in the introduction to this volume, the First World War marked the beginning of an extended period in which German political, military, and economic interests became more closely interconnected and were advanced in a more frankly aggressive and semicolonial fashion. Several decades of intense German interest in dominating the Balkan peninsula began with the war, meaning that the ways in which the war changed German perceptions deserve closer attention. In the case of Romania, German politicians, bankers, and military men became deeply attached to the transformation of Romania into a vassal state as a result of the wider shifts in global economic power, market structure, and commercial policy. The ways in which the British, and later the Americans, were able to organize and exploit global resources and markets represented an enduring challenge to German power. The other powers' simultaneous ability to effectively eject Germany from those global markets represented a dangerous weapon in the hands of rivals. The expressed willingness of the British and others to continue an "economic war after the war" threatened the ability of the German state to stabilize not only Europe, but German society after even a victorious war.[4] In the context of the remarkable transformation of the global economic order created by the Anglo-Americans during the war, the German state began looking for politically reliable markets, especially sources of raw materials. Military victory and geography made Romania (and eastern Europe more generally) the logical object of those ambitions. The 1918 Treaty of Bucharest was, then, a product not of Germany's prewar ambitions or simply the logical consequence of military victory, but rather reflected the country's efforts to grapple with an emerging global order that deeply threatened Germany. Those efforts came at a steep cost for Romania as Germany transformed Romania into a sort of imperial dependency assigned the role of producing low-cost raw materials for German consumption.

BEFORE THE WAR

To make this argument, some attention must be paid to German policy toward Romania before the First World War. The political relationship between Romania and Germany was rooted in an alliance between Romania, Austria-Hungary, and Germany. The purpose of the alliance was to contain Russian influence and expansionism in the Balkans generally and toward the Turkish straits specifically. When proposing the alliance with Romania in 1883, for example, Bismarck observed to his ambassador to Austria-Hungary, Heinrich VII, Prince Reuss, that "there is no state in all of Europe other than Russia and France that is not now in favor of the maintenance of peace."[5] That is to say, Bismarck sought closer links with Romania as a part of his larger project of hemming in Russia. Similarly, Bismarck's successor, Leo von Caprivi, argued in 1891 that "the whole military-political situation in the Southeast changes as soon as Romania decides for Russia, to the utmost disadvantage of our ally [Austria-Hungary]."[6] For Romania's part, King Carol I would explain in 1888 that "relations with Russia ... are a difficult problem for our foreign policy. We do not wish to challenge Russia. Indeed, we want to do everything in our power to avoid a war. But in view of the danger which a powerful Russia poses to us, we need the backing of the Central powers."[7] The threat from Russia was felt particularly keenly in Romania because of Russia's links to neighboring Bulgaria. The Romanian architect of the alliance, Ion Brătianu, imagined Romania existing "between Russia and its Bulgarian provinces."[8]

German state relations with Romania developed as a response to Russian influence and were understood in politico-military terms. This set of assumptions continued during the tumultuous years of the Balkan Wars, when the relationship between Romania and the Central powers frayed. Austria-Hungary had sought to use a Bulgarian alliance as a useful tool to hem in Serbia and Serbian ambitions. The Romanians, however, saw Bulgaria as a rival and a threat, and so eventually aligned themselves in the Second Balkan War with Serbia against Bulgaria. The ensuing peace treaty, the 1913 Treaty of Bucharest, created a new Balkan territorial order on an anti-Bulgarian basis. Austria-Hungary opposed it; Romania supported it. As Ion Brătianu's son, Ion I. C. Brătianu, would explain to Russian foreign minister Sergei Sazonov, "The mistakes of Austro-Hungarian diplomacy have damaged the relationship between Romania and the Double Monarchy."[9]

The ways in which the alliance was discussed betray the broadly political and military nature of the relationship. Note, for example, how Kaiser Wilhelm II spoke of the role Romania might play during his "War Council" in December 1912. The kaiser was confident that if Romania and Bulgaria "sided with Austria, then we would be free to use all our might against France."[10] As Romania came to identify its interests with the 1913 Treaty of Bucharest, Austria-Hungary came to see Romania as part of its Balkan problems. From the German perspective, a hostile Romania created substantial new military difficulties for the Central powers. For several decades, the Austro-Hungarians and Germans had assumed that the Russians would have to deploy a force to the Prut River to guard against the Romanians, even if Romania did not formally enter a war between Russia and the Austro-Hungarian Empire. Now, Habsburg statesmen assumed that the Russians would not need to bother with an observation force for the Romanians. Instead, it might be the Habsburgs who had to leave a force in Transylvania, just in case. The Russians were increasingly in a position to concentrate their forces against Austria-Hungary, while the Habsburgs were forced to contemplate further dispersal of their army.[11]

Broadly speaking, then, German state interests in Romania revolved around protecting the security of their ally, Austria-Hungary. It was this interest that brought the Germans to first accept an alliance with Romania. In November 1912, during the messy days after the First Balkan War, Foreign Minister Alfred von Kiderlen-Wächter would repeat the same broad logic:

> By and large we are only secondarily implicated in the present crisis. We have, consequently held back as much as possible. . . . It has been often said [most notably by the kaiser directly to Kiderlen-Wächter—DH] that Germany does not have to fight for the Albanian or Adriatic interests of Austria or even for Durazzo. But that is not the question. The purpose of our alliance is to ensure that the great central European monarchy bordering us remains unquestioned in its Great Power status, so that we do not one day, as Prince Bismarck expressed it, find ourselves nose to nose with Russia with France at our back.[12]

Germany's interests in the Balkans were ultimately driven by Germany's interest in Austro-Hungarian security.

Although the political framework of German and Romanian relations frayed in the years immediately preceding the First World War, economic relations between the nations remained strong, and indeed became stronger. The Romanian state continued to access international capital markets through a consortium led by Disconto Gesellschaft, one of the largest German banks. Local affiliates of German and Austrian banks continued to play important and profitable roles in organizing Romanian grain sales and financing for local infrastructure. Deutsche Bank owned one of the largest oil companies in Romania; Disconto Gesellschaft owned several others. And German exports to Romania dwarfed those from other countries.[13]

It is tempting to argue that German foreign policy followed the interests of German capital; this was very much Fritz Fischer's argument.

Instead, we see in Romania during the run-up to the First World War a sort of parting of the ways. Although German diplomats struggled (unsuccessfully) to contain the damage to Germany's relations with Romania from the collapse of Romanian-Habsburg relations, German capitalists continued to expand investment in and trade with Romania. German engagement with Romania before the First World War was manifold, encompassing both an increasingly fraught diplomatic relationship and a deepening economic connection.

It is also crucial to keep in mind that Germany's relationship with Romania existed not in some narrow sort of bilateral relationship but rather as elements or nodes of complex networks. German investments in Romanian state bonds were predicated on the ability of Romanian grain to be sold at profit in western European markets, and German oil investments were based on the presumption of sales to French and British markets.[14] Similarly, German diplomatic relations with Romania can only be understood in the context of Austro-Russian competition in southeastern Europe and how Bulgarian, Serbian, and French policy influenced those dynamics. Romania was often able to use the multiple actors within those networks to its own advantage, whether courting various great powers in the crisis years before the war or securing investment from an international consortium of German, French, and Belgian banks led by Disconto Gesellschaft.

THE FIRST WORLD WAR

The First World War occasioned a far-reaching reorganization of global markets. The scale of the Allied war-effort—the ways in which the British and later the American states organized networks of supply that spanned the globe—was unprecedented. Adam Tooze and Ted Fertik refer to a "repurposing and reorganization" of the global economy. The British Empire "turned its far-flung commercial and financial networks into the world's first truly global military mobilization apparatus."[15] Indian jute, South African gold, Malayan tin, and American cotton were all organized into a supply system feeding the war effort against Germany. That commercial power, operating in the context of reasonably open markets, effectively aligned the economies of neutral states with the Western allies. The reach of Entente economic power was thereby expanded, and the choices available to neutral states were severely reduced. The very idea of neutrality was open to question in the context of the economic mobilization of the First World War.

The "repurposing" of the global economy to defeat Germany was worrisome enough for German statesmen. At the same time, however, the British and later the Americans were able to leverage not merely their naval power but their commercial and financial power to progressively exclude the Germans from those same global markets. The blockade by the Royal Navy was supplemented by preemptive purchasing, controls over bunker coal, the leverage created by the vast and irreplaceable British merchant marine, as well as a global commercial intelligence collection system.[16] The result, when coupled with Germany's own economic mobilization for the war effort and the effects of the significantly wetter and colder weather in the later years of the war on agricultural production, was endemic shortages in Germany and Central Europe. Shortages of raw materials impacted the German war effort in many ways. They limited the production of gunpowder, sharply limited heating and lighting, and left civilians starving, cold, and ill-dressed. As a direct consequence, political pressure mounted to seek an early end of the war.

Germany's place in the global economy, then, was very much a factor in the course of the war. It also threatened to be a substantial issue after the war. In June 1916, leaders of the Entente met in Paris to discuss economic questions. One outcome of the conference was a commitment to a variety of measures that would extend the wartime reorganization of the global economy into the postwar period. Raw materials and shipping would be organized to prioritize allied and neutral needs, while German exports would be denied most-favored-nation status and would thus be, effectively, discriminated against in the principal consumer markets of the world.[17]

Initially, many Germans tended to dismiss the threatened "economic war after the war." The peace treaty that ended the war would include provisions outlawing such discriminatory measures, they thought. The self-interest of the Entente and powerful neutrals, most argued, would create strong incentives to revive prewar markets.[18] By 1918, however, anxiety among leading German businessmen, academics, and politicians had grown. The ways in which the United States had taken up economic warfare, the moves of the British government to raise export taxes on colonial goods or to exclude German interests through laws like the Non-Ferrous Metal Industry Act of 1918, seemed to point to a high level of political commitment. British self-interest increasingly seemed to point to an effort to prevent Germany from reentering global markets.[19] A number of short semi-academic books (written by academics for a university-educated audience) appeared, for example, warning of the threat of continuing economic warfare.[20] A final report based on inquiries made by the Imperial Economics Office among German businessmen opened with the observation that the question of acquiring raw materials is one of the most crucial for the reconstruction of our economy. The solution is all the more difficult because we are reliant on supplies of essential materials from enemy countries or countries themselves dependent on our enemies. The enemy knows what a weapon it has against us. Their statesmen have repeatedly declared that they will make use of this weapon in the most brutal manner.... By cutting the importation of raw materials, the life's blood of our industry would be eliminated, the spine of the German national economy broken and its reconstruction made impossible.[21]

Similarly, at a July 1918 conference chaired by the state secretary of the Economics Office, Freiherr Hans Karl von Stein, a number of figures from Carl Duisberg (the head of Bayer Chemical) to Karl Helfferich (then the coordinator of economic terms of the peace agreements) warned that a return to prewar market society was highly unlikely. Helfferich feared that the West had reorganized the world economy to its own benefit and was unlikely to give up that advantage. Moreover, he added, Germany could be excluded from many markets by the action of private interests, such as trusts and corporations, operating outside of any state treaty and thus all but untouchable by any peace agreement. The efforts of Albert Ballin, director of the Hamburg-Amerika shipping company, to encourage a swift return to the prewar model of open markets was met with disbelief and ridicule.[22]

Thus, as German officials contemplated the postwar world in 1918, they were unconvinced that the prewar system of international markets would be revived. Rather, it seemed that the "repurposing" of global markets during the war would leave the German economy struggling to find necessary raw materials as well as export markets needed to generate the revenue required for the purchase of raw materials should these be available. Given that possibility, the idea of securing politically dependent markets was deeply attractive.

THE TREATY OF BUCHAREST

The 1918 Treaty of Bucharest needs to be seen against this background. Romania had entered the war in August 1916, only to see its armies forced into precipitous retreat and its Wallachian districts occupied from December 1916. In December 1917, when the new Bolshevik Russian government sought an end to the war, the Romanians were forced to seek terms themselves. The Romanian Army was simply incapable of continuing the war against Germany and Austria-Hungary without the assistance of the Russians. As a result, representatives of the Romanian government entered into negotiations with the Central powers.

While the Bulgarians and Hungarians had worried about territorial provisions,[23] German negotiators had focused on control of Romanian petroleum, finances, and control over transportation. Their purpose was to tie the Romanian economy tightly to that of Germany as a supplier of raw materials.

A central element of German ambitions in Romania was the oil industry. Petroleum had assumed an increasingly significant role over the course of the war. Most obviously, this was because U-boats relied on diesel fuel. Other notable uses included industrial lubrication, fuel for trucks, and illumination in the trenches, for railways, and in rural areas (particularly for farmers doing morning milking sessions in winter). Shortages of petroleum had sparked increasingly frantic discussions inside the German government, prompting civilian members of the government to begin openly challenging the priorities of the military, suggesting that more of the declining petroleum supplies should be assigned to civilians rather than to the navy. As the head of the War Food Office, Wilhelm von Waldow, put it in a July 1918 meeting about petroleum shortages, "The longer the war lasts, the more the military must adapt to the needs of the civilian population."[24]

Petroleum was becoming an essential issue for the German state, one that increasingly pitted domestic economic activity against the war effort. The long-term solution to this supply problem was widely seen to be securing control over Romanian oil. A number of plans were developed to transfer Romanian petroleum interests to Germany. In the summer of 1917, for example, the Military Administration of Romania created the legal apparatus to nationalize Western-owned oil companies and transfer them to the German oil companies operated by Deutsche Bank and Disconto Gesellschaft.[25]

The German oil companies had lobbied for their own visions of a future Romanian oil industry. Both Deutsche Bank and Disconto Gesellschaft submitted plans to transfer Western oil interests in Romania to German ownership. Deutsche Bank contemplated creating a company jointly owned by Deutsche Bank, the German Empire, and the Romanian state, but which would be operated by Deutsche Bank in order to ensure that the business was run in a properly commercial, profitable manner. Disconto preferred that the state take no ownership role at all. Similarly, the oil companies hoped that the peace treaty would include long-term leases for petroliferous lands owned by the Romanian state. Both banks looked toward a return to international markets at some point after the war, believing the ability to buy and sell petroleum globally was essential to the efficient operation of any oil production company given the peaks and valleys in production and movements in global prices.[26]

The German state, however, feared that the interests of private oil companies operating according to market incentives might not align with those of the state. As a result, not only the Western oil companies but also leases for Romanian state land were to be awarded to a soon-to-be-created oil company, the Central European Oil Company, which would be largely owned and completely dominated by the German state. As Paul von Koerner, ministerial director at the Foreign Office and a lead negotiator for the Treaty of Bucharest, argued, "The interests of the state and of the country as a whole . . . are difficult to reconcile with the interests of the banks and private corporations."[27]

The repeated efforts of the German state to sideline the private oil companies point to a larger uncertainty about the future of transnational markets. The very fact that the private oil companies might find it desirable to sell petroleum on global markets in the search for higher profits made them unreliable. After all, in the context of a postwar economic war, the Entente Powers might easily simply offer higher prices. It would be a version of the wartime preemptive purchases, and one that a peace agreement between Germany and her opponents would be hard-pressed to prevent. So, the Reich found itself differentiating between the interests of German companies and those of the German state, and saw state ownership as an essential tool in protecting German interests.

Anxiety that simple market incentives would not direct petroleum to where the German state thought it was most needed led German negotiators to insist on several additional conditions, which brought home the subordinate position Romania was to play in this postwar arrangement. First, to ensure that the most petroleum possible was exported, the Germans insisted on a petroleum sales monopoly in Romania, one which would be dominated by German capital interests, with a majority of voting rights. A central purpose of this monopoly would be to reduce Romanian consumption of petroleum, "particularly for heating and illumination purposes, which would indirectly generate an increase in export quantities."[28] In addition, the new Central European Oil Company would be exempt from Romanian law, Romanian labor regulations, and Romanian taxation. In effect, these stipulations drastically reduced Romanian state influence over one of its most important economic sectors, carving out a sphere within Romania in which the German state would have the decisive voice. In many respects, the terms resembled the terms of oil concessions that the European powers would extract from Middle Eastern states in the interwar period.[29] The terms also very much anticipated Nazi petroleum policy in Romania during the Second World War.[30]

Taken together, the terms of the 1918 Treaty of Bucharest with regard to petroleum ensured that the German state would have substantial influence over the Romanian oil industry, an influence that would empower Germany to continue delivering petroleum to Central Europe regardless of market conditions, the preferences of Romania, or the policies of the Western powers.

The financial provisions of the treaty had a similar thrust. To understand German financial policy toward Romania, we must briefly explore the problems that German war debts were expected to create. Two types of debt were at issue. The first and more immediately threatening was short-term debt issued by the neutrals in their own currencies to facilitate German purchases abroad during the war. This debt was structured such that payments began shortly after the war ended. To service these debts, Germany would require a substantial flow of foreign currency. At the same time, planners expected a surge in long-deferred imports of products ranging from coffee to fertilizer to copper. As a consequence, the German financial authorities expected an intensely painful payments crisis, as German demand for foreign currency to pay others far outstripped its own ability to secure foreign currency. The result would be continuing shortages of consumer goods and industrial raw materials into peacetime.[31] Needless to say, this suggested a postwar domestic political crisis of some sort. The German state had, then, unusually substantial incentives to seek opportunities to hoard ready currency.

The second type of debt was the war debt held by Germans in marks, amounting to around 51 billion marks in the summer of 1918.[32] This debt was less immediately dangerous, since it could be repaid in marks and ultimately Germany's central bank, the Reichsbank, could make the marks required available. The resulting inflation, however, would act as a (substantial) tax on savings held by the propertied classes in Germany. Such a policy choice carried with it substantial political risk. Without recourse to inflation, the German state would be expected to seek to generate additional revenues, for example, by substantial increases in taxation. Such increases would necessarily result in higher domestic prices, potentially undercutting the ability of the German economy to rapidly increase exports, which were of course needed to stave off a severe international payments crisis. This war debt too, then, implied a high risk of domestic political consequences after the war.

The initial objects of German financial policy were the 226 million marks held at the Reichsbank in accounts owned by the Romanian state from before the war as well as the many hundreds of million marks held in accounts at the Reichsbank from the sale of Romanian grain and oil during the occupation (this was variously estimated as 580 million, 800 million, and 1.1 billion marks). In the German debates about the fate of these sums, at a minimum, 806 million marks (226 million plus 580 million), we can see once again, the question of private versus state interests at play. German holders of Romanian state bonds sought to have the debt they held redeemed immediately, using money held in those Romanian state accounts. The German state (outside of the Reichsbank, which sided with its banking stockholders in internal deliberations), however, preferred to have that money transferred to the German government.[33] And as with the oil question, we see once again that the state privileged its own interests. The larger account generated by sales of Romanian products was awarded to the Central powers. The remaining accounts would be used as security for debt service payments to nationals of the Central powers.[34]

More interesting than the determination of the German state to use Romanian resources was the way that German officials began to speak about Romanian state indebtedness. Karl Helfferich, former economist and banker that he was, went through the available figures carefully. He outlined twelve separate charges the Central powers were proposing. They totaled 2.46 billion lei (1 leu = 0.8 mark), not counting the 800 million owed Germany and Austria-Hungary for debts incurred before August 26, 1916. Helfferich thought it prudent to strike a 200 million line item intended as compensation to Western oil companies for the assets seized under the terms of the Treaty of Bucharest, which was either an accounting trick or an assumption that Romania would enduringly break with Western markets. In any case, that left a total of 3.06 billion owed to the Central powers.

In addition to those sums owed the Central powers, the Romanians owed another 800 million lei for other debts contracted before August 1, 1914, and another 4.5 billion lei for loans contracted since the beginning of the war. These figures are striking testimony to the ruinous financial consequences of the war for all concerned, especially since Romania was a noncombatant for most of the war. Of that 5.3 billion lei, 3.3 billion were owed to the Entente and 2 billion to Romanians. There was also the 1.7 billion lei owed to the Romanian National Bank, and the expected demand for capital to resuscitate the railroads and claims by private German and Austro-Hungarian citizens, which Helfferich estimated to require 1.1 billion lei in new loans. By Helfferich's math, excluding the non-interest-bearing charges, the Romanian state would have annual interest charges of 440 million lei. If Romania declared a partial bankruptcy and repudiated its debt to the Entente and neutrals (something the Germans very much hoped would happen as it would both harm the Entente and tie Romania more firmly to Germany), Romania would expect to owe 7.75 billion lei with annual interest charges of 275 million lei.

Helfferich noted that "it would be expected that Romania would be in position to bear these burdens if it were permitted the unlimited exploitation of its principal national products, particularly petroleum. But that is impossible."[35] Romania would instead have to rely on taxes and domestic consumer monopolies to service its debt. Even that was problematic since the monopolies would likely have to be mortgaged to secure future loans. The Romanian state would then be under exceptional financial strain that would push it toward seeking ways to avoid financial impositions through bankruptcy. Helfferich therefore thought the Romanian accounts at the Reichsbank should serve as a security deposit (which obviously meant they could not be used to pay off the state or private citizens). He also suggested that a loan should be offered, if not by private banks then by the German state itself, conditioned on fulfillment of the other terms of the treaty. If Romania did not fulfill those terms, not only could there be no loan, but "to the contrary, in light of the German financial position we must unconditionally demand an indemnity of many billions."[36] In fact, the many separate charges already to be levied on the Romanians were an explicit effort to hide an indemnity. It was the indemnity that dare not speak its name. As the Bavarian representative in Berlin explained to the Bavarian minister-president Otto Ritter von Dandl, "The absence [of an indemnity] is only an illusion."[37]

The effect of such heavy indebtedness would be to force additional domestic taxation in Romania, and thus raise domestic prices, and consequently to depress domestic consumption. Meanwhile, the need to service external debt would encourage exports to earn foreign currency, particularly marks if Romania did indeed default on its debts to the Entente. The financial sections thus tended to reinforce the general interest in seeing Romania primarily as a provider of raw materials. There was little interest in Romania's potential as an export market. The trade arrangements mostly kept tariffs at the same level so that the Romanian state could generate the income needed to service its debt. The only major reference to exporting German material was in terms of the reconstruction of the rail system, a crucial element of Romania's export economy. The contrast with Germany's efforts to start exporting to Russia in order to generate foreign exchange is remarkable.[38] Instead, Romania would be disproportionately selling its products abroad and then using the income derived from exports to service debt held by the Central powers. As the Romanian minister of agriculture put it in the summer of 1918, "It will be indispensable for us to produce in the country the largest possible amount of things that we require domestically.... We must try to produce the utmost possible quantity and to export the utmost possible quantity."[39] Moreover, to the extent that Romanian debt was held in marks, it was in Romanian interest to export to Germany in particular to earn the marks necessary to service Romanian debt. If anything, the pressure to export grain in particular would be increased by the fact that much of the profit from petroleum sales to Germany would not be repatriated but rather circulate between the German state and its commercial allies in the Central European Oil Company. As a consequence, Romania was to provide Germany with a steady flow of raw materials. The proceeds from the sale of those raw materials would be recycled back to Germany either as retained earnings or as debt service payments, thereby strengthening a German mark that was expected to be under substantial pressure after the war as a result of the expected shortage of foreign exchange.

German ambitions for controlling Romanian petroleum and grain both turned on the ways in which those materials could be transported to Central Europe. The petroleum discussion in particular emphasized the need to bring petroleum directly to Germany without using the oceans dominated by the Royal Navy. The blockade led Germany to perceive a strategic necessity in reshaping and controlling the physical links between Romania and Germany.

A key to that vision was improving the water links between Germany and the Balkans. Water transport offered a much cheaper means of moving bulky items, such as wheat or oil. To that end, many Germans, and particularly the Bavarian state, committed themselves to a massive infrastructure project to link the Danube to the Rhine, Main, and Elbe Rivers through a network of high-capacity canals. They also hoped to deepen, straighten, and generally make the Danube more navigable for larger vessels. A coalition of south Germans and commercial interests had already pressured the Reich into co-funding preliminary studies, and the Foreign Office was pushing the Habsburgs hard to commit to expensive improvements to the Austrian sections of the Danube needed to permit much larger barges to navigate from Bavaria to the south. The army, too, was keenly interested in the possibility of increasing the carrying capacity of the Danube. The OHL (Oberste Heeresleitung, i.e., the army's high command), for example, had made the physical improvement of the waterways in Austria-Hungary and their connection to German canals a condition of accepting the Austro-Polish solution (the proposal to attach conquered Russian Poland to Galicia and place it under Habsburg sovereignty) in late 1917.[40]

The plans to improve the navigability of the Danube and to integrate it into a network of German waterways aimed to dramatically reduce transportation costs in ways that would reshape economic incentives. In effect, this was a vision of commercial arteries that were to restructure the economic geography of the Balkans, creating a more integrated economic unit for the benefit of Germany (a development Austria-Hungary sought to obstruct through inaction for fear of German competition). Waterways would begin to create a homogenized market space dominated by Germany.

Germans also hoped to profit by controlling what went on the waterways. Georg von Hertling, in his capacity as minister-president of Bavaria, contacted both Berlin and Bucharest on January 9, 1917, a month after the fall of Bucharest, about the necessity of leasing landing facilities to Bavarian Lloyd (a joint shipping venture between the Bavarian state and Deutsche Bank) "in the interests of the future development of the Danube commerce with Romania and the strengthening of the position of the Bavarian Lloyd vis-à-vis non-German shipping companies" (in what was certainly a reference to the Austrian and Hungarian shipping companies).[41] After all, "shipping companies are more or less power instruments in the economic policies of their countries."[42] This thought was reflected in the determination of the German negotiators to divide Romanian port facilities and Romanian shipping between the victors, and the prolonged struggle with Austria-Hungary over the proper disposition of those assets.[43]

A few months later, Hertling once again petitioned the Reich, this time emphasizing that proper economic integration would benefit from creating a "unified" system of interior waterways, focusing particularly on the Danube. The Danube should be subject to a single administrative system that would standardize weights, tolls, and docking systems, and that would open the river as a whole to all riparian states. Hertling's model was the Bern International Convention concerning the Carriage of Goods by Rail of 1890.[44] Western, non-riparian states would be excluded from the regulatory bodies (a break from the system created by the Treaty of Paris in 1856). Germany and Austria-Hungary were to have multiple votes by virtue of including riparian component parts of their states, specifically Bavaria and Hungary. It was further hoped that Germany could establish a river authority with the power to levy a centralized system of tolls, the receipts from which would be distributed to member states. Romania and Serbia would be forced in their respective peace agreements to join the reformed Danube Commission, which was charged with facilitating the regulation of commerce on the river across the various states.[45] The German ambition was to narrow the number of states that could have a claim to organize the Danube and then to establish an administrative system which would permit Germany and Austria-Hungary to shape the relevant domestic policies and economies of the Balkan states. A public corporation would serve as an attractive means of skirting the political difficulties surrounding the limits to be placed on Balkan states' sovereignty.

The other crucial transportation system was the railroad. Romania's rail system had been a collaborative effort between Romania and Germany and had served as the opening that brought German capital interests into Romania before the war. During the war, that rail system had been severely damaged, tenuously restored, and then operated at the edges of capacity. Nonetheless, the rail system was a crucial element of moving grain and petroleum about the country, as well as supplementing the Danube in moving materials in and out of Romania. The railroads were a crucial element in the economic organization of Romania.

German policy aimed to control this instrument. The Germans argued that given the substantial damage and the shortage of locomotives and wagons, it would be in everyone's interest, especially Romania's, if German officials were installed in prominent positions in the Romanian rail system and given decisive voices, particularly over pricing. The head of the army's rail branch (Chef des Feldeisenbahnwesens) thought it would be wiser to parallel German plans in Belgium, Poland, and Serbia, whereby the Romanian rail system, hitherto state-owned, would be turned into a private company, of which the German Reich would own two-thirds and the Romanian state one-third. The War Office, by contrast, foresaw a German loan of 400 million marks, and an undertaking to deliver four hundred locomotives and one thousand wagons, as well as other sundry equipment. In return, the Germans would name a commissioner, who would appoint the general director and have general oversight.[46]

Under Helfferich's direction, the demands on the Romanian railways were reduced. The demand for ownership was dropped. Instead, Germans would seek a negotiated tariff agreement, a long-term delivery agreement, and trust that influence would flow from the fact that Romanian locomotives and equipment would require German spare parts and replacements. To this would be added a German commissioner who would exercise an oversight function. Erich Ludendorff insisted that such a figure was a crucial shield again "Romanian chicanery."[47] In this way, German influence could be exerted inside the rail system as well as through its supply base.

Through control of both railways and waterways, German planners hoped to establish a transport network that would redirect Romanian economic activity away from Western markets and reorient it toward Central Europe. German influence would be wielded directly within Romanian institutions to shield German sources of supply from the influence of western European capital and Romanian political ambitions.

German policy toward Romania, as revealed in the Treaty of Bucharest, was not the realization of prewar policies and was not oriented toward the needs of private German capitalists, as Fritz Fischer claimed. Before the war, the relationship had existed in the context of multiple, overlapping networks. The relationship between the states had focused on security questions, and commercial relations had assumed profitable sales to western Europe. During the war, however, the German state took note of Allied economic policy, both their actual wartime interventions and their statements about postwar policy, and responded. As a result of the war, Germans sought to impose a radically simplified structure of relations. This entailed the reduction of Romania into the status of something like an imperial dependency. Romanian sovereignty would be relativized through a system of controls inside Romania, ranging from the commercial monopoly on petroleum sales to the commissioner inserted in the Romanian state railway to a revised Danube Commission. Meanwhile, Romania would be tied to the German domestic economy through the Central European Oil Company and state debt and perhaps expanding waterways, so that materials that might once have come from the United States or the British Empire would now come from Romania. The result was, as German foreign minister Richard Kühlmann put it, to make Romania "a colony of the Central powers."[48] This was a position that anticipated the vision of *Grossraumwirtschaft* sketched by German economic planners in the Third Reich. Romania escaped the slow expropriation the treaty entailed only through the defeat of Germany in November 1918.

CHAPTER 2

A NEW LIGHT ON YUGOSLAV-GERMAN TRADE RELATIONS AND ECONOMIC ANTI-SEMITISM

The Ethnic German Poultry Product Cooperative
in the Vojvodina during the 1930s

BERND ROBIONEK

When dealing with the economic history of southeastern Europe during the latter half of the 1930s, one can hardly avoid the topic of the German trade offensive.[1] Already in the late 1930s, a controversy arose over whether Nazi Germany was exploiting the agricultural produce– and raw material–supplying countries in the southeast, or if they were beneficiaries of the intensified trade with the Third Reich. After the Second World War, this controversy continued in scholarly circles.[2] Since the late nineteenth century, Berlin's guiding idea behind an economic penetration of the southeast followed German industrial business interests by establishing asymmetric trade relations and creating a quasi-colonial hinterland.[3] At the beginning of the 1930s, when the global depression was in full swing, Western countries replaced free trade with bilateral regulations, allowing them to protect their domestic markets and to adjust imports from predominantly agricultural countries like Yugoslavia to their own advantage. German state officials utilized this new way of handling commodity exchange to meet strategic foreign policy goals. After the international trade networks had broken down during the First World War, leading German economic circles expected to gain a new access to the promising markets in eastern Europe through the German ethnic minorities living there.[4] What part the German minorities took in the updated strategy that was pursued by the "motherland" in the 1930s remains an open question. Some scholars assume that the minorities were extraordinary beneficiaries of their host countries' intensified trade with Germany.[5]

We can assume that ethnic German actors had their own agendas, which were rooted in regional requirements and sometimes differed from the agendas of their co-ethnics in Germany. Although a bottom-up view promises new insights, this perspective has been neglected so far. Did moments occur when the interests of minority representatives contradicted those of the decision-makers in the motherland? This chapter focuses on one enterprise, namely the "Avis" poultry product marketing section of the ethnic German cooperative union in Yugoslavia, or more precisely in the Vojvodina, a multiethnic region north of Belgrade.[6] This microstudy allows us to understand how an ethnic enterprise functioned under the changing foreign trade conditions in the 1930s. It addresses the agency of the ethnic German entrepreneurs by introducing an analysis of three basic behavioral categories: logic, dynamic, and motive. Avis was run by minority leaders and situated between ethnic Germans, Jews, and Slavs, as well as Yugoslav policy makers. We will also see how the running of an economic enterprise related to the growing tensions among these ethnic groups during the 1930s. The regional context hints at an answer to the question of why the business was maintained in spite of its failure from a strictly economic point of view.

Avis was an offspring of a cooperative system that had developed owing to the influences of German foreign policy aims in eastern Europe, especially the revisionist drive toward Poland.[7] Since the mid-1920s, the semiofficial Deutsche Stiftung (German Foundation) in Berlin, an organization administering loans to German minority organizations abroad, stimulated the spread of ethnic German cooperatives, the number of which was estimated at seven thousand in the early 1930s.[8] By granting large funds to minority cooperative banks in eastern Europe, the administration in Berlin planted outposts into the economic landscape. One of the most dynamic minority cooperatives of the interwar period was the "Agraria" in the Vojvodina. This venture expanded through its banking section, which was established in 1927, and from the early 1930s through its branches for marketing animal produce.[9]

THE BIRTH OF AVIS:
OFFERING A SOLUTION FOR A LARGE-SCALE ECONOMIC PROBLEM

In the early 1930s, the German minority in the Vojvodina numbered approximately 377,000 people.[10] Eighty-four percent of the "Swabians" (regional term for ethnic Germans) were inhabitants of rural communities.[11] After 1918, Novi Sad emerged as the geographical center of the movement for promoting a pan-German identity. At the beginning of the 1920s, the cultural organization Kulturbund and the Party of the Germans (Partei der Deutschen) were founded. The post-1918 land reform excluded the ethnic Germans, who in many cases did not possess enough land to make a living, from property distributions.[12] In this situation, the Party of the Germans promised to care for the vital interests of its target group. In the longer run, however, the adherents of the political minority movement made up only a relatively small proportion of the population.[13]

In the fall of 1922, the organized ethnic German movement entered the cooperative scene in Yugoslavia. Minority activists, first among them the prominent politician Stephan (Stefan) Kraft (1884–1959), who had attended a business school while studying law in Vienna,[14] founded the Agraria, a cooperative for trading agricultural utilities and field crops.[15] The Agraria formed a union by integrating already existing cooperatives. Since 1925, it established its own local branches, the Bauernhilfen (literally: Peasants' Aid). Step by step, a diversified cooperative system developed. In 1927, the financial section of the Agraria was outsourced to the newly formed Agricultural Central Credit Bank (Landwirtschaftliche Zentral-Darlehenskasse, LZDK). One of the crucial tasks of the LZDK was to carry out the frequent audits of all local and central cooperatives belonging to the ethnic German union.[16] Kraft, who had been removed from the top of the Agraria but had gained the presidency of the LZDK, inaugurated the additional founding of a pig farming cooperative in 1930 and the Avis egg producing cooperative in June 1931.[17]

The logic behind the move into livestock raising lay in countering the low prices for grain sales on the international markets. Many small farmers were severely hit by the drop in grain prices, which had been cut in half by strong overseas competition. Because many small farmers accumulated debts, the public discourse mirrored the situation by talking about an ongoing crisis.[18] As a common crisis can lead to decay, it sets an imperative of forcing the leaders in society to react. In this case, the appeal of the counterstrategy, widely known as "Denmarkization," was catchy: instead of dumping the grain on the world market, it would be more profitable to use it for feeding livestock. Animal produce was not challenged to the same extent by global competition, and the prices remained relatively stable. "Denmarkization" meant specializing in exporting animal produce to industrialized countries. In order to keep up with producers in competing countries, a rationalization of the methods of production was envisioned.[19] This plan was pursued by Kraft and his collaborators in the cooperative system. The leading figures carried out an ambitious publicity campaign through the German press in the Vojvodina, calling for the regional improvement of stockbreeding and thus preparing the foundation of the Avis. On the drawing board, the plan presented a tempting impression. Requiring far less effort than hard field work, the profit from livestock raising was assessed at a high rate. According to the regulations introduced by Avis, participants had to bring in a share of 100 dinars and were enabled to buy one hundred breeding chickens at the price of 500 to 600 dinars. The chickens, after being bred in the innovative central incubator, were expected to bring in a profit of 750 dinars after just three months. The proposal was made that cooperative members had to deliver their eggs in good quality within five days.[20]

The logical reasons behind Avis were not determined only by economic factors. Moreover, its creation aimed to include as many co-ethnics as possible into the German cooperative system.[21] After the Party of the Germans, among other political parties in Yugoslavia, was forced to close down in 1929 due to an overall authoritarian shift in domestic politics, and the continuation of the Kulturbund itself was at stake, ethnic entrepreneurship seemed to offer organizational sanctuary.[22] With regard to Avis, the auditing department of the LZDK declared the "continued existence and expansion of our economic cooperatives ... an absolute necessity for our ethnic community [*Volk*]."[23] Max Siebold, who later became the director of Avis, imagined the egg production cooperative as attracting hitherto-neglected parts of the population to organized Germandom.[24] In the 1930s, some 45 percent of the ethnic Germans were landowners who formed the traditional base of agricultural cooperatives. Two-thirds of the farmers, however, possessed less than ten hectares of land.[25] In terms of socioeconomic groups, almost half of the population belonged to the (predominantly agricultural) workers (30 percent) and craftspeople (18 percent). A middle class emerged in the urban centers.[26] As poultry keeping does not rely on having extensive farmland, people like rural workers, craftspeople, shop owners, and other individuals who had some chickens pecking in their yard gained a new importance.

However, this ambitious plan failed for several reasons. First of all, it received a rather lukewarm response among the German population. When potential participants had some money left, they preferred to deposit it safely in the LZDK rather than risk an investment in professional poultry keeping. Soon, the application of systematic measures in order to increase the efficiency of chicken farming came to a halt.[27] An illustration of the lack of commitment by the target group was the case of the central incubator, which was placed at the disposal of the cooperative members. After a while, they lost interest in using the device.[28] Avis was not able to change the fact that poultry keeping was only a sideline of Swabian agriculture and conducted in rather primitive conditions. It was aimed primarily at supplying one's own household. The surplus of eggs was mostly sold by housewives on local markets.[29]

NEWCOMER ON THE INTERNATIONAL MARKET: DISILLUSIONMENT BY REGIONAL CONDITIONS

Despite the poor response, Avis traded considerable amounts of eggs. Since the backbone of Avis was the complicated export business, unprofessional production posed a grave problem. Most of the commodity was delivered to Germany. Facing the high quality standards demanded by the foreign market, it was not a decisive advantage that the German embassy in Belgrade had succeeded in lifting the tariff on egg imports when Avis started operating.[30] The receiving companies in the motherland acted strictly against the shortcomings of Avis, which had to pay penalties for late or flawed deliveries.[31] The reputation of the cooperative suffered so much that it began to lose customers on the crucial German market.[32] Moreover, adverse domestic conditions in the field of egg production prevailed. For instance, one expert, who had been sent from Germany in order to modernize poultry keeping among the Germans in the Vojvodina, became so frustrated by the disinterest of the regional target group that he eventually resigned.[33]

Avis was designed as a production cooperative. Its headquarters were located in Novi Sad, and it had three regional branches: Avis A in Veliki Bečkerek (later renamed Petrovgrad), Avis B in Velika Kikinda, both in the Banat, and Avis C in Novi Vrbas (Bačka). As can be seen from data for district A, Avis was affected by the commercial division of the regional market. Professional traders, who bought produce from farmers, had their strongholds in the central areas of the Vojvodina.[34] Only the more remote areas at the border with Romania, which required a bigger effort in transportation, were left to Avis.[35] Another negative factor was the ethnic principle on which the choice of commodity sources was based. According to Avis's regulations, members were obliged to bring the produce to certain local spots for further delivery to the branch compound, but farmers' phlegmatic behavior was so widespread that Avis commissioned collectors who used horse-drawn vehicles. As the settlements with an ethnic German population were partly scattered, the collectors frequently rode seventy kilometers (forty-five miles) to reach all of the associated Swabians interested in selling eggs to Avis.[36]

From a strictly commercial standpoint, the luxury of conducting an ethnic economy was nonsense, because the collectors systematically ignored the high potential of supplies in a series of Serbian villages along the way, only because the people living there belonged to a different ethnic group. Not only did expenses increase, but the quality suffered due to the long distances covered. In fact, the collectors worked as intermediaries who were paid in relation to the number of eggs they were able to purchase. Avis B was challenged by the competition of regional traders who reacted by raising prices. Instead of a broadly based production cooperative, Avis turned into a trading enterprise. Due to the lack of working capital, as the registered members (numbering some 2,300) almost entirely failed to pay their dues, Avis relied on other departments of the cooperative system, especially the LZDK, to cover its deficit.[37]

BETWEEN THE MILLSTONES OF BILATERAL TRADE REGULATIONS

Avis faced serious trouble when the Yugoslav trade agreement with Germany expired in March 1933 due to a preliminary cancellation by the German side.[38] From then on, high tariffs had to be paid, stymieing the flow of shipments.[39] Hard times were ahead, because the industrialized countries, in order to protect their domestic agricultural producers by synchronizing supply with demand, replaced free trade with fixed import quotas.[40] Due to these restrictions on the international market, the business of agricultural exporters—such as Avis—turned into a permanent challenge. While being severely affected by the trade limitations, domestic affairs in the motherland seemed to improve the position of Avis. In April 1933, the Nazis reinforced their nationwide campaign against Jewish businesses.[41] For Avis, the supply gaps that occurred from the discrimination against Jewish traders on the German market opened new sale opportunities.[42] On the other hand, an impediment turned up in May 1933, when Germany introduced a minimum weight for import eggs. According to an estimate by Avis, less than 30 percent of the production in the Banat met the requirements.[43] Nevertheless, Avis clung to the German market, where its prospects remained precarious. The management was looking forward to trade negotiations between Belgrade and Berlin.[44] At the end of July 1933, the two governments concluded a provisional agreement, raising hopes for Avis to acquire a considerable share of the total amount of eggs to be allowed into Germany.[45] Awaiting this export option, Avis started to stockpile large quantities of eggs. Several weeks passed before access to the German market could be restored, causing considerable losses due to the perishable nature of the commodity.[46]

Finally, in October 1933, Avis obtained the desired certificates valid for the rest of the year. Avis had to fulfill the export quota set by the export license in order to avoid penalties and prove reliability as an experienced exporter, because the allocation of future quotas depended on past accomplishments. Failure would have led to the dwindling of Avis's business foundation. Hence, its agents combed the purchase areas, engaging in a costly competition with the commercial traders.[47] At the end of the year, when Avis was again running out of licenses for deliveries to the Reich, the management pleaded its vital interests to the German decision makers by using its special Berlin connections.

DRAWING THE LINE BETWEEN "US" AND "THEM"

In early December 1933, the Pontus agency, which had been established to administer clandestine credits to economic associations of German minorities in southeastern Europe, submitted a letter to the Auswärtiges Amt (German Foreign Office, AA) on behalf of Avis, which presented itself as a bulwark against communist influence and as a victim of Jewish businessmen:

> Ever since, keeping poultry has its very special meaning among our German population, because not only farmers, but also persons carrying on a trade, workers, and smallholders [Kleinhäusler] are taking part in it. It is characteristic of our region that nowadays these poorer people likewise own a cottage or a piece of land, thus having the possibility to take on intensive poultry farming. In the past few years, Marxist propaganda started just within this lower stratum of our German population. The leadership of the German organizations in Yugoslavia decided effectively to combat this development by founding our cooperative and uniting the poorer people.... Another reason was that, since then, the outcome of poultry production was taken over by Jewish wholesalers in an exploitative manner.... It was predictable that Jewish wholesalers would immediately recognize the danger of an association based on equal social standing and, relying on the accumulated capital of decades, would begin to fight the cooperative to the utmost.[48]

By creating an image of the enemy in accordance with the ideology that recently began its reign in the motherland, Avis demanded from the officials in Berlin an extra export quota of six thousand quintals. Support came from the German ambassador in Belgrade.[49] The AA's trade affairs desk consulted the Reich Ministry of Agriculture.[50] Promising prospects emerged when the German administration envisioned buying at least two hundred million eggs from foreign markets by mid-1934.[51] Stephan Kraft, who was on a trip to Berlin at the beginning of February, pushed the urgent request forward.[52] Although expressing concerns due to unsatisfactory experiences with earlier imports from Avis, the Ministry of Agriculture agreed to the idea under the condition that complications with the Yugoslav authorities were avoided.[53] Kraft convinced the relevant officials that there were no troubles to fear.[54] Finally, in mid-February 1934, the Ministry of Agriculture accepted the extra quota and even afforded Avis the exclusive right to deliver eggs of lower quality.[55] Facing the import restrictions of the industrial countries, the Yugoslav government had little choice but to tolerate these export rights granted to Avis.

However, soon the special treatment given to Avis by the motherland became public knowledge, when the news leaked from the pages of the ethnic German cooperative paper *Der Landwirt*.[56] The privilege given to the ethnic German enterprise provoked business circles in the Vojvodina, who protested to the Yugoslav office in charge of controlling livestock exports (Ured za kontrolisanje izvoza stoke), a department of the Yugoslav Trade Ministry.[57] Outraged by the exceptional quota awarded to Avis, Daka Popović (1886–1967), former governor of the Danube Banovina (*banovina*: an administrative entity on the state level) and managing committee member of the Novi Sad chamber of commerce, issued a memorandum to the royal government, criticizing the strong position of the ethnic German cooperatives that were apparently "organized exclusively along ethnic lines [and], thanks to political and economic connections, nowadays prosper to the detriment of the domestic Slavic cooperatives, because they take the lead in commercializing and placing their products in foreign countries."[58] The protests resulted in pressure from the authorities urging Avis to stop purchases from non-members, who frequently were not of German ethnicity and whose number roughly equaled the registered participants, making together "some 5,000."[59] In compliance with the official rule on including only cooperative members, the Slavs were left out while Avis elevated the price level in ethnic German settlements: "In our German communities of the 'B' district [northern Banat] the trader always spends three to five Paras [one hundredth part of a dinar] more [per egg] than in the neighboring settlements of the Serbian war veterans."[60]

This remark touched upon a sensitive issue. Several areas of the Yugoslav borderlands with Hungary and Romania were colonized by Slavic settlers, many of them former volunteers in the Serbian army, the *dobrovoljci*. By the mid-1920s, some 6,700 *dobrovoljci* families, often from the mountainous Lika or Montenegro, had settled in the Bačka and the Banat.[61] They encountered serious difficulties due to the lack of local infrastructure, rejection by neighboring compatriots, and inexperience in extensive field cultivation. Many of these settlers who were designated to serve the Yugoslav national project by reinforcing the Slavic element at the state borders suffered from poor living conditions. The constant fear that the territorial gains Yugoslavia had made at the end of the First World War remained vulnerable became apparent when, for instance, district officials in the Vojvodina informed their superiors in 1930 that Hungary "pursues with maximum power the revision of the peace treaties."[62]

While discontent grew among the newcomers,[63] the long-established ethnic Germans seemed to be better off. Already in 1927, Serbian colonists from the village of Vojvoda Stepa had complained to the Yugoslav Ministry of Agriculture against the discrimination they felt in comparison to the ethnic Germans from the neighboring village of Nemačka Crnja in the northern Banat.[64] Being ethnically German could be advantageous. Against the background of the desperate economic situation in 1933 and 1934—when rural proletarians roamed about the country, seeking jobs in return for meager meals and scanty shelter[65]— every extra dinar earned was welcome.[66] Sometimes the gains from poultry produce sales generated the decisive asset that gave Swabian farmers a modest financial surplus.[67] This went hand in hand with the exclusion of the non-German population from the benefits of Avis. After Yugoslav officials cracked down on informal purchases from nonmembers, the chances of Slavic people to join the attractive business venture practically sank to nil. For many people, the economic situation continued to be hard. As late as 1937, when grain prices rose again, an average family had to work a whole day for a loaf of bread. Considering the small profit per capita of only half a dinar daily, every financial gain achieved through selling animal produce proved to be vital.[68] Under these conditions, the poultry keepers Saveta Laković, Žarko Rakić, and Svetozar Žilitj applied for acceptance to Avis B, but the supervising department of the LZDK refused their petition: "With reference to your letter, we inform you that we cannot approve the applications for membership, since we basically only want to have persons of German extraction [Volkszugehörigkeit] in our cooperatives."[69]

With the circle of Avis's primary suppliers closing, the yield of the commodity worsened. After Avis had only been able to handle the export quota in the fall of 1933 with a supreme effort and frequent purchases from nonmembers, it was clear that the special quota granted in early 1934 was much larger than available supplies, particularly given that it comprised one-third of the entire Yugoslav contingent for egg exports to Germany.[70] Understandably, the Yugoslav Trade Ministry as well as the German state monopoly on agricultural products, which had to cope with the substandard commodity delivered by Avis, wanted to get rid of the arrangement. Hence, the opportunity to sacrifice the special quota to a higher purpose was welcomed by both sides when they started negotiating a new treaty in April 1934.

A NEW TRADE AGREEMENT AND CHANGES IN GERMAN MINORITY POLITICS

For more than a year already, the AA had tended to undermine the Little Entente, the alliance between Czechoslovakia, Romania, and Yugoslavia, which opposed the revisionist claims of Hungary.[71] The officials of the French Foreign Ministry saw the Little Entente as a cornerstone for the maintenance of the international order in Europe as laid down after the First World War. France, however, failed to underpin diplomacy by economic means. While Paris intended to protect domestic farmers who were affected by the crisis of agricultural prices, the politicians in Belgrade began to disassociate from France as their traditional ally.[72] Despite all political reservations, Yugoslav government circles began to turn with interest toward Berlin in the expectation of sufficient export opportunities. The redistribution of the huge export quota enjoyed by Avis encouraged the Yugoslav representatives to come to the negotiating table. Not surprisingly, already in the run-up to the bilateral treaty of May 1934, the livestock department of the Yugoslav Trade Ministry concluded an agreement with the German state monopoly on eggs.[73] Later on, however, the Yugoslavs were not satisfied with the quantity earmarked for the treaty of May 1934, but putting the allocation of the export quotas back into Yugoslav hands provided a strong impulse to accept the conditions as suggested by the German side.[74] The May treaty contained three essentials:

1. Official delegations met on an annual basis to define the trade quotas.
2. A clearing agreement provided that the payments from traders on both sides had to pass through the national banks. Thus, transactions were centralized. Instead of directly paying the exporter, the recipient settled the bill at his national bank, which credited the sum to the national bank of the partner country. But the latter national bank did not simply hand the money over to the exporter. It waited for an equivalent value to come in, which meant that an appropriate import had to be made first. In principle, the clearing procedure was designed to create a balance of reciprocal trade.
3. Preferential prices granted by Germany contributed to the accumulation of a Yugoslav reichsmark surplus in Berlin. In fact, Yugoslavia supplied Germany with agricultural products on credit. Exporting industrial goods to Yugoslavia was less attractive for German companies because, in comparison to foodstuffs, there was a higher demand on the world market. This asymmetry resulted in Yugoslav economic dependency on Germany.

Regardless of all reservations against making common cause with Germany, the economic situation in Yugoslavia was so desperate that the agreement was widely welcomed among political leaders as well as the public.[75] At least the blockade of badly needed exports seemed to have been overcome. However, the managers of Avis were anything but enthusiastic about the treaty. Not only were they affected by complicated and unfavorable transaction rules—a problem they shared with other Yugoslav exporters—but they were stripped of their exclusive access to the

German market. Karl Fütterer, a young expert on cooperatives who once had been sent from Germany as an assistant to the Agraria, submitted Avis's claim for compensation to the AA. As in late 1933, it seemed appropriate to the authors of this claim to adopt an anti-Semitic tone: "After we have, in defiance of the attacks from the Jewish egg wholesalers, established direct business connections with the central agency of the German egg commerce, giving up for our young and financially weak organization the tempting advantages of the moment, we are now, by the cancellation of the contract, forced to seek good relations with those people."[76]

The reason why, despite the drastic manner in which the Avis board of directors in Novi Sad presented its request, the ideological inflection failed to produce the desired result this time was rooted in the quarrels that emerged among Nazi officials over the matter of ethnic German affairs after the Nazis had come to power. Fütterer acted on behalf of Avis. He applied to Carl Clodius, who ran the foreign economic policy desk at the AA, for "friendly mediation at the Reichsnährstand."[77] The Reichsnährstand (statutory corporation of farmers) was the Nazi Party–controlled umbrella organization in charge of agricultural matters in the Third Reich. Accordingly, the anti-Semitic tone should have rung a bell. It was, however, Fütterer's mistake to label himself the "chief of the economic office of the VDA," because at that time, the VDA (Volksbund für das Deutschtum im Ausland, National Union for Germandom Abroad), an established mass organization, was curtailed by the Reichsnährstand's claim to the leading position over ethnic German affairs in the rural parts of eastern Europe.[78] The Reichsnährstand tended to avoid disturbances when it came to siding with the Nazi-affiliated segments of German minorities.[79] For this reason, Fütterer appeared as a disruptive element. He had issued a report to the AA disproving of Stephan Kraft's Nazi-inclined rivals, the so-called *Erneuerer* ("renewers"), who in many cases were well-educated younger activists of the German *Volksgruppe* (ethnic community) in Yugoslavia. As their prospects for advancement in Yugoslav society were generally unsatisfactory, the *Erneuerer* were eager for leading positions in the minority movement.[80] Against this political background, it came as no surprise that the Reichsnährstand rejected Avis's claim for compensation.[81]

HOMEGROWN PROBLEMS AND ANTI-SEMITIC PATTERNS

Despite the setback of the compensation claim, Avis kept Karl Fütterer busy. In the absence of monetary means, he used his soft skills. This was facilitated by Carl Clodius, who did not want to disappoint his economic partners in Novi Sad. In advance of the annual Yugoslav-German trade talks in February 1935, he asked Fütterer what kind of favors the ethnic German cooperative union in the Vojvodina expected from the AA. Fütterer expressed the idea of enabling Avis to engage in large-scale exports of poultry to Germany. After Clodius consented, the official delegates from Berlin lifted the limit on poultry purchases. Throughout 1935, poultry sales from Avis to the motherland increased by 1,565 percent, reaching 532,000 kilograms (1,170,000 lb.).[82] The cooperative press continuously announced high prices.[83] Not without self-interest, Max Siebold, the chief executive of Avis, was optimistic for the extended demand on the German market to last.[84] Since he was the owner of the Tisa poultry processing compound in Stari Bečej, he personally benefited from improved market access through Avis.[85] Everybody seemed satisfied. The poultry-keeping members of Avis were pleased with making an easy dinar and even sold young chickens by the bundle.[86] In his internal correspondence, Clodius proudly compared the effect of his decision to a "suction pump."[87] But the export boom was only a flash in the pan. In 1936, Avis's turnover of poultry dropped to one-third of its 1935 output.[88] In vain had the auditing department of the LZDK pointed to the negative effect of the rash sellout, calling it "only a seeming success, because it has to result in a decrease in egg production. This way of acting can be compared to an industrial enterprise which sells its machinery in order to obtain working capital."[89]

In 1936, when egg sales to Germany could proceed without quantity restrictions,[90] Avis was able to export only 46 percent of the amount its exports had reached in 1934.[91] Especially in the Bačka, the yield fell to one-third of the pre-1935 amount,[92] urging Siebold to admit "that [even] the domestic requirements could hardly be met."[93] Now, the electric incubator could have done a great service, but due to its insufficient use far below capacity, it had been transferred from Novi Vrbas (Avis C, the Bačka) to Petrovgrad (formerly called Veliki Bečkerek, the Banat).[94] Avis tried to devise a countermeasure for the lack of hens by setting up its own rearing facility. The initiative turned out to be a disaster when the animals died at a rate of "a hundred per day" because the feeding device had been handled improperly. From an economic standpoint, the declining business size pointed in the right direction, because every egg traded by Avis brought a little loss. Regardless of a prosperous business climate, in 1935 Avis was heavily indebted at the LZDK (to the tune of some 1.25 million dinars), and it continued to accumulate losses.[95]

It would have been appropriate to shrink the business to a reasonable size or even to cease operating,[96] but management still followed the imperative of bulk sales in order to maintain the basis of the enterprise by serving and thus securing the export quotas. Regarding the massive breakdown of egg production among the regional Swabians, without falling back on merchandise from commercial traders, it was impossible to fulfill the foreign trade obligations. Already in 1934, the supervising department of the ethnic German cooperative union admonished Avis to stop purchasing from external sources. Avis replied that a prevention of "emergency completions," as these purchases from private companies were called by the management, would endanger the essential export business.[97] Despite repeated appeals to the ethnic Germans not to give up the egg deliveries to the cooperative in favor of short-term advantages granted by the local traders, Avis "could not necessarily count on the loyalty of its members."[98] Bridging the gaps caused by the deficit of member-based egg production was inevitable. Prices on the open market were, of course, higher than expenses for direct purchases from primary sellers. While seeking solutions to the insufficient member-based supply, some Avis managers took the opportunity to line their own pockets. Johann Awender, chief executive of Avis A, acted as an intermediary between the A branch and the traders. This way, he made a fortune of 174,224 dinars by the end of 1936.[99] The chief executive of Avis B in Velika Kikinda, who had been praised by the central management of Avis as a shining example of how to counter the "unscrupulous trade" with his apparently "unyielding diligence,"[100] made a personal profit by charging Avis two dinars for each box of eggs he had previously bought from regional traders.[101]

Samuel Frenkel, a trader in poultry products with a branch office in Kikinda, was one of many Jewish owners of grocery firms. One-third of the Yugoslav Jews worked in commerce. Together they managed more than two-thirds of the whole country's foodstuff business.[102] Avis maintained a sort of symbiotic competition with the Jewish-dominated free trade. In May 1935, the auditing department of the ethnic German cooperative system complained about "constant business connections with Jewish merchants."[103] By contrast with Avis, Jewish middlemen like Oskar Šosberger in the central Banat or Hartman & Conen in Subotica (the upper Bačka) took advantage of their indifference to the ethnicity of their suppliers.[104]

In early 1934, Germany concentrated all egg production under its agricultural state monopoly. Despite efforts to intensify domestic production, the repression of Jewish food traders resulted in shutdowns and supply shortages.[105] Livestock merchants abroad occasionally profited from the Nazis pushing German Jews out of business. While in April 1936, *Der Angriff*, the daily newspaper of the Nazi labor union, the Deutsche Arbeitsfront (German Labor Front), proudly announced sufficient supplies to satisfy domestic demand with "Aryan Easter eggs,"[106] Jewish companies abroad were able to increase their deliveries. Throughout

1936, Hartman & Conen sent twice as many eggs to Germany than Avis did.[107] Therefore, the news of the "Aryan eggs" was a complete propaganda hoax.[108]

Since the bottleneck of the international clearing procedure usually caused delays in realizing profits, domestic sales in Yugoslavia from commercial traders to Avis partly spared the former from financial troubles. Avis suffered severely from the belated payments in return for deliveries to Germany.[109] This, among the aforementioned problems, contributed to a permanent financial loss that reached 1.8 million dinars by mid-1938.[110] Without the backing of the LZDK, Avis would have gone bankrupt already in 1937.[111] One issue that strained Avis's financial resources was the self-serving mentality of many of its managers. Since the early years of Avis, executive personnel had received considerable advance payments.[112] Exaggerated daily allowances became a longstanding problem.[113] An obvious case of embezzlement occurred when goose feathers worth 15,000 dinars disappeared from a storehouse. Bookkeeping was negligent. Serious financial manipulations took place (e.g., exchange rates assessed at an exaggerated value) in order to disguise the deplorable state of the cooperative's internal affairs. An accountant who had been chartered by Pontus and sent to Novi Sad noted the allegedly "known fact that the Swabian peasants are paying little attention to the breeding of poultry and to the production of eggs."[114]

Avis acted like an ordinary trade company. However, the authorities turned a blind eye to the commercial character of Avis, obviously conscious of the fact that some Yugoslav trade companies indirectly profited from the export certificates issued to Avis. Privatization efforts were made in 1939, because, as an auditor put it, "most of the merchandise comes from the market, provided by traders."[115] Josef Frantner, cashier of Avis B, informed the internal auditing department of his disapproval of advance payments to egg peddlers, because his employer had already lost 5,000 dinars through this kind of generosity. On this occasion, Frantner issued a complaint: "So much for the administrative work of this German-Jewish cooperative [sic], where, for certain reasons, deals are preferably made quite shamelessly with Jews, yes with Jews, who by all means try to harm and mock the whole German cooperative system."[116]

Someone had to be held responsible for this desolate situation. Following the anti-Semitic scapegoat scheme, Frantner's anger over unsatisfactory conditions found an outlet. This way, he avoided dealing with the professional lapses of his colleagues and refrained from substantial criticism, which could have served as a precondition for addressing and solving the actual problems. However, never did the accountant, who reported on behalf of the Berlin-based apparatus in charge of subsidies for German minority cooperatives, mention any Jewish machinations. According to this expert, the shortcomings emanated from the "incapability of acquiring the special requirements for this commercial sector as well as [from a deficiency in] realizing and using the favorable moments [of the export business]."[117] In comparison to experienced trade enterprises, Avis behaved like an amateur in the face of complicated export procedures. Nevertheless, instead of pulling the emergency brake, Stephan Kraft's LZDK extended the credit limit to 2.5 million dinars.[118] At the time, Kraft was the only ethnic German member of parliament in Belgrade. As the most prominent politician of the German minority in Yugoslavia and president of Avis, he defended the cooperative regardless of its inefficiency, by emphasizing its "social repercussions" in times of crisis. According to his announcement, Avis made an annual expenditure of 600,000 dinars for its staff and collectors, mostly paid "to people from the poorer social strata who earn their living this way."[119] In addition to benefiting the workers, prices rose significantly in areas where Avis agents showed up, increasing the incomes of poultry-keeping households.[120]

CONTRADICTIONS OF AN ETHNIC ECONOMY

As a part of the Agraria cooperative system, Avis was designed as an ethnic economic organization. Structurally this aim was met, although on a practical level—due to business requirements—significant deviations occurred. The enterprise's development was deeply influenced by the changing export regimes, because it was tied to the German market. Avis arguably was relevant as a prelude to forming a sphere of German economic domination against Yugoslavia and her allies in the Little Entente. In order to gain advantage, the managers of Avis demonstrated political attachment to their German partners by placing themselves on the side of National Socialist anti-Semitism.[121] This seemed to work as long as the power struggle among the Nazi organizations in the field of German minority politics did not create an obstacle. In the background, however, it was Jewish traders who ensured that Avis was able to fulfill its export obligations. The anti-Semitic references of Avis personnel served to ensure two functions: benefits from Berlin and distraction from their own failures.

Whereas Avis contributed to the reinforcement of ethnic boundaries, the national function of the cooperative was ambiguous. Avis connected Yugoslav citizens (Swabians), who lived in peripheral areas along the border with Romania, through the urban centers of the Vojvodina, to foreign markets. Before the division of the Banat between Yugoslavia and Romania in the aftermath of the First World War, these trade routes often went in the direction of Timișoara, not Novi Sad. Thus, from a spatial point of view, Avis played a constructive role in the economic integration of the young Yugoslav state. Once Avis was set into motion, the question remains what allowed the enterprise to cut deeper and deeper into the budget of the LZDK.

This can be explained on three levels. First, the logic of LZDK bankrolling Avis derived from the ideological background of the cooperative system, which was assigned the task of including as many ethnic Germans as possible. Second, the dynamic was fueled by the bilateral trade regime, compelling Avis managers to maintain a high level of deliveries. And third, the motives were manifold, depending on the type of person who participated in the project. To the management, Avis offered tempting amenities, such as commissions or other forms of allowances, not to mention the parasitic methods of some functionaries. Yanni Kotsonis's controversial finding that cooperatives were primarily influenced by the interests of the upper class is corroborated in this case by the example of the director, Max Siebold, who used the ethnic label of Avis as a gateway to foreign markets.[122] Likewise, Stephan Kraft, the president of Avis, had a personal interest in maintaining the enterprise despite its constant financial losses. At the time, he was seriously challenged by the *Erneuerer*, and the advantages Avis afforded to the poultry-keeping Swabians enhanced his popularity as a minority politician. However, the most striking conclusion remains that Avis played a key role in Yugoslav-German trade relations by paving the way for the May 1934 agreement. In spite of this role, it failed to gain a lasting financial advantage from the intensified trade between the two countries.

CHAPTER 3

RACIALIZING THE BALKANS

The Population of Southeastern Europe in the Mind of German and Austrian Racial Anthropologists, 1914-1945

CHRISTIAN PROMITZER

This chapter deals with the question of to what degree the population of southeastern Europe became a subject of German racial anthropology. Racial theory was one of the buttresses of the Nazi doctrine concentrated on acquiring new "living space" (*Lebensraum*) for the "German master race" (*deutsche Herrenrasse*). This was a peculiar and gruesome concept of settler colonialism that focused on eastern Europe (Poland, the Baltic states, and the European parts of the Soviet Union). It implied the extermination of the Jewish population as well as the displacement and partial extermination of the other ethnic groups living there (mainly Poles, but also other Slavs and Romani people).[1] The Balkan Peninsula, in turn, was not a primary object of the Nazi concept of *Lebensraum*; it was rather foreseen as a so-called *Ergänzungsraum*, a "complementary space" that had to be economically penetrated and whose agricultural and other resources were to be exploited by the German war machine.[2] As a result, the place of the Balkan Peninsula in the Nazi worldview was different from that foreseen for eastern Europe, which was mainly inhabited by members of a Slavic population who were considered "subhuman" and consequently subjected to cruel measures. The population of the Balkans, however, was characterized by an abundance of small ethnic groups, if we exclude the Romanians. German anthropologists considered the so-called Dinaric "race" the "racial" backbone of the Balkans; they assessed it to be below the Nordic "race," but far above the so-called "Eastern race," predominant in eastern Europe. This assessment did not prevent the German occupiers of the former Kingdom of Yugoslavia from treating the Serbian population as badly as they did the Poles and Russians in eastern Europe. The Bulgarians and Croats, in turn, with their alleged non-Slavic Nordic and Turk racial admixtures, were encouraged to follow the example of the Slovak satellite state and were to be treated as subaltern allies. The Nazi racial doctrine pretended to proceed from empirical assessments of physical commonalities, but in practice turned out to be a bundle of constructed social distinctions in the service of the Nazi brand of white supremacism. Slavs and other ethnic groups in the region were subjected to "constant improvisation" with regard to their status: "Opportunity and ideology shaped one another."[3]

This chapter first focuses on the close reading of a volume, entitled *The Nations and Races of Southeast Europe*. Its authors were the sociologist and anthropologist Wilhelm Emil Mühlmann (1904–1988), the ethnographer Karl Christian von Loesch (1880–1951), and Gustav Adolf Küppers (1894–1978), who after 1933 became known as a journalist working in the Balkan region. The book, which comprised about one hundred pages, dealt with the racial and ethnic composition of southeastern Europe and was published in Nazi Germany two years after the defeat of the Kingdom of Yugoslavia in 1941.[4] This work allows us to grasp the central categories of German racial thinking about the inhabitants of the Balkan Peninsula; the volume furthermore summarizes the contemporary anthropological knowledge about this region in a concise manner. Beginning with this text, it will be easier to go back in time at least to the period of the First World War and to elaborate the basic assumptions about the composition of the "races" that German and Austrian anthropologists tried to assess in the Balkans. With respect to German racial anthropology, which its propagators later on would term "racial science" (*Rassenkunde*), since the early 1900s there has been a trickling, though continuous, side stream of academic interest in the Balkans.[5] After the Nazi takeover, concomitant with the increasing economic ties of the Third Reich with the countries of the region, some aspects of this racial interest in the Balkans would find their way into the minds of the German public. I argue that German racial anthropology dealing with the Balkans was characterized by continuities from the periods before and after the Nazi seizure of power in Germany (in 1933) and Austria (in 1938), and particularly after the attack on Yugoslavia (1941), when the authorized stakeholders of official Nazi ideology would finally seize on and propagate concepts of racial anthropology on the Balkans. This chapter focuses solely on German "racial science" in the narrower sense of the meaning—that is, it concentrates on anthropological research that put the physical traits of the examined population at the center of its study;[6] it deals less with the then-flourishing research on the supposed character or folk psychology of individual nations living in the Balkans, for which the elaboration of the heroic Balkan human type, which was at the center of the intellectual efforts of Gerhard Gesemann (1888–1948), is a prominent example.[7] In terms of geography, the focus is on the core regions of the Balkans south of the Danube and Sava Rivers, but always from the viewpoint of German racial science and not by dealing with its offshoots in the region.⁸ Since my leading question is directed toward the racial classification of the "other" in the Balkans and not toward the issue of the "own"—meaning, how closely the German minorities of southeastern Europe, namely in Slovenia, Slavonia, the Banat, and Transylvania, were related to the bulk of the German nation in terms of racial anthropology—this chapter does not deal with the German minorities of southeastern Europe.⁹ Also, the Jewish inhabitants of southeastern Europe are addressed only as far as racial anthropologists mention them in comparisons with the local non-Jewish population.

THE NATIONS AND RACES OF SOUTHEASTERN EUROPE IN THE *VÖLKISCH* VIEW

In 1943, the publishing house Volk und Reich, which had acquired a dubious glory in the *völkisch* scene already before the Nazi seizure of power, released the aforementioned study on the "nations and races" of southeastern Europe. The book was based on an idea of Gustav Adolf Küppers, who was looking for experts who were able to interpret the footage of several thousand photos he had taken in the Balkans with the methods of racial anthropology. Wilhelm Emil Mühlmann and Karl Christian von Loesch finally agreed to collaborate with Küppers, to evaluate the photographs with the methods of racial anthropology, and to give a general survey about the ethnic and racial composition of southeastern Europe.¹⁰

Already as a student of Eugen Fischer (1874–1967) and Fritz Lenz (1887–1976), who in 1921 together with Erwin Baur coauthored the notorious bible of racial hygiene, *Grundlagen der menschlichen Erblehre* (Basics of Human Genetics), Mühlmann had come in touch with "racial science." During the 1930s, he became a member of the SA (Sturmabteilung)—the Nazi paramilitary wing—and the NSDAP (Nationalsozialistische Deutsche Arbeiterpartei) and worked as head curator of the ethnographic collection at the Anthropological Institute of Egon von Eickstedt (1892–1965) in Breslau (today Wroclaw in Poland's Silesian Lowlands).¹¹

Karl Christian von Loesch was in the 1920s chairman of the Deutscher Schutzbund für das Grenz- und Auslandsdeutschtum (German Defense League for German Affairs in Border and Foreign Regions) and cofounder of the Institut für Grenz- und Auslandsstudien (Institute for Border and Foreign Studies) in Berlin, where he developed an early sympathy for independence activists of Ukrainian, Slovak, Macedonian, and in particular Croatian origins. He became a member of the NSDAP in 1933.¹²

The works of the three authors cover different areas of a broad thematic field: von Loesch deals with the folklore and the ethnology of the peoples of the Balkan Peninsula, but he shows that he is versed in Nazi "folk" history, the principles of which he applies to the history of the

Balkan nations.[13] Mühlmann, in turn, applies himself to several aspects of the physical anthropology and the racial composition of the Balkan peoples,[14] while Küppers tries to blend all these different aspects by giving them a personal touch on the basis of his own experiences.[15]

When the volume was released, the turn of the Second World War was already in full swing; at the end of January/beginning of February 1943, the Wehrmacht had been defeated before Stalingrad, and eight months later Fascist Italy capitulated. The Jews of a large part of Yugoslavia had already become victims of the Holocaust, and over the course of 1943 Jews from Thrace, Macedonia, and Greece were also transported to the extermination camps. That year was also the last year during which the strained economic capabilities of the German Reich, despite increasing negative impacts and constraints due to the ever more intensifying war, still allowed scholars who were loyal to the regime to carry out noteworthy publication activities, such as to publish a magnum opus within the framework of Nazi doctrine.

As indicated previously, the Balkan Peninsula originally only represented a secondary site for the military plans of the Third Reich. However, two years earlier, Benito Mussolini's miscarried Italian campaign against Greece had made an intervention by his German ally necessary; in April 1941, Hitler's army invaded both Yugoslavia and Greece. So there was only a short time during which it was possible to publish essential academic works with a focus on the Balkan Peninsula. Consequently, individuals with expertise on a region that had not yet been the focus of the intended Greater Germanic Reich took center stage, as was the case with Gustav Adolf Küppers, while others, who had academic expertise as ethnographers (von Loesch) and anthropologists (Mühlmann), had to work out a regional expertise in a hurry. Karl Christian von Loesch possessed at least some earlier knowledge about Croatia and the German minorities in southeastern Europe.[16] These were the conditions under which the 1943 volume *The Nations and Races of Southeast Europe* was published. It showed the flexibility and efficacy of individual scholars who succeeded in underpinning the provisional policy of the Third Reich in the Balkans within a short time frame with central catchwords of the Nazi doctrines—in particular with respect to their racial theories.

Although von Loesch had been attached to the Nazi regime since its beginnings, he came more and more into conflict with the SS over the years; the latter would finally take over his institute in 1943. His turning away from the regime went so far that he would seek contact with the conspirators of the July 1944 plot.[17] However, if we read his 1943 contributions about the peoples of southeastern Europe, we will not find any significant deviation from mainstream Nazi thinking. Out of the corpus of the text, this chapter concentrates on his remarks about the Serbs and the Croats. The conflict between these two nations indeed had defined the ethnic tensions in the interwar Yugoslav state, which in April 1941 came under blitzkrieg and was eliminated by the Wehrmacht. Von Loesch, of course, would support the foundation of the "Independent State of Croatia" by the fascist Ustašas, who were totally dependent on the Third Reich. Within weeks they started to take pains to either—at worst—exterminate the autochthonous Serb community in Croatia and Bosnia with fire and sword or to assimilate them at best. About these mass crimes von Loesch did not spare a single word; he only noted that many of the Serbian Orthodox parishes expressed their affiliation to the Croat nation by signing up for the Roman Catholic Church.[18] Thereby he withheld the fact that these conversions happened in conditions of direct and structural violence for pure reasons of self-protection.

Concerning the Serbians within the former Yugoslav context, von Loesch contended that they had failed their historical leadership role, since they could not master the space they had to govern. Similarly, the Yugoslav army, which was led by them, quickly disintegrated during the German attack on Yugoslavia.[19] Von Loesch also claimed that the Croat population should not be put on the same level with the other South Slavic nations by reminding the reader that the government of the "Independent State of Croatia" in its first proclamation had referred to the Gothic-Germanic origin of the Croats, whose descendants only subsequently had adopted the Slavic language.[20]

It is therefore no wonder that von Loesch also followed the official Nazi doctrine with respect to the local Jewish population, whose autochthonous character he denied. He rather claimed that the agglomerations of Jews in the states of southeastern Europe were of recent origin and, in spite of all deployed resistance measures, much more threatening than their respective concentrations in Vienna and Berlin, since in southeastern Europe the social cohesion of the nations, the numbers of non-Jewish inhabitants, and the economic power of the latter were less pronounced vis-à-vis the "Jewish masses."[21] One has to add that these remarks which described the presence of a large Jewish population in the region were anachronistic when they were published in 1943. As mentioned earlier, at the time the mass killing of the local Jews in the death camps was already underway.

RACIAL SYSTEMATIZATION AND RACIAL PHOTOGRAPHY

If von Loesch's contribution to the volume was more oriented toward the immediate strategic relevance of the nations of southeastern Europe for the Third Reich and took the line of the then-fashionable spirit of generalized völkisch scholarship, which claimed to understand the most profound incentives of the individual nations, Wilhelm Emil Mühlmann's part of the book was more concretely attached to German racial anthropology and its traditions since the nineteenth century. Although Mühlmann had not conducted empirical fieldwork in the region, he self-evidently summed up the state of research about the population of the region and interpreted the photo footage Küppers provided within the defaults of the most recent update of the Nazi worldview for the Balkans. This assertiveness was possibly an expression of blunt opportunism—during this period, with respect to his academic career, Mühlmann was engaged with overcoming the resilience of full-on Nazis who resented his attempts to attach sociological reflections to the dominant racial approach in the field of anthropological research.[22] It is in this gloomy light that we also have to regard his opportunist participation in the Osttagung deutscher Wissenschaftler (Conference of German Scholars on the East) in 1942, where parts of the Generalplan Ost, which foresaw the ethnic cleansing and colonization of east-central and eastern Europe by Germans, were discussed.[23]

In the present text, Mühlmann argues from the start that, due to lack of research and to unfavorable conditions, a precise picture of the racial composition of southeastern Europe is still lacking. Herewith, he also echoed a recent contribution of the notorious social and racial hygienist Heinrich Reichel (1876–1943) from the University of Graz on the complex "racial fabric" of this part of Europe.[24] The reasons for this complexity, Mühlmann continued, could be found in the complicated course that racial history had taken in southeastern Europe; this region was characterized by tremendous racial entanglements, which in turn were the result of the manifold historical processes of migration and assimilation throughout the area's history. This resulted in a racial diversity that would render clear ethnic affiliation difficult, since it would be hardly possible, if not utterly impossible, to determine the respective historical moments when identifiable separate racial elements came together.[25] According to Mühlmann, the racial composition of the Balkan Peninsula would only allow for a rough classification into four types:

1. The Atlanto-Mediterranean race, which he described as tall, dolichocephalic (i.e., having a relatively long skull), and dark-haired. This type would be the oldest identifiable racial breed of southeastern Europe. It had arrived on the Balkan Peninsula peacefully by way of trade, traffic, and urban colonization, and was still to be found among the populations of Bulgaria, eastern Serbia, Macedonia, and Greece.[26]

2. The East European or Eastern Baltic race, which had brought along several hereditary traits from Central Asia, reminiscent of Mongoloid and Caucasoid forms, and often containing admixtures of the so-called Turanid race. This type, according to Mühlmann, was of small stature and had ash-blond hair. Turanid admixtures were present in Hungary, the Dobruja, Bessarabia, and Bulgaria, where remnants of once-settled Tartar peoples—Huns, Avars, the Proto-Bulgars, Pechenegs, and Kumans—were to be found.[27] Among the Bulgarians, Mühlmann claimed, one could find a tendency toward military discipline and order—an attitude that had its origin in the ancient Bulgarians. Was this, he continued, only the (sociological) result of political dominance, education, and tradition, or the continuing (genetic) influence of the old Turanid master race?[28]
3. The Nordic race, whose well-known characteristics and their unquestioned position at the top of the racial hierarchy are notorious. Therefore, we only want to highlight Mühlmann's remark that peoples from the North—Celts, Germanic peoples, and, not least, the aboriginal Slavs—as neighbors of the ancient urban civilizations of the south, had introduced varying degrees of Nordic blood into the population of the Balkan Peninsula.[29]
4. Finally, the Dinaric or Dinarid race, which for Mühlmann figures as a major puzzle of Balkan racial science. This type was characterized as being big-boned, very tall, and brachycephalic (i.e., having a relatively broad, short skull). Being widespread in the Balkan Peninsula, its distribution coincided with that of pastoralism in the mountainous regions (Carpathians, Transylvanian Alps, northern Albania, Montenegro, Dinaric Alps). It was not assigned to any particular people, but most likely to the ancient Illyrians and Thracians.[30] Mühlmann regarded this type as the physical manifestation of Gesemann's heroic breed, but was not short on his own characterization: "These rough fellows are less concerned with agriculture and trade, they are better with war or theft of sheep."[31]

Mühlmann was undecided whether the Dinaric race was sui generis or the hybrid result of crossbreeding. In the latter case, he could not discount the possibility that one of the two initial breeds had been the Nordic race, but he doubted that such an intermixture of the "master race" with another type would have led to racial improvement; thereby he pointed to sporadic pathological cases such as oxycephaly and acromegaly (i.e., having a skull of abnormally pointed or conical shape).[32] From there, he did not need to reach far to contend portentously: "Something is wrong with the Dinaric race."[33] In any case, Mühlmann went on, one could observe that racial mixtures between Dinarid types and those with a certain degree of Nordic elements had led to *Entnordung*, that is, to a degeneration of the Nordic elements and in particular of dolichocephalism, which was generally interpreted as the essential Nordic racial element. *Entnordung* had its imprint on the South Slavs in particular: The aboriginal Slavs that had settled on the Balkan Peninsula had owned a high share of Nordic elements, although with Atlanto-Mediterranean and eastern European admixtures. This high degree of Nordic elements was still present among the Croats who happened to finish their formation as a distinct ethnic group by being surrounded by Germanic tribes. Consequently, the Croats, in terms of race, had the closest connection with the mostly Nordic populations of central Europe.[34] Not by accident, this anthropological assessment coincided with the alliance of the Third Reich with the "Independent State of Croatia."[35]

According to Mühlmann, the process of *Entnordung* would shape the fate of the other South Slavs. Upon their arrival in the Balkans, the already-present ancient Thracian-Illyrian population, supposedly of the Dinaric type, would adopt Slavic language and lifestyles, but in turn imprint its racial elements on the arriving Slavs, so that they would become "Dinarized." Consequently, by pointing to the different racial destiny of the Croats, Mühlmann questioned the concept of a South Slavic commonality and even showed his disdain for the term "South Slavs," which for him was only a "comfortable label" hiding the extraordinarily complex processes of ethnogenesis and resting on historical legends, which were misused for political reasons in order to foster the ideology of Yugoslavism. For him, the Croats, in particular, did not belong to the "South Slavs."[36]

This shows how Mühlmann, a prominent representative of German racial anthropology, was ready and willing to adopt the most recent geopolitical and strategic changes on the Balkan Peninsula, happening in the first six months of 1941, and to translate them into the language of "racial science," which could be erroneously understood as part of natural science and therefore as presenting objective and ingrained facts. But, to the contrary, we just have to remember that during the winter of 1940–1941 Hitler had struggled to win over both Yugoslavia and Bulgaria for his Tripartite Pact, in order to secure his southern flank for the assault on the Soviet Union. In this period, German media consequently did not put the commonality of the Yugoslav peoples (Serbs, Croats, and Slovenes in that time) under a question mark. Only the subsequent coup on March 27, 1941, in Belgrade would lead—literally overnight—to a U-turn in Hitler's policy and his crushing attack on the Kingdom of Yugoslavia ten days later.[37] If this had not been the case, and the Kingdom of Yugoslavia, like that of Bulgaria, had joined the Tripartite Pact, the racial narration of South Slavic commonality would have taken a different path. The hitherto published studies on the racial anthropology and the logics of Nazi racial theory suggest that in such a counterfactual view the Dinaric race would have prominently figured as an ally of the Nordic master race.

But let us return to the original source: Mühlmann based his theses on several thousand photographs of various "racial types" occurring in southeastern Europe. Gustav Adolf Küppers had taken them between 1935 and the onset of the Second World War during five expeditions to the Balkans, each trip lasting several months. Only a small sample of close to a hundred photographs found their way into the volume itself.[38] On his expeditions, Küppers, among others, searched for the remnants of "Germanic blood in the Balkans" from the migration period of the fourth to the sixth centuries.[39] Thereby he got support from the Museum für Völkerkunde (Museum of Ethnology) in Berlin and the Kaiser-Wilhelm-Institut für Anthropologie, menschliche Erblehre und Eugenik (Kaiser Wilhelm Institute for Anthropology, Human Heredity, and Eugenics). The latter was responsible for the scientific legitimacy of Nazi racial doctrine and instructed Küppers to obtain anthropological handprints made with the help of soot.[40] Already in that period, fear of the long arm of the Third Reich's authorities was prevailing among the politically aware members of southeastern Europe's population; this became apparent when individuals often were not willing to get their hands dirty for the effort, since they associated the hand-printing procedure with being equated with criminals. In the Romanian Black Sea port of Constanța, Küppers was even confronted with the accusation that Germany was searching for the culprits of the Reichstag fire.[41]

With respect to his results, Küppers claimed: "In vain we looked around for the Balkan man as such. Nor did we find the very ethnic type of the Magyars, the Serbs, the Bulgarians, or the Romanians.... Instead of the expected ethnic and racial types, we found local and regional varieties of often surprisingly uniform character."[42] The same regional type with an externally discernible, fairly Nordic look could be found among the Croats of Dalmatia, on the one hand, but also among the inhabitants of the Montenegrin-Albanian border region, as well as around Lake Ohrid and in the Bulgarian part of the Balkan mountain range. But the similarity of these types was only superficial; intrinsically they would be separated by an anthropological threshold, which also severed the Balkans from the West.[43]

THE BROADER BACKGROUND: THE FIRST ANTHROPOLOGICAL EXAMINATIONS OF THE BALKANS

How did von Loesch, Mühlmann, and Küppers arrive at the concepts they used to describe the populations of southeastern Europe and wherefrom—apart from Küppers's photographs—did they get other information on which they based their theses? Depictions of the outward appearance of the local population in the Balkans can occasionally be found already in early modern travelogues and other treatises that touch on this part of Europe. One of the most striking examples of this kind of publication is the so-called Austrian *Völkertafel* or "Tableau of Nationalities," which was painted in the early eighteenth century. Besides depictions of a German, a Frenchman, an Englishman, and so forth, the tableau in its final column also includes a representative of the inhabitants of the Balkans labeled as "Turk or Greek" ("Tirk *oder* Griech" in German dialect). This ambiguousness in the designation probably should have indicated that the population of the European part of the Ottoman Empire mainly consisted of Muslims ("Turks") and affiliates of the Greek Orthodox Church ("Greeks").[44]

With increasing knowledge about the Balkan Peninsula, both the number and the verbosity of these interpretations increased. Above and beyond the many travelogues and geographical treatises, starting in the second half of the nineteenth century in Germany and Austria-Hungary, but also in France and Great Britain, the anthropological study of the Balkan Peninsula became fashionable. This interest was triggered by the wish to learn more about the aspirations of local Christian populations to free themselves from Ottoman rule and to create their own nation states. Thus, in 1877, at a time when the Russian-Ottoman war on the fate of Bulgaria was at its apex, the renowned German pathologist and liberal Rudolf Virchow (1821–1902), who was also interested in anthropology, gave a lecture to the Berlin Society for Anthropology, Ethnology, and Prehistory titled "On the National Position of the Bulgarians." At that time, Virchow's anthropological considerations about the Bulgarians rested only on the study of a few skulls of deceased Bulgarians, which he had not even measured himself.[45]

In German-speaking lands, anthropology was considered a natural science; it focused on the physical and morphological aspects of the examined persons and put emphasis on the measurement of their skulls (craniometrics) and assessment of their complexion. In the 1880s, Virchow would conduct a mass examination of German schoolchildren that differentiated between "German" and "Jewish" individuals and implies the further development of physical anthropology toward its manifestation under the name of "*Rassenkunde*" ("racial science"). In that it assessed the physical characteristics of humans, deindividualized them as "racial types," and applied an unequivocal doctrine of racial hierarchy, it is questionable whether racial anthropology ever had a phase of "innocence."[46] German racial anthropology rather early had its repercussions in the Balkans: already during the 1890s, anthropological mass examinations of soldiers and pupils were also undertaken in Greece and Bulgaria.[47]

Since the 1880s, anthropologists started to replace the older term "Aryan race," which had its origin in linguistics, with the more anthropological-sounding designations "Nordic type" or "Nordic race." But be it "Nordic," as the anthropologists used to say, or "Aryan," as was the more profane usage of various mystics of the extreme right and eventually the Nazis, both terms absolutely designated the "master race," to whom all other varieties like the Dinaric, the Atlanto-Mediterranean, and the Eastern or Eastern-Baltic races were inferior. All these terms were introduced by the Russian-French anthropologist Joseph Deniker (1852–1918), who presented a corresponding systematization of the European racial types at the turn of the twentieth century.[48] Shortly thereafter, the Serbian geographer Jovan Cvijić (1865–1927) used Deniker's term "Dinaric" in order to describe a psychological (rather than racial) type prevailing in the mountainous zones of the Balkan Peninsula, distinguished by its heroic and noble character compared to other types on the peninsula, and which was common among Serbs and Albanians.[49] Whatever Cvijić's intention may have been—to underpin Serbian national ideology or to lay the ideological foundations for a future Yugoslav state—the notion of the "Dinaric" type or race would have long-term repercussions among Austrian and German anthropologists such as Gustav Kraitschek (1870–1927) and Hans F. K. Günther (1891–1968). It challenged the moral high ground claimed by the "Nordic race," and therefore these anthropologists tried to show the inferior character of the "Dinaric" one.[50]

RACIAL ANTHROPOLOGY AND PRISONERS OF WAR

The laboratory for a more thorough racial-anthropological study of the Balkan Peninsula's population were the Austrian and German POW camps during the First World War, in which anthropologists of the Central powers found abundant opportunities to conduct systematic racial anthropological examinations. Rudolf Pöch (1870–1921) and his assistant Josef Weninger (1886–1959) from Vienna as well as Felix von Luschan (1854–1924) and his colleagues Otto Reche (1879–1966) and Egon von Eickstedt (1892–1965) from Berlin carried out the majority of these measurements. The subjects of their study were prisoners from the Russian army as well as captured soldiers from the African and Asian colonies of the French and British imperial armies, but also POWs from the armies of Serbia and Montenegro.[51] The results of their examinations would only be published after the war. Thus it would take until 1934, long after the death of Pöch, before Weninger—now Pöch's successor as professor of anthropology—finally published his *Racial Examinations of the Albanians* on the basis of the material collected during the war years. Weninger considered his study a "contribution to the problem of the Dinaric Race," as ran its subtitle. He did not trust in anthropometrics alone but preferred to apply his own sense of proportion in order to determine the shape of the nose. This way, he believed he could clearly delineate the "Dinaric" nose from the "Jewish" one.[52] In the long run, Weninger had the bad luck that the concept of racial categorization of which he was an adherent would finally be directed against his intimate surroundings after the Nazi takeover of Austria in March 1938. Because his wife was Jewish, he was removed from his university chair. Later on, he barely managed to save his mother-in-law from deportation to the death camps.[53]

Pöch's and Weninger's data from the First World War also formed the basis for the doctoral dissertation of Anton Rolleder (1910–1976) in the academic year 1938–1939 at the Medical Faculty of the University of Vienna. Rolleder dealt with the racial composition of the Serbs.[54] He had been a member of the NSDAP in Austria since 1930, while his father was active as a judge for the Nazi regime.[55] As in the case of Weninger's monograph, Rolleder had only anthropological measurement sheets and photographs available for his dissertation. The number of Serbs examined was 293. Rolleder recognized four somatic types; he refrained, however, from assigning them to certain racial types according to one of the then-established anthropological classification systems of races. His greater intention was namely "to prepare a uniform picture of all the peoples who live in this space in which we locate the center of the Nordic race."[56] However, this endeavor was not realized, because his time was consumed by his activities as a member of the SS medical corps, as head of the Subdivision of Eugenics and Racial Policy within the Gau Office for Public Health in Vienna, and as lecturer in forensic medicine at the University of Vienna.[57]

The Viennese anthropologist Viktor Lebzelter (1889–1936) was another scholar whose subsequent career would be deeply influenced by the anthropological research he carried out during the First World War. Namely, in 1926, Lebzelter became collaborator and in 1934 head of the anthropology department of the Viennese Museum of Natural History. Having earned his doctorate in anthropology at the University of Vienna, in 1916, Lebzelter, together with the Viennese folklorist Arthur Haberlandt (1889–1964), undertook a research trip to Montenegro and northern Albania, which had just been conquered by the Austro-Hungarian army. Independently from Pöch's research but based on its methodology, they took physical measurements of the male Albanian population.[58] In the same year, during a stay in the POW camp of Dąbie close to Kraków, Lebzelter conducted anthropological examinations of prisoners from the Serbian army as well as civilian internees from Serbia. Of the total of 300 persons from the Balkans, about 196 of them were Serbs from northwestern Serbia and the Morava Valley, and 41 were Romani—likewise from northwestern Serbia—whom Lebzelter called "sedentary gypsies of Greek Orthodox faith." According to Lebzelter, in terms of "sociobiology," this group tended to behave like all other peoples of the Balkan Peninsula in abiding by the "national mentality" shared by all Balkan peoples, which prevented interethnic mating. This, however, contradicts his contention that the Romani originally had been dolichocephalic, but having mixed themselves with the surrounding populations they had partially lost this trait. As for the sedentary Romani of the Muslim creed, Lebzelter believed that they had practiced interethnic mating, since they had lost their dark pigmentation and in their surroundings they were consequently referred to as "white gypsies." Lebzelter also noticed that the Romani showed a better resistance to tuberculosis than the other Serbian prisoners of war, as this was an indirect indication of the bad sanitary conditions in the camp.[59] After the end of the First World War, Egon von Eickstedt too dealt with the evaluation of anthropological measurements of Serbian Romani who had been imprisoned in German POW camps.[60]

Lebzelter's diverse and lengthy treatise on body measurements is largely descriptive and without any moral judgements. This reveals a professional reticence that was absent from the work of his contemporaries. Lebzelter's strict professionalism went along with his repudiation of the concept of a Nordic master race, and he was also a critic of Hans F. K. Günther and Otto Reche's negative assessments about racial mixture. Such an approach was possibly influenced by Lebzelter's worldview as a Christian conservative and Habsburg loyalist.[61] His moderate approach was also visible in the presentation of his findings on the anthropological examinations of the Serbs. He did not endorse his own data as definitive and was less guided by presuppositions when creating "race types" than his colleagues. He allowed himself only one significant statement, when he mentioned that among the Serbs the Dinaric type showed a mixture with a "fair type" and therefore posed the question whether this latter type was attributable to either the Nordic or the Eastern race, or even to "an unknown racial element."[62] Lebzelter's restraint with regard to racial theories popular in Germany and Austria even enabled him to present his views about the origin of the South Slavs in 1929 in the pages of the journal of the Croatian Archeological Society.[63]

NAZI RACIAL ANTHROPOLOGY ON THE BALKANS

After the Nazis took power in Germany in 1933, one discerns at least three schools of thought with their respective approaches in the field of racial anthropology, if we set aside Hans F. K. Günther, whose professional contributions were considered among his peers as less novel than promotionally effective. The first one was represented by the aforementioned Kaiser-Wilhelm-Institut für Anthropologie, menschliche Erblehre und Eugenik, led by Eugen Fischer (1874–1967), then, from 1942, by Otmar Freiherr von Verschuer (1896–1969). Certainly the central institution, which embodied the academic base for racial theory and racial hygiene in the Third Reich, in cooperation with the notorious SS doctor Josef Mengele (1911–1979), a pupil of Verschuer, it would play a fatal role in the scientific exploitation of the Holocaust by desecrating human body parts from concentration camps for the purpose of proving Nazi racial theories. However, until now its role in southeastern Europe has not been researched in detail. We know of a study trip in 1935–1936 undertaken by one member of the institute, Wolfgang Abel, in order to study the "cross-breeding" of the Romani population of Romania, and of Verschuer traveling shortly thereafter to instruct German physicians in Transylvania. The institute otherwise was active in the hosting of guest scholars from the region—in the years from 1929 till 1939, one visitor came from Yugoslavia and three from Romania, and thereafter one person each from Bulgaria, Croatia, and Romania.[64] The second institution was the Institut für Rassen- und Völkerkunde (Institute for Racial Science and Ethnology) at the University of Leipzig, which was led by Otto Reche and had a focus on blood group serology. The third school of thought was the circle around Egon von Eickstedt at the University of Breslau, which by methodology appeared to prolong a radicalized variant of traditional racial anthropology.

The University of Leipzig was also the seat of the Südosteuropa-Institut (Institute on Southeast Europe), which since 1937 edited the *Leipziger Vierteljahrsschrift für Südosteuropa* (*Quarterly for Southeast Europe*). It is therefore not coincidental that the journal's first issue contained an article on the "The Racial History of Southeast Europe within the Framework of Blood Group Research." Its author was Michael Hesch (1893–1979), a Transylvanian Saxon, who during the First World War had been a collaborator of Rudolf Pöch in his mass examinations of POWs. Hesch later became assistant to Reche. At the time when he published the article, he was already a member of the SS and an expert adviser on racial issues in the Division for Cultural Policy of the Leipzig branch of the NSDAP.[65] In his article, Hesch emphasized that blood group A, which he assigned to the "Nordic" and "Western" races, was sufficiently represented among the populations of southeastern Europe, while the Asian proportion, which was reflected in blood group B, was here essentially weaker than in eastern Europe. In keeping with the Nazi program for the search for *Lebensraum*, which focused on the suppression of the "inferior" local populations in Poland, Ukraine, and the European part of Russia proper, Hesch could state: "With respect to East Europe, which has undoubtedly received its share of blood group B, largely by direct route from Central Asia, Southeast Europe exhibits fewer elements of Eastern blood."[66] Hesch furthermore emphasized the importance of blood group research for political objectives, as well as for biological research into racial entities (*Volkskörper*) and for the cultural study of national characters (*Volkstumsforschung*). Thus he pointed out that the lower proportion of blood group B among Transylvanian Saxons, compared to Hungarians, Szeklers, and Romanians, would prove that the Saxons had hardly mixed with non-German populations settling in their vicinity.[67] Thereafter, Hesch would not pursue his interest in southeastern Europe any further, instead he concentrated on issues related to the occupation of Poland. He would make his further career in the SS Race and Settlement Main Office, where he was to train examiners of "racial aptitude," that is, persons who had the power to decide whether Polish children would be eligible for Germanization.[68]

Compared to the approaches of Reche and Fischer, who concentrated on genetics (*Erbbiologie*), Egon von Eickstedt in Breslau advocated methods that were more oriented toward anthropometric parameters, whereby classical craniometrics were enhanced by a subtle selection of additional measurements and indices as well as by the attempt to capture mental "race characteristics." By doing so, Eickstedt and his circle nevertheless toed the line of National Socialist racial doctrine.[69] What is more, their classical approach made it possible for anthropologists from southeastern Europe itself, such as Božo Škerlj (1904–1961) and Branimir Maleš (1897–1968) from Yugoslavia, as well as Metodi Popov (1881–1954) from Bulgaria, to appear as contributors in Eickstedt's journal *Zeitschrift für Rassenkunde* (*Journal of Racial Science*). The contacts with and the participation of experts from southeastern Europe suggested a scholarly exchange on equal terms. However, it was clear that German *Rassenkunde* defined the standards of the research field and claimed to be of global (catholic) scope, with the Nordic master race on top. Southeastern European versions of racial anthropology did not have such aspirations and mostly remained on a parochial level.[70] A key representative of this school was a woman anthropologist, Ilse Schwidetzky (1907–1997), who studied the previously mentioned process of *Entnordung* (the loss of Nordic racial elements) among the South Slavs.[71]

Within the framework of our research questions, two magazines have to be mentioned, which reached beyond academia and aimed more toward an interested general public. The first one was the periodical *Volk und Rasse* (*People and Race*), which sometimes published articles on southeastern Europe. Its editors were the Reichskomitee für öffentlichen Gesundheitsdienst (Reich Committee for Public Health Service) and the Deutsche Gesellschaft für Rassenhygiene (German Society for Racial Hygiene). In a representative 1935 article in this journal, which paid respects to Gerhard Gesemann's notion of the masculine heroic culture of the Balkans, Heinz Wülker (1910–1943), a young "racial biologist" and collaborator of Walther Darré (1895–1953), the Reich minister of Food and Agriculture and Reichsbauernführer (Reich farmers' leader), wrote about the Montenegrin pastoral warrior tribes as noteworthy elite groups, whose organization into clans and centuries-long struggle against the Turks had made them an exemplary breed.[72] The second journal was *Volkstum im Südosten* (*Nationality and Folklore in the Southeast*), which was published in Vienna and specifically dealt with affairs in southeastern Europe. In its pages, the focus was mainly on völkisch ideology, but racial issues were addressed, too. For example, after the German attack on Yugoslavia, Egon Lendl (1906–1989), a geographer from Salzburg, repeatedly picked up the theses of the Gothic and Iranian descent of the Croats as they were propagated by the Ustaša government in the Independent State of Croatia, in order to disassociate the Croatian nation from the other South Slavs.[73]

ON THE MALLEABILITY OF "RACIAL SCIENCE"

After the Second World War and the end of Nazism, all of the aforementioned anthropologists with expertise on southeastern Europe passed the process of denazification; in most cases, they were able to pursue their professional careers and to go on with racial categorization.[74] After the end of the war, Egon von Eickstedt became professor of anthropology at the University of Mainz. Together with Ilse Schwidetzky he established a new Anthropological Institute there. In 1961, Schwidetzky would inherit his university chair until her retirement in 1975. Both carried on the affirmative use of the notorious term "race" in the sense of biological essentialism—including, for Schwidetzky, in a 1979 volume she edited on the "racial history" of southeastern Europe.[75]

How can we comprehend the impact of racial science on the Balkans and its conceptual claims about the inhabitants of this region during the culmination of the Third Reich's influence on this part of Europe, namely in the first half of the 1940s? Comparing the volume of von Loesch, Mühlmann, and Küppers with the earlier work of German and Austrian anthropologists on the racial composition of the Balkans, we can observe a thin, but nonetheless visible line of tradition, starting with the examination of prisoners of war during the First World War. Apart from the exception of Viktor Lebzelter, this tradition led directly into the fields of "racial science" (*Rassenkunde*) and genetics (*Erbbiologie*), which became ideological strongholds of the Nazi doctrine in academic circles.

With respect to the Balkans, we can see that the concept of the Dinaric race, characterized by its heroism, formed an ambiguous ideological challenge that the German and Austrian advocates of the alleged Nordic master race had to address. However, we should not treat racial ideology as the most important propellant of Nazi policy toward the Balkans. The racial assessment of a nation was malleable and—as the cruel treatment of the Serbs shows—often a consequence of the resistance a nation showed against the Third Reich.[76] One should also not overestimate the role of southeastern Europe in the development of German racial science. The Balkans were not the main focus of the Third Reich's racial and spatial planning. The attack on Yugoslavia in April 1941 and the other military operations of the Wehrmacht in southeastern Europe at the time brought this part of the continent only briefly into the center of Nazi interest, before the campaign against the Soviet Union in the summer of 1941 and the mass murder of the European Jews, which affected all regions under the military control of the Third Reich, drew the Nazis' attention again to other fields of operation. While von Loesch, Mühlmann, and Küppers prepared their volume on the nations and races of southeastern Europe, the Jews of Thessaloniki and other cities of southeastern Europe were transported to the extermination camps. Within a Jew-free new Europe under Nazi rule, certain nations of southeastern Europe, like the French of the Régime de Vichy in western Europe and the Slovaks in central Europe, would be allowed to occupy a subordinate, but stable position, if they followed the völkisch principles. This was especially true of Bulgaria, Romania, and Croatia; compared to other regions of southeastern Europe, which were occupied by the Italian Army and the Wehrmacht, these three were allowed to remain as semiautonomous states dependent on the Third Reich. Von Loesch, Mühlmann, and Küppers's book was intended to codify this new situation in the region by means of racial anthropology. Due to wartime circumstances, although they could not boast regional expertise, von Loesch and Mühlmann became the main authors of this volume, instead of researchers who had been engaged in the racial anthropology of southeastern Europe in preceding years. Only Küppers had worked since the mid-1930s as a photographer in the region.

On the whole, the theses of the volume were in the service of the provisional Nazi policy in the Balkans after the German attack on Yugoslavia. If Yugoslavia, according to Adolf Hitler's wish, had submitted to the Axis after the example of Bulgaria, and the coup of March 27, 1941 and the German attack had not taken place, the political reorganization of this part of Europe by the Third Reich would have taken another path, with a compliant, authoritarian, pro-German Yugoslav state. Under such circumstances, the role of the Dinaric race would have been much more positively treated than proved to be the case. But within the factual political framework in the region that came into being after the dismemberment of the Yugoslav kingdom, German racial science instead tried to emphasize the alleged positive influence of the remnants of the Nordic race in the region; it furthermore tried to find arguments for the genetic difference between the Serbs and Croats, in order to deliver an ideological foundation for the "Independent State of Croatia" and to legitimate its mass crimes on behalf of national homogenization.

The volume by von Loesch, Mühlmann, and Küppers became an outstanding and authentic example for Nazi racial policies toward southeastern Europe, since due to the intensification of warfare, essential reduction of research, and paper rationing, other publishing endeavors of this kind came to an end in late 1943. The German crimes committed against the Jewish, Serbian, and Romani populations in the Balkans largely took place without involvement of the racial experts discussed here. Some of them were nevertheless engaged with their racial anthropological expertise in Nazi deportation and extermination policies elsewhere, namely in Poland, Czechoslovakia, and the Soviet Union.

CHAPTER 4

"MY LIFE FOR PRINCE EUGENE"

History and Nazi Ideology in Banat German Propaganda in World War II

MIRNA ZAKIĆ

The French-born Habsburg general Eugene of Savoy (1663–1736) fought in a succession of wars against France and the Ottoman Empire, starting with the Siege of Vienna in 1683 and culminating in the conquest of Belgrade in 1717. He also distinguished himself as an administrator, head of the Imperial War Council, and patron of the arts. His campaigns to wrest control of Wallachia, the Banat, the Bačka, and Belgrade from the Ottomans expanded Habsburg territory and increased Habsburg influence in southeastern Europe. Eugene and the governor he selected for the Banat, Count Claude Florimond de Mercy (1666–1734), shored up these conquests through the expansion of the Military Border and the organized settlement of German-speakers from central Europe, as well as Serbs, Romanians, and others, in order to tie the Banat and neighboring areas to the Habsburg Empire through economy, administration, and military security.[1]

The historian Charles Ingrao echoed some of the panegyrics written in Eugene of Savoy's honor by proponents of the Habsburg imperial legacy and descendants of the German-speaking settlers who colonized the southeast, when he described Eugene as a brilliant and multifaceted military leader. However, Ingrao also placed Eugene's Balkan conquests within the context of eighteenth-century continental power politics and argued that the territorial expansion in the southeast had been a somewhat lesser priority for the Habsburg Empire than the contemporaneous show of strength in western Europe. Only with the balance of power vis-à-vis the French relatively secure was the empire able to focus on pushing back the Ottomans in the southeast, in what would prove to be the only war in three centuries in which the Habsburg Empire won a clear-cut victory without significant help from an ally.[2]

Far from following a single-minded goal of imperial expansion across the centuries, the complex and sometimes-haphazard accretion of territories under the rule of the House of Habsburg better befitted the moniker of "accidental empire."[3] While Eugene of Savoy's Balkan campaigns were the result of extensive planning to secure the empire's southern border, they also demonstrated the unpredictable long-term consequences of policies of imperial expansion. The twentieth-century descendants of the German-speakers, whom Eugene wanted settled in the southeast, interpreted their historic presence in the region as a part of a long-term, nationalist, *völkisch* program of national and racial consolidation.

While the Nazis' instrumentalization of scholarship and history to justify their racial policies and plans for Europe is well-known,[4] the case of Eugene of Savoy's reputation among the ethnic Germans (Volksdeutsche) in southeastern Europe illustrates the latter's ability to interpret Nazi ideology in ways that furthered Nazi goals but also supported the ethnic Germans' own communal sense of self as a German minority. Eugene's posthumous fortunes revealed the tensions evident in German nationalism between region and nation-state, between *Heimat* in the narrow sense of one's area of residence and the broader sense of national home, and between conceptions of national belonging emanating from a Nazified Germany and those embraced by German minorities in other countries.[5]

With reference to this volume's major themes of migration, memory, and German imperialism in the Balkans by means of both trade and warfare, Nazi propaganda could and did claim continuity with the colonization project that Eugene of Savoy had spearheaded. While German imperial incursion into the region in the twentieth century may have been new in the aftermath of earlier Habsburg and Ottoman incursions, Eugene of Savoy's later reputation shows how the Habsburg legacy could be molded and (mis)remembered so as to justify German claims over the Balkans. As to ethnic German invocation of Eugene's name and legacy, his centrality to their historical mythologizing allowed the Banat Germans specifically to connect their historical experience and home area—on which the German state created in 1871 could not lay even the most tenuous claim—with the supposed racial unity and historical continuity of the German Volk in which they claimed membership.

In 1918, the historic Banat region of the defunct Austro-Hungarian Empire was split between Romania and Serbia. In the period between the western, Serbian Banat's occupation by German forces in April 1941 and its liberation in October 1944, the ethnic Germans of this region engaged in many forms of collaboration with the Nazis. Although they were only 20 percent of the Serbian Banat's population, the Banat Germans enjoyed a position of relative privilege under Nazi rule and administered and policed their home area on the Third Reich's behalf. They made significant economic contributions to the Nazi war effort. They actively participated in the persecution of the Jews, Roma, and Serbs, as well as the Aryanization of Jewish property in the Banat. Starting in spring 1942, they were recruited into the Waffen-SS division "Prinz Eugen" and took part in brutal anti-partisan operations in Serbia proper, Bosnia, and Croatia. Finally, Banat German leaders spearheaded the official Nazification of education and public discourse in their home region.

Eugene of Savoy featured prominently in print propaganda and speeches by leaders of this ethnic German minority. The Banat Germans' Nazified version of their own past, with Eugene of Savoy as a central figure, instrumentalized history in order to convey the notion of a unified, racialized, eternal German Volk, defined by the same parameters in the eighteenth as in the twentieth centuries. The Banat Germans tried to fit their historical experiences into the broader patterns of European and German history, while retaining their self-image as a community related to yet separate from that of Germans from the Reich (Reichsdeutsche). The rhetoric about Eugene of Savoy as the "father of their homeland," the model for a Waffen-SS division created specifically for the Banat Germans, and a historic trailblazer on par with Adolf Hitler allowed the Banat Germans to claim a place in the Nazi New Order as both Germans and *Banat* Germans.

THE GREAT MAN IN HISTORY AND THE "GERMAN" EMPIRE'S BORDERS

Eugene of Savoy held a central position in the romanticized historical memory of the Banat Germans before, during, and even after the Nazi period. Rather than a servant and champion of a multiethnic empire, Eugene—in the narratives of his life and achievements peddled by Banat German propaganda—stood out as the quintessential great man in history, unfettered by the historical and ideological context of his time, a self-made and self-perpetuating genius sprung fully formed from the accumulated legacy of his Germanic ancestry. "His life was a long chain of great victories," ran a typical bit of breathless praise.[6] Far from being just one of his many successes on behalf of the empire, Eugene's conquests and endorsement of colonization of the southeast by German-speakers were extolled as his most important and glorious achievements, a living legacy for the later-day Germans in the southeast to nurture and live up to. Moreover, Eugene occupied a pinnacle in the historical development of the German people, preceded as well as followed by periods of alleged decadence and stagnation, yet also heralding the inevitable future rise of the Germans to renewed greatness—under the leadership of Adolf Hitler as another authentic, historic genius.

In short, in ethnic German memory Eugene of Savoy was not merely an important historical figure. Rather, his stature approached that of a folk hero: invincible, incorruptible, and wise, truly fortune's favorite. A history textbook written for use in Banat German schools during the occupation actually described him as the "last great folk hero [*Volksheld*]" of the First Empire.[7]

This adulation of Eugene's legacy predated the Nazi period. The anonymously composed "Song of Prince Eugene" ("Prinz-Eugen-Lied"), first recorded in 1719, which recounts the 1717 Siege of Belgrade in the tradition of heroic verse, referred to Eugene as the "noble knight"—a grandiose moniker suggestive of belonging to a long tradition of military prowess and nobility of spirit.[8] In ethnic German folktales, the Habsburg general featured as a messianic figure bringing the promise of salvation to a land overrun by Turkish heathens. He shared the hard life of his men on campaign and set an example for them with his martial zeal. Like Moses, he opened springs of fresh water in a swampy, pestilential landscape. He and his armies enjoyed God's special grace as they survived grave misfortunes and slaughtered the enemy by the tens of thousands.[9]

By the early years of the twentieth century, Eugene's legacy had gained a nationalist dimension. Echoing the nationality politics in the Dual Monarchy, the "Song of the Banat Germans" ("Banater Schwabenlied"[10]) by the Romanian German poet Adam Müller-Guttenbrunn portrayed German-speaking colonists in the southeast as inheritors of Eugene's military glory; as hardworking peasants, who transformed a devastated region into a blooming, peaceful Eden; and as champions of German nationalism in the face of Hungarian assimilationist pressure.[11] Whereas Eugene's colonization project had been intended to further the dynastic influence of the House of Habsburg, this later interpretation depicted the supposedly eternal German nation extending its sway and preserving its uniqueness in foreign lands.

In the Nazi period, especially during the wartime occupation of the Banat, ethnic German propaganda built on this mythology surrounding Prince Eugene. Writers from both the Serbian and the Romanian Banat as well as writers from the Third Reich deployed a trope from the "Song of Prince Eugene" and routinely described him as the "noble knight"[12]: role model, precursor, and pinnacle, all at once. The ethnic German community in occupied Belgrade was organized officially into County (Kreis) "Prinz Eugen." The 225th anniversary of Eugene's final expulsion of the Ottomans from the region in 1717 was celebrated with great pomp in 1942. The following year, an ethnic German cast performed a play about the Habsburg general's Balkan campaigns, written by a member of the Waffen-SS division "Prinz Eugen," at the National Theater in Belgrade.[13]

Propaganda posited Eugene of Savoy as a model for all toiling and fighting Germans in the Danube region. The two centuries that separated the Banat Germans from Eugene's time were bridged in rhetorical flights of fancy, which suggested that the intervening years mattered less than the greatness, which the ethnic Germans of the early 1940s borrowed from the "father of our homeland," who "stands at the beginning of our history."[14] Neatly eliding the complex ethnic and cultural history of the Balkans, ethnic German propaganda claimed that the region's true history began with Eugene and the settlement of German-speakers, who colonized it (in both the physical and the cultural sense) in the 1700s, bringing civilization to what had been a wilderness of backward people or a wholly depopulated land.

Propaganda claimed that Prince Eugene's victorious campaigns in the southeast won him an indelible place in the annals of history. Josef "Sepp" Janko, the Nazified ethnic German leader (*Volksgruppenführer*) in occupied Serbia and the Banat, stressed in his speeches that Eugene had been the "first [field] marshal of the empire" ("*erster Marschall des Reiches*"), making him sound like a Nazi general more than a Habsburg imperial commander.[15] The ethnic German county leader (*Kreisleiter*) in occupied Belgrade, Christian Brücker asserted that Eugene's expulsion of the Ottomans had accomplished nothing short of the salvation of the empire and earned him a place as "one of the greatest generals in the history of the German Volk."[16]

Hyperbole and provincial myopia went hand in hand as Nazified ethnic Germans developed a narrative that placed them and their historical experience at the center of major, continent-spanning events, rather than relegating them to the periphery of both the defunct Habsburg Empire and Adolf Hitler's plans for the future of Europe. Some Reich Germans who wrote about the ethnic Germans in the Danube region tapped into the same rhetorical vein. One triumphal narrative of the "German" Banat's history and its 1941 "return to the Reich" called Eugene: "one of the greats of German history. . . . [T]his inventive soldier and politician . . . hounded—in the name of the emperor of the erstwhile Holy Roman Empire of the German Nation—the Turks out of Europe and thereby dealt, at the same time, a blow to arrogant France, which was in league with the Turks. Thus did Prince Eugene's deeds attain world-historical significance."[17]

Eugene's putative greatness stemmed not only from his military prowess and the common touch, which ensured his men loved him and followed his commands with joy as well as dutifulness,[18] but also from his vision for the future of southeastern Europe and its ties to the Germanic heartland. Eugene's persuasive argument in favor of settling loyal imperial subjects from central Europe in the southeast, to cultivate the land and fortify the Habsburg Empire's new southern border, was reinterpreted to better suit later ideas about German history and German national identity.

The concept of *Reichsidee* (imperial idea), which encompassed justifications for territorial expansion, the divine right of monarchs, and the civilizing benefits of imperial rule, gained a new lease on life as Nazified scholars and propagandists—ethnic German and Reich German alike—used it to connect the imperial past with the Nazi present. If the *Reichsidee* had been Eugene's "guiding star and signpost" and its realization Eugene's role in history,[19] then it was no dusty remnant of a dead past. In 1943, the Austrian historian Heinrich von Srbik argued that Eugene's *Reichsidee* remained relevant to the present and the future, as a resurrection of the old imperial ties between Vienna and Budapest and as a model for the New Order in Europe, thus eliding differences between Habsburg imperial government and Nazi (and Hungarian) domination in the wartime Balkans.[20]

What had Eugene's armies fought for? To what purpose had they expelled the Ottomans from territories north of the Danube and from Belgrade? According to the Nazified version of history, Eugene's armies had fought to save Europe, Christendom, and Western civilization itself from the backward, Oriental, Muslim Turks.[21] In line with narrative tropes characteristic of the Nazi worldview, the Habsburg Empire had been in every sense a *German* empire, albeit plagued by external threats and internal corruption and impoverishment. The French-born Eugene was its effective ruler thanks to his natural charisma, his ease with the sword, and his skill in popular government.[22] He reclaimed the empire's destined greatness and set in motion events that led to the long-term arrival of German settlers and, hence, the extension of the natural, if not always the political, borders of Germany.

Sometimes these ideologically inflected accounts of the past briefly tended toward historical veracity, such as when they acknowledged that Eugene's plans for the newly conquered territories included their being placed under the rule of the court in Vienna, rather than the Kingdom of Hungary. However, far from wanting the southeast ruled from Vienna due to some putative proto-nationalism, Eugene wished to secure these territories as the "most extreme border and bulwark of all Christendom"[23] and of the Habsburg Empire,[24] not some imagined, racially-defined Germany coterminous with the empire.

More often, Nazified history tended to equate the empire with Europe and with German nationalism as understood by the Nazis. All three were contrasted with the supposedly alien Turkish (Ottoman) presence expelled from a region over which it had held no natural claim and on which it had left no permanent trace. Christian Brücker insisted that the "German sword" and "German reforms"—military conquest followed by peaceful government—had taken other Balkan peoples under their protection and rescued their national characters from foreign influence by bringing them back to the European fold.[25] When the news of his victories against the Ottomans spread, a "wave of elation and joy swept through Europe, [and] the knight Prince Eugene was seen as the savior of all civilized mankind,"[26] wrote Brücker.

The lip service paid to eighteenth-century "Germans" as protectors and champions of oppressed ethnic groups and to Eugene of Savoy's own understanding of his mission in the southeast as military, imperial, and Christian (Catholic) was folded into anachronistic exaltation of his campaigns as a comprehensive, German triumph. In his account of Danube German history, Hans Diplich, the wartime headmaster of the German-language lyceum in the Banat town of Bela Crkva / Weisskirchen, insisted that Eugene's conquest of the northern Balkans was tantamount to a purely German victory since the "Habsburg emperor was also the German emperor," for the "people recognized in him [Eugene] the uncrowned, secret emperor."[27] Diplich further argued that the subsequent colonization of the area transformed the urban landscape of Timişoara / Temeschburg and Belgrade into German cities, civilized and made prosperous the countryside, and turned the whole area into a so-called bulwark of Christendom in German hands: "The whole Middle Danube region gained a German stamp through the deeds of settlers in the Southeast, which Prince Eugene had planned and introduced. German became the trade language of the whole Balkans. Thus what took place here was, in the best sense of the word, an all-German achievement. German soldiers conquered the land, German peasants and burghers colonized it, and German border troops occupied the gateway to Turkish lands."[28]

In language reminiscent of imperialist narratives that erased or downplayed the importance and, even, the presence of people other than the conquerors, this passage drew together several threads which run through Nazified narratives about Eugene and his legacy: the notion that the region's true history began with the permanent "German" presence in the eighteenth century; the identification of the Habsburg imperial project with a nationalist and, even, racial definition of Germanness; and the exaltation of both military conquest and colonization as the twentieth-century ethnic Germans' inheritance, tantamount to a civilizing influence in a savage land.

Sepp Janko echoed these sentiments in many of his speeches, usually while emphasizing the ethnic Germans' martial heritage as a direct link to the events of Eugene's time. Banat German propaganda touted the ideal of the ethnic German as not merely a peasant (*Bauer*), but a peasant-soldier (*Bauer-Soldat, Wehrbauer*), harkening back to the ethnic Germans' erstwhile role on the Habsburg Military Border. Janko produced the following biased account of the founding of the Military Border:

> Prince Eugene was the one who realized that one of the most dangerous portals for invasion out of the East must be closed once and for all in this very area, in order to preserve the Reich from further attacks. Therefore, he strove to have peasants settled here, peasants who knew how to use both plow and sword. . . . He knew that only German peasants could be settled in such a polluted region, menaced by enemies from within and from without, the very peasants who made this land into what it is today—the granary of Europe.[29]

In this account, the noble knight of mythologized history became an early precursor of the Nazi project to unite all racial Germans in a Greater Reich, while colonization for the purpose of securing the new borders of the Habsburg Empire in the 1700s was tied directly to Nazi efforts to rearrange Europe's ethnic map in accordance with their racist ideas. The ambiguous position of multiethnic regions like southeastern Europe in the Nazi worldview overlapped uneasily and imperfectly with this deliberately anachronistic, ideologically inflected interpretation of past events.

FROM EUGENE TO HITLER

While Count Mercy was often ranked as Eugene's equal in terms of administrative skill and strength of vision for what the southeast could become under "German" leadership, Eugene of Savoy took pride of place in ethnic German memory as conqueror, visionary, and trailblazer.[30] Panegyrics to Eugene's achievements routinely referred to his conquests in the southeast as the beginning of the Banat Germans' own history.[31]

Nazis from the Reich dreamed of a Germanic east as the crucible in which German racial greatness would be tested, proven, and secured.[32] In Nazified Banat propaganda, as the settlers moved from central Europe to its outskirts and worked hard for generations, changing a neglected, pestilential landscape of morasses and uncultivated wilderness (the legacy of the supposedly backward Ottoman reign), they were themselves transformed into a stronger, hardier, somehow more German people. Christian Brücker painted an idyllic picture of an orderly, fruitful, very German landscape and people as the inheritors of those hardy colonists:

> Our ancestors were a hard and hardworking sort. They shrank from neither hardship nor death, but knew only their work and their duty. They asserted themselves through harsh struggle and made a beautiful homeland [*Heimat*] for their descendants. Across the Sava and the Danube, where fertile fields stretch as far as the eye can see, where German villages with straight streets and smart houses festoon the broad flatlands, where our peasants stride across the fields with vigilance and care as the eternal guardians of our soil, where our German customs rule and our German songs ring out, here is the Danube Swabians' homeland, the legacy of the great prince.³³

Brücker's rhetoric echoed an oft-quoted proverb, which summed up the ethnic German narrative of ancestral suffering, struggle, and triumph: "For the first [generation, there was only] death; for the second, hardship; for the grandchildren only—bread."³⁴

On more than one occasion, Sepp Janko emphasized the image of bread as both nourishment and achievement for ethnic German peasants, both essential foodstuff and symbol of their rootedness in the soil. Furthermore, he denied that the German settlers initially had been alien to the region which they colonized, by claiming that they had merely moved from one part of the empire to another, again blurring all distinctions between the Habsburg era and the Nazi view that every place with an ethnic German presence could be claimed for the expanded German Reich. Janko implicitly likened German-speaking settlers of the 1700s to the ethnic Germans resettled in Hitler's "empire" in the 1900s. Moreover, Janko asserted the Banat Germans' preeminent claim on their home area, at the expense of all other groups, implying that the Germans alone had done the hard work and borne the sacrifices of making the Banat the fruitful area it eventually became:

> Our ancestors, who came once to this area, did not move to a strange land as emigrants [*Aussiedler*] from the empire, no, they merely resettled from one part of the empire to another. They turned deserted soil into fertile fields, and the bread, which has grown through their sour sweat from this earth ever since, was and is German bread. This is so, whether others try to claim otherwise or no. They [the settlers] did not come here to eat foreign bread, but to make [their own] bread. Thus, even today, no one can claim that our Volksgruppe here eats other than German bread.³⁵

On another occasion, Janko suborned biblical metaphor to the service of Nazi rhetoric, when he referred to Eugene as the "bread giver . . . we have him to thank that we have our daily bread [*Brotgeber . . . ihm danken wir es, dass wir unser tägliches Brot haben*]."³⁶ Another text described the Petrovaradin / Peterwardein fortress by the Bačka city of Novi Sad /

Neusatz as "'Petros,' a rock in the tossing sea of ethnicities," upon which Austrian rule over the southeast was built.[37]

The Banat Germans claimed that Eugene belonged, in a sense, more to them than to any other part of the Volk, "as not merely a great general and wise statesman, but first and foremost as liberator and father of our homeland."[38] His deeds in the southeast marked the pinnacle of Habsburg/German imperial power, after which followed a long period of decline, in line with the Nazi obsession with perceived racial and national weakness and the need for rebirth.

Underlining the ways in which Nazi ideology shaped ethnic German historical memory, Janko claimed in a 1942 speech: "[The colonization of the southeast] was an all-German achievement and meaningful as such. . . . For Prince Eugene, the empire was a natural whole in the center of Europe, shaped by nature and by destiny. Austria could only fulfill the empire's European tasks when it held the leadership position in the empire."[39] Janko went on to argue that even later colonization waves, which occurred in the reigns of Maria Theresa (1717–1780) and Joseph II (1741–1790), happened haphazardly, without a unifying vision, so that the colonists gradually lost contact with the Germanic heartland and the rest of the Volk, the "all-German community of destiny [*Schicksalsgemeinschaft aller Deutschen*]."[40]

According to Janko, only the fact that they were peasants with close ties to the soil prevented the further erosion of the Banat Germans' communal sense of self as a part of this greater community of Germans. They were Germans rooted in the (German) soil, which belonged to them by dint of both nature and hard work. The promise that racial greatness would be reclaimed allegedly came true with Nazi Germany's rise to a dominant position in Europe, which marked both the recovery of the special destiny shared by the ethnic Germans—Eugene's "children"— and a renewed impetus for them to prove their Germanness.

During the war, the walls of the soldiers' rest home in the Banat town of Pančevo / Pantschowa were decorated with scenes from the romanticized version of ethnic German history: from Eugene's triumphant campaign, through the arrival of the first settlers, to the unification of the roles of peasant and soldier during the Military Border's existence. The last mural showed three generations of an ethnic German family standing in a freshly plowed field: an old man, his adult son eagerly saluting a recruitment officer on horseback, and the little grandson saluting like his father. The painting illustrated the proverb about the three generations needed to transform a pestilential wasteland into a fertile, cultivated landscape, and drew a parallel between the continuity of the seasons in a peasant's life and the continuity between generations. Overlooking all was a portrait of Adolf Hitler, symbolically bringing the ethnic Germans full circle, back to the German Reich.[41]

The advent of Nazism was supposed to be the high point of ethnic German historical development, greater even than the inception of their historical presence in the southeast in the wake of Eugene's campaigns. Sepp Janko assured his conationals that they could lay their collective fate safely in Hitler's hands.[42] In 1943, the Banat German daily newspaper, the *Banater Beobachter*, reported on the celebration of the Nazi regime's tenth anniversary in the village of Kačarevo / Franzfeld: "The residents of Franzfeld have shown yet again . . . *how great their love is for the man who was and is our rescuer and liberator, who guides with determination and a sure hand the fortunes of the German people, and leads us all into a new and better future* [emphasis in the original]."[43]

Eugene of Savoy and Adolf Hitler served as the two signposts of historical continuity in the Nazified version of Banat German history, the past and the future united: rescuers and liberators, military leaders and conquerors, the one having made possible the settlement of German-speakers in the Banat, while the other led them to political and military triumph. Ethnic Germans were supposed to feel an especially strong connection to Hitler, who had lived outside Germany's borders and was, therefore, meant to understand the issues facing ethnic Germans. Speaking in 1942, on the occasion of Hitler's fifty-third birthday, Sepp Janko did not dare to go so far as to claim Hitler himself belonged to the ranks of the Volksdeutsche, but Janko did assert that Hitler at Germany's helm meant even more to ethnic Germans than to Reich Germans, since the former's need of him was implied to be greater.[44]

Hans Diplich embraced hyperbole when he claimed that, of all the Germans, those living on the Middle Danube retained the purest and clearest "consciousness of the all-German mission."[45] He urged the ethnic German pupils studying their history in school to bear in mind the ways in which their past, present, and future were connected, confirming the greatness that he claimed was naturally theirs as well as urging them to prove themselves worthy of that greatness: "Prince Eugene's achievement stands at the very beginnings of the Danube Germans. More recently, he was the source of a new awareness of the German task in the Southeast. We have become the heirs and the bearers of this task."[46]

Other ethnic German authors also tied Eugene's achievements and legacy to the Nazi regime, with varying degrees of explicitness. They claimed that Germany's new rise to greatness made remembrance of past greatness easier,[47] or that the two meanings of the word *Reich* as both the lost empire and the Nazi regime redoubled the necessity for ethnic

Germans in the southeast to secure the Reich's borders once and for all against incursion by foreign elements.[48]

Reich Germans too linked the Banat's place in Hitler's Europe to Eugene of Savoy's imperial colonization project, interpreted as an early attempt at consolidating the German Volk. A German Foreign Ministry memo from November 1942 stated: "[T]he importance of the former 'Austrian Military Border' . . . cannot be overlooked in the politics of the Reich. Following the rebuilding of the Greater German Reich, the historico-political means used by Reich Marshal Prince Eugene regarding the incorporation of Southeast Europe into Greater Central Europe seem particularly pertinent."[49] A few months earlier in 1942, Ulrich Greifelt, the chief of staff of the Reich Commissariat for the Strengthening of Germandom (one of the major offices within Heinrich Himmler's bailiwick, in charge of remaking the ethnic and political map of Europe along Nazi racial principles), credited early efforts at German colonization of the east and southeast to the campaigns of Frederick II and Eugene of Savoy, "who opened up new settlement areas for German peasants in the Southeast through his feats of arms."[50]

Yet Reich Germans were in no doubt as to which historical figure came first in the ranks of great men in German history. Greifelt wrote: "But it was the Führer's work and [great] idea that first imbued the timeless German task in the East with a new meaning and a youthful strength. For the first time in history, this task will advance out of the Volk's imagination, in order to lead to a final solution [*einer endgültigen Lösung*] with the Volk and for the Volk."[51]

For the Reich Germans, Eugene of Savoy was but a harbinger of Hitler's coming. For the ethnic Germans, Eugene was a hero of particular importance and Hitler's historic peer.

Nazi rhetoric acclaimed the manifold roles played by the eighteenth-century colonists and their descendants in the southeast—as peasants, colonizers, producers of food for the German armed forces in World War II, racial kin to Reich Germans—and in the course of the war, Banat German collaboration with the Third Reich took many forms: economic, administrative, policing, and persecution of the few Banat Jews and the legalized plunder of their property.[52] Yet one aspect of their legacy and experience eventually proved more important than all the others: namely, the military service they could render to the Third Reich, in a secondary theater of war, for which the troops much needed in the Soviet Union could not be spared. Spring 1942 saw the formation of the 7th Volunteer Mountain Division "Prinz Eugen" of the Waffen-SS, into which most able-bodied Banat German men were conscripted, and which was deployed in anti-partisan operations in Serbia proper, Croatia, and Bosnia in 1942–1945. Composed predominantly of Balkan ethnic Germans, it was both unique and anomalous within the Waffen-SS as a whole.[53]

Ethnic German propaganda played up the historical and ideological connections and parallels between the settlers and border soldiers of Eugene's era and the ethnic German soldiers in Hitler's war.[54] "Your ancestors' work in the German Danube region is a major achievement of German blood," intoned *Volksdeutsche Stunde*, a regular German-language propaganda program on Radio Belgrade. "[W]e do not scoff at foreign peoples, we have simply never underestimated our enemies, and have always faced them like true knights."[55]

This Banat German narrative depicted the ethnic Germans as an idealized community of peasants and soldiers (or peasant-soldiers) and the centerpiece of Hitler's plans for the future German colonization of the east (and southeast). The Banat Germans thus allegedly continued and preserved both Eugene's mission to secure the racial as well as the political borders of the German Reich *and* the ethnic Germans' cherished notion of Eugene's Balkan campaigns as the paramount aspect of his service to the Habsburg Empire and their own military service as central to the Nazi war effort in Europe.

Possibly the most elaborate depiction of this historical elision—leaping over two hundred years of intervening history, from Eugene to Hitler, from border soldiers to Waffen-SS soldiers, both pioneers and representatives of an eternal Germandom, unified by blood, destiny, and uniforms worn on behalf of a German Reich in all its guises, sanctified by both God and Volk—can be found in the Nazified version of the "Song of Prince Eugene." The new lyrics set to the old tune are worth quoting in their entirety:

> To a land, an unknown,
> Unnamed land without people,
> Prince Eugene was once sent.
> With his army, he defeated
> All the enemies who were there,
> And made a new, German land.
>
> Settlers came to the Southeast,
> To stand here at their posts,
> As the farthest watch of the Reich.
> German will then accomplished
> What no other could before:
> A new homeland for our people [*Volk*].

But the others [*Fremden*] wished
That we would raise our children
In a spirit that would ruin us.
But we fought against this,
We have always sung German [songs],
Defiant, as a true master should.

Enduring through this long struggle,
We have had the good fortune
To become again frontline soldiers.
Once much-lauded border soldiers and peasants,
The Führer has shown us
What the times demand of us.

Now we make a pledge,
Mustered all together,
Eternal love to this land.
Adolf Hitler, we pledge to thee
Today a new oath of loyalty
As Prince Eugene's soldiers![56]

The "Prinz Eugen" division's predominantly ethnic German recruits, its name and the odal rune chosen as its emblem, the propaganda content to which its men were exposed, and even the practice of allowing the men home leave at harvest time all served to affirm the connection between the figure of the "noble knight," the recruits' peasant *Heimat*, and the *Grenzer* (border soldiers) tradition of the eighteenth-century colonists.[57] In the field, "Prinz Eugen" distinguished itself by its brutal persecution of civilians suspected of harboring resistance members. This was a deliberate tactic decreed by the division commander, the Romanian ethnic German and SS lieutenant general Arthur Phleps, who insisted that a Slavic population unwilling and unable to pay the odal rune the proper respect and submit to its rule deserved no mercy, but rather violent retribution.[58] The division participated in numerous massacres and thus cemented in the minds of its surviving victims the culpability of all those who identified as Germans for the Third Reich's criminal violence.[59]

AFTER 1945

In the aftermath of the Third Reich's defeat and the mass expulsion and flight of ethnic Germans from eastern and southeastern Europe, Eugene of Savoy as military leader, pioneer of colonization, and proto-Nazi was reinterpreted again in exculpatory writings produced by ethnic German expellees in West Germany. As Nazi anti-communism was transformed into Cold War anti-communism and the so-called lost German territories in the east and southeast became loci of sentimental attachment and implicit historical and moral vindication, expellees were able to claim a place for themselves in the postwar narrative of German suffering, which both acknowledged and dodged responsibility for Nazi crimes.[60]

Even those expellee works that made the most explicit references to the Waffen-SS division "Prinz Eugen," and claimed a share in the historical Eugene's glory, tended to appeal coyly to a superhuman justice for final judgment on the division's legacy, implying that it deserved treatment separate from and more favorable than the Nazi regime as a whole.[61] The expellees wished to see themselves as innocent of any involvement in Nazi crimes, despite their wartime agency and active collaboration. They portrayed their postwar mistreatment and loss of their ancestral homes as particularly unjust. When their narratives of ethnic German history echoed Nazi-era descriptions of Ottoman rule in southeastern Europe as fundamentally alien to European (Western, German) civilization and the Ottomans as violators of the innocent, implicitly Germanic Banat, these dramatic descriptions evoked the distant past but also reflected more recent experiences: the violence which Soviet troops and Communist resistance members in Yugoslavia had inflicted on the ethnic Germans at war's end.[62]

Sometimes expellee narratives downplayed Eugene's role in the settlement of German-speakers on the Habsburg Empire's borders.[63] More often, they repeated the same old tropes about the noble knight, the epoch-making man in history, the military genius and shrewd administrator who had made two hundred years of German life in the southeast possible.[64]

The most striking change was evident in the expellee perspective on Eugene's goals with regard to conquest and colonization of the Balkans. Overtly rejecting politically sensitive references to Volk, eternal Germandom, and blood, soil, and destiny, expellee authors insisted that Eugene's loyalties had been imperial and religious, devoted to the defense of the West, albeit still in service to a "German emperor."[65]

Sepp Janko's memoirs, written in exile in Argentina, continued to emphasize the preeminent role Germans had played in protecting, cultivating, and dying in defense of the Balkans—yet Janko also contradicted his wartime record with a bit of sophistry, claiming that Eugene and Mercy had seen colonization by German-speakers and other ethnicities as a "tool of population policy, not Volk policy."[66] Paradoxically, this interpretation hewed somewhat closer to the reality of Eugene's worldview and motivations, but it was inspired less by a newly discovered desire for historical objectivity than by the need, in the brave new postwar world, to whitewash, conceal, and reject erstwhile collaboration with the defeated Nazis.

After World War II, Eugene became the champion of a "large, supranational empire . . . reaching from the Adriatic to the Belt, from the Mosel to the Carpathians. The Savoyard did not desire a nation-state, for thinking in narrowly national terms was foreign to him, but an empire under the emperor in Vienna as the protector of Christendom."[67] The parallel was obvious between this vision of Habsburg imperial power and the German national anthem, the "Deutschlandlied" ("Song of Germany"), which describes a Germany dreamed up by nineteenth-century nationalists, stretching from the Tyrol to the Fehmarn Belt and from the Meuse (Mosel) to the Neman.[68] The rhetoric looped in on itself, affirming German nationalism and the idea of a Germany embracing the whole organic unity of its people scattered among several post-1945 states, while also seeming to deny any connection with the Nazi attempt to craft a Greater German Reich.

Expellees idealized and willfully misinterpreted their historical record as identical with the Christian West and the defense thereof, and with a continued desire to see their nationalist dreams of belonging to an expanded Germany realized.[69] Thwarted in the latter since the expulsions, they stressed the former, with the added benefit of presenting themselves as victims of an eternal, Slavic savagery in its newest, communist guise, rather than as exponents of an eternal Germany unified by ties of language, culture, blood, (Nazi) ideology, and history. Yet their rhetoric still echoed Nazi tropes and attitudes as well as the enduring complexity of German nationalism at the crossroads of nation-state and regionalism, the Nazi legacy and (re)building a national identity in the Cold War.

The difficulty of ever fully coming to terms with the Nazi past was reflected in the ethnic German expellees' continued attachment to the figure of Eugene of Savoy, seen through the lens of later ideologies. Once fêted as a precursor to Nazism, Eugene and his legacy—even after the Nazi defeat—remained associated with the blurring of distinctions between imperial colonization and Nazi-era resettlement, dynastic loyalty and racial ideology, and military service to Kaiser and to Hitler.

CHAPTER 5

NAZI GERMANY AND THE HOLOCAUST IN THE INDEPENDENT STATE OF CROATIA, 1941-1945

MARK BIONDICH

The Axis invasion of Yugoslavia in April 1941 led to the rapid demise and partition of that state. The largest occupation entity to emerge on its territory was the Independent State of Croatia (hereafter NDH, *Nezavisna Država Hrvatska*) governed by Ante Pavelić's Ustaša movement. The NDH was a Greater Croatian state comprised of much of Croatia, all of Bosnia and Herzegovina, and the province of Sr(ij)em, but was in fact an Italo-German condominium.[1] The NDH authorities were complicit in the Holocaust and between April 1941 and the summer of 1942 possessed considerable latitude in implementing anti-Jewish measures, from legislation and economic expropriation to mass arrest, deportation, and mass murder in camps. Neither Berlin nor its representatives in the NDH shaped the overall thrust of anti-Jewish policy in the first year of the NDH's existence. Only after January 1942 did the Third Reich's European-wide Final Solution converge with the Ustaša regime's autonomous agenda into a joint genocidal enterprise.

The Holocaust in the NDH was thus shaped by multiple factors: the politics of collaboration, which in Croatia were driven by the Ustaša regime's desire to consolidate an ethnically homogeneous nation-state; native anti-Semitism and exclusionary definitions of the nation; armed resistance and insurgency, which acquired an ideological character; and the politics of occupation and of the Third Reich. As in the case of German policies in the occupied east and elsewhere in the southeast, where the image of "Jewish Bolshevism" served as an important prerequisite for German annihilation policies, a somewhat analogous situation prevailed in the NDH, where the Ustaša regime viewed Jews as agents of communism. In the context of occupation and war, which was at once an ideological conflict against communist Partisans and a struggle for the preservation of Croatian statehood at any cost, this stereotype in due course facilitated genocide. While it may appear at first glance that Ustaša compliance with the Third Reich's anti-Jewish policies was driven by the NDH's status as a satellite, in actual fact German occupation simply enabled a native anti-Semitism to become operative and ultimately genocidal.[2] Of the thirty-six thousand to thirty-nine thousand Jews in wartime Croatia, roughly thirty thousand perished in the Holocaust: among them, approximately twenty-three thousand in Croatian camps and reprisal executions, and seven thousand in Auschwitz-Birkenau.[3] And of the one million Yugoslavs who perished in the Second World War, approximately 60 percent died on the NDH's territory.[4]

THE NDH AND THE ROLE OF THE ITALO-GERMAN OCCUPATION REGIMES

On April 10, 1941, shortly after the Wehrmacht entered Zagreb, a senior Ustaša official, Slavko Kvaternik, proclaimed the NDH's establishment. As Adolf Hitler had already agreed to cede a preponderant political influence to Fascist Italy in Croatia, and since Pavelić was deemed to be Italy's protégé, Berlin quickly acknowledged the Ustaša claim to power. In Italy at the time of the Axis invasion, Pavelić was hurriedly transported with a small group of supporters to Zagreb where, Rome erroneously anticipated, he would embody Fascist Italy's interests. While the Axis powers were the NDH's midwives, the Third Reich had not prearranged the Ustaša ascent to power. Nevertheless, the NDH became an integral component of the Axis order in the former Yugoslavia. Although Fascist Italy and Nazi Germany treated the NDH as de jure a sovereign state, their forces de facto behaved like occupation armies. A demarcation line divided the country into German and Italian spheres of interest,[5] with the Italian sector further subdivided into three zones (Zones I, II, and III); the first covered those territories annexed by Italy, while II and III together encompassed the territories between Zone I and the Italo-German demarcation line. The Italian military formally exercised executive authority in Zones II and III,[6] and enforced it after September 1941 in Zone II and parts of Zone III by expelling the Ustaša militia from these areas.

The German and Italian occupation authorities pursued competing policies and often had opposing objectives. As the Partisan insurgency gained ground in fall 1941,[7] the German and Italian military authorities adopted different strategies. The Italian military, whose presence in the NDH was more pronounced than the Wehrmacht's between 1941 and 1943, provided protection to Serbs and Jews fleeing Ustaša persecution. Although Italy had supported the Ustašas since the early 1930s, Italo-Croatian relations soured with the Rome Accords (May 1941), which formalized Italy's annexation of much of Dalmatia and imposed an Italian monarch on the country. Fascist Italy exerted considerable but more limited influence in the NDH than the Third Reich, and relentlessly remained on guard against German encroachments.[8] Italian actions generated considerable animosity within the Ustaša regime, which steadily sought (and generally failed) to leverage the anti-Italian sentiments of German officials in the NDH to strengthen its own hand. The Italian military limited the scope of Ustaša activities and undermined the project of Croatian statehood.[9]

THE GERMAN POLICY OF OCCUPATION

The German sphere of influence in the NDH was larger than Italy's and encompassed the NDH's economically more developed regions. Most of Croatia's Jews lived in the German-occupied zone and its three largest cities; Zagreb (with 12,000 Jews), Sarajevo (10,000), and Osijek (2,500) together accounted for more than half the NDH's Jewish population. Apart from its embassy in Zagreb, the Third Reich maintained two consulates (in Dubrovnik and Sarajevo) and a plenipotentiary (in Mostar) who oversaw the local bauxite mines, in addition to a German military commander. Soon after the Axis partition of Yugoslavia, however, the Wehrmacht withdrew its main battle elements from the NDH in preparation for the invasion of the Soviet Union. By midsummer 1941, the Wehrmacht had fewer than eight thousand troops in the NDH, consisting largely of older, poorly trained and equipped reservists.[10] German foreign policy in the NDH was concerned primarily with securing the Reich's economic interests (raw materials such as bauxite) needed for the war effort, which required public order, stability, and the control of key lines of communication.[11] The Croatian economy was under broad German control, and the new Croatian currency, the kuna, was pegged to the reichsmark (RM) at a 20-to-1 exchange rate. In order to clear its share of Yugoslavia's debt, Croatia had to supply Germany with raw materials and pay for the upkeep of Wehrmacht units stationed in the NDH.[12] The Croatian authorities also agreed to provide more than one hundred thousand laborers to the Third Reich, a target that was exceeded by May 1942; thereafter they agreed to provide an additional fifty thousand workers.[13] The presence of Italian forces notwithstanding, the absence of a significant Wehrmacht or SS presence in the NDH initially provided the Ustaša authorities with considerable latitude. What altered matters significantly was the communist insurgency, which gradually acquired a mass character because of the Ustaša regime's murderous policy toward its Serb population. As the Italian military enforced its prerogatives in its occupation zones and pursued an accommodative policy toward the Serb nationalist resistance, by the winter of 1941–1942 much of the NDH had descended into chaos. The perilous security environment compelled greater German military involvement.

The two main German institutions in the NDH in 1941 were the Wehrmacht and the Foreign Ministry. The former was represented by the Plenipotentiary General Edmund Glaise von Horstenau. Although a critic of the Ustaša regime's Serb policy,[14] he supported its anti-Jewish measures and shared its anti-Italian views. The Wehrmacht's regional commanders, whether in the NDH or Serbia, were largely averse to the Ustaša regime and likely would have preferred a military occupation. The Wehrmacht struggled to cope with the insurgency in the NDH and attributed the blame to the violence and incompetence of the Ustaša authorities. By November 1942, the Germans had obtained Zagreb's reluctant consent to gain full control over Croatian military forces in their occupation zones.[15]

German occupation policy in the NDH was often characterized by institutional rivalry. The German ambassador, Siegfried Kasche, was pro-Ustaša, and his views often differed markedly from those of the Wehrmacht representatives. The SS and the Reich Security Main Office (RSHA), which increased their presence in the NDH beginning in 1942, were also at odds with Kasche. While Kasche worked to consolidate the Ustaša regime and assessed that domestic disorder stemmed partly from the Italian military's policies, his influence waned as his superiors viewed him as too sympathetic to the regime. The SS increasingly asserted its prerogatives in the NDH under its police attaché, SS-Sturmbannführer Hans Helm, the RSHA's representative at the German embassy in Zagreb. Apart from the Jewish question, on which they concurred, Helm and Kasche rarely saw eye to eye on the NDH's internal problems. Compounding the matter was the SS's decision to recruit forces in the NDH. The Ustaša authorities opposed the plan as an infringement on their already fragile sovereignty and were supported by Kasche, while the SS merely disregarded this opposition. By 1942, the SS operated its own units in the NDH, drawn at first primarily from ethnic Germans (*Volksdeutsche*) and after 1943 from Bosnian Muslims.[16] In March 1943, following a series of high-level meetings between the Wehrmacht, SS, and police officials, Hitler ordered the formation of a mixed German-Croatian SS police and gendarmerie to bring about the NDH's "pacification." Thereafter, the Ustaša police were placed under SS command and control; SS brigade leader and major general of police Konstantin Kammerhofer, another critic of the Ustaša regime, served as the highest SS police official in the NDH from March 1943 to May 1945.[17] The insurgency in the NDH obligated Berlin to commit ever greater military and police resources; between November 1942 and March 1943, the Croatian military and police were under German command. In September 1942, the Croatian ambassador to Berlin, Mile Budak, informed Zagreb of mounting criticism of the NDH in Berlin, which believed "that we have demonstrated too little ability in the organization of the state."[18]

Although German representatives in the NDH were often critical of the regime, Berlin undeniably contributed to the chaos in the country and was implicitly implicated in the violence. From the outset, the Ustašas were preoccupied with and determined to force a resolution of the so-called "Serb question." Guided by visions of a violent cartography of ethnic homogenization, Ustaša leaders directed the brunt of their violence at the NDH's two million Serbs. In mid-May 1941, the German Foreign Ministry noted that the Croatian government was "anxious to be able to reduce the exceedingly strong Serbian minority in Croatia."[19] On June 4, 1941, a Croato-German "resettlement" agreement was concluded, wherein the parties agreed that by October 1941 the NDH would accept 170,000 Slovenes from German-occupied Slovenia in exchange for "transferring" a corresponding number of Serbs to Serbia.[20] Two days later, Pavelić traveled to Salzburg for his first audience with Hitler. When their conversation turned to the NDH's nationality composition and the agreement to resettle nearly 350,000 people by year's end, Hitler admitted that "this type of resettlement was naturally painful at the moment, but was better than lasting harm." He pointedly remarked that "if the Croatian State was to be really stable, a nationally intolerant policy had to be pursued for fifty years."[21] Pavelić must have concluded that the German authorities would not interfere with his "nationally intolerant policy." In late June 1941, the Ustaša militia began a systematic "cleansing" of Serb-populated regions.

The German occupation authorities' assessments of the NDH's precarious security situation were occasionally clouded by their own ideological and other prejudices. While they frequently blamed the Ustašas for instigating chaos and then undermining German "pacification" efforts, many German officials, especially the large Austrian contingent that had served in the Habsburg officer corps, harbored anti-Italian views and blamed the Italian military for undermining stability. Others interpreted the violence in the NDH through their own anti-Semitic lens and even attributed blame for the escalating disorder to Jewish machinations. This only played into Pavelić's hands.[22] Even as German officials urged the Croatian authorities to moderate their anti-Serb policies in 1941–1942 and forced some senior personnel changes in the Ustaša leadership, the Reich leadership undermined these efforts. When Pavelić met with Hitler on April 27, 1943, the latter ranted about Serb treachery and seemingly vindicated the Croatian leader's positions.[23] German views of and behavior in the NDH confirm a salient point raised by Christopher

Molnar and Mirna Zakić in the introduction to this volume, namely, that even as German elites maintained derogatory perceptions of local regimes and peoples they increasingly viewed the region as an integral component of their putative "informal economic empire" and source of key raw materials.

THE HOLOCAUST IN CROATIA

For the first year of its existence, the Ustaša regime implemented anti-Jewish policies autonomously from the Third Reich. Prewar Ustaša propaganda and internal party documents had, since at least 1936, developed several anti-Semitic themes, typically characterizing Jews as foes of Croat liberation, as capitalist plutocrats and social parasites, but also increasingly as agents of international communism.[24] This last theme became by far the most salient in wartime Ustaša anti-Semitism. Although the Ustaša regime's citizenship and race laws largely borrowed from existing Nazi legislation, the legal segregation of Croatian Jews, the expropriation of Jewish property (seldom referred to as "Aryanization" in Ustaša documents, as most confiscated properties were Serb-owned), and the arrest and deportation of Jews were almost entirely in Croatian hands. Only in 1942–1943 was there extensive coordination between Zagreb and Berlin.

Notwithstanding the Ustaša authorities' considerable latitude in Jewish policy, in the first weeks of the occupation they observed and built upon the behavior of the German occupation forces, which established a new threshold for violence. In April 1941, Wehrmacht units demolished synagogues in several towns, desecrated Jewish cemeteries, and defaced several properties across the NDH. The Wehrmacht occasionally compelled Jews to perform forced labor. Already in mid-April 1941, the Gestapo seized several Jewish community offices and conducted its own arrests and interrogations of prominent Jews in Zagreb, Sarajevo, and elsewhere.[25] Jewish-owned industrial enterprises were seized for the war effort, while Jewish art collections were systematically looted.[26] Pavelić and his inner circle, who had virtually no contact with Berlin prior to April 1941 and had to determine what parameters of violence would be acceptable to the German authorities, must have realized very quickly that anti-Jewish measures would be not only tolerated but even welcomed. The Ustaša movement's anti-Semitism notwithstanding, the adoption of harsh anti-Jewish measures enabled Zagreb to ingratiate itself with Berlin and gain potential support against Italian encroachments on the NDH's sovereignty.

It is difficult to determine precisely when the Ustaša authorities decided on the systematic mass murder of their Jewish population. Ivo

Goldstein has argued that already by May 1941, a small inner circle of Ustaša leaders around Pavelić and his senior police official Eugen "Dido" Kvaternik "knew clearly what they would do with the Jews," implying that genocide was the goal.[27] Alexander Korb has suggested that for much of 1941 the Croatian authorities still presumed that Berlin was interested in a "territorial" solution to the Jewish question—as Hitler told the visiting commander of the Croatian Home Guard, Marshal Slavko Kvaternik, in late July 1941—and were keen to transfer as much of the Jewish population as possible to German-occupied territory, either in Serbia or the General Government in Poland. This "territorial" solution would have mirrored but been smaller in scope than the June 4 resettlement plan. The Croatian authorities proposed to Berlin on two occasions (October 1941, May 1942) that the NDH's Jews be resettled to German-occupied east central Europe.[28] The RSHA rejected the first proposal, as it came before the Wannsee Conference of January 20, 1942. Beginning in early 1942, however, the RSHA began coordinating with the Croatian authorities the deportation of its Jewish population to Auschwitz-Birkenau; this reflected not only the decisions reached at Wannsee but also the RSHA's concerns about Jewish flight to the Italian occupation zones.[29] According to Korb, the Ustaša regime's internal deportations of Jews should be viewed against the backdrop of its larger demographic project of national homogenization. The Ustaša regime murdered nearly two thousand Jews (one-quarter of whom were women and children) between June and mid-August 1941 at its main killing sites (Jadovno and Pag), before opening the Jasenovac camp system.[30] In September 1941, as they began deporting Jews in larger numbers to the camps, the Ustašas may have still believed in the possibility of expulsion. As the camps became the final destination for Croatia's Jews, by early 1942 the Croatian authorities decided on the annihilation of the Jewish population. At that point, Jewish women and children were deported to and systematically murdered in Stara Gradiška prison, Camp V of the Jasenovac system.[31] The deportations to Nazi-run death camps between August 1942 and May 1943 were the logical continuation of this strategy. In early 1942, the Ustašas crossed the threshold separating mass detention from systematic mass murder.[32] This was hardly a massive leap for the Ustašas, who had already employed mass violence against Serbs in 1941.

LEGAL SEGREGATION AND EXPROPRIATION

In May 1941, the Ustaša authorities created a "Jewish Section" (*Židovski odsjek*) under their police directorate in Zagreb. Originally responsible only for the capital, in September 1941 the section's mandate was extended to the entire NDH. Led by Ivica Baraković and Vilko Kühnel, it was subordinate to the Directorate of the Ustaša Police (RUR, Ravnateljstvo Ustaškog redarstva), which in turn reported to Dido Kvaternik, the head of the Directorate for Public Order and Security (RAVSIGUR, Ravnateljsvto za javni red i signurnost) and one of Pavelić's confidants. From that point until fall 1942, the Jewish Section was tasked with the coordination of all anti-Jewish measures and synchronized closely with the Ustaša Supervisory Service (UNS, Ustaška nadzorna služba), the NDH's security service overseeing the camp administration.

It was in this context that the authorities defined citizenship and provided a legal and ideological basis for the exclusion of Jews. On April 30, 1941, the Ustaša authorities issued the NDH's citizenship law,[33] which limited nationality to persons of Aryan descent; according to its ideology, the regime regarded Croats as "Aryans." As Jews were regarded as non-Aryans, they were de jure stripped of citizenship. The race law, also issued on April 30, limited Aryan status to persons "who are members of the European racial community." Article 6 provided a loophole, however: Jews who had, before April 10, 1941, served the interests of the Croat nation, "especially for its liberation," could apply for honorary Aryan status.[34] The German embassy in Zagreb estimated that, of the more than four thousand Croatian Jews who applied for honorary Aryan status, only between five hundred and six hundred received the exemption.[35] Pavelić's deputy, Ademaga Mešić, claimed in mid-1942 that he had interceded with Pavelić about granting Aryan status to a Jewish associate, but that Pavelić had told him that he had personally granted Aryan status only to about sixty Jews, mainly those with Catholic wives and children.[36] The race law was accompanied by a separate legal decree relating to "the protection of Aryan blood and honor of the Croat nation," forbidding intermarriage between Aryans and Jews, quarter-Jews (otherwise defined as Aryans), and other non-Aryans.[37] On June 4, 1941, a "Decree on the Protection of National and Aryan Culture of the Croat Nation" excluded Jews from participation in a range of cultural institutions. It was accompanied by an order that Jews had to wear yellow insignia with the letter "Ž" (*Židov*, Jew).[38] On June 5, a decree was issued vetting the racial status of public officials and members of the academic community.[39] In the words of the Croatian foreign minister, Mladen Lorković, these decrees collectively ensured that "Croat blood is protected from defilement by the Jewish race."[40] Pavelić remarked to a German journalist that "the Jewish question will be solved radically from the racial and economic viewpoints."[41] Many local officials issued auxiliary directives within the general framework of the legislation decreed by Zagreb.[42]

Between April and July 1941, following the arrest of the most prominent Jewish citizens, Ustaša officials demanded a financial contribution or ransom from the local Jewish community for their release. In late April 1941, the Ustašas arrested several prominent Jews in Zagreb, demanding five hundred kilograms (later one thousand kilograms) of gold. It is estimated that in 1941 the Jewish community of Zagreb may have paid the monetary equivalent of approximately one billion Yugoslav dinars in gold to the Jewish Section.[43] Similar ransoms were demanded in Sarajevo, Osijek, and elsewhere.[44] The Croatian authorities also issued decrees on the expropriation of Jewish property. On April 18, 1941, the Ustaša regime abolished all major business transactions involving Jews in the two months preceding the NDH's creation. A decree against sabotage empowered the authorities to confiscate businesses whose proprietors were deemed insufficiently loyal to the regime.[45] In late April 1941, the Croatian authorities formed the Office for the Renewal of the Economy within the Ministry of National Economy, which was tasked with expropriating Jewish businesses and appointing commissioners to oversee their operations. In early June 1941, Croatian Jews were ordered to register their properties with this office.[46] It was superseded on July 1 by the State Directorate for Economic Renewal[47] and on September 15, 1941, by the State Directorate for Renewal. This last entity was authorized in October 1941 to nationalize Jewish businesses and private property in the interests of the national economy.[48] In late December 1941, the expropriation process was taken over by the State Treasury's Office of Nationalized Property.[49]

The institutional chaos accompanying expropriation only confirmed its arbitrary nature. Although the Croatian Parliament's Treasury Committee assessed in April 1942 that expropriation would enable the Croatian state to generate "extraordinary revenues," conceivably running into the billions of Croatian kuna,[50] both the state treasurer, Vladimir Košak, and the director of the Office of Nationalized Property, Ante Barić, acknowledged that outright plunder by Ustaša officialdom and others had undermined the process and threatened the state's interests.[51] Nevertheless, Barić claimed that by 1942 the state had generated 600 million Croatian kuna in revenue and was still owed 2 billion by buyers. Large industrial enterprises were not sold but retained by the state.[52] A formal decree nationalizing all Jewish property in the NDH was not issued until October 30, 1942; the timing was not fortuitous, as it came when most Croatian Jews were already in Ustaša camps and the first deportations had occurred to Auschwitz-Birkenau.[53]

THE GERMAN WAR IN THE EAST AND NDH'S JEWISH POLICY

The German invasion of the Soviet Union on June 22, 1941, represented an important turning point in the intensification of the NDH's anti-Jewish measures. Pavelić's "Extraordinary Legal Decree and Command" of June 26, 1941, disseminated widely in the press and read over Croatian State Radio, explicitly accused Jews of spreading disinformation intended to "disturb" the population and implicated Jews as a fifth column.[54] Henceforth, Jews were arrested in larger groups, deported to camps, and, in some cases, executed in reprisal for acts of communist sabotage. The intensification of anti-Jewish measures and rhetoric in the summer of 1941 was linked closely to the escalation of armed insurrection and mounting disorder in the country. Pavelić remarked ominously on August 24, 1941, that the Jews "will be finally liquidated in the shortest time."[55] The tenor of the regime's rhetoric became decidedly more aggressive, with overt references in the state press to "liquidation."[56]

The Ustaša propaganda apparatus characterized the war as a struggle against "Jewish Bolshevism."[57] The German war in the east was "a struggle for the integrity of the European soil and for the soul of Europe."[58] According to the state secretary for propaganda, Josip Milković, it was a struggle for the fate of European civilization.[59] In July 1941, Pavelić issued an appeal to the Croat nation, calling for volunteers for the eastern front in a war to defend Europe from "Judeo-Bolshevik savagery."[60] In a September 1941 speech to Ustaša militiamen, Pavelić's language was laced with recurrent references to "Judeo-Bolsheviks" and "Jewish Bolshevism."[61]

THE CAMP SYSTEM: ARREST, DEPORTATION, AND MASS MURDER

The citizenship and race laws of April 30, 1941, and a host of related decrees collectively facilitated the Jewish community's exclusion from economic, social, and cultural life and marked the first step in its destruction. The majority of the NDH's Jews died not in pogroms or in massacres by roving Ustaša death squads, but in the Croatian camps. Within weeks of the NDH's formation, the authorities developed a nascent camp network. Several temporary facilities, often designated as "collection camps," were formed in prisons, factories, schools, and other buildings and served as transit camps. The largest of these was the Danica camp in Koprivnica, but others existed at Kerestinec near Zagreb, on the grounds of the Zagreb Assembly, and elsewhere. They included also the Kruščica camp in central Bosnia (operational from August to early October 1941), Loborgrad near Zagreb (August 1941 to August 1942), and Đakovo (December 1941 to July 1942), which were used primarily for Jewish women and children.[62] The so-called "labor camps" were concentration camps and mass killing sites. The earliest of these were located at Jadovno near Gospić as well as at Slana and Metajna on the Adriatic island of Pag; these out-of-the-way sites operated between May and

August 1941 but were hastily closed when the Italian military occupied Zone II. At that point, Jasenovac became the main concentration camp and pivot of the camp system, although initially only for male inmates.[63] This made possible the incarceration of ever larger numbers of prisoners after August 1941.[64] The Ustaša authorities' November 26, 1941 decree about the deportation of "undesirable elements" to camps retroactively authorized the mass deportation of Jews and others to these sites.[65]

The timing of the mass incarceration of Croatia's Jews varied from region to region, occurring in phases between the summer of 1941 and summer of 1942, and depended on local circumstances and the size of the local Jewish community. The Croatian authorities determined the timing of the arrests and the fate of those detained.[66] Between April and June 1941, prominent Jews were arrested individually or in small groups, often to extract a financial contribution from the Jewish community.[67] Mass arrests and deportations to Ustaša camps and so-called "reprisal executions" began after the German invasion of the Soviet Union on June 22. In Zagreb, they occurred between late June and September 1941; over this three-month period, nearly three thousand Jews (roughly one-quarter of its Jewish population) were arrested and, in numerous cases, deported to collection camps. Many were killed at this time either at Jadovno or on Pag. From late September 1941 until January 1942, there were no mass arrests in Zagreb.[68] Mass confinement was extended to Sarajevo and some parts of Bosnia between September 1941 and January 1942, and to Osijek and eastern Croatia in the first months of 1942. In Zagreb, arrests originally included mostly Jewish men (and occasionally their families), but in Bosnia after September 1941 they included men, women, and children alike, with men deported to Jasenovac, and women and children to collection camps in central Bosnia (Kruščica) or central and eastern Croatia (Loborgrad, Đakovo). In Osijek, mass arrests began in the spring of 1942 and led first to ghettoization and then to deportation.[69]

From the beginning, the Croatian authorities associated the communist insurgency with the Jewish population, which was manifested in so-called reprisal executions. On July 23, 1941, the Ustaša Police Directorate in Zagreb ordered local police authorities to arrest known communists and sympathizers; Serb and Jewish communists were to be deported to Gospić (and then the Jadovno or Pag camps), while Croat and Bosnian Muslim prisoners (the latter regarded by the regime as Croats) were to be detained in local prisons. After two explosions damaged the railyards in Sarajevo on the night of July 29–30, 1941, the local authorities executed twenty-eight men, at least eight of whom were Jewish.[70] On September 22, 1941, the Ustaša police in Zagreb published a notice that fifty "communists and Jews" had been court-martialed and executed in reprisal for an explosion at Zagreb's central post office. In mid-September 1941, an Osijek court sentenced nine Jewish men to death for supposed involvement in communist activities.[71]

These executions occurred at a time when an incipient insurgency had engulfed much of the NDH, provoked by the Ustaša regime's massacres of Serbs. Both the Yugoslav communists and Serb nationalist groups sought to tap into the initially inchoate resistance; by late summer 1941, as desperate Serb peasants fled to the forests to avoid massacres or deportation to Serbia, organized resistance began its ascent. By fall 1941, large parts of the NDH were already in the hands of Partisans or Serb nationalist detachments known as Četniks. The communist insurrection also provided the Ustaša authorities with a pretext to "evacuate" the Jewish population to Croatian-operated camps.

In the reports cited here to the central Ustaša administration, local officials of all sorts—civilian administrators, but more frequently regular Croatian military (Home Guard) and Ustaša party and militia bosses—habitually linked Jews to the communist insurgency, adding momentum and an even greater sense of urgency to Zagreb's anti-Jewish measures. They asserted that Jews sympathized with and even financed and led the insurgency; they thus urged the central authorities to move quickly with "evacuation" and a "solution" to the Jewish question. One can point to other factors in these same reports, besides alleged "security" considerations, most notably logistical issues such as food and housing shortages in towns where Jews comprised a large share of the population. Some officials blamed Jews for the rapid proliferation of the black market and the hoarding of foodstuffs.

Already on June 14, 1941, the Home Guard Command reported that the Jews "secretly conspire through the communists and freemasons."[72] Weeks later, a Home Guard Command assessment of the security situation in Croatia concluded that "our young State has many hidden enemies." Jews played a prominent role in this regard, as they "are undoubtedly collaborating with and financing the actions of the communists."[73] On July 21, 1941, the Home Guard Command again reported that the communists "are certainly aided by the Jews."[74] Regional military and police authorities echoed these reports. On August 8, 1941, the commander of the Third Gendarmerie Battalion in Banja Luka (Bosnia) reported that he had issued strict orders to his subordinates to monitor the activities of local Jews, who numbered around four hundred, "as all of them are partial to communism."[75] The number of reports alleging subversion increased in the fall of 1941, as the insurgency spread territorially and grew in intensity. On October 26, 1941, the commander of the

Fourth Gendarmerie Battalion in eastern Bosnia remarked that "there are legitimate suspicions that they [Jews] are financing the current insurrection."[76] In mid-December 1941, the deputy commander of the Croatian Home Guard in eastern Bosnia concluded that Jews who had abandoned the towns "now play a vital role, largely as political commissars, in Partisan units."[77] Many officials began calling for harsher measures.[78]

Considering the precarious security situation and poor state of civilian administration in large parts of the NDH, the proposals of local police and military commanders contributed to the trajectory toward mass murder. The alleged "Judeo-Bolshevik" threat—Jews as a fifth column, commissars, saboteurs, and financers of the insurgency—invariably became linked to anti-Partisan operations. In at least one case, an Ustaša unit perpetrated massacres without any clear central directive. On December 10 and 17, 1941, a unit of the Ustaša militia murdered 350 Jews, half of them Austrian refugees, in the town of Brčko (Bosnia), whose southern environs had been overrun by the Partisans in early November.[79] In this case, the communist insurgency served as a pretext not for deportation but outright murder. The Brčko massacre was atypical in that it occurred outside the camp system, however it demonstrated how local Ustaša militias could act by fiat to implement mass murder.[80] Repression was instigated and encouraged by the central authorities, but local officials often had considerable scope to direct the persecution of Jews as they deemed fit.

It is not coincidental that deportations came early and were most far-reaching in Bosnia, the communist insurgency's center of gravity. When mass arrests began in Sarajevo in September 1941, they encompassed the entire Jewish population regardless of age or gender, in contrast with Zagreb, where mostly adult men were arrested. The first mass incarceration of Jews began on the night of September 3–4, 1941, followed by deportations to Jasenovac and Kruščica. The arrests and deportations were evidently ordered by Jure Francetić, the Ustaša commissioner in Sarajevo. On October 20, 1941, RAVSIGUR's Dido Kvaternik dispatched the Jewish Section's Vilko Kühnel to Sarajevo to coordinate further action. This occurred during a second wave of arrests in Sarajevo between October 16 and 24, 1941, when another fourteen hundred Jews were deported to camps. Only those Jews in mixed marriages or otherwise deemed necessary to the local economy were spared at this time. Another three thousand Jews were arrested in Sarajevo on the night of November 15–16, 1941, and then deported to the camps.[81]

At this point, however, the Interior Ministry in Zagreb halted the deportations. On November 21, 1941, Francetić sought clarification from the ministry, claiming that the deportations had "helped immensely to clear the air."[82] The deportations were evidently halted because many deportees were destined for Osijek, whose administration protested the plan. It claimed that it could not house these people, whose "presence would endanger the already difficult food supply of the city, which now has thousands of Jews who are unreliable and dangerous for the public order." The Osijek administration claimed that it could not feed its own poor "and therefore cannot in any way spend its limited supplies for such a large number of undesirable Jews."[83] In late November 1941, the Jewish Section ordered the local police to locate a facility for the Bosnian Jews, and to accept 300 Jewish children who were to be cared for by local Jewish families. The Osijek police turned to an abandoned industrial plant in the town of Đakovo; on December 2, 1941, this site became a camp for 1,865 Jewish women and children. By early March 1942, the Đakovo camp held more than 3,000 predominantly Bosnian Jewish women and children.[84] The deportations between September and December 1941 affected most of the Jewish population of Sarajevo. By that point, an unknown number, likely close to 2,000, had found refuge in the Italian occupation zone. The final wave of arrests in Bosnia would occur in late August 1942; the UNS ordered the registration and arrest of all remaining Sarajevo Jews, with few exceptions, and their deportation to the Loborgrad camp near Zagreb, from where they were deported to Auschwitz-Birkenau.

As Bosnian Jews were arrested, deported, and confined in camps, the Ustaša authorities' attention shifted to Osijek.[85] Here too the local Croatian military commanders and Ustaša officials urged the central authorities to move quickly against local Jews despite logistical concerns raised by civilian administrators. For example, on October 8, 1941, the local Home Guard command reported to Zagreb that "the measures taken against [local] Jews are insufficient, as they continue to maintain contact with broad sectors of the population." On November 17 the same commander reported that the local Jewish population should be "totally removed from Croatian society."[86] The reports and policy suggestions of local military commanders became more urgent after the Jewish Section ordered the resettlement of Bosnian Jews to Osijek's environs.[87]

In late 1941, the Jewish Section instructed the regional authorities in Osijek to consider local options for the confinement of the Jewish population. The regional prefect, Stjepan Hefer, the Osijek city administration, and local police authorities began negotiations with the Jewish community of Osijek on the construction of a local ghetto. On March 23, 1942, Hefer reported to Zagreb that a ghetto would be established in the village of Tenje near Osijek by June 1942; it was to be financed by the Jewish community, built using Jewish labor, and administered by

Žiga Volner of the Jewish community. Construction began in April 1942 under the supervision of the Ustaša police, and by May 1942 the first two barracks were constructed. That same month, Baraković of the Jewish Section informed the Home Guard Command that Osijek's Jews were in the process of being ghettoized.[88] In June 1942, over a period of only a few days, the Ustaša police supervised the deportation of Osijek's Jews to Tenje, which was still under construction. The Jews of the neighboring towns and hamlets were also sent to the Tenje camp, which by July 1942 had approximately three thousand inmates.[89] On August 14, 1942, SS officers arrived in Tenje to coordinate with Croatian police officials the deportations to Auschwitz. Three transports were organized between August 15 and 22, by which point almost the entire Jewish population of Osijek and its environs had been removed.[90]

THE RSHA AND DEPORTATIONS TO AUSCHWITZ-BIRKENAU

In the spring of 1942, the Croatian authorities' hitherto autonomous Jewish policy converged with the Third Reich's Final Solution, becoming a joint enterprise under RSHA direction. This followed the January 20, 1942 Wannsee Conference, where senior Nazi Party and Reich government officials agreed to a Final Solution for German-controlled Europe and the deportation of Jews on all Axis territory to death camps. The RSHA appointed SS-Sturmbannführer Franz Abromeit as the commissioner for Jewish affairs at the German embassy in Zagreb, whose role was to coordinate the deportations with the Croatian authorities.[91] Although the Croatian interior minister Andrija Artuković told the Croatian Parliament on February 24, 1942 that the Jewish question in the NDH had been resolved, from the RSHA's perspective this was hardly the case. By this stage, a majority of the Jewish population had already been detained and was in camps. It was not the RSHA's policy, however, to rely on other Axis governments to "solve" the Jewish question as conceived by the Third Reich. Although the RSHA had rejected the Croatian authorities' proposal of October 1941 to transfer the Jewish population to Poland, in spring 1942 it was the German embassy in Zagreb that submitted a formal request to the Ustaša government regarding the deportation of its remaining Jews to the Third Reich.[92] The only significant complication was the policy of the Italian military in the NDH, whose commanders refused to surrender Jews in their occupation zones; this inevitably led to tensions between the Germans and Italians.

Between May 1 and June 1, 1942, the Croatian State Information and Propaganda Office organized a widely publicized exhibition on the so-called Jewish question (entitled simply *The Jews*) at Zagreb's Art Pavilion.[93] The exhibition was attended by an official delegation of the

NSDAP's Auslandsorganisation in Croatia and other representatives of the German embassy.[94] As the NDH was a predominantly peasant society where most Croats had little or no contact with the urbanized and middle-class Jewish population, the exhibition was intended for "the instruction of the broader masses in an anti-Jewish spirit."[95] By emphasizing the allegedly exploitative nature of Jews and attributing to them the ills of the old social order, the exhibition played to existing and often inchoate cultural and religious stereotypes.[96] In this respect, it laid the groundwork for the deportations that followed in the summer of 1942. The exhibition also screened a German trilogy of anti-Semitic films including Fritz Hippler's *Der ewige Jude*, Erich Waschneck's *Die Rothschilds*, and Veit Harlan's *Jud Süss*. The Croatian State Information and Propaganda Office produced its own short film, *Židovi* (*The Jews*), which was screened in Zagreb theaters in May 1942.[97] The exhibition also emphasized the importance of the struggle "which unified Europe, under the leadership of the Great German Reich, is conducting against Jewry and plutocracy."[98] Between June and September 1942, the exhibition traveled to Karlovac, Osijek, and Sarajevo.[99]

In the summer of 1942, the Croatian authorities agreed to the German request for deportations. In July 1942, Abromeit and the SS police attaché Helm worked with the German embassy and the RSHA to plan the operation, as Croatian officials in the Jewish Section directed another registration of Jews in Zagreb and Sarajevo between July 29 and 31. Between August 8 and August 13, approximately 1,200 Jews in Zagreb were arrested by the Ustaša security police. The Jews arrested in Zagreb, Sarajevo, and other towns were joined by the Jewish women interned in the Loborgrad camp and the Jews of Tenje ghetto.[100] The Croatian State Railways provided the trains for the deportations, which were conducted between August 13 and 27, 1942; according to the RSHA, 4,927 Jews were deported to Auschwitz that month. The Croatian state treasurer Košak agreed in October 1942 to cover the cost of the deportations and to pay an additional thirty RM to Berlin for every deportee; in exchange, Croatia retained the deportees' property.[101]

It is hardly surprising that the Croatian government agreed to Berlin's request for deportations. Deportations from Croatia, which Zagreb had proposed in October 1941, represented a logical continuation of its policy of internal deportations and confinement in camps. This was an opportunity for the Croatian authorities to rid themselves of a community they had deemed "undesirable" from the beginning. When Pavelić traveled to Vinnitsa (Ukraine) to meet with Hitler in late September 1942, he remarked that the Jewish question in Croatia had for all intents and purposes been "solved," apart from those Jews in the Italian-occupied zones.

Hitler agreed with Pavelić that Jews were closely linked to the Partisan threat, and that those in the Italian zones should be removed. After this meeting, the German foreign minister Joachim von Ribbentrop instructed the German embassy in Rome to raise the matter with the Italians.[102] Pavelić evidently hoped to exploit the Jewish question in order to gain German support to limit the despised Italian influence in the NDH.[103]

This helps to explain why, even after the deportations of August 1942, the RSHA remained engaged in the NDH's affairs. German engagement proved problematic, however, as Berlin's policy since April 1941 had been based on deference to Italian political interests in the NDH. From mid–1942, German officials began raising the issue with Rome.[104] The Croatian authorities were in no position to make demands on the Italians. On June 8, 1942, the Italian embassy in Zagreb delivered a diplomatic note to the Croatian government blaming it for the mass flight of Jews to the Italian zone.[105] On July 18, 1942, the inspector general of the Reich's engineering conglomerate Organisation Todt reported to the German Foreign Ministry that in Mostar (Herzegovina), Jews were the most dangerous source of unrest but enjoyed the protection of the local Italian commander.[106] In late July 1942, Kasche visited Berlin and informed the Foreign Ministry that Italian officials refused to cooperate in the matter of Croatia's Jews.[107] In late August 1942, the Italian ambassador to the NDH, Raffaele Casertano, told the Croatian foreign minister Mladen Lorković that Kasche had raised the Jewish issue with him but simply noted that the decision would be made in Rome.[108] At that same time, the commander of the Italian Second Army in Croatia, General Mario Roatta, advised a Croatian delegation to pursue the matter with the Italian embassy in Zagreb.[109] Only after Pavelić's meeting with Hitler in late September 1942 did Ribbentrop take up the matter personally. When Casertano traveled to Rome in February 1943, he briefed Benito Mussolini personally on the deteriorating Italo-Croatian relationship.[110] Although Mussolini relented under growing German diplomatic pressure, the Italian military in Croatia refused to hand over the Jews in its occupation zone.[111]

As the German Foreign Ministry pressed the issue with Rome, on January 19, 1943, the RSHA emissary in the NDH, Abromeit, concluded an agreement with the Ustaša police officials Filip Crvenković and Vilko Kühnel on the deportation of Croatia's remaining Jews. Abromeit's staff personally supervised the arrest of seventeen hundred Jews in Zagreb and another three hundred across the NDH; they were deported on May 5 and May 10, 1943. In July 1943, the RSHA broadened its resettlement request to include an estimated eight hundred Jewish women and children still in the Jasenovac camp.[112] These operations did not go smoothly, however. SS officials remained distrustful of their Ustaša counterparts and felt that they had been denied access to Jewish inmates in Jasenovac, while Abromeit and Helm, his direct superior at the German embassy in Zagreb, even suspected some Croatian politicians of interceding on behalf of individual Jews.[113] In large part, these frustrations may have simply reflected German disdain for Ustaša officialdom. In spring 1943, the SS deployed Einsatzgruppe E to Croatia, whose task was to arrest Jews in the formerly Italian-occupied zones following Italy's capitulation in September 1943.[114] From that point forward, there would be no additional deportations to the Reich; Jews arrested in the NDH were sent to the Jasenovac camp. In late April 1944, Kasche and Helm sent a joint report to the German Foreign Ministry stating that the Jewish question had been solved in Croatia. They identified three general exceptions: Jews recognized as honorary Aryans by the Croatian authorities, Jews in mixed marriages, and *Mischlinge* (those of mixed birth). In a separate report, Helm indicated he still believed that several Croatian officials had family ties with Jews or were shielding Jews but oddly he never mentioned Jews in Partisan-controlled territory.[115] By that stage, however, nearly thirty thousand Jews had already been arrested, deported to camps, and in most cases murdered, an overwhelming majority of them in the Ustaša camps.[116]

CONCLUSION

Much of the literature on the Holocaust in the NDH, whether in socialist Yugoslavia or Western studies until quite recently, has emphasized the intentionalism of the Ustaša movement/regime. This argument is sustainable vis-à-vis the Serb question in the NDH, but the Ustaša regime's Jewish policy in 1941 was to a significant extent an improvised affair even as it rapidly escalated in its ferociousness. It was inspired to a significant extent by the Third Reich, and the Ustašas certainly hoped to ingratiate themselves with Berlin, but the Third Reich hardly dictated affairs. As Wendy Lower has recently argued, the history of the Holocaust has been losing its center in Germany and has become a subject especially of eastern European history. This has forced scholars increasingly to rethink "the distribution of power in the Nazi system, the imperial dynamic of the center and periphery, as well as the relations between the occupier and occupied."[117] German policy in the NDH reminds us that, as much as the Third Reich unleashed extraordinary acts of violence and was the driver of the Final Solution, it never completely controlled the killing process from start to finish.

Three-quarters of the NDH's Jewish population died in the Holocaust.[118] The Croatian case demonstrates that, as decisive as Berlin's intentions were for the implementation of the Final Solution, realities on the ground often shaped how genocide was implemented. Berlin did not always control the killing process on its periphery. The Ustaša authorities had substantial scope in shaping the nature of their own Jewish policy. The Third Reich's direct influence on this policy was initially minimal. That is not to suggest that Ustaša conceptions of the "Jewish question" were originally identical to Nazi views. There were broad similarities, but notwithstanding their wartime rhetoric the Ustašas never conceived of the Jewish question in the same racial terms. For much of 1941, the Ustaša authorities may have believed they could rid themselves of their Jewish population by deporting them to the Reich. Zagreb's abortive proposal of October 1941 that the Third Reich take all its Jews—similar in scope to the resettlement agreement of June 1941—may have reflected its belief that Berlin would entertain a similar solution to the Jewish question. As the Croatian authorities intensified their own campaign of arrests and deportations, the camps became the destination of the Jewish population. The logic of Ustaša policy escalated rapidly toward systematic mass murder and converged in 1942 with the Nazi Final Solution.

From a German perspective, however, the NDH was not only an improvised affair but a disastrous experiment in occupation politics. If the wider objectives of German policy in the NDH were to secure raw materials for the war effort and lines of communication at minimal military cost, then these went unrealized. Notwithstanding its collaboration in the Final Solution, the NDH became an arduous investment, requiring ever greater military commitments from the Reich, which it met by ruthlessly exploiting local resources. This included the recruitment of the Volksdeutsche and Bosnian Muslims by the Waffen-SS and Croats by the Wehrmacht and German police; the growing use of locally recruited forced labor; callous exploitation of economic resources; and an anti-Partisan counterinsurgency, which victimized growing numbers of noncombatants regardless of nationality, gender, or age. Although Wehrmacht references to its own violence repeatedly emphasized its technocratic and clinical nature—"pacification" for the purposes of establishing "order"—and routinely contrasted it with the "primitive" and "uncivilized" violence of the Ustašas, in the end both wreaked enormous havoc and indiscriminately claimed the lives of tens of thousands of noncombatants.[119] Nor was the violence of the Ustašas conceivable without the German occupation apparatus, which generally established a low threshold for meting out harsh reprisals. The NDH thus became the scene of multiple genocides, resistance movements, and occupation regimes, a veritable whirlwind of violence.

CHAPTER 6

GERMAN COLLECTIVE GUILT IN THE NARRATIVES OF SOUTHEASTERN EUROPEAN HOLOCAUST SURVIVORS

KATEŘINA KRÁLOVÁ AND JIŘÍ KOCIÁN

The events of World War II left an indelible mark on European memory in general and on Holocaust survivors in particular. The incorporation of the Holocaust into a pan-European narrative dates back as far as 1989 and became one of the most influential historical-cultural processes, even to the point of giving a new imperative to European integration with regard to the Eastern Bloc countries.[1] As Tony Judt puts it, "Holocaust recognition is our contemporary European entry ticket."[2] However, since the publication of Judt's *Postwar* in 2006, little attention has been paid to the community of memory consisting of Holocaust survivors from southeastern Europe. At first glance, it may seem that the Holocaust and the persecution of the Jews have been overshadowed by the military actions and political turmoil in southeastern Europe during World War II. After the war, the specific case of Jewish suffering was intentionally merged with grand national narratives of the anti-fascist fight, whereas commemoration of the Holocaust was limited to the Jewish community or family practices of remembering.[3] As Saul Friedländer stated in the late 1970s, for Holocaust victims and for society as such, commemoration is of the utmost importance in the process of reconciliation.[4]

The extermination of European Jewry, however, affected not only the target group but also the perpetrators. Soon it became the constitutive element of the notion of "collective guilt" (*Kollektivschuld*), a term that Carl Gustav Jung had already coined in 1945.[5] This term soon transcended its original psychological definition and became applied in the broader sense as a collective responsibility of Germans for the horrors and violence of World War II. As such, over the past seventy years, the concept of collective guilt has become a hallmark of German historiography and has stimulated philosophical, political, and legal debates. Our chapter aims to use testimonies of Holocaust survivors in order to find narratives of German collective guilt and to put them into a historical and regional context. We argue that German collective guilt became a common pattern in the memory of Holocaust survivors and their positioning of Germans, which only slightly recedes according to communal and personal experiences during World War II. In doing so, we further assert that the collective guilt narrative present in the majority of the survivors' interviews documents the hardship of overcoming the trauma of the Holocaust. The survivors draw on memories of their personal agency while facing mass violence during the war and how these experiences and attitudes persisted into the postwar period. The analysis of these phenomena provides us with a better understanding of the individual stances toward German collective guilt and the formative processes behind them.

Simultaneously, we examine whether and under what conditions the shift occurred from Germans being constructed as colonizers of southeastern Europe who persecuted Jews with the ultimate aim of extermination to the Germans being conceptualized only as representatives of a decentralized collective. As such, they might be expressing regret or even be regarded just as individuals with various attitudes, motivations, and values. As the year 1945 symbolizes the ultimate turning point in the historical narratives of World War II and the Holocaust, we can observe how the two aforementioned constructs were utilized depending on internal narrative temporality (prewar, war, and postwar periods) and the geographical allocation.

Based on interviews from the USC Shoah Foundation Visual History Archive with survivors from Romania, Bulgaria, Yugoslavia, and Greece, this empirical study presents a rich mosaic of Jewish attitudes toward Germans before, during, and after World War II and illuminates the origins of these attitudes. Despite the fact that Jews in southeastern Europe became the target of similar or equal policies of racial persecution, as was the case with the rest of Europe, the specific political situation in the region during the war resulted in distinct survival trajectories and narratives that we seek to illuminate. For a general understanding of the sources we used and the methodology we developed for this purpose, we initially elaborate on the sources with which we worked and how we employ them. The following analytical section, from which we draw our conclusions, is divided into three chronologically ordered parts: the first covers prewar Jewish-German interactions, the second contrasts the experiences of Jews with German persecutors and with other perpetrators, and the third covers the application of this personal and collective experience in the postwar attitudes of Holocaust survivors toward Germans.

METHODOLOGY AND TESTIMONIES FROM SOUTHEASTERN EUROPE

The USC Shoah Foundation Visual History Archive (VHA) is the world's most extensive electronic database of video-recorded oral history testimonies, focusing mainly on the remembrances of Holocaust survivors. Currently, it contains more than 54,000 interviews in more than 30 languages that amount to around 115,000 hours of video material.[6] When creating the sample used for the purpose of this study, we limited our broader search to Holocaust survivors who were born in the countries of interest to us. This preselection was made with the intention of providing us with narration that would also cover the interwar period. As a result, we had at our disposal 3,422 interviews for Romania, 866 for Yugoslavia, 613 for Greece, and 676 for Bulgaria. These numbers roughly correspond to the sizes of the respective Jewish populations in these countries before World War II: in interwar Romania approximately 750,000 (4.2 percent of the overall population), in Greece 80,000 (1.2 percent), in Yugoslavia 70,000 (0.49 percent), and in Bulgaria 50,000 (0.8 percent).[7]

For the next step, we chose the keyword "attitudes toward Germany and/or Germans," which appears in 4,947 testimonies in total and is defined as "feelings toward, and/or opinions about, Germany and/or the German people."[8] We used this keyword to filter our preselection sample since we are further looking into narratives about people whom the interviewees considered to be Germans (indifferently encompassing various groups such as local Germans, German citizens, German soldiers, etc.). In this way, we limited our focus group to 198 interviews for Romania, 71 for Greece, 45 for Yugoslavia, and 11 for Bulgaria. We narrowed these down to the final sample of the most appropriate interviews according to their content: 4 each for Romania, Greece, and Yugoslavia, and 3 for Bulgaria.[9]

When processing these interviews, we kept to the standard oral history methodology.[10] Our point of interest lay exclusively in using the interviews as a source of memory and narration. Such an approach served best for our research interest of examining narratives instead of using the interviews as a supplementary source to reconstruct historical events.[11] To present our results, we resorted to the "fragmentization" of the interviews into shorter excerpts while contextualizing and commenting upon them in order to highlight our key themes.[12]

The Jewish population in southeastern Europe featured an immense diversity of cultural, religious, and political inclinations and characteristics. Because of this diverse background, attempting to coherently define a typical, generic community within southeastern Europe is quite futile because the reality of the situation was that such a community did not exist; it is much more proper to think of a varied cluster of communities.[13] Another factor that contributed to the diversity among these groups was the long-lasting cultural and political influence of the two regional empires, the Austro-Hungarian and the Ottoman Empires, which created further cleavages.[14] Nevertheless, it is possible to think about the whole group of Jewish survivors providing their testimonies to VHA as a specific "community of memory." The act of providing testimony not only represents a technological extension of individual and collective memories but also contributes to the formation of constitutive narratives of such a community (those we are interested in) that impact further remembering.[15]

The situation during World War II also differed dramatically from state to state: Romania and Bulgaria retained their political independence, though as satellite states of Nazi Germany; Greece and Yugoslavia experienced German, Italian, and Bulgarian occupation, in the latter case also the creation of the fascist Independent State of Croatia (Nezavisna Država Hrvatska—NDH). In general, it can be stated that the Jews in German-occupied territories (Yugoslavia and Greece, after 1943 including the former Italian territories) and the NDH were exposed to extermination policies equal to those in the rest of German-occupied Europe. In the old Romanian state (unlike in the areas this state occupied and Northern Transylvania, which was controlled by Hungary) and the old Bulgarian state (without its occupation zone in Greece, Macedonia, and South Serbia), the chances of survival were much better.[16]

THE INTERWAR PERIOD AND CONTACT WITH GERMANS

The fact that only Romania and Yugoslavia had large German minorities[17] in the interwar period, both roughly half a million people in size, determined different levels of interaction during the interwar period among Jews and Germans. In Bulgaria and Greece, it was mostly traders, businessmen, and intellectuals who represented the German language and culture.[18]

During this period, this reality influenced the interactions between Jews and Germans, and there was also the possibility of studying at prestigious local schools with a partial or complete curriculum in the German language. When the parents of the narrators in question made the choice to send their children to these schools, they might have been motivated by practical prospects the successful graduates of these schools would go on to find, or the cultural and language preferences of their families. Toward the outbreak of World War II, Jewish-German relationships were increasingly complicated as the Nazi ideological indoctrination of German minorities progressed.[19]

Lili A., born in Belišće near Osijek in Yugoslavia in 1923, fled from forced labor under the Ustaša regime to Budapest, surviving there until the end of the war by concealing her Jewish identity. She attended a high school that included the whole ethnic spectrum of the local population and remembers the last years before the war:

> Already before the war, one could feel certain [anti-Jewish] movements, there was a big German settlement, the *Volksdeutscher* [ethnic German].... You knew that in the city [Osijek] the *Neustadt*[20] was the *Volksdeutscher* [*sic*]. And these organized themselves already before the war and have had their so-called *Kulturbund* [Cultural Association of Germans in Yugoslavia founded in 1920 in Novi Sad[21]].... And then the *Volksdeutsche* began to slowly orient themselves toward Hitler and National Socialism.[22]

Lili further reflects on the increasing influence of Nazism in her close environment and her age group. The difficulties of becoming ostracized and bullied by former friends and classmates at schools, especially those attended by local Germans, usually represents a narrative overture of the actual experiences of the war and the Holocaust.

Similar recollections can be found in the narration of Max G., who was born in the Transylvanian town of Bistriţa in Romania in 1923 and spent the war in a forced labor battalion in the Bucharest area. He emphasizes the linguistic background of his family as the motivation for the choice of school:

> I went to a Saxon school and my first cultural language was German, at home we spoke Yiddish.... Shortly after the Spanish Civil War in 1933 [*sic*], the Saxons started changing their attitude, some of them became overnight anti-Semitic..., but not all of them, I have to compliment some of them they did not give in.... At a later point he [the teacher] called my mother and advised her to take me out from the Saxon school, that it is not good for me that already some children heard at home about Hitler and they started molesting [bothering] me.[23]

Despite describing negative experiences from school, the accentuation placed on his personal encounters with Germans and their differences of opinion when it came to Hitler and Nazism, which is documented in this case by his teacher, is significant for Max G.'s entire interview. He himself attributes this ambiguity to his cultural awareness, local community relationships, and, furthermore, to the wartime aid providers in a way that conflicts with the collective guilt narrative, as will be demonstrated in the next part of our chapter.

Professional training and education in the German language was nonetheless a trend that was not limited to states with significant ethnic

German populations. Izidor D., born in 1910 in Sofia, Bulgaria, had an older brother who studied in Leipzig, while he went to university in Munich. In his interview, Izidor states that he knew German very well from high school. This enabled him to enroll in an engineering degree program at the University of Munich, where he met other Jewish and non-Jewish students from Bulgaria. After finishing his studies in 1934, he moved to Vienna before coming back to Bulgaria and serving in a forced labor battalion during the war. About his time in Germany, he notes, "I got to know a lot of Bavarians, people of Munich, the Bavarian dialect and the country, the mountains very well [before the war] there was an atmosphere like before the storm ... about the things [events of World War II] makes not much sense to talk about, there was enough told and written about them."[24]

Izidor's story documents the effects of the active German economic and foreign policy in the Balkan Peninsula between the wars, which facilitated intellectual and business contact between Germans and Jews and which made it desirable to acquire qualifications as he did. Besides these pragmatic factors, for many interviewees, Germany also seemed to have projected a particular image of a cultural and civilizational stronghold.

Ivonne K., born in 1924 in Thessaloniki, Greece, came from an upper-middle-class family living in the affluent part of the city center and survived the war under a false identity in Athens. She recalls her family's affinity toward German culture: "The Jews of Thessaloniki were Germanophiles. You know my mother, during the war of '13 [Second Balkan War], my grandfather brought them a German teacher ... and all the children spoke German. My dad and all the brothers, they were ten brothers, all went to a German school. We were Germanophiles because there was nothing against them [Germans]."[25]

Similar positive family attitudes toward the German language and culture appear in the recollections of Frenty A. He was also born into the upper social strata in Thessaloniki in 1924, and his father owned a company involved in the glass industry and trade. Frenty recalled that he "went to German movies because we were employing a German lady, a *Fräulein* [miss], at home who wanted to see them.... Father lived in Vienna for three years. Therefore, he had a strong personal and professional attachment to the German-speaking environment."[26] During the war, Frenty A. passed through the Bergen-Belsen concentration camp, and then the Nazi regime sent him and his family, along with other Jews from Thessaloniki, to Palestine.[27] Another narrator who remembers German cultural traits in Greece is Elias C., born in Volos in 1924. After he went from being in hiding to joining the partisans, he had to undergo a leg amputation in a partisans' hospital: "We saw many movies, so to say usually, dramatic ones, those related to war. There were many movies but one impressed me a lot, a German movie and it was pacifistic.... And I say [said] ... bravo to the Germans."²⁸ In this example, Elias points to the expectations raised by the assumed high standards of German culture, and he further elaborates on the complete negation of this, which was brought by the events of the war. A shock suffered from the mechanically executed brutality of the Germans in contrast with the positive cultural stereotype they enjoyed appears in some form in the majority of the interviews.

It can be asserted that contact with Germans, the German language, and German culture played an ambiguous role in the life stories of the narrators. It is hardly possible to draw correlations between interwar experiences and postwar attitudes without more profound knowledge of specific local and individual contexts. For some survivors, their German-language skills became crucial in facilitating their survival during the war. Also, this provided some of them with a different perspective that relativized the notion of German collective guilt and responsibility for the Holocaust. For many others, the stark contrast between the interwar perception of Germans and Germany and their Holocaust experiences amplified the shock they experienced. Nonetheless, for Jews in southeastern Europe, the political and ideological shift toward National Socialism among Germans in and beyond Germany ushered in the tragic turn of events during World War II.

RECOLLECTIONS OF WORLD WAR II ENCOUNTERS AND THE HOLOCAUST

The different fates of Balkan Jews during World War II were to a great extent determined by the state they were living in at the outbreak of the conflict. As discussed above, German military actions and the following occupations struck Greek and Yugoslav Jews the hardest. Revekka A. was born in 1920 on the island of Corfu and during the war survived the Auschwitz-Birkenau and Bergen-Belsen concentration camps. Recalling the German occupation and her Auschwitz experience, she noted: "The Germans are not to be described with any words.... Kicking me and throwing me in the lake that I was not working.... What was I? A puppy? I was, a little girl.... They destroyed me for all my life. What else should I tell you about the Germans, [they are] the most cruel, resilient, evil people. Human life had no value for them. He gave you one with the pistol, killed, no harm, no foul."²⁹

In this account, Revekka A. emphasizes her individual personal experiences and generalizes them for all Germans. In relation to the collective guilt narrative, this excerpt thematizes two fundamental elements typical for the interviews: dehumanizing representation of the collective German perpetrator and the long-lasting impact of personal traumatic experience.

On the other hand, Ivonne K., who spent the occupation with a false identity in Athens, mentions that during the war she had limited information about the horrors of the concentration camps and Jewish suffering. Thus, she reflects on them from a perspective of collective suffering: "We had no experience [with the Germans]. We did not know anything. But we knew that something very serious was happening, something bad, something tragic. But we did not know the evolution of these things.... How is it only possible they bind children together, one-by-one, the Germans, and throw them into the lake, one-by-one tied them and threw them into the lake. Who thinks of this? Nobody."[30]

Though Ivonne previously refers to a German caretaker serving in their household prior to the war, this person is omitted from the general narrative. This suggests a dichotomy present between the collective *Germans* and the individual direct childhood experience, which was accompanied by a particular sentiment.

The shock of the German occupation of Greece[31] was also present in Frenty A.'s narration: "No one could imagine how the occupation would continue, the starvation, the misery of the people. The population had to fear.... They started to execute people.... At any rate, no reason.... The German passed, he did not like your face, bam!"[32] In these testimonies, *the German* or *the Germans* are present as collective perpetrators; no apparent distinction is made between civilians, the Wehrmacht, or SS units. The occupation of Greece and the ensuing transports to concentration camps organized by the German occupation administration and armed units left an indelible mark on the attitude of the Greek Jews toward Germans.

In her interview, Bellina A., born in 1931 in Huși in what is now Romanian Moldova, is more specific and remembers the positive impression the German soldiers made on her at first: "They were so sharp and elegant; back then we did not know what happened to other Jews—we knew they were deported but just rumors."[33] As Romania did not apply such strict policies with regard to its local Jewish population, Bellina A. managed to survive with her parents in her hometown until the end of the war. Nevertheless, during the royal coup d'état when King Michael deposed the pro-Axis military dictator Ion Antonescu on August 23, 1944, German forces occupied Romania to suppress the coup. Bellina remembered how Jews from other towns were being deported, but her parents, still not knowing anything about the Holocaust and the general treatment of the Jews, were accommodating several families in their house. She recollects a story of her mother's bravery in the face of German occupational forces: "There was a girl 17 or 18.... The Germans said to her mother... 'bring the girl here,' and she did. [My mother] went to the German officer and . . . she said [to the officer] 'you are a civilized country, you are very cultured people, I know we are occupied . . . but this is not right, let the girl go.'"[34]

In her testimony, Bellina repeatedly confronts the image of German high culture with the reality of war atrocities and also thematizes the memory of personal agency. This experience of spontaneous action would prove influential in later interactions with Germans after the war, as will be discussed later in this chapter.

A different account of the German military personnel comes from Max G. during the time of his service in the forced labor battalion. Yet, he again highlights personal agency when he recounts one of his interactions with Germans. He describes a moment that fundamentally changed his situation and living conditions during the war and also, as elaborated later in his interview, facilitated his refusal of the collective guilt narrative:

> And then comes . . . the turning point in my life . . . it changed my impression of Germans and Germany. . . . Suddenly I hear above [a] tremendous argument in dual language[s], one was shouting in Romanian, one was shouting even louder in German, and I just had to laugh . . . I realized they do not understand each other, so I gathered my courage . . . because this Romanian officer was a very nice guy, why shall he be shouted down like this, I raised my head, I stood up and in the best military German I said 'this man cannot understand you.'"[35]

At the time, Max G.'s knowledge of German he gained at school came to his benefit, a common feature for many narratives. He describes his further involvement with the German officer mentioned in the previous episode, for whom he worked as a translator and interpreter for the rest of the war and who surprised him very much with his political views: "I was under his command . . . then these three soldiers . . . the first two always warned me of the third one. . . . 'Yeah, we know you are Jewish, and you be careful, don't say [that] about the Soviet Union etc.' . . . They were youngsters, social democratic Germans, workers' sons; . . . a year later . . . I discovered that Herr Leutnant Ripke was the one who had this spirit and he finally got courage to talk to me one day, immediately after Stalingrad, he was asking me and smiling 'You don't know what happened?'"[36]

Max G. then elaborates on his recollections and argues for a more nuanced stance toward German collective guilt while emphasizing individual merits and opposing the dominant narrative: "We read about righteous men who did a great deal for Judaism. So, like Schindler, he saved thousands [of] people, that's unique, absolutely outstanding. But then they are officers, German officers, even if they saved one human being or two, or their attitude is also significant." Max even extends his positive notion of ethnic Germans onto Romanian king Michael I, who was of the Hohenzollern dynasty: "And what about this German king, who saved [a] hundred thousand of souls by bringing the third army to a collapse. They had no time to start executing Jews or catching them."[37]

Izidor D. also served in a forced labor battalion after his return to Bulgaria from Austria. He takes a rather similar stance to the previous narrator when recounting how he got a relatively safe administrative position thanks to his language skills: "There was this [German] colonel who comes and asks me if I know German] 'we need a translator, we do [pretend] not [to] know who you are [a Jew], you will be satisfied. We always talked like equals. He was not an SS man, he was an army colonel."[38] In this case, a clear distinction is made between the positive figure of an army officer and members of the SS, whom Izidor regards as perpetrators.

Unlike narrators from Romania and Bulgaria, narrators from Yugoslavia and Greece subjected members of the German armed forces and other Germans to a direct comparison with the other occupying force operating in the country, the Italian army. Revekka A. offers her firsthand reflection as a Greek Jewish survivor from the Ionian Islands, which historically belonged to and were later occupied by Italy: "The Italians were not for war. The Italians were all perfume, song, and dance.... The Italians were party animals.... The Germans broke the door, went in, found girls, they did what they wanted and what they liked in the house, they took it. And in the end, they beat you up and left. These were other people, the Germans."[39]

Elias C. from Volos, a city that belonged in the Italian occupation zone until the Italian surrender in September 1943, had similar views: "If he [German soldier] was on duty you who were his friend and drank tsipouro [Greek wine brandy] together, on duty, he could kill you." The depiction of Germans as dehumanized executors of orders, with the narrators frequently alluding to or explicitly comparing them to robots or killing machines, is as good as omnipresent in the accounts. As is the case of Elias C. and before that Revekka A., this is frequently contrasted with the depiction of the relaxed, even sympathetic Italians not worrying about Jews: "I encountered this patrol, an Italian one. I knew a little Italian because I was speaking fluent Spanish, and this is a similar language. Eh, I say 'I want to go home,' like that."[40]

The image of Italians as friendly and with no anti-Jewish prejudices also appears in the testimony of Beruria S., who was born in 1926 in Zagreb, Yugoslavia. In 1941, she emigrated with her parents to Abano

Terme in Padua, Italy, after the German occupation and the creation of the NDH. In this excerpt, she reflects on the situation in Italy while contrasting it with her opinion about the Germans:

> I mean I speak German, but I don't want to hear the German language. . . . It was Italy . . . children were being brainwashed from young age into the Fascist Party except that you can't brainwash Italians, because Italians are not that kind of a people to be as brainwashed as the Germans, into becoming militaristic like that . . . they are not the same type of people, they are human and Germans are like beasts in my opinion. . . . I blame the Germans because they are, I shouldn't say all of them, . . . but a great majority of them are a very horrible people and I will not back away from that. And maybe they have certain aspects of great culture, but I cannot give them credit for it.[41]

This excerpt also documents the narrator's awareness of the fact that applying collective guilt is problematic, though she refuses to abandon it and projects a plethora of traces and arguments similar to other narrators. The refusal of German language usage, the dehumanizing view of the perpetrator, the stark contrast between the image of German high culture and the reality of the Holocaust all underline the recollections in both direct and mediated ways.

When discussing discrepancies between Jewish attitudes toward Germans in regard to the World War II period, narrations that deal directly with the situation in the concentration camps must also be examined. Even among Jewish Holocaust survivors, we do not find a singular narrative of collective guilt. In contradiction to some of the previously discussed testimonies, Edith F., an Auschwitz survivor born in Oradea, Romania, in 1922, talks about aid given to her by labor camp guards: "The camp [in Pürschkau, which she reached after Auschwitz in 1944] was run by this *Organisation Todt* [a German military construction work organization], they had yellow uniforms and *Hakenkreuze* [swastikas]. I do believe they were wounded soldiers, mostly they lacked one arm, . . . they were supervising, and there were also men, who I do believe evaded war because of their age—they were over fifty . . . many of them were very decent, they suffered when they saw us."[42]

Yet again, the narrator differentiates between the Germans based on the armed forces branch to which they belonged. In this context, she describes how a compassionate commanding officer who belonged to the Wehrmacht shared his bread with the Jewish prisoners, which enabled her to project a certain empathy toward Germans. This attitude is further supported by a memory of German peasants who hid her after she had escaped from a death march at the end of the war.

Helen S., born in 1928 in Sofia, remembers the assistance she received from a guard in the Dachau camp for several months. In her account, she rejects any account of collective guilt with the following argument: "In a concentration camp, there were Germans who hid away children and families, and they got caught by their neighbors . . . one German tell[s] on the other German. They went to [a] concentration camp, so you cannot hate all the Germans."[43] In this case, the narrator transcends the image of Germans as aid givers to depict Germans as victims of Nazism. Despite the fact that we can observe several of these shifts emerging in the testimonies (Germans as aid givers, anti-Nazi individuals, victims of Nazism), collective guilt remains the dominant common denominator in the context of the events of World War II when narrated by the Holocaust survivors' community of memory.[44]

REFLECTIONS ON THE POSTWAR: JEWISH ATTITUDES TOWARD GERMANS

In contrast to most memoirs of Holocaust survivors, which outline foremost an idealized version of reality prior to anti-Jewish persecution and then elaborate extensively on Holocaust-specific experiences, ending abruptly with the liberation,[45] as well as taking into account their informal structure, the VHA testimonies are a far better source on postwar attitudes of Jews and the experiences they underwent after the actual war had ceased on the European continent. When assessing their position toward Germans, many survivors ground their collective guilt narrative in the aspects of the Holocaust that they witnessed, or rather what Jews in general had to withstand and overcome as a collective of victims. For example, Ivonne K., a medical doctor by profession, reflects on dehumanizing medical experiments: "One has to admit that this people [the Germans] made death science. What I did [as a] doctor on rabbits with anesthesia they did without on people. . . . I hate this on my son and on everybody else. . . . He should judge himself how to think and how to proceed with Germans."[46] An apparent disapproval of her son's attitude in the last segment points to Ivonne K.'s regret that she was not able to transmit the notion of German collective guilt to the next generation and make it the general understanding of Germans.

Revekka A. emphasizes the wartime violence and extermination camps. By doing so, she forms a bond between herself and not only Jews but also all of humankind. The bond she discusses is united under a real or imagined German oppression, yet she further stigmatizes Germans as the ultimate oppressors in the process:

> No discussion with the Germans. Nor could you predict . . . bombardment, fires, incendiary bombs, they killed a lot of people, and in the villages they

were shooting peasants working in the fields. . . . Just like this, because they wanted to! Why did they walk us into crematoriums? Did we do anything to them? They just wanted to! They thought they would rule the whole world, and they will kill them all and make all Jews disappear from the surface of the Earth. . . . There are no more horrible, cruel, and inhuman people than the Germans. Never let anyone experience this thing.[47]

The position Revekka A. takes toward Germans is in opposition to Tullia Santin's claims. The latter's research, which is based on memoirs, argues that the survivors' attitudes toward Germany do not strictly correspond with the factual Holocaust experience. To support this, in the case of Greece, she contrasts the strict rejection of anything German by one Jewish child survivor with the much more moderate stance of two Auschwitz survivors.[48] Similarly, Elias C. also expresses the incomprehensibility of the Holocaust by making a distinction between expectations and actual experience: "We did not think the German people could have reached this level. . . . This was done nowhere. . . . In the twentieth century, to burn people. To burn a little child in the oven. What is this? However much hatred you had at this point? . . . The Germans agreed with Hitler one hundred percent. And if there were some who did not think so, one could count them on the hand, on the fingers of one hand. One, not two. So, they all agreed."[49]

On many occasions, the survivors considered cruelty and violence to be inborn, genetically transferred attributes of the Germans. The survivors who take this position often realize how dangerous and irrational it is. For instance, Ivonne K. states:

> For me there are no good Germans, I am ashamed to say so. . . . Because their chromosomes are like this. They are the same. It is in their cells. These people cannot be blamed . . . when these people grow up and grow older, they cannot but let the evil come out of them. They have no power to stifle it. I do not trust them. Right now, you say I am a racist. Yes, I'm a racist, what to do? But with those who made me, so much evil, and bad, how to say it. I cannot.[50]

Leslie P., born in 1921 in Oradea, Romania, had a similar position. Having served in forced labor battalions in Hungary and then surviving in hiding, he extends the framing of his position into imperial history: "They didn't need Bismarck or Kaiser [emperor] to make them superior, it's born in them, it comes in their blood."[51] When asked about the young people who grew up after the war, he responded by relativizing the transfer of collective guilt: "I have a [sic] mixed feeling[s]. . . . You see the educated one[s] have a bad feeling and are apologetic . . ., but they don't feel they owe an apology because it is not their generation . . . they [feel they] do not have to be responsible for the fathers' generation."⁵²

In light of her positive experiences with one of the guards in Dachau, Helen S. tries to remain rather moderate. Even though she still uses "Germans" as a general perpetrator category equivalent to "Nazis," she differentiates between those who persecuted Jews and those who did not: "I don't have hatred for them, first of all hatred will eat you up, you will eat yourself up with it, I can't hate people I don't know. . . . Now I never gonna forgive the Germans for what they did, let God do that, I am not a judge, but if there is a Nazi, he should be taken and sent to prison and maybe executed."⁵³

On the other hand, Mirjam D., who was born in 1940 in Slavonski Brod in Yugoslavia and who survived the Holocaust hiding in Vukovar, openly criticizes generalizations and the collective guilt narrative: "For many years, there was this aversion against German tourists, a lot of them came . . . but it makes no sense to generalize between nations, it is exactly what happened to the Jews."⁵⁴ A similar critique comes from Max G.: "Recently I saw, read about a book from Goldhagen,⁵⁵ condemning all the Germans en masse, but . . . it is not true, you have many individuals who behave differently."⁵⁶

It appears that the main factors leading Jewish survivors to either accept or reject the German collective guilt narrative were their individual wartime experiences and developments in their countries of origin, which affected both themselves and their relatives. For many, negative attitudes toward Germans created a mental block that persisted but at the same time was a testament to their personal agency. To quote Frenty A. on this matter: "Something, you will tell me now that it's ridiculous, I never buy a German car. I have a Swedish car. . . . You can tell me that the German industry is not going to break down if Fred A. does not buy German products. But it is something. I never forgive them. Never."⁵⁷ While this quote may seem to build upon the rigidity of preconceived ideas based on trauma, it illustrates a commitment to personal agency. On the symbolic level it contests the course of historical events and to a certain extent repudiates the image of a Jew as a passive victim, though in a very individualized manner.

One of the issues that appears in many of the testimonies is the attitude of survivors toward traveling to or settling in Germany. This prospect, together with the mere sound of German being spoken, often remains traumatizing. Ivonne K. is quite determined in this respect: "I have never been to Germany, ever. One time I went because I had to and I spent three days there, and I left in a hurry. To German Switzerland, to Zurich, I went twice, I stay a little and go away in a hurry. I cannot hear

German."⁵⁸ Vera H., born in 1936 in Novi Sad in Yugoslavia, survived the war in the ghetto in Budapest, where she was one of those who received aid from Raoul Wallenberg, a Swedish diplomat who helped Jews by issuing them neutral country passports. She reflected on an inner conflict experienced during her business assignment in Germany during the 1950s and how she suffered from being assigned there: "I was sent from Israel by an Israeli tour operator to Frankfurt for two years, promoting Israeli tourism.... I could live anywhere in Europe and actually in Germany I felt awful.... When I came to Frankfurt, it was amazing how comfortable I felt and how guilty I felt and how I hated it that I feel good."⁵⁹

She further adds that even traveling to Switzerland and Austria put her at ease compared to in West Germany, which she perceives as the homeland of Nazism. Therefore, while living in Germany, she used every chance to leave the country.

Some survivors did decide to move permanently to Germany after the war for personal or economic reasons, and this posed a similar challenge. Lili A. migrated to Germany in 1966 to reunite with her husband, who had been sent there as a business representative a year earlier. Despite having doubts, she tried to rationalize the potential threat of anti-Semitism. She describes that crossing the border and seeing German uniforms shook her confidence from the first moment, but she also used a specific way of coping with her fears of being exposed to racist prejudice or verbal attacks:

> Some of my good friends in Belgrade, Jews, asked me: "Can you go to Germany?" I thought about it and said "Anti-Semitism is everywhere, not only in Germany, unfortunately. I do not know who was a Nazi and who was not, I hope I will find my way around." ... Slowly I got used to it [her fears], in the beginning, I always wore my necklace with the Star of David, so that everyone could see right away that I was a Jew. So that no one would make any remarks about the Jews when I came somewhere.⁶⁰

It is noteworthy that Lili A. chose a strategy to openly express her Jewish identity, to make clear her status as a survivor by trying to implicitly force the Germans she met into concealing possible manifestations of anti-Jewish attitudes they may have had.

Edith F. moved to Germany from Romania in 1986, also following her family. She explains that as a Holocaust survivor, she lost her attachment to any homeland, in her case Hungary and Romania, so moving to Germany was not difficult because of this kind of sentiment. Nevertheless, she could not stop looking out for perpetrators among the Germans: "The bad thing here [in Germany] is when you think about ...

my generation, in the beginning, now I try to avoid that, not to [see] somewhere the *Oberscharführer* [senior squad leader] from my camp or the lady-guard. That feels a bit bad, but my kids live here."[61]

The experience of personal encounters with Germans was another important issue that was repeatedly stressed by the narrators. For those living in Germany, it was an everyday necessity they needed to get accustomed to. In many cases, not even living side by side in the time of peace could overcome their reservations. Lily A. describes her doubts about the ability of the older generation to fully comprehend the real extent of the Holocaust and express sufficient regret. She extends these feelings implicitly even onto young Germans, which makes her reserved and socially isolated: "We made friends with Yugoslavs mostly. Somehow, until today, I do not have close German friends. I have acquaintances and I must say they are really good people, some are even younger than me, they did not have a chance to be Nazis, but still, I cannot befriend them as much as other people."[62]

The general German understanding of the Holocaust is also contested by Frenty A., who paid a visit to the Bergen-Belsen concentration camp in 1995. He states that the memory site is well established and well kept, but the context of the surroundings, which simply do not reflect on history, is still very disturbing to him: "Around the camp, there were small farms with pigs, with sheep, with happy Germans who lived there with their children, with their wives, all of them. And because I speak German, I approached a house and I say, 'Nice village you have here.' He says, 'Yes.' 'Is it recent?' 'No, it's my 150-year-old village,' he says. This means it was there.... They ate, drank, and could not care less. And they knew very well what was going on inside.... Of course, I did not tell him that we were neighbors a few years ago."[63]

The perceived lack of care and compassion from the German population demonstrated by this story supported Frenty A.'s opinion that Germans had offered minimal opposition to Hitler during the Third Reich, and they did not counteract the anti-Semitic policies, even if all this was happening at their doorsteps.

Leslie P. had already lived for decades in the United States at the moment of his interview in 1990. His encounter with Germans overseas reaffirmed his belief that the Germans have an inborn sense of superiority: "I know because I talk to them on trains, I speak perfect German.... They think the Americans have no culture, ... the French are dirty ... and only the Germans are perfect.... They still believe that they are the super-people."[64]

A different perspective can be found in an interview with Mimi P., born in 1927 in Gradets, close to Vidin (Bulgaria), who participated in the leftist resistance during the war. A decorated partisan fighter and veteran who remained in the country, she recalls a meeting with a former German soldier in the postwar era, through which she challenges the notion of German collective guilt: "There [at a meeting of Bulgarian war veterans] was this German guy, a deputy of *Bundestag* [German parliament], and you know what he told me, that he can't say if the winners live worse than the losers. Imagine, they disappeared for seventeen years into Siberia as German fascists, and this German who was a kid [back then] tells us how the winners can live worse than the losers."[65]

Mimi's usage of terms such as "German fascism" corresponds with the official interpretation of the war during the communist era, which also effaced Bulgaria's alliance with the Axis during World War II. Besides that, another stance opposing the idea of German collective guilt emerges from this interview. As she humanizes the former enemy, who was a child at the time of the war, and describes his long struggle for survival following its end, Mimi P. empathizes with the German(s) who was as a conscript presumably forced into compliance with the fascist regime.

During the postwar period, some of the survivors presented in this chapter tried to overcome the events of the Holocaust and World War II, rejecting the idea of German collective guilt; this was often motivated by positive individual experiences with Germans during the war. Still, the majority of narrators from southeastern Europe struggled to contain negative emotions toward Germans as a collective and considered them all to be responsible for the horrors and suffering during World War II, often related not only to the persecution of Jews. This perception undermined most attempts at reconciliation, social engagement, or even random casual interactions between these Jewish survivors and Germans.

In many of the postwar reflections on the perception of Germans by Holocaust survivors, considerations of contemporary political developments and threats appear. Their sensitivity to racial or religious hatred emanating from their societies is understandably higher considering their past experiences. In this respect, Frenty A.'s warning and prophetic statement from 1998 about the rise of neo-Nazism is symptomatic: "The Nazis ... Germans and Greeks, of Golden Dawn. In a tavern ... they were all dressed up in the same way, they were wearing a swastika, that is hooked cross, and they were singing and making speeches and so on.... These people. You would not think 150 poisonous ones arrived there, but there are 150 thousand if not much more than that."[66] In this way, he reacts to the news of an undisturbed meeting where Greek and German neo-Nazis gathered close to Thessaloniki. While the mention of the former—the Greek neo-Nazis—refers to the racist party Golden Dawn, represented until 2019 in the Greek Parliament, the presence of the latter, German neo-Nazis, is a mere assumption on his part, probably due to the principle of collective guilt.

COLLECTIVE GUILT AND INDIVIDUALIZED VICTIM-PERPETRATOR NARRATIVES

Holocaust survivors from southeastern Europe providing their reflections on the events of World War II offer diverse takes on the attribution of collective guilt to Germans. Based on our sample, it seems that the most important determinant for attitudes toward Germans was whether the speaker's country of origin was occupied by Nazi Germany.[67] Despite the fact that the prewar presence of a strong German minority in these countries has had a limited influence on the process of their stereotypization, in postwar reflections "the Germans" were generalized regardless of the previous demographic situation. Thus we can assume that the collective memory of the trauma, to which local Jewish communities were exposed, takes to a certain extent precedence over the personal layer of individualized victim-perpetrator narratives. This includes all varieties of these narratives, which typically construe Jewish-German relations.

It was mostly narrators from Yugoslavia and Greece who perceived Germans as dehumanized collective perpetrators born with a tendency toward hatred and violence. They represented the collective guilt narrative individually or collectively on behalf of all the Jewish victims with similar attitudes in similar contexts, such as the memories of violence during the occupation, concentration camps, torture, and medical experiments. They did not see a possibility for reconciliation after the war and refrained from direct contact with Germans, the German language, and Germany. In many cases, they tried to transmit their perception of the Germans onto the second generation, directly or indirectly, despite being aware of the generalization and the fact that it is superficial and discriminatory.

For the most part, narrators born in Romania and Bulgaria tended to relativize or reject the principle of collective guilt. Such attitudes usually stemmed from positive experiences gained at the time of war. These narratives presented Germans as aid givers, opponents of the National Socialist ideology, uncommitted to the National Socialist cause, and therefore not intentionally partaking in the persecution of Jews but even as victims of the Nazi regime's persecution. Knowledge of German and cultural proximity helped some of the Jews survive the war, but it was not a decisive factor in constituting their general attitude toward Germans, as many of the narrators who supported the collective guilt narrative also possessed these advantages.

TABLE 6.1 LIST OF INTERVIEWS

Name (gender)	Archival reference	Date of birth	Place of birth	Date of recording	Place of recording	Language
BULGARIA						
Helen S. (F)	ID 36035	6-2-1928	Sofia	12-6-1997	Lubbock, Texas (US)	English
Izidor D. (M)	ID 46806	12-20-1910	Sofia	6-5-1998	Sofia, Bulgaria	Bulgarian
Mimi P. (F)	ID 38790	9-6-1927	Gradets (near Vidin)	2-19-1998	Sofia, Bulgaria	Bulgarian
GREECE						
Elias C. (M)	ID 48297	2-26-1924	Volos	11-27-1998	Larissa, Greece	Greek
Frenty A. (M)	ID 47797	10-3-1924	Thessaloniki	11-3-1998	Athens, Greece	Greek, French
Ivonne K. (F)	ID 41963	6-10-1924	Thessaloniki	3-17-1998	Athens, Greece	Greek
Revekka A. (F)	ID 45239	10-1-1920	Kerkira	6-23-1998	Corfu, Greece	Greek
ROMANIA						
Bellina A. (F)	ID 20080	9-16-1931	Huși	9-29-1996	Toronto, Canada	English
Edith F. (F)	ID 9502	12-24-1922	Oradea	1-31-1996	Hesse, Germany	German
Leslie P. (M)	ID 52426	1921	Oradea	3-31-1990	Palo Alto, California (US)	English
Max G. (M)	ID 25547	5-6-1923	Bistrița	2-1-1997	Hilo, Hawaii (US)	English
YUGOSLAVIA						
Beruria S. (F)	ID 33668	7-27-1926	Zagreb	9-21-1997	Setauket, New York (US)	English
Lili A. (F)	ID 12825	2-26-1923	Belišće	3-27-1996	Frankfurt am Main, Germany	German
Mirjam D. (F)	ID 20374	9-10-1940	Slavonski Brod	10-3-1996	Samobor, Croatia	Croatian
Vera H. (F)	ID 54894	1936	Novi Sad	8-26-1998	Houston, Texas (US)	English

Source: USC Shoah Foundation Visual History Archive, accessed December 21, 2017, http://vhaonline.usc.edu.

In what could be described as the general community of memory, given the Holocaust and post-Holocaust experience as well as the age of the survivors, we can observe two different tendencies in relation to the constitutive narrative of German collective guilt in the context of the occupied and independent countries. This happens despite the fact that southeastern Europe was not generally considered as the German Lebensraum. The less forgiving of these two tendencies, nevertheless, dominates, and therefore documents how the events of the Holocaust, even after fifty years, remained embedded in the collective consciousness of this community in southeastern Europe and probably elsewhere as well.

Reconciliation with Germans in the form of forgetting or forgiving—not as amnesia but in terms of coping with the trauma—was not possible for most survivors. They emphasize their personal agency during the war, but also how it persisted into the postwar period and further influenced their daily lives. For the first generation after the war, their agency became inextricably linked to their Jewish identity as Holocaust survivors. In general, this pattern demonstrates an inability on behalf of the victims of mass atrocities to ever fully cope with their trauma. This often takes the form of collective guilt projected onto the group held responsible for their suffering, even if only a portion of this group was actually responsible.

II
AFTERSHOCKS AND MEMORIES OF WAR

CHAPTER 7

MULTIPLY ENTANGLED

The Gottschee Germans between Slovenia, Austria, Germany, and North America

JANNIS PANAGIOTIDIS

Anna, Alois, and Frieda Klun were born in Lienfeld, Lower Carniola, Austria in 1897, 1905, and 1908 respectively. None of them died there. Alois was the first to leave home: in 1928, he emigrated from what, by then, had become the village of Livold in the Slovenian part of the Kingdom of Serbs, Croats, and Slovenes (soon to be renamed the Kingdom of Yugoslavia) to Canada, and from there onward to the United States of America, where he settled in New York.[1] Anna and Frieda continued to live in their native village until late 1941, when German authorities relocated them from their Italian-occupied home to the Brežice (Rann) region of German-occupied Lower Styria as part of the ongoing *"Heim ins Reich"* ("back home to the Reich") campaign of Nazi Germany, which sought to resettle German minorities within the borders of the Greater German Reich. There, the sisters' ways parted: since Frieda was married to an ethnic Slovene, Josef (Jože) Krajec, the Nazi authorities deemed her unworthy of becoming a frontier settler against "Slavdom." Therefore, in 1943, Frieda, Josef, and their two children were sent to Germany in its 1937 borders—the so-called *Altreich*—and settled in the town of Sontra near Kassel, where they had another daughter. Meanwhile, Anna lived in Brežice until June 1945, when the victorious Yugoslav Partisans expelled her and her fellow resettlers to Austria, where she eked out an existence as a kitchen hand in a nunnery in Graz.[2] In 1950, she was able to join her brother Alois—by then known as Louis—in New York.[3] There, at almost sixty years of age, she married Max Scheschareg, whom she knew from back home in Slovenia; he had been from the neighboring village of Grafenfeld (Dolga Vas). Anna died in Pennsylvania in 1993, aged ninety-six. Louis had already passed away in his Florida home in 1983. Frieda, the youngest, outlived both of her siblings. She died in 2005 at the age of ninety-seven in Hünfeld, Germany.

These moving biographies are not chosen at random: Frieda Klun was my grandmother; her German-born daughter is my mother. Yet this chapter is more than an exercise in family history. These three stories of multiple migrations and displacement are quite typical for people born at that particular time in that particular place. The Kluns were Gottscheers, part of the German-speaking minority living in the Gottschee/Kočevje (Kočevska region) region in the predominantly Slovenian-speaking southern marches of the Austrian Empire. The presence of this linguistic minority in the region went back to the settlement of Carinthian, Tyrolian, Franconian, and Thuringian peasants in the densely wooded area in the fourteenth century.[4] Over the centuries, they developed into what *völkisch* scholars in the past would have called a *Sprachinsel*, a "linguistic island."[5] Yet, contrary to the impression of isolation that the "island" image conveys, the life trajectories of the Klun siblings point to the multiple entanglements of the Gottscheers between their home region, the Habsburg Empire, Yugoslavia, Austria, North America, Germany, and for a short while even Italy. These entanglements were the result of repeated movement of both people over borders and borders over people.

I will use the example of the Klun siblings and the other inhabitants of their native Lienfeld/Livold to look at how Gottscheers moved through time and space in the course of the twentieth century.[6] As a result of mass labor migration, forced displacement, and refugee resettlement, this linguistic minority has virtually disappeared from its home region. Yet, unlike the members of other former German minorities in eastern and southeastern Europe, who in their vast majority merged into the populations of postwar Germany and Austria, the Gottscheers and their descendants nowadays mainly live in the United States and Canada. This resulted from the multiple historical entanglements of the Gottscheers and the interdependency between different migratory movements at different points in time. I will show this by focusing on the situation after the Second World War, when the majority of Gottscheers became "prisoners of the postwar" in Austria.[7] As will be seen, the transatlantic networks that most Gottscheers possessed due to massive emigration from the region in the late nineteenth and early twentieth centuries were instrumental in directing their postwar movement across the ocean. Their connections thus showed them the way out of their Austrian impasse—though, as will become clear, not without obstacles.

To build a sample of "Lienfelders on the move," I combine three different yet complementary sets of sources. The first is the list of resettlers compiled by the Nazi resettlement authorities in 1941, which provides a complete inventory of the people moved from the Gottschee to Lower Styria.[8] This list provided the basis for research in the digital archive of the International Tracing Service (ITS) in Bad Arolsen, Germany (now known as the Arolsen Archives), which holds a variety of records on people displaced in the course of wartime and postwar events.[9] As the original purpose of the ITS archive was to trace individuals, its records are sorted and searchable according to name, making it possible to search for every single individual from the resettler list. Among the ITS records, the most important material was the so-called Care and Maintenance (CM/1) files of the International Refugee Organization (IRO), which constitute a treasure trove for researching individual migration trajectories and reconstructing migrant networks.[10] They are complemented by emigration data on people resettled overseas under international schemes.[11] A third important source is the extensive genealogical database at www.ancestry.com, containing among other things US census data, passenger lists, and naturalization records, which are particularly useful for the reconstruction of transatlantic migrations.[12]

Straddling the rupture of 1945, this chapter contributes to this volume's migration theme by following these people through their varied fortunes of the interwar, wartime, and postwar periods, situating their movements within the context of German empire building, war, and global connections. As will be seen, despite their designation as a "German" minority, the Gottscheers hardly considered Germany an important point of reference until the interwar period, when German empire building started to encroach on their lives. Assisted by young Nazi activists from among the minority, German authorities then removed the Gottscheers from their homes during the war to merge them with the main body of the German nation while using them as frontier settlers. After the Nazi defeat, resettlement resulted in flight and expulsion to Austria, where the Gottscheers attempted to receive assistance from the international refugee care organizations active in the country. Drawing on individual case files, I examine their—largely unsuccessful—attempts to change national affiliation after the war and to claim Slovenian rather than German identities, thereby exploring the limits of ethnic and national hybridity, ambiguity, and fluidity in the region. Expanding this volume's focus on the entangled history of Germany and the Balkans, I finally look at the way the Gottscheers were eventually able to capitalize on their transatlantic connections to achieve the desired aim of emigration, both by using preexisting family networks and by creating new emigration chains in the process.

THE GOTTSCHEE AND MIGRATION

As the misleading and discredited metaphor of the "linguistic island" already indicated, the danger of "ethnicizing" or "nationalizing" history is inherent in writing about multilinguistic territories and linguistic minorities.[13] The designation of the Gottscheers as Gottschee "Germans" is a product of the "nationality struggles" in the Habsburg Empire since the second half of the nineteenth century, and later on of the impact of German diaspora politics. Historically, the Gottschee region had been settled by both German- and Slovenian-speaking colonists.[14] As the widespread presence of Slavic family names among the Gottscheers suggests, there was no significant dividing line between different linguistic groups.[15] Language as a criterion of nationality became important when the Habsburg census started to register the language of daily use (*Umgangssprache*) of each individual in 1880. For the court district (*Gerichtsbezirk*) Gottschee, the 1880 census revealed 14,323 German-speakers and 5,622 Slovenian-speakers, for a total population of 19,976 individuals.[16] Lienfeld was linguistically rather homogenous, registering 95 percent German-speakers (607 of 638 inhabitants) in 1890.[17]

Historically, mobility played an important role in the lives of the inhabitants of the Gottschee region. For centuries, they were known as peddlers, whose trading routes would take them the length and breadth of the Habsburg Empire as far as Salzburg and Prague, and even into Poland and Russia.[18] Even so, the majority of people in the region gained their subsistence by farming smallholdings and working in forestry. These traditional trades, never the source of great riches, by the late nineteenth century could not sustain the growing population anymore, making the Gottschee region a prime source of overseas emigration. At the time, emigration from the Habsburg Empire as a whole took off. Between 1876 and 1914, more than 3.5 million people left Austria-Hungary.[19] Importantly for the issue of entanglement, return migration was substantial as well: of the 1.2 million who emigrated between 1908 and 1913, for instance, 460,000 or almost 40 percent returned.[20] The province of Carniola, to which the Gottschee belonged, was among the regions with the greatest population losses due to emigration: between 1900 and 1910, the net migration loss amounted to 6.7 percent of the population, the highest rate among the Austrian provinces of the empire together with Galicia.[21] In the Gottschee, the population shrank by almost 10 percent between 1880 and 1910.[22] In absolute numbers, 76,195 persons emigrated from the Carniola province between 1892 and 1913. Of those, almost a quarter—17,566 individuals—came from the District Captaincy (Bezirkshauptmannschaft) of Gottschee, which also included the almost exclusively Slovenian-speaking court districts of Grosslaschitz (Velike Lašče) and Reifnitz (Ribnica), and had had 41,409 inhabitants in 1880.[23] Emigration continued after the First World War, though at a lower rate due to immigration restrictions in the United States. In the 1930s, there were some 16,000 Gottscheers living abroad, as opposed to an estimated 14,000 living in the Gottschee in 1937.[24] Thus, by the eve of the Second World War, more Gottscheers lived in the United States than in the Gottschee itself—most were in New York (Brooklyn and Queens) and Cleveland.[25]

ENTANGLEMENTS WITH AUSTRIA AND GERMANY AFTER THE FIRST WORLD WAR

The state order established after the First World War added further nodes to the web entangling the Gottscheers. These new entanglements had less to do with the movement of people over borders—though that continued—and more to do with the movement of borders over people. When Habsburg imperial space was reorganized imperfectly according to the principle of nationality after the First World War, the Austrian Republic became an "external homeland" for German-speaking subjects of the now-defunct Habsburg Empire. These people included the Gottscheers, who were now part of the German-speaking minority in the Kingdom of Serbs, Croats, and Slovenes. Article 80 of the 1919 Treaty of Saint-Germain granted them and all other former Habsburg citizens the right to choose their ethno-nation over their home regions: "Persons possessing rights of citizenship in territory forming part of the former Austro-Hungarian Monarchy, and differing in race and language from the majority of the population of such territory, shall within six months from the coming into force of the present Treaty severally be entitled to opt for Austria, Italy, Poland, Roumania, the Serb-Croat-Slovene State, or the Czecho-Slovak State, if the majority of the population of the State selected is of the same race and language as the person exercising the right to opt."[26]

Thousands of German-speaking inhabitants of Slovenia, especially from among the urban elites, opted to leave the country under these provisions.[27] While exact numbers are hard to come by, it appears that the predominantly rural Gottscheers in their majority did not embrace the Austrian option. Instead, they soon resumed their overseas emigration activities—like Alois Klun, who bypassed US immigration restrictions by taking a detour through Canada.

Of increasingly greater importance than the Austrian neighbor, however, was Germany. According to a 1937 report by the Austrian consul on the political stance of the German-speaking minority in Slovenia, their relation toward Yugoslavia was "indifferent" and toward Austria "platonic."[28] Most Slovenian Germans were of a *großdeutsch* persuasion by then, that is, oriented toward a greater German empire. Especially in the case of the youth, this increasingly implied an orientation toward

National Socialism.²⁹ To be sure, German irredentism had not been an invention of the Nazis. Pan-German (*alldeutsch*) visions went back to the *Kaiserreich* and did not subside in the Weimar Republic, where they became paired with territorial revisionism fueled by defeat and territorial loss.³⁰ The Nazis, however, took the outreach to German (or rather, German-speaking) minorities in eastern and southeastern Europe to a new level, tying them to the Reich and hierarchically organizing them as *Volksgruppen* ("ethnic groups") according to National Socialist precepts, often with the help of radical activists from the younger generation.³¹

In the Gottschee, the most prominent representative of the radical National Socialist youth was Wilhelm Lampeter, born in 1916. He rose to power in the Gottscheer *Volksgruppe* in 1938, sidelining the old leaders, Father Josef Eppich and the lawyer Dr. Hans Arko, who had been loyal to the Yugoslav state.³² The new leadership directly responded to orders from the Reich government, thereby de facto politically dissociating the Gottscheers from Yugoslavia and tying their fate to the German Reich.

Lampeter was well aware that despite this firm political attachment to Germany, the actual ties of most Gottscheers lay across the ocean. From a National Socialist viewpoint, this was a problem. In his 1942 analysis of the situation of the Gottscheers during the interwar period, Lampeter stated that "peasant thinking has been covered by Americanism, and people are convinced that it is impossible to survive in the homeland (*Heimat*) without the influx of Dollars. . . . The liberal-capitalist worldview has an annihilating influence on the economy."³³ Consequently, the ideological instruction of the Gottscheers by the *Mannschaft*—a paramilitary organization formed in 1939 for all males between twenty-one and fifty years of age—was meant to counter these "negative influences of America on the Gottscheer *Volksgruppe*." In particular, these influences included:

1. Excessive emigration
2. Negative selection [i.e. the loss of the young and fit through emigration]
3. Negative influence on relatives remaining behind through letters, pictures, and visits
4. Confusion through the tasteless American clothes sent to relatives back home as gifts
5. Negative effects of the Dollar on the *Volksgruppe*.³⁴

These American influences were to be countered by instructing the *Mannschaft* members, among other things, about "the German people," "Adolf Hitler and his people," "genetics as a cornerstone of National Socialist ideology," "the Nordic man," "the peasant in the National Socialist

Reich," and "German culture and the German peasant."[35] The aim was to inculcate "a peasant way of thinking tied to soil and blood [*bäuerliches, erd- und blutgebundenes Denken*] into the heart and soul of the German man. This way of thinking shall burn out of the German man the liberal-capitalist confusion about the almightiness of some yellow metal and some ragged shreds of paper called money."[36] In other words, the Gottscheers were to be mentally disentangled from America and made to embrace the "German"—that is, National Socialist—way of thinking.

RESETTLEMENT TO LOWER STYRIA

The forced entanglement of the Gottscheers with Germany reached its high point in the wake of the German invasion of Yugoslavia in 1941. After its quick defeat, the country was divided between the Axis powers, with Croatia becoming a nominally independent state. Slovenia was divided between Germany, Italy, and Hungary.[37] The Gottschee ended up under Italian occupation, making the German-speaking Gottscheers once again a minority. Given Nazi Germany's plans for the "reordering of ethnographic conditions" of Europe, which Hitler had announced in a Reichstag speech in October 1939, this implied the resettlement of the Gottscheer *Volksgruppe*.[38] By 1941, there had been a series of precedents for such collective movements of people between Germany and its allies, with the aim of disentangling ethnically mixed populations in central, eastern, and southeastern Europe, thereby clearly demarcating the respective spheres of influence by removing ethnic minorities as possible irritants. In October 1939, Germany and Italy had signed a resettlement treaty regarding the German-speaking minority in Italian South Tyrol. About 90 percent of the South Tyrolians opted for Germany, with approximately 75,000 persons actually leaving their homes for the expanded German Reich. The near-total resettlement of German-speaking minorities from Estonia and Latvia followed in late 1939 and early 1940. Other ethnic Germans were removed from Soviet-occupied Poland (Eastern Galicia and Volhynia) and Romania (Northern Bukovina and Bessarabia) as well as from independent Romania (Southern Bukovina and Dobruja). By 1940, the number of *Heim ins Reich* settlers amounted to some 500,000 individuals.[39]

Despite repeated initiatives since 1939 by the Gottscheer *Volksgruppe*'s National Socialist leaders for their region to be annexed to the Greater German Reich, the Gottscheers were no exception to the new rule of creating ethnically homogenized spheres of influence by moving minorities.[40] They were to be "united" with the Reich and become German citizens, yet outside of their home region and not as a distinct group, but as part of the homogenized German *Volkskörper*. Like the other resettled German minorities, the Gottscheers were to become settlers in territories already annexed to the German Reich.[41] While Germans from northeastern and eastern Europe were installed in occupied Polish territories of the so-called "Warthegau," the Gottscheers were not supposed to move very far from home: their assigned territory was in Lower Styria, in the so-called "Ranner Dreieck," also known as "Save-Sotla strip," the region around the town of Brežice (Rann) between the Sava and Sotla Rivers, at the southeastern tip of German-occupied Slovenia. As in the better-researched case of occupied Poland, this necessitated the prior displacement of the local non-German population, in this case Slovenes.[42] After the failure of plans to move them to the Independent State of Croatia, where in a "domino effect" they were supposed to replace Serbs earmarked for deportation to German-occupied Serbia, some thirty-seven thousand Brežice Slovenes were eventually put in camps in the German *Altreich* (Silesia, Brandenburg, Thuringia, and Württemberg), where they spent the remainder of the war.[43] Following a well-known mechanism, the forced disentanglement of populations implied entangled resettlements, as it were.

The Gottscheers, meanwhile, were supposed to be resettled. This involved a process of selection by the Einwandererzentralstelle (EWZ), the main Nazi agency tasked with assessing the suitability of individuals for resettlement and the awarding of German citizenship based on physical, racial, social, and political criteria.[44] Through a mechanism of co-optation called "self-selection" (*Selbstauslese*), the EWZ was heavily assisted by the Gottscheer Nazi leadership (*Volksgruppenführung*), which proactively asked for ethnically mixed families, politically unreliable individuals, and "unfit" smallholders to be excluded from compact resettlement with the rest of the *Volksgruppe*.[45] The co-optation by the authorities provided the *Volksgruppenführung* with significant leverage over their opponents from among the Catholic clergy and bourgeois circles, who opposed the resettlement. The option was officially announced on October 20, 1941; the deadline for registration was November 20.

Despite propagandistic efforts, by November 13 far from all Gottscheers had registered for resettlement. In some districts, up to 25 percent of the population refused to do so.[46] This was arguably due to family ties with the Slovenian population, the influence of local priests opposed to resettlement, and the fact that the Gottscheer population had been kept in the dark about their prospective destination. As a consequence, the resettlement authorities also permitted ethnically mixed families and political opponents of the *Volksgruppenführung* to register.[47] A few days before the deadline, on November 17, the authorities for the first time publicly announced the Ranner Dreieck as the Gottscheers' destination and promised compensation for property left behind. At the same time, it was made clear that the option for German citizenship would be a one-time opportunity—whoever was left behind now would not have a chance to join the *Volk* later.[48]

The "sticks and carrots" strategy worked: of the 12,487 Gottscheers counted in the June 1941 census of the *Volksgruppe*, 12,093 eventually opted for resettlement and becoming German citizens.[49] At the time, 211 of them resided in Lienfeld. In all of the Gottschee, only 300 to 600 individuals chose to stay behind, including the former community leader Father Josef Eppich.[50] Including children, 11,747 individuals appeared before the EWZ commission for screening. The commission decided whether applicants were to become settlers in Lower Styria (so-called *St-Fälle*), be resettled in the *Altreich* (*A-Fälle*), or be rejected altogether. The vast majority of Gottscheers satisfied the EWZ's selection criteria: 94.6 percent (11,110 individuals) were classified as *St-Fälle*. By contrast, only 4.9 percent (571 individuals) were deemed *A-Fälle*, and 66 individuals were rejected. While 79 percent of those deemed *St-Fälle* were classified as "pure ethnic German" (*rein volksdeutsch*), the same was true for only 30 percent of *A-Fälle*. "Mixed" individuals and families were thus most likely to be earmarked for resettlement in the *Altreich*.[51]

Frieda Klun and her family were among those latter cases. She and her Slovenian husband, Josef, had already registered for resettlement during the first week of the registration period. They received certificates of German citizenship and resettler IDs (*Umsiedlerausweise*), which, however, were marked "valid only in the *Altreich*."[52] Even so, they initially moved to Lower Styria with the other resettlers. They reached Rann on December 29, 1941, and moved into a house outside of town, which they occupied together with Frieda's sister Anna. In late spring of 1942, they got their own home. It was not until a year later that they were taken to Blankenburg in Thuringia, where they spent four weeks in a transit camp. In late May 1943, they settled in the town of Sontra near Kassel, where Josef received an accountant job in the local mines.[53] There, they safely lived to see the end of the war.

In an ironic twist of fate, the classification as an *A-Fall*—which Frieda even years later considered to be a personal insult—turned out to be a blessing in disguise. The other Gottscheers, including Frieda's sister Anna, stayed in the Rann region, which was exposed to attacks by Yugoslav Partisans resisting the Nazi occupation and by April 1944 also became the target of Allied bombing raids.[54] At the end of the war, the German authorities did not permit evacuation from Rann to the Reich until May 8, 1945, the very day of the German capitulation. Some people, including Anna, managed to escape to Austria by train—in her case reportedly after hiding from the Partisans in her Slovenian neighbors' oven.[55] Many others fleeing north by train or wagon were overtaken by the Partisans and imprisoned. By the fall of 1945, they were released and expelled to Austria.[56]

TRYING TO PASS FOR SLOVENE IN POSTWAR AUSTRIA

After their evacuation and forced expulsion from Yugoslavia, the Gottscheers became part of the diverse population of refugees and displaced persons (DPs) in Austria, which had returned to independence after the German defeat. There, the Gottscheers found themselves in a legal limbo: the Nazi authorities had provided them with German citizenship during the resettlement, but it was anything but clear what these legal acts were worth in the postwar situation. At any rate, during the first postwar years, there was no sovereign German state to offer them protection, and Yugoslavia had not been covered by the Potsdam Agreement, which made expellees from Poland, Czechoslovakia, and Hungary Germans by default after expulsion. Moreover, though any Gottscheer born before 1918 had been an Austrian imperial citizen by birth, the Republic of Austria did not recognize any legal obligation toward them or any of the "Old Austrians" gathered in its territory. Return to Yugoslavia, where they had lost all property and which stripped members of disloyal minorities of their Yugoslav citizenship, was not an option either.[57] They were, to use Tara Zahra's phrase, "prisoners of the postwar."[58]

Given the family ties most Gottscheers had to North America, a logical way out of this "prison"—which in actuality consisted of refugee camps or private accommodation in Styria and Carinthia—seemed to point overseas. After repatriation had turned out to be unfeasible for many DPs from the newly Communist countries of eastern and southeastern Europe, emigration also became the evolving international community's preferred solution to the greater postwar refugee problem.[59] The International Refugee Organization (IRO), which assumed responsibility for the European DP population in July 1947, tried to organize the continental or overseas resettlement of its clients. This was a cumbersome effort, as its success depended on the good will of intended host states, most of which were reluctant to accept greater numbers of refugees and applied strict selection criteria.[60] The United States, which was the desired destination for many eastern European DPs, did not open its gates until the passing of the DP Act in June 1948, granting access only to a limited number of DPs.[61]

The Gottscheers had an additional problem: international care and assisted resettlement schemes were exclusively directed at non-German refugees. The 1948 DP Act did include a small quota for ethnic Germans, who were to make up 50 percent of the German and Austrian immigration contingents of roughly twenty-seven thousand persons.[62] Emigration was thus theoretically possible. Yet prospective emigrants of German ethnic origin did not enjoy the same status as DPs and were not granted IRO support. As the 1948 IRO constitution stated, "Persons who will not be the concern of the Organization" included: "Persons of German ethnic origin, whether German nationals or members of German minorities in other countries, who a) have been or may be transferred to Germany from other countries; b) have been, during the second world war, evacuated from Germany to other countries; c) have fled from, or into, Germany, or from their places of residence into countries other than Germany in order to avoid falling into the hands of Allied armies."[63]

This definition excluded the Gottscheers, who were of German ethnic origin. Or were they? After all, "ethnic origin" was hardly an objective condition. Already in the past, sifting people according to nationality in the multiethnic lands of southeastern Europe had been a challenge for different state authorities, be they Habsburg, Yugoslav, or Nazi. Habsburg jurisdiction had distinguished between *Willensmerkmale* and *Wesensmerkmale* to define national belonging, that is, the subjective will to belong to a nationality on the one hand, and "objective" criteria like language and culture on the other.[64] The Nazis, too, referred to a mix of subjective and objective markers in the sorting of (non-Jewish) populations, for instance in occupied Czechoslovakia.[65] All these criteria were hardly straightforward in their application, given that people were often "nationally indifferent," could switch their national self-identification, and were in many instances multilingual.[66]

In the tense atmosphere of "nationality struggles" in interwar nation states, and even more so in the face of Nazi population policy, "national indifference" had become ever more difficult to sustain, as people in multiethnic regions were forced to choose sides. The Gottscheers, who had been offered a resettlement option under duress, were no exception. Yet, in quite a few instances, people were allowed to switch back after the war. The most famous case was arguably the "rehabilitation" of Polish "autochthones"—ethnically ambiguous Slavic-speaking inhabitants of the Polish-German borderlands—who had been registered in the German *Volksliste* introduced in occupied Poland.[67] In Slovenia, too, Slovenes from German-occupied Lower Styria, who had opted for membership in the local equivalent of the *Volksliste*—the Steierischer Heimatbund—could return to their previous identification as Slovenes.[68] For Gottscheers, too, switching allegiance and trying to pass for a nationality other than German could appear like a viable option when dealing with the international care organizations.[69]

Remarkably, this option did not originally occur to the first Lienfelders who registered with the international refugee authorities starting in mid-1947. Instead, they displayed astonishing honesty regarding their ethnic belonging. The first documented applicant, in June 1947, was Stefan Poje, a native of Eben (Ravne), who had married a woman from Lienfeld and had been resettled from there in 1941. In his registration with the—soon to be dissolved—Intergovernmental Committee on Refugees, he claimed his nationality to be "jugoslawische (V.D.)," V.D. meaning "volksdeutsch" or "ethnic German."[70] Ordered according to fluency, he listed German and Slovenian as his languages, claiming good reading and writing skills for German, but no writing skills for Slovenian. His wife, Elisabeth, though only claiming Yugoslav nationality, also listed German as her first language.[71] Their daughter, Rosina, claimed no knowledge of Slovenian at all, just fluent German and good English (!).[72] The Pojes were not alone in their frankness: with few exceptions, the Lienfelders, who claimed international assistance until late 1948, stated their nationality as "volksdeutsch," often explicitly stressing that they could not return to Yugoslavia because they had been expelled as Germans.[73] The latter might point to a lingering fear of being sent back to Yugoslavia—although involuntary repatriations to Communist countries had ceased by 1946, memories of the forced return of anti-Communist Yugoslavs shortly after the war might still have been present.[74] Yet while no Gottscheer was sent back to Yugoslavia, the way into IRO care and toward emigration was also blocked: all these applications by "*Volksdeutsche*" were placed "in suspense" or they were deemed ineligible straightaway.

By early 1949, word seems to have spread among the Lienfelders that telling the truth about one's origins was not an effective strategy to attain the desired goal: IRO assistance and, ultimately, resettlement overseas.[75] Hence, the stories began to change, and Lienfelder applicants began to claim that they were and had always been, in fact, Slovenes. The change is most obvious for those who had previously made declarations to the contrary in their registrations. The same Stefan Poje, who in his 1947 registration had claimed to be *volksdeutsch* and professed no knowledge of written Slovenian, in his February 1949 application for assistance to the IRO claimed to be a fluent speaker of Slovenian and German, with only slight reading and writing skills in German. His wife, who now called herself Elizabeta, only claimed slight knowledge of German, while daughter Rozina (now spelled with a more "Slavic-looking" z), who in 1947 had spoken no Slovenian at all, now was allegedly fluent in Slovenian and German. Stefan Poje attributed his resettlement to Lower Styria to the difficult conditions under Italian occupation.[76] The eligibility officer, however, did not buy this story and placed the application "in suspense," given that "1) Names of children and surname [are] typically German; 2) [He] availed himself of the 'Umsiedlung' to Brezice [*sic*] in 1942. Consequently no reason to doubt V.D."[77] Stefan Poje appealed against this decision, claiming that: "I am no *Volksdeutscher* but a *Nationalslovene*. Proof: my name, my language. I have not resettled from Italian-occupied Slovenia to German-occupied Slovenia (Brezice-Rann) as a VD, but because the Italians persecuted me as a *Nationalslovene*."[78]

The irony is obvious in Stefan Poje pointing to his name, which the eligibility officer had held against his claim to be Slovene, as evidence of this very claim. And, in a way, they were both right: while the surname was widespread among Gottscheers—the resettlement list holds no fewer than 119 Pojes, twenty of whom were from Lienfeld—it could easily be Slovenian, too, and thus hardly made for convincing evidence either way. At any rate, Stefan Poje's appeal remained without success and his application remained "in suspense."[79]

Anna Klun, too, attempted to pass for Slovene. The story she presented in May 1949 to convince the eligibility officers of her Slovenian identity was significantly more elaborate than Stefan Poje's. Obviously aware of the importance of names for appearing to belong to a particular nationality, she spelled her first name "Ana," to make it look more Slavic. Aware of the importance of language as a criterion for nationality, she stated Slovenian to be her first language, claiming fluent speaking, reading, and writing skills. Describing her experiences during the war, she alleged to have been resettled by the Italians (rather than the Germans) in 1941, and then expelled by the Partisans in 1945 for lack of right of residence (*Heimatrecht*) in Brežice. She had no family left in Slovenia: an aunt had supposedly been kidnapped by the Italians, her cousin and her sister-in-law killed by the Partisans, and her sister and family had been taken away by the Germans.[80]

Arguably because of doubts arising among the deciding officers, An(n)a added more detail to her story in June: the Italians had pressured her family to leave because they wanted the best plots of land. Hence she left, together with the whole village. In addition, the Italians had been causing her trouble at the inn she was running, so that she preferred to be resettled than be taken to Italy. She once again declared to be Slovenian. Her father allegedly hailed from near Ribnica, a predominantly Slovenian region west of the Gottschee, where no *Volksdeutsche* lived. The Kluns had come to the Gottschee region through buying land there, but even though it was a German region, they had remained Slovene. The interviewer added that the applicant spoke good Slovenian. And indeed, An(n)a Klun managed to convince the eligibility officer of her

"Slovenianness"—on June 23, 1949, he deemed her "Within the mandate of the I.R.O.," adding a handwritten remark that "Impression from personal interview confirms above."[81]

A historian is not often in a position to judge the veracity of such personal accounts found in official sources. Nor is it necessarily his or her primary task to "catch" historical actors lying. Yet in this case, my privileged access to information about Anna Klun's case allows me to check certain elements of her story presented to the IRO for accuracy. Her good Slovenian language skills, for instance, which the interviewer mentions in his report, could not be confirmed by her niece and nephew—my mother and uncle—who recalled her to only have basic Slovenian from her job as an innkeeper in Lienfeld.[82] Her account of wartime events also took a creative approach to the facts. The alleged kidnapping of her sister and family by the Germans clearly referred to Frieda Klun's resettlement from Brežice to the German *Altreich*, which, though involuntary, was a relatively comfortable affair. The other alleged kidnappings and killings in the family were apparently invented.[83] Unfortunately, family memory does not reach back far enough to assess Anna's claim regarding her father's origins from Ribnica. This is possible, considering that the surname Klun was rare among Gottscheers but appears more frequently in the ITS archives among DPs from Trieste, the Italian-Slovenian borderlands of Venezia-Giulia, Croatia, and other parts of Slovenia, including Ribnica.[84] It is therefore quite plausible that the Klun family had only recently been assimilated into the Gottscheer minority.

Be that as it may, less decisive for Anna's IRO status than her ancestral origin was her wartime behavior, which was subject to further scrutiny. While her application for resettlement was placed "in suspense" since October 1949 because of her advanced age (fifty-two at the time), she was declared "Not within the mandate of the I.R.O." in January 1950, as it had been established that she had become a German citizen in May 1942, and a member of the Kulturbund, the association of ethnic Germans in Yugoslavia, in 1943.[85] These acts of allegiance, rather than real or presumed cultural traits and ethnic origins, were eventually decisive for the failure of Anna's application for IRO assistance. Unlike claims about subjective belonging and language skills, these facts could be easily checked, as the IRO had access to the naturalization files of the Einwandererzentralstelle (EWZ).[86] At the time, the Gottscheers had presented themselves as Germans to the EWZ, in order to become citizens of the Third Reich. Now these very files were held against them in their quest to be recognized as Slovenian DPs. This, then, points to a metaphorical entanglement of the Gottscheers: they became entangled in the web of stories they told—or had to tell—about themselves in different contexts, in order to get by during the upheavals of wartime and the postwar period.

These cases of unsuccessful national conversion, which were the rule rather than the exception among the Lienfelder sample, also highlight the limits of ethnic and national hybridity, ambiguity, and fluidity in the region. Despite her initial success before the IRO eligibility officer, there was not much ambiguity about someone like Anna Klun, who in fact barely spoke Slovenian (the eligibility officer probably spoke none at all), had joined the Nazi resettlement campaign, and eventually could not make a compelling case for not being German. The same was true for many other Gottscheers, who in their majority were no "amphibians" like the ones described by Chad Bryant in a Czech context, but occupied a distinct place in Slovenian prewar and wartime society.[87] This does not mean that there had been no "conversions" in the past, as evidenced by the many Slavic family names among the Gottscheers, and no "mixing" in the present, as can be seen, for instance, from Frieda Klun's marriage to Jože/Josef Krajec. But intermarriage did not necessarily imply "hybridization": despite being married to a Slovene, Frieda did not speak Slovenian, and neither did her children. Thus, while certainly not an "island," the Gottscheers were a recognizable minority within the Yugoslav state, which prevented most of them from retroactively claiming themselves into the Slovenian nation when it appeared convenient.

EMIGRATION AND NETWORKS

That said, at least one Lienfelder family did successfully pass for Slovenian. Janez Cerne (born in Lienfeld in 1890); his wife, Paulina Cerne née Jonke (born in Hornberg, Gottschee, in 1901); and their five children were determined eligible for IRO support in June 1949 and sailed from Bremerhaven to New York on the *General Muir* on December 16, 1949.[88] On the Nazi resettlement list, they had been listed as Johann and Pauli Tscherne. Unfortunately, their IRO application has not been preserved, making it impossible to determine the story they told to convince the eligibility officers of their Slovenianness. Whatever it was, they managed to emigrate before their credentials could be double-checked.

But passing for Slovene in order to gain international assistance was only one element of the emigration project. The other crucial ingredient was a sponsor in the United States, which points to the importance of family networks. In fact, the IRO was very much aware of this importance: its application forms invariably asked about relatives abroad, which most of the Lienfelders did have, mostly in the United States, and in a few cases also in Canada.

Regarding emigration along family networks, the Tscherne-Jonke family is a fascinating case, as they tapped into preexisting networks while creating new ones in the process of migration. Johann/Janez and Pauli(na) Tscherne/Cerne were sponsored by Pauli's older sister, Julia Plesche née Jonke, born in Hornberg in 1891, who had already emigrated to the United States before the First World War.[89] She had settled in the Gottscheer neighborhood of Ridgewood, Queens, and had become a US citizen in 1944.[90] Now she helped to bring her sister to the United States, where Pauli herself had already spent time during the early 1920s under her maiden name.[91]

In late 1949, two of Johann's siblings—his brother Heinrich Tscherne (born in Lienfeld in 1897), with his wife, Josefa, and their four children, and his sister Maria Marn née Tscherne (born in Lienfeld in 1892)—were still in Europe. Unlike Johann, neither had been able to convince the IRO that they were Slovenes. Maria had been among the early applicants for IRO assistance in January 1948 and had naively admitted to being ethnically German—a mistake she was subsequently unable to correct.[92] On her CM/1-form, she had originally stated the desire to join her husband, Josef Marn, in Toronto, Canada. (Unfortunately, the available sources do not reveal how he had gotten there.) On February 15, 1950, she informed the IRO review board that she was no longer interested in emigration.[93] Two weeks later, on February 28, 1950, she took an airplane (!) from Amsterdam to New York.[94]

It appears that, like her older brother, Johann, Maria too benefited from the Hornberger Jonke network, that is from the aid of her brother's in-laws. Her destination address in Ridgewood was the house where the Plesche-Jonke family had lived in 1930, and which still in 1940 had been home to another Jonke sister, Lina Schager née Jonke (born 1889).[95] In August 1951, a year and a half after Maria's arrival, her younger brother Heinrich's sons, Heinrich Jr. and Albert, emigrated by ship from Bremerhaven to the same address, where Maria would still be living when she was eventually naturalized in 1955.[96]

But the Tschernes did not leave it at using the Jonke network—they also created a migration chain of their own. This was the case in 1956, when Johann and Pauli's by then twenty-three-year-old son Alfred sponsored the immigration of his uncle Heinrich and his family (wife Josefa and two underage daughters), who left by plane from Munich airport on Christmas Eve 1956.[97] Postwar emigration projects were, thus, not entirely dependent on preexisting networks but could also be self-sustaining.

That said, the preexisting networks resulting from the multiple Gottscheer emigrations during the interwar period or even before the First World War were usually decisive for the success of the resettlers' later emigration. While the Tscherne-Jonke family is an example of how different sponsors could combine their efforts to create an efficient migration network, sometimes it was just one very active individual who managed to reunite a scattered family. A case in point is Pauline Schleimer, who after the war helped her father and four siblings immigrate to the United States. Pauline was born in Lienfeld in 1899 and arrived in the States on February 1, 1921, where she was soon joined by her sisters Theresia (born 1902) and Hilda (born 1900).[98] While Theresia stayed and continued to share a home with Pauline, Hilda returned to her native Lienfeld. During the resettlement campaign in 1941, she was sharing a house with her parents, Max Sr. (born 1868 in Upper Silesia) and Maria Schleimer née Rankel (born 1866 in Windischdorf, Gottschee); her younger brother, Max Jr. (born 1908), and his wife Helena (née Preiditsch), and their children Helena and Maria (born 1940 and 1941, respectively). Another two sisters had moved away from the village: Helena (born 1905) lived in Windischdorf with her husband, Josef Handler, and Klara (born 1910) was working in Stuttgart. After the resettlement, Klara joined her parents and brother Max in Lower Styria in 1943, and after the war worked in her brother's household in Kalsdorf bei Graz in Styria, Austria.[99] The Handler family and Hilda Schleimer found refuge in Klagenfurt, Carinthia.[100]

In September 1949, Pauline inquired with the IRO about her family members. Her handwritten letter revealed not only concern for her family, but also a remarkable degree of preparation for their resettlement overseas: "I would be very grateful if you could give me some information in regard to my family in Austria. . . . I bought a [sic] 81 acre farm with a ten room house to give them all a chance to reestablish themself [sic]. Now Sir, have they a chance to come over? If not I will have to sell and try something else. Please give me an answer. Respectfully, Pauline Schleimer."[101]

While the effect of this letter on the IRO authorities remains unclear, other sources reveal that the Schleimers started moving to the United States soon after: in March 1950, Helene Handler and her family sailed from Genoa to New York on the SS *Italia*.[102] Max Jr. and his family as well as Klara Schleimer followed on the same ship in May 1950.[103] Max Sr., by then eighty-two years of age, was awarded the luxury of an airplane ride via London and joined the family in June (his wife had presumably passed away).[104] For reasons not evident in the available source material, Hilda only came over with a considerable time lag, in January 1957.[105]

We may assume that the financial means available to the Schleimer family played a significant role in expediting the migration process. As Pauline's letter reveals, she had been able to buy a large farm and house

TABLE 7.1 OVERSEAS EMIGRATION OF RESETTLERS FROM LIENFELD

Year	By ship	By plane	Total individuals
1948	1	—	1
1949	10	—	10
1950	18	4	22
1951	8	—	8
1952	19	—	19
1953	1	—	1
1954	—	—	—
1955	18	1	19
1956	10	5	15
1957	1	—	1
1958	—	—	—
1959	—	1	1
Year uncertain	...	...	15
Total	86	11	112*

* Total numbers in this last row do not add up because of the fifteen individuals whose year of travel and means of transportation are unclear.

Source: Numbers are compiled from the emigration records of Lienfelders contained in the International Tracing Service archive in Bad Arolsen, Germany, as well as on www.ancestry.com.

in Pennsylvania. Her sister Hilda's CM/1 application further mentions a sum of $5,600 available in a Brooklyn bank account, from her time in the United States.[106] People with such means could afford passage on a ship—and even air travel—as soon as the United States opened its gates to ethnic German immigration. The same was true for Anna Klun, whose passage in tourist class on the *Queen Mary* from Cherbourg in May 1950 most certainly had to do with her brother's sponsorship (in every sense of the word) and arguably outweighed any possible concerns regarding her age and her Kulturbund membership.[107]

All in all, the available records show that at least 112 Lienfelders (including fourteen children born to Lienfelder families after the resettlement) emigrated overseas in the late 1940s and throughout the first half of the 1950s. At least half of the 1941 resettlers thus found new homes in North America after the war.

It remains an open question what determined the timing of each emigration, whether it was financial or legal and bureaucratic issues, or if there were other factors at play. The legal framework for emigration from Europe and immigration to the United States kept evolving during the first half of the 1950s. The revised DP Act of June 1950 had a special quota for German expellees, which amounted to one-sixth of the total contingent of 341,000 DPs to be accepted in the United States.[108] The Refugee Relief Act (RRA) of August 1953 permitted the immigration of 55,000 ethnic Germans residing in Germany and Austria, provided they had affidavits, close relatives in the States, and preferably a useful profession. Their transportation cost was covered by the United States and the International Committee for European Migration (ICEM), which succeeded the IRO in 1951.[109] Following the passage of the RRA, affidavits were increasingly supplied by institutional actors like churches or immigrant associations.[110] In the case of the Gottscheers, this was the National Catholic Welfare Council (NCWC). One of its constituent organizations was the Gottscheer Relief Association, which had supported the Gottscheer DPs since its foundation in May 1945.[111] All the Lienfelders who emigrated during the years 1955–1957 did so under NCWC sponsorship.

While the reasons for the timing of particular emigrations remain unclear, it is clear that the destination of these emigrations was determined by previous movement of people and the resulting networks. Most of the displaced Lienfelders found their new home in the Glendale and Ridgewood neighborhoods in Queens, New York, the Gottscheers' American base since the first half of the twentieth century. There were exceptions: alternative destinations included Cleveland, Ohio—another common site of Gottscheer migration—Fort Wayne, Indiana, and Kitchener, Ontario. But by and large it appears that people were not sent just anywhere.[112] The majority of those who crossed the ocean ended up living within a few blocks of each other. While the important role of networks and migrant communities is well-known in migration history, it deserves to be highlighted that the same mechanisms also applied in the case of forced migrants like the Gottscheers, thus blurring the boundaries between different types of voluntary and involuntary migrations.[113] As naturalization records show, many of the Lienfelder emigrants became American citizens within a few years—Anna Klun, for instance, in January 1956.[114]

What about those who stayed in Europe? While documentation on them is much less readily available, it is safe to assume that they mostly stayed in Austria, and in particular in the Carinthia and Styria regions, where they had first settled after the war.[115] They officially received the right to acquire Austrian citizenship in 1954.[116] Their temporary shelter turned into a permanent home. A minority also lived in West Germany (in the case of former *Volksgruppenführer* Wilhelm Lampeter, also in East Germany), having settled there before, during, or after war.[117] The West German state finally recognized the validity of the German citizenship the Nazis had awarded them in 1955.[118] For instance, from among the Lienfelders, Friedrich and Franz Kresse had moved to Munich before the war, in 1936 and 1939, respectively.[119] Johann Stimitz, who had served in the German army during the war, came to Germany in 1952, after spending almost four years in American and Yugoslavian captivity and another three and a half years in Austria. His sister Maria also lived in West Germany.[120] For those who moved to Germany during the war, I refer once again to my grandparents, the Krajec-Klun family, whose supposed lack of political trustworthiness as an ethnically mixed couple and resulting resettlement in the *Altreich* saved them from many wartime and postwar misfortunes. Moreover, their overseas connections and the resulting flow of luxury goods like coffee and cigarettes from America that could be traded on the black market ensured them a relatively comfortable existence during the difficult postwar years in West Germany.[121]

In this chapter, I have explored the multiple entanglements of a German minority from southeastern Europe in the twentieth century. Until the interwar period, Germany was hardly important as a point of reference for the German-speaking Gottscheers. Their focus was, rather, on the United States as a destination for both temporary labor and permanent emigration. German influence did not prevail until the ascent of the Nazis to power, and in particular in the course of wartime resettlement, which was intended to make the Gottscheers part of the extended German Reich. Yet when it came to finding a new home after the Second World War, the established transatlantic ties turned out to be more important for shaping Gottscheer life trajectories. This points to the importance of a global perspective when discussing the entangled history of German minorities from the Balkans, and from central, eastern, and southeastern Europe more generally.

Initially, a precondition for being able to utilize these transcontinental networks for emigration was access to IRO resettlement schemes, which were originally reserved for non-German refugees. Resulting attempts by Gottscheers to shed their "*volksdeutsch*" past and claim a Slovenian national identity before the international refugee bureaucracy largely remained unsuccessful, as they often lacked the necessary cultural traits—in particular language skills—and had damning documentary evidence about their wartime behavior held against them. Contrary to the idea that ethnic and national identities are essentially infinitely malleable, fluid, and exchangeable, in the case of the Gottscheers they had hardened to the extent that attempts at strategic conversion failed.

The importance of established migrant networks for the postwar emigration of the resettled and displaced Gottscheers, finally, reveals some more general insights for the study of refugee migration and refugee management. In a worst-case scenario, the Gottscheers could have stayed in a perpetual legal limbo, with no chance of social and political integration. They also could have been resettled just about anywhere, far away from relatives and outside of established communities. Yet, fortunately for them, in the majority of cases those who were resettled overseas were allowed to utilize their own networks, join established emigrant communities, and become US citizens soon after, allowing them a relatively smooth integration into a new society. The same happened in Austria and Germany. In that sense, refugee resettlement is no different from other types of migration, provided that migrant agency and networks are integrated into the resettlement schemes.

CHAPTER 8

WE HAD TO LEAVE OUR REALLY GOOD DOG

American Gottscheers and the Memories of World War II in Slovenia

GREGOR KRANJC

The homeland of the Gottscheers, a six-hundred-year-old unique German linguistic island in the heart of Slovene ethnic territory,[1] began to disappear in the fall of 1941, following the Axis invasion and occupation of Yugoslavia in April that year. The vast majority of the community decided or was coerced by Nazi German officials and the Nazified local leadership of the Gottscheers into resettling from their now Italian-occupied villages into the Third Reich (the resettlement ran from November 14, 1941 to January 23, 1942), a part of the Nazis' wider "ingathering" of ethnic Germans, or *Heim ins Reich* (back home to the Reich) foreign policy.[2] By "began," the author is acknowledging that the process of physical (human) and especially cultural destruction was a long one, extending beyond the period of Nazi and Fascist predominance from 1941 to 1945, to the postwar communist era (1945–1991), which witnessed the expulsion of almost all ethnic Germans from Yugoslavia and the systematic destruction of virtually all traces of the Gottscheer presence—a process that has only been arrested (and in a few rare cases reversed) since Slovenia's 1991 independence from Yugoslavia.

World War II and its immediate aftermath is, thus, the critical caesura in Gottscheer history. Similar to other ethnic German communities, like the Baltic or Volhynian Germans, who were also first resettled by the Nazis (in their case to Poland) and then expelled by newly liberated eastern European peoples and the victorious Allies, the Gottscheer existence today is almost entirely a diasporic one, as the population of Germans in all of Slovenia stood at 499 out of a total population of 1,964,036, according to the 2002 census.[3] Consequently, Gottscheer connections to their homeland are today principally founded upon memories. For an ever-dwindling number, these memories are based on lived experiences in the former homeland, while for most they are secondhand experiences, such as stories from their parents, grandparents, or community members, written accounts, and heritage tourism to the homeland. This chapter explores how the traumatic end of the Gottscheer presence in Slovenia has been remembered primarily by Gottscheers in the United States, who account for the majority of the global Gottscheer diaspora. The point is less the always elusive attempt to ascertain "what exactly happened" in those years, and more how digesting this history through "narration and oral history may form integral pieces of an identity jigsaw within a family context" or that of a broader community, remembering that memory "shape[s] and give[s] life to our positioning as people, communities and nations, and [is] . . . couched within context-specific identity narratives."[4]

The chapter begins with a brief historical survey of the Gottscheer experience from 1941 to 1945, before exploring how this era has been remembered in the testimonies and writings of American Gottscheers. While the author approaches the oxymoronic "collective memory" with caution, recognizing "that a uniform, univocal, and unambiguous version of events does not (and cannot) exist," the analysis reveals a striking sense of shared victimhood in Gottscheers' memories and commemorations of the war. The Gottscheers saw themselves as victims at the hands of the prewar Yugoslav government and Slovene society; (somewhat less so) at the hands of the Nazi regime, their Italian allies, and Reich settlement officials; as well as at the hands of the Partisans and the Communist postwar government of Josip Broz Tito.[5] The postwar expulsion of Gottscheers from Yugoslavia is recognized as the crescendo of their suffering. What is largely glossed over in these wartime memories are Gottscheers' experiences of the critical wartime years between their resettlement in late 1941/early 1942, and their final expulsion from Slovenia in 1945. It is during these years that the Gottscheer postwar mantra of victimhood, an outlook shared by many expelled Germans after World War II, comes up against the inconvenient truth that they too were part of the machinery of Nazi oppression—living in the homes and working the fields and businesses of ethnically cleansed Slovenes. As much as Gottscheers saw themselves as distinct from their Slavic neighbors, only heightened by the fact that Slovenes ignominiously cast them out of their homeland, the Gottscheers do share in what scholars have identified as a peculiar east central European perception, conditioned by suffering under two totalitarian regimes from either side of the ideological spectrum, "of themselves as victims who were thus unable to have been perpetrators of oppression."[6]

THE HISTORICAL RECORD: PREWAR, WARTIME, AND POSTWAR

The Gottschee region (Kočevje in Slovene)[7] lies some 50 kilometers (ca. 31 miles) southeast of the Slovene capital of Ljubljana. The March 1941 census revealed a German-speaking population of 12,498 individuals (2,754 families) residing in about 170 villages, with some two-thirds of Gottscheer families employed in agriculture and livestock rearing, followed by crafts.[8] To underscore the impact the ensuing decade would have on the Gottscheer presence, the 1953 census recorded only 94 Germans in the Gottschee, or 1.3 percent of the prewar number.[9] The Gottschee's demographic realities since the late nineteenth century—of increasing Gottscheer emigration to the Gottscheer diaspora (especially in the United States), the moving in of Slovenes, and interwar assimilationist policies—suggested to at least one scholar that the Gottschee would have been "Slavified"[10] by the end of the twentieth century. Be that as it may, it is undeniable that World War II and its aftermath eliminated the physical presence of Gottscheers in Slovenia.

The Gottscheers' wartime experiences can be divided into three periods or phases. The first, lasting from the April 1941 invasion until early 1942, was dominated by the resettlement, as almost all Gottscheers opted to move, leaving Gottschee largely void of its former German-speaking inhabitants. The second phase ran from early 1942 until early 1945, and saw the Gottscheers attempting to carve out new lives in the resettlement region of the so-called Rann (Brežice) Triangle located in the German-occupied Slovene region of Štajerska (Styria). During the third phase, from liberation in early May 1945 to the end of the year, virtually all Gottscheers (and Germans) fled Slovenia or were expelled by the new communist government, which had emerged from the successful wartime Partisan resistance movement. The Gottscheers' remaining cultural heritage would be either systematically destroyed or neglected in the ensuing decades.

Less than a week after the Axis invasion of Yugoslavia began on April 6, 1941, the Nazified local leadership of the Gottscheers led by Wilhelm (Willi) Lampeter, the head of the enclave's Kulturbund,[11] took control in the vacuum left by the retreating Royal Yugoslav Army. Young Gottscheers like Lampeter, who was only twenty-three at the start of World War II, were particularly receptive to Nazi ideals in the lead-up to the war. Some came under Nazi influence while completing their higher education in 1930s Nazi Germany. Lampeter, for example, completed his education in Stuttgart after his nationalist activism got him expelled in 1935 from the secondary school in the town of Gottschee, the largest settlement in the region of Gottschee (3,231 inhabitants in 1936).[12]

Historian and journalist Alenka Auersperger chronicles the enthusiasm with which young Gottscheers greeted the Anschluss of Austria, and the pilgrimages taken by some to see the Führer.[13] The younger generation's assumed obedience to Nazi dictates, and their opposition to what they saw as the older Gottscheer leadership's passiveness in the face of Slovene assimilation and their willingness to cooperate with Yugoslav institutions and regulations, was recognized in Berlin. In November 1938, the Volksdeutsche Mittelstelle, the Reich office responsible for links with Germans abroad, replaced Hans Arko, the relatively moderate longtime head of the Gottschee Kulturbund, with Lampeter.

However, one must also avoid reading too much into the divide between young and old Gottscheers. Arko, for example, was still a self-professed Nazi supporter (since 1927, he claimed), who saw the Slovenes as intellectually inferior to Gottscheer Germans.[14] Arko's sense of German superiority was not unique; other Germans of the former Habsburg Empire had to struggle after 1918 with their relegation—and that of their Austro-German *Hochkultur* (high culture)—to minority status in new east central European states often ruled by peoples who had historically been considered "peasant peoples." As historian Mirna Zakić observed, the founders of the pre-Nazi-era Kulturbund in Yugoslavia "recognized Yugoslavia's legitimacy," at the same time that "they cherished a certain Habsburg nostalgia . . .[,] emphasized cultural and linguistic ties to Germany," and stoked ethnic Germans' "idealized historical memory of colonization" and their role as "a civilizing influence in a supposedly savage land."[15] According to Arko, his most important contribution to the Nazification of Gottscheers was his ability to convince the Yugoslav government to resume Gottscheers' fifteenth-century "peddling rights" in Germany from 1933 to 1936: "Under the cover of peddling, 25 to 30 young farmers were sent annually to the Reich where they gathered in a camp during the winter months for training in Nazi ideology."[16]

In any event, Lampeter appeared to live up to the trust placed in him by Berlin. For example, in a September 1939 secret meeting, Lampeter and the Gottscheer leadership agreed to organize an armed *Volksdeutsche Mannschaft* militia.[17] Modelled upon the Nazi *Sturmabteilung* (Storm Detachments—SA), the Mannschaft was the muscle behind Lampeter's organization. Dressed in an SA-like uniform of boots, riding pants, and gray shirt, every man between the ages of eighteen and fifty served mandatorily in the Mannschaft.[18] Fortunately for Lampeter, such pro-Reich activities were increasingly tolerated by Yugoslav authorities, who after the start of World War II and the effective Axis encirclement of Yugoslavia, did all they could to avoid giving Nazi Germany a pretext to invade or interfere in the country.

Despite the enthusiasm with which Lampeter and many Gottscheers awaited the arrival of the Germans in April 1941, hoisting garlands and swastikas in Gottscheer villages, it was the Italians who marched into the town of Gottschee. They immediately removed Lampeter from his position.[19] In May 1941, Italy officially annexed the Gottschee and the surrounding regions of the Notranjska and Dolenjska, including the capital of Ljubljana. Germany occupied—and for all practical purposes annexed—the wealthier northern Slovene regions of the Gorenjska and the Štajerska, while Hungary completed the trisection of Slovenia with its absorption of the eastern region of the Prekmurje. Swallowed by its three Axis neighbors, Slovenia ceased to exist.

The decision to resettle the Gottscheers can be traced back to Adolf Hitler's October 6, 1939 Reichstag speech, in which he promised, in the wake of the occupation of Poland: "to establish a new order of ethnographic conditions, that is to say, resettlement of nationalities in such a manner that the process ultimately results in the obtaining of better dividing lines than is the case at present. In this sense, however, it is not a case of the problem being restricted to this particular sphere, but of a task with wider implications, for the east and south of Europe are to a large extent filled with splinters of the German nationality, whose existence they cannot maintain."[20]

Himmler conveyed the news to the Gottscheer leadership on April 20, 1941, that the "Sawa-Sotla" region was "their future home," a message that Hitler confirmed to Lampeter when they met during Hitler's visit to the Slovene city of Maribor—a visit made infamous by his demand to "make this land German again."[21] An additional meeting, to organize the resettlement, was held between the Gottscheer leadership and the Office of the Reichskommissariat for the Strengthening of Germandom (RKFDV) in Berlin in May 1941.[22] The location of the resettlement was indeed the Slovene Sava-Sotla region (or Lower Sava region) of Štajerska, some seventy kilometers (forty-four miles) east of the Gottschee, just inside the frontiers of Nazi-occupied Slovenia. Shaped like a triangle—hence the term Rann Triangle—the German-occupied Lower Sava faced both the frontiers of Italian-annexed Slovenia and the puppet Independent State of Croatia. The Gottscheers were thus envisaged to become the human racial border of the expanded southern frontiers of the Reich, as their resettlement along the Lower Sava would be possible only with the ethnic cleansing of the existing Slovene population.

With the order for resettlement passed down, the question remains—why would the vast majority of Gottscheers leave their home of six centuries in favor of an uncertain future? Or, as historian Norman Naimark noted in his study of twentieth-century ethnic cleansing, "People do not leave their homes on their own. They hold on to their land and their culture, which [are] . . . interconnected."²³ The reasons for the resettlement are numerous and overlapping. Moreover, because the Gottscheers were not ethnically cleansed, but left their homeland voluntarily as seemingly privileged members of the German master race, the motivations to resettle were also very personal, as there was still choice, however constrained, in the matter. Some left out of ideological conviction that only the Führer knew best. Others left for many of the same reasons that many of their own relatives and neighbours had for decades—the promise of a better economic future than subsistence farming in the Gottschee.

Such motivations could perhaps explain the movement of a large minority of Gottscheers, but not virtually the entire population. Duplicity was employed. In the spring 1941 meetings between the Gottscheer leadership and Reich officials, the former requested that the final destination of the resettlement not be made known to the masses, as it suspected—correctly, as it would turn out—that the Gottscheers would be far from enthusiastic about moving into Slovene lands that were economically comparable to their current situation. Historian Hans Hermann Frensing summarized Lampeter's strategy thus: "At first, the population shall exercise the option [to resettle], only then—when there is no return—shall the farmers be notified of the settlement region."²⁴ This was indeed the case, as the pro-Lampeter *Gottscheer Zeitung* only announced on November 17, 1941, that the Rann Triangle was the chosen destination for resettlement, which came after the October deadline to "opt" for resettlement, and after the first transports began to relocate Gottscheers.²⁵ The November announcement also insisted that the Slovenes that were moved to make way for the Gottscheers were "well supplied" and were "looking to the future full of hope."²⁶

The Gottscheer leadership also spread false rumors, for example, that the Italians would relocate all Gottscheers who did not opt for resettlement to Abyssinia or southern Italy.²⁷ Intimidation was also employed, not by Reich officials and soldiers, who had only a minimal presence in the Italian-occupied Gottschee, but rather by Lampeter's *Mannschaft*. In one reported case, a Gottscheer from Masern (Grčarice) who allegedly professed that "my home is here" was struck in the face by a *Mannschaft Sturmführer* (lieutenant) who retorted, "You are denying your German roots."²⁸ Resistance to resettlement, as Naimark's dictum predicts, was present, particularly among older Gottscheers and some members of the Catholic clergy, who were additionally irked by Nazism's anti-Catholicism. For example, Father Joseph Gliebe, who refused resettlement, called the young Gottscheer leaders *Rotzbuben* (snot boys) and helped collect signatures opposing resettlement.²⁹ Lampeter responded by drawing up a detailed list of politically untrustworthy Gottscheers, which included Gliebe and other clerics, as well as threatening those resisting relocation with deportation.[30]

Judging by the numbers of those who opted for resettlement, however, resistance was largely contained by Lampeter and the Gottscheer leadership. With a resettlement agreement reached between the Italians, Germans, and the Gottscheer leadership on August 31, 1941, preparations for resettlement accelerated. The German Resettlement Company (Deutsche Umsiedlungs Treuhandgesellschaft—DUT) took over immovable Gottscheer property and sold it to the Italian real estate company Emona. Gottscheers were allowed to take their movable personal possessions and one-third of their livestock (at a minimum at least one animal).[31] Most Gottscheers from outlying villages were driven in trucks to the town of Gottschee and then transported by train to the Rann Triangle (they were given their German citizenship on the train). To make way for the incoming Gottscheers, some 37,000 Slovenes were hastily and violently deported to camps in Germany, with those deemed racially fit earmarked for Germanization.[32] By the end of the resettlement in January 1942, a total of 135 trains resettled 11,509 Gottscheers (2,833 families).[33] An estimated 350–600 Gottscheers, some married to Slovenes, did not resettle.[34] Almost all of the resettlers were deposited in the 100-kilometer-long (63-mile-long) and 10–15-kilometer-wide (6–10-mile-wide) Rann Triangle (later they would be joined by approximately 1,000 ethnic Germans from Romania and South Tyrol), while some 200 families were moved to Germany.[35] Significantly, some 8,000 Slovenes, for pragmatic—especially economic—reasons, were not expelled from the Lower Sava and were instead redefined as "Windisch"—a people who spoke a dialect of Slovene but who were "really" German-oriented.[36]

Upon arrival in Brežice, the Gottscheers were assigned the homes and businesses of the expelled Slovenes. Initial housing assignments were often only temporary as a more "methodological" distribution of the population occurred in July 1942, in which the resettlement officials attempted to match the Gottscheers' economic skills with their place of residence (craftsmen into urban areas, peasants into the countryside), although the records reveal considerable reassignments of properties until 1945.[37] Former village communities were intentionally broken up and their members scattered in order to erode local patriotism, in preparation for what Nazi racial experts hoped would be the quick dissolution of the unique Gottscheer culture (along with all Volksdeutsche "splinters") into a homogenized German identity.[38] The Gottscheer leadership and communal organizations, once they had fulfilled their task of a successful resettlement, were largely ignored by Reich officials. Lampeter, who in three reports to Berlin complained of unsatisfactory conditions in the Rann Triangle shortly after the resettlement, was demoted by Himmler.[39] Lampeter condemned the negative impact that the resettlement had had on the Gottscheers' "rare form of social organization," as well as resettlement officials' denigration of the Gottscheer language as a "gypsy language."[40] "It has to be concluded," Lampeter lamented, that "after a few weeks' residence in the Reich, the Gottscheer Germans have been entirely deprived of the very self-possession that made possible their survival over six hundred years amongst the Slovenes."[41] Lampeter left the Rann Triangle in the spring of 1942, only returning briefly in 1945.

Parallel to the Reich's "Germanization" of the Gottscheers, historian Helga Harriman also noted a "quite solicitous" attitude by Reich settlement officials and their associated welfare organizations toward the incoming Gottscheer settlers, concluding that the "health and happiness of the German vanguards on the border were of utmost concern to Hitler's officers."[42] Support mechanisms included the provision of special courses in maternal health and childcare for the Gottscheers. Gottscheers dissatisfied with their assigned properties were compensated with "financial or other assistance, loans, [and] agricultural machinery,"[43] while settlement officials embarked upon ambitious renovations of homes, with more than five hundred persons so employed as late as 1943 in the Rann Triangle.[44]

As for Slovene-Gottscheer relations in Rann, some Gottscheers complained to settlement officials about the several thousand Slovenes who were not deported: "We thought that we were leaving for Germany, but ended up among Slovene bandits. Did we not resettle to get away from them and now we are again surrounded by them?? And even worse; there are now 'Windische' and other Slovenes in administrative positions giving orders as equals."[45]

Reich officials attempted to cocoon Gottscheers from any "unpleasant contacts" with expelled Slovenes by passing a decree forbidding expellees from ever reentering the Rann Triangle.[46] Other reports attest to the Gottscheers' "worse than bad" attitude toward the property and possessions left behind by the deported Slovenes.[47] For example, the regional resettlement headquarters in Brežice reported that winter solstice celebrations in December 1941 had their bonfires fueled by the splintered furniture of Slovene expellees, concluding that they "do not take care of the property that was left behind by the resettled Slovenes, which they ruin without reason."[48] Many Slovenes returning to their homes at the end of the war found that the departing Gottscheers had completely pilfered all remaining furniture and possessions.[49]

The removal of 95 percent of the German-speaking population of the Gottschee left wide swaths of the region, with the exception of the town of Gottschee and a few other more ethnically mixed settlements, deserted. Not surprisingly, the emerging Slovene Liberation Front (Osvobodilna fronta—OF) resistance and its armed partisan units found a ready-made base of operations, with empty homes providing billets as well as a space to organize free of the prying eyes of unsympathetic locals, while the Gottschee's considerable forests offered places to hide. Even a handful of Gottscheers who refused resettlement were persuaded to join the OF.[50] The Italians attempted to eliminate the nascent OF in their infamous 1942 summer offensive, which hit the eastern Gottschee around Kočevski Rog (Gottscheer Hornwald) particularly hard, with mass arrests and numerous villages burned so as to deny accommodation and sustenance to the resistance. While never reaching the same intensity as the summer of 1942, similar patterns of retaliation for partisan activity in the Gottschee would characterize Italian occupation policies until their capitulation in September 1943, and would be repeated during the German reoccupation that followed (1943–1945). Allied bombing raids would also severely damage the town of Gottschee. The Slovene historian Mitja Ferenc offered a depressing itemization of the war's impact on the Gottschee: of 176 settlements in the Gottschee, 89 were uninhabited in July 1945, and almost two-thirds of the region's houses (2,548 of 3,945) were damaged or destroyed, twice the average for the rest of Slovenia. Ferenc concluded unequivocally that damage "on such a scale had not been sustained by any other Slovene region or district."[51]

Partly as a result of the more formidable German military presence, the resettled Gottscheers in the Rann Triangle mostly avoided partisan attacks until 1944, when the OF, which viewed Gottscheer colonists as justified targets, made permanent inroads into the Štajerska. In the last weeks of the war, the Germans ordered the Gottscheers to retreat north toward the Austrian frontier. They needed little persuading, as a November 21, 1944 decree by the supreme legislative body of the Yugoslav Partisan movement stripped Yugoslav citizens of "German ethnicity" of their citizenship and property. The Rann Triangle was one of the first regions to be cleansed of its German residents by the feared communist secret police, the Department for the Protection of the People (Odeljenje za zaštitu naroda—OZNA), beginning in May 1945 and continuing through midsummer.[52] Gottscheers who evaded capture by the Partisans were housed in Austrian displaced-persons (DP) camps, avoiding the fate of their less fortunate compatriots who were imprisoned in a number of Yugoslav concentration camps. The Strnišče (Sterntal) camp was perhaps the most notorious for its treatment of ethnic Germans. In addition to facing the cruelty and sadism of a number of guards, the inmates—men, women, and also some children—were given starvation rations, which, combined with rampant communicable diseases, resulted in high mortality levels. The camp was closed in October 1945, in part through the intervention of the Red Cross, and its remaining inmates were deported to Austria.[53]

Of those few hundred who remained in the Gottschee in 1941, very rough estimates—"rough" because professing oneself a German was a potentially lethal identification—placed their number at around one hundred at liberation. Of these, some forty were expelled soon after liberation, accused of having fraternized with the enemy.[54] A number of karst sinkholes in the largely deserted Kočevski Rog area of the Gottschee also provided Tito's regime with an "ideal" location to conceal the executions of thousands of Yugoslav Axis collaborators (mostly Slovene Home Guards, Croatian Ustašas, and Serb Četniks) in May and June 1945. While a few Gottscheers were alleged to have been executed in Kočevski Rog, the majority of Gottscheers escaped the worst of Yugoslavia's postwar politicide. It is estimated that some one thousand Gottscheers perished during the war, which includes those killed in action in German uniform and in Partisan attacks and postwar retribution.[55] Two-thirds of the expelled Gottscheers, some seven thousand, eventually emigrated to the United States, while roughly three thousand remained in Austria and some fifteen hundred moved to Germany.[56]

With the expulsion of almost all Gottscheers by 1946, all that remained of their centuries-old presence was the ruins of their homeland's sacral and vernacular architecture. The postwar communist regime continued this process by systematically destroying Gottscheer villages in and around Rieg (Kočevska Reka) in western Gottschee, which became a restricted military zone beginning in the early 1950s as underground bunker complexes were constructed to protect the republic's communist leadership in the event of war. Between 1953 and 1956, all twenty-seven remaining churches, nine of twelve cemeteries, and dozens of chapels and roadside shrines were destroyed in the restricted zone.[57]

Despite several attempts by the communist regime to create a model socialist economic system in the relative clean slate of the Gottschee, it was unable to attract sufficient labor to the area. Consequently, agriculture was eventually abandoned, except in the valleys in and around the town of Gottschee that held the bulk of the Gottschee's population. Forestry was deemed an important sector, and forests would engulf the agricultural lands surrounding depopulated and deserted villages. Forest cover, which accounted for 41.5 percent of the Gottschee's surface area at the turn of the twentieth century, increased to 82 percent by the 1970s, and today exceeds 90 percent.[58] All that remains of former Gottscheer habitation is fruit trees in the forest, the foundations of houses and wells, and some five hundred tombstones in the remaining Gottscheer cemeteries.

NARRATIVES OF MEMORY

While it is important to recognize that "groups do not have memories in the neurological sense and thus there is no organic basis to the term 'collective,'" collective memories are shaped by what historian Dan Stone describes as an individual's "social setting,"[59] and "originate from" what memory scholar Wulf Kansteiner notes are "shared communications about the meaning of the past that are anchored in the life-worlds of individuals who partake in the communal life of the respective collective."[60] Clearly World War II was a life-changing and traumatic experience for American Gottscheers. What also emerges from this brief historical survey is how collective these experiences were: virtually all Gottscheers left their homeland at the same time in 1941–1942; almost all resettled in the Rann Triangle; and almost all were forced to flee or were expelled under similar conditions of duress. Arriving in Austria and sheltered in DP camps, the Gottscheer experience would now become integrated into the wider saga of the thirteen million Germans expelled after the war from eastern Europe.[61] American Gottscheer and Catholic organizations in the United States, chief among them the Gottscheer Relief Organization of New York, formed in 1945, were critical in the eventual relocation of most Gottscheer DPs to the United States in the early 1950s, with 1952 witnessing the arrival of the largest number of DPs.[62] These groups collected donations to feed and sustain Gottscheer DPs in Austria and lobbied for the relaxation of US postwar quotas on German and Austrian immigration. Community and family connections in the United States, as well as the country's postwar economic opportunities, made America a desirable destination for Gottscheer DPs.

Having shared the trauma of resettlement and expulsion, American Gottscheers are remarkable for having sustained their unique Gottscheerish dialect and customs, and enjoy a rich communal existence in their community newspapers, conferences and gatherings, and heritage tourism to the homeland. While Gottscheers and their descendants can be found across the United States, the community was historically centered in two urban areas—Cleveland, Ohio, where they lived in the same districts as the even larger Slovene ethnic community, and the Ridgewood neighborhood of the New York borough of Queens. For many, particularly those who experienced the war years in the Gottschee, World War II formed the basis of the Gottscheer "American Dream," as recounted by the granddaughter of an expellee during a 1993 Gottscheer celebration in Ridgewood: "The Gottscheers came here with just the clothes on their backs, worked very hard, emphasized education for their children and succeeded. We're the typical 'American Dream' story."[63]

While it is understandable that the horror of World War II could be optimistically interpreted by some American Gottscheers as ultimately providing the privilege of a prosperous postwar American life, how did Gottscheers remember or characterize the *actual* war years? Patterns in collective memory, gleaned from archival testimonies and writings in Gottscheer community newspapers,[64] emerge for each of the three phases introduced in the historical survey—resettlement, life in the Rann Triangle, and expulsion—accompanied by examples of dissonance and ruptures within commonly shared memory narratives that generally emphasized collective victimhood and downplayed any role in the system of Nazi oppression in occupied Slovenia.

OCCUPATION AND RESETTLEMENT

The decision to leave the Gottschee was an evidently difficult one, and most Gottscheer testimonies and writings focus inordinately on the few short months between the announcement of the resettlement in the spring of 1941 and the actual resettlement in late 1941. Interwar assimilation of the Gottscheers by the Slovene and Yugoslav governments, and the disappointment caused by the Italian rather than the expected German occupation of Gottschee, was often foregrounded as the main motivation for why so many Gottscheers departed. One witness twinned anticipated Italian cultural oppression with that already experienced under the interwar Yugoslav government: "We did not like this arrangement [resettlement], but it was preferable to again having to serve a strange government, again having to worry about our culture and language."[65] Other witnesses regurgitated the contemporary threat that Italy would have deported recalcitrant Gottscheers to southern Italy or Abyssinia, without identifying these "threats" as false rumors that had been issued by their own Gottscheer leadership to persuade Gottscheers to opt for resettlement. Some accounts provided an equally erroneous interpretation of the resettlement as Hitler kowtowing to a dominant but "timber-poor" Italy in need of the Gottschee's forests: "The relocation was a political decision meant to placate the Italians who always wanted the western part of Yugoslavia as their own. It was Hitler's way to satisfy Mussolini."[66] Far more historically accurate was American Gottscheer John Tschinkel's dissenting observation that Italians "had little to say on the emigration issue," adding that this insistence upon Italian culpability was consistent with the Gottscheers' tendency to blame others, rather than themselves, for the resettlement.[67]

While the Gottscheer resettlement was instigated as part of the Nazis' wider *Heim ins Reich* foreign policy, Nazi Germany's guiding role in the resettlement is noted in only a few Gottscheer recollections. Indeed, the words "Nazism" and "Nazis" are rarely mentioned; speakers prefer "Germans" or the "Reich" when speaking of the Third Reich. When Nazi Germany's role was recognized in the testimonies, it was often to underscore the Gottscheers' complete lack of agency in a resettlement that they in actuality *opposed*: "A majority of Gottscheers did not like it [resettlement], but they had no other choice! Germany was a dictatorship under Hitler. 'Open your mouth too wide,' or otherwise resist, often meant a permanent move to concentration camps, or worse, if that is possible."[68] Another witness stated that locals began to spit on the ground when the announcement to resettle was made, "to show their anger and disgust at this betrayal. But we knew that there was nothing we could do—so slowly we became resigned to what was to follow."[69]

However, such claims that a majority of Gottscheers were opposed to resettlement and were overridden by a brutal dictatorial Nazi Germany appear rather convenient and somewhat lacking in verifiable evidence—other witnesses claimed that Gottscheers were enthusiastic about moving to Germany proper, while a few hundred Gottscheers were allowed to stay in the Gottschee and were not deported against their will to Germany. Moreover, such retrospective resistance to the Nazis overlooks the arguably even more important role that the local Kulturbund, led by Lampeter, his militia, and the pro-Nazi newspaper, the *Gottscheer Zeitung*, played in persuading or coercing Gottscheers to move—a fact that was acknowledged by none of the accounts surveyed, with the exception of Tschinkel's.

At the other end of the spectrum—and throwing much-needed cold water on the historian's penchant for always trying to find the political in circumstances that were confusing and often contradictory—was the testimony of Albert Stiene, who stated that, as a nine-year-old boy in 1941, he did not recall much about why they left Gottschee, but gave a very nine-year-old picture of the times: "I don't remember much about it, except that we had to leave our really good dog, Waldman, behind. We left him with our Slovenian neighbor in house number 4."[70]

LIFE IN THE RANN TRIANGLE

Of the three periods, the Gottscheers' existence in the Rann Triangle was chronologically the longest. Unlike the resettlement phase that was concluded less than a year after the April 1941 invasion, or the postwar expulsions that were effectively executed within six months, Gottscheers spent three years in the Rann Triangle, from late 1941/early 1942 to the spring of 1945. Moreover, as this was the only phase in which Gottscheers were sedentary, and not on the move, reminiscences of this phase could offer perhaps the best window into daily life under German occupation. Unfortunately, the period is largely glossed over in almost all Gottscheer accounts. Generally noteworthy is the initial reaction to their new living conditions in the Rann Triangle, the expulsion of its Slovene inhabitants, the settlers' livelihood in the region, and growing Partisan attacks. The recollections emphasize an unwillingness of the Gottscheers to see themselves as colonists or representatives of the "master race," and a pronounced discomfort with the expulsion of the Slovenes.

Only about half of the examined witnesses and writings mentioned the fact that some thirty-seven thousand Slovenes along the Lower Sava were expelled to make room for the incoming Gottscheers—surprising given that the Nazi expulsion of Slovenes, which lasted from October 24, 1941 to July 30, 1942, overlapped with the incoming Gottscheers.[71] Acknowledgement of the expulsion of Slovenes was most often made in short matter-of-fact statements, for example that the Slovenes "were removed/expelled/evacuated/forced to leave their homes and migrate" or the vague "where Slovenes had previously lived."[72] The perpetrators of these expulsions are rarely mentioned. Only one witness other than Tschinkel offered some indication of the terrible conditions of the Slovene expulsions: "The German SS had driven out the local [Slovene] inhabitants with great cruelty."[73] While one witness stated that "German-friendly Slovenians, mostly farmers, were forced to leave their own beloved homeland," he then attempted to explain why Gottscheers should not be held accountable, reverting to the familiar Gottscheer narrative of powerlessness: "Even if we had held out and stayed in our homeland, this cruel injustice to the Slovenians in Lower Styria would have happened anyway. This is because it was intended to keep the border between Germany and Italy free of Slovenians and to settle the area with ethnic Germans from South Tyrol, Bessarabia, and Bulgaria. We, as a small sliver of a people, had no influence on these world events."[74]

The same witness, a pro-resettlement Catholic priest, went as far as stating that Yugoslavia's rejection of the Tripartite Pact on March 27, 1941 in a coup d'état was responsible for the expulsion of Slovenes, telling a Slovene expellee: "Look, there is a war going on and there are a lot of injustices. You are innocent, but your people (politicians and students) in Laibach [Ljubljana] and Belgrade have shouted, 'We would rather have war than a treaty.' Now that war has broken out, you must leave, while they have resettled us here."[75]

One witness made the rather unbelievable assertion that the expulsion of Slovenes "was unknown to the Gottscheers," a statement clearly not borne out by the testimonies of many Gottscheers.[76] One in particular recalled moving all of a former Slovene shop owner's belongings into one room, in case he returned.[77] Tschinkel noted that upon his family's arrival in the village of Veliko Mraševo, "it was obvious that the former residents had been forced to leave not much more than a few days ago," and that "some Slovenes were being expelled even long after" the Gottscheers had been resettled.[78]

Thus, among those Gottscheers who acknowledged the expulsions of Slovenes, the most common narrative is one in which Gottscheers were not responsible for the fate of the original Slovene inhabitants. This assumed powerlessness in the expulsion of Slovenes is not immune to challenge—while the Nazis undoubtedly orchestrated and carried out the expulsions, the majority of Gottscheers *opted* for resettlement, and if some were duped as to their resettlement destination, they were duped by their own community's sons and leaders. Crudely put: they came, they saw, they stayed. Gottscheer responses to the ethnic cleansing of Slovenes in the Lower Sava folds into a common theme that runs throughout Gottscheer memories of World War II—a view of Gottscheers not as agents of Nazi oppression against Slovenes, but as victims of the Third Reich. While this theme certainly finds firm ground in the postwar expulsion and mistreatment of Gottscheers, it is rather flimsy during the period of the Gottscheers' existence in the Rann Triangle, when the Nazis' racial hierarchy was policy.

Indicative of this are the witnesses' almost unanimously negative first impressions of the resettlement zone. One witness described the "dilapidated" home she was assigned as "dreadful"; another received an apartment with a leaky roof instead of a promised house; a third was allocated a wooden, "freezing" home; while another complained that the soil was sandy and made it difficult to grow anything.[79] While the irony of complaining about the poor condition of homes that belonged to Slovenes who were forcibly uprooted to make room for the Gottscheers was apparently lost on some of the witnesses, the testimonies hint that such complaints did not fall on deaf ears—three of the four witnesses listed above were able to request, and soon received, better houses and/or businesses that also formerly belonged to Slovenes. In short, while the Gottscheer testimonies rarely acknowledge this fact, the difficult housing conditions appeared to be merely temporary in the chaos of the resettlement and the German government's end goal was to provide better conditions for their resettlers.

Similarly, some Gottscheers painted a picture of their livelihood in the Rann that was almost equated to forced labor. One noted that she was "ordered to work" in the fields by officials of the German Settlement

Association (Deutsche Ansiedlungsgesellschaft—DAG) (this witness's position improved after she received the grocery store business of an expelled Slovene), while another lamented that the "once-independent farmers were now nothing more than workers for the Resettlement Commission under the auspices of the new government."[80] Another witness highlighted the coercion employed, noting that if one refused DAG work assignments more than three times, that individual was punished by being transported to Germany to work in the armaments industry.[81]

However, in recalling the challenging labor conditions faced by the resettled Gottscheers, the witnesses omit the underlying cause; namely, that too many Slovenes were expelled and not enough Germans were resettled to make up for the resulting labor shortage. Reich officials attempted to ameliorate this problem by allocating to the Gottscheers Slovene forced laborers—many from the Maribor region—as well as additional forced laborers from outside of Slovenia. As Tschinkel notes, the Nazis "were loyal to their blood brother and had no intention of turning the newly in-gathered citizens of the Third Reich into slaves."[82] Indeed, Tschinkel was the only source to describe these Slovene laborers for what they were—forced laborers—and noted that a few were assigned to his father's farm in the Rann Triangle and were housed in DAG-built barracks.[83] Other Gottscheer recollections were far coyer, including one who was assigned what she described as a "nice compulsory-service girl" to help raise her newborn in 1944.[84] Another source, noting that her family was given *too much land and vineyards to cultivate* in Bistrica ob Sotli, was "helped" by "workers . . . from factories in Marburg (Maribor) and Celje (Cilli)" and "later . . . got a maid from the countryside and a farm laborer."[85]

Indeed, even examples that Gottscheers put forth as signs of good wartime neighborly relations with Slovenes revealed the Nazis' racial pecking order. For example, one witness stated that "we had very good relationships with our Slovenian neighbors. In school, I tried to help the students, mostly Slovenians, because of my fluency in German. I also spoke Slovene fairly well."[86] While his "assistance" was duly noted, what was left unsaid was the perversity of a Slovene-speaking majority prohibited from speaking their mother tongue and forced to learn German.

Life in the Rann eventually became quite dangerous, particularly with the increase in Partisan attacks upon the resettled Gottscheers in 1944, along with Allied bombing raids, a fact recalled in almost all reminiscences and writings. As described, Partisan raids primarily aimed to steal food and other resources, while some were of a "terrorist nature," including the "disappearing" of Gottscheers, killings, and torture.[87] Almost none of the narratives asked why the Partisans attacked

Gottscheer communities during the war, a question that would have forced the Gottscheers to grapple with their own role in the machinery of Nazi occupation. One source that did address this issue described the Partisans' and Gottscheers' mutually exclusive interpretations of the Gottscheer resettlement in the Lower Sava—the Partisans believed the Gottscheers had "robbed" (and the source places the term in quotations in the text, perhaps to underscore his incredulity toward this perspective) the Slovenes of their homes in the Lower Sava, while the Gottscheers believed they had had to resettle to preserve their cultural identity and had made a "fair exchange" with the expelled Slovenes: "They [the Gottscheers] never really understood the hatred which they had incurred in Slovenia because of their resettlement."[88] Once again, the Gottscheers are granted almost childlike ignorance of their role in German occupation policies in Slovenia and additionally exonerated by what the author claims was their culturally defendable reason for resettling into Slovene homes. In short, by highlighting partisan wartime atrocities—similar to the already-noted highlighting of unpleasant housing and labor requirements in the Rann Triangle, and the downplaying of the expulsion of Slovenes—Gottscheer testimonies preserve their understanding of themselves as primarily victims of the war who, lacking any agency, were "swept up by the tidal wave of the Third Reich and carried along its path of self-destruction."[89]

POSTWAR EXPULSIONS

The brutal and indiscriminate expulsion by the new communist Yugoslav regime of all Gottscheers (and indeed all Germans) from Yugoslavia confirmed for traumatized Gottscheers their status as victims of World War II. Not unexpectedly, this third phase received the most attention in wartime recollections. Few Gottscheers were left unscathed by the expulsions. The most "fortunate" were able to escape Yugoslavia with only some personal belongings; the least fortunate were captured by the Partisans and imprisoned in concentration camps, the most notorious of which was Sterntal. Perhaps most heart-wrenching was the story of one witness who lost both of her children, aged two years and six months, to disease and malnutrition while imprisoned in Sterntal.[90]

However, the ferocity of the retribution against the Gottscheers led, as did the postwar killings at dozens of execution sites across Slovenia of tens of thousands of alleged Axis collaborators and other opponents of Tito's new regime, to an overshadowing and at times forgetting of the fascist crimes that preceded—and in part conditioned—the postwar backlash. The same witness who lost her two children in Sterntal weighed fascist and communist crimes, indicating that she was perhaps aware to some degree already in 1945 of Nazism's atrocities. Reacting to the comment of a Partisan guard that "we must never forget what the Germans did to us," she recalled responding: "What they [the Germans] could not do in four years, you could do in four months. I never hurt anyone, but you buried my last child somewhere yesterday." Another Gottscheer imprisoned in Sterntal claimed that the conditions in the camp were akin to an "extermination camp."[91] Such hyperbole, while certainly indicative of the witness's traumatic experience, also serves to blur the distinction between atrocities committed by Germans from 1939 to 1945, and those atrocities suffered by Germans in 1945. Sterntal's imprisoned Gottscheers endured horrible condition and privations, and a number perished, but Sterntal was not Auschwitz—unlike Auschwitz, the camp was eventually inspected and closed through the intervention of the Red Cross, and its inmates were deported to a safe country (Austria) to start a new life. This "comparative trivialization,"[92] to borrow Holocaust historian Michael Shafir's term, aims to further Gottscheer (and indeed German) victimhood by diminishing through ill-matched comparisons the suffering inflicted by Germans during the war.

The expulsions and the diasporic focus on them as a sort of "year zero," from which the American Gottscheer community only recovered through hard work, perseverance, and devotion to their community, also eroded the ability of Gottscheers to admit that fellow Slovenes suffered. While this observation has already been highlighted in witnesses' awkward acknowledgement of the expulsion of the Slovenes from the Lower Sava, it manifested perhaps most surprisingly in the experience of Max Mische, an American Gottscheer community activist, who, unlike most in his community, developed close relationships with Slovene scholars of the Gottschee, including Mitja Ferenc. Only after Ferenc "kidnapped" Mische during the latter's visit to Slovenia for a Gottscheer gathering in 1999 and took Mische on a tour of the former Rann Triangle and its museums of expelled Slovenes in Brežice and Brestanica, two towns in the Lower Sava region that served as collection points for Slovenes expelled by the Nazis, did the scales fall from Mische's eyes: "My journey to Brežice and what I saw there had given me much to think about, possibly for years to come. One thing was for certain: my perspective had been altered, as I now realized that two great injustices had been perpetrated during the last war. One was against the Gottscheers, and the other against the Slovenes."[93] Similarly, a witness stating that "it is a harsh truth" to admit that "both the Gottscheers and the Slovenians were victims" of World War II underscores the gulf that opened up between the two communities, owing in no small part to the collective postwar punishment meted out against Gottscheers.[94]

However, since Slovenia's independence in 1991, Gottscheer and Slovene victims of postwar communist violence, particularly those of a Catholic and anti-communist persuasion, have come to haltingly recognize each other's suffering. As the enforced public silence that surrounded the postwar killings eroded in 1980s communist Yugoslavia, Gottscheers were confronted by the unlikely sight of Victor Michitsch, the chairman of the *Gottscheer Landsmannschaft* (Homeland Association) based in Klagenfurt, Austria, standing alongside the bishop of Ljubljana, Alojzij Šuštar, in a 1989 ceremony marking the restoration of a Gottscheer church, while declaring: "All of us suffered an unhappy past, which is evident in many common aspects."[95] Since then, American Gottscheers have attended the annual Catholic masses, held since 1990, in Kočevski Rog, to commemorate the victims of postwar killings.[96] The two communities were also represented at the fiftieth anniversary commemoration, held in 1999, of the women's penal camp that was located in the Gottscheer village of Verdreng (Podlesje), while the Slovene Catholic Church has been supportive of the restoration of the destroyed and damaged sacral architecture of Gottschee, and has welcomed Gottscheer heritage tourists from the United States.[97]

Yet, while the acknowledgement of shared victimhood between Slovenes and Gottscheers reflects the historical record better than a myopic Gottscheer-centered victimhood, the fact remains that the vast majority of Gottscheers still characterize their experience during World War II as one of victimization. The postwar expulsions force the question—if Gottscheers were merely victims, then why were they expelled? Ferenc's response is instructive: "Undoubtedly the pro-Nazi stance of the majority of the Germans, and their collaboration with the occupation forces against the Slovene population during the war [led many to] believe in the collective guilt of the German people."[98] For Ferenc, and indeed for the majority of Slovenes, the Gottscheers—not all, but many—sided with the Nazis and in the process contributed to "German fascist policy [that] aimed at eliminating the Slovene people as an ethnic group."[99] The chronology of abuse matters to Ferenc—Nazi abuses gave way to communist retaliation. While one could argue about the proportionality of the Tito regime's response—and Ferenc describes it as "vicious" and "fraught with intolerance"—it did not come out of nowhere.[100]

The unwillingness to search within the community for at least part of the reason for the expulsions manifested in some cases in conspiratorial musings. One source, who likened the fate of the Gottscheers to that of North America's indigenous populations, claimed that the "Western Allies felt ethnic cleansing [of Germans] in Yugoslavia was the best way to lure Tito into becoming democratic."[101] Another source employed an outdated and anachronistic nineteenth-century Romantic nationalist perspective, linking the expulsion of Gottscheers to the "1,000 year struggle with the Slavs," which the author believed the Germans lost across eastern Europe: "In 1945, all of the Volksdeutsche in East Europe shared a similar aim in life—to flee from the Slavic advance. It was nothing less than a *Drang Nach Osten* [Drive to the East] in reverse."[102]

Tschinkel critiques the diasporic Gottscheer reply to the question "why did you leave your country," which was most often "we fled from communism" or "we were displaced by postwar Yugoslavia under Tito because we were anti-communist," an answer that "produced admiration and sympathy for many decades of the Cold War" and was worn "as a badge of honor." While this was "convenient" for Gottscheers, Tschinkel stated that "we knew that our explanation was not correct. We chose this explanation because we were embarrassed to tell the truth," which was that "we were expelled at the end of the war by Yugoslavia because we were identified by the liberating forces as being part of the occupying power of Nazi Germany. We were identified as such because we allowed ourselves to come under the Nazi spell during the prewar years."[103] While Tschinkel's dissenting response is underpinned by an overly simplistic division between a young Nazified Gottscheer leadership that bears the blame for "turning" the largely blameless community, it remains a more historically comprehensive answer for why the Gottscheers were expelled than the community's anti-communist consensus.

Yet, Tschinkel also glosses over an important factor in the construction of postwar memory narratives—the age of the witnesses. Indeed, Tschinkel was himself impacted by this. Born in 1931, Tschinkel was only ten when the war broke out in Yugoslavia. It is Tschinkel's generation, Gottscheers who were mostly children during World War II, that have been among the most active in collecting and publishing oral narratives of Gottscheer experiences during the war, in part because of the passing of their parents' generation and the need to preserve in writing their experiences. The first issue of the *Gottschee Tree*, the American Gottscheer genealogical and community journal from which many of the testimonies for this chapter were acquired, only appeared in 1987 and almost three-quarters of the gathered testimonies were by witnesses who were children or teenagers in 1941. As children, agency in historical events is circumscribed, with history understood *as something that happened to them*, rather than *something they took part in*. As historian Michelle Mouton noted in her study of German children's memories of the Nazis' Expanded Programme to Send Children to the Countryside (*Erweiterte Kinderlandverschickung*—EKLV), "They were not burdened by the guilt that frequently encourages memory revision."[104] Thus, the sense of victimhood in the testimonies of Gottscheers who were only children during the war was less, to borrow Tschinkel's words, a result of "embarrassment of the truth" that they had "come under the Nazi spell," or to conceal nefarious activities they had committed in the name of Nazi hegemony in occupied Slovenia. Rather, this victimhood comes from a more genuine place shared by all child refugees from war, in which the only world that they had ever known—their homes and lives in the villages of Gottschee—were taken away from them. Yet, with evidently shakier memories of the war years, Gottscheer children were, like children everywhere, prone to fill in the missing spaces with the remembrances and narratives provided by their parents and their community.

An interrogation of a cross-section of Gottscheer written representations of their past should not be interpreted as a scolding of how far the community has erred from more-or-less accepted scholarly versions of the Gottscheers' historical experiences during World War II. The ultimate goal is to explore how Gottscheers, "as a trauma-affected group,"[105] attempted to craft an understanding of their past that reflected each individual's unique experience of the war (whether firsthand or secondhand), while also accommodating the collective memories of the Gottscheer diaspora within which they lived and which sustained the richness of their new lives in the United States. Thus, it is not surprising to find that many Gottscheers who were willing to testify about their wartime personal experiences were also active within the Gottscheer diaspora, offering an answer to Michel de Certeau's query: "Of all the things everyone does, how much gets written down?"[106]

On the other hand, there were consequences for those who tested and critiqued the veracity of collective memories. Tschinkel felt obligated to resign his membership in Gottscheer organizations that had become, in his view, too conciliatory to former right-wing elements, including the 1997 decision by the *Gottscheer Landsmannschaft* to award Lampeter an honored membership. A perusal of the online commentary war between Tschinkel and community members who find him "one-sided ... dogmatic" and "less than factual," reveals that interpretive differences of a distant past still cut to the core of how Gottscheers see themselves and their families, and are thus highly personal.[107]

This is not to suggest that only "memory dissidents" like Tschinkel understood what really happened to Gottscheers during the war, while the rest of the community was either duped or consisted of secret Nazi sympathizers in cleaving to the collective memory consensus. Tschinkel, along with some Slovene historians, underemphasizes certain relevant factors. For example, prewar assimilation by the Yugoslav and Slovene governments did much to make the Gottschee, and especially its young who were at the receiving end of educational Slovenianization, receptive to Nazism. The Gottscheers in the 1930s did not sugarcoat their words, but instead warned that the Slovenes wanted to "exterminate" and "destroy" the German minority.[108]

Rather than play the role of historical judge for the crimes of the right and of the left, this chapter has attempted to identify which elements of collective remembering are either plucked out of, or forced back into, the quicksand of memory, and the vastly more difficult question of why this is so. Prewar assimilation by Ljubljana and Belgrade, a resettlement that was *forced* upon them by everyone but their own community members, a colonization scheme punctuated by Reich Germans' false promises and lethal Partisan attacks, and the culminating horror of the postwar expulsions feature prominently in most Gottscheer accounts of the war. Of course, what is missing from Gottscheer narratives also speaks to how Gottscheers represent the past—what sociologists Chana Teeger and Vered Vinitzky-Seroussi typologize as "covert silence in the domain of memory," in which "certain issues come to be ignored and silenced in the aim of memory . . . curtail[ing] the eruption of conflict over representations of shameful and contested pasts."[109] Such covert silences, undoubtedly also influenced by the young age of some of the witnesses during the war, pepper Gottscheer narratives: the almost complete absence of any role for the Gottscheer leadership in the 1941 resettlement, the glossing over of the ethnic cleansing of Slovenes, a dearth of insight into how the daily life of Gottscheers in the Rann Triangle revealed their newfound prominence in the Nazi racial hierarchy, and explanations of the 1945 expulsions that largely ignored the Nazi crimes that preceded them.

Gottscheer narratives offer the historian a window into how decisions that were made in Nazi corridors of power to metaphorically "garden,"[110] in sociologist Zygmunt Bauman's understanding, the region between Berlin and the Bosporus, transplanting valuable Germanic seedlings and expelling (and in some cases eliminating) those peoples considered to be weeds, were experienced on the grassroots level by one of the "chosen breeds." In the battle over memory, however, the *Heim ins Reich* policies largely escape close scrutiny in Gottscheer memory narratives. "J'accuse" is directed principally at the postwar triumph of a genocidal communism, while the war forms a mere backdrop—a "memory antechamber" of sorts leading to the great caesura of 1945. However, the continuing centrality of wartime and postwar events in explanations of who Gottscheers were and are underscores both the "'groupness' of traumatic injury and its memory" and its continuing indivisibility from Gottscheer identity.[111]

CHAPTER 9

FROM MODEL TO WARNING

Narratives of Resettlement "Home to the Reich" after World War II

GAËLLE FISHER

Between 1939 and 1942, the National Socialist regime organized the transfer of more than half a million ethnic Germans, putative Germans living beyond the borders Germany, in the context of what came to be known as "resettlement 'home to the Reich'" (*die Umsiedlung "Heim ins Reich"*).[1] This experience constitutes a contentious issue in the history and memory of Nazism and World War II. In their seminal work on German memory of the set of events now widely known as "the expulsions," Eva and Hans Henning Hahn describe this episode as a "repressed" aspect of the history of World War II in the Federal Republic and argue that resettled Germans never obtained their "due place" in the postwar context.[2] As other scholars have shown, even as it happened, for many ethnic Germans, resettlement was an ambivalent experience, associated with high hopes and expectations, but soon followed by a series of disappointments and a deep sense of betrayal.[3]

In effect, the expression "resettlement 'home to the Reich'" stood and stands for a bundle of different experiences. In retrospect especially, resettlement was not the straightforward and benign population transfer the infamous National Socialist slogan suggested. This transfer consisted of distinct phases, corresponding to more or less violent experiences of displacement and settlement, all intertwined in complex ways with the history of Nazism, World War II, and the Holocaust. Ultimately, this experience was decisive for the character and framing of these people's postwar lives, too, as they negotiated the meaning of home, homeland, Germanness, and belonging in postwar Germany and Europe. This episode thus displays especially well the entanglement of German and Balkan histories in the twentieth century and exposes the significance of a range of powerful continuities across 1945 with respect to prewar modes of identification, wartime experiences, and postwar processes of identity formation in West Germany in particular.

The Nazi policy of resettlement was duplicitous from the outset. Officially, its purpose was both humanitarian and ideological: since most of those affected lived in areas that came under Soviet control following the Molotov-Ribbentrop agreement of the summer of 1939, it was a matter of evacuation—rescue from life under Soviet rule. But as Hitler himself explained, it was also a matter of giving "unsustainable groups of Germans" the possibility to return to the motherland to live "as Germans among Germans."[4] As Elizabeth Harvey has argued, this policy made for a perfect "propaganda story,"[5] and it was exploited for this purpose extensively and effectively.[6] Those affected were told they may be "losing the homeland [Heimat]," but they would be "gaining the fatherland,"[7] and many ethnic Germans appear to have indeed thought of Germany as the "promised land."[8] Even to skeptical outside observers, the operation offered a stereotypical display of the legendary German zeal for organization and efficiency.[9] And since, in the official wording, resettlement was described as "voluntary" (*freiwillig*) for all those above fourteen years of age, the fact that the vast majority of those who could, chose to leave made it look like a huge plebiscite in favor of Hitler.

Yet after being brought "home to the Reich," the "returnees" (*Heimkehrer, Rückkehrer*) or "resettlers" (*Umsiedler*), as they came to be known, were ideologically screened, racially categorized, and ultimately deployed wherever they were needed most from the perspective of Germany's war effort and the vision of the Nazi New Order.[10] In most cases, this meant being sent to areas conquered and occupied by the Nazis in central and eastern Europe, and compensated with the goods and properties of ethnic "others," such as expelled and murdered Jews and Poles. Not only was the process in itself chaotic and badly managed, but at the end of the war, when the tables turned, these same people were also among some of the first to flee from their new homes. Displaced once more, albeit this time more violently, most of them then ended up in what remained of the Reich—a devastated, divided, and occupied land.

As many of the historians working on the topic have concluded, ethnic German "resettlers" found themselves in a highly ambivalent position: as "the human material for a project of settler colonialism," they were both "privileged" and "vulnerable"—simultaneously victims of the Nazis and "beneficiaries of plunder and genocide."[11] Resettlement was to serve "the consolidation of the German nation" (*die Festigung des deutschen Volkstums*) abroad, but this "deployment of people," as the guidelines euphemistically described the transfer, was nothing short of exploitation.[12] As Doris Bergen has argued, despite the praise, resettlers were often treated as "third rate Germans."[13]

Adding to the sensitive character of this experience retrospectively—and this is something that has often been overlooked—is the fact that the rationale for resettlement was not so much challenged as reinforced by the circumstances of the end and immediate aftermath of World War II. For one, the policy of resettlement itself can be seen as a justification and a precedent for the expulsions of Germans from central and eastern Europe on a wider scale at the end of the war.[14] This transfer certainly contributed to legitimizing the reorganization of Europe on the basis of ethnicity rather than borders after 1945, not least because it "hardened" conceptions of ethnicity and community among all of those involved.[15] Moreover, the spread of communism and the Cold War vindicated the existence of a Soviet threat from which the Nazis had, as they themselves claimed, "saved" ethnic Germans.[16] Last but not least, since most resettlers ended up in West Germany after 1945, the promise of returning to Germany to "live as Germans among Germans" was effectively realized and the experience therefore also remained central to their claim to belonging in that country after the war was over.

The experience of resettlement thus not only highlights the challenge of measuring the degree of agency of individuals under difficult circumstances, but also that of assessing the extent to which National Socialist policies, categories, and ideas continued to shape postwar social realities and beliefs. Indeed, the legacies and aftermath of this experience raise a number of questions: How did resettlers engage with the combined legacies of victimhood and complicity in war and genocide after World War II? How did they tell this story in different, changing postwar environments and in light of the experiences of others? In other words, how did they come to terms with this specific experience of displacement, framed in and enacted on racist terms?

BUKOVINA-GERMAN RESETTLERS AS A COMMUNITY OF EXPERIENCE

This article focuses on the postwar narratives of one particular group of resettlers, namely ethnic Germans from the historical region of Bukovina or so-called Bukovina Germans.[17] Once the easternmost province of the Austrian half of the Habsburg Empire, Bukovina became part of Romania in 1918 before being divided between Romania in the south and the Soviet Union in the north during World War II. In Romanian, interwar Bukovina, ethnic Germans represented less than 10 percent of the population: the Romanian census of 1930 registered 75,000 Germans. At the time of resettlement, however, non-German spouses, acquaintances, and employees were often included on the lists. In fall 1940, therefore, after the Soviet Union invaded the north of the region, a total of 95,770 people were resettled from North and South Bukovina to the Reich.[18]

With regard to the history of resettlement, Bukovina Germans are an intriguing example for a number of reasons. Firstly, the Germans living in the south of the region chose to be resettled, too, despite the fact that their homeland was not occupied by the Soviets in 1940. For this purpose, Romania even signed a separate, additional agreement with Nazi Germany. This embodied the "voluntary" (*freiwillig*) and quasi-plebiscitary character of resettlement. Secondly, as one of the last groups to be resettled, Bukovina Germans were rather badly treated by the Nazi authorities. Many lived in resettlement camps for years; thousands were even still living in camps, waiting to be resettled, when the war ended. Those who were resettled were then dispersed across the occupied territories including Wartheland, Danzig-Westpreußen, Upper Silesia, and Alsace-Lorraine without any regard for their backgrounds or existing communities. Finally, stemming from a remote, traditional, economically backward, and ethnically highly diverse area, their group identity was not as strong as that of others (especially Bessarabian or Baltic Germans) and their "Germanness" was therefore often put into question by the Nazis.[19] Among Bukovina Germans, a relatively high percentage (half of the northern Bukovinians and a third of southern Bukovinians) were categorized as "A-cases"—namely "ethnically or politically unreliable."[20] This meant they were to be "resettled among Germans" in the *Altreich* (Germany within the borders of 1937, Austria, and the Sudetenland). Indeed, only those regarded as "racially pure" were categorized as "O-cases," with the O standing for the east (*Ost*), and meaning they were considered fit for the "Germanization" of conquered areas, namely resettlement among non-Germans. This policy thus scattered and divided not only many Bukovina-German communities but also families. By 1944, 7,267 Bukovina Germans deemed "racially inferior," "ungermanizable," and therefore unworthy of citizenship had even been categorized as "S-cases," standing for *Sonderfälle* (special cases), and sent back to Bukovina or settled in the *Generalgouvernement*.[21] Bukovina Germans therefore experienced the distinction between ethnic Germans (*Volksdeutsche*) and Reich Germans (*Reichsdeutsche*), and their dismissal as "second-class Germans" by the Nazi authorities, in an especially stark manner.

Notwithstanding (or perhaps therefore), after the war, resettlement became *the* foundational experience for this group. This is reflected in the way many Bukovinians presented their past after World War II and narrate their lives to this day.[22] One could even argue that "Bukovina German" after World War II became synonymous with—and eventually reduced to—the notion of "resettler." The way resettlement was narrated, however, changed drastically over time. In what follows, I distinguish three main phases: the 1950s, during which the majority of Bukovina

Germans established themselves in West Germany and when resettlement was essential to claims to belonging in this society and rationalized as "a good idea, badly carried out"; the period from the 1960s to the 1980s, during which the experience was barely discussed at all and was dismissed as "ultimately for the best" in order not to challenge the Cold War status quo; and finally, the period after 1989, when narratives of resettlement experienced an unprecedented boom and Bukovina Germans were depicted as having been "at the mercy of tyrants."

To a large extent, this chronology reflects the known conjuncture of German memory culture.[23] For instance, Pertti Ahonen has argued that, for decades, a "distorted memory" placing the blame for the destruction of the diversity of central and eastern Europe on the communists alone remained dominant in West Germany.[24] Many others have noted the paradigm shift relating to the history of Nazism, the Holocaust, and the concept of collective guilt in the 1980s.[25] In the early 2000s, Norbert Frei even pointed to the contemporary morally loaded way of asking about this history and argued that drawing on the statements of the last witnesses of National Socialism to understand how this period was experienced was highly problematic and misleading with regard to the issue of historical veracity.[26] Rather than concentrating on these narratives' historical truth, however, I argue here that these shifts might be able to tell us about something different. Focusing on one particular "community of experience" gives privileged insight into why this change was possible, namely the associated changing purpose of this narrative for different members of the group in different postwar settings and moments. In other words, it draws attention to the relationship between this "community of experience" and shifting, later "communities of identification."[27] Indeed, each phase brought with it a new way of framing the experience of resettlement. By analyzing the shifts to the narrative and paying attention to who is speaking, it is possible to highlight not just the adaptation of the discourse but also its changing uses for individuals and for the community to which they sought to belong. Beyond echoing existing conceptualizations of trends in German memory discourse, therefore, this case study sheds light on the relationship between experiences made in the war and the different postwar modes of identification of both Bukovina Germans and of those identifying as Germans after World War II in general.

A "GOOD IDEA, BADLY CARRIED OUT": JUSTIFYING RESETTLEMENT IN WEST GERMANY IN THE IMMEDIATE AFTERMATH OF WORLD WAR II

An estimated seventy thousand Bukovina Germans, who had been resettled by the National Socialists in 1940, survived World War II. When the war came to an end, some seventeen thousand of them, those classified as "A-cases" or "O-cases" who had not yet been resettled, were living in Germany. But most of them, more than fifty thousand people, having spent the war in occupied territories, fled behind the front lines to the reduced territory of Germany in the last weeks and months of the war.[28] Men were often absent, having been conscripted, been taken prisoner, or fallen. Remaining family members were often split apart, as women with young children could go by train, but others had to go on foot. Once they had arrived, they found themselves among millions of other ethnically German and foreign refugees. These included millions of Germans who had been expelled from their homelands behind the Oder-Neisse line or their ancestral homelands in central and eastern Europe, who came to be known as "expellees of the homeland" (*Heimatvertriebene*), and former slave and foreign workers and Holocaust survivors, so-called displaced persons (DPs).[29] Most Bukovina Germans did not want to go back to Bukovina but they did not know where to go in Germany either, or even what this "Germany" might look like.

In general, in view of the number of uprooted people in Germany at this time, the future of Bukovina Germans in Germany was very uncertain. In the western zones of Germany and the later Federal Republic of Germany, therefore, where most Bukovina Germans ended up or wanted to go, the experience of resettlement became the key to Bukovina Germans'—as with other resettled Germans'—claim to belonging in the country.[30] Indeed, aside from helping members of the community find each other, convincing the German authorities and the Allies that their presence and establishment in Germany (what they called *Seßhaftmachung*), and their entitlement to citizenship, were legitimate was one of the main tasks of the group's leadership and the institutions, such as the Self-Help Organization of German Resettlers from Bukovina (*Hilfskomitee der deutschen Umsiedler aus der Bukowina*), founded in the immediate aftermath of the war.[31] The continued use of the Nazi term *Umsiedler* (resettlers) rather than the terms *Flüchtlinge* (refugees) or *Vertriebene* (expellees) in the names of their organizations and official correspondence was no coincidence.[32] As they argued, their German "ethnic belonging" (*Volkszugehörigkeit*) had been assessed and certified already in 1940–1941 when they had been granted German citizenship for the first time. This might have happened under the Nationalist Socialist regime, but they were determined for it to remain valid.

Defending not just the outcome but also the basic tenets of resettlement was of fundamental importance to the leadership of the Homeland Association of Resettlers from Bukovina (*Landsmannschaft der deutschen Umsiedler aus der Bukowina*), from 1952 the Homeland Association of

Bukovina Germans (*Landsmannschaft der Buchenlanddeutschen*), which was officially founded in October 1949 after the Allies lifted their ban on political organizations. The topic was, for instance, central to the speeches given at the first postwar national meeting (*Bundestreffen*) which took place in Darmstadt in 1951.[33] The speakers acknowledged Bukovinians' present hardship but reminded them that life in Bukovina had not been easy either. Participants were encouraged to welcome the return "to the womb of the old and faithful mother" who "keeps her children on her knees and is one with them in terms of language and disposition [*Herzensbildung*]."[34] This alone, the speaker insisted, was "worth a lot of effort" (*viel Mühsal wert*).[35] The use of religiously infused language and images to describe experiences and suffering was quite common among expellees at this time. However, this statement also captures that many Bukovina Germans conceived of their relationship to the state and the nation in terms of kinship and subordination. In effect, these were similar arguments to those used in the Nazis' resettlement propaganda just a few years earlier.

By embracing the current situation, the leaders not only aimed to lessen the sense of disorientation among Bukovinians, but they also sought to defend their own past stances and actions. Most of the leaders had been members of the former intellectual elite in Bukovina and had either explicitly supported or even helped implement the policy of resettlement in an official capacity. Rudolf Wagner (1911–2004), for example, a historian by training and a former member of the SS, who would turn out to be the postwar community's most important figure, had been a staff manager (*Stabsleiter*) of the so-called Resettlement Commission in Bukovina in 1940.[36] In his postwar accounts of these events, including the speech he held at the meeting in 1951, he emphasized that the ensuing suffering should not detract from the fact that resettlement in 1940, in the face of the communist threat, had been a rational decision.[37] As Wagner explained in more detail in another text he published on the subject in 1955, "wanting to go to Germany" was by no means an indication of being "a Nazi": the Soviets had been "on the doorstep," and the homeland (*Heimat*) "no longer recognizable."[38] He argued that even Jews would have joined if they had been able to.[39] German Bukovinians from the region's northern half had therefore been forced out and those from the south had been compelled to follow because with the loss of the regional capital, Cernăuți (in German: Czernowitz), which was in the north, they had been robbed of their "spiritual and cultural epicenter."[40] Bukovina Germans had constituted an organic group and leaving was the only way of remaining a member of the German people.[41] In this sense, Wagner concluded, not only had resettlement not been "voluntary" (*freiwillig*), but Bukovina Germans had effectively been the "first expellees" of World War II.⁴²

This echoed both the Nazis' own humanitarian justification for resettlement and the stance of other expellee leaders on the subject after the war and demonstrates how the inherited National Socialist anti-Bolshevism conveniently aligned with the dominant anti-communist attitude of the early Federal Republic.⁴³ However, the most remarkable aspect of this interpretation was not so much what was said, as what was missing. While Wagner listed many of the people involved and details of the transfer, and even briefly referred to Bukovina Germans' current situation, he rapidly glossed over their experiences in Poland. Although he bemoaned evasively that the Bukovinians' "experiences in dealing with members of other ethnicities" were not "put to better use," he made no mention of the treatment of the resettlers by the National Socialists or of the others affected by the policy of resettlement, such as the Jews and Poles, whose houses Bukovina Germans had obtained in the annexed and occupied territories during the war.⁴⁴ The categorization of Bukovinians into A-, O-, and S-cases and their respective fates were not discussed at all. In other words, there was no critical discussion of the policy of ethnic engineering and Germanization. A shortened version of Wagner's text was the contribution on the subject published in the *Dokumentation der Vertreibung*, the major state-funded multivolume project on the resettlement and expulsion of Germans during and immediately after World War II.⁴⁵ Wagner's was one of just two contributions by Bukovina Germans; this was therefore the version of events that was to be saved for posterity.

In this respect, the accounts dating from this period written by individuals with less of a stake in the matter and an experience of resettlement "from below" had a slightly different tenor. In his short history of Bukovina Germans published in 1955, the young Hugo Weczerka (b. 1930), for instance, did mention the expulsion of Poles and Jews and even noted that moving into their houses had been an "embarrassing process" (*ein peinlicher Vorgang*) for Bukovina Germans "who had lived in harmony with members of many ethnic groups in their *Heimat*."⁴⁶ However, as he went on to explain: "In the end, it was simply a replacement for the goods they had left behind and for which the German state was either owed compensation, or the newly acquired goods were paid for correctly [*regelrecht bezahlt*]."⁴⁷ This was a rather strange interpretation of the circumstances under which goods were acquired in the occupied territories. Moreover, in the end, Weczerka concluded: "The losses are upsetting, the hardship today still considerable, and the dispersion depressing. Yet had the Bukovina Germans not reached the salvaging shores of the

German motherland on time, the catastrophe would have been total!"[48] Weczerka thus regarded resettlement as both necessary and fortunate. As in other written sources from this period, no link was established between the war and the policy of resettlement or between its premise and its consequences or outcome.[49]

For the sake of comparison, the interviews conducted by the ethnologist Johannes Künzig with some twenty Bukovinians in the early to mid-1950s constitute a further interesting source.[50] Künzig's main aim had been to record the accents, dialects, and traditions of different German minority groups. However, in the process, many of his interview partners spoke about their recent experiences. These conversations therefore offer privileged insight into how ordinary, less educated individuals of various ages viewed what had happened to them and their current situation, and these narratives of resettlement present interesting differences from the elite discourse. Firstly, in general, the majority of the Bukovina Germans interviewed identified themselves primarily as victims. They described repeatedly their successive displacements as "blows of fate" (*Schicksalsschläge*) and emphasized their "misfortune" (*Unglück*). The way they spoke also indicated they largely viewed themselves as completely helpless in the face of what had happened. Resettlement was discussed with passive phrases and expressions such as "We were resettled" or framed as an obligation: "We had to resettle." From their perspective, there had been no choice. None of the interviewees recalled feeling any enthusiasm or mentioned political indoctrination. As in the texts of the Homeland Association, if anyone was given explicit responsibility for resettlement, it was the Soviets. But it had not been a clever or strategic decision—just a hopeless situation.

Secondly, a number of statements made clear that the experience of resettlement had been associated with a range of expectations, which largely echoed the Nazi propaganda: better land and larger houses; more peace and less hardship; and, last but not least, a German neighborhood. This was even the source of some resentment. In a discussion between two interviewees, for instance, one of them explained that leaving the Bukovinian homeland had been "difficult" and had only been possible because they had hoped they would "join German surroundings [*in den deutschen Lebenskreis kommen*]," "live among German people," and not, as they had until then, "always have to live among foreign peoples." In response to this, however, the second interviewee exclaimed: "Yes, but then we did not, as you say, come to live among Germans! We first were put into camps, and we had to sit there for nine months, and then we were settled in Silesia, in Polish farmhouses, and first we had to clear these Polish farmyards, then rebuild them, obtain machines and everything else.

And then this was all thrown out of the window, we had to leave everything behind and leave again."⁵¹ The first speaker then concurred: "Yes, that is right. We had to leave again and we have been moving around like this, homeless, for ten years!"⁵² This exchange captures both the faith in the German promises and the real sense of disappointment and instrumentalization many resettlers felt after these were not honored. In contrast to the elite, neither the fact that things could have been worse, nor the fact that they had returned to the motherland functioned as a real consolation for the suffering, the losses, and the feelings of deception.

Yet, there were considerable gaps and silences here as well. Although some interviewees mentioned boredom in the resettlement camps, others discussed the poor quality of the food, and many complained that the houses they had received had not met expected standards, the years of *Ansiedlung* (settlement) and the process of resettlement itself (racial screening and so on) were not dealt with in much detail at all. While the departure from Bukovina and the flight at the end of the war were emotional, most accounts of this phase were succinct and matter-of-fact. As one interviewee for instance typically explained: "I left home at fourteen and then we were in a range of camps. First, we left with the train through Poland in 1940, then we went to a camp in Upper Silesia, and from there to a barrack camp [*Barakenlager*] in Pomerania with over one thousand people. We were there for two years, and in 1942, we went back to Upper Silesia and my father got a farm. We settled in well there."⁵³

Such a concise account and generally positive assessment of the time in Poland was not unusual. A number of interviewees expressed satisfaction with their lot during the war. In view of the situation of Bukovina Germans as refugees in the early Federal Republic, where the chances to obtain a house and acquire land were extremely limited, some even looked back longingly on this period and property in Poland.⁵⁴ This compared favorably to their current situation.

In particular, however, while some responders discussed social relations in Bukovina in detail, hardly anyone said anything, for example, about everyday life in Poland or the relationship to their new neighbors. A couple of Künzig's interviewees mentioned partisans or the difficulties faced by the women after their husbands had been conscripted and they were left to work on the farm alone with often-hostile local Poles.⁵⁵ But no one, for example, addressed how the houses were obtained, the fact that they had been confiscated, or the handling of members of other ethnicities by the Germans, let alone the proximity of their homes to concentration camps. In some cases, complaints about the circumstances or the goods obtained were even framed in an ethnocentric or racist manner. Previous owners might, for instance, be blamed for the poor state of the farms. Jakob M., for example, stressed that while the Germans had made the best of the land, the Poles before them had "worked badly" (*die Polen haben schlecht gearbeitet*).⁵⁶

This supports Elizabeth Harvey's claim, based on wartime documents, that "plenty of evidence testifies to [resettlers'] disappointment with their situation." However, as she goes on to argue, "How much of their dissatisfaction was caused by unease and anxiety at the fact that their welfare was being sustained at the expense of the non-German population is harder to assess."⁵⁷ Similarly, Markus Krzoska has commented that although some of the resettlers might have worried about the fate of members of other ethnicities, "indifference and rejection were undoubtedly much more widespread."⁵⁸ This remained the case when narrating the experience soon after the war, as well. There was no real reevaluation of the resettlers' experience from a moral standpoint and in light of new knowledge or information. If anything, former resettlers' current hardship made them focus even more on their own sense of victimhood. This resulted in what others have called a form of "communicative silence" or at least an incomplete discussion of what they had gone through.⁵⁹

In general, Künzig's interviewees only dared voice muted criticism of National Socialist policies and deeds. They did not name complicit individuals or question the underpinning logic of the Germanization project for which they were exploited. As Doris Bergen has argued, resettlers might not have felt comfortable criticizing their experiences under National Socialism among postwar West Germans: in view of the perceived continuity between the notion of "German" and "National Socialist," they may not have wanted to appear ungrateful and thereby endanger their own claim to belonging in postwar Germany.⁶⁰ Indeed, whatever their grievances, all of the interviewees remained convinced that their situation was better in the FRG than it would have been in the "old home" in Bukovina. Not only did many believe that they had long been treated like "second-class citizens" in Romania, but they had also been told about the drastic circumstances for Germans there since 1945. In their eyes, therefore, postwar anti-communism and the division of Europe had only reinforced the legitimacy of their displacement, despite the hardship they experienced during and even after the war. Echoing the way many Germans viewed National Socialism in general, resettlement was therefore presented and perceived as "a good idea" that had simply been "badly carried out."⁶¹

"ULTIMATELY FOR THE BEST": SILENCING RESETTLEMENT DURING THE COLD WAR

The early postwar period established how resettlement was to be narrated for the following decades. Yet, over time, it became increasingly difficult to speak of resettlement, not to mention of wartime "settlement" (*Ansiedlung*) in occupied territories, which was at the core of the Nazis' wider occupation regime and Germanization project, as a "good idea." In fact, with time, it became increasingly contentious to speak of the experience of resettlement "home to the Reich" at all. This had two main causes: On the one hand, generational change, a growing awareness of the crimes of National Socialism, and pressure for Germans who had lost their homes during the war to assimilate into German society during the Cold War all contributed to marginalizing the discussion of their experiences and victimhood.⁶² On the other, while knowledge about the character of the Nazi regime grew, no one wanted to endanger the status quo by asking awkward questions.⁶³ Like most West Germans, whose priority was to enjoy in peace the country's new prosperity, what mattered most was that Bukovina Germans had found a new and safe home in the Federal Republic. How they had gotten there was not important: it was best left unmentioned.

The few accounts of resettlement published in the 1960s are indicative of this stance. Rather than focusing on the suffering or "ordeal" (*Leidensweg*) of resettlers as in the 1950s, the focus was now placed ever more exclusively on the outcome: the escape from Soviet rule and the obtaining of a new home. This even made it possible to present resettlement itself as a great achievement. This was the case with Wagner's ultimate, lengthier, and more detailed account of the unfolding of resettlement, published in 1961, in which he proudly outlined his own role in the process and even described resettlement as "a great success" (*ein voller Erfolg*).⁶⁴ Some passages of this essay are identical to his previous texts, but some information was removed and some new elements were added. Although he still stressed the compulsion to leave, he foregrounded the role of members of the German community rather than Nazis, toned down his anti-Soviet rhetoric, and even argued that the German minority was threatened with disappearance already in interwar Romania.⁶⁵ In particular, in this text Wagner not only mentioned that many Jews had wanted to join resettlement to escape the Soviets, but also that falsified papers (baptism certificates) were printed to enable many non-Germans (including baptized so-called "half Jews") to leave, too, and that both Bukovina Germans and members of the resettlement commission had supported this practice—something which he suggestively argued "spoke in their favor."⁶⁶ Mixing older ideas with more recent arguments about "integration," he also discussed the separation of the resettlers in A- and O-cases "according to the established degree of their belonging to the German culture" and "the speed at which they could assimilate." But he also explained that some people "of pure German blood" were resettled in the *Altreich* due to their competences and that these individuals had eventually "gotten the better deal" since they were not expelled.⁶⁷ Finally, here again, he bemoaned that the specific experiences and background of Bukovina Germans "had not been put to better use" by the Nazis but pointed out that today, thanks to the *Landsmannschaft*, they continued to cherish these traditions in West Germany.⁶⁸ He concluded by mentioning the gift, a silver cigarette box and amber cigar holder, he had received on behalf of Molotov in 1940 "for the good work" and described these days as "colorful" (*bunt*).⁶⁹ The text not only captured Wagner's ability to adapt his discourse to the mood of the times but also the lasting pride and excitement with which he remembered this event and period. In the end, therefore, the fate of Bukovinians no longer sounded tragic at all; what took place was ultimately for the best.

In the case of less prominent Bukovinians, who were also less of an authority on the subject, the focus on the outcome simply dispensed with the need to discuss the details of resettlement any further. What was clear was that the end had justified the means. There was therefore no point in speculating by asking questions that did not need to be posed or could not be answered. In the homeland book of the Bukovinian village of Ilișești, for example, which appeared in 1960, the author stated the following: "Whether, with regard to the resettlements, the wellbeing of the people was the motivation or whether they were the result of cold political calculation will not be discussed here and Germany will not be asked about it either. The whole idea of resettlement, based on the assumption of a victory in the war, is still far too hazy for us to be able to judge it clearly today."⁷⁰ The author then went on to explain that despite all that had happened during the war, "after the collapse [of Nazi Germany], it became clear that the resettlement of the Germans from southern Bukovina was a blessing of fate, because it prevented greater loss of life and perhaps even their disappearance as a people."⁷¹ He thus concluded, emphatically: "It is therefore our duty to thank Germany."⁷² In short, though he conceded resettlement had had negative aspects, these had been compensated or neutralized by the good ones, and there was therefore no need to discuss them. In the process, the earlier "blows of fate" had become strikes of luck.

This intriguing discourse of gratefulness lasted until the end of the Cold War and even survived the resurgence of interest in the history of World War II and "the expulsions"—and therefore the experience of resettlement, too—in the 1980s.⁷³ On the day of Pentecost in 1980, at a meeting of Bukovina Germans, for example, the Bukovinian Catholic priest Norbert Gaschler delivered a long speech on the topic.⁷⁴ For someone close to the leadership of the Homeland Association, Gaschler adopted an uncommonly open and critical stance. He described the different stages of resettlement in considerable detail, including the range of reactions, from enthusiasm to despair, to the announcement of resettlement in Bukovina itself. He spoke of the difficulties faced by Bukovina Germans (particularly those who were religious) in the resettler camps, the disappointment felt by many, and what he described as small acts of resistance. Gaschler nevertheless reached the conclusion that resettlement had been "for the best." According to him, Bukovinians were now fully "integrated" as members of society in the Federal Republic of Germany, and if one took their contemporary situation into account, it was quite clear that resettlement had been a good thing. As he explained: "Not only were we spared much hardship and suffering, but we have also found a nicer, more comfortable and more peaceful home."[75]

Moreover, while Gaschler sought to distance himself from National Socialism, he did not, as a number of passing statements and anecdotes show, fundamentally question National Socialist methods, principles, and intentions. He, for instance, expressed indignation about his classification as an "A-case," to be resettled to the *Altreich* and therefore deemed, according to the Nazi logic, unfit to Germanize or live among "ethnic others." As Gaschler pointed out, the rest of his family had been classified as the more politically reliable "O-cases." The reason for his being labeled an A-case was probably his faith and profession. However, as of 1980, Gaschler still believed this was due to an administrative error. According to him, as a "real German," he had been mis-categorized: "What and who is responsible that I was not allowed to go to the East and was separated from my relatives and acquaintances, neighbors, and friends? Apparently, only healthy, purely German and politically reliable resettlers were given citizenship for the East [*für den Osten eingebürgert*]. But this was not always the case. There were shocking cases, which clearly showed that the process was sometimes wholly arbitrary."[76] Although Gaschler discussed National Socialist practices, he did not challenge their basic logic. He failed to see that what he called "arbitrary" and "shocking" was the result of the regime's fundamentally authoritarian and racist principles. This blindness prevented the acknowledgement of the bankruptcy of the system and its criminal character and, with this, any discussion of resettlers' complicity in its project.

Depicting Bukovina Germans as completely separate historical actors from the National Socialists, as Gaschler had done, was a common and convenient deflection strategy. It constructed a convenient dichotomy between "us" and "them," and implied resettlers had been devoid of any agency. However, this also resulted in intriguing contradictions. For example, in the homeland book of the village of Poiana Micului (in

German: Buchenhain; Polish: Pojana Mikuli), published in 1986, one of the few such books published in this period, the author, Josef Neuburger, granted the Bukovinians a curious mixture of power and helplessness.[77] On the one hand, he emphasized the positive traits of Buchenhainers: they were "clear headed" and a "particularly healthy type of people."[78] Yet, on the other hand, he spoke of the attractiveness of National Socialist propaganda, including the genuine enthusiasm some of the resettlers felt for the "departure" (*Umbruch*), and emphasized the pressure they had been under and their lack of room for maneuver: "There was not much time to mull things over"; they had had "hardly any time to think about their critical situation"; "no one could go against the tide."[79] Neuburger's discussion of their complicity in criminal policies was equally apologetic. Regarding the obtaining of Jewish and Polish property, he explained: "One day before the settlers could take over the farmyards they had been assigned to, the Polish owners were thrown out of or, rather, expelled from their native or inherited homes. They could only take a few belongings with them, whatever they could carry. Many Buchenhainers had already been the witnesses to such a violent expulsion. Did they perhaps think back to their own—though in their case nonviolent—departure from their native [Bukovinian] homeland Pojana in the year 1940? They too had to leave behind the things they loved and move into an uncertain future!"[80] Although Neuburger described explicitly what happened to the Poles, their situation was directly linked to the vulnerability of the Bukovinians themselves. The author thereby equated the fate of Bukovinians with that of the National Socialists' other victims. The situation of Jews, in turn, was entirely omitted.

The mention of the concentration camp Auschwitz, which was near the Buchenhainers' wartime area of settlement in Silesia, followed the same pattern. Despite the fact that the resettlers had lived just a few kilometers away from the camp, Neuburger explained that the Buchenhainers had only heard of the camp from their Polish neighbors who were "terribly scared" of it.[81] The Buchenhainers themselves had apparently not been aware of the camp until the end of the war, when they had encountered inmates on what is known as death marches during their own flight from the region: "For many Buchenhainers, the short encounter with the poorest of the poor on the flight to the West remained unforgettable. Later, those who fled spoke only reluctantly about these inhuman experiences. Maybe they too were tortured by the parable of the 'good Samaritan'? Had they not seen fellow human beings who were tired and weakened to death and walked on without offering their help?"[82] This amounted to an admission of at least moral responsibility. Yet the rhetorical questions, as in the previous quote, left the task of answering them and the interpretation of the circumstances to the reader. Moreover, by emphasizing how this vision had disturbed them, weighed on their consciences, and even constituted an "inhuman experience," the author made Buchenhainers, once more, sound like the actual victims of this situation.

Neuburger concluded this chapter in his book by saying that in Poland, the Buchenhainers had not been able to "feel really happy"[83]: they had "never truly felt at home."[84] Nevertheless, he emphasized that they had "accomplished the tasks they had been given with great care,"[85] and that, thanks to them, "a number of Polish villages had been given a complete makeover."[86] These last statements resembled strongly those made in the interviews from the 1950s. With the ongoing Cold War, the substance of the narratives had changed rather little. Resettlement was still conceived of as the closing chapter of a two-hundred-year collective history, which, on the whole, was to be evaluated positively. The priority remained to tell a constructive version of how Bukovinians had avoided the communist yoke and become valued and valuable West German citizens. Even in the few academic works on the subject, anti-communism continued to determine the assessment of the events' outcome.[87] From this perspective, Bukovina Germans had simply made the best out of a bad situation.

"AT THE MERCY OF TYRANTS": REMEMBERING RESETTLEMENT AFTER 1989

In 1990, the Homeland Society of Bukovina Germans published a book entitled *Mit Fluchtgepäck die Heimat verlassen . . . 50 Jahre seit der Umsiedlung der Buchenlanddeutschen* (*Leaving home with no more than one could carry . . . 50 years since the resettlement of Bukovina Germans*).[88] Consisting of a series of pictures and short texts by different authors, it presented different aspects of Bukovina Germans' resettlement "home to the Reich." Half a century after the events, it aimed both to describe and to commemorate this foundational experience for the group. Now that there was no more doubt as to where Bukovinians belonged, it was possible to speak openly about what had happened to them. This was, after all, what distinguished them from other groups of "expelled" Germans.

On the one hand, therefore, the book was solidly in the tradition of what preceded. It had a quasi-celebratory tone. With hindsight, 1940 had not only been the end of something but also the beginning of something new, and almost all of the contributors adopted the view that resettlement had been "for the best." However, on the other hand, the sole focus on resettlement and its framing, not as a "return" or the end of the collective history of Bukovina Germans abroad, but rather as a historical episode in its own right, was new. Furthermore, the individual contributions reflected a shift toward personal memories of the event rather than the kind of group narrative that had been offered until then. Last but not least, while the use of the word "flight" in the title resonated with the growing discussion in Germany of the victims of "flight and expulsion" and cast Bukovina Germans as victims, too, the printed pictures featuring members of the SS and swastikas—something not seen since the propaganda publications of the 1940s—visibly captured the involvement of the National Socialist regime in the operation.

This book was therefore both emblematic of the discourse in the late 1980s and symptomatic of the conflicting ways in which the recent German past would be reframed and reevaluated in the following decade.[89] Indeed, while in this period the ever-closer scrutiny of the history of the Third Reich spurred unprecedented debates about German guilt and responsibility for the war and the Holocaust, over the course of the 1990s many Germans simultaneously recalled ever more publicly their own suffering in the war.[90] After 1989, the topic of resettlement was "rediscovered" within a context where the role of ethnic Germans in central and eastern Europe was being reconsidered from the perspective of examining "Germans as perpetrators." Yet, simultaneously, many Bukovina Germans felt increasingly confident putting forward their personal stories of victimhood.

The post-1989 narratives of resettlement thus developed in two dramatically different directions. On the one hand, new academic work brought with it a reevaluation of resettlement as a policy and placed it in a completely new framework. Most notably, in a book published in 1991, the historians Götz Aly and Susanne Heim posited a direct link between the policy of resettlement and the Final Solution.[91] In general, resettlement came to be viewed as an aspect of National Socialist foreign policy and as embedded in the wider process of destruction of central and eastern Europe's diversity during World War II.[92] This inevitably raised new questions about resettlers' roles and choices within this wider system and setting. On the other hand, however, Bukovina Germans and their representative organization, which gained increased visibility in reunified Germany, continued to focus on the experience of the resettlers themselves, advocate Rudolf Wagner's "first expellees" argument, and emphasize their suffering. The 2005 book *Die Umsiedler* (*The Resettlers*) by the former director of the Bukovina Institute in Augsburg, Ortfried Kotzian, for example, not only highlighted the specificity of the experiences of resettlers among the wider group of ethnic German expellees but also presented their case alongside that of other victims of genocide and ethnic cleansing.[93] For Kotzian, resettlement was a chapter like any other in the wider "century of expulsions."

The public attention suddenly drawn to this event and to experiences during World War II in general prompted many individual Bukovina

Germans to share their own versions of events. In issues of the Bukovinian *Landsmannschaft*'s newspaper, *Der Südostdeutsche*, dating from the late 1990s and the early 2000s, so-called witness accounts or "accounts of experience" (*Erlebnisberichte*) dealing with resettlement appeared ever more frequently. By 2001, at least one article per issue discussed the experience of resettlement. These articles were often combined with reproductions of resettler identity cards (*Umsiedlerkarten*) and certificates of citizenship (*Einbürgerungsurkunden*), or contemporary photographs. Such documents, together with historical letters and diaries, surfaced repeatedly in private collections and were eagerly brought to public attention by those who found them.[94] The motives for these activities ranged from the psychological need to confide life experiences in old age to the desire to share results of genealogical research by members of the "second generation" after the parents passed away.[95] A certain fascination with Nazism unquestionably also played a role. But many also genuinely regarded the circumstances of their own or their ancestors' displacement as unknown, forgotten, or misconstrued, and wanted to set the historical record straight.

Although the history of resettlement was not actually unknown, the fact that new questions were being asked made it feel as though it were. Indeed, for those interested in the topic at this point, the main issue with respect to resettlement—and the history of Bukovina Germans in general—was not whether Bukovina Germans as a group had been "saved" as a result of the transfer or not, but rather: Under what circumstances did they leave? What had the intentions of the Nazis been? How did the resettlers feel? In other words, how did resettlement relate to Nazi doctrine and ideology? By questioning what had previously been taken for granted, the topic was indeed discovered anew. This was true of the treatment of the subject in popular history and academic research but also in how individual Bukovina Germans conceived of their own biographies.

A close reading of personal accounts from the 2000s makes the shift in focus particularly evident.[96] These accounts often began in the year 1940, or at the earliest with the witnesses' childhood in the interwar period, and not, as they previously had, with their ancestors' emigration from central to eastern Europe in the eighteenth and nineteenth centuries—something that had often made resettlement seem a mere closing of the circle of migration. Moreover, the deceitful intentions of the National Socialists constituted the story's premise rather than its conclusion. Many of these authors placed the ideological backdrop, which before was deemed irrelevant and often omitted completely, in the foreground or even made it the primary focus of attention. Some, for instance, hinted at the euphemistic nature of the expressions "home to the reich" or even "resettlement" and "resettler." Besides, they no longer accepted the methods of the National Socialists uncritically, but commented on them or even derided them directly. One woman, for instance, declared: "We were 'deloused.' This was a procedure, which I can still laugh about today, but that really was not nice."[97] Another Bukovina German, whose mother, because she was a Pole, had been categorized as an "O-case" rather than an "A-case," dismissed this categorization as "absurd."[98] Many noted the irony that the A-cases, long regarded as belonging to a dishonorable class insofar as this categorization indicated being considered "racially inferior" or "politically unreliable," had been the lucky ones, since they had not had to flee at the end of the war. As such, being classified as "A" and therefore ineligible for the east was no longer shameful but fortunate. In itself, the open discussion of A- and O- but also S-cases—the "special cases," which, until the 2000s, were hardly ever mentioned in such accounts—reflected the fact that these categories were no longer taken at face value or as taboo.

Similarly, the way the National Socialists had treated the resettlers was no longer simply, as Josef Neuburger had abstractly and somewhat benignly argued, "the tide of the times" one could not counter, but rather a gross transgression of human norms. Some even suggested that, at least from an ideological standpoint, the treatment of resettlers could be compared to that of Jews.[99] Indeed, Bukovina Germans increasingly drew on Holocaust imagery to explain what they had experienced, in particular with respect to the transports, life in the resettlement camps, their relationship to the SS who ran the camps, and the racial assessment.[100] In effect, many viewed their collective handling, previously presented as their rescue, as downright criminal or even inhumane. The central role given to resettlers' treatment by the German authorities meant that the Soviets, who had been so crucial in the 1950s, completely disappeared from the picture.[101] Anti-communism itself no longer mattered. The persecution of the Jews, in turn, became a key part of these stories. In the midst of the so-called memory boom in Germany in the early 2000s and what many have described as hegemonic Holocaust memory, the fact that many of the places Bukovinians had been resettled to were key locations on the map of the Holocaust could no longer be ignored. At this time, those exploring the topic specified their questions further in this direction. These queries included: How were the houses obtained? How did ethnic Germans relate to their new neighbors? Where did they work? Considering the proximity of the ghettos and camps, what did resettlers see, do, and know?

Many Bukovina Germans themselves reassessed their experiences in light of what they now knew about the Holocaust. In her short account,

Regina Schröcker, who was born in 1932 in Poiana Micului, mentioned that her family had lived just six kilometers (less than four miles) from the concentration camp Auschwitz. As she explained, they had therefore lived "close to death."[102] Many authors of these accounts mentioned encounters with Jews during the war and witnessing aspects of Jewish persecution, although they often also qualified this by saying they did not know what they were seeing at the time. Berta Vogel, for example, remembered seeing "people" wearing yellow signs or stars on their clothes and avoided using the word "Jew" in order to emphasize her cluelessness.[103] Edith Schütrumpf, who was born in Kotzman (in Ukrainian: Kitsman) in 1928 and lived in the GDR after the war, and who had spent time as a resettler in Łódź (in German: Litzmannstadt) during the war, said in an interview from 2004 that she recalled seeing the Jewish ghetto in the city. She then compared her memory with scenes from the films *Schindler's List* and *The Pianist* and claimed that only when seeing the films had she made sense of what she had witnessed. Yet, Schütrumpf also argued she had nevertheless felt "burdened" (*belastet*) by this and that it burdened her until the present.[104] By the beginning of the twenty-first century, therefore, the murder of the European Jews not only cast a shadow over the experience of resettlement and the war, and even Bukovina German memories of life in Bukovina before the war; in many cases, it appeared to have cast a shadow over the rest of their lives, too.[105]

These narrators were admittedly very different people than those who spoke previously: they were mostly women from a younger generation, most of them had no or little personal memory of prewar Bukovina, most of them had no or only tenuous links to the *Landsmannschaft*,[106] and most of them had led humble lives. These were the Bukovinians who were still alive by the turn of the millennium and those who had not yet spoken, and their testifying also reflected a broader change in gender norms and social visibility—whose history mattered or who would be heard. Becayse they offered seemingly less rehearsed and more authentic accounts, interviewers were most eager to speak to such people who were able to provide the kind of redemptive narratives that many younger Germans wanted to hear.[107] Indeed, the fact that many of these narrators were female, elderly, and had been children at the time of the events reinforced both the sense that they were being honest and had indeed had limited insight and agency. This gave credibility to excuses or claims of ignorance and helplessness. In the end, the vast majority did not incriminate their older relatives either.[108] But these new interlocutors nonetheless offered a narrative in tune with the contemporary German and European "politics of regret."[109]

The last change in tenor of narratives of resettlement can therefore be explained less with the uncovering of new evidence and facts than with a new framing of the events and with what Emily Kneightly and Michael Pickering have described as the changing ethics of a period and the notion of "appropriate response."[110] This shift was indicative of a wider shift in what it meant to be German in general. As Gabriele Rosenthal has argued, by the 1980s, for most Germans, narratives about the war were also always narratives about *Vergangenheitsbewältigung* (dealing with the past).[111] In a reunified Germany, being German became ever more closely associated with taking responsibility for the past and embracing a discourse of guilt and contrition.[112] By the 2000s, even for a group like Bukovina Germans, with an established, essential, and fundamentally positive mode of identification as Germans, none of what had happened under National Socialism was defensible any longer. It became impossible to conclude, as before, that resettlement had been "all for the best after all." Instead, many Bukovina Germans presented themselves as having been at the mercy of tyrants, not simply because they were victimized, but also because they were seduced and fooled by them. "Bukovina German" thus largely became synonymous with "resettler" and resettler with "unfortunate and unknowing witness of violence, dictatorship, and genocide;" the narrative of resettlement, integrated into broader life narratives, was interpreted anew as a warning from the past. This interpretation remained in many ways somewhat incomplete and simplistic. But it at least resonated with present political and ethical concerns in Germany and Europe, and this was therefore how Bukovinians made sense of their experiences.

Narratives of resettlement and the memories connected with this event shifted considerably over time. These changes reflected different ways in which the event was given meaning by individuals of different ages, generations, genders, levels of education, and types of experience, as well as the changing institutional and collective narrative frames and contexts within which the story was told and deployed. With this, the narratives also took different forms, from public and collective political stances to individual and personal statements.

Looking at the narratives of resettlement over time makes it possible to identify different patterns and phases but also to focus on the narratives' different purposes. In the immediate postwar period, in the context of competing claims to victimhood among the war's different victims and uncertainty about the future, Bukovina Germans spoke about their losses frequently and in detail. Yet since there was no real framework to discuss National Socialism critically and Bukovinians were required to defend their claim to belonging in West Germany, resettlement was defended as a legitimate attempt to bring Bukovina Germans "home." Ironically, the postwar situation appeared to have accomplished the Nazis' plan and the Cold War provided a lasting rationalization for the undertaking. With the establishment of this narrative early on, the specifics of the event were not scrutinized again for several decades and the circumstances were rarely discussed. Even as most West Germans began to distance themselves more decisively from National Socialist ideas, when it came to resettlement, the end was still thought to have justified the means. What mattered was that resettlers had avoided a more tragic fate and ultimately been spared, as a group, from life under communism. It took until 1989 for the narrative to shift significantly. With new knowledge and the emergence of a new kind of consensus about the character of Nazism, with the end of the Cold War and the division of the European continent, and as a result of further generational and societal changes, many people started paying more attention to the ideological underpinnings of resettlement. It became increasingly difficult to cast Bukovina Germans solely as victims, let alone to celebrate their resettlement as a "rescue operation." Resettlement's multifarious connections with other events during the war, the violent policies of occupation, Germanization, and last but not least the murder of European Jews were increasingly the focus of attention. Seeking to draw lessons from history, understandings of the Holocaust in particular shaped the meaning given to resettlement and narratives about the past, identity, and memory in reunified Germany and Europe more generally. Such a stance was possible because it did not threaten, by this point, to challenge Bukovinians' claim to belonging in Germany and identification as Germans. While the new narratives were not always particularly complex, they nonetheless both reflected and contributed to a new form of engagement of Bukovinians and Germans with their own and Germany's entangled history with other countries, societies, and regions.

The story of resettlement was thus, in the space of sixty years, turned on its head, from success to disaster—from model *German* population transfer to *European* warning for the future. In this sense, narratives of resettlement were symptomatic of the West German approach to National Socialism in general. But looking at this example, this particular community of experience, shows that this was not simply a transition from a "distorted" to a correct or from an "amoral" to a moralistic version of the past. What changed over time were the speakers and the listeners, the questions that were asked about the past, and the framework within which experience was placed for the sake of the present and identification. What changed was why the story was being told and the associated meaning of "being Bukovinian" and "being German." The narratives therefore were always true in their own setting because the change was not about truth but the meaning.

CHAPTER 10

COMMEMORATING THE LOST *HEIMAT*

Germans as *Kulturträger* on the Monuments
of the Danube Swabians

JEFFREY LUPPES

Wolfgang Wippermann has shown that the theory of Germans as bearers of culture (*Kulturträgertheorie*) was a key element of the ideology of the German *Drang nach Osten* (Drive to the East). This ideology encompassed an anti-Slavic stance that justified the expansion of German influence eastward into Polish territory from the Middle Ages to the Third Reich.[1] Especially vis-à-vis the Poles, the theory has applied historically to legitimate Teutonic possession of lands and dominance over Slavic populations. In essence, this view implied that "foreign" control of Polish territory was justified because of the cultural, political, and technological superiority of the Germans.

This theory has been brought to bear in other geographic contexts and used to raise implicit territorial claims to areas not contiguous to the German Empire, particularly in the German settlements along the Danube and in the Balkans. The perceived cultural accomplishments of the Germans who settled there were nicely summarized in a contribution to the *Festschrift* compiled for the consecration of a monument to German expellees in Geislingen, Baden-Württemberg, in 1950.[2] In this text, Fritz Heinz Reimesch, at the time the chairman of the Association of Transylvanian Saxons in Germany, referred to the German settlers in this region as "pioneers" who transformed the areas of the Carpathians, Bessarabia, and the Black Sea region—until the arrival of the Germans, allegedly inhabited only by "nomads"—into the flourishing breadbasket of Europe.[3] An important aspect to note when the *Kulturträger* theory is applied to southeastern Europe is the belief that the land was hitherto unexploited, and that earlier inhabitants—if the area was not completely unpopulated—were primitive and had no lasting connection to the land. While the founding of cities, towns, and villages and the creation of farms were certainly worth mentioning, Reimesch noted, those architectural achievements and the other "material assets" amassed over generations were "but a part of their accomplishments, certainly the most visible, but probably not the most important, because in addition to these agricultural and commercial deeds stand those of the mind, which first and foremost led to the return of the nomadic Southeast—since Roman times overrun by the Asiatic mentality and won back after the Turkish Wars— to the Christian West. That was mostly German work."[4] Never did the original German settlers and their descendants attempt to force their way of life on their non-German neighbors; rather they "endeavored to be good role models and honest instructors." No other *Volk*, Reimesch suggested, could have done the same.[5]

The Germans as bearers of culture theory is featured on a number of the monuments erected in (West) Germany to commemorate the homelands in central and eastern Europe, from which Germans were forced to leave in the months around the end of the Second World War. The roughly fifteen hundred monuments are located in easily noticeable areas of bustling big cities and quiet small villages, along bike paths, in tranquil cemeteries and churchyards, as well as in well-visited town squares and city halls. In fact, the first major comprehensive study of the monuments identified the loss of *Heimat* and the concomitant territorial claims it engendered as one of the monuments' two main thematic clusters.[6] These monuments bemoan the forfeiture of territory as a consequence of Nazi Germany's war of aggression and express the desire to reacquire it. Influential expellee organizations erected these monuments, particularly but not exclusively in the first twenty-five years after the war, in the pursuit of "concrete politics": societal recognition and legal definitions of the expellees, material compensation for their losses, and ultimately, the revision of the postwar border status quo.[7]

Within this cluster, some of the most fascinating expellee monuments are those erected by the Danube Swabians and other ethnic Germans who were forced to leave their homelands in the Balkans. Few commemorative objects reveal the entanglement of German-Balkan histories more than the monuments of the Danube Swabian expellees. Like all other expellee monuments, these memorials commemorate the lives lost as a result of the forced exodus and establish links to the *Heimat* left behind. Unlike the monuments of other expellee groups, which have often raised unconcealed territorial claims to regions long a part of German territory, such as Silesia and East Prussia, however, the monuments of the southeast European Germans memorialize the forfeiture of territory that had never belonged to a German nation-state. Surprisingly, it has been the ethnic Germans from southeastern Europe—in particular, the Danube Swabians—who have most conspicuously employed the *Kulturträger* theory to raise their claims.

This chapter investigates how the flight and expulsion of Danube Swabians and other ethnic Germans from the Balkans has been commemorated publicly in the form of monuments. More specifically, it analyzes the forms, inscriptions, and iconographies of these monuments to reveal the commemorative strategies employed by their initiators. It argues that the more understated yet unmistakable territorial connectedness the monuments display has been premised on the notion of Germans as "bearers of culture": as people, who by virtue of their resourcefulness, hard work, and stalwartness—that is, because of innate characteristics associated with their ethnicity and cultural heritage—were able to carve out a flourishing *Heimat* from a desolate, unfruitful, and generally backward region. Therefore, the land—though governed by others—had become unquestionably German. In addition, this chapter investigates why these expellee groups in particular—and not others—have chosen this motif to represent and commemorate their wartime experiences and the loss of their homeland. Finally, this contribution aims at revealing the lasting imprint of this region in the minds of the ethnic Germans who once lived there.

THE DANUBE SWABIANS: A HISTORIC OVERVIEW

Donauschwaben ("Danube Swabians") is an umbrella term to describe the roughly 1.5 million ethnic Germans who lived along and near the Danube in the Pannonian Basin, in the successor states of the Austro-Hungarian Empire—in particular in Hungary, Romania, and Yugoslavia—prior to the Second World War. As G. C. Paikert noted, "The German populations of the basin were widely scattered, constituting partly sizable, cohesive ethnic blocs, where Germans lived in large numbers (enclaves), and partly isolated diasporae, small ethnic islands in the sea of the other nationalities."[8] The term "*Donauschwaben*" is not a historic term and only gained currency after Robert Sieger coined it in 1922.[9] According to Mirna Zakić, the term "signaled that they saw themselves as a unique German-speaking group, emphasizing both their affinity with the German nation and their regional specificity as residents of the Danube basin."[10] Not all ethnic Germans in southeastern Europe were Danube Swabians. Significant numbers also lived in Transylvania (the Transylvanian Saxons) and in what is now Slovakia (the Zipser Germans). As an umbrella term, the moniker encompasses people with different experiences as minorities in various countries during the interwar period as well as with different degrees of involvement later with the Nazi regime, including conscription into the Wehrmacht, during the war. Similarly, not all Danube Swabians, who under German law are considered "expellees,"[11] were forced to leave their homes in the same way, as will be discussed here.

At any rate, the moniker applies to the ethnic Germans who made their way down the Danube during the three great *Schwabenzüge* (Swabian treks) during the seventeenth and eighteenth centuries. The Hungarian-speaking populations called these settlers "Swabians," although many had originated in Alsace-Lorraine, Austria, Hessen, the Rhineland, and Westphalia, in addition to the Swabian region of what is today southwest Germany. The Hungarian nobility encouraged settlement in the areas devastated and depopulated after decades of conflict with Ottoman armies. As is often emphasized in Danube Swabian memoir literature, the establishment of ethnic German communities did not come about with the sword as some sort of "manifest destiny." Instead, as Konrad Gündisch notes, "It is particular of the German settlement of the Southeast that it did not occur as a conquering land grab but proceeded rather in a peaceful manner to each side's mutual advantage with colonists and land donors appearing as partners."[12]

More than two hundred years after the first arrivals, the departure of the Danube Swabians occurred with far more discord. Some Danube Swabians evacuated their homes with the retreating German army, while others fled near the end of the war in fear of the rapidly advancing Soviet war machine. Thus, the Danube Swabians joined the millions of Germans in central and eastern Europe uprooted by the war and its aftermath. It is important to note, however, that the Hungarian government was the only one formally to expel its ethnic German population. Romania did not force its German minorities to leave the country en masse but instead deported large numbers to the Soviet Union for forced labor. Thousands did not survive. As for many of those who remained, the postwar Romanian government confiscated properties and collectivized their farmland before forcing them to resettle in the Bărăgan Plain region of the country. In Yugoslavia, ethnic Germans lost their citizenship and were interned in forced labor camps such as Gakovo and Rudolfsgnad by Tito's communists. Thousands perished.[13]

While there is no question that countless ethnic Germans from southeastern Europe endured unspeakable suffering, it is also clear that at least some previously had cast their lot with their ethnic compatriots and the National Socialism these espoused.[14] Representations of the flight and expulsion of Germans from central and southeastern Europe—especially as commemorated by monuments—rarely offer historical context.[15] Far more often, they portray the expellees as the hapless victims of hardships and brutalities meted out by rampaging Soviet soldiers or murderous partisans and vengeful former neighbors. The monuments of the Danube Swabians are no exceptions. However, it is clear that the ethnic Germans in southeastern Europe had acted in ways that would make their non-German neighbors question their loyalty. About the motivations for the removal of the ethnic German populations from Hungary, Romania, and Yugoslavia, Paikert (somewhat awkwardly) writes, "The volume of Swabians who manifested a negative attitude toward the state in which they lived, and of those who were engaged in outright anti-state or anti host-nation activities and offenses, made the avoidance of extremely serious consequences practically impossible once the tide turned. Though a large proportion of the Swabians was, indeed, indifferent or downright opposed to Nazism, yet they acquiesced in the total Nazification of their people without substantial resistance."[16] Bedraggled and dispossessed, the surviving Danube Swabians streamed primarily into occupied Germany, although some remained in Austria. Others settled as far away as Australia, Brazil,[17] Canada,[18] and the United States.[19]

THE MONUMENTS OF THE DANUBE SWABIANS

Initiators have emplaced more than one thousand expellee monuments of all kinds in cemeteries, city halls, parks, along bike paths, and in many other public places throughout the Federal Republic of Germany. The monuments are key components of the expellee organizations' visual and discursive repertoire. Through them, expellee activists have sought to ensure that their side of history will never be discounted. Taken as a whole, these concrete examples of cultural production constitute an important and substantial part of Germany's memory culture and make unequivocal but often-overlooked statements about the expellees' understanding of their war experience.[20]

As far as the monuments go, the locations of the specifically Danube Swabian monuments point toward an interesting aspect of expellee culture in the Federal Republic: in general, the Germans from the East initially came to reside in areas of West Germany that corresponded geographically to their ancestors' regions of origin. That is, the expellees from northern regions (e.g., Pomerania or East Prussia) generally ended up in the northern *Länder* of the Federal Republic (e.g., Schleswig-Holstein or Lower Saxony), while many from central areas of the East (e.g., the Silesians) settled in the middle of West Germany (e.g., North Rhine-Westphalia or Hessen). Accordingly, the vast majority of the Danube Swabian monuments are geographically bound, as most expellees from the Southeast found new homes—at least initially—in the south, particularly Baden-Württemberg.[21]

Baden-Württemberg, as "*Urheimat*" of many of the Danube Swabians, has cultivated a special relationship with all ethnic Germans from southeastern Europe. The state government "adopted" all Danube Swabians in a *Patenschaft* in 1954.[22] Individual cities and towns have also adopted other groups of southeastern European Germans. For example, Stuttgart adopted the Bessarabia, Germans in 1954, Sindelfingen adopted the Germans from Yugoslavia in 1964, and Gerlingen and Backnang jointly adopted the Hungarian Germans in 1969 and 1971, respectively. In all, twenty-seven communities in Baden-Württemberg have entered into a *Patenschaft* agreement with Danube Swabian cities in southeastern Europe. As a result, Baden-Württemberg is home to the most Danube Swabian monuments. Although less likely to be seen in other parts of Germany, these monuments are more than just a marginal phenomenon. Smaller numbers are located in the neighboring southern *Länder* of Bavaria and Rhineland-Palatinate, as well.

What follows is an examination of typical Danube Swabian monuments that reveal the entangled history of the Germans from the Balkans by focusing on the elements of the theory of Germans as bearers of culture.

ULM

Ulm—the city from which many of the Germans who eventually settled in southeastern Europe embarked on their journey down the Danube—is a good point of departure for examining these local monuments. For this reason, the city adopted the *Landsmannschaft* (Homeland Society) of Danube Swabians. The city is also home to the Central Danube Swabian Museum. The two main expellee monuments in this city of approximately 120,000 are situated on the historic city wall, along a well-travelled bicycle path that follows the Danube, the southeastern European Germans' "*Schicksalsstrom*" (river of fate) from its source, through neighboring Bavaria, and into Austria, traveling all the way to Vienna. The first of the two monuments, the *Ahnenauswandererdenkmal* (Ancestral Emigrant Monument), was dedicated on the occasion of the third *Tag der Donauschwaben* (Day of Danube Swabians), August 8, 1958. Coincidently, the festivities took place the very month the sentences for the defendants in the highly publicized Ulm *Einsatzgruppen* trial were pronounced.[23]

The size of the dedication ceremony and the number of high-ranking political figures who participated that day reveal the commemorative significance of this memorial. According to published reports, approximately forty thousand people attended the *Tag der Donauschwaben* festivities that weekend, one of the key events of which was the unveiling of the new monument. Contingents of Danube Swabians from overseas, including the United States, made the long journey to Ulm to participate. Underscoring the fact that this was no small-scale, insignificant event, the city's Lord Mayor Theodor Pfizer spoke at several of the events, including the dedication ceremony, and state-level cabinet members were also in attendance. Moreover, telegrams and well-wishes were sent by several prominent national and regional government officials, including Eugen Gerstenmaier (president of the Bundestag), Ludwig Erhard (federal economics minister and later federal chancellor), and Gebhard Müller (minister president of Baden-Württemberg).

Originally bearing a single inscription ("From Ulm, German settlers traveled on the Danube to Southeast Europe in the 18th century. Their descendants, expelled by fate, returned to the land of their fathers"),[24] the four-meter-high white stele designed by Erich Koch features a smaller bronze statue of a man, woman, and young child in a boat with an oversized cross for a mast, which symbolizes the arduous river journey to their new *Heimat*. Beyond the brief clause ("expelled by fate"), the actual forced migration of the Danube Swabians is not the primary commemorative focus of this monument. In fact, the expulsion usually plays an ancillary role on the monuments of the Danube Swabians. However, the word *Schicksal* (fate) suggests, as is usually the case on all types of expellee monuments, that Germans fell victim to events out of their control and had no hand in what befell them. Instead, this memorial celebrates the expellees' origins and honors both Ulm as the specific site of departure for many of the intrepid original German settlers and the region as the source of this migration. In other words, the inscription and the intent make clear the origins not only of the settlers (clearly labeled "Germans"), but also demonstrate the "Germanness" of those who returned after the Second World War to what became the Federal Republic ("the land of their fathers"—*Vaterland*) despite their prior citizenship in countries outside of the Reich.

The monument thus links the expellees' "new *Heimat*" to the "old *Heimat*" (referred to elsewhere as the "*Urheimat*"). The city government rechristened the area the "*Donauschwabenufer*" (Banks of the Danube Swabians) in 1962 and added an additional inscription after a renovation in 1974: "Several thousand surviving returnees emigrated to other European countries and overseas due to hardship and desperation and became respected citizens. They are also to be honorably commemorated."[25]

As memorialized by the *Ahnenauswandererdenkmal*, the colonizers who departed Ulm for southeastern Europe were part of the civilizing mission discussed above, which supposedly brought German customs to underdeveloped and uncivilized areas. Through their industriousness and ingenuity, flourishing outposts of Western culture were established. These became a bulwark against incursions from the east. The monument does not mention, however, the new *Heimat* the settlers created. To honor these communities, expellee activists created another monument just a short distance away. Fastened onto the ancient city wall, this collection of twenty-five plaques (as of 2016) has steadily grown in number since the initial unveiling thirty years prior. The plaques have three main objects of memorialization: the large collectives of southeastern European German settlers (Danube Swabians and Banat Germans—the two largest plates), individual settlements in the region, and communities of Danube Swabians in Australia and Brazil (the two newest plates, dedicated in 2016). The plaques contain visual clues that clearly corroborate the theory of Germans as bearers of culture.

The first of the two larger plates was part of the original configuration and features the vague framing inscription: "Danube Swabians: To the dead of the Heimat, of war, and of the expulsion."[26] In a smaller font, the names of cities of the region (Ulm, Vienna, Buda, and Pest, and a handful of new settlements downriver) mark points along the Danube.[27] In addition, the plaque exhibits in slightly larger lettering the terms "Emigration" referring to the departure from Ulm for points southeastward along the Danube, "Settlement" referring to the arrival in and establishment of the "new *Heimat*" in southeastern Europe, and "Return" referring to the expulsion and the arrival back in Baden-Württemberg.[28]

The plaque is festooned with symbolic artistic renderings of key historical events and activities emblematic of the bearers of culture theory. For example, in reference to the emigration, the plaque shows an "*Ulmer Schachtel*"—the elongated, shallow, wooden barge traditionally used to carry goods down the Danube, but which was also the main mode of transporting the Danube Swabians on the precarious journey to their new homes. Because the craft were unable to sail against the river's current, they were dismantled upon arrival and either sold as lumber or used to create temporary homes for recent arrivals. In other words, those who left for southeastern Europe did not plan to return home, rather to create a new one. Thus, by their nature, the boats enhance the territorial claims of those who sailed on them. What is more, the use of this symbol once again celebrates the local origin of many of these Germans by linking them historically to Ulm and the region—important for the integration of the expelled Danube Swabians back into the "*Urheimat*" after the Second World War. The eighteenth-century image of the Ulm cathedral wrapped by the city wall serves the same purpose.

The images on the plaque portraying the settlement display more directly the hallmarks of the bearers of culture theory. Representing the creation from scratch of a new *Heimat*, recently arriving figures with few belongings and walking sticks are shown joining their countrymen already hard at work together constructing new homes. The nearly completed structure in the foreground stands in a row of houses, revealing the cooperative hard work and resourcefulness of the settlers in adapting German architectural styles in a planned and systematic manner. The new homes were to be the first permanent reminders of the German imprint on the region, which up to that point had supposedly been occupied by nomads with no lasting connection to the land. Below this image, one sees two rows of gravestones in the shape of small crosses. In this context, the crosses depict another cultural contribution, namely, the spread of Christendom into the area by German settlers as well as the piety of the deceased. The image of gravestones indicates, moreover, the passing of generations and attests to the longevity of the settlement. As we will see, many monuments in this category include dates of settlement and expulsion, or other references to the passage of time expressing the prolonged existence and enduring influence of German settlement.

Organized geographically, with the right side representing the east, the image on the plaque's left side refers to the return of the Danube Swabians to western Germany because of the expulsion. Defoliated trees in the background reveal the devastation wrought by war and the end of the land's bounty. The bare trees no longer produce fruit. The initiators selected a caravan of horse-drawn covered wagons heading west to portray the fate of the descendants of the original settlers. To the left, a man carries an indistinguishable person piggyback. To the right, a mother leaves the *Heimat* on foot cradling a young child. Dispossessed and cast out of their homeland, what the Danube Swabians had achieved culturally and economically over generations had come to an abrupt end.

Unveiled in 1996, the other large plate—dedicated specifically to the *Banater Schwaben* (Swabians of the Banat) is a complement. The inscription on the plaque's bottom reads: "A half million Germans found a *Heimat* in Banat for almost 300 years."[29] As usual, the text contains more than meets the eye. Just as the inscription invokes the concept of *Heimat* in order to demonstrate the Germanness of a particular region, explicitly stating the longevity of German settlement is a method of attesting a temporal connection to the land. As with the plaque to its left, the designer organized the plate chronologically and geographically. An *Ulmer Schachtel* and the words "18 JH ULM" (Ulm eighteenth century) on the left side, with an arrow pointing to the right, indicate the direction of the initial migration.

Emphasizing the settlers' contributions in cultivating a supposedly once-barren landscape, the plaque depicts an overfilled cornucopia and a settler behind a horse-drawn plow tilling the soil. In addition, the symbol of iron mining commemorates the wealth created by the industrialization of the area and the exploitation of natural resources. Here as well, one sees further examples of superior German architecture: more modest dwellings as well as the Cathedral Church of Timișoara. Strikingly, but not surprisingly, the German designations for the cities of this multiethnic, polyglot area along the Danube are used instead of their contemporary names (e.g., Temeschburg instead of Timișoara), even though the plaque was added in 1996. The plaque does not mention the other inhabitants of the area, such as the Romanians, Hungarians, Serbs, Croats, and Jews. Indeed, because of regular shifts of political borders at the hands of neighboring great powers throughout the nineteenth and twentieth centuries, the plaque emphasizes the region's natural boundaries—its rivers and mountains—thus suggesting the insignificance of such political developments.³⁰ Quite clearly, according to the Homeland Society of Banat Danube Swabians, because of the duration of the settlement and the cultural contributions their ancestors made there, this area was made German and still is claimed to be German regardless of the nation-state currently in control. Their coat of arms is found in the upper left corner. Because the ethnic Germans of the Banat were not formally expelled and actually remained in Romania in large numbers until the 1980s and 1990s, the expulsion is not depicted.³¹ With an arrow pointing westward, a lone figure carrying a rucksack symbolizes their return to the land of their predecessors.

In-depth analysis of each of the rest of the twenty-three smaller plaques would exceed the scope of this essay. Suffice it to say, the other plaques exhibit similar imagery and reiterate the themes articulated by the larger plates. For example, renderings of important civic and architectural achievements (e.g., city seals, churches, and cathedrals, or other significant man-made landmarks) and symbols of the rewards reaped thanks to agricultural ingenuity and diligence highlight German cultural and economic contributions in establishing a new *Heimat*. Demonstrating the longevity of the German settlement, most plaques feature the years various cities and towns were founded. Some provide further description—for instance, the plaque for Novo Selo/Neudorf an der Donau, which reads ERSTE DEUTSCHE ANSIEDLUNG IN DER BATSCHKA (First German settlement in the Batschka/Bačka/Bácska),³² and for Torschau, which reads ERSTE DEUTSCHE PROTESTANTISCHE GEMEINDE IN DER BATSCHKA (First German Protestant community in Batschka). The villages were founded in 1734 and 1784, respectively. Accentuating the suddenness and unexpectedness of their ending, the year of the communities' uprooting (either 1944 or 1945) is also included. What precipitated the end of these vibrant communities, however, is not. It appears as if they simply ceased to exist. The expulsion is sparingly mentioned on just a few plaques. Likewise, and particularly worth noting, are the plaques dedicated to the communities in Gakovo (Batschka) and

Rudolfsgnad (Banat). Both share the typical features described above but also display the text: 1944–1948 INTERNIERUNGSLAGER TODESSTÄTTE TAUSENDER DONAUSCHWABEN (1944–1948 Internment camp, Place of death for thousands of Danube Swabians). The initiators of the plaques deemed it not necessary to provide further historical context.

KARLSRUHE

An equally conspicuous example is the monument to the German community of Billed (Banat—today Biled in Romania); the marker is located at the main city cemetery in Karlsruhe, Baden-Württemberg. Unveiled on Pentecost Sunday and consecrated a few weeks later in 1987, the cross-shaped monument made of Greek marble was placed in a section of the unusually scenic and tranquil graveyard provided free of charge by the city government. The inscriptions on each side are telling, but the text on the right side is especially pertinent: "Billed was founded by German colonists under Empress Maria Theresia in 1765. After a difficult beginning, the community grew and developed into a blooming Swabian village. Due to nationalist and political pressure, the Germans returned to their motherland after 200 years."[33] To consecrate the site further, the initiators buried a capsule at the foot of the monument containing soil from both cemeteries in Billed, from the war memorial there, and from a field in Billed. Inlaid stones taken from Billed's main landmark, the *Kalvarienberg* (calvary hill), and from the village's church provide the monument's foundation.

Even more revealing, however, is the monument's main feature, the relief prominently built into the cross on its front side. This work of art displays the typical characteristics of the *Kulturträger* motif and presents a pictorial narrative in six images of what Peter Krier, a Banat German functionary, called in his introduction of the monument at the dedication ceremony the community's *"Werden-Sein-Vergehen"* ("Becoming—Existing—Elapsing").[34] Krier described in detail what each of the six images signifies. First, two figures, a father and son, whose clothing makes them recognizable as Germans, are in the upper-left image. With few possessions, the two look resolutely upon the desolate land that they intend to turn into a new, free, and blessed homeland for themselves and their descendants. The second image, labeled by the speaker the central figure of the relief, depicts a man plowing the soil in this "desolate, swampy, and uncultivated" land. Krier stated, "With the plow, our ancestors created a blossoming cultural landscape—a breadbasket, a blessed land—in Southeast Europe, on the eastern border of the German Reich." The third image, a church in a field of wheat, stands as the symbol of the community's time of prosperity. According to Krier, eight generations of Germans in Billed were baptized and married in the church. At the bottom left, the fourth image, the calvary (*Kalvarienberg*)—Billed's most notable landmark—reminds all who see it that the symbol of the cross belongs to the life and history of all people. Billed had its own cross to bear, and each of the smaller crosses represents a time of hardship in the village's life. Addressing the Second World War and its ramifications for the community more directly, the barbed-wire fence in the fifth image symbolizes the bondage and disenfranchisement that followed for the prisoners of war, for those deported for forced labor to the Soviet Union and forcibly transferred by communist authorities to the Bărăgan Plain in central Romania in the early 1950s. The woman gazing over the fence, the speaker stated, stands for the mothers and women waiting for their loved ones to return home and for those waiting for their freedom. The last image, according to Krier, represents the evacuation from their homeland. A female figure looks upon the graves the Germans regrettably had to leave behind, while a male figure looks at the setting sun in the west, where his family would once again have to create a new *Heimat*.

There are a number of other monuments in Baden-Württemberg (e.g., in Bad Schönborn-Langenbrücken, Beuren, Görwihl, Herrischried, Reutlingen, Stuttgart, or Winnenden, to name just a few), Bavaria (e.g., Munich), and Rhineland-Palatinate (e.g., Frankenthal or Landau), which lead to similar conclusions. In fact, the monuments of the Danube Swabians display perhaps the least amount of variation of all the expellee monuments. Like the others, the *Donauschwabenufer* in Ulm and the Billed monument provide examples of the visual documentation of the cultural contributions made by Germans during the extended period of their settlement in this southeastern European region. They record and display an understanding of history in which Germans transformed a barren landscape into bounteous fields of plenty and transferred German customs to the far reaches of Europe, becoming models of stability and achievement for their neighbors. These colonizers created a *Heimat*, an island of exceedingly prosperous German territory in an inhospitable climate, in lands outside of the German Reich, thereby offering unusually compelling evidence of the entanglement of German-Balkan histories.

Why did these expellee groups choose the Germans as bearers of culture motif to represent and commemorate their experience of flight and expulsion and the loss of their homeland? Why are monuments of this type so prevalent among the southeastern European Germans and not among the expellees from other regions, especially Poland, where the political ideology associated with this theory was traditionally most relevant? The answers to these questions speak to other commonalities among these monuments. For instance, with the notable exception of the *Ahnenauswandererdenkmal* in Ulm (1958), expellee organizations did not erect these monuments during the peak period of local expellee monument construction in the early 1950s, that is, at the time when political agitation for a border revision (regardless of its plausibility) peaked.[35] Not only were local branches of the expellee organizations actively campaigning for border revision, but it was also a topic of regular discussion among all major political parties at the national level. The reestablishment of a German state in its 1937 borders was improbable after 1945. Nevertheless, many expellees and other Germans did not view it as impossible. For Germans from areas that had never been a part of the unified Reich, particularly for the Danube Swabians, however, a beneficial alteration of the territorial status quo was out of the question.[36] Thus these monuments are devoid of the unconcealed territorial demands seen on expellee monuments elsewhere.[37]

For many expellees, as the sentiments captured by these monuments indicate, there was little question that the former eastern provinces, such as Silesia and East Prussia, had always been and would always remain a part of Germany. One cannot say the same thing about the formerly German communities in the Balkans. Therefore, as an alternative to the unmistakable, overt territorial claims made by Silesians and East Prussians, the monuments of the Danube Swabians contain a more understated territorial connectedness. Furthermore, the initiators of monuments that display the Germans as bearers of culture motif dedicate them to specific groups or communities, and not to *all* expellees.

Similarly, the justification for their connection to this territory is not the injustice of the expulsion per se (as it is elsewhere) but rather the creation of a *Heimat*. For the Germans expelled from parts of the Third Reich, the *loss* of their homelands entitled them to their territorial claims. For the ethnic Germans from southeastern Europe, it was the establishment of a *Heimat* that entitled them to territorial claims. In fact, the expulsion is not the centerpiece of these Danube Swabian narratives of the past but is instead a single event—one of several key events—in the historical trajectory of these communities. Equally important are the initial arrival of the German settlers, the foundation of the communities, and the period thereafter when these cities and towns flourished. Nevertheless, the forced migration of the Germans terminated once thriving municipalities and marked the abrupt end of German cultural contributions to the southeast. In pictorial form, this is represented by long, westward traveling caravans. In textual form, it is oftentimes marked with an inscription of the year 1944 or 1945. The commemorative thrust of the monuments is therefore equally on German toil and the settlers' resultant successes, recognizable in the renderings of local landmarks and agricultural themes. In other words, the justification of the southeastern European Germans' strong identification with the Balkans is not the expulsion alone, but rather the longevity of the settlement and the distinctly German cultural and economic achievements they made there.

Furthermore, the monuments of the Danube Swabians are a part of a preemptive effort to affirm the Germanness not only of these areas along the Danube—the *Heimat* created by these German settlers—but also the Germanness of those who resettled in what became the Federal Republic immediately following the war and in the decades since.[38] The monuments thus link the ancestors of the Danube Swabians and others with the "*Urheimat*," while concomitantly connecting them and their descendants both to the *Heimat* they created within the frontiers of other states and to the new *Heimat* in what became the Federal Republic. Thus, these ethnic German expellees are placed on an equal footing with other expellees, whose homelands had unquestionably been within the boundaries of the German Reich. Of course, this points toward unpleasant divisions not only among Germans themselves, but also among the various expellee groups.[39]

CHAPTER 11

CROATIAN ÉMIGRÉS, POLITICAL VIOLENCE, AND COMING TO TERMS WITH THE PAST IN 1960S WEST GERMANY

CHRISTOPHER A. MOLNAR

On November 29, 1962, in broad daylight, more than twenty members of a Croatian Catholic youth organization with roots in Croatia's wartime fascist regime marched up to the Yugoslav Trade Mission in Mehlem, a district in the West German capital of Bonn. Shouting anti-communist slogans and carrying a banner that read "long live freedom and self-determination for all people," they forced their way into the building, shot and killed the Serbian doorman, and brazenly destroyed much of the building with explosives. As they ran from the building, a few of them unfurled a banner, written in German, which read "this is how you get rid of the Berlin Wall." Instead of disappearing into the city, most of the Croats allowed themselves to be arrested without resistance.[1] In doing so, they signaled that they wanted a trial. They intended to use the attack and trial as part of a propaganda campaign to portray Yugoslavia as a brutal totalitarian state that sought the annihilation of the Croatian people. Their goal was to win West German and international support for the Croatian national cause.

This chapter examines the West German response to the attack and the subsequent trial, and argues that the German response both reflected and contributed to the emergence of a new and more critical perspective on the history of the Third Reich and World War II in West Germany. The Mehlem attack and trial also represented a major turning point in German attitudes toward the sizeable Croatian émigré community. This was because Croats had asked Germans to explore the wartime history of the Yugoslav state at the very time that Germans had begun to more critically examine their own history during the Third Reich and World War II. By the early 1960s, many West Germans were no longer content to see themselves as a nation of innocent victims, as they had portrayed themselves during the conservative 1950s. When the West German media, prompted by the Mehlem attack, looked into the history of the Yugoslav lands during World War II, they portrayed Croats not as a nation of victims, but as a nation that had been allied with the Third Reich and committed genocide against Serbs and Jews. More than that, the German media highlighted the clear connections between Croatian wartime fascism and the Croatian émigré community in West Germany.

Finally, this study shows that memory, so often understood to be deeply rooted in a specific locality, has also been shaped historically by the movement of peoples, often as a result of war, which was such a hallmark of the twentieth century.[2] In the Federal Republic of Germany, migration frequently functioned as a sort of social site of memory, giving Germans occasion to consider and reconsider their own experiences during World War II. The history of the Croatian attack in Bonn, and the German response to it, shows that the process of *Vergangenheitsbewältigung*—of coming to terms with the past—did not just redefine West Germany's relationship to the Nazi past, it also reshaped German attitudes toward foreigners in their midst.

SETTLING IN GERMANY: CROATIAN ÉMIGRÉS FROM WORLD WAR TO COLD WAR

In order to understand the Croatian radicals' attack on the Yugoslav Trade Mission, as well as their efforts to defend themselves, we must first turn to the very end of World War II in Yugoslavia and Croatian émigrés' arrival and treatment in early Cold War West Germany. As World War II came to a close in Europe in early May 1945, the fighting continued unabated within Yugoslavia. With minimal outside support, Josip Broz Tito's Partisans had liberated Yugoslavia from its German occupiers and all but destroyed the Independent State of Croatia (Nezavisna Država Hrvatska, NDH), the fascist puppet state that Germany had established in 1941. On May 7, 1945, when Ante Pavelić, the leader of the fascist Ustaša movement and the NDH, learned that Germany would surrender unconditionally, he ordered his forces to continue fighting the Partisans while retreating northwards toward British-held Austrian territory.[3] Pavelić's forces formed part of a mass movement of peoples—among them retreating German soldiers, Serbian Četniks, and thousands of Slovenian, Croatian, and other civilians—seeking to reach Austrian soil in order to surrender to the British and to thereby save themselves from a final encounter with the Partisan army.[4] Tens of thousands did make it to Austria—many surrendering at the Austrian border town of Bleiburg—but the British delivered all South Slavic prisoners to the Partisans, who on May 15, 1945, began a weeks-long series of massacres of anti-communist forces, most of whom had never reached the Austrian border.[5] In this explosion of violence, the Partisans killed around seventy thousand people, perhaps fifty thousand of them Croats.⁶

Many Croats, including Pavelić and much of the NDH leadership, evaded capture at the end of World War II and found safe havens, particularly in South America and Western Europe. Pavelić, for example, sought to carry on the Ustaša movement from his exile in Perón's Argentina.⁷ Within Europe, West Germany became the most important stronghold of the Croatian émigré community. About thirteen thousand Croatian émigrés had settled there by the early 1950s. They established numerous organizations, many of which remained loyal to Pavelić and Ustaša ideals and called for the recreation of a territorially expansive Croatian nation-state.⁸ Living in Germany, Croatian émigrés presented themselves as innocent victims of World War II. Despite the NDH's collaboration with the Nazis and the mass murder of Jewish, Roma, and especially Serbian civilians, émigrés portrayed themselves as Catholic anti-communists who had fought only for the freedom of their long-desired national homeland.⁹ They made a simplified and greatly exaggerated retelling of what they called the "Tragedy of Bleiburg" the centerpiece of their claim to victim status. In their recounting of the "Tragedy of Bleiburg"—which one Croatian priest called a genocidal massacre without historical precedent—hundreds of thousands of innocent Croatian martyrs gave their lives defending their faith and fatherland against godless communists.¹⁰

Croatian émigrés' depiction of themselves as innocent victims of communist terror, who were driven from their homeland at the war's conclusion, resonated with many West Germans, especially during the conservative 1950s. Germans had likewise suffered terribly during the war and its aftermath, particularly through Allied air raids, the Red Army's brutal occupation of eastern Germany, and the expulsion of between twelve and fourteen million Germans from eastern Europe.¹¹ Of course Germany had started World War II and carried out horrific crimes against Jews, Roma, Russian prisoners of war, homosexuals, and other groups. But as Robert Moeller and other historians have shown, at least until the early 1960s, most West Germans chose to remember their own suffering, rather than the violence they inflicted on others. Like Croatian émigrés, they thus came to see themselves as the true victims of the war.¹²

In this environment, and in the context of the early Cold War, many influential West Germans—particularly expellees, conservative politicians, and leaders of the Catholic Church—came to view Croatian émigrés as reliable Cold War allies and as a community worthy of sympathy and support.¹³ By the early to mid-1950s, federal and local officials in

West Germany recognized that the Croatian émigré community was led by people with deeply compromised pasts. They also knew that many émigrés still swore allegiance to Pavelić and the Ustaša movement.[14] But in an era in which West Germans were not inclined to probe too deeply into their own pasts, most Germans also proved uninterested in Croatian émigrés' politics or wartime experiences.[15] Their reliable anti-communism trumped any other concerns. For the most radical Croatian émigrés in West Germany, the sympathy and support Croats found in the Federal Republic, together with what they saw as the West's failure to take on Tito's Yugoslavia, emboldened them to take measures into their own hands. These considerations led them to launch the attack on the Yugoslav Trade Mission in Bonn.[16]

YUGOSLAVIA ON TRIAL

The vast majority of the Croatian attackers were arrested and taken into custody shortly after the assault. With the attackers in custody and a trial set for spring 1964, an important question immediately arose for the Croatian émigré community. How, exactly, would they defend themselves? How could an undeniable act of political violence be used to win sympathy and support from the West German people? In planning their defense, Croatian émigrés did not have to start from scratch. The attackers and the wider émigré community turned to a playbook that émigrés had developed and deployed with great effect during the 1950s. Croatian émigrés had wanted a trial, but they were determined that, rather than those who carried out the attack, it would be the Yugoslav state and its wartime record that would be put on trial.

The Croatian émigré community in West Germany had always been characterized by political dissension, the splintering and reforming of émigré groups, and heated personal rivalries. The Mehlem attack threw the émigré community into even greater disarray. But the disarray was only evident where most Germans could not see it, primarily at émigré gatherings and in Croatian-language publications.[17] In the public eye, Croatian émigrés—moderates and radicals, intellectuals and military men—came together as they had never done before.

In January 1963, just weeks after the attack, leading Croatian émigrés from the most important organizations gathered in Cologne and formed a Joint Committee for the Defense of the Croatian Patriots.[18] The day that it was established, the committee published a declaration that foreshadowed, in many respects, the Croats' defense strategy, both during the trial and in the court of public opinion. The "demonstration" in Mehlem, the declaration began, was "provoked by the annihilation of the Croatian people and its thousand-year-old culture in so-called Yugoslavia" and "spontaneously carried out by Croatian patriots." The attack, it continued, "is the response to the attempted annihilation of a nation" and a warning to the world and those who support "the illegal regime in Croatia and thereby contribute to the destruction of the Croatian people." The declaration ended by noting that all Croatian émigré groups in West Germany stood firmly behind the attackers.[19] The resolution highlights the émigrés' belief that Yugoslavia was an illegal and criminal state that denied Croats their national self-determination and actively sought the complete biological destruction of the Croatian people. Moreover, it shows that Croatian émigré groups, far from denouncing or distancing themselves from the attack, defended it as a noble and patriotic act.

In their propaganda campaign leading up to the 1964 trial, Croatian émigré organizations published and distributed numerous booklets and flyers defending the "Croatian patriots" and describing the criminal nature of Tito's Yugoslavia. Written in German, they were clearly meant to sway German public opinion. The central argument of all of the publications was that the attack on the Yugoslav Trade Mission should be understood as a noble and morally defensible uprising of the entire Croatian people against their "Serbo-communist" oppressors, who were waging a genocidal war against the Croatian nation.

Berislav Deželić, nominally a member of the moderate Croatian Peasant Party, but actually a leading figure in a number of much more radical and revolutionary Croatian organizations, was one of the most active defenders of the "Croatian patriots." In a 1963 pamphlet entitled "Who Is to Blame for the Mehlem Attack?" he wrote, for instance, that "280,000 Croatian officers and soldiers were liquidated at Bleiburg and in the 'death march' from Maribor to Vršac during the first three months of the communist reign of terror."[20] The persecution of Croatians, he claimed, had never ceased, as the "communist-Serbian-totalitarian regime in Belgrade" sought to achieve the "biological, economic, cultural, and religious extermination of the Croatian people."[21] Because they were facing a genocidal regime, Deželić argued that the Mehlem attack "should not be viewed as a malicious act, and also not as an act stemming from base motives, but rather as a political and patriotic reckoning with the odious enemy. If the formality of the law speaks against these young men, moral law is on their side!"[22]

Stjepan Hefer, a leading Ustaša official during World War II who succeeded Pavelić as the leader of the Croatian Liberation Movement in Buenos Aires, published a German-language booklet at the very outset of the trial that made similar arguments. Under written law, Hefer admitted, the Mehlem attackers were guilty. But he maintained that unwritten law, the law upon which the great American and French revolutions were built, holds that "the holiest obligation is to overthrow—with force if necessary—every tyranny."²³ Like Deželić, he contended that Tito's Yugoslavia had carried out a genocidal war against the Croatian people, most notably by slaughtering half a million Croats at Bleiburg and other sites in the immediate aftermath of the war, and that the war of destruction in Croatia continued into the present.²⁴ The Mehlem attackers, Hefer concluded, were therefore more than justified; Croats were *obligated* to strike out against the Yugoslav state. For him, the Mehlem attackers were not misguided fascists, but revolutionary patriots and freedom fighters working in the tradition of the liberal American and French revolutions. Moreover, Hefer was convinced that the West German courts and the "freedom-loving German public" would find that the "Croatian patriots" had acted in accordance with a higher natural law that trumped formal law.²⁵

Croatian émigrés emphasized, however, that the Mehlem attack was about more than just the long history of Croatian suffering and the Croatian people's struggle for freedom. They argued that Tito's Partisans, and eastern European communism more generally, had claimed many other victims, and threatened to claim still more. On March 11, 1964, the opening day of the trial, Croats distributed thousands of German-language flyers in all of West Germany's major cities, in which they set the Mehlem "demonstration" in this larger perspective. The flyers proclaimed that "the bloody wave of communism has flooded over half of Europe! Germany is divided by the shameful wall, and Croatia suffers under the yoke of the Serbo-Communist tyrants." The Mehlem attack, then, was intended as a warning and wake-up call to the whole civilized world, which must be made to realize that "the communists are striving for world domination."²⁶ In his booklet, Stjepan Hefer likewise described the attack as the result of Croats' "unconquerable drive for freedom" and a warning to the people in the free world that communism also threatened their freedom.²⁷ Croatian émigrés portrayed themselves as freedom fighters working to usher in a new peaceful world order. Peace and order, Deželić wrote, can only reign on earth when the "principles of democracy, ethics, law, and love are observed," and therefore "émigrés are the strongest weapon against communism, because they defend those values."²⁸

In addition to casting Yugoslavia as a genocidal regime and the Croats as noble patriots fighting for their own freedom and the destruction of world communism, Croatian émigrés also shrewdly tapped into Germans' own conception of themselves as a nation of victims. During World War II, Danube Swabians (*Donauschwaben*), ethnic Germans whose ancestors had settled in the Yugoslav lands centuries earlier, had collaborated with the Nazis. In late 1944, Tito's liberation movement stripped Danube Swabians of their rights and property and began a brutal assault on them that ended with the near destruction of the centuries-old ethnic German community in Yugoslavia.[29] Just as they had done during the 1950s, Croatian émigrés pointed to Yugoslav violence against Danube Swabians in an effort to gain support in West Germany.[30] In typically exaggerated fashion, Deželić claimed in another pamphlet that, in addition to atrocities against Croatian soldiers, civilians, and priests, Tito's communists had slaughtered 250,000 Danube Swabians and 70,000 ethnic German prisoners of war.[31] Adopting the language of genocide so common in both German and Croatian victim discourses, he wrote that Tito's regime had "exterminated 250,000 members of the German minority in concentration camps."[32] Virtually all defenders of the "Croatian patriots" echoed Deželić on this point.[33]

As part of the propaganda offensive, Branimir Jelić, cofounder of the Ustaša movement and the powerful leader of the Croatian National Committee in West Germany, wrote and widely distributed his own booklet, "An Overview of Croatia's Historical Development to the Present Day," in which he praised and defended the "Croatian patriots" who had bombed the Yugoslav Trade Mission. In a wide-ranging tract, he touched on all of the usual points: Croats' Catholicism, their history of close friendship with the German people, Croatian suffering under the murderous Serbo-communists, and Yugoslav communists' brutal slaughter of German POWs and *Volksdeutsche* during and after World War II. On this last point, however, Jelić added a new twist. He claimed that Momčilo Popović, the Serbian doorman who died as a result of the Mehlem attack, had been "a famous extermination camp commander ... who gassed and incinerated 5,000 *Volksdeutsche* children."[34] By using imagery straight from the Holocaust in this invented story, Jelić linked Tito's regime with Hitler's notorious crimes, only this time Germans were the ones being annihilated. How could Germans, Jelić seemed to be asking, do anything but embrace the Croatian freedom fighters who only wanted to bring down Tito's criminal regime?

The defendants used these same strategies during the trial. Defendant after defendant acknowledged their role in the attack, but then quickly swiveled to claim that their family members had been murdered because they were Croats and that Yugoslavia was a criminal state. Vladimir Murat, one of the young attackers, exclaimed from the witness stand that "Tito is Eichmann number two. He not only had 500,000 Croats slaughtered, but also had just as many Germans exterminated after the end of the war."[35] The Croatian defense strategy can be seen clearly in the testimony of Rafael Medić-Skoko, the Ustaša priest who masterminded the attack. On the witness stand he stated that he regretted that Croats had broken German law and abused German hospitality, but did not regret the attack itself. When asked if he was sorry for the murder of the Serbian doorman Popović, he responded that: "I feel sorry for my mother, who was beaten so severely that for fifteen years she could neither live nor die; I lament the 75,000 Croats who were murdered; I lament the 280,000 Croatian soldiers who were massacred at the end of the war; and finally, I am sorry for the 5,000 innocent [German] children whom Popović gassed. If I also lamented his death, then I would be a bandit like him."[36] The entire defense strategy, from the pretrial propaganda blitz to the trial itself, centered on the depiction of Croats and Germans as innocent victims who had suffered terribly at the hands of communists in the closing years of the war and its aftermath. Rife with fabrication and exaggeration, the defense nonetheless drew upon emotions and historical arguments that resonated deeply with West Germans in the first postwar decades. The émigrés' energetic defense of the "Croatian patriots" and appeals to German officials and the German people suggest that they fully believed they could count on German sympathy even when Croatian émigrés carried out brazen acts of political violence on West German soil. They were wrong.

REDISCOVERING CROATIAN FASCISM

Despite their best efforts, the émigrés' strategy for securing German sympathy and support for the Croatian cause failed. A German expellee group with roots in southeastern Europe publicly stood behind the Mehlem attackers and hired a right-wing lawyer to help raise funds for their defense, but otherwise little German support was forthcoming.[37] The court also remained unswayed. The defendants were convicted and sentenced to short prison terms.[38] Even the right-radical, anticommunist *Deutsche Soldaten-Zeitung*, while expressing sympathy for the Croatian cause, concluded that the Croats had "unforgivably abused our hospitality."[39] Most Germans likely agreed with a trial report in *Die Zeit*, which stated that "conflicts are not to be resolved by explosives, but only through negotiations."[40] Rather than earning German support, the Mehlem attack and trial represented a turning point in West German attitudes toward Croatian émigrés. Thenceforth, Germans adopted a much more critical perspective toward the Croatian émigré community, which ultimately led to their political isolation in West Germany.

One of the early consequences of the attack was that the West German intelligence and security services quickly began to devote more attention to the Croatian émigré community. Before the Mehlem attack, the Landesämter für Verfassungsschutz (State Offices for the Protection of the Constitution) had only monitored immigrant organizations when they were suspected of being communist or anti-Semitic movements. In a direct response to the Mehlem attack, the Ministry of the Interior recommended in 1963 that each state have its Office for the Protection of the Constitution carry out covert surveillance of extremist émigré groups within their jurisdiction.[41] The increased scrutiny from West German intelligence agencies brought to light the extensive radicalization of the Croatian émigré community. In 1963, German authorities banned the Croatian Crusaders Brotherhood, the organization responsible for the Mehlem assault. A Federal Office for the Protection of the Constitution report from that year noted that, of the eight nationalist émigré organizations in West Germany that utilized terroristic and conspiratorial methods, seven were Croatian. Another report from the same office in late 1964 largely confirmed this picture.[42] Thus, the attack and subsequent propaganda campaign, which Croatian émigrés had hoped would bring German and international attention to the suffering of the Croatian nation and its national aspirations, ended up highlighting the troubling radicalism of a significant swath of the Croatian émigré community in West Germany.

The West German response to the Mehlem attack as described so far—the denunciation of violence as a political tool, condemnation of Croats for abusing German hospitality, and increased surveillance of émigré organizations—likely would not have differed considerably even had the violence occurred earlier, say during the more conservative early 1950s. Indeed, the West German response to the attack was in some ways similar to Germans' reaction to violence carried out by anti-communist Russian émigrés in the early years of the Weimar Republic. Germans had tolerated and often expressed sympathy for the sizeable Russian émigré community, centered in Berlin, primarily because of its experience of loss in the Bolshevik Revolution and Civil War and because it was reliably anti-communist.[43] This changed quickly when two Russian monarchist émigrés assassinated the liberal Russian émigré V. D. Nabokov, the father of the writer Vladimir Nabokov, in the Berlin Philharmonic in 1922. The German press universally condemned the assassination and highlighted the potential dangers of having a large Russian émigré community resident in Germany. Annemarie Sammartino writes that "the German press reaction was unanimous; by carrying out the assassination on German territory, the Russian assassins—and by extension, the émigré community as a whole—had failed to respect the borders of *Gastrecht*, the set of formal and informal expectations that governed the conduct of foreign guests and their German hosts."[44]

This focus on law and order, and specifically the violation of *Gastrecht*, was also evident in the West German response to the Mehlem attack and trial. But the more critical stance toward the Croatian émigré community was not simply an issue of law and order; it was intimately bound up with the transformation of West German memory of the Third Reich. During the 1950s, West Germany was gripped by a sort of collective amnesia about the crimes Germans had committed during the war. Remaining mostly silent on their own crimes, Germans stressed that they were victims of the war.[45] But in the late 1950s and early 1960s, a number of developments challenged this silence about the Nazi past.[46] In 1959, West Germans were shocked and dismayed by the widespread appearance of anti-Semitic graffiti, a development that raised uncomfortable questions about the relationship between the Nazi past and the democratic present. Soon thereafter, a series of highly publicized trials against German war criminals, most notably the trial of Adolf Eichmann in Jerusalem in 1961 and the trial of German Auschwitz guards in Frankfurt, which ran from 1963 to 1965, confronted Germans with the reality that they had perpetrated terrible and undeniable crimes during the war. According to Devin Pendas, the Auschwitz trial was "a cultural watershed . . . a focal point and a wellspring for the politics of memory in the Federal Republic."[47] During this era, television stations also began to run popular documentary series that, despite overly simplistic descriptions of the Nazi era, nonetheless laid bare the crimes of the Third Reich.[48]

This memory boom also affected historical scholarship. In the early 1960s, federal officials refused to publish a major federally funded research project on the fate of German POWs in eastern Europe because it portrayed Germans too one-sidedly as victims of Soviet barbarity.[49] At the same time, a new generation of young historians, often associated with the Institute of Contemporary History in Munich, began grappling with the history of the Third Reich, the Holocaust, and fascism more generally. One of the first books that the institute published was Martin Broszat's landmark study, *The Croatian Ustaša State*. Published the same year that the Croatian attackers stood trial, it presented a damning portrait of Croatian fascism and noted the cozy relationship that Branimir Jelić—the public face of the Croatian émigré community in West Germany—had enjoyed with Nazi elites during the 1930s.[50] Croatian émigrés believed they could vindicate the Mehlem attackers and the wider émigré community by emphasizing Croatian suffering at the hands of Yugoslav communists during World War II and its aftermath. But in doing so, they invited Germans to explore a period of history that they had only recently begun to mine more deeply and critically than they had during the 1950s. Croatian émigrés would soon regret turning the trial into a referendum on Yugoslavia's wartime history.

In the fifteen months between the attack and the beginning of the trial, the press coverage of the attack, while occasionally noting that most Croats in West Germany were not radicals, treated the attackers unsympathetically and frequently drew attention to the fascist roots and ideals of many of the leading émigré organizations.[51] Some of these stories explored the links between Croatian fascism during World War II and the Croatian émigré community in remarkable detail. A story in *Der Spiegel*, for example, stated that Croatian émigré organizations' strident anti-communism masked the reality that their members came primarily from among those who "collaborated with Hitler in the independent Croatian state."[52] The article then recounted how Hitler created the Independent State of Croatia and named Pavelić its leader; that Pavelić immediately began murdering Jews and Serbs; that Croatian archbishop Alojzije Stepinac supported the Ustaša movement and that Croatian priests enthusiastically took part in murdering Serbs; and that the Croatian émigré community in West Germany remained essentially loyal to Pavelić and Ustaša ideals.[53]

The popular television news program *Panorama* aired two stories about the attack during this period. The second, much longer broadcast, from April 1963, was especially hard-hitting.[54] It began by surveying the death and destruction wrought by "Croatian terrorists" in Mehlem and then immediately "turned the wheel of history back twenty-two years," to the Nazi invasion of Yugoslavia and the establishment of the Independent State of Croatia. It emphasized again that the Independent State of Croatia owed its existence to Adolf Hitler and then graphically detailed the extreme brutality of Pavelić and the Ustašas. The report showed footage from Jasenovac, the notorious Croatian concentration camp, complete with barbed wire, armed guards, and camp inmates, and then flashed to piles of mutilated corpses that recalled the disturbing images of liberated Nazi concentration camps at the end of World War II. It also noted that independent Croatia's last interior minister, Mate Frković, had participated in the murder of Croatia's Jews and was now a leading member of an émigré group in Munich. Croatian émigrés did not help their cause when, in a number of interviews in the *Panorama* piece, some explained that they were still loyal to Pavelić and that they supported the use of violence to achieve their goals. During this period, politicians on the West German left also began to draw connections between wartime fascism and the Croatian émigré community, such as when a Social Democratic representative in the Bundestag asked the interior minister if he believed that "the residency and activity of previously active foreign

Nazis and fascists in Germany would become intolerable if they sought to become active again—in the old spirit—here by us?"[55]

The bad publicity and the focus on the émigrés' wartime pasts only intensified during the trial, which ran from March through June 1964. The trial in Bonn was itself a spectacle. The court was packed with observers from Germany and throughout the world. Fearing an attack by Croatian extremists, more than forty German police and security officials guarded the entrances to the courtroom, checked everyone's identification, and searched all who entered, observers and reporters alike, for bombs and other weapons.[56] The links between Croatian fascism and the émigré community were discussed not only on the witness stand, but also outside of the courtroom. A trial report in the *Frankfurter Allgemeine Zeitung* noted that at the entrance to the court building, young Croatian supporters of Pavelić got into heated arguments with those who disagreed with them. With great fervor, the Pavelić supporters repeated over and over again that "Pavelić was not a fascist. He was the spiritual leader of Croatian Christianity."[57]

Another journalist wrote that, while the attackers looked more like a school class than a group of extremists, the Croatian émigrés in the audience spread a "whiff of danger" throughout the courtroom. The same journalist reported that, at an émigré press conference after a day in court, Croats loudly proclaimed that "Croatian history knows no terror," but that she would not have been surprised if "two black-masked Ustašas suddenly appeared at the door with machine guns at the ready."[58] During the trial, an extended article in *Der Spiegel* called the "almost without exception radical" Croatian émigrés in West Germany the "legacy of Dr. Ante Pavelić," and informed readers that the Ustašas "slaughtered Serbs, Jews, Gypsies, and disliked Croats so barbarically that even the German military administration registered its concerns with the Foreign Ministry."[59] This article, like many others, drew a straight line running from the Mehlem attack to Croatian wartime fascism, Adolf Hitler, and the Nazis.

The press surrounding the Croatian émigré community after the Mehlem attack was overwhelmingly negative. A 1963 report from the Bavarian Office for the Protection of the Constitution, for instance, began by noting that since the attack, Croatian émigrés had been written about in black and white terms and denounced as a gang of Nazis and neofascists.[60] The Croatian émigré community also recognized that it had lost its case in the media. The émigré press complained about the "concentrated attacks" of the leftist press—"members of the German fifth column"—among which they counted mainstream news outlets such as *Panorama* and the *Süddeutsche Zeitung*. Émigrés were so outraged that they had been depicted as "Ustašas, Nazis, and fascists" that they even physically assaulted the *Panorama* journalist who had covered the Mehlem attack.[61]

Croatian émigrés had sought to make the trial about the history of World War II and its aftermath. They portrayed Tito as a brutal leader whose crimes against Croats and Germans were comparable to Nazi crimes, and who had to be fought against, with violence if necessary. The West German media followed the émigrés' lead by tracing the roots of the Mehlem attack back to World War II, but it discovered and publicized a very different story. Collectively, it suggested that if any party from the Balkans was comparable to the Nazis, it was the Ustaša movement during World War II, members of which now formed the core of the émigré community in West Germany. Media coverage of the attack and trial thus made it abundantly clear that the Croatian émigré community was worthy of neither sympathy nor support.

Once supported because of their fervent anti-communism and their portrayal of themselves as a nation of victims, Croatian émigrés became toxic after Mehlem. Most Germans likely did not follow the trial, but traditional supporters of the Croatian émigré community—German expellees, the Catholic Church, and conservative politicians—could not have missed the negative publicity. In an era in which West Germans had begun to plumb the depths of their own national past, few West German elites welcomed an association with radical Croatian nationalists, whose compromised pasts had just been exposed by the media. This public distancing from the Croatian émigré community became even more pronounced when it soon became evident that the Mehlem attack was not an isolated incident. Rather, it was only the beginning of a wave of political violence that Croats would carry out against representatives of the Yugoslav state on West German soil.[62]

The German condemnation of radical Croatian émigrés was shaped by the era in which the Mehlem attack and trial took place. Growing interest in the history of the Third Reich, World War II, and the Holocaust made the German media better prepared and more willing to examine and condemn the wartime history of the Independent State of Croatia and the Croatian émigrés who sought to recreate that state. The German response to the Mehlem attack was a minor episode in the long West German process of "coming to terms with the past." But we must resist a reading of this episode that is too congratulatory toward Germans for grappling with the dark chapters of their recent history.

In the same year that Croatian émigrés attacked the Yugoslav Trade Mission in Bonn, the Office of the State Prosecutor in Hamburg opened an investigation into Reserve Police Battalion 101's actions in

German-occupied Poland during World War II.⁶³ The German men in this battalion were complicit in the murder of tens of thousands of Jews, and yet in their postwar testimony, they forcefully condemned the Polish collaborators who had helped them round up Jews.⁶⁴ Christopher Browning suggests that "these men must have found considerable psychological relief in sharing blame with the Poles." He goes on to note that "Polish misdeeds could be spoken about quite frankly, while discussion about Germans was quite guarded. Indeed, the greater the share of Polish guilt, the less remained on the German side."⁶⁵ In other words, denouncing eastern European collaborators was easy: it did not offend or implicate Germans, and it was satisfying to share the blame for mass murder. West German journalists earnestly excavating the wartime record of the Croatian émigré community cannot be lumped together with perpetrators of the Holocaust, but there are obvious parallels between the press coverage of the Mehlem attack and the exculpatory testimony of Browning's "ordinary men." West German journalists covering the Croatian émigré community did not seek to deny Germany's crimes during World War II, but like the men of Reserve Police Battalion 101, they found it politically unproblematic and morally satisfying to condemn violent Slavic peoples for wartime crimes.

Many Germans actively followed the war-crimes trials in the first two decades after the end of World War II, from the International Military Tribunal in Nuremberg in the immediate postwar years to the Frankfurt Auschwitz trials from 1963 to 1965. Yet the focus on Nazi elites or particularly monstrous perpetrators during these trials allowed "ordinary" Germans to distance themselves from the brutal crimes that were the focus of the trials.⁶⁶ Along the same lines, most Germans must have been able to distance themselves from the atrocities in wartime Croatia that the Mehlem trial brought to the surface, even though the Ustaša regime was a fascist puppet state created by the Third Reich. Nonetheless, like the war-crimes trials in West Germany, this trial, although receiving much less attention, created a space for the discussion of Germany's difficult past and its impact on the rest of Europe.⁶⁷ Even if the West German media focused on Croatia—its genocidal wartime regime and the links between the Ustaša movement and West Germany's Croatian émigré community—the more general denunciation of fascism, in both German and foreign variants, came through unmistakably.

After the Mehlem attack in November 1962, Croatian émigrés presented themselves and Germans as innocent victims of a genocidal communist regime in Yugoslavia and argued that freedom-loving peoples are obligated to fight against tyrants, with force if necessary. Croats never denied the attack in Bonn; they simply argued that it was justified historically. These sorts of arguments—couched in the language of victimization and anti-communism—had earned radical Croatian émigrés significant German support in the 1950s. But Croatian radicals and leaders of the émigré community had made two fundamental miscalculations. First, they failed to realize that most West Germans, including their supporters among expellees, conservative politicians, and the Catholic Church, would not countenance the use of political violence by foreigners on West German soil. Second, and perhaps more importantly, they failed to recognize that West German society was changing. The victim discourses and silences about the war, which had dominated the conservative 1950s, gave way, tentatively and unevenly to be sure, to a more robust confrontation with the Nazi past in the 1960s. The emergence of a more complex public memory of the Third Reich created an environment in which the Croatian émigrés' attempts to use history to vindicate themselves and to bring attention to the Croatian national cause were bound to fail. As a result of the attack and trial, Croatian émigrés lost nearly all of the support they had previously enjoyed in West Germany, and this was, to a great extent, because of the intensive historical examination of the history of World War II in the western Balkans that the émigrés' attack and trial had invited. Having presented themselves as anti-communists and innocent victims of communist terror, Croatian émigrés now found themselves depicted in the media as living relics of the fascist past.

CHAPTER 12

PHOTOGRAPHIC (RE)MEMORY

The Holocaust and Post-World War II Memory in Yugoslavia

AMILA BECIRBEGOVIC

> Der Tod ist ein Meister aus Deutschland, er ist gerade ein Weltmeister aus Bosnien.
> (Death is a German champion and a Bosnian outright world champion.)
>
> Saša Stanišić in *How the Soldier Repairs the Gramophone*

As Jacques Derrida notes, the question of memory is not just a question of the past; instead memory is entangled with future generations and representations.[1] This entanglement is evident through the recycled Holocaust imagery utilized in the immediate post–World War II period and during the 1990s genocide in Bosnia and Herzegovina. The Bosnian atrocity images mirror the same composition and reproduce the same aesthetic framework as the now infamous concentration camp liberation photographs from April 1945. By staging the Bosnian photos to look like the Holocaust images through color composition, number of inmates, and the iconic barbed wire, the journalists and photographers set up a parallel between the past and the present, thus aesthetically entangling the Holocaust with Bosnia. James Young emphasizes that *what* is remembered of a genocide depends on *how* it is remembered.[2] Simply put, Holocaust memories from the past can deeply influence future genocide imagery. In this chapter, I explore the representational (re)memory of the Holocaust through the memory of the Bosnian War (1992–1995). The now infamous images of the Serb-run concentration camp in Trnopolje entangles Bosnian memory with the Holocaust by utilizing collectively acknowledged histories as gateway tropes into the present, allowing the contemporary witness to engage in modes of memory transference.

I examine how the same past can be represented in various ways, specifically via visual memorialization. Hence, the shape that these often visual products ultimately take can determine how and even whether we remember a particular event. These memorialization efforts are constructed with a particular time and space in mind, as well as being contingent on specific, socially manifested, historical, political, and aesthetic expectations of the collective. My periodization focuses on post-1945 entanglement and memory, but my early analysis of Holocaust memorials and Tito's caricature ties back to the understanding of various Balkan states and ethnic groups before and during occupation by Nazi Germany. This is a vital jumping-off point, as earlier contributions about war and empire in the Balkans have already highlighted via the analysis of national identity, anthropology, and economics. My chapter showcases how Germany is tied up with the history and identity of the Balkans, specifically via the memory of the Third Reich, through media and representation. During my later analysis of the 1990s images from the Bosnian camps, I address the aesthetic of various racial ideologies, thus intertwining ideology and stereotypes through my focus on images. This chapter looks at the politics of identity, through monuments as well as print media and news broadcasts, to showcase the entanglement of Yugoslavian-German identity politics. What ties all of the contributions together in the second half of this volume is the investigation of war memories and who bears the responsibility for and memory of World War II.

Through my analysis of visual media, I seek to question not only who bears the responsibility for the memory of these atrocities, but also how the memory of the Holocaust serves as a recycled trope, both aesthetically and politically. Representation often designates how we view the past. It is through representation, whether in the form of museums, artifacts, or photographs, that we pass on memories of events which would otherwise be inaccessible to younger generations. Just as Gerd Gemünden argues for breaking with a narrowly constructed German memory, I too argue for "acts of memory that connect the present with the past in profitable ways" through complexity and multicultural engagement.[3] In other words, the images that I analyze approach the German past differently, from a Yugoslavian perspective, and engage with Germany's National Socialist past through a multicultural lens.

This comparative approach can be tremendously beneficial. The reemergence, or what I call (re)memory, of the Holocaust forged connections between Germany and Bosnia through post–World War II photographic conventions and their captions. Photographs play an essential role in multicultural engagement and can determine which genocides get forgotten and which gain international recognition. Roland Barthes notes that photography produces an effect within the viewer that restores what has been abolished by time. The image serves to attest that what is being observed has indeed existed in the past.[4] This is particularly effective when viewing images of histories that are not already well established in the public sphere. Thus the comparison to well-known historical cases through established photographic conventions can be crucial in highlighting parallels between events. A desire for the "presence" of the past in contemporary genocide cases intensifies, and new technologies render old media obsolete, often solely privileging the visual. Thus photos act as communicative bridges between generations, becoming ever more prevalent, so much so that, as Ernst Jünger expressively puts it, we no longer recognize war without visual representation.[5] In fact, since the liberation of Nazi-run concentration camps, a visual Holocaust rhetoric established widely held photographic conventions, which have since been applied to many other contemporary genocide cases, most notably in Bosnia.

MEMORY AND PHOTOGRAPHY: VISUALIZING THE PAST

Genocide has become a recognizable meme for contemporary audiences through the recycled memory—or (re)memory—of the Holocaust, resulting in a hyper-mediated form. The (re)memory of Holocaust signifiers aids in seeing the past through the lens of the present. Through the hybridized remediation of historical referents, we are able to examine how the contemporary viewer experiences the Holocaust, resulting in a more socially complex view of genocide as a shared cultural memory among audiences who vary greatly in ethnic, cultural, and generational background. I focus on three distinct, yet interrelated, structures of memory transference: postmemory, prosthetic memory, and (re)memory.

Postmemory, a term coined by Marianne Hirsch, outlines the relationship that the generation after bears to the traumatic memory of those who came before.[6] According to Hirsch, images can become historical access points that allow the second generation to understand the context of the historical events. I draw on Hirsch's postmemory model and focus on the contemporary generation's dependence on familiar tropes, icons, or cultural myths as historical anchors, in order to gain access to the past. An image can signal to the viewer what the past looked like and provide an essential affective link and an edge of specificity. Over time, these signifiers become iconic and come to stand for an entire history. Such reductive and reifying signifiers inevitably reinforce and amplify normative constraints regarding what we should remember and how we should remember it. Yet, as Hirsch theorizes postmemory, these signifiers can also act as shorthand cues that allow the past to come alive in the present. In turn, this illustrates how iconic images of the Holocaust, used over and over again to shape collective cultural memory, can become historical access points that allow the second and third generations to understand both the context of the survivor generation and the historical events.

Alison Landsberg elaborates on the transference of memory from one generation to the next, noting that memory has changed as a result of technology (e.g., cinema) and mass culture, and introduces her term, prosthetic memory, which relies on a memory that does not come from a familial connection or from a person's lived experiences.[7] Landsberg focuses instead on how different forms of media, chiefly television and film, create a visceral memory likened to a lived experience of the events that are portrayed, thereby providing a point from which listeners and viewers can access a past to which they otherwise would have no personal connection.[8] Thus the viewer takes on the memory of an event, "wearing" it like a prosthesis.[9]

(Re)memory is a term that I borrow from Toni Morrison's 1987 novel *Beloved*. This model of memory is linked more immediately to the present, rather than the past, and can best be described as a haunting intruder, a spectral memory that unexpectedly reintroduces the past into the present. Morrison's *Beloved*, set after the American Civil War, follows the protagonists, Margaret Garner and Sethe, two former slaves who escape from Kentucky to Ohio, a free state. The narrative is an amalgamation of their memories, specifically Sethe's, who encounters a (re)memory in the form of her dead daughter's ghost. Morrison uses (re)memory to look back in time through Sethe's own experiences, slowly unveiling the horrors of the past in order to transform and translate them in the present. Thus (re)memory is a fitting term not only to express the fraught history of the American Civil War, but also Germany's National Socialist past and contemporary genocide cases.

In (re)memory, the past can get transmitted through various mnemonic devices, from images and text, to places and even music. Most importantly, through (re)memories, the past interacts with and is alive in the present. Additionally, contemporary generations also have a stake in engaging with the past and can in some cases even utilize the tropes of the past in such a way that they are able to express their own contemporary feelings simultaneously. Much like Hirsch's model of postmemory, (re)memories are transferable from one generation to the next. And similar to Landsberg's notion of prosthetic memory, (re)memories are visceral experiences of the past. The memory itself feels real to the contemporary reader, who embodies and wears it much like a prosthesis. However, what is different about (re)memory is that it ultimately serves as a jumping-off point to start a discussion, not just about the past, but also about contemporary events and issues. (Re)memory recycles tropes, making them not only affectively real, but also topically important to the present moment.

ENTANGLED MEMORY:
THE HOLOCAUST AND WORLD WAR II MEMORY IN YUGOSLAVIA

The outbreak of the Yugoslavian war in the early 1990s, the worst fighting in Europe since World War II, brought with it an influx of ex-Yugoslavian refugees, primarily Bosnian Muslims, into Germany. Former Yugoslavia encompassed present-day Croatia, Bosnia and Herzegovina, Serbia, Montenegro, Macedonia, and Slovenia. These six states made up socialist Yugoslavia in 1945 and slowly began to disintegrate after the death of Yugoslavian leader Josip Broz Tito in 1980. As Tito's reign was nearing an end, apprehensions grew due to economic hardships and religious and political tensions that had begun to boil within Yugoslavia, primarily between Orthodox Christian Serbs, Bosnian Muslims, and Catholic Croats. In 1991, Slovenia and Croatia quickly gained independence, distancing themselves from Yugoslavia. As a reaction, especially to Croatia's independence, the Serbian government waged an all-out war in its effort to secure dominion over Yugoslavia.

Tito's political influence tied Yugoslavia immediately to Holocaust memory. From 1943 until his death in 1980, Tito led Yugoslavia, drawing on practical and philosophical ideologies present in both communism and socialism, later dubbed Titoism.[10] The political term and the system's power and legitimacy originally derived from Tito's Partisans' liberation of Yugoslavia from Nazi rule independently of the Soviets, which resulted in Yugoslavia being the only east European country to remain socialist, but independent, after World War II. However, because of the Tito-Stalin split of 1948, the Soviets and their satellite states often accused Yugoslavia of both Trotskyism and fascism, with countless Soviet propaganda attacks depicting Tito both as the reincarnation of Hitler, and also, paradoxically, as a US ally against the Soviets.

In the Soviet satirical magazine *Krokodil* (Crocodile), which featured predominantly political cartoons and propaganda, Tito was often portrayed as a barbarian, resembling a bumbling bulldog, covered in swastikas and SS insignia, as well as dollar signs, the US flag, and other American paraphernalia. The magazine was founded in 1922 and named after Fyodor Dostoyevsky's satirical short story *The Crocodile*. It was branded as a lighthearted inquiry into Soviet society and was given considerable license to lampoon political figures and current events. Nonetheless *Krokodil* stayed within censorship boundaries and only lightly made fun of average Soviet middle-class workers, focusing predominantly on problems associated with rowdy workers and men drinking on the job. The real criticism and satirical work was done in connection to caricatures of capitalist countries, focusing primarily on leaders who opposed the

FIG. 12.1. Serpent Tito, *Krokodil*, September 1949.

Soviet Union. Early in 1949, *Krokodil* published an image of Tito, dressed as an SS officer, wearing a swastika on his left arm. Tito was represented as the embodiment of Hitler, laying a bloody ax nonchalantly to his side, while also holding out his hat to receive American money.[11]

Tito inspired repeated Soviet satirical representations precisely because he was seen as a political threat and as a leader who undermined Soviet power outright. His insistence on remaining independent from US and Soviet influences, and Yugoslavia's geographic proximity to the USSR, alarmed Soviet leaders. These early Soviet propaganda attempts tie my work to the earlier periodization of this book and its focuses on German military influence during both world wars, which ultimately shaped political and cultural representations after World War II. Thus, this form of Soviet propaganda is a representation of the memory of World War II and a direct embodiment of the experience of the Cold War, focusing directly on Soviet and German relations and less on the Yugoslavian experience. This is an important early representation of Yugoslavian-German entanglement and serves as a reminder that these Nazi and Holocaust parallels were not established in a vacuum and that the later representations are a (re)memory of these earlier conflicts.

In September 1949, Tito was depicted again as Tito-Hitler in *Krokodil*, but this time more blatantly as a snake, surrounded by three other snakes that bear the words "terror," "spy," and "betrayal" in Russian. The snake most obviously signifies the biblical representation associated with the serpent from the Garden of Eden. However, the snake does not only embody capitalistic temptation, but also a political allegory. The image of the snake is frequently used as a religious and moralistic symbol and is thus often employed in political propaganda. Jews, for example, were often linked to serpents, rats, and other "parasitic" animals and pests by the Nazis. Tito's snake body is simultaneously covered in dollar signs and swastikas, hinting at both a moralistic and a political "Other," as well as a religious and ethnic parasitic "stranger." *Krokodil* manages to integrate commentary on the perceived relationship between fascism and capitalism through one image. Tito's snake body symbolizes a perceived betrayal by not pledging alliance to Stalin and to the Soviets. Thus, Tito literally becomes not only a "snake in the grass," but at the same time also a Nazi figure in allegiance with the "Other side."

Clearly, the Soviets were not pleased with Tito's stand against Stalin, so much so that they continued this depiction of Tito, using Hitler and accompanying Nazi insignia as a visual trope to draw parallels between Yugoslavia and their own contemporary political moment. It didn't take long for these caricatures to develop in the immediate post–World War II period, with Hitler becoming not only a representational icon of the enemy but also quickly developing into a general signifier that stood in for "evil." The Soviets latched on to this shorthand and reappropriated Hitler as a satirical (re)memory in the war against the West. Tito-Hitler points not only to the global phenomenon of endlessly caricaturing Hitler's visage, but also to a deeper historical entanglement that Yugoslavia has in connection to Germany's National Socialist past. In fact, this Hitler comparison was produced so often in the immediate post–World War II period precisely because of Croatian involvement with the Nazi regime.

In August 1941, the Croatian government established a concentration camp in the marshlands at the confluence of the Sava and Una Rivers near the village of Jasenovac in Croatia. Jasenovac was most

FIG. 12.2. Stone Flower Memorial, Jasenovac, Croatia.

predominately an extermination camp designed to house ethnic Serbs and Jews, but soon evolved into an SS hub in southeastern Europe. The camp was established and run by the governing Ustaša regime in Croatia and was among the largest camps in the area throughout the war.[12] The Ustašas were aligned with the Nazis in an effort to ethnically cleanse the area of Serbs and Yugoslavian Jews, anti-fascist Croats, Roma, and Bosnian Muslim resistance fighters (i.e., Partisans or their sympathizers, categorized by the Ustašas as communists).[13]

In early 1941, the Croatian government actively began to commission recruitment propaganda for the Croatian SS, seeking to recruit Yugoslavian SS members with the straightforward call: "Croats! Sign up for the volunteer SS division." Most of these officers were stationed at Jasenovac, which was run almost exclusively by Croatian SS guards and widely regarded as one of the most efficient satellite camps in eastern and southern Europe. Liberated by the Partisans in April 1945, Jasenovac is still widely regarded as the main camp in Yugoslavia responsible for the near total annihilation of Yugoslavian Jews.[14]

In an attempt to memorialize and "work through" the atrocities committed by the Ustaša regime, Tito erected countless memorials throughout Yugoslavia. The most famous of these memorials is the "Stone Flower," designed to commemorate the victims at Jasenovac. Although these retro-futuristic concrete monuments, often in the shape of abstract flowers and trees, throughout Croatia, Serbia, and Bosnia were designed to commemorate the victims, they primarily served as a political *Wiedergutmachung* (restitution) technique and exemplified the Yugoslavian ploy to make things right again.[15] Tito's intent in commissioning socialist Yugoslavian artists to erect memorials at Jasenovac and other camps like Sajmište in Serbia was aimed primarily at showcasing Partisan resistance and expunging the memory of Croatia as a Nazi satellite state. In an effort not to alienate entirely the Croatian people and former Ustaša members, these monuments elided all victims into one amorphous mass, without truly addressing why Jews were victimized, what other groups were imprisoned, and who oppressed them. Thus, each one of Tito's glib memorialization attempts paid little actual attention to the commemoration of the victims and problematically focused almost exclusively on the Yugoslavian resistance.

It was in part this convoluted attempt at coming to terms with Yugoslavia's tarnished past that led to the Yugoslavian war in the 1990s. Apprehension grew as Tito's reign neared its demise, due to economic hardships as well as religious and political tensions, which resurfaced between Orthodox Serbs and Catholic Croats. Following Tito's death on May 4, 1980, Croatia and Slovenia sought independence, setting off tensions that grew more persistent throughout the 1980s, eventually leading to the genocide in Bosnia from 1992 to 1995. The Serbian militia used the Tito-Hitler trope as an excuse to wage war against both Croats and Bosnians. The Serbian president Slobodan Milošević became the outspoken political leader at the forefront of masterminding not only the war against Croatia, but also the genocide of thousands of Bosnian Muslims.

Serbian political leaders and Serbian extremist organizations operated under the irredentist and fiercely nationalistic ideology of a Greater Serbia, similar to the Nazi vision of *Lebensraum* (living space) or the expansion of territory and national boundaries into other countries.[16] Behind this quest for national space was a deeply embedded nationalistic ideology, which defined the Serbs as a unified front against a historical myth based on the defeat of Serbia by the Ottoman forces at the Battle of Kosovo in 1389, and, most recently, based on the genocide committed against Serbs during World War II at the hands of the Croatian extremists. Thus the enemy was presented as both Bosnian Muslims, who had converted to Islam under the Ottoman Empire, as well as the Croatian Ustašas, who had exterminated Serbs at Jasenovac during the 1940s. The basis for ethnic cleansing in the 1990s was rooted in this belief that Bosnian Muslims who converted to Islam after 1389 and the Croatian Ustašas of the 1940s were still the same enemy in the 1990s as in the past. However, genocide is rarely solely based on the perceived notion of ancient ethnic hatreds. Thus it is important to note that although ethnic cleansing is often based on the fear of an ethnic "Other," this perceived fear is merely an effective tool to engage the general population and mobilize them in an effort to exterminate the "Other" from society. Hence, in their effort to wage war against these two groups, the Serbian authorities relied heavily on the media as a primary weapon in their military campaign aimed at enticing Serbian citizens into becoming vehement followers.

From 1986 to 1987, Milošević actively attempted to gain control over the major Serbian and Yugoslavian newspapers, as well as several public television networks and radio broadcasters, such as RTS (Radio Television of Serbia). His methods of controlling the media included creating strategic shortages of paper, interfering with or stopping supplies and equipment, and confiscating newspapers from being printed without proper "licenses." He also often would freely fire, promote, or demote journalists and government employees, thus taking control of the networks and determining what was said and how it was said. In an attempt to reappropriate the racial rhetoric associated with World War II, Milošević set out to depict Croats as Nazis, and Bosniaks as the reincarnated "other."

One of the most famous examples of such racially driven media tactics was a falsified black and white image of a young boy lying on a Christian grave site surrounded by crosses. The image was passed off as a photo accompanied by a heart-wrenching narrative and a caption that reads: "Serbian boy mourning the loss of his entire family killed by Bosnian Muslims." The caption hints clearly at past atrocities and invokes the Ottoman Empire and the forceful takeover by Turkish troops of Serbian and Bosnian villages during the late 1380s. In yet another interpretation of the image, the caption reads: "Croats leave an orphaned boy behind." In this case, the caption connects the extermination of Serbs and Jews during World War II with the falsified image. Published by the Belgrade newspaper *Večernje Novosti* (Evening News), the propagandistic photo was actually the 1888 realist painting *Siroče na majčinom grobu* (*Orphan on Mother's Grave*) by the Serbian artist Uroš Predić. While the subject matter deals with an orphan, because of the time period and circumstances of the original painting, it had nothing to do with World War II, Croats, or Bosnians.

WILLKOMMEN IN BOSNIA: HOLOCAUST (RE)MEMORY IN THE BOSNIAN GENOCIDE

Can a photo save lives? The case of the now infamous images from the Trnopolje concentration camp near Prijedor, Bosnia, provide an example of the power of the photograph: its ability to save lives. In the summer of 1992, Britain's Independent Television News (ITN) set out to photograph the camps in Bosnia, so as to rouse the international community into action. The crew set out to photograph the camp conditions in Omarska, one of the most horrific camps at this time, where prisoners were greeted with the phrase "Willkommen in Omarska" in German as a sadistic reminder that they would not make it out alive.[17] Although ITN reporters initially set out to photograph Omarska, they were confronted with staged interactions with prisoners and denied access to much of the camp. On the way back through the Bosnian countryside, though, the ITN crew stumbled upon camp Trnopolje and immediately latched on to a post–World War II representational trope, drawing comparisons between the Nazi concentration camp Buchenwald and Trnopolje. The images that were published include the covert photographs from the camp at Omarska and the barbed-wire images from the camp at Trnopolje. When we view documentary photographs and atrocity images for contemporary cases, such as Bosnia, we often default to and use our memories of the Holocaust as our context, against which to appropriate these more contemporaneous instances of horror.

The photographically mediated image was central in the initial construction of the collective memory of World War II.[18] In fact, subsequent atrocities rely heavily on the symbolic visual tropes established in the aftermath of World War II. Barbie Zelizer comments on the now-iconic Holocaust images taken during the liberation of the camps in 1945, noting that the wide availability of cameras for the first time resulted in a manic desire for photographic images of the atrocities. "The atrocity photos taken by the U.S. and British photographers streamed in so quickly that the press back home had little time to debate their impact. Turning out roll after roll of black-and-white film, photographers relentlessly depicted the worst of Nazism in stark, naturalistic representations of horror: bodies turned at odd angles to each other, charred skulls, ovens full of ashes, shocked German civilians alongside massive scenes of human carnage."[19]

What was so problematic and allowed for this pure power of personal photographic agency was that these photographers were given "few guidelines about which shots to take or how to take them," producing an open range for personal style development and the agency to construct the guidelines for an atrocity photograph.[20] The photographs streamed in so rapidly that the press as well as the audience back home had little time to think about their impacts, due to the wide range and accessibility of photos coming in. This large pool of incoming photographs generated a "generalization factor."[21] The photographs no longer had specific captions and information attached to them, but represented a general notion of suffering, bearing witness to the atrocity on a mass scale. These generalized captions of Nazi horror also eventually turned into nonsequential visual depictions and facilitated the use of "visuals to illustrate the broader strokes of the atrocity rather than the contingent details of one specific instance of violence."[22] This phenomenon helped turn Holocaust photographic conventions into a general atrocity trope, often necessitating the depiction of nameless emaciated bodies, unspecified mass graves, and a focus on the inhumane living conditions of the victims and survivors.

This photographic trope was replicated in countless future atrocities, most predominately in contemporary representations of the Holocaust. Marianne Hirsch uses the term "postmemory" to describe how the children of survivors gain a powerful, highly affective, and ethically engaged sense of memory of traumatic events through the mediation of photographs. Hirsch's visual paradigm of postmemory can also be applied to the case of the 1990s genocide in Bosnia. The now-infamous images of the Serb-run concentration camp in Trnopolje visually entangle Bosnian memory with the Holocaust.

Trnopolje, a small village at the base of the Kozara Mountains, with the Mrakovica memorial commemorating the Partisan resistance during World War II looming in the distance, is located in the greater municipality of Prijedor, Bosnia. It was a quiet and peaceful village, with one school and one supermarket, largely inhabited by Bosnian Muslims. In the summer of 1992, all of that changed as Serbian troops forcefully moved into the region, burning homes, destroying neighborhoods, and building several concentration camps in the surrounding area, most notably Keraterm, Omarska, Trnopolje, and Manjača. Bosnian Muslim women, men, and children were housed in these camps under the pretense of political imprisonment. Swanee Hunt captures through various testimonies and interviews the conditions that these inmates endured, revealing that these inmates were routinely beaten, raped, experimented on, and made to enact degrading and despicable acts.[23] As historian Noel Malcolm points out in his analysis of post–World War II Bosnia, by 1992 the annihilation of Bosnian Muslims at the hands of extremist Serbs had reached an alarming new height, so much so that the international community began to send investigative reporters, who actively sought to compare Bosnia to the Holocaust.[24]

Britain's ITN wanted to rouse the international community to action through journalism. On their way back from a staged visit at Omarska, an ITN crew stumbled upon the Trnopolje camp and immediately latched on to a post–World War II representational trope, drawing direct comparisons between Buchenwald and Trnopolje. In an effort to illustrate what was really happening in these camps, ITN reporters asked one

FIG. 12.3. Buchenwald inmates, by Margaret Bourke-White, *Life* magazine, May 1945.

FIG. 12.4. Trnopolje, Independent Television News footage by Penny Marshall and Ian Williams, August 1992.

of the more physically emaciated inmates, Fikret Alić, to step forward and to remove his shirt, in order to highlight his emaciated frame, all the while continuing to film the interactions between the ITN crew and the Trnopolje inmates.²⁵ ITN asked Alić and fellow inmates to come closer to the barbed wire and strategically directed Alić and the other inmates how to position their bodies and stand by the barbed wire. While the footage, which was subsequently turned into a still image, was certainly staged, the subjects really endured these horrific conditions, undergoing months of starvation and physical torture, which were not necessarily captured on camera by ITN or other journalists.²⁶

The Trnopolje image was so powerful that ITN was able to immediately rouse international interest, with subsequent publications in the US, Britain, Germany, France, and Canada. In forcing this photographic comparison along, the *Daily Mail*, *Time*, and *Der Spiegel* linked the Bosnian images directly to the Holocaust by pairing the photograph with photographs of well-known German camps, adding captions like "Belsen '92" and "Horror of the New Holocaust." The reemergence, or what I call (re)memory, of the Holocaust forged connections between Germany and Bosnia through post–World War II photographic conventions and their captions. This (re)memory was achieved in two ways. First, the initial representation of the atrocity had to be simplistic, thus drawing parallels to already "worked-through" atrocities like the Holocaust and presenting simple binary narratives (victim v. perpetrator, Bosnians v. Serbs). Second, the visual (re)memory needed to contain the brutally grotesque (e.g., emaciated bodies) in order to portray the enormity and impact of the atrocity.

The conventions surrounding photographic (re)memories function by replicating the Holocaust in a contemporary setting, often by reformatting images to black and white, in order to invoke a 1940s aesthetic. In addition, the most important aspect of visual (re)memory relies on "props," like the barbed wire, the housing barracks, and the focus on the emaciated body, as tools to illustrate the general conditions of the inmates, functioning as proof of suffering and genocide.

Photographs depicting the living quarters where the Bosnian inmates were held exemplify the prevalence of the visual component in (re)memory. In this set of images, malnourished male inmates are depicted at camp Manjača as they stand, lie, and sit within their living quarters. Manjača was a mountain near the city of Banja Luka, located roughly seventy-five kilometers southeast from Prijedor. According to Human Rights Watch and the Red Cross, there were just under four thousand prisoners held at Manjača.²⁷ Prisoners were photographed with their shoes off inside the barracks so as not to dirty the blankets they were

FIG. 12.5. Manjača inmates, courtesy of International Crime Tribunal for the former Yugoslavia (ICTY).

sitting on. These photographs "quote" iconic images from Buchenwald and other World War II liberation photos once again in various ways, for example in the number of male subjects shown in the composition and in their industrial, cramped, dirty, and inhumane living spaces. The Manjača images can also be said to quote the era—the historical time— of the iconic Holocaust atrocity photos. Provided by the International

FIG. 12.6. "Logor—Zabranjen Ulaz," Manjača concentration camp gate, courtesy of ICTY.

Crime Tribunal for the former Yugoslavia (ICTY), the photos of Manjača were originally in color but were ultimately changed and often reproduced by the ICTY as black-and-white images. The ability to transform these colored photographs into black and white retrojects them into the mid-1940s.

The sign displaying the slogan "Arbeit macht frei" (Work makes you free) provides another example of how the past can be rendered present in photographic (re)memory—and not only where the perspective of victims is at issue, but also that of perpetrators. Hirsch uses her concept of postmemory to defend the reproduction of the infamous Auschwitz gate as a visual tool that brings the past into life for the postmemory generation. The same phenomenon can be tied, not just to intergenerational memory transfer—a second generation's response to the traumas of the first—but also to the dynamics of cross-cultural photographic (re)memories. Thus, this same ironic and sadistic portrayal of nationalistic slogans was used in Serb-run camps, in Manjača and Omarska, where victims were often greeted with the German phrase "Willkommen in Bosnia" (Welcome to Bosnia), as a reminder that they had just entered into a modern-day Auschwitz. Exhibiting a similar display as the "Arbeit macht frei" sign, Serbs put up signs that read "Logor—Zabranjen Ulaz" (Concentration Camp—Prohibited Entry), further drawing parallels between Auschwitz and Bosnia. Witnesses and perpetrators alike forged links between the Bosnian images and the Holocaust. It was precisely the visual (re)memories enacted in the Bosnian photos, in particular in the context of the Yugoslavian war-crimes tribunals, which "succeeded in rousing moral outrage."[28] These photos were crucial in mobilizing the public to send aid and help shut down the camps; they eventually led to the end of the war and Germany's acceptance of thousands of Bosnian refugees.

In her eloquent book *Regarding the Pain of Others*, Susan Sontag asserts that the possibility to view images of such atrocities in the immediate post–World War II period was new and fascinating, but now, more than ever, our ability to observe the horrors of atrocities at a distance, through modern mass media, including photography, television, and online, may only feed our morally questionable appetite for abjection.[29] Sontag draws our attention to the moral perils that accompany memory formation in the age of mass media, when images of even contemporary atrocities, not just past ones, can take on a life of their own, disconnected from the very real and historically specific events they mediate. The paradigm of what I call (re)memory is rife with such dangers—trivialization of specific atrocities, the flattening out of historical particularity, and the reduction of historical and moral complexity. However, (re)memory also has very significant capability for keeping alive meaningful connections to past genocides and for mobilizing acutely needed action in support of contemporary victims. The effects of hyper-mediated memory are neither all good nor all bad, but rather full of dangers and great potential at the same time.

When we take into consideration the contemporary moment, we can see that bridging the gap between cross-cultural and cross-generational memory is a significant component in the European (2014–present) and US refugee crises (2016–present). What Michael Rothberg calls multidirectional memory formations allow memories of different traumatic events, anchored in different times, to inform each other mutually (e.g., the Bosnian war and the Holocaust, or the Turkish migrant experience and the post–World War II Jewish migrant experience).[30] Such multidirectional entanglements of memory include, but also go far beyond, the sort of visual rhetoric I have analyzed. Indeed, a wide variety of tropes associated with collectively acknowledged histories can serve as gateways into the present, allowing the contemporary witness to engage in modes of memory transference.

While the Bosnian images, overall, serve a necessary function as proof of the atrocities and managed to incite the international community into action, resulting in the rapid liberation of the camps, they simply lack the nuance and specificity to truly create cross-generational bridges that affectively bring the past and the contemporary moment into dialogue with one another. The images express a strong message about the atrocities and move the people to action, yet they do not tell us much about the connection between the past and the present, between Germany and Bosnia. This is where the role of other media outlets, from films and comics to other artistic outlets, such as art, poetry, and music, comes into play.

MEMORY MIGRATION: THE FUTURE OF YUGOSLAV-GERMAN ENTANGLEMENT

The Dayton Peace Agreement brought the Yugoslavian war to an official end in 1995. However, as Robert Bideleux and Ian Jeffries point out in their political and economic analysis of post–World War II Bosnia, the Dayton agreement also divided Bosnia into two federations, the Republic of Srpska and the Federation of Bosnia.[31] The agreement established a state of Bosnia with internal divisions, mini "Berlin Walls" that separate one community from another to this day. Although the agreement played a vital role in ending the war and slowly reestablishing peace in the region, it also continues to play a role in the aftermath and the current political situation. More than twenty years after the Dayton Peace Agreement, nearly half of the refugees and displaced Bosnian citizens remain away from their prewar homes.

In 2005, the Bosnian Ministry of Human Rights and Refugees estimated that there were still more than half a million persons temporarily residing abroad. The majority of these refugees have at one point resided in or are still living in Germany. According to the Federal Statistical Office of Germany, in the early 1990s about 345,000 refugees from Bosnia found temporary protection in Germany. This population of displaced Bosnian Muslims sought refuge in Germany, particularly in former West Germany, as many Bosnians had relatives who were already living there due to their role as guest workers and migrants since the 1960s.[32] The atrocities during World War II remain a powerful reference point for refugees who left Bosnia either for or via Germany and provide a constant point of comparison for the Bosnian war of the 1990s.

What is unique about the experience of ex-Yugoslavian migrant workers and refugees in Germany is that they have seamlessly integrated into German society and continue to actively engage with German national memory politics, particularly in relation to World War II and the Holocaust. The Yugoslavian refugees' migrant experience is thus of particular historical interest since it has gone largely unnoticed, partially due to the fact that ex-Yugoslavians contrast less conspicuously culturally and in appearance with the dominant sociocultural populations of Western Europe, making them seem less threatening, despite their multiethnic and multireligious makeup, which includes Catholic Croats, Orthodox Serbs, Yugoslavian Roma, Yugoslavian Jews, and Bosnian Muslims. However, political friendliness abroad toward Yugoslavian refugees is primarily tied to an attempt at maintaining positive relations with Serbia and Bosnia, as many of the former Yugoslavian countries are viewed as the European gateway to the east. In addition, Germany's own experiences after World War II and the memory politics that ensued in the immediate post–World War II period have also heavily influenced the treatment of Yugoslavian refugees in Europe.

Representation becomes the raw material of history—it is the living source from which history is drawn, occupying a place between construction and reconstruction—and literary and historical truths may not always be separable. Now more than ever, our ability to remember the past is facilitated by mediated memory. These representations ultimately also help to stabilize and anchor collective memory. This can be extremely problematic, because ultimately only what gets memorialized gets remembered. Thus, when confronting contemporary representations, the audience also has to consider what is forgotten, glossed over, and left out. Although the (re)memory of Trnopolje and Omarska can be seen as a superficial comparison between the Bosnian war and the Holocaust, what these representations attempt to do is to bring the reality of the war in Bosnia into a thinkable context. The (re)memory of these visual tropes serves as a gateway both into Germany in the 1940s and also into the more immediate present.

Thus the comparison to the Holocaust is an attempt at coming to terms with Germany's National Socialist past and also with the Bosnian past. These visual signifiers serve as reminders that there are active parallels between the Holocaust and the Bosnian genocide of the 1990s, which continue to entangle Yugoslavia with German memory in profound ways. In the case of Bosnia, which is widely regarded as one of the more "successfully" worked-through contemporary genocides, with international crime tribunals established at the Hague and a permanent exhibit about the atrocities at the United States Holocaust Memorial Museum in Washington, DC, this comparison proved to be vital in spreading international awareness of the genocide. However, there are still many memory gaps. Although the images published in 1992 helped rouse moral outrage and mobilized intervention, the narrative about the Bosnian genocide has struggled to get out from underneath the shadow of this initial comparison. Nonetheless, the initial comparison was vital, not only in educating the international community, but in saving the lives of countless Bosnians.

CHAPTER 13

THE POLITICS OF SCREEN MEMORY IN NICOL LJUBIĆ'S *STILLNESS OF THE SEA*

ANNA E. ZIMMER

The fall of the Berlin Wall in November 1989 and the subsequent collapse of the Iron Curtain led to the disintegration of physical and ideological borders in Europe, in particular, and between the East and West, in general. Nevertheless, the war that brewed in Yugoslavia tempered these positive developments. In the early 1990s, as most of Europe celebrated the end of the Cold War and the relative absence of ethnic conflict in Europe since the end of World War II, ethnic cleansing was being carried out in southeastern Europe, in Yugoslavia, and further abroad genocide was being committed in Rwanda.[1] Furthermore, the recently reunited Germany struggled to balance its role as a NATO member with its fraught history of deploying German troops. As Christopher A. Molnar and Mirna Zakić claim in the introduction to this volume, "The violent breakup of Yugoslavia in the 1990s reinvigorated—but did not resolve— issues of suffering, loss, and identity, and the question of whose memories dominated public discourse and media representation of violence in the Balkans."[2] Literature also offered a venue in which to reevaluate the representation of both collective and personal memories of distant and more recent wars.

In this chapter, I examine the work of Croatian-German author Nicol Ljubić, who recognizes the power of collective memory to inform decision-making in contemporary politics, while also analyzing and interrogating parallels drawn between catastrophic events of the 1990s and national pasts dominated by the memory of World War II. In his 2010 novel, *Meeresstille: Roman*[3] (translated into English by Anna Paterson as *Stillness of the Sea* in 2011[4]), Ljubić complicates the political parallels drawn between ethnic cleansing in the former Yugoslavia and the Nazi-perpetrated Holocaust through the articulation of personal and familial stories of war and migration. Ljubić's reassessment of the cogency of Germany's dominant post–World War II identity exposes the myth of a postnational Germany that has overcome its Nazi past, challenged by memories of more recent violent conflicts in the Balkans.

Germany's attempts at *Vergangenheitsbewältigung* (overcoming the past) have long been more substantial than those of other nations. As Richard Ned Lebow explains, "The Federal Republic has gone further than its neighbors in confronting its past for many reasons. One of them, ... is its longstanding cultural practice of using the past as a resource to frame thought about the present. This goes back at least as far as the late eighteenth century and early nineteenth, when German idealists and romantics (e.g., Hölderlin, Schelling, Hegel) sought to use their highly stylized understanding of ancient Greece as a model for contemporary ethics, aesthetics, and politics."[5] The formation of the Federal Republic of Germany after World War II was founded on a rejection of Nazism, a strong anti-militarism, and an assertion that the new democratic nation must acknowledge its World War II guilt in order to move into a more just future. *Stillness of the Sea* challenges this foundational myth by revealing how this memory blinded Germany when making foreign policy decisions in the late 1990s, thus highlighting the messy aftershocks of war half a century later.

My analysis of *Stillness of the Sea* explores the use of the memory of Germans as World War II perpetrators as a means to argue for the 1999 NATO intervention in the former Yugoslavia. Of particular interest is the way in which the memory of past wars and military interventions is utilized as a frame of reference to understand, criticize, or support current political action. It is important to note that there are different memories of World War II and the lessons drawn from them: Germany's responsibility for the Holocaust and Germany's disregard for the sovereignty of other nations. In the 1990s, confronted with ethnic cleansing in Yugoslavia, Germany's politics of regret for the genocide of Europe's Jews won out, but rather than precluding military action against a sovereign nation, this memory was utilized to argue for Germany's participation in the NATO-led air strikes against Serbian cities.

TRANSNATIONALISM AND THE MEMORY BOOM: RESUSCITATING NATIONAL IDENTITIES OR ACKNOWLEDGING GLOBAL CONNECTIONS?

Historical memories, especially World War II memories, have played a central role in the formation of a postwar German national identity. Since 1945, however, the memory of World War II has become increasingly multifaceted and encompasses not only Nazi perpetration and the Holocaust, but also includes expulsion, exile, the complicity of average citizens, the crimes of the *Wehrmacht*, and the Allied bombing campaigns. Moreover, since German reunification in 1990, the influence of war memories upon discourses of national identity has become even more dynamic and uncertain due to the heightened connectivity of people across national borders and the increasing heterogeneity of nations, a search for new certainties and moral yardsticks in the post–Cold War era, and the changing nature of war. Many contemporary novels, including *Stillness of the Sea*, are an integral part of this "memory boom" and insert themselves into these discourses.[6] Ljubić's novel narrates complex transnational memories that reflect increasingly porous boundaries between nations, while also acknowledging and problematizing the continued impact of official national memories upon domestic and foreign policy.

Attempts to strengthen shaken national identities after the dismantling of the clearly bifurcated Cold War world order are partially responsible for the memory boom.[7] The renewed interest in the past has often been attributed to a desire to counter the erosion of national identities due to the receding economic and social significance of nations and their increasingly heterogeneous populations, through the articulation of national memories.[8] In an age of globalization, a strengthening of local memories can lessen fear of cultural homogenization and the disintegration of national identities and traditions. While Ljubić attends to local specificities, he also depicts the dynamic interplay of memories from around the world that can at times serve to forge empathy across national lines, and at other times create divisions. As such, I argue that *Stillness of the Sea* acknowledges what sociologists Daniel Levy and Natan Sznaider refer to as the cosmopolitanization of memory.

Levy and Sznaider depart from a widespread understanding of collective memory as located within the nation and argue that during this age of globalization the boundaries of nations are becoming more porous, as are the confines of collective memory: "Rather than restricting the conceptualization of collective memory to a national context . . . it is possible, and necessary, to uncover memoryscapes that correspond to emerging modes of identification in the global age."[9] Expanding upon Ulrich Beck's conceptualization of cosmopolitanism, they assert the emergence of cosmopolitan memory and suggest that "national and ethnic memories are transformed in the age of globalization rather than erased."[10] This distinction is important, as many conceptualizations of globalization and cosmopolitanism erase the importance of national pasts in their future-oriented imaginations and often wrongfully overestimate the homogenizing effects of globalization.[11] In comparison, Levy and Sznaider argue, "The cosmopolitanization of Holocaust memories . . . involves the formation of nation-specific and nation-transcending commonalities."[12]

In my textual analysis, attention to the cultural and historical specificities of the novel uncovers the extent to which nation-states still function as real or imagined coordinates of our world and the memories thereof.

SCREEN MEMORY: REPRESSING THE PAST OR THE PRESENT?

Examining German literary texts about the former Yugoslavia, many literary scholars have questioned to what extent the Balkans are portrayed fairly—or even subjected to balkanization, with an emphasis on the supposed primitive and barbarian nature of the region[13]—and whether the war-torn region is simply used as a screen onto which German-speaking Europe projects its own questions of identity and lessons from the past.[14] *Stillness of the Sea*'s main character, a German of Croatian descent, whose "Germanness" is often highlighted, criticizes this type of projection in the political sphere, but in his private life projects his own insecurities and fears onto his girlfriend, a Serb from Bosnia studying in Berlin. The post-Yugoslav wars could therefore be understood as screen memories (*Deckerinnerungen*) in the Freudian sense.[15] While Freud was primarily concerned with individuals' memories and the ways in which comforting memories can block painful memories from view, the concept of screen memory is nevertheless applicable to collective memory as well. Comparisons between two events (oftentimes both traumatic) can function as screen memories, repressing memories of the past that are closer to home or blocking insight into local histories. Miriam Hansen and Andreas Huyssen have done important work exploring the Holocaust as a screen memory in which the Holocaust functions as a displaced referent for the United States' own national traumas such as the Vietnam War or the mistreatment and displacement of Native Americans. In addition, they demonstrate the Holocaust's power as a universal signifier that eschews historical specificity when used as a moral yardstick to measure the severity of another catastrophe.[16] As these examples demonstrate, a screen memory can be projected upon an event in the past or present.[17]

While Hansen and Huyssen primarily view screen memory as negative, Michael Rothberg highlights its multidirectionality. Rothberg claims that "the displacement that takes place in screen memory (indeed, in all memory) functions as much to open up lines of communication with the past as to close them off."[18] Rather than emphasizing the covering up of memory suggested by the original term *Deckerinnerungen* (literally, "cover memories"), Rothberg points out the aptness of the English translation "screen memory" since it highlights two understandings of a screen, which can function as a barrier (through which something may still get through) and as a site of projection or illumination.[19] In discussing Freud's concept of screen memory, Rothberg favors cooperation rather than competition: "While screen memory might be understood as involving a conflict of memories, it ultimately more closely resembles a remapping of memory in which links between memories are formed and then redistributed between the conscious and unconscious."[20] While I do not disagree with Rothberg's overall assessment of screen memory, the novel under consideration often depicts screen memories that displace, silence, or overshadow other memories, unlike the productive articulations of multidirectionality that allow for the forging of empathy between groups. I argue that *Stillness of the Sea* portrays and criticizes two different types of screen memory: in the first type, the memory of World War II and postwar national identities obfuscate local historical and cultural specificities in Yugoslavia, and in the second type, recent events such as the post-Yugoslav wars function as displaced referents for—or at the very least, distractions from—German domestic challenges, such as the tribulations of reunification in the new Berlin Republic and xenophobia. Moreover, I assert that while *Stillness of the Sea* opens up important lines of communication with the past and exposes the dangerous repercussions of screen memories in international politics, at times it also closes off lines of communication with largely forgotten pasts.

NICOL LJUBIĆ'S *STILLNESS OF THE SEA*: REMEMBERING THE BALKANS IN BERLIN

Nicol Ljubić was born in 1971 in Zagreb, Croatia, to a Croatian father and a German mother. Due to his father's profession as an airplane technician for Lufthansa, Ljubić spent very little of his life in Croatia, but rather grew up in Greece, Sweden, Russia, and Germany, where he completed his *Abitur* in Bremen. In Hamburg, he studied political science and journalism at the Henri-Nannen-Schule. He now lives in Berlin, where he works as a professional journalist and has published multiple literary works.[21] *Stillness of the Sea*, his third novel, was nominated for the prestigious German Book Prize (2010), secured a place on the list of the twenty best German novels of 2010, and was awarded the Adelbert-von-Chamisso-Förderpreis in 2011, a literary prize awarded to German-language authors whose work is shaped by a change of culture (many prizewinners' mother tongue is not German). For his research during the book project, the Robert Bosch Foundation sponsored Ljubić with a *Grenzgänger Stipendium* (border-crosser stipend), which supports international research trips of artists committed to challenging existing stereotypes about societies.

Stillness of the Sea tells two parallel stories: a love story set in Berlin and the trial of an accused war criminal at The Hague. Robert, a Croatian-German, whose father came to Germany as a *Gastarbeiter* (guest worker),[22] shows little interest in his family's past until he meets Ana, a Serbian student studying German literature in Berlin on a scholarship awarded to the children and grandchildren of victims of National Socialism.[23] As Ana pushes Robert to explore his Croatian roots, Robert becomes curious about Ana's father, who he later learns is on trial, having been accused of killing more than forty Muslims in Višegrad, Yugoslavia, in 1992. By bringing to life clashes between personal stories and public histories from Germany and the former Yugoslavia in the early twenty-first century, *Stillness of the Sea* calls into question the validity of politicizing memories of the Nazi-perpetrated Holocaust to argue for the NATO intervention in Yugoslavia, including the 1999 bombing of Serbian cities.

BEYOND THE EASTERN TURN IN GERMAN LITERATURE

Ljubić joins a number of authors who write in German about topics related to eastern Europe and the former Yugoslavia, thus contributing to what Irmgard Ackermann has called the *Osterweiterung* (eastern expansion) of German-language literature, or what Brigid Haines terms the "Eastern Turn" in German literature.[24] Like *Stillness of the Sea*, a number of texts that belong to the Eastern Turn grapple with the collapse of the former Yugoslavia and its aftermath.[25] For example, in Hungarian author Terézia Mora's German-language novel *Alle Tage*[26] (translated into English by Michael Henry Heim as *Day In Day Out*[27]), the protagonist's trauma due to the conflict in the Balkans functions as a warning to Berlin against naïve celebration of ethnic and religious diversity. Swiss musician and author Melinda Nadj Abonji's *Tauben fliegen auf*[28] (translated into English by Tess Lewis as *Fly Away, Pigeon*[29]), winner of the 2010 German Book Prize, grapples with the collapse of the former Yugoslavia and its effects on the Hungarian minority in northern Serbia, while also exposing the racist tendencies in Swiss society in the 1990s. As such, *Fly Away, Pigeon*, much like *Stillness of the Sea*, acknowledges ethnic and cultural tensions at home and abroad. In addition, German lawyer and writer Juli Zeh's travelogue, *Die Stille ist ein Geräusch: Eine Fahrt durch Bosnien*[30] (*Silence Is a Sound: A Trip through Bosnia*), traces Zeh's 2001 trip through Bosnia and Herzegovina and paints a portrait of a country about which the West hears few stories following the war. Finally, Hans-Christian Schmid's 2009 film, *Sturm* (*Storm*), interrogates the strengths and weaknesses of the International Criminal Tribunal for the Former Yugoslavia (ICTY). Much like Ljubić, Schmid puts a trial on trial, asserting the importance of the tribunal, while also questioning whether the tribunal is successful in bringing individual war criminals to justice and justice to victims.[31] While many of these texts share thematic similarities with *Stillness of the Sea*, they lack the mnemonic focus of Ljubić's novel.

However, *Stillness of the Sea* shares its focus on tensions between familial memories and official histories with Turkish-German author Zafer Şenocak's *Gefährliche Verwandtschaft*[32] (translated into English by Tom Cheesman as *Perilous Kinship*[33]). Şenocak's novel plays with the intersection of Germany's Nazi past, the Armenian genocide, and Turkish migration to Germany. Leslie Adelson offers an astute analysis of the configuration of genocide and taboo in *Perilous Kinship*: "When figural Turks and Jews make contact in German narratives alluding to stories of victimization and genocide, these narratives become 'touching tales' of Turks, Germans, and Jews. They function as such, in part, because they evoke a culturally residual, referentially nonspecific sense of guilt, blame, shame, and danger."[34] denocak's text therefore reads the Holocaust through the lens of the Armenian genocide (and vice versa) and raises questions about the importance of family and national histories, victim-perpetrator dichotomies, and living in the present in light of the past.[35] In comparison, Ljubić's narrative grapples with the post-Yugoslav wars and ethnic cleansing through the lens of a German understanding of World War II and the Holocaust. *Stillness of the Sea* indeed presents "touching tales" of Germans, Serbians, Croatians, and Muslims. These tales at times evoke a sense of guilt and shame that is nonspecific in its reference, while at other times, these stories are shown to move from the realm of memory and storytelling directly into the realm of foreign policy decision-making as precedent for the justification of current actions.

Finally, due to *Stillness of the Sea*'s consideration of the extent to which the youngest postwar generation may carry responsibility for the horrors of the past and the degree to which young Europeans must confront their roles (even as mere observers) in war and peacetime, the novel shares important characteristics with an earlier West German genre: *Väterliteratur* (literature of fathers). Especially popular among the rebellious 1968er generation, *Väterliteratur* in the 1970s and 1980s confronted the personal and political past of the fathers (less frequently of the mothers) of young men and women who were born during or shortly after World War II. In this primarily autobiographical fiction, the narrator attempts to come to terms with the tainted National Socialist past of his or her parents and to reckon with the ways in which the parents' past shaped the child's identity.[36] In *Stillness of the Sea*, two generations removed from World War II, Robert tends to relegate war to an older generation. Ana, on the other hand, experienced war firsthand as a child in the 1990s and must come to terms with the crimes of which her own father has been accused. Ana's life is overshadowed by the presumed guilt of her father: "He [Ana's father] has turned them [the whole family] into victims. . . . Victimized, they will spend the rest of their lives in the perpetrator's shadow."[37] Ana refuses, however, to let her father's past dictate her present, claiming: "Come on, you can't inherit guilt. You can still be a wonderful human being, even if your father killed someone. Maybe just because of it, you'd do all you could to be different."[38] While Ana speaks here of the actions of individuals, her statements could also describe how West Germany responded to its National Socialist legacy and attempted to create a new identity after 1945, or the challenges faced by Serbs in present-day Europe.[39] Admittedly, *Stillness of the Sea* focuses more on the protagonists' attempts in the present to lead meaningful lives despite their familial pasts rather than reflecting upon the causes of individual acts of violence in the former Yugoslavia.[40]

Like many texts that could be classified as *Väterliteratur*, *Stillness of the Sea* attempts to collect information about a father figure in the hopes of understanding the past and the narrator's identity in the present. While Ana is willing to share playful anecdotes such as receiving her first Shakespeare play from her father, the stories she tells about her family do not go beyond her rosy childhood. Due to the fact that Ana is unwilling to talk about the war, Robert resorts to detective work. He invades Ana's privacy, going to The Hague where Ana's father, Zlatko Šimić, is on trial, in the hopes of reconciling his love for Ana with the fact that her father is most likely a vicious criminal. Robert never questions the righteousness of his actions and seems unable to accept that he might be in love with the daughter of a criminal. During the trial, Robert spends less time listening to the witnesses and lawyers than he does daydreaming and imagining what he might say to Šimić, were they to meet. In an imagined letter to Šimić, Robert writes, "You're always a good man in the stories Ana tells about you. I admit there were times I wished you were my father. I fantasized about the day I would meet you for the first time.... When I listened to what you were charged with, I wished you weren't where you are—I wished that the man in the dark suit, who toyed with his tie while a woman spoke of her family burning, was not Ana's father."[41] While at the trial, Robert learns more about Šimić, but is unable to reconcile this gruesome past with his own relationship with Ana in the present. The Šimić character displays striking similarities with Nikola Koljević, the Bosnian Serb politician, university professor, and Shakespeare scholar, who served as a representative abroad for the Bosnian Serb nationalists and as a deputy to Radovan Karadžić, who was himself indicted by the ICTY and forced from power.[42] Koljević died in 1997 of self-inflicted gunshot wounds. In *Stillness of the Sea*, the details of Šimić's life, as presented at the trial at The Hague, do not match the true story of Koljević exactly, but by putting him on trial in the novel, Ljubić can pose questions not only about bringing outspoken war criminals such as

Slobodan Milošević and Karadžić to justice, but also explore the complexity of determining the innocence or guilt of those politicians who did not carry out ethnic cleansing themselves, but were likely accomplices. Furthermore, it blurs the line between victim and perpetrator. Or, as Ana puts it, "But because I'm a Serb, everyone thinks of me as a potential culprit, even though they know nothing about my life. And meantime they all forget that there were victims among the perpetrators and that some of the victims would have turned into perpetrators, given half a chance."[43]

THE LEGACY OF WORLD WAR II: HUMANITARIANISM AND ATONEMENT FOR AUSCHWITZ

Robert, a PhD candidate in history, initially seems to have the necessary qualifications to tackle the complex task of understanding the interwoven stories and histories of Germans, Croatians, Serbs, and Muslims in present-day Europe. However, his academic training in history proves insufficient to disentangle the multifaceted histories. Stories that Robert viewed as the purview of academic historians become personal as he interacts with Ana, researches his own family history, discusses the historical dimensions of the post-Yugoslav wars with colleagues, and meets young Muslims directly impacted by war at The Hague and later in Sarajevo. Each character brings a new level of complexity to Robert's understanding of war, guilt, military interventions in the name of human rights, and connections between the personal and the historical. However, the novel's primary focus upon Robert—either by the third-person narrator or through inner monologue, in which Robert relates his own thoughts—prevents the multifarious memories of perpetration and loss from interacting dialectically. Simply put, while the narrative structure switches between the love story and the trial at The Hague, thus offering multiple perspectives, the overarching narrative remains one-sidedly focused on Robert and Germany, thus missing important opportunities for communication and intercultural understanding. Instead of leading to solidarity between people of different nations, the articulation of different violent pasts creates ruptures between Robert and Ana.

Robert's relationship with Ana not only brings to light problems of repressing the past and the dangers of silence about past wars during peacetime,[44] but also highlights the difficulty of extracting the personal from the political. In addition, Robert's self-absorption demonstrates his inability to see beyond himself and leads the reader to question whether Germany has likewise suffered from a self-absorbed foreign policy. While he wants to know more about Ana and her past, Robert does not want to confront the fact that Ana's experiences may be connected to larger political events and that she might still be traumatized. After a discussion in bed with her, the narrator relates Robert's thoughts: "He had wanted to know what she had gone through because he sensed that she was still living with it. But she was giving the whole thing a political dimension, which seemed unfair and wrong in their situation, alone with each other and together in bed. Above all, it wasn't justified, given the reason for his question, which was that he cared for her very much."[45] Here, one can detect Robert's narcissism and annoyance as the object of his academic work, history, invades the confines of his private life.

Later in the novel, Ana finally tells Robert about her experience of being bombed in Belgrade in 1999: "Do you realise what it was like? No, how could you know? You've never experienced bombs falling on your home town. It's not like on television."[46] Ana claims that as a German, Robert, who experiences the war only through the medium of television, cannot understand her experiences. Rather than asking her what it felt like, Robert feels personally attacked and the narrator's focus switches from Ana quickly back to Robert: "This sounded like an accusation. It wasn't his fault, but he felt complicit. How could she blame him for observing the war from afar? Did this mean that he wasn't competent to speak about it?"[47] In Robert and Ana's relationship, screen memories prevail. In particular, Robert's obsession with understanding Ana, not through conversation with her, but primarily through the means of his profession—research, observation, and even a little detective work—only get him slightly closer to understanding her complicated past. The novel reveals that he is actually more concerned with his own identity. Ana and Robert's conversation ends in misunderstanding and does not allow for a discussion of the connection between the NATO bombing of Belgrade in 1999 and the legacy of the war in Bosnia and Herzegovina, which officially ended in 1995 and was the reason Ana and her mother fled Višegrad.

On another occasion, during a discussion of the NATO bombing of Serbian cities in 1999, the political tensions between Germany and Serbia are mirrored by the conflict brewing between Robert and Ana. Robert finds it absurd that the memory of the post-Yugoslav wars could interrupt his relationship with Ana, but also begins to question whether the NATO-led bombing of Belgrade was justified and considers how it affected his lover's family: "After all, the NATO attack on Serbia was driven by Germany's guilty conscience, its historic culpability. The German Minister for Foreign Affairs [Joschka Fischer] said he had learnt a lesson: no more Auschwitzes. And so bombs rained down on the city where Ana lived with her family and friends. What was their connection to Auschwitz?"[48] Here Robert acknowledges what journalist Hans Kundnani refers to as the "historical narcissism" of German politics. Kundnani claims that "because of the power of collective memory—in particular about the Third Reich and World War II—in Germany, foreign policy debates have had a tendency to become somewhat narcissistic ones that are as much about German identity as about the fate of the people and places on which they appear to center."[49] While Kundnani does not utilize the term screen memory, his analysis of the German debate surrounding the Kosovo War reveals that screen memories of World War II shielded Germany from a complete understanding of the politics in the present. During the political debate, the collective memory of Germans as World War II perpetrators was often invoked, a viewpoint that supported Joschka Fischer's argument for NATO intervention.[50] Kundnani argues that this historical narcissism leads to a focus on the identity of Germans and the role of Germany in the world rather than on the political, historical, and cultural background of the countries or people Germany purports to help. In the novel, Robert seems to recognize Germany's altruism as misguided by facile historical comparisons, but he fails to understand the historical complexity and tackle his own narcissism. Furthermore, while Germany's role as perpetrator is remembered, World War II memories of German victimhood, such as the Allied bombing of German cities and the rape of German women by the Russian army, are alluded to in Ana's memories, but do not inform German foreign policy.

Ana and Robert also discuss the effects of Holocaust imagery upon their understandings of more recent conflicts. Specifically, they discuss the ways in which the screen memory of the Holocaust is literally projected onto photos of a Serbian camp for Bosnian prisoners (a topic that Amila Becirbegovic explores in detail in the previous chapter of this volume). As Ana explains, "The problem is that here in Berlin, in Germany, people don't know what went on during the war. Their ideas come from a handful of images, like the emaciated men behind a barbed-wire fence. Or people running away from snipers. And so forth. Any judgement they make is going to be unreliable. It's like picking up a few pieces of a thousand-piece jigsaw, taking a look at them and then deciding you know the whole picture. If they'd seen different images, they might well have reached different conclusions."[51] In the original German, the novel's use of judicial language is more predominant in this last sentence: "Hättet ihr andere Bilder gesehen, wäre euer Urteil vielleicht anders ausgefallen."[52] The use of the word "Urteil" rather than "conclusions" evokes the multiple meanings of the word, which could be translated as "verdict" or "judgment," for example. Unfortunately, emphasis on the legal process is lost in the English translation. In this passage, Ana speaks of photos taken by a British television crew in 1992 at the Serbian-run Trnopolje camp, which depict emaciated Bosnian Muslims behind barbed wire.[53] Robert remembers the photos: "He knew that some kind of concentration camp had been constructed in Trnopolje and that these images, of a kind bred into the bone of German people, had caused huge outrage."[54]

As the passage above demonstrates, Holocaust iconography functions as a screen memory, dictating the interpretation of these images in Bosnia and pushing NATO politicians, not only in Germany but also in the United States and Great Britain, to act in the name of preventing another genocide. While that is a noble goal, the photos also short-circuited discussion and debate about a proper response by appealing to Holocaust tropes. These seemingly familiar images prompted reflexes, rather than leading to reflection. The legacy of the Holocaust was used to bemoan the world's lack of reaction to the genocide in Rwanda and later to justify the NATO airstrike of Serbian cities. While these are honorable objectives, critics such as media scholar Philip Hammond present the dangers of the discourse of humanitarianism and the "moral vocabulary" that dominated the 1990s.[55] Hammond explains that "The moralistic media consensus which developed in favor of intervention in the Balkans was premised on the notion that Western action to uphold human rights should override established principles of international law, particularly that of non-interference in the internal affairs of sovereign states. This development has been driven by the felt need of Western societies to discover some new moral purpose in the post–Cold War world, despite the disastrous consequences of intervention for those on the receiving end of their benevolence."[56] Robert acknowledges that Ana is a recipient of such "benevolence" and rightfully admits that such action was perhaps not justified in order to release Germans from their World War II guilt. Yet, while Ljubić presents the complicated legacy of the Holocaust in the present, Ana and Robert's conversation—like so many in the novel—ends abruptly. The novel therefore eschews the hard work of reflecting critically upon the role of Holocaust memory or the power of Holocaust imagery as a global signifier of evil, or upon Germany's attempts to develop a new identity as a nation trusted enough to undertake military intervention.

Furthermore, while Ljubić does not dismiss the importance of human rights, the various understandings of the past he presents certainly call the means of protecting them into question. On one occasion, he alludes to important debates about reconciling the human rights regime, an amorphous and elaborate global system to promote human rights, with state sovereignty. Ana reminds Robert that NATO invaded a sovereign nation and alludes to the presumed moral superiority of Westerners: "If it were true that the court [the tribunal at The Hague] is as unbiased as everyone says, they would've put Clinton and Schröder on trial and all the other western politicians as well. Everyone who was responsible for bombing a sovereign state. Which is what Serbia was, you know."⁵⁷ Robert responds with silence, yet again cutting off lines of communication. Despite the fact that dialogue is cut short on the level of the plot, the brief mention of the entangled histories of Germany and Serbia nevertheless invites the reader to further reflect upon the positive and negative repercussions of the multidirectionality of these memories.

The memory of Germans as perpetrators also plays an important role in *Stillness of the Sea*. Much like Germans, who for several generations were educated to shoulder the burden of an identity as perpetrators, Serbs bear a similar label following the post-Yugoslav wars. Philip Hammond explains that Serbs, much like earlier generations of Germans, were demonized following the 1990s wars and often equated with Nazis. Years later, however, Germans reversed the roles: "The conflict in Yugoslavia offered a self-flattering view of the West—as a beacon of democracy and civilization—and portrayed Yugoslavs, particularly the Serbs, as barbarians. However, many argued that the view of the Balkans as characterized by 'ancient ethnic hatreds' provided a convenient excuse for Western governments."⁵⁸ The violence in Yugoslavia, much like that in Rwanda, was seen as a natural event, and therefore did not require explanation since it seemed to spring from an immutable ethnic or racial "nature."

Furthermore, the media often portrayed the conflict as a simple battle between good and evil, and while many different ethnic groups committed atrocious acts, Serbs were disproportionately labeled as cruel perpetrators, or even fascists. Ana bemoans this fact and emphasizes the arbitrary nature of national identities: "I often feel that war defines all of us—Serbs, Croats and Bosnians. Who did what? Who has experienced what and where? Where does the guilt lie? Given the same time and place, I could easily have been born a Bosnian. I would be the same woman, but you would see me differently, because you would perceive me as a victim. But because I'm a Serb, everyone thinks of me as a potential culprit, even though they know nothing about my life."⁵⁹ This passage also emphasizes the power of wartime memory to dictate the identity of an entire ethnic group. Ana rightfully complains that such screen memories and one-sided understandings of history can at times silence the memories of individuals, explaining to Robert, "You know what it's like here ... When people find out I'm a Serb, they think I'm fascist if I don't admit to my guilt or, at least, the guilt of my people. They've no patience with any 'buts.' And that hurts me, because it denies me my own life story, my experiences. And it provokes me too. I end up defending something that I don't want to defend in the slightest."⁶⁰ Despite the fact that Ana feels her side of the story is ignored—and it is subordinated to Robert's story—it does find a voice in *Stillness of the Sea*. Robert's story as screen memory indeed partially blocks Ana's story from view, but the novel nevertheless allows some of her memories to shine through. While power dynamics may prevent the articulation of multidirectional memories in public discourse, literature can begin to pry open the power-laden gates of official memories. Rather than favoring one memory of World War II and of the post-Yugoslav wars over others, Ljubić's novel allows the memories to exist alongside each other, albeit in a tense and uneven relationship.

In addition to aligning Ana with the perpetrators due to her nationality, the novel complicates her status as victimizer by alluding to her as a rape victim during the war. Referring to Ana's insider knowledge about why her father may have ordered the death of more than forty people, Robert muses: "It's unimaginably tragic that you're probably the only one who knows why your father did what he did. You believe that he did it for you. Ana, you taught me about that passage, 'I will grind your bones to dust, And with your blood and it, I'll make a Paste, And of the Paste a Coffin I will rear . . .' It's Titus Andronicus, who speaks of the revenge he will take for the violation of his daughter."[61] This further muddles her classification as either victim or perpetrator, and sheds light upon her hesitance about sharing her experience with Robert. While Ana and Robert do not discuss it, Robert's understanding of Šimić as a loving father acting out of revenge, rather than as a nationalistic criminal, complicates the reader's indictment of Šimić. During another scene, Robert's friends celebrate Radovan Karadžić's indictment, but Ana explains that there is little to celebrate because the war is far from over: "'You believe that it's all over now,' she said. 'But it's not over. And it won't be over even when they tick the last name off their list.'"[62] Aisha, a young Muslim woman from Višegrad who sought asylum in Germany as a child, and whose friends died during the war—possibly at the hands of Ana's father—echoes Ana's claims. After meeting Robert at The Hague, she urges him to travel to Bosnia to better understand: "'You should go,' she tells him. 'People like you, who haven't lived there, have only watched the war on TV, you can't understand what it's really like. . . . People outside looking in might think that the war is over. . . . You'll learn that the people who lived through the war lead two lives, the one they have during the day and the other one, which starts when they go to bed and try to sleep.'"[63]

Robert does later travel to Sarajevo, where he meets Alija, a Muslim who offers to show him around Bosnia. As they stand on the bridge over the Drina River in Višegrad, where bodies were dropped en masse into the water during the civil war, Alija detects Robert's guilty feelings:

"'These are not your memories,' he [Alija] said. 'You lead your own life, deal with your own sorrows.'"[64] With these lines, *Stillness of the Sea* underscores a tension created throughout the novel concerning the responsibility of a peaceful Western Europe toward the rest of the world and the confusion that results from screen memories.[65] Ljubić does not present definitive conclusions, but highlights both the benefits and the adverse side effects of humanitarian intervention and the challenge of determining which memories and histories will inform decision-making in the present.

EXPORTING THE PAST OR LEARNING LESSONS AT HOME?

As Robert becomes obsessed with Ana's past in a distant country, *Stillness of the Sea* also exposes the legacy of National Socialism in Germany today. Unlike the political debates surrounding the NATO-led bombing of Serbia in 1999, the novel not only demonstrates how lessons of the Nazi past impacted Serbia, but also how memories of the war in the former Yugoslavia and the resulting migrations are shaping life in Europe today—even in Germany. For example, on a trip to the North Sea with Ana, neo-Nazis force Robert to pull over and then question him about his nationality, stating, "You look a bit like an Eyetie or a Yugo."[66] Robert does not acknowledge his Croatian roots, claiming only his German identity, and the neo-Nazis leave. The novel does not offer further reflection upon this occurrence, and Ana and Robert do not discuss it. However, the hatred shown toward minority groups in Germany in this scene brings a domestic problem to the forefront: xenophobia in Germany. While the screen memory of National Socialism is projected upon the Balkans, the legacy of this tainted past within Germany today is sometimes overlooked. Immigrants, in particular, "often find themselves confronted with the ghosts of the past at the same time that they experience the prejudices of the present."[67] *Stillness of the Sea* alludes to the historical legacy of these present domestic prejudices, but also reveals how these injustices are often overshadowed by distant foreign conflicts.

In *Stillness of the Sea*, Ljubić draws many historical analogies between Germans, Croatians, Serbs, and Muslims, thus creating an intricate network of intertwined histories. However, more often than not, these memories lead to competition or simply resignation due to the complexities and pain associated with the different memories. By the end of the novel, Robert and Ana are no longer on speaking terms, as they are unable to reconcile their pasts in the present. This is primarily due to Robert's inability to fully understand Ana's experience of war, which he claims leads her to act as though she were morally superior: "Your wartime experiences... don't confer moral superiority, you know."[68] Yet again, Ana and

Robert's disagreement does not lead to further discussion of their different experiences, but rather to silence: "Her lips moved, and he realised that she had been about to say something, but then changed her mind."[69] In addition, despite the fact that the novel provides sufficient information to indict Ana's father, he goes free due to the ICTY's inability to produce the evidence needed to convict him. Both the dissolution of the romance and the release of Šimić come as disappointments to the reader. While the novel portrays challenges to the productive interaction of memories of violent pasts and the difficultly of bringing the guilty to justice, readers are left to their own devices to imagine more just futures.[70]

Through the articulation of memories that exceed the confines of a single nation-state, Nicol Ljubić's *Stillness of the Sea* calls into question a German postwar national myth, namely the myth of a post-national Germany that has overcome its Nazi past. *Stillness of the Sea* complicates political parallels drawn between the Nazi-perpetrated Holocaust and ethnic cleansing in the former Yugoslavia through the articulation of personal and familial stories of war and migration. In particular, the novel raises important questions about tensions between the human rights regime, respect of national sovereignty, and how the past should or should not inform foreign policy decisions. It depicts a nation blinded by its post–World War II identity and by an emphasis on foreign conflicts, rather than pressing domestic concerns, such as Germany's relative negligence in combating right-wing extremism and neo-Nazism. Despite the methodological challenges of writing about "ultracontemporary literature,"[71] I nevertheless assert the importance of such an endeavor, as it allows for scholarly focus not only upon the past or imaginings of the future, but also upon the artistic articulation of present-day societal concerns. It is my hope that my analysis of Ljubić's novel illuminates a number of complexities surrounding historical analogy and memorial networks in literary texts about German-Balkan encounters.

While *Stillness of the Sea* succeeds in exposing screen memories and initiating conversations about the nature of international politics and memory in the late twentieth and early twenty-first century, I argue that the novel nevertheless often closes off dialogue rather than foster dialogic exchange between memories of violence around the world. *Stillness of the Sea* is largely characterized by silences (as the German title *Meeresstille* suggests) and unanswered questions, and full of abruptly ended conversations and repressed memories. Upon completion of the novel, the reader is left to navigate the silences of repressed or forgotten memories and the cacophony of a crowded memorial landscape.

NOTES

INTRODUCTION: GERMAN-BALKAN ENTANGLED HISTORIES IN THE TWENTIETH CENTURY

1. Otto von Bismark and Horst Kohl, *Die politischen Reden des Fürsten Bismarck*, vol. 6, *1873–1876* (Stuttgart: J. G. Cotta, 1893), 461. For more than a century, Bismarck's statement has been mistranslated into English as referring to "the whole of the Balkans" rather than the more accurate "the entire Orient." Nevertheless, Bismarck was discussing developments in the Balkans when he made the statement. See Margaret Lavinia Anderson, "'Down in Turkey, far away': Human Rights, the Armenian Massacres, and Orientalism in Wilhelmine Germany," *Journal of Modern History* 79, no. 1 (March 2007): 110–11, 111n116.

2. On the so-called Eastern Crisis of 1875–1878, see A. L. Macfie, *The Eastern Question, 1774–1923*, rev. ed. (New York: Longman, 1996), 34–45.

3. Bismarck's Balkan and Ottoman policy during these years was focused not on German gains in the region, but on using diplomacy to avoid a major European war over control of the region. See Sean McMeekin, "Benevolent Contempt: Bismarck's Ottoman Policy," in *War and Diplomacy: The Russo-Turkish War of 1877–1878 and the Treaty of Berlin*, ed. Peter Sluglett and M. Hakan Yavuz (Salt Lake City: University of Utah Press, 2011), 79–85.

4. Lothar Gall, "Die europäischen Mächte und der Balkan im 19. Jahrhundert," in *Der Berliner Kongress von 1878: Die Politik der Grossmächte und die Probleme der Modernisierung in Südosteuropa in der Zweiten Hälfte des 19. Jahrhunderts*, ed. Ralph Melville and Hans-Jürgen Schröder (Wiesbaden: Franz Steiner Verlag, 1982), 1–16.

5. Lothar Gall, *Bismarck: The White Revolutionary*, vol. 2, *1871–1898*, trans. J. A. Underwood (London: Allen and Unwin, 1986), 48–55.

6. Henry Cord Meyer, *Mitteleuropa in German Thought and Action, 1815–1945* (The Hague: Martinus Nijhoff, 1955), 30–32.

7. Paul Dehn, *Deutschland und die Orientbahnen* (Munich: G. Franz'sche h.b. Hof- Buch- und Kunst-handlung [J. Roth], 1883), 42.

8. On German plans to gain influence in the Balkans in the late nineteenth and early twentieth century, see Stephen G. Gross, *Export Empire: German Soft*

Power in Southeastern Europe, 1890–1945 (Cambridge: Cambridge University Press, 2015), 34–44. On the Berlin to Baghdad railway, see Sean McMeekin, *The Berlin-Baghdad Express: The Ottoman Empire and Germany's Bid for World Power, 1898–1918* (London: Penguin, 2010).

9. Ulf Brunnbauer and Klaus Buchenau, *Geschichte Südosteuropas* (Ditzingen: Reclam, 2018), 284–285; R. J. Crampton, "The Balkans," in *Twisted Paths: Europe, 1914–1945*, ed. Robert Gerwarth (New York: Oxford University Press, 2007), 268; and Tony Judt, *Postwar: A History of Europe since 1945* (New York: Penguin Books, 2005), 17–18.

10. Mark Biondich, *The Balkans: Revolution, War, and Political Violence since 1878* (Oxford: Oxford University Press, 2011), 151–153.

11. Albania also broke with the Soviet Union and the Warsaw Pact over the course of the 1960s, but unlike Greece and Yugoslavia, it remained internationally isolated.

12. In the section of this volume dealing with the postwar era, the focus is on the Federal Republic's relationship with the Balkans. There is currently little historical scholarship on East Germany's relationship with the Balkans. See, however, Friederike Baer, *Zwischen Anlehnung und Abgrenzung: Die Jugoslawienpolitik der DDR 1946 bis 1968* (Cologne: Böhlau, 2009).

13. On German settlement in eastern Europe, see Martyn Rady, "The German Settlement in Central and Eastern Europe during the High Middle Ages," in *The German Lands and Eastern Europe: Essays on the History of Their Social, Cultural and Political Relations*, ed. Roger Bartlett and Karen Schönwälder (New York: St. Martin's Press, 1999), 11–47; and Roger Bartlett and Bruce Mitchell, "State-Sponsored Immigration into Eastern Europe in the Eighteenth and Nineteenth Centuries," in *German Lands*, ed. Bartlett and Schönwälder, 91–114.

14. Michael Burleigh, *Germany Turns Eastwards: A Study of Ostforschung in the Third Reich* (Cambridge: Cambridge University Press, 1988), 4.

15. Important studies of Germany and the east, broadly conceived, include Bartlett and Schönwälder, *German Lands*; Burleigh, *Germany Turns Eastward*; Charles W. Ingrao and Franz A. J. Szabo, eds., *The Germans and the East* (West Lafayette, IN: Purdue University Press, 2008); Vejas Gabriel Liulevicius, *The German Myth of the East: 1800 to the Present* (Oxford: Oxford University Press, 2009); Annemarie H. Sammartino, *The Impossible Border: Germany and the East, 1914–1922* (Ithaca, NY: Cornell University Press, 2010); Gregor Thum, ed., *Traumland Osten: Deutsche Bilder vom östlichen Europa im 20. Jahrhundert* (Göttingen: Vandenhoeck & Ruprecht, 2006); Wolfgang Wippermann, *Der "deutsche Drang nach Osten": Ideologie und Wirklichkeit eines politischen Schlagwortes* (Darmstadt: Wissenschaftliche Buchgesellschaft, 1981); and Wolfgang Wippermann, *Die Deutschen und der Osten: Feindbild und Traumland* (Darmstadt: Primus Verlag, 2007).

16. For a brief overview of this literature as well as a critique of the continuity thesis, see Winson Chu, Jesse Kauffman, and Michael Meng, "A *Sonderweg* through Eastern Europe? The Varieties of German Rule in Poland during the Two World Wars," *German History* 31, no. 3 (September 2013): 318–344, especially 318–24.

17. This literature is now enormous. Important recent studies include Chad Bryant, *Prague in Black: Nazi Rule and Czech Nationalism* (Cambridge, MA: Harvard University Press, 2007); Winson Chu, *The German Minority in Interwar Poland* (Cambridge: Cambridge University Press, 2012); Benjamin Frommer, *National Cleansing: Retribution against Nazi Collaborators in Postwar Czechoslovakia* (Cambridge: Cambridge University Press, 2005); Brendan Karch, *Nation and Loyalty in a German-Polish Borderland: Upper Silesia, 1848–1960* (Cambridge: Cambridge University Press, 2018); Vejas Gabriel Liulevicius, *War Land on the Eastern Front: Culture, National Identity, and German Occupation in World War I* (Cambridge: Cambridge University Press, 2000); Wendy Lower, *Nazi Empire-Building and the Holocaust in Ukraine* (Chapel Hill: University of North Carolina Press, 2005); Burkhard Olschowsky and Ingo Loose, eds., *Nationalsozialismus und Regionalbewusstsein im östlichen Europa* (Munich: De Gruyter Oldenbourg, 2016); Eric C. Steinhart, *The Holocaust and the Germanization of Ukraine* (New York: Cambridge University Press, 2015); John C. Swanson, *Tangible Belonging: Negotiating Germanness in Twentieth-Century Hungary* (Pittsburgh, PA: University of Pittsburgh Press, 2017); Gerhard Wolf, *Ideologie und Herrschaftsrationalität: Nationalsozialistische Germanisierungspolitik in Polen* (Hamburg: Hamburger Edition, 2012); and Tara Zahra, *Kidnapped Souls: National Indifference and the Battle for Children in the Bohemian Lands, 1900–1948* (Ithaca, NY: Cornell University Press, 2011).

18. This growing literature is referred to throughout the introduction and especially in the individual chapters. See also Carl Bethke, *Deutsche und ungarische Minderheiten in Kroatien und der Vojvodina 1918-1941: Identitätsentwürfe und ethnopolitische Mobilisierung* (Wiesbaden: Harrassowitz, 2009); Gaëlle Fisher, *Resettlers and Survivors: Bukovina and the Politics of Belonging in West Germany and Israel, 1945–1989* (New York: Berghahn, 2020); Emily Greble, *Sarajevo, 1941–1945: Muslims, Christians, and Jews in Hitler's Europe* (Ithaca, NY: Cornell University Press, 2011); Mariana Hausleitner, *"Viel Mischmasch mitgenommen": Die Umsiedlungen aus der Bukowina 1940* (Berlin: De Gruyter Oldenbourg, 2018); and Caroline Mezger, *Forging Germans: Youth, Nation, and the National Socialist Mobilization of Ethnic Germans in Yugoslavia, 1918–1944* (Oxford: Oxford University Press, 2020).

19. Liulevicius, *German Myth*; and Wippermann, *Die Deutschen und der Osten*. See also Kristin Kopp, *Germany's Wild East: Constructing Poland as Colonial Space* (Ann Arbor: University of Michigan Press, 2012); and James E.

Casteel, *Russia in the German Global Imaginary: Imperial Visions and Utopian Desires, 1905–1941* (Pittsburgh, PA: Pittsburgh University Press, 2016).

20. Larry Wolff, *Inventing Eastern Europe: The Map of Civilization on the Mind of the Enlightenment* (Stanford, CA: Stanford University Press, 1994), 4.

21. Maria Todorova, *Imagining the Balkans* (Oxford: Oxford University Press, 1997). See also Larry Wolff, *Venice and the Slavs: The Discovery of Dalmatia in the Age of Enlightenment* (Stanford, CA: Stanford University Press, 2001).

22. Eliga H. Gould, "Entangled Histories, Entangled Worlds: The English-Speaking Atlantic as a Spanish Periphery," *The American Historical Review* 112, no. 3 (June 2007): 76. See also Jürgen Kocka, "Comparison and Beyond," *History and Theory* 42, no. 1 (February 2003): 39–44. For recent examples of this approach in the broad field of German-Russian history, see Timothy Snyder, *Bloodlands: Europe between Hitler and Stalin* (New York: Basic Books, 2010); and Michael David-Fox, Peter Holquist, and Alexander M. Martin, eds., *Fascination and Enmity: Russia and Germany as Entangled Histories, 1914–1945* (Pittsburgh, PA: University of Pittsburgh Press, 2012).

23. Stevan K. Pavlowitch, *A History of the Balkans, 1804–1945* (New York: Routledge, 2014), 4–14.

24. Todorova, *Imagining the Balkans*, 162.

25. Friedrich Naumann, *Central Europe*, trans. Christabel M. Meredith (New York: Alfred A. Knopf, 1917), 1.

26. Naumann, *Central Europe*, 2–3. Naumann was purposefully vague about which states would constitute part of Mitteleuropa, but it is clear that he viewed the Balkans as a key part of his plans.

27. Meyer, *Mitteleuropa*, 203. See also David Hamlin, *Germany's Empire in the East: Germans and Romania in an Era of Globalization and Total War* (Cambridge: Cambridge University Press, 2017), 161–62.

28. Biondich, *Balkans*, 88–89; Jonathan E. Gumz, *The Resurrection and Collapse of Empire in Habsburg Serbia, 1914–1918* (Cambridge: Cambridge University Press, 2009); John R. Lampe, *Balkans into Southeastern Europe, 1914–2014: A Century of War and Transition*, 2nd ed. (New York: Palgrave Macmillan, 2014), 39–43; and Pavlowitch, *History of the Balkans*, 220. On the German occupation of Romania, see Lisa Mayerhofer, *Zwischen Freund und Feind: Deutsche Besatzung in Rumänien, 1916–1918* (Frankfurt: Peter Lang, 2010).

29. Borislav Chernev, *Twilight of Empire: The Brest-Litovsk Conference and the Remaking of East-Central Europe, 1917–1918* (Toronto: University of Toronto Press, 2017); David Hamlin, "'The World Will Have a New Face': Germans and the Post–World War I Global Economic Order," *Central European History* 52, no. 2 (June 2019): 233–51; Hamlin, *Germany's Empire*, 8–11, 281–306; Jesse Kauffman, *Elusive Alliance: The German Occupation of Poland in World War I* (Cambridge, MA: Harvard University Press, 2015); Lampe, *Balkans into Southeastern Europe*, 46–47; Liulevicius, *War Land*; and Adam Tooze, *The Deluge:*

The Great War, America and the Remaking of the Global Order, 1916–1931 (New York: Penguin Books, 2014).

30. Gross, *Export Empire*, 2. See also Carl Freytag, *Deutschlands "Drang nach Südosten": Der Mitteleuropäische Wirtschaftstag und der "Ergänzungsraum Südosteuropa" 1931–1945* (Göttingen: V&R Unipress, 2012).

31. Gross, *Export Empire*, 3, 15, 17–18, 22–23; Lampe, *Balkans into Southeastern Europe*, 136–37, 146–48; and Mary C. Neuburger, *Balkan Smoke: Tobacco and the Making of Modern Bulgaria* (Ithaca, NY: Cornell University Press, 2013), 135, 139–41.

32. Biondich, *Balkans*, 130, 135.

33. Mark Mazower, *Inside Hitler's Greece: The Experience of Occupation, 1941–44* (New Haven, CT: Yale University Press, 1993), xiii, 23–52; and Gross, *Export Empire*, 292–329.

34. For a brief summary of resistance movements in Yugoslavia and Greece, see Lampe, *Balkans into Southeastern Europe*, 161–68; and Biondich, *Balkans*, 145–49.

35. Mazower, *Inside Hitler's Greece*, xiii, 155. See also Kateřina Králová, *Das Vermächtnis der Besatzung: Deutch-griechische Beziehungen seit 1940*, trans. Odysseas Antoniadis and Andrea Schellinger (Cologne: Böhlau Verlag, 2016), 50–58.

36. Ben Shepherd, *Terror in the Balkans: German Armies and Partisan Warfare* (Cambridge, MA: Harvard University Press, 2012).

37. Radu Ioanid, "Occupied and Satellite States," in *The Oxford Handbook of Holocaust Studies*, ed. Peter Hayes and John K. Roth (Oxford: Oxford University Press, 2010), 333; and James Frusetta, "The Final Solution in Southeastern Europe: Between Nazi Catalysts and Local Motivations," in *The Routledge History of the Holocaust*, ed. Jonathan C. Friedman (New York: Routledge, 2011), 266.

38. Mirna Zakić, *Ethnic Germans and National Socialism in Yugoslavia in World War II* (Cambridge: Cambridge University Press, 2017), 161–84.

39. Biondich, *Balkans*, 132; Frusetta, "Final Solution," 264–65, 268–71; and Ioanid, "Occupied and Satellite States," 326–29, 331.

40. Ivo Goldstein and Slavko Goldstein, *The Holocaust in Croatia* (Pittsburgh, PA: University of Pittsburgh Press, 2016); and Alexander Korb, *Im Schatten des Weltkriegs: Massengewalt der Ustaša gegen Serben, Juden, und Roma in Kroatien, 1941–1945* (Hamburg: Hamburger Edition, 2013). On Slovene collaboration with the Axis, see Gregor Joseph Kranjc, *To Walk with the Devil: Slovene Collaboration and Axis Occupation* (Toronto: University of Toronto Press, 2013).

41. Biondich, *Balkans*, 135–42, quotation on p. 136.

42. Lampe, *Balkans into Southeastern Europe*, 178–96. On the Greek Civil War, see Stathis N. Kalyvas, *The Logic of Violence in Civil War* (Cambridge: Cambridge University Press, 2006).

43. Jordan Baev, "The Establishment of Bulgarian–West German Diplomatic Relations within the Coordinating Framework of the Warsaw Pact,"

Journal of Cold War Studies 18, no. 3 (Summer 2016): 158–80; and William Glenn Gray, *Germany's Cold War: The Global Campaign to Isolate East Germany, 1949–1969* (Chapel Hill: University of North Carolina Press, 2003), 140, 180, 183–84.

44. West Germany established diplomatic relations with Romania in 1967 and Bulgaria in 1973; see Baev, "Bulgarian–West German Diplomatic Relations," 164, 173. Yugoslavia and West Germany established diplomatic relations in 1951, but West Germany severed these relations in 1957. The two states reestablished diplomatic relations in 1968; see Marc Christian Theurer, *Bonn, Belgrad, Ost-Berlin: Die Beziehungen der beiden deutschen Staaten zu Jugoslawien im Vergleich, 1957–1968* (Berlin: Logos-Verlag, 2008). West Germany and Albania did not establish diplomatic relations until 1986. On the Hallstein Doctrine, see Gray, *Germany's Cold War*.

45. Lampe, *Balkans into Southeastern Europe*, 226.

46. Neuburger, *Balkan Smoke*, 200–202.

47. Lampe, *Balkans into Southeastern Europe*, 226; and Mogens Pelt, *Tying Greece to the West: US-West German-Greek Relations, 1949–74* (Copenhagen: Museum Tusculanum Press, 2006).

48. Matthew Frank, *Making Minorities History: Population Transfer in Twentieth-Century Europe* (Oxford: Oxford University Press, 2017), 125; and Valdis O. Lumans, *Himmler's Auxiliaries: The Volksdeutsche Mittelstelle and the German National Minorities of Europe, 1933–1945* (Chapel Hill: University of North Carolina Press, 1993), 171–76. On Germany's racial resettlement program more generally, see Isabel Heinemann, *"Rasse, Siedlung, deutsches Blut": Das Rasse- und Siedlungshauptamt der SS und die rassenpolitische Neuordnung Europas* (Göttingen: Wallstein Verlag, 2003).

49. R. M. Douglas, *Orderly and Humane: The Expulsion of the Germans after the Second World War* (New Haven, CT: Yale University Press, 2012), 62–63, 110–13, 116, 122–23, 151; and Mathias Beer, *Flucht und Vertreibung der Deutschen: Voraussetzungen, Verlauf, Folgen* (Munich: C. H. Beck, 2011), 86–93.

50. On expellees and West German memory culture, see Robert G. Moeller, *War Stories: The Search for a Useable Past in the Federal Republic of Germany* (Berkeley: University of California Press, 2001), 51–87; and Gilad Margalit, *Guilt, Suffering, and Memory: Germany Remembers Its Dead of World War II*, trans. Haim Watzman (Bloomington: Indiana University Press, 2010), 186–220. On postwar trials and West German memory of the Third Reich, see Devin O. Pendas, *The Frankfurt Auschwitz Trial, 1963–1965: Genocide, History, and the Limits of the Law* (Cambridge: Cambridge University Press, 2006); Caroline Sharples, *West Germans and the Nazi Legacy* (New York: Routledge, 2012); and Rebecca Wittmann, *Beyond Justice: The Auschwitz Trial* (Cambridge, MA: Harvard University Press, 2005).

51. Ulrich Herbert, *Geschichte der Ausländerpolitik in Deutschland:*

Saisonarbeiter, Zwangsarbeiter, Gastarbeiter, Flüchtlinge (Munich: C. H. Beck, 2001); and Geoffrey Swain, *Tito: A Biography* (London: I. B. Tauris, 2011), 6.

52. On the origins of the West German labor recruitment program, see Herbert, *Geschichte der Ausländerpolitik*, 202–16; and Rita Chin, *The Guest Worker Question in Postwar Germany* (Cambridge: Cambridge University Press, 2007), 33–41.

53. Maren Möhring, *Fremdes Essen: Die Geschichte der ausländischen Gastronomie in der Bundesrepublik Deutschland* (Munich: Oldenbourg, 2012), 313–83.

54. Alexander Clarkson, *Fragmented Fatherland: Immigration and Cold War Conflict in the Federal Republic of Germany, 1945–1980* (New York: Berghahn, 2013), 126–27.

55. Christopher A. Molnar, "Imagining Yugoslavs: Migration and the Cold War in Postwar West Germany," *Central European History* 47, no. 1 (March 2014): 159–66.

56. Richard Caplan, *Europe and the Recognition of New States in Yugoslavia* (Cambridge: Cambridge University Press, 2005), 41–43; and Brendan Simms, "From the Kohl to the Fischer Doctrine: Germany and the Wars of the Yugoslav Succession, 1991–1999," *German History* 21, no. 3 (July 2003): 400–401.

57. Christopher A. Molnar, *Memory, Politics, and Yugoslav Migrations to Postwar Germany* (Bloomington: Indiana University Press, 2018), 161–90.

58. Daniel Levy and Natan Sznaider discuss Holocaust memory and the Kosovo War under the chapter subheading "Germany Liberates Auschwitz in Kosovo," in *The Holocaust and Memory in the Global Age*, trans. Assenka Oksiloff (Philadelphia: Temple University Press, 2006), 166–70. See also Simms, "Kohl to the Fischer Doctrine," 404–8; Hans Kundnani, *The Paradox of German Power* (Oxford: Oxford University Press, 2015), 50–53.

59. Claudia Sternberg, Kila Gartzou-Katsouyanni, and Kalypso Nicolaïdis, *The Greco-German Affair in the Euro Crisis: Mutual Recognition Lost?* (London: Palgrave Macmillan, 2017), especially 46–60; and Klaus Neumann, "German Debts: Entangled Histories of the Greek-German Relationship and Their Varied Effects," *German Politics and Society* 34, no. 3 (Autumn 2016): 77–99.

60. Frank Decker, "The 'Alternative for Germany': Factors Behind Its Emergence and the Profile of a New Right-Wing Populist Party," *German Politics and Society* 34, no. 2 (June 2016): 1–16; Gregory J. Goalwin, "Population Exchange and the Politics of Ethno-Religious Fear: The EU–Turkey Agreement on Syrian Refugees in Historical Perspective," *Patterns of Prejudice* 52, nos. 2–3 (2018): 121–34; and Federico Giulio Sicurella, "The Language of Walls along the Balkan Route," *Journal of Immigrant and Refugee Studies* 16, nos. 1–2 (2018): 57–75.

61. Quoted in "Sasa Stanisic wins German Book Prize, criticizes Nobel winner Peter Handke," *DW.com*, October 14, 2019, www.dw.com/en/sasa-stanisic-wins-german-book-prize-criticizes-nobel-winner-peter-handke/a-50830275.

CHAPTER 1. "A COLONY OF THE CENTRAL POWERS"

1. Richard Kühlmann, *Erinnerungen* (Heidelberg: Verlag Lambert Schneider, 1948), 555–56.

2. Peter Borowsky, *Deutsche Ukrainepolitik 1918: Unter besonderer Berücksichtigung der Wirtschaftsfragen* (Lübeck: Matthiesverlag, 1970); Fritz Fischer, *Germany's Aims in the First World War* (New York: W. W. Norton, 1967); Fritz Fischer, *War of Illusions: German Policies from 1911 to 1914* (New York: Chatto & Windus, 1975); Fritz Fischer, "Weltpolitik, Weltmachtstreben und deutsche Kriegsziele," *Historische Zeitschrift* 199, no. 2 (October 1964): 265–346; Martin Kitchen, *The Silent Dictatorship: The Politics of the German High Command under Hindenburg and Ludendorff, 1916–1918* (London: Croom Helm, 1976); Wolfgang J. Mommsen, "The Debate on German War Aims," *Journal of Contemporary History* 1, no. 3 (July 1966): 47–72; and Claus Remer, *Die Ukraine im Blickfeld deutscher Interessen: Ende des 19. Jahrhunderts bis 1917/18* (Frankfurt: Peter Lang, 1997).

3. Winfried Baumgart, *Deutsche Ostpolitik 1918: Von Brest-Litovsk bis zum Ende des Ersten Weltkrieges* (Vienna: R. Oldenbourg Verlag, 1966); Wolfdieter Bihl, *Österreich-Ungarn und die Friedensschlüsse von Brest-Litovsk* (Vienna: Verlag Böhlau, 1970); and Oleh Fedyshyn, *Germany's Drive to the East and the Ukrainian Revolution, 1917–1918* (New Brunswick: Rutgers University Press, 1971).

4. For more on this, see David Hamlin, "'The World Will Have a New Face': Germans and the Post–World War I Global Economic Order," *Central European History* 52, no. 2 (June 2019): 233–51.

5. Roy Bridge and Roger Bullen, *The Great Powers and the European State System* (New York: Routledge, 2004), 214–16, 224; and Otto von Bismarck to Ambassador in Vienna, Heinrich VII, Prince Reuss, August 19, 1883, in *Die grosse Politik der europäischen Kabinette, 1871–1914*, vol. 3 (Berlin, 1922–1927), 263.

6. Leo von Caprivi to Reuss, March 26, 1891, *Die grosse Politik*, vol. 7, 158–60. See also Memorandum of Chancellor von Caprivi, May 11, 1890, *Die grosse Politik*, vol. 9, 28–33, and von Caprivi's assertion that Russia's only secure path to the Dardanelles was through Romania, Memo of Chancellor von Caprivi, October 29, 1891, *Die grosse Politik*, vol. 7, 170–71. For more on German military policy, see Terence Zuber, *German War Planning, 1891–1914: Sources and Interpretations* (Suffolk: Boydell Press, 2004).

7. King Carol of Romania to Bernhard von Bülow, 1888, quoted in Gheorge Nicolae Cazan and Serban Radulescu-Zoner, *Rumänien und der Dreibund, 1878–1914* (Bucharest: Editura Academiei Republicii Socialiste Romania, 1983), 61, more generally on conclusion of the alliance, 50–77.

8. Bismarck to Reuss, September 8, 1883, *Die grosse Politik*, vol. 3, 265–68.

9. Sasanow Memorandum for Tsar Nicholas II, June 11, 1914, in *Die Internationalen Beziehungen im Zeitalter des Imperialismus: Dokumente aus den Archiven der Zarischen und der Provisorischen Regierungen, Reihe 1, 3. Band, 15 Mai bis 27 Juni* (Berlin: Reimar Hobbing, 1933), 293–99. See also Julius von Waldthausen to AA, November 2, 1912, *Die grosse Politik*, vol. 33, 266–67; Tschirschky report, November 13, 1912, *Die grosse Politik*, vol. 33, 413; Bericht aus Bukarest, November 14, 1912, in *Österreich-Ungarns Aussenpolitik: Von der Bosnischen Krise 1908 bis zum Kriegsausbruch 1914 (ÖUA), Band IV* (Vienna: Österreichischer Bundesverlag, 1930), 870–72; Waldburg to Theobald von Bethmann-Hollweg, July 3, 1914, Politisches Archiv des Auswärtigen Amtes (hereafter PA AA), R9.655; and Katrin Boeckh, *Von den Balkankriegen zum Ersten Weltkrieg: Kleinstaatenpolitik und ethnische Selbstbestimmung auf dem Balkan* (Munich: R. Oldenbourg Verlag, 1996), 282–84. On Austro-Hungarian distaste for the Treaty of Bucharest, see John Leslie, "The Antecedents of Austria-Hungary's War Aims: Policies and Policy-Makers in Vienna and Budapest before and during 1914," *Wiener Beiträge zur Geschichte der Neuzeit* 20 (1993): 335–36.

10. Walter Goerlitz, ed., *Der Kaiser ... Aufzeichnungen des Chefs des Marinekabinetts Admiral Georg Alexander v. Mueller über die Ära Wilhelms II* (Berlin: Musterschmidt Verlag, 1965), 124–25.

11. Waldthausen to Bethmann-Hollweg, April 19, 1914, *Die grosse Politik*, vol. 39, 502.

12. Kiderlen, November 28, 1912, Yale University, Kiderlen-Wächter Papers, Box 10, Folder 0040185.

13. Jahresbericht über den Gang des Handels im Jahre 1901, April 8, 1902, Bundesarchiv Lichterfelde (hereafter BL) AA, 53484, bl. 215–16; Kaiserliche Konsulät Bucharest, May 12, 1913, "Die rumänische Petroleumindustrie im Jahre 1912," BL, R3101/2306, bl. 35–53; Waldburg to Bethmann-Hollweg, October 19, 1913, National Archives and Records Administration (hereafter NARA), Captured German Records Collection, T-136, Reel 87, AA Finanzen Rumäniens 1910–1914; Rosenberg memorandum, November 11, 1913, NARA, Captured German Records Collection, T-136, Reel 87; "Die deutschen Auslandsbanken am Balkan," *Balkan Revue* 1, no. 1 (April 1914): 11–22; "Deutschlands Handel mit den Balkanstaaten," *Balkan Revue* 1, no. 1 (April 1914): 490; "Rumänische Geld- und Bankwesen im Jahre 1913," *Balkan Revue* 1, no. 12 (March 1915): 753–58; and Karsten Steinke, *Die Internationalisierung britischer, französischer und deutscher Kreditinstitute aus historischer Sicht: Von der industriellen Revolution bis zur Gegenwart* (Aachen: Shaker Verlag, 2000), 84.

14. Jahresbericht 1899, January 1901, BL AA, Microfilm 53483, bl. 119–20; "Zur wirtschaftliche Lage Rumäniens," *Kölnische Zeitung*, August 4, 1909, BL R901/1976; Kaiserliche Konsulät Bucharest, May 12, 1913, "Die rumänische Petroleumindustrie im Jahre 1912," BL, R3101/2306, bl. 35–53; Jean-Mircea Nicolescu, *Das Währungsproblem in Rumänien in der Nachkriegszeit* (Bucharest:

Graphisches Institut Vremea, 1935); and Maurice Pearton, *Oil and the Romanian State* (London: Clarendon Press, 1971), 68-69.

15. Adam Tooze and Ted Fertik, "The World Economy and the Great War," *Geschichte und Gesellschaft* 40, no. 2 (June 2014): 220. For a fuller treatment of the British mobilization of the global economy, see Adam Tooze, *The Deluge: The Great War, America and the Remaking of the Global Order, 1916-1931* (New York: Viking, 2014).

16. A. C. Bell, *A History of the Blockade of Germany and of the Countries Associated with Her in the Great War: Austria-Hungary, Bulgaria, and Turkey* (London: H. M. Stationery Office, 1961); Nicholas Lambert, *Planning Armageddon: British Economic Warfare and the First World War* (Cambridge, MA: Harvard University Press, 2012); and Eric W. Osborne, *Britain's Economic Blockade of Germany, 1914-1919* (London: Routledge, 2004).

17. *Conférence économique des Gouvernements Alliés tenue à Paris les 14, 15, 16 et 17 Juin 1916: Programme* (Paris, 1916); "Der Wirtschaftskrieg nach dem Kriegsende. Die Pariser Wirtschaftskonferenz und ihre Folgen für Deutschland," November 1916, BL, R3010/1854, bl. 12-112; and Willi Prion, *Die Pariser Wirtschaftskonferenz* (Berlin: Heymann Verlag, 1917).

18. See press clippings in BL, R901/4172, bl. 2-12; Dr. W. Prion an der Deutsche Weltwirtschaftlichen Gesellschaft betr. Pariser Wirtschaftsbeschl., November 23, 1916, BL, R901/4172, bl. 89-92. See also "The Allies' Economic Combine," *The New Republic*, July 8, 1916, 239-40.

19. Karl Helfferich to Trautmann, Legationsrat AA, December 28, 1917, BL, R704/26, bl. 2-3; Metallgesellschaft to Regierungsrat Dr. Hertel, Reichswirtschaftamt, March 25, 1918, BL, R3101/1854, bl. 335.

20. E.g., Prion, *Pariser Wirtschaftskonferenz*; Friedrich Kahl, *Die Pariser Wirtschaftskonferenz vom 14. bis 17. Juni 1916 und die ihr voraufgegangenen gemeinsamen Beratungen der Ententestaaten über den Wirtschaftskrieg gegen die Mittelmächte* (Jena: Gustav Fischer Verlag, 1917); Otto Jöhlinger, *Der britische Wirtschaftskrieg und seine Methoden* (Berlin: Julius Springer, 1918); and Peter Heinrich Schmidt, *Der Wirtschaftskrieg und die Neutralen* (Zurich: Schultess & Co., 1918).

21. Schlußbericht zu der Zusammenstellung der Ergebnisse, die die bisherigen Erhebungen des Reichswirtschaftsamts über die Sicherung des Rohstoffbezug gebat haben, June 29, 1918, BL, R3101/20804, bl. 22.

22. Besprechung vom 17. Juli 1918 über die Veranstaltung einer Erhebung zur Vorbereitung des Wirtschaftsfriedens, BL, R3101/20804, bl. 66-87.

23. Otto Czernin (Consul in Sofia) to Czernin, February 17, 1918, and Pallavicini to Czernin, February 18, 1918, Österreichisches Staatsarchiv, Haus- Hof- und Staatsarchiv (HHStA), MdÄ PA 1, 1055 Krieg 70/14; Lersner to Kühlmann March 15, 1918, BL, R3101/1890, bl. 208; Kühlmann, *Erinnerungen*, 552-59; and Elke Bornemann, *Der Frieden von Bukarest 1918* (Frankfurt: Peter Lang, 1978).

24. "Besprechung über die Versorgung der deutschen bürgerlichen Bevölkerung mit Leuchtöl im Winter 1918-19," July 26, 1918, BL, R703/76, bl. 26-29. The document says June 26, but the content and the invitations make clear the document is from July.

On the projected impact of petroleum shortages on food supplies, see also "Aufzeichnung der im Reichswirtschaftsamt (RWA) Besprechung über Petroleumverteilung," November 14, 1917, BL, R3101/7743, bl. 222; and RWA, "Denkschrift über die Versorgung der deutschen bürgerlichen Be völkerung mit Leuchtöl im Winter 1918-19," early July 1918, BL, R703/76, bl. 11-14.

25. Aktenvermerk über eine Besprechung mit Vertreter des Wirtschaftsstabes in Rumänien, Hauptmann Dr. Hopf, undated, BL, R3101/7743, bl. 401-4. See also Hopf, Denkschrift betrf. Nutzbarmachung der rumänischen Erdölindustrie im deutschen Interesse für die Zeit nach dem Krieg, September 1917, BL, R3101/7743, bl. 404.

26. "Vorschläge über Konsolidierung der deutschen und rumänischen Interessen in der rumänischen Petroleum-Industrie unter Zusammenwirken der Regierung der beiden Länder und Beteiligung von Österreich-Ungarn," November 24, 1917, and "Aufzeichnung über die Fortsetzung der Besprechung über Liquidation feindlicher Erdölunternehmungen in Rumänien," December 8, 1917, BL, R31010/7744, bl. 67-74, 44-48; and Dr. Georg Solmssen to Wirklich Geheimrat Körner, March 5, 1918, BL, R3101/1891, bl. 40-57.

27. "Entwurf des Auswärtigen Amts, abgeändert auf Grund der kommissarischen Beratung vom 15 Dez 1917," BL, R3101/1422, bl. 43-49; Helfferich memorandum of February 19 meeting, BL, R3101/1890, bl. 158-168; report of February 18, 1918, discussions, Herr von Rosenberg to Herr Göppert, March 22, 1918, BL, R704/71, bl. 45-47, 99; and Gerald D. Feldman "German Business Interests and Rumanian Oil in the First World War," *Germany and Southeastern Europe— Aspects of Relations in the Twentieth Century*, ed. Roland Schönfeld (Munich: Südosteuropa-Gesellschaft, 1997), 23-26.

Further examples of state suspicion of private oil interests in Aufzeichnung einer Besprechung am 6. Dez betr. Liquidation feindlicher Rohölunternehmungen in Rumänien, BL, R3101/33151, bl. 15-20; and "Aufzeichnung über die Fortsetzung der Besprechung über Liquidation feindlicher Erdölunternehmungen in Rumänien," December 8, 1917, BL, R3101/7744, bl. 44-48.

28. "Entwurf des Auswärtigen Amts, abgeändert auf Grund der kommissarischen Beratung vom 15 Dez 1917," BL, R3101/1422, bl. 43-49.

29. Forderungen der M. Verw. in Rumänien vom Dez. 1917, "Entwurf des Auswärtigen Amtes für den Friedensvertrag mit Rumänien. Forderungen betreffend die Erdölindustrie," December 20, 1917, BL, R704/71, bl. 23-24, 4-10; III. Teil Wirtschaftliche Sicherungen, BL, R3101/1890, bl. 40-47; Anlage 1.A. Forderungen betreffend die Erdölindustrie, BL, R3101/1890, bl. 66-70; and Staatssekretär des Reichsschatzamtes to Helfferich, March 2, 1918, BL, R704/71, bl. 51-55.

On concessions in the Middle East, see George Lenczowski, *Oil and the State in the Middle East* (Ithaca: Cornell University Press, 1960), 64–67.

30. Dietrich Eichholtz, *Krieg um Öl: Ein Erdölimperium als deutsches Kriegsziel, 1938–1943* (Leipzig: Leipziger Universitätsverlag, 2006).

31. Reichsbank-Direktoriums, Havenstein and Glasnap to Reichskanzler, March 8, 1918, BL, R2/3889, bl. 5–16.

32. Gerald Feldman, *The Great Disorder: Politics, Economics, and Society in the German Inflation, 1914–1924* (Oxford: Oxford University Press, 1993), 49. See also Staatssekretär des Reichsschatzamtes Graf Roedern und Präsident des Reichsbank-Direktoriums Havenstein to Reichskanzler, July 29, 1918, BL, R2/3889.

33. Reichsbank-Direktoriums, Havenstein and Glasnap to Reichskanzler, March 8, 1918, BL, R2/3889, bl. 5–16; Reichsbank (Glasnap) to State Secretary's Economic Office, January 26, 1918, BL, R3101/1890, bl. 154–156; and Helfferich to Wirtschaftsamt, February 16, 1918, BL, R3101/845, bl. 36–37.

34. Deutsch-Rumänischer rechtspolitische Zusatzvertrag, Articles 2, 11, BL, R3101/1891, bl. 73–74, 87. See also commentary appended to treaty, BL, R3101/1891, 113–16, 122–23.

35. Helfferich on AA proposals, undated, probably January 1918, BL, R3101/1890, bl. 91–104.

36. Helfferich on AA proposals, BL, R3101/1890, bl. 91–104.

37. Helfferich memorandum of February 19 meeting, BL, R3101/1890, bl. 158–168; and Schoen to von Dandl, April 2, 1918, Bayerische Hauptstaatsarchiv (hereafter BayHStA), MA 97679.

38. E.g., Aufzeichnung über die Besprechung vom 1. Januar 1918 im Auswärtigen Amt über das Ergebnis der bisherigen Verhandlungen, BL, R2/2559, bl. 123–29; Reichsbank Direktorium to Kühlmann, April 29, 1918, BL, R901/81086, bl. 151.

39. Quoted in David Mitrany, *The Land and the Peasant in Romania: The War and Agrarian Reform, 1917–1921* (Oxford: Oxford University Press, 1930), 108.

40. For more on this, see David Hamlin, "Water and Empire," *First World War Studies* 3, no. 1 (Winter 2012): 65–85.

41. Hertling to Reichsamt des Innern/Auswärtiges Amt, January 9, 1917, and Hertling to "Kaiserlich Deutsche Generalgouvernement in Bukarest," January 9, 1917, BayHStA, MF 67588.

42. Bavarian Ministry of Finance to Hertling, February 5, 1917, BayHStA, MF 67588.

43. Chef des Generalstabes des Feldheeres to Reichswirtschaftsamt, April 4, 1918, BL, R3101/0845, bl. 36; Erich Ludendorff memorandum, undated, presumably April 1918, BL, R3101/0845, bl. 85; Chef des Generalstabes des Feldheer to Kapitänleutnant Boehner, Leiter des Schiffsausgleichs, April 5, 1918, BL, R3101/0845, bl. 39; Dr. von Schön, Bavarian Consulate in Berlin, to Chef des

Feldeisenbahnwesens, April 9, 1918, BL, R5/1596; and Protokoll of August 8, 1917, meeting in Bucharest regarding Romanian shipping, Aktenvermerk drafted by Chef des Feldeisenbahnwesens, August 17, 1917, BL, R5/1596.

44. Bavarian Minister President Graf Hertlin to AA, Reichsamt des Innern, April 17, 1917, BL, R5/1596.

45. Preliminary meeting for August 9 meetings in Vienna, August 1, 1917, PA AA, R21.832; see also Ergebnis der Besprechung im Auswärtigen Amt am 12. Mai 1917, PA AA, R21.832; and Program for discussions in Vienna, August 9, 1917, BL, R5-1596.

46. Militärverwaltung in Rumänien, III. Teil Wirtschaftliche Sicherungen, undated, probably January 1918, BL, R3101/1890, bl. 40-47; "Aufzeichnung über das Ergebnis der Sitzung am 2. Januar d.J., betreffend Forderungen auf dem Gebiete der Erdölindustrie und der Eisenbahnen bei den Friedensverhandlungen mit Rumänien," BL, R901/81059, bl. 210-16; and Kriegsamt plan for Romanian RR, March 3, 1918, BL, R3101/1890, bl. 173-78.

47. Helfferich memorandum of February 19 meeting, BL, R3101/1890, bl. 158-68; Erläuterungen für die Eisenbahnbestimmungen zu den Friedensverhandlungen mit Rumänien, February 20, 1918, BL, R3101/1890, bl. 149-51; Ludendorff to Helfferich, February 24, 1918, BL, R3101/1890, bl. 136.

48. Quoted in Manfred Nebelin, *Ludendorff: Diktator im Ersten Weltkrieg* (Munich: Siedler Verlag, 2011), 380.

CHAPTER 2. A NEW LIGHT ON YUGOSLAV-GERMAN TRADE RELATIONS AND ECONOMIC ANTI-SEMITISM

The author would like to thank Fernando Zamola for his comments on the first draft of this chapter.

1. David E. Kaiser, *Economic Diplomacy and the Origins of the Second World War: Germany, Britain, France, and Eastern Europe, 1930-1939* (Princeton, NJ: Princeton University Press, 1980).

2. William S. Grenzebach Jr., *Germany's Informal Empire in East-Central Europe: German Economic Policy toward Yugoslavia and Rumania, 1933-1939* (Stuttgart: Franz Steiner, 1988); Alan S. Milward, "The Reichsmark Bloc and the International Economy," in *Der "Führerstaat": Mythos und Realität. Studien zur Struktur und Politik des Dritten Reiches*, ed. Gerhard Hirschfeld and Lothar Kettenacker (Stuttgart: DVA, 1981); Roland Schönfeld, "Zur Entstehung der deutschen 'Clearingverschuldung' gegenüber Südosteuropa in der Weltwirtschaftskrise," in *Südosteuropa im Entwicklungsprozeß der Welt: Festschrift für Professor Dr. Hermann Gross*, ed. Walter Althammer and Werner Gumpel (Munich: Olzog, 1979); Hans-Jürgen Schröder, "Südosteuropa als 'Informal Empire' Deutschlands 1933-1939: Das Beispiel Jugoslawien," *Jahrbücher für Geschichte Osteuropas* 23 (1975): 70-96; Hans-Jürgen Schröder, "Der Aufbau der deutschen Hegemonialstellung

in Südosteuropa 1933-1936," in *Hitler, Deutschland und die Mächte: Materialien zur Außenpolitik des Dritten Reiches*, ed. Manfred Funke (Düsseldorf: Droste, 1978); and Vuk Vinaver, *Svetska ekonomska kriza u Podunavlju i nemački prodor 1929-1934* (Belgrade: Institut za savremenu istoriju, 1987).

See also Paul Einzig, *Bloodless Invasion: German Economic Penetration into the Danubian States and the Balkans* (London: Duckworth, 1938), 5: "The German invasion of the Danube basin did not begin with the entry of the Reichswehr troops into Austria on March 12, 1938. . . . Ever since the advent of the Nazi régime Germany has been engaged in a bloodless conquest of the countries of Central and South-Eastern Europe. . . . The process is gradual. There is nothing spectacular about it."

3. Cf. Klaus Thörner, *Der ganze Südosten ist unser Hinterland: Deutsche Südosteuropapläne von 1840 bis 1945* (Freiburg: Ça ira, 2008).

4. Stephen Gross, "Selling Germany in South-Eastern Europe: Economic Uncertainty, Commercial Information and the Leipzig Trade Fair 1920-40," *Contemporary European History* 21, no. 1 (February 2012): 19-39; and John Hiden, "The Baltic Germans and German Policy towards Latvia after 1918," *Historical Journal* 13, no. 2 (June 1970): 295-317.

5. Sabine Bamberger-Stemmann, *Der Europäische Nationalitätenkongreß 1925 bis 1938: Nationale Minderheiten zwischen Lobbyistentum und Großmachtinteressen* (Marburg: Verlag Herder-Institut, 2000), 13n2; Carl Bethke, *Deutsche und ungarische Minderheiten in Kroatien und der Vojvodina 1918—1941: Identitätsentwürfe und ethnopolitische Mobilisierung* (Wiesbaden: Harrasowitz, 2009), 251-52; and Mirna Zakić, "The Price of Belonging to the Volk: Volksdeutsche, Land Redistribution and Aryanization in the Serbian Banat, 1941-1944," *Journal of Contemporary History* 49, no. 2 (April 2014): 320-40.

6. The term Vojvodina as used here contains southern Baranja and Bačka, the western Banat, and the eastern part of Srem. On the ethnogenesis of the "Swabians" see Mirna Zakić, *Ethnic Germans and National Socialism in Yugoslavia in World War II* (Cambridge: Cambridge University Press, 2017), 27-30.

7. Norbert Krekeler, *Revisionsanspruch und geheime Ostpolitik der Weimarer Republik: Die Subventionierung der deutschen Minderheit in Polen* (Stuttgart: Deutsche Verlags-Anstalt, 1973).

8. Günter Wehenkel, "Deutsches Genossenschaftswesen im osteuropäischen Raum," *Der Auslanddeutsche* 14 (1931): 182. It is hard to determine whether this figure given by Wehenkel includes only cooperatives that were associated with the cultural and/or political leadership of the German minorities, or those that operated independently from the German minority movements in the east. See Bernd Robionek, "Ethnic-German Cooperatives in Eastern Europe between the World Wars: The Ideology and Intentions behind an Ethnic Economy," in *National Economies: Volks-Wirtschaft, Racism and Economy in Europe between the*

Wars (1918–1939/45), ed. Christoph Kreutzmüller, Michael Wildt, and Moshe Zimmermann (Newcastle upon Tyne: Cambridge Scholars Publishing, 2015), 212–28.

9. Nikola L. Gaćeša, "Privreda Vojvodine između dva svetska rata," *Zbornik za istoriju* 22 (1980): 107; and Rüdiger Müller-Stock, *Volkstum und Genossenschaftswesen* (Stuttgart: Kohlhammer, 1938), 24. Unfortunately, the Serbian/Yugoslav historiography has paid little attention to the German cooperative union. Cf. Mihailo Vučković, *Istorija zadružnog pokreta u Jugoslaviji 1918–1941* (Belgrade: Kultura, 1966).

10. Calculation based on figures from Zoran Janjetović, "Die Konflikte zwischen Serben und Donauschwaben," *Südost-Forschungen* 58 (1999): 132n94.

Still very insightful for the history of the German minority in Yugoslavia, though mostly based on the writings of minority representatives, is the work of Hans-Ulrich Wehler, *Nationalitätenpolitik in Jugoslawien: Die deutsche Minderheit 1918–1978* (Göttingen: Vandenhoeck & Ruprecht, 1980). For a comparative study of the German minorities in both halves of the Banat, see Mariana Hausleitner, *Die Donauschwaben 1868–1948: Ihre Rolle im rumänischen und serbischen Banat* (Stuttgart: Franz Steiner Verlag, 2014). Political developments are examined in Johann Böhm, *Die deutsche Volksgruppe in Jugoslawien 1918–1941: Innen- und Außenpolitik als Symptome des Verhältnisses zwischen deutscher Minderheit und jugoslawischer Regierung* (Frankfurt: Peter Lang, 2009).

11. Wehler, *Nationalitätenpolitik*, 17–18.

12. Nikola Gaćeša, "The Germans in the Agrarian Reform and Land Ownership Patterns in the Vojvodina Province during the Period from 1919 to 1941," in *The Third Reich and Yugoslavia 1933–1945*, ed. Života Anić et al. (Belgrade: IRPS, 1977), 145–70.

13. In the late 1930s, only 10 percent of the ethnic Germans were members of the Kulturbund. Zoran Janjetović, "National Minorities in Yugoslavia 1918–1941," *Review of Croatian History* 8, no. 1 (2012): 72.

14. Jugoslovenski godišnjak, *Ko je ko u Jugoslaviji*, 2nd ed. (Belgrade: Nova Evropa, 1928), 72.

15. Zoran Janjetović, *Nemci u Vojvodini* (Belgrade: INIS, 2009), 123–24.

16. Andreas Dammang, *Die deutsche Landwirtschaft im Banat und in der Batschka* (Munich: Reinhardt, 1931); cf. Bernd Robionek, "Im Gravitationsfeld des 'Mutterlandes': Deutsche Genossenschaften in Nordbosnien zwischen den Weltkriegen," in *"Nijemci" u Bosni i Hercegovini i Hrvatskoj—Nova istraživanja i perspektive*, ed. Enes S. Omerović (Sarajevo, Zagreb, and Tübingen: Institut za istoriju u Sarajevu/Hrvatski institut za povijest/Zentrum zur Erforschung deutscher Geschichte und Kultur in Südosteuropa an der Universität Tübingen, 2015), 219–40.

17. Jovan Durman, "Zadrugarstvo Nemaca u Jugoslaviji do Drugog svetskog rata," *Zadružni arhiv* 2 (1954): 115–32.

18. Dragan Aleksić, *Država i privreda u Kraljevini SHS* (Belgrade: INIS, 2010), 73; Jacob B. Hoptner, *Yugoslavia in Crisis 1934–1941* (New York: Columbia University Press, 1962), 94; Jaša Janjić, *Poljoprivredna kriza, njeni uzroci i posledice: Predavanje održano 19. septembra 1929. na kongresu Saveza srpskih zemljoradničkih zadruga u Novom Sadu* (Novi Sad: Štamparija Jovanović i Bogdanov, 1929); Trgovačko-industrijska i zanatska komora u Novom Sadu, *Privreda Vojvodine u 1929 godini* (Novi Sad: Jovanović i Bogdanov, 1930), 5–6; and Nikola Vučo, *Agrarna kriza u Jugoslaviji 1930–1934* (Belgrade: Prosveta, 1968), 87.

19. Cf. Anu Mai Köll, *Peasants on the World Market: Agricultural Experience of Independent Estonia 1919–1939* (Stockholm: Centre for Baltic Studies, 1994).

20. "Geflügelzucht und Verwertungsgenossenschaften," leaflet issued by Avis (central cooperative), Novi Sad, 1931, Bundesarchiv (hereafter BA), R57neu/Jugoslawien 1071/51, 28790.

21. Cf. Torsten Lorenz, "Introduction: Cooperatives in Ethnic Conflicts," in *Cooperatives in Ethnic Conflicts: Eastern Europe in the 19th and Early 20th Century*, ed. Torsten Lorenz (Berlin: BWV, 2006), 9–44.

22. Bernd Robionek, "Zwischen Anspruch und Wirklichkeit: Das deutsche Genossenschaftswesen in der Vojvodina (1922–1941)," *Jahrbuch des Bundesinstituts für Kultur und Geschichte der Deutschen im östlichen Europa* 20 (2012): 519–27.

23. LZDK (auditing dept.) to Avis (Riester), Novi Sad, June 22, 1936, Arhiv Vojvodine (hereafter AV), 111/34.

24. Max Siebold, "Die soziale und wirtschaftliche Bedeutung der Kleintierzucht," in *Die Geflügelhaltung: Sonderbeilage des "Deutschen Volksblattes" anläßlich der II. Internationalen Geflügelausstellung in Novisad vom 30. Nov. bis 4. Dez. 1930*, Novi Sad, December 1930.

25. Janjetović, *Nemci*, 120.

26. Wehler, *Nationalitätenpolitik*, 18.

27. LZDK (auditing dept.) to Avis (central cooperatives), February 13, 1933, AV, 111/34.

28. "Auszug aus dem Geschäftsbericht," Avis (central cooperative), October 22, 1932, AV, 111/34; "Bericht über die Geschäftstätigkeit der Kreisgenossenschaften für Geflügelzucht und Eierverwertung im Jahre 1933," *Der Landwirt*, September 23, 1934, 318.

29. Cf. "Geschäftsbericht 1934," Avis, AV, 111/34; Hans Gehl, "Nebenzweige der Landwirtschaft," in *Schwäbische Familie: Beiträge zur Volkskunde der Banater Deutschen*, ed. Hans Gehl (Timişoara: Facla-Verlag, 1981), 21; and Francis Pine, "'The Cows and Pigs are His, the Eggs are Mine': Women's Domestic Economy and Entrepreneurial Activity in Rural Poland," in *Socialism: Ideals, Ideologies, and Local Practice*, ed. Christopher M. Hann (London: Routledge, 1993), 238–39.

30. Hans-Paul Höpfner, *Deutsche Südosteuropapolitik in der Weimarer Republik* (Frankfurt: Peter Lang, 1983), 299–300.

31. "Auszug aus dem Geschäftsbericht," Avis, October 22, 1932, AV, 111/34; and Auditing report (Avis), April 1935, AV, 111/34.

32. Entwurf der Eierverordnung, Reich Ministry of Agriculture (v. Imhoff), Berlin, March 11, 1932, Politisches Archiv des Auswärtigen Amtes, Berlin (hereafter PA AA), R118091; "Auszug aus dem Geschäftsbericht," Avis (central cooperative), October 22, 1932, AV, 111/34; Royal Ministry of Finances, *Statistika spoljne trgovine Kraljevine Jugoslavije za 1932 godinu* (Belgrade: Državna štampa, 1933), 24; "Revisionsbericht über die 'Avis' Zentralgenossenschaft," LZDK (Heidenfelder), Novi Sad, February 9, 1933, AV, 111/34; "'Avis' Zentralgenossenschaft für Viehzucht," auditing report of the Serbian cooperative union (copy), Belgrade, 1934, PA AA, R30321, 332–334; auditing report (Avis), April 1935, AV, 111/34; "Revisions-Bericht über die 'Avis,' Zentralgenossenschaft für Geflügelzucht, reg. landwirtschaftliche Produktivgenossenschaft m.b.H., Novisad, pro 1937," Kontrofina (Roellin), Zurich, April 30, 1938, 3, BA, R2/15706, 194–248; Walther Güttges, "Der deutsche Eierhandel: Nach dem Stande vom 30. Juni 1937" (PhD dissertation, Cologne University, 1938), 142; and Karolin Steinke, *Simon Adler: Eierhändler in Berlin* (Berlin: Centrum Judaicum, 2011), 38–39.

33. "Durchführung der Eierkontingentierung" (copy), Reich Ministry of Agriculture (Köhler) to AA, Berlin, January 20, 1934, PA AA, R118094; and LZDK (auditing dept.) to Avis (central cooperative), Novi Sad, February 13, 1933, AV, 111/34.

34. "Sveža jaja u ljusci god. 1936. Izvoz svežih jaja u ljusci u Nemačku," Royal Ministry of Trade and Industry document compilation, Belgrade, January 16, 1937, Arhiv Jugoslavije (hereafter AJ), 65/253/756.

35. Avis (central cooperative) to LZDK (auditing dept.), Novi Sad, March 12, 1934 (re. Avis A), AV, 111/34.

36. Calculated after "Ausweis der Eier-Anlieferungen bis 31.XII.1932," Avis A, AV, 111/34.

37. Auditing report (handwritten), LZDK, Novi Sad, June 18, 1932, AV, 111/34; "Auszug aus dem Geschäftsbericht," Avis (central cooperative), October 22, 1932, AV, 111/34; "Revisionsbericht über die 'Avis' Zentralgenossenschaft," LZDK (Heidenfelder), Novi Sad, February 9, 1933, AV, 111/34; Avis (central cooperative) to LZDK (auditing dept.), Novi Sad, March 12, 1934 (re. Avis B), AV, 111/34; "Auszug aus dem Warenskontro [*sic*]," Avis C, Novi Vrbas, March 31, 1936, AV, 111/34; Bogumil Hrabak, "Ruralna privreda Banata 1919–1931. godine," *Zbornik Matice srpske za istoriju* 63/64 (2001): 271.

38. "Ministar trgovine i industrije o otkazu trgovinskog ugovora s Nemačkom: Zadatak budućih pregovora," *Politika*, September 14, 1932, 2.

39. "Eiermarktbericht," *Der Landwirt*, March 19, 1933, 90; and Grenzebach, *Germany's Informal Empire*, 24.

40. Jozo Tomasevich, *Peasants, Politics, and Economic Change in Yugoslavia* (Stanford, CA: Stanford University Press, 1955), 630–33; cf. Ivan T. Berend, *Markt und Wirtschaft: Ökonomische Ordnungen und wirtschaftliche Entwicklungen in Europa seit dem 18. Jahrhundert* (Göttingen: Vandenhoeck & Ruprecht, 2007), 44–113; and Slavcho Zagorov, Jenö Végh, and Aleksandr D. Bilimovič, *The Agricultural Economy of the Danubian Countries, 1935–45* (Stanford, CA: Stanford University Press, 1955), 321.

41. Hannah Ahlheim, *"Deutsche, kauft nicht bei Juden!" Antisemitismus und politischer Boykott in Deutschland 1924–1935* (Göttingen: Wallstein Verlag, 2011), 246; Avraham Barkai, *Vom Boykott zur "Entjudung": Der wirtschaftliche Existenzkampf der Juden im Dritten Reich 1933–1943* (Frankfurt: Fischer Verlag, 1988), 30; and Michael Wildt, *Volksgemeinschaft als Selbstermächtigung: Gewalt gegen Juden in der deutschen Provinz 1919 bis 1939* (Hamburg: Hamburger Edition, 2007), 120.

For a more reciprocal approach, see Moshe Gottlieb, "The Anti-Nazi Boycott Movement in the United States: An Ideological and Sociological Appreciation," *Jewish Social Studies* 35, no. 3/4 (July–October 1973): 198–227; Richard A. Hawkins, "The Internal Politics of the Non-Sectarian Anti-Nazi League to Champion Human Rights, 1933–1939," *Management & Organizational History* 5, no. 2 (Summer 2010): 251–78; and Sibylle Morgenthaler, "Countering the Pre-1933 Nazi Boycott against the Jews," *Leo Baeck Institute Year Book* 36, no. 1 (January 1991): 127–49. See also Martin Dean, *Robbing the Jews: The Confiscation of Jewish Property in the Holocaust, 1933–1945* (Cambridge: Cambridge University Press, 2010).

42. "Mitteilungen der 'Avis,' Zentralgenossenschaft für Geflügelzucht. Kühlhauseier," *Der Landwirt*, April 16, 1933, 128; and "Bericht über die Geschäftstätigkeit," *Der Landwirt*, September 23, 1934, 318.

43. "Mitteilungen der 'Avis,' Zentralgenossenschaft für Geflügelzucht: Neue Eierverordnungen in Deutschland," *Der Landwirt*, May 13, 1933, 164.

44. "Eiermarkt-Bericht," *Der Landwirt*, February 19, 1933, 47; "Eiermarktbericht vom 13. Juni 1933," *Der Landwirt*, June 18, 1933, 214; and "Eiermarkt. 11. Juli 1933," *Der Landwirt*, July 16, 1933, 250.

45. "Jugoslawisch-deutsches Handelsabkommen," *Der Landwirt*, August 13, 1933, 281; and "Jugoslawische Eierausfuhr nach Deutschland," *Der Landwirt*, September 10, 1933, 313.

46. "Eiermarktbericht. 27. September 1933," *Der Landwirt*, October 1, 1933, 338; "Eiermarktbericht vom 4. Oktober 1933," *Der Landwirt*, October 8, 1933, 345; and "Eiermarktbericht vom 11. Oktober 1933," *Der Landwirt*, October 15, 1933, 353. Cf. "Eiermarktbericht 19. Oktober 1933," *Der Landwirt*, October 22, 1933, 361; "Eiermarktbericht vom 24. Oktober 1933," *Der Landwirt*, October 29, 1933, 370; "Eiermarktbericht vom 31. Oktober 1933," *Der Landwirt*, November 5, 1933, 382; and "Revisionsbericht, über die 'Avis' Zentralgenossenschaft für

Geflügelzucht und Eierverwertung, Novisad," LZDK (Heidenfelder), December 1933, AV, 111/34.

47. "Eiermarktbericht vom 8. November 1933," *Der Landwirt*, November 12, 1933, 393; "Eiermarktbericht vom 15. November 1933," *Der Landwirt*, November 19, 1933, 401; "Mitteilungen der 'Avis,' Zentralgenossenschaft für Geflügelzucht. Eiersammlung," *Der Landwirt*, October 29, 1933, 367; and "Eiermarktbericht. Vom 12. Dezember 1933," *Der Landwirt*, December 17, 1933, 440.

48. Avis (Siebold, Riester) to AA (Seiler), Novi Sad, December 2, 1933, PA AA, R118094.

49. "Telegramm Nr. 86," German Embassy Belgrade (von Heeren) to AA, Belgrade, December 27, 1933, and esp. "Im Anschluss an Telegramm Nr. 86 vom 27. Dezember v.J," German Embassy Belgrade (von Heeren) to AA, January 2, 1934, PA AA, R118094.

50. AA (Ulrich) to German Embassy Belgrade, January 6, 1934, PA AA, R118094; and AA (Benzler) to Reich Ministry of Agriculture, Berlin, January 4, 1934, PA AA, R118094.

51. Reich Ministry of Agriculture (Moritz) to Reich Ministry of Finances, Berlin, April 5, 1934, BA, R2/18082.

52. AA (Ulrich) to AA, Berlin, January 4, 1934, and AA (Ulrich) to Reich Ministry of Agriculture (Walter), January 4, 1934, PA AA, R118094.

53. "Durchführung der Eierkontingentierung" (copy), Reich Ministry of Agriculture (Köhler) to AA, Berlin, January 20, 1934, PA AA, R30321, 207.

54. Kraft to AA (Kiewitz), Novi Sad, February 17, 1934, PA AA, R118095.

55. "Einfuhr von Eiern aus Jugoslawien" (copy), Reich Ministry of Agriculture (Bose) to Reich Egg Processing Ltd., Berlin, February 15, 1934, PA AA, R118095.

56. "Eiermarktbericht. 31. Jänner 1934," *Der Landwirt*, February 4, 1934, 48.

57. "Svoj svome—ili kako Nemci iz Rajha pomažu naše Nemce," *Jugoslovenski dnevnik*, February 22, 1934, 2; cf. "Eiermarktbericht. 14. Feber 1934," *Der Landwirt*, February 18, 1934, 64; and "Eiermarktbericht. 20. Feber 1934," *Der Landwirt*, February 25, 1934, 72.

58. Quoted after Janjetović, "Die Konflikte," 143n168.

59. "Auszug aus dem Geschäftsbericht," Avis (central cooperative), October 22, 1932, AV, 111/34.

60. Avis (central cooperative) to LZDK (auditing dept.), Novi Sad, March 12, 1934, AV, 111/34.

61. Milivoje Erić, *Agrarna reforma u Jugoslaviji 1918-1941 god.* (Sarajevo: Veselin Masleša, 1958), 478.

62. Quoted after Šandor Mesaroš, *Mađari u Vojvodini 1929-1941* (Novi Sad: Institut za istoriju, 1989), 44-45; cf. Vuk Vinaver, *Jugoslavija i Mađarska 1918-1933* (Belgrade: Narodna knjiga, 1976), 189-202.

63. Gojko Malović, ed., "Optiranje i naseljavanje Srba u Mađarskoj 1920–1931," *Arhiv* 2, no. 1 (2000): 215–32.

64. Miodrag Cvetić, "Nastanak, naseljavanje i depopulacija tzv. 'dobrovoljačkih naselja' u severnom Banatu," *Rad Muzeja Vojvodine* 41/42 (1999/2000): 119.

65. Marie-Janine Calic, *Sozialgeschichte Serbiens 1815–1941: Der aufhaltsame Fortschritt während der Industrialisierung* (Munich: R. Oldenbourg Verlag, 1994), 394–95.

66. "Mitteilungen der 'Avis,' Zentralgenossenschaft für Geflügelzucht. Genossenschaftliche Eiersammlung," *Der Landwirt*, December 17, 1933, 439.

67. Gehl, "Nebenzweige," in *Schwäbische Familie*, ed. Gehl, 21; cf. Helmut Wolpert, "Deutsche Wirtschaft in der jugoslavischen Wojwodina" (PhD dissertation, Berlin University, 1939), 173–74.

68. Jovica Luković, "'Es ist nicht gerecht, für eine Reform aufkommen zu müssen, die gegen einen selbst gerichtet ist': Agrarreform und das bäuerliche Selbstverständnis der Deutschen im jugoslawischen Banat 1918–1941—ein Problemaufriss," in *Kulturraum Banat: Deutsche Kultur in einer europäischen Vielvölkerregion*, ed. Walter Engel (Essen: Klartext, 2007), 148–49.

69. LZDK (auditing dept.) to Avis (central cooperative), April 21, 1937, AV, 111/34.

70. "Sitzung des Handelspolitischen Ausschusses vom 19. Dezember 1933. Anlage 2: Eier in dz (Vertraulich!)," AA Sonderreferat W (Ritter), Berlin, December 20, 1933, PA AA, R118094.

71. Günter Wollstein, ed., "Eine Denkschrift des Staatssekretärs Bernhard von Bülow vom März 1933: Wilhelminische Konzeption der Außenpolitik zu Beginn der nationalsozialistischen Herrschaft," *Militärgeschichtliche Mitteilungen* 13, no. 1 (1973): 77–94.

72. Milica Bodrožić, "Spoljna politika Kraljevine Jugoslavije u vreme vladavine Jugoslovenske nacionalne stranke 1932–1934. godine," *Zbornik Matice srpske za istoriju* 63/64 (2001): 281–82; Vladimir Lj. Cvetković, *Ekonomski odnosi Jugoslavije i Francuske 1918–1941* (Belgrade: Institut za noviju istoriju Srbije, 2006), 130; Kaiser, *Economic Diplomacy*, 45; Bogdan Krizman, *Vanjska politika jugoslavenske države 1918–1941: Diplomatsko-historijski pregled* (Zagreb: Školska knjiga, 1975), 79; Lazar Pejić, "Ekonomske ideje dr Milana Stojadinovića i balkanski privredni problemi," *Balcanica* 7 (1976): 260–61; and Vuk Vinaver, *Jugoslavija i Francuska između dva svetska rata: Da li je Jugoslavija bila francuski "satelit"* (Belgrade: Institut za savremenu istoriju, 1985), 204–5.

73. Contract between Reich Egg Processing Ltd. (Hambrock) and Ured za kontrolisanje izvoza stoke (Petrović), Belgrade, April 21, 1934, PA AA, R118096.

74. Memorandum, "Politische und wirtschaftliche Bedeutung des Handelsvertrags mit Jugoslawien," AA (Ulrich), Berlin, June 21, 1934, PA AA, R105941.

75. Zoran Janjetović, "'Narodno blagostanje' i nemačka privreda 1933–1936. godine," *Istorija 20. veka* 13, no. 1 (1995): 111–26; and Ministère des Relations Extérieures, ed., *Documents Diplomatiques Français, 1932–1939*, series 1, vol. VI (Paris, 1972), 433.

76. Avis to Reichseierverwertung, October 15, 1934, PA AA, R118096.

77. Fütterer to AA (Clodius), Berlin, October 15, 1934, PA AA, R118096.

78. For a general overview of the quarrels between various departments in the Reich concerning authority over the ethnic minorities abroad, see Tammo Luther, *Volkstumspolitik des Deutschen Reiches 1933–1938: Die Auslanddeutschen im Spannungsfeld zwischen Traditionalisten und Nationalsozialisten* (Wiesbaden: Franz Steiner Verlag, 2004).

79. Reichsnährstand (Staff office) to Darré (office), Berlin, February 20, 1936, BA, N1094 III/5. On National Socialist influence on the German minority in the Vojvodina, see Zoran Janjetović, "Die Donauschwaben in der Vojvodina und der Nationalsozialismus," in *Der Einfluss von Faschismus und Nationalsozialismus auf Minderheiten in Ostmittel- und Südosteuropa*, ed. Mariana Hausleitner and Harald Roth (Munich: IKGS Verlag, 2006), 219–35.

80. Cf. Mariana Hausleitner, "Der Einfluss des Nationalsozialismus bei den Donauschwaben im rumänischen und serbischen Banat," *Spiegelungen* 9, no. 2 (2014): 62.

81. AA (Seiler) memorandum, Berlin, December 21, 1934, PA AA, R30321, 375; and LZDK (auditing dept.) to Avis (central cooperative), June 22, 1936, AV, 111/34.

82. Arno Oebser, *Das deutsche Genossenschaftswesen in den Gebieten der ehemaligen Tschecho-Slowakei, in Rumänien, Südslawien und Ungarn* (Stuttgart: Kohlhammer, 1940), 227.

83. "Geflügelmarktbericht," *Der Landwirt*, June 2, 1935, 238; cf. "Geflügelmarktbericht vom 19. September 1935," *Der Landwirt*, September 21, 1935, 382.

84. Max Siebold, "Fleischerzeugung in der Geflügelhaltung," *Der Landwirt*, June 16, 1935, title page.

85. Kosta Mihailović et al., *Proizvodne snage NR Srbije* (Belgrade: Ekonomski institut NR Srbije, 1953), 544; cf. Max Siebold, "Geflügelzucht," *Deutsches Volksblatt: Landwirtschaftliche Sonderbeilage*, December 17, 1929, 8.

86. "Geflügelmarktbericht 13. Juni 1935," *Der Landwirt*, June 16, 1935, 258.

87. Quoted after Gustavo Corni and Horst Gies, *Brot, Butter, Kanonen: Die Ernährungswirtschaft in Deutschland unter der Diktatur Hitlers* (Berlin: Akademie-Verlag, 1997), 371.

88. Oebser, *Das deutsche Genossenschaftswesen*, 227.

89. Presiding Committee of the Agricultural Central Credit Bank, *Tätigkeitsbericht der deutschen landwirtschaftlichen Genossenschaftsorganisationen Jugoslawiens für das Jahr 1934* (Novi Sad: self-published, 1935), 7, 18.

90. Grenzebach, *Germany's Informal Empire*, 55.

91. "Erfolgreiche Tagung der deutschen Genossenschaften in Novisad," *Der Landwirt*, December 5, 1936, 406–7; cf. Oebser, *Das deutsche Genossenschaftswesen*, 227. Of the total 6.5 million eggs Avis sold in 1934, 86 percent went to Germany (Balance sheet [Avis], December 31, 1934, AV, 111/34).

92. Avis C to LZDK (auditing dept.), Novi Vrbas, May 22, 1936, AV, 111/34.

93. Quoted after "Erfolgreiche Tagung der deutschen Genossenschaften in Novisad," *Der Landwirt*, December 5, 1936, 406–7.

94. "Geschäftsbericht 1934" (Avis), AV, 111/34.

95. "Revisions-Bericht über die 'Avis,' Zentralgenossenschaft für Geflügelzucht, reg. landwirtschaftliche Produktivgenossenschaft m.b.H., Novi Sad, pro 1937," Kontrofina (Roellin), Zurich, April 30, 1938, 2, 11–12, 23, BA, R2/15706, 194–248.

96. LZDK (auditing dept.) to Avis C, March 12, 1936, AV, 111/34.

97. Avis (central cooperative) to LZDK (auditing dept.), Novi Sad, March 12, 1934 (re. Avis B), AV, 111/34.

98. "Mitteilungen der ‚Avis' Zentralgenossenschaft für Geflügelzucht," *Der Landwirt*, December 17, 1933, 439.

99. "Revisions-Bericht über die Landwirtschaftliche Zentral-Darlehenskasse als Verband Deutscher Kredit- und Wirtschaftsgenossenschaften im Königreich Jugoslavien, reg. Gen.m.b.H., Novi Sad (L.Z.D.K.) Teil I," Kontrofina (Roellin), Zurich, May 30, 1938, 147, BA, R2/15707/78–268.

100. Avis (central cooperative) to LZDK (auditing dept.), Novi Sad, March 12, 1934 (re. Avis B), AV, 111/34.

101. Report of LZDK (auditing dept.), April 1935, AV, 111/34.

102. "Sveža jaja u ljusci god. 1936," January 16, 1937, AJ, 65/253/756; Milan Koljanin, *Jevreji i antisemitizam u Kraljevini Jugoslaviji 1918–1941* (Belgrade: Institut za savremenu istoriju, 2008), 64–67; and Nebojša Popović, *Jevreji u Srbiji 1918–1941* (Belgrade: Institut za noviju istoriju Srbije, 1997), 35–36, 101–16.

103. LZDK (auditing dept.) to Avis, Novi Sad, May 22, 1935, AV, 111/34.

104. Report of the LZDK (auditing dept.), April 1935, AV, 111/34.

Hartman & Conen, founded by two Jewish partners in 1885, had been a pioneer in meat stock export with branch offices in Berlin and Hamburg. Stevan Mačković, "Od 'Hartman és Conen R.t.' do '29. Novembra,'" *Ex Pannonia*, no. 6/7 (2003): 25–31.

105. Anne Paltian, "Eiergroß- und Einzelhandlung Jacobowitz & Co.," in *Verraten und Verkauft: Jüdische Unternehmen in Berlin 1933–1945*, ed. Aktives Museum Faschismus und Widerstand Berlin e.V. (Berlin: self-published, 2010); and Steinke, *Simon Adler*, 40–44.

106. "Wieder 'arische' Ostereier," *Der Angriff*, April 10, 1936, 11.

107. "Sveža jaja u ljusci god. 1936," January 16, 1937, AJ, 65/253/756.

108. The absurdity of the announcement is hardly diminished by the fact that the junior boss of Hartman & Conen, who kept contact with business

partners in Germany, was baptized, like his mother, who was in a mixed Jewish-Christian marriage, and that the majority of the workers in the company were Catholics. Wilhelm Conen, *Unmenschen, die sich für Halbgötter hielten* (self-published, 1979), 12–26; cf. Koljanin, *Jevreji*, 443n158. Also see Christoph Kreutzmüller, Michael Wildt, and Moshe Zimmermann, "Foreword," in *National Economies*, ed. Kreutzmüller, Wildt, and Zimmermann, x: "The paper did not need to explain what made eggs purchased to be eaten on the most important Christian holiday 'Aryan.' The readers seemingly understood. There is no record of them finding the announcement laughable."

109. "Schwierigkeiten bei der Eierausfuhr," *Deutsche Zeitung*, July 19, 1934, 4; "Geflügelmarktbericht 7. Mai 1935," *Der Landwirt*, May 12, 1935, 214.

110. "Nachtrag zum Revisionsbericht der 'Kontrofina,' Zürich, vom 30. April 1938 über die 'AVIS,' Zentralgenossenschaft für Geflügelzucht, reg. Landwirtschaftliche Produktivgenossenschaft m.b.H., Novi Sad," Kontrofina (Roellin), Zurich, November 16, 1938, 2, BA, R2/15707/436–442.

111. LZDK (Orth) to Avis C, AV, 111/34.

112. LZDK (auditing dept.) to Avis (central cooperative), December 7, 1933, AV, 111/34; "Revisionsbericht, über die 'Avis' Zentralgenossenschaft für Geflügelzucht und Eierverwertung, Novisad," LZDK (Heidenfelder), December 1933, AV, 111/34.

113. Auditing report (LZDK), April 1935, 3, AV, 111/34.

114. "Revisions-Bericht über die 'Avis,' Zentralgenossenschaft für Geflügelzucht, reg. landwirtschaftliche Produktivgenossenschaft m.b.H., Novi Sad, pro 1937," Kontrofina (Roellin), Zurich, April 30, 1938, 8–12, 26, 48, BA, R2/15706, 194–248.

115. Handwritten report on Avis C (LZDK, auditing dept.), June 1939, AV, 111/34.

116. Handwritten note from Avis B (Frantner) to LZDK (auditing dept.), Velika Kikinda, December 26, 1939, AV, 111/34.

117. "Revisions-Bericht über die 'Avis,' Zentralgenossenschaft für Geflügelzucht, reg. landwirtschaftliche Produktivgenossenschaft m.b.H., Novi Sad, pro 1937," Kontrofina (Roellin), Zurich, April 30, 1938, 46, BA, R2/15706, 194–248.

118. "Revisions-Bericht über die 'Avis,' Zentralgenossenschaft für Geflügelzucht, reg. landwirtschaftliche Produktivgenossenschaft m.b.H., Novi Sad, pro 1937," Kontrofina (Roellin), Zurich, April 30, 1938, 23, BA, R2/15706, 194–248. Cf. Hans Rasimus, *Als Fremde im Vaterland: Der Schwäbisch-Deutsche Kulturbund und die ehemalige deutsche Volksgruppe in Jugoslawien im Spiegel der Presse* (Munich: Arbeitskreis für Donauschwäbische Heimat- und Volksforschung in der Donauschwäbischen Kulturstiftung, 1989), 404–5.

119. "Geschäftsbericht 1934," (Avis), AV, 111/34; cf. "Jahrestagung der deutschen Hauptgenossenschaften," *Der Landwirt*, June 30, 1935, 280.

120. "Bericht über die Geschäftstätigkeit," *Der Landwirt*, September 23, 1934, 318; cf. Presiding Committee of the Agricultural Central Credit Bank, *Tätigkeitsbericht der deutschen landwirtschaftl. Genossenschaftsorganisation Jugoslawiens für das Jahr 1933* (Novi Sad: self-published, 1934 or 1935), 20.

121. Here I will touch only briefly upon the issue of structural anti-Semitism in the (German) cooperative movement. Already in the 1920s, cooperative banking among the ethnic German settlements in Bosnia was connected with the alleged liberation scheme of the peasantry from "usurious Jews" ("Anlage 2 zum Bericht J. Nr. 537 vom 30. September 1927. Abschrift," Mr. Voll, Petrovopolje, July 28, 1927, PA AA, R30320, 28–30). Cf. David Peal, "Antisemitism by Other Means? The Rural Cooperative Movement in Late Nineteenth-Century Germany," in *Hostages of Modernization: Studies on Modern Antisemitism 1870–1933/39*, vol. 3, *Germany—Great Britain—France*, ed. Herbert A. Strauss (Berlin: De Gruyter, 1993), 128–49; and Jonathan Zatlin, "The Usurious Jew: Wilhelm Roscher and the Developmental Role of the Homo Economicus Judaicus," in *National Economies*, ed. Kreutzmüller, Wildt, and Zimmermann, 18–32.

122. Cf. Yanni Kotsonis, *Making Peasants Backward: Agricultural Cooperatives and the Agrarian Question in Russia, 1861–1914* (New York: St. Martin's Press, 1999).

CHAPTER 3. RACIALIZING THE BALKANS

1. Michael Burleigh, *Germany Turns Eastwards: A Study of* Ostforschung *in the Third Reich* (Cambridge: Cambridge University Press, 1988); and Götz Aly and Susanne Heim, *Vordenker der Vernichtung: Auschwitz und die deutschen Pläne für eine neue europäische Ordnung* (Frankfurt: Fischer Verlag, 2013).

2. Milan D. Ristović, *Nemački "novi poredak" i Jugoistočna Evropa: 1940/41–1944/45: Planovi o budućnosti i praksa*, 2nd ed. (Belgrade: Službeni glasnik, 2005); and Carl Freytag, *Deutschlands "Drang nach Südosten": Der Mitteleuropäische Wirtschaftstag und der "Ergänzungsraum Südosteuropa," 1931–1945* (Göttingen: V & R Unipress and Vienna University Press, 2012).

3. John Connelly, "Nazis and Slavs: From Racial Theory to Racist Practice," *Central European History* 32, no. 1 (March 1999): 4.

4. Karl C. von Loesch, Wilhelm E. Mühlmann, and Gustav Adolf Küppers, *Die Völker und Rassen Südosteuropas* (Amsterdam: Volk und Reich, 1943).

5. Paul Weindling, "Racial Expertise and German Eugenic Strategies for Southeastern Europe," in *Health, Hygiene and Eugenics in Southeastern Europe to 1945*, ed. Christian Promitzer, Sevasti Trubeta, and Marius Turda (Budapest: CEU Press, 2011), 27–54.

6. Benoit Massin, "From Virchow to Fischer: Physical Anthropology and 'Modern Race Theories' in Wilhelmine Germany," in *Volksgeist as Method and Ethic: Essays on Boasian Ethnography and the German Anthropological*

Tradition, ed. George W. Stocking Jr. (Madison: University of Wisconsin Press, 1996), 79–96; Benoit Massin, "The 'Science of Race,'" in *Deadly Medicine: Creating the Master Race*, ed. Dieter Kuntz (Chapel Hill: University of North Carolina Press and United States Holocaust Memorial Museum, 2004), 89–125; Richard McMahon, "The History of Transdisciplinary Race Classification: Methods, Politics and Institutions, 1840s–1940s," *British Journal for the History of Science* 51, no. 1 (March 2018): 41–67; and Robert Proctor, "From Anthropologie to Rassenkunde in the German Anthropological Tradition," in *Bones, Bodies, Behavior: Essays on Biological Anthropology*, ed. George W. Stocking Jr. (Madison: University of Wisconsin Press, 1988), 138–79.

7. Christian Töchterle, "Wir und die 'Dinarier'—Der europäische Südosten in den rassentheoretischen Abhandlungen vor und im Dritten Reich," in *Südostforschung im Schatten des Dritten Reiches: Institutionen—Inhalte—Personen*, ed. Mathias Beer and Gerhard Seewann (Munich: R. Oldenbourg Verlag, 2004), 170–72.

8. For a survey of German racial science, see the individual contributions to Marius Turda and Paul J. Weindling, ed., *Blood and Homeland: Eugenics and Racial Nationalism in Central and Southeast Europe, 1900–1940* (Budapest: CEU Press, 2007), and Anton Weiss-Wendt and Rory Yeomans, ed., *Racial Science in Hitler's New Europe, 1938–1945* (Lincoln: University of Nebraska Press, 2013).

9. Tudor Georgescu, *The Eugenic Fortress: The Transylvanian Saxon Experiment in Interwar Romania* (Budapest: CEU Press, 2016); Isabel Heinemann, *"Rasse, Siedlung, deutsches Blut": Das Rasse- und Siedlungshauptamt der SS und die rassenpolitische Neuordnung Europas* (Göttingen: Wallstein Verlag, 2003); Markus Leniger, *Nationalsozialistische "Volkstumsarbeit" und Umsiedlungspolitik 1933–1945: Von der Minderheitenbetreuung zur Siedlerauslese* (Berlin: Frank & Timme, 2006); Christian Promitzer, "Täterwissenschaft: Das Südostdeutsche Institut Graz," in *Südostforschung im Schatten des Dritten Reiches*, ed. Beer and Seewann, 93–113; Alexa Stiller, "On the Margins of *Volksgemeinschaft*: Criteria for Belonging to the Volk within the Nazi Germanization Policy in the Annexed Territories, 1939–1945," in *Heimat, Region, and Empire: Spatial Identities under National Socialism*, ed. Claus-Christian W. Szejnmann and Maiken Umbach (Basingstoke: Palgrave Macmillan, 2012), 235–51; and Michael Wedekind, "Besatzungsregime, Volkstumspolitik und völkische Wissenschaftsmilieus: Auf dem Weg zur Neuordnung des Alpen-Adria-Raumes (1939–1945)," in *Zweiter Weltkrieg und ethnische Homogenisierungsversuche im Alpen-Adria-Raum*, ed. Brigitte Entner and Valentin Sima (Klagenfurt: Drava, 2012), 22–43, 174–93.

10. Ute Michel, "Wilhelm Emil Mühlmann (1904–1988)—ein deutscher Professor," in *Jahrbuch für Soziologiegeschichte 1991*, ed. Carsten Klingemann et al. (Opladen: Leske + Budrich, 1992), 90.

11. Michel, "Wilhelm Emil Mühlmann," 72, 76, 80.

12. Hans-Werner Retterath and Alexander Korb, "Karl Christian von Loesch," in *Handbuch der völkischen Wissenschaften*, ed. Michael Fahlbusch, Ingo Haar, and Alexander Pinwinkler (De Gruyter: Berlin 2017), 447–48.

13. Karl C. von Loesch, "Die Völker Südosteuropas," in von Loesch, Mühlmann, and Küppers, *Die Völker und Rassen Südosteuropas*, 7–37.

14. Wilhelm E. Mühlmann, "Das rassische Bild," in von Loesch, Mühlmann, and Küppers, *Die Völker und Rassen Südosteuropas*, 38–56.

15. Gustav Adolf Küppers, "Völkerkundliche Bilder von fünf Balkanreisen," in von Loesch, Mühlmann, and Küppers, *Die Völker und Rassen Südosteuropas*, 97–104.

16. Retterath and Korb, "Karl Christian von Loesch," 450.

17. Retterath and Korb, "Karl Christian von Loesch," 450–51.

18. Von Loesch, "Die Völker Südosteuropas," 19.

19. Von Loesch, "Die Völker Südosteuropas," 31.

20. Von Loesch, "Die Völker Südosteuropas," 31.

21. Von Loesch, "Die Völker Südosteuropas," 36.

22. Michel, "Wilhelm Emil Mühlmann," 81–84.

23. Michel, "Wilhelm Emil Mühlmann," 93–95.

24. Heinrich Reichel, "Das Rassengefüge des europäischen Südostens," in *Deutschland und Südosteuropa: Die natürlichen, völkischen, kulturellen und wirtschaftlichen Beziehungen des Deutschtums mit den Völkern des Südostens* (Graz: Steirische Verlags-Anstalt, 1942), 44–52.

25. Mühlmann, "Das rassische Bild," 38–39.

26. Mühlmann, "Das rassische Bild," 40–42.

27. Mühlmann, "Das rassische Bild," 42.

28. Mühlmann, "Das rassische Bild," 55.

29. Mühlmann, "Das rassische Bild," 40–41.

30. Mühlmann, "Das rassische Bild," 43–45.

31. Mühlmann, "Das rassische Bild," 44.

32. Mühlmann, "Das rassische Bild," 43–44.

33. Mühlmann, "Das rassische Bild," 44.

34. Mühlmann, "Das rassische Bild," 48–50.

35. See the discussion of these racial theories in Aristotle Kallis, "Recontextualizing the Fascist Precedent: The Ustasha Movement and the Transnational Dynamics of Interwar Fascism," in *The Utopia of Terror: Life and Death in Wartime Croatia*, ed. Rory Yeomans (Rochester, NY: University of Rochester Press, 2015), 275.

36. Mühlmann, "Das rassische Bild," 50–51.

37. Christian Promitzer, "The South Slavs in the Austrian Imagination: Serbs and Slovenes in the Changing View from German Nationalism to National Socialism," in *Creating the Other: Ethnic Conflict and Nationalism in Habsburg Central Europe*, ed. Nancy Wingfield (Oxford: Berghahn, 2003), 204–5.

38. Küppers, "Völkerkundliche Bilder," 97–98.

39. Küppers, "Völkerkundliche Bilder," 103.

40. Küppers, "Völkerkundliche Bilder," 97, 99.

41. Küppers, "Völkerkundliche Bilder," 99.

42. Küppers, "Völkerkundliche Bilder," 101.

43. Küppers, "Völkerkundliche Bilder," 100.

44. Zoran Konstantinović, "'Tirk oder Griech': Zur Kontamination ihrer Epitheta," in *Europäischer Völkerspiegel: Imagologisch-ethnographische Studien zu den Völkertafeln des frühen 18. Jahrhunderts*, ed. Franz K. Stanzel (Heidelberg: Winter, 1999), 299–314.

45. Rudolf Virchow, "Die nationale Stellung der Bulgaren," *Verhandlungen der Berliner Gesellschaft für Anthropologie, Ethnologie und Urgeschichte* (Sitzung vom 11. Februar 1877) (1877): 74–75.

46. Compare the different views of Andrew Zimmerman, *Anthropology and Antihumanism in Imperial Germany* (Chicago: University of Chicago Press, 2001) and Andrew D. Evans, *Anthropology at War: World War I and the Science of Race in Germany* (Chicago: University of Chicago Press, 2010), as well as Britta Lange, *Die Wiener Forschungen an Kriegsgefangenen 1915–1918: Anthropologische und ethnografische Verfahren im Lager* (Vienna: Österreichische Akademie der Wissenschaften, 2013), 21–27.

47. Sevasti Trubeta, *Physical Anthropology, Race and Eugenics in Greece (1880s–1970s)* (Leiden: Brill, 2013), 59; and Christian Promitzer, "Physical anthropology and ethnogenesis in Bulgaria, 1878–1944," *Focaal: Journal of Global and Historical Anthropology* 58 (2010): 52.

48. Joseph Deniker, *Les races et les peuples de la terre: Éléments d'anthropologie et d'ethnographie* (Paris: C. Reinwald, 1900), 390.

49. Jovan Cvijić, "Kulturni pojasi Balkanskog poluostrva," in Cvijić, *Govori i članci*, 2nd ed. (Belgrade: Srpska akademija nauka i umetnosti, 1991), 79–80.

50. Hans F. K. Günther, *Rassenkunde Europas: Mit besonderer Berücksichtigung der Hauptvölker indogermanischer Sprache* (Munich: J. F. Lehmann, 1929), 79–80; and Gustav Kraitschek, *Rassenkunde mit besonderer Berücksichtigung des deutschen Volkes, vor allem der Ostalpenländer* (Vienna: Burgverlag, 1923), 38–41, 55, 59–60, 112, 114. See also Brigitte Fuchs, *"Rasse," "Volk," Geschlecht: Anthropologische Diskurse in Österreich 1850–1960* (Frankfurt: Campus, 2003), 250–52.

51. Margit Berner, "Forschungs-'Material' Kriegsgefangene: Die Massenuntersuchungen der Wiener Anthropologen an gefangenen Soldaten 1915–1918," in *Vorreiter der Vernichtung: Eugenik, Rassenhygiene und Euthanasie in der österreichischen Diskussion vor 1938. Zur Geschichte der NS-Euthanasie in Wien Teil III*, ed. Heinz Eberhard Gabriel and Wolfgang Neugebauer (Vienna: Böhlau, 2005), 167–98; Margit Berner, "Die 'rassenkundlichen' Untersuchungen der Wiener Anthropologen in Kriegsgefangenenlagern 1915–1918," *Zeitgeschichte* 30 (2003): 124–36; Andrew D. Evans, "Science Behind the Lines: The Effects of World War

I on Anthropology in Germany," in *Doing Anthropology in Wartime and War Zones: World War I and the Cultural Sciences in Europe*, ed. Reinhard Johler, Christian Marchetti, and Monique Scheer (Bielefeld: Transcript, 2010), 99–122; Maciej Gorny, "'Asiatisches Barbarentum' in der Ethnopsychologie und Rassenanthropologie im Ersten Weltkrieg," in *Der erinnerte Feind: Kritische Studien zur "Türkenbelagerung,"* vol. 2, ed. Johannes Feichtinger and Johann Heiss (Vienna: Mandelbaum, 2013), 285–99; Maciej Gorny, "Bone & Soul: Physical Anthropology, the Great War and Nationalism in Eastern Europe," *Cuadernos de Historia Contemporánea* 36 (2014): 239–58; and Lange, *Die Wiener Forschungen an Kriegsgefangenen*.

52. Josef Weninger, *Rassenkundliche Untersuchungen an Albanern: Ein Beitrag zum Problem der dinarischen Rasse* (Vienna: Antropologische Gesellschaft in Wien, 1934); and Lange, *Die Wiener Forschungen an Kriegsgefangenen*, 214.

53. Ingrid Arias, *Die Wiener Gerichtsmedizin im Nationalsozialismus* (Vienna: Verlags-Haus der Ärzte, 2009), 32; and "Josef Weninger," https://www.oeaw.ac.at/online-gedenkbuch/gedenkbuch/personen/q-z/josef-weninger/, accessed August 29, 2018.

54. Anton Rolleder, "Rassenkundliche Forschungen an Serben," *Verhandlungen der Deutschen Gesellschaft für Rassenforschung* 9 (1938): 132–40.

55. Ernst Klee, *Das Personenlexikon zum Dritten Reich* (Frankfurt: S. Fischer, 2003), 506; and Arias, *Die Wiener Gerichtsmedizin*, 30–34, 59–60, 124–25.

56. H. (Hans) Grimm, "Rolleder, A., Rassenkundlichen Forschungen an Serben," *Südostdeutsche Forschungen* 4, no. 1 (1939): 220–21; and Arias, *Die Wiener Gerichtsmedizin*, 32.

57. Arias, *Die Wiener Gerichtsmedizin*, 33–34, 59–60.

58. A. (Arthur) Haberlandt and V. (Viktor) Lebzelter, "Zur physischen Anthropologie der Albanesen," *Archiv für Anthropologie* NS 17 (1919), 123–54.

59. Viktor Lebzelter, "Zur physischen Anthropologie der serbischen Zigeuner," *Mitteilungen der Anthropologischen Gesellschaft in Wien* 52 (1922): 27, 29, 34.

60. Lange, *Die Wiener Forschungen an Kriegsgefangengen*, 133.

61. Fuchs, *"Rasse," "Volk," Geschlecht*, 283–84.

62. Viktor Lebzelter, "Beiträge zur physischen Anthropologie der Balkanhalbinsel. I. Teil: Zur physischen Anthropologie der Südslawen," *Mitteilungen der Anthropologischen Gesellschaft in Wien* 53 (1923): 48.

63. Viktor Lebzelter, "Zur Rassengeschichte der Jugoslaven," *Vjesnik Arheološkog muzeja u Zagrebu* 15, no. 1 (1928): 25–30.

64. Hans-Walther Schmuhl, *The Kaiser Wilhelm Institute for Anthropology, Human Heredity, and Eugenics, 1927–1945: Crossing Boundaries* (Dordrecht: Springer, 2008), 55, 76, 167, 171, 214, 283, 358–59; and Weindling, "Racial Expertise," in *Health, Hygiene and Eugenics*, ed. Promitzer, Trubeta, and Turda, 52–53.

65. Katja Geisenhainer, *"Rasse ist Schicksal": Otto Reche, 1879–1966, ein Leben als Anthropologe und Völkerkundler* (Leipzig: Evangelische Verlagsanstalt,

2002), 477; and Paul J. Weindling, "Race, Eugenics and National Identity in the Eastern Baltic: From Racial Surveys to Racial States," in *Baltic Eugenics: Bio-Politics, Race and Nation in Interwar Estonia, Latvia and Lithuania 1918-1940*, ed. Björn M. Felder and Paul J. Weindling (Amsterdam: Rodopi, 2013), 42.

66. Michael Hesch, "Die rassengeschichtliche Stellung Südosteuropas im Lichte der Blutgruppenforschung," *Leipziger Vierteljahrsschrift für Südosteuropa* 1, no. 3 (1937): 26-28.

67. Hesch, "Die rassengeschichtliche Stellung Südosteuropas," 29-30.

68. Richard Weikart, "Hitler's Struggle for Existence against Slavs: Racial Theory and Vacillations in Nazi Policy toward Czechs and Poles," in *Eradicating Differences: The Treatment of Minorities in Nazi-Dominated Europe*, ed. Anton Weiss-Wendt (Newcastle: Cambridge Scholars Publishing, 2010), 67-68.

69. On Eickstedt and his circle, see Dirk Preuß, *"Anthropologe und Forschungsreisender": Biographie und Anthropologie Egon Freiherr von Eickstedts (1892-1965)* (Munich: Utz, 2009); and Andreas Lüddecke, *Rassen, Schädel und Gelehrte: Zur politischen Funktionalität der anthropologischen Forschung und Lehre in der Tradition Egon von Eickstedts* (Frankfurt: Peter Lang, 2000).

70. Christian Promitzer, "The Body of the Other: 'Racial Science' and Ethnic Minorities in the Balkans," *Jahrbücher für Geschichte und Kultur Südosteuropas/History and Culture of South Eastern Europe: An Annual Journal* 5 (2003): 27-40.

71. Ilse Schwidetzky, *Rassenkunde der Altslawen* (Stuttgart: Enke, 1938).

72. H. (Heinz) Wülker, "Dinarische Hirtenkriegerstämme in Montenegro als Beispiel für die Bildung von Auslesegruppen," *Volk und Rasse* 10, no. 5 (1935): 152-55.

73. Egon Lendl, "Entwicklung und Schicksal des kroatischen Volksbodens," *Volkstum im Südosten* 3 (1941): 86-90. On the journal itself, see Petra Svatek, "Volkstum im Südosten," in *Handbuch der völkischen Wissenschaften*, ed. Fahlbusch, Haar, and Pinwinkler, 2140-43.

74. For individual postwar biographies, see Wolfgang Böhm, "Gustav Adolf Küppers," in Böhm, *Biographisches Handbuch zur Geschichte des Pflanzenbaus* (Munich: K. G. Saur, 1997), 175-76; Michel, "Wilhelm Emil Mühlmann," 101-2; and Retterath and Korb, "Karl Christian von Loesch," 450-51. On Michael Hesch, see Arias, *Die Wiener Gerichtsmedizin*, 124-25. On Eickstedt and Schwidetzky, see Lüddecke, *Rassen, Schädel und Gelehrte*.

75. Ilse Schwidetzky, ed., *Rassengeschichte der Menschheit. Teil 6: Europa IV: Ungarn, Rumänien, Bulgarien, Jugoslawien, Albanien, Griechenland* (Munich: R. Oldenbourg Verlag, 1979).

76. Cf. Connelly, "Nazis and Slavs," 21-22.

CHAPTER 4: "MY LIFE FOR PRINCE EUGENE"

Title is borrowed from Walter Schreiber, *Mein Leben für Prinz Eugen: Deutsche Bauern siedeln im Banat* (Berlin: Steiniger Verlage, 1941).

1. Karl Werner Holy, "Die Kolonisation des Grafen Mercy," in *Mosaik Europas: Die Vojvodina*, ed. Horst Haselsteiner and Doris Wastl-Walter (Frankfurt: Peter Lang, 2011), 33–47; Karl A. Roider and Robert Forrest, "German Colonization in the Banat and Transylvania in the Eighteenth Century," in *The Germans and the East*, ed. Charles Ingrao and Franz A. J. Szabo (West Lafayette, IN: Purdue University Press, 2008), 89–104; Márta Fata, "German Settlers (*Donauschwaben*) in Southeastern Europe since the Early Modern Period," in *The Encyclopedia of Migration and Minorities in Europe: From the 17th Century to the Present*, ed. Klaus J. Bade, Pieter C. Emmer, Leo Lucassen, and Jochen Oltmer (Cambridge: Cambridge University Press, 2011), 444–47.

2. Charles W. Ingrao, *The Habsburg Monarchy, 1618–1815* (Cambridge: Cambridge University Press, 1994), 82–83, 119–20.

3. Pieter M. Judson, *The Habsburg Empire: A New History* (Cambridge, MA: Harvard University Press, 2016), 16.

4. Ingo Haar, *Historiker im Nationalsozialismus: Deutsche Geschichtswissenschaft und der "Volkstumskampf" im Osten* (Göttingen: Vandenhoeck & Ruprecht, 2000); and Ingo Haar and Michael Fahlbusch, eds., *German Scholars and Ethnic Cleansing, 1919–1945* (New York: Berghahn Books, 2005).

5. Celia Applegate, *A Nation of Provincials: The German Idea of Heimat* (Berkeley: University of California Press, 1990); David Blackbourn and James Retallack, eds., *Localism, Landscape, and the Ambiguities of Place: German-Speaking Central Europe, 1860–1930* (Toronto: University of Toronto Press, 2007); and Claus-Christian W. Szejnmann and Maiken Umbach, eds., *Heimat, Region, and Empire: Spatial Identities under National Socialism* (Basingstoke: Palgrave Macmillan, 2012).

6. Christian Brücker, *Deutsche Spuren in Belgrad* (Betschkerek: Buchreihe der Deutschen Volksgruppe im Banat und in Serbien, 1944), 32.

7. Hans Diplich, *Deutsche Geschichte*, Schulungsdienst der deutschen Volksgruppe im Banat und in Serbien, Folge 5 (Grossbetschkerek: Schulungsstelle des Kulturamtes, 1942), 34.

8. "Prinz-Eugen-Lied," in *Donauschwäbisches Liederbuch*, ed. Konrad Scheierling (Straubing: Donauschwäbisches Archiv, 1985), 2.

9. "Prinz Eugen bei Zenta," "Prinz Eugen, der Streiter des Herrn," and "Der Prinz-Eugen-Brunnen," in *Donauschwäbische Sagen, Märchen und Legenden*, ed. Hans Diplich and Alfred Karasek (Munich: Verlag Christ Unterwegs, 1952), 23–24.

10. The Banat Germans were routinely referred to as—and referred to themselves as—the Banat Swabians, due to the notion that most of their ancestors had come from Swabia. Eighteenth-century colonists actually came from diverse parts of the Holy Roman Empire.

11. Adam Müller-Guttenbrunn, "Banater Schwabenlied," in *Deutsches Volk auf fremder Erde: Auswahl aus volksdeutschem Schrifttum*, vol. 1, *Deutschtum*

Jenseits der Reichsgrenzen, ed. Wilhelm Albert (Leipzig: Verlag Ernst Wunderlich, 1936), 88.

12. Hans Diplich, "Prinz Eugen—der Heilbringer," in *Kalender der Deutschen Volksgruppe im Banat und in Serbien für das Jahr 1943*, ed. Sepp Janko (Grossbetschkerek: Banater Druckerei und Verlagsanstalt Bruno Kuhn und Komp, 1943), 43; Hans Herrschaft, *Das Banat: Ein deutsches Siedlungsgebiet in Südosteuropa*, 2nd ed. (Berlin: Verlag Grenze und Ausland, 1942), 56, 65; Sepp Janko, "Zur Prinz-Eugen-Feier des Kreises Temesch," speech in Sečanj / Petersheim on August 24, 1941, in Sepp Janko, *Reden und Aufsätze* (Betschkerek: Buchreihe der Deutschen Volksgruppe im Banat und in Serbien, 1944), 82; Nikolaus Kahles, "Prinz-Eugen-Feier in Grosskikinda," *Banater Beobachter*, August 19, 1942, 5; and Karl von Möller, *Deutsches Schicksal im Banat* (Vienna: Adolf Luser Verlag, 1940), 22.

13. Kahles, "Prinz-Eugen-Feier in Grosskikinda," 5; Erich Queisser, "'Prinz Eugen in Belgrad': Eine Uraufführung im Belgrader National-Theater," *Banater Beobachter*, March 3, 1943, 5.

14. "Prinz Eugenius der edle Ritter," *Volkswacht*, August 16, 1942, 1.

15. Sepp Janko, "Zur Prinz-Eugen-Feier des Kreises Donau," speech in Pančevo / Pantschowa on August 15, 1941, in Janko, *Reden*, 77.

16. Brücker, *Deutsche Spuren in Belgrad*, 44.

17. Herrschaft, *Das Banat*, 59, 65.

18. Brücker, *Deutsche Spuren in Belgrad*, 34–39.

19. Brücker, *Deutsche Spuren in Belgrad*, 31, 44.

20. "Kulturbericht Südosteuropa," November 1–7, 1943, Bundesarchiv Berlin, R 58, file 537, fiche 1, fr. 3.

21. Franz Thierfelder, "Auf den Spuren Eugens: Peterwardein," in *Kalender*, ed. Janko, 44.

22. Diplich, *Deutsche Geschichte*, 34–35.

23. Thierfelder, "Auf den Spuren Eugens," 44.

24. Richard Bahr, *Deutsches Schicksal im Südosten* (Hamburg: Hanseatische Verlagsanstalt, 1936), 13–14.

25. Brücker, *Deutsche Spuren in Belgrad*, 29.

26. Brücker, *Deutsche Spuren in Belgrad*, 39.

27. Diplich, *Deutsche Geschichte*, 34, 35. Sepp Janko did not bother with fine distinctions: in a 1941 speech, he simply referred to the Habsburg emperor as the "German emperor" as a matter of course. Janko, "Zur Prinz-Eugen-Feier des Kreises Temesch," 82.

One year later, Janko blurred the issue further when he offhandedly claimed that, in Prince Eugene's era, Austria had "held the effective leadership of the German Empire." Sepp Janko, "Millekerfeier," speech in Vršac / Werschetz on July 5, 1942, in Janko, *Reden*, 128.

28. Diplich, *Deutsche Geschichte*, 34.

29. Janko, "Zur Prinz-Eugen-Feier des Kreises Donau," 77.

30. Herrschaft, *Das Banat*, 63–64; von Möller, *Deutsches Schicksal im Banat*, 23–24; and Viktor Wagner, *Das Banat im Spiegel der Geschichte* (Novi Sad: Schwäbisch-Deutscher Kulturbund, 1930), 5–6.

31. Diplich, *Deutsche Geschichte*, 36; and Herrschaft, *Das Banat*, 59.

32. Vejas Gabriel Liulevicius, *The German Myth of the East: 1800 to the Present* (Oxford: Oxford University Press, 2009), 171–202.

33. Brücker, *Deutsche Spuren in Belgrad*, 46.

34. Kahles, "Prinz-Eugen-Feier in Grosskikinda," 5.

35. Sepp Janko, "Zur Grosskundgebung des Kreises Hennemann," shortened version of speech held in Vršac / Werschetz on August 10, 1941, in Janko, *Reden*, 73.

36. Janko, "Zur Prinz-Eugen-Feier des Kreises Donau," 77.

37. Thierfelder, "Auf den Spuren Eugens," 44.

38. Brücker, *Deutsche Spuren in Belgrad*, 44.

39. Janko, "Millekerfeier," 128–29.

40. Janko, "Millekerfeier," 129. Ethnic German folktales about Joseph II—while they portrayed him in a relatively positive light as the peasants' emperor and protector from greedy nobles, bandits, and corrupt administrators—did not ascribe to him any martial prowess, quasi-supernatural powers, or special divine protection, as they did to Eugene of Savoy. See "Ein Kaiser zieht verkleidet durch das Land," "Der Kaiser und seine Soldaten," "Immer Neun Uhr," and "Kaiser Josef und die Hajduken," in *Donauschwäbische Sagen*, ed. Diplich and Karasek, 27–30.

41. Josef Beer, "Aus dem Soldatenheim in Pantschowa: Bilder, die zu uns sprechen," *Volkswacht*, November 1, 1942, 4.

42. Janko, "Zur Prinz-Eugen-Feier des Kreises Donau," 81.

43. "Eindrucksvolle Feierstunde am 30. Januar in Franzfeld," *Banater Beobachter*, February 4, 1943, 5.

44. Sepp Janko, "Rede zum Geburtstag des Führers," April 20, 1942, in Janko, *Reden*, 120.

45. Diplich, *Deutsche Geschichte*, 35–36.

46. Diplich, *Deutsche Geschichte*, 36.

47. Brücker, *Deutsche Spuren in Belgrad*, 31.

48. Janko, "Zur Prinz-Eugen-Feier des Kreises Temesch," 83–85; and anonymous, "Dies Land ist deutsch!," in *Volkswacht*, August 30, 1942, 5.

49. Abteilung Deutschland to Joachim von Ribbentrop, November 5, 1942, quoted in Walter Manoschek, *"Serbien ist judenfrei": Militärische Besatzungspolitik und Judenvernichtung in Serbien 1941/42* (Munich: R. Oldenbourg Verlag, 1993), 27.

50. Ulrich Greifelt, "Ein neuer Abschnitt deutscher Ostgeschichte," *Deutsche Arbeit*, vol. 6/7, June–July 1942, 163.

51. Greifelt, "Ein neuer Abschnitt deutscher Ostgeschichte," 163.

52. Mirna Zakić, *Ethnic Germans and National Socialism in Yugoslavia in World War II* (Cambridge: Cambridge University Press, 2017), 80–184.

53. Thomas Casagrande, Michal Schvarc, Norbert Spannenberger, and Ottmar Traşcă, "The *Volksdeutsche*: A Case Study from South-Eastern Europe," in *The Waffen-SS: A European History*, ed. Jochen Böhler and Robert Gerwarth (Oxford: Oxford University Press, 2017), 251.

54. Anonymous, "Die SS" in *Kalender*, ed. Janko, 38; Diplich, "Prinz Eugen—der Heilbringer," 43; and Diplich, *Deutsche Geschichte*, 64.

55. "Ein Wort über Ehre, Blut und Boden," in *Volksdeutsche Stunde: Eine Auswahl aus Rundfunk-Feierstunden*, by Johannes L. Schmidt (Betschkerek: Buchreihe der Deutschen Volksgruppe im Banat und in Serbien, 1943), 55.

56. Nikolaus Britz, "Prinz-Eugen-Lied," printed in Kahles, "Prinz-Eugen-Feier in Grosskikinda," *Banater Beobachter*, August 19, 1942, 5.

57. Casagrande et al., "The *Volksdeutsche*," 232; Otto Kumm, *"Vorwärts Prinz Eugen!" Geschichte der 7. SS-Freiwilligen-Division "Prinz Eugen"* (Osnabrück: Munin-Verlag, 1978), 40.

58. Arthur Phleps, "Taktische Grundsätze für die Führung des Kleinkrieges," April 27, 1942, Bundesarchiv Militärarchiv, RS 3-7, file 15, 151–154.

59. Casagrande et al., "The *Volksdeutsche*," 246–47; Aleksandar Jakir, "Die 7. SS-Gebirgs-Division 'Prinz Eugen' in Dalmatien," in *Nationalsozialismus und Regionalbewusstsein im östlichen Europa*, ed. Burkhard Olschowsky and Ingo Loose (Oldenbourg: De Gruyter, 2016), 369–71, 378–86; and Zakić, *Ethnic Germans and National Socialism*, 227–38.

60. Andrew Demshuk, *The Lost German East: Forced Migration and the Politics of Memory, 1945–1970* (Cambridge: Cambridge University Press, 2012); Norbert Frei, *Adenauer's Germany and the Nazi Past: The Politics of Amnesty and Integration*, trans. Joel Golb (New York: Columbia University Press, 2002); and Robert G. Moeller, *War Stories: The Search for a Usable Past in the Federal Republic of Germany* (Berkeley: University of California Press, 2001).

61. Kumm, *"Vorwärts Prinz Eugen!,"* 401–2.

62. Hans Diplich, "Das Banat als Kulturlandschaft," in Hans Diplich, *Essay: Beiträge zur Kulturgeschichte der Donauschwaben* (Homburg: Verlag Ermer KG, 1975), 16; Nikolaus Hans Hockl, "Der Türke im Land," in *Wir Donauschwaben*, ed. Hans Diplich and Hans Wolfram Hockl (Salzburg: Akademischer Gemeinschaftsverlag, 1950), 36; and Anton Valentin, *Die Banater Schwaben: Kurzgefasste Geschichte einer Südostdeutschen Volksgruppe mit einem Volkskundlichen Anhang* (Munich: Veröffentlichung des Kulturreferates der Landsmannschaft der Banater Schwaben, 1959), 23.

63. Josef Beer, *Donauschwäbische Zeitgeschichte aus erster Hand* (Munich: Donauschwäbische Kulturstiftung, 1987), 15.

64. Diplich, "Das Banat als Kulturlandschaft," 16–17; Hans Wolfram Hockl, "Prinz Eugen," in *Heimatbuch der Donauschwaben*, ed. Hans Wolfram Hockl

(Baden-Württemberg: Donauschwäbischer Heimatverlag and Südostdeutschen Kulturwerk, no year), 51–53.

65. Hockl, "Prinz Eugen," 52.

66. Sepp Janko, *Weg und Ende der deutschen Volksgruppe in Jugoslawien* (Graz: Leopold Stocker Verlag, 1982), 13. By way of contrasting the ostensible goals of Germans and those of other groups in the southeast, another expellee author could not resist a snide aside that replicated Nazi anti-Slav attitudes: "[The Germans'] task [in the Balkans] was primarily economic or cultural, and their fulfillment thereof was exemplary. They had no political or military mission, unlike the Serbs." Joseph Volkmar Senz, "Die Donauschwaben als Nachbarn der Serben und Kroaten," in *Ein Leben für die Donauschwaben: Ein Porträt von Josef Volkmar Senz und seinem Werk*, ed. Rotraud Senz and Ingomar Senz (Munich: Verlag der Donauschwäbischen Kulturstiftung, 1999), 140.

67. Hockl, "Prinz Eugen," 53.

68. Margarete Myers Feinstein, *State Symbols: The Quest for Legitimacy in the Federal Republic of Germany and the German Democratic Republic, 1949–1959* (Boston: Brill, 2001), 87–89.

69. Hans Sonnleitner, *Symbole der Donauschwaben: Wappen, Wappenspruch, Fahne und Hymne* (Munich: Donauschwäbisches Archiv, 1982), 268–73.

CHAPTER 5. NAZI GERMANY AND THE HOLOCAUST IN THE INDEPENDENT STATE OF CROATIA, 1941-1945

1. On the Ustaša movement, see Rory Yeomans, *Visions of Annihilation: The Ustasha Regime and the Cultural Politics of Fascism, 1941–1945* (Pittsburgh: Pittsburgh University Press, 2013); and Alexander Korb, *Im Schatten des Weltkriegs: Massengewalt der Ustasa gegen Serben, Juden und Roma in Kroatien 1941–1945* (Hamburg: Hamburger Edition, 2013).

2. On the Holocaust in the NDH, the standard work is Ivo Goldstein and Slavko Goldstein, *Holokaust u Zagrebu* (Zagreb: Novi liber, 2001). For older studies, see Ognjen Kraus, ed., *Antisemitizam, holokaust, antifašizam* (Zagreb: Židovska općina, 1996); Zdenko Levntal, *Zločini fašističkih okupatora i njihovih pomagača protiv Jevreja u Jugoslaviji* (Belgrade: Savez jevrejskih opština, 1952); Jaša Romano, *Jevreji Jugoslavije 1941-1945: Žrtve genocida i učesnici narodnooslobodilačkog rata* (Belgrade: Jevrejski istorijski muzej, 1980), 91–134; Jaša Romano and Lavoslav Kadelburg, "The Third Reich: Initiator, Organizer and Executant of Anti-Jewish Measures and Genocide in Yugoslavia," in *The Third Reich and Yugoslavia, 1933–1945*, ed. Života Anić et al. (Belgrade: Institut za savremenu istoriju, 1977), 670–90; and Aleksandar Stajić and Jakov Papo, "Ubistva i drugi zločini izvršeni nad Jevrejima u Bosni i Hercegovini u toku neprijateljske okupacije," in *Spomenica: 400 godina od dolaska Jevreja u Bosnu i Hercegovinu*, ed. Samuel Kamhi (Sarajevo: Odbor, 1966), 205–47.

3. The last prewar Yugoslav census of March 1931 enumerated the population based on language and religion; according to this census, Yugoslavia had 68,405 Jews. The size of the Jewish community in 1941 can only be estimated and would need to include Jewish refugees from central Europe. Vladimir Žerjavić, "Demografski pokazatelji o stradanju Židova u NDH," in *Antisemitizam, holokaust, antifašizam*, ed. Kraus, 133–35. See also Harriet Pass Freidenreich, *The Jews of Yugoslavia: A Quest for Community* (Philadelphia: The Jewish Publication Society of America, 1979).

4. On wartime population losses in Yugoslavia, see Bogoljub Kočević, *Žrtve Drugog svetskog rata u Jugoslaviji* (London: Veritas Foundation Press, 1985); and Vladimir Žerjavić, *Gubici stanovništva Jugoslavije u Drugom svjetskom ratu* (Zagreb: Jugoslavensko viktimološko društvo, 1989).

5. Jozo Tomasevich, *War and Revolution in Yugoslavia, 1941–1945: Occupation and Collaboration* (Stanford, CA: Stanford University Press, 2001), 233. The demarcation line was determined by the German and Italian foreign ministers on April 21–22, 1941, when they also agreed on their respective spheres of influence. The primary German interest during these negotiations was to secure the main communication lines between the Third Reich and Greece and to secure a majority of Yugoslavia's raw materials.

6. While the Italian and German Foreign Ministries negotiated the demarcation line, the subdivision of the Italian sphere of influence was stipulated in the Rome Accords between Rome and Zagreb. See Tomasevich, *War and Revolution in Yugoslavia*, 269.

7. The literature on the resistance is extensive. For recent treatments, see Marko Attila Hoare, *Genocide and Resistance in Hitler's Bosnia: The Partisans and the Chetniks, 1941–1943* (London: British Academy, 2007); Vjeran Pavlaković, "Yugoslavia," in *Hitler's Europe Ablaze: Occupation, Resistance, and Rebellion during World War II*, ed. Philip Cooke and Ben H. Shepherd (New York: Skyhorse, 2014), 213–42; and Stevan K. Pavlowitch, *Hitler's New Disorder: The Second World War in Yugoslavia* (New York: Columbia University Press, 2008).

8. On Italian occupation policies, see H. James Burgwyn, *Empire on the Adriatic: Mussolini's Conquest of Yugoslavia, 1941–1943* (New York: Enigma Books, 2005); Davide Rodogno, *Fascism's European Empire: Italian Occupation During the Second World War* (Cambridge: Cambridge University Press, 2006); and Tomasevich, *War and Revolution in Yugoslavia*, 234–68.

9. On the Italian rescue of Jews, see Daniel Carpi, "The Rescue of Jews in the Italian Zone of Occupied Croatia," in *Rescue Attempts during the Holocaust: Proceedings of the Second Yad Vashem International Historical Conference*, ed. Yisrael Gutman and Efraim Zuroff (Jerusalem: Yad Vashem, 1977), 465–525; and Jonathan Steinberg, *All or Nothing: The Axis and the Holocaust, 1941–1943* (London: Routledge, 1990).

10. Korb, *Im Schatten des Weltkriegs*, 109.

11. During Pavelić's April 27, 1943 audience with Hitler, the latter reiterated the Third Reich's three main interests in Croatia: the provision of bauxite, secure lines of communication, and the removal of Wehrmacht units in the shortest possible time. See Nada Kisić Kolanović, *Mladen Lorković: Ministar urotnik* (Zagreb: Golden, 1998), 284.

12. On German economic policy in the NDH, see Holm Sundhaussen, *Wirtschaftsgeschichte Kroatiens im nationalsozialistischen Großraum 1941–1945: Das Scheitern einer Ausbeutungsstrategie* (Stuttgart: Deutsche Verlags-Anstalt, 1983).

13. Kisić Kolanović, *Mladen Lorković*, 161–62.

14. On his extensive criticism of the NDH leadership, see Peter Broucek, *Ein General im Zwielicht: Die Erinnerungen Edmund Glaises von Horstenau*, vol. 3 (Vienna: Böhlau, 1988).

15. Tomasevich, *War and Revolution in Yugoslavia*, 278.

16. On SS recruitment of the *Volksdeutsche* and Bosnian Muslims, see George Lepre, *Himmler's Bosnian Division: The Waffen-SS Handschar Division, 1943–1945* (Atglen, PA: Schiffer Publishing, 1997); Enver Redžić, *Muslimansko autonomaštvo i 13. SS divizija: Autonomija Bosne i Hercegovine i Hitlerov Treći Rajh* (Sarajevo: Svjetlost, 1987); and Mirna Zakić, *Ethnic Germans and National Socialism in Yugoslavia in World War II* (Cambridge: Cambridge University Press, 2017).

17. Tomasevich, *War and Revolution in Yugoslavia*, 290.

18. Cited in Kisić Kolanović, *Mladen Lorković*, 234.

19. *Documents on German Foreign Policy, 1918–1945* (hereafter DGFP), Series D, vol. xii (Washington, DC: US Government Printing Office, 1962), doc. 525, pp. 830–31.

20. DGFP, Series D, vol. xii, doc. 589, pp. 957–58.

21. DGFP, Series D, vol. xii, doc. 603, pp. 977–81.

22. Korb, *Im Schatten des Weltkriegs*, 362–63.

23. According to the Croatian readout of the talks, see Kisić Kolanović, *Mladen Lorković*, 287.

24. See Pavelić's November 15, 1940 message to his followers in Croatia, in Mijo Bzik, *Ustaška pobjeda u danima ustanka i oslobođenja* (Zagreb: Promičbeni ured, 1942), 43. Pavelić's German-language memorandum, *Die kroatische Frage* (1936), which was later published as *Dr. Ante Pavelić riešio je Hrvatsko pitanje*, intro. by Ivo Bogdan (Zagreb: Europa, 1942), links Jews to international communism.

NB: Variations in orthography are due to many of the citations of Croatian source material from the NDH period not corresponding to modern literary Croatian.

25. Goldstein and Goldstein, *Holokaust u Zagrebu*, 249.

26. Korb, *Im Schatten des Weltkriegs*, 165–66.

27. Goldstein and Goldstein, *Holokaust u Zagrebu*, 251.

28. Christopher R. Browning, *The Final Solution and the German Foreign Office: A Study of Referat D III of Abteilung Deutschland, 1940–43* (New York: Holmes & Meier 1978), 93.

29. Korb, *Im Schatten des Weltkriegs*, 204–5.

30. The figures are taken from Žerjavić, "Demografski pokazatelji," 136, and Narcisa Lengel-Krizman, "Logori za Židove u NDH," *Antisemitizam, Holokaust, Antifašizam*, ed. Kraus, 91–103. Ivo Goldstein has argued that 2,500 Jews passed via Gospić through the Jadovno-Pag camp complex, where most were likely killed. See Goldstein and Goldstein, *Holokaust u Zagrebu*, 276.

31. Korb, *Im Schatten des Weltkriegs*, 400.

32. Korb, *Im Schatten des Weltkriegs*, 200–201, 206.

33. "Zakonska odredba o državljanstvu," *Narodne novine*, April 30, 1941, 1.

34. "Zakonska odredba o rasnoj pripadnosti," *Narodne novine*, April 30, 1941, 1.

35. Korb, *Im Schatten des Weltkriegs*, 141–42.

36. "Zapisnik XLVIII. sjednice stalnog odbora za rizničarske poslove, održane dana 27. lipnja 1942," Hrvatski Državni Arhiv (HDA), Fond 211, Hrvatski državni sabor NDH, Box 21, 5.

On June 27, 1941, Pavelić's office issued a press statement cautioning against "visits to the Poglavnik [Leader] with respect to ... the recognition of Aryan character." "Upozorenje Ureda Poglavnika," *Hrvatski narod*, June 28, 1941, 16. According to Narcisa Lengel-Krizman, in the case of mixed marriages the authorities typically granted Aryan status if the Jewish partner had consented to a Catholic marriage and if the children were baptized. See Lengel-Krizman, "Logori za Židove u NDH," 93–94.

37. "Zakonska odredba o zaštiti arijske krvi i časti hrvatskog naroda" and "Naredba o zabrani zaposlenja ženskih osoba u nearijskim kućanstvima," *Narodne novine*, May 6, 1941, 1. For a comparison of German and Croatian race laws, see Raul Hilberg, *The Destruction of the European Jews*, vol. 2 (New York: Holmes & Meier, 1985), 708–18; and Stajić and Papo, "Ubistva i drugi zločini," 219.

38. "Naredba o promjeni židovskih prezimena i označavanju židovskih tvrtki," *Narodne novine*, June 4, 1941, 1.

39. "Naredba o utvrđivanju rasne pripadnosti državnih i samoupravnih službenika i vršitelja slobodnih akademskih zvanja," *Narodne novine*, June 5, 1941, 1.

40. Cited in "NDH pod vodstvom Poglavnika i dalje će u postojanom i neumornom radu znati svladati svaku zapreku," *Hrvatski narod*, October 11, 1941, 5.

41. Pavelić's comments were reprinted in "Židovsko će se pitanje radikalno riješiti," *Hrvatski narod*, May 6, 1941, 1.

42. On the decrees issued in Sarajevo between April and July 1941, see Stajić and Papo, "Ubistva i drugi zločini," 220–22.

43. "Zapisnik 113. sjednice stalnog odbora za rizničarske poslove," December 12, 1942, HDA, Fond 211, Box 23, 16–20.

44. See Lengel-Krizman, "Logori za Židove u NDH," 91–93; Romano, *Jevreji Jugoslavije*, 93, 126; and Stajić and Papo, "Ubistva i drugi zločini," 227–28.

45. "Zakonska odredba o redovitom poslovanju i sprečavanju sabotaže u privrednim poduzećima," *Narodne novine*, June 5, 1941, 1; and "Zakonska odredba o sačuvanju hrvatske narodne imovine," *Narodne novine*, April 18, 1941, 1.

46. "Zakonska odredba o obaveznoj prijavi židovskog imetka" and "Zakonska odredba o spriječavanju prikrivanja židovskog imetka," *Narodne novine*, June 5, 1941, 1.

47. "Zakonska odredba o osnutku Državnog ravnateljstva za gospodarstvenu ponovu," *Narodne novine*, July 1, 1941, 1.

48. "Zakonska odredba o podržavljenju imetka Židova i židovskih poduzeća," *Narodne novine*, October 9, 1941, 1.

49. On expropriation, see Korb, *Im Schatten des Weltkriegs*, 230–40.

The state treasurer, Vladimir Košak, claimed in April 1942 that he intervened with Pavelić because of his concerns with how expropriation was being conducted. "Zapisnik IV. sjednice stalnog odbora za rizničarske poslove," April 16, 1942, HDA, Fond 211, Box 20, 2–9.

50. "Zapisnik II. sjednice stalnog odbora za rizničarske poslove," April 13, 1942, HDA, Fond 211, Box 20, 5–7. The Croatian Foreign Minister claimed in October 1941 that expropriation would eventually help the Croatian authorities solve a host of economic problems. See "NDH pod vodstvom Poglavnika," *Hrvatski narod*, October 11, 1941, 5. According to Fikreta Jelić-Butić, who based her estimate on the work of the postwar Yugoslav war crimes commission, the value of confiscated Jewish property in the NDH was between 20 billion and 25 billion Yugoslav dinars (in 1939 dinars). Fikreta Jelić-Butić, *Ustaše i Nezavisna Država Hrvatska, 1941–1945* (Zagreb: Školska knjiga, 1977), 184.

51. Besides Ustaša functionaries, several private entities and workers' groups encouraged the process of expropriation and staked their claim. Eventually, the state used the "Industrious Croat" and "Progress" to conduct the sales of nationalized businesses. "Zapisnik XVI. sjednice stalnog odbora za rizničarske poslove," May 11, 1942, HDA, Fond 211, Box 20, 3–4, 10.

52. "Zapisnik 100. sjednice stalnog odbora za rizničarske poslove," November 25, 1942, HDA, Fond 211, Box 23, 1, 9–11, 16.

53. Stajić and Papo, "Ubistva i drugi zločini," 224. See also "Zakonska odredba o podržavljenju židovske imovine," *Narodne novine*, October 30, 1942, 1.

54. See "Poglavnikova izvanredna zakonska odredba i zapovijed," *Hrvatski narod*, June 27, 1941, 1; "Red i poštenje: Smisao izvanredne Poglavnikove odredbe," *Hrvatski narod*, June 28, 1941, 2.

55. Cited in Jelić-Butić, *Ustaše i Nezavisna Država Hrvatska*, 181.

56. See "Hrvatska u borbi protiv Židova," *Hrvatski narod*, November 24, 1941, 4.

57. "Reich je u ratu sa Sovjetskom Unijom," *Hrvatski narod*, June 23, 1941, 1.

58. "Pravi smisao rata protiv Moskve," *Hrvatski narod*, July 23, 1941, 1.

59. "Zašto smo nacionalisti, a ne komunisti," *Hrvatski narod*, August 1, 1941, 5–6. See also "Boljševizam—djelo Židova," *Hrvatski narod*, July 9, 1941, 4; and "Protiv kapitalizma i boljševizma," *Hrvatski narod*, June 30, 1941, 2.

60. "U borbu protiv židovsko-boljševičke Moskve!," *Hrvatski narod*, July 3, 1941, 1.

61. "Nema Hrvata, koji nije spreman za Hrvatsku život dati," *Hrvatski narod*, September 17, 1941, 1–2.

62. See Narcisa Lengel-Krizman, "A Contribution to the Study of Terror in the So-Called Independent State of Croatia: Concentration Camps for Women in 1941–42," *Yad Vashem Studies* 20 (1990): 1–51.

63. Lengel-Krizman, "Logori za Židove u NDH," 94. On the Croatian camp system, see Mirko Peršen, *Ustaški logori* (Zagreb: Globus, 1990), 328–29.

64. The tempo of deportations to Jasenovac increased between September and November 1941, as thousands of Jewish men from Zagreb, Sarajevo, and elsewhere in Bosnia were deported there. See Korb, *Im Schatten des Weltkriegs*, 201–2.

65. On November 26, 1941, the Ustaša regime issued the "Legal Decree Regarding the Sending of Suspect and Dangerous Persons to Forced Labor in Collection and Labor Camps" ("Zakonska odredba o upućivanju nepoćudnih i pogibljenih osoba na prisilni boravak u sabirne i radne logore"), which provided a legal framework for the camp system. See Lengel-Krizman, "Logori za Židove u NDH," 97.

As the Ustaša regime began forming its embryonic camp system, it turned to the Nazi Security Service (SD, Sicherheitsdienst) under SS-Sturmbannführer Wilhelm Beisner, who in June 1941 organized a trip to Berlin for several Ustaša leaders, including the senior police official Dido Kvaternik. The Croatian delegation visited the SS headquarters in Oranienburg and toured the Sachsenhausen concentration camp. See Korb, *Im Schatten des Weltkriegs*, 153.

66. Only in a few isolated cases involving prominent Jewish figures, such as Sarajevo's chief rabbi Dr. Moric Levi, and the president of Sarajevo's Zionist organization, Dr. Leon Perić, did the German authorities conduct their own arrests and interrogations in April 1941. See Stajić and Papo, "Ubistva i drugi zločini," 232.

67. The only exception was the April 27, 1941 arrest of 165 Jewish students between the ages of eighteen and twenty-one in Zagreb. On May 20, they were transported to the Danica camp (in Koprivnica) and then to Jadovno, where most of them were killed. Lengel-Krizman, "Logori za Židove u NDH," 94.

68. Goldstein and Goldstein, *Holokaust u Zagrebu*, 259–65.

69. As often seemed to be the case in the NDH, there was a certain element of arbitrariness to the timing of the arrests. For example, while most of Osijek's Jews were forced into a ghetto in early 1942, those in neighboring Vukovar were arrested in August 1941. Jews in certain professions were exempted, but the fate of their families varied from case to case. See Lengel-Krizman, "Logori za Židove u NDH," 94.

70. Stajić and Papo, "Ubistva i drugi zločini," 232–34.

71. Ravijojla Odavić, "Sabirni logor Tenje," in *Slavonija u narodnooslobodilačkoj borbi*, ed. Martin Kaminski (Slavonski Brod: Historijski institut Slavonije, 1967), 210.

72. Cited in *Zločini na jugoslovenskim prostorima u Prvom i Drugom svetskom ratu: Zbornik dokumenata* (hereafter, *Zločini*), Tome I, Book 1: Zločini Nezavisne Države Hrvatske 1941 (Belgrade: Vojnoistorijski institut, 1993), doc. 58, p. 101. The Croatian Home Guard, like the regular bureaucracy, filed routine reports that discussed, inter alia, the "Disposition of the People," broken down by nationality.

73. *Zločini*, I/1, doc. 90, pp. 170–71. See also *Zločini*, I/1, doc. 116, p. 308.

74. *Zbornik dokumenata i podataka o narodnooslobodilačkom ratu jugoslovenskih naroda* (hereafter, *Zbornik NOR*), Tome V, Book 1: Borbe u Hrvatskoj 1941. godine (Belgrade: Vojnoistorijski institut, 1952), doc. 92, p. 268.

75. *Zbornik NOR*, Tome IV, Book 1: Borbe u Bosni i Hercegovini 1941. god. (Belgrade: Vojnoistorijski institut, 1951), doc. 250, p. 557, and doc. 140, p. 419.

76. *Zbornik NOR*, IV/2, docs. 122 and 166, pp. 355, 589.

77. *Zbornik NOR*, IV/2, doc. 182, p. 511. Echoed in January 1942 by the commander of the Second Home Guard Corps, *Zbornik NOR*, IV/2, doc. 139, p. 405.

78. For example, on April 1 and again on June 19, 1942, the prefect of Lekenik commune (Sisak district) urged the Jewish Section to authorize the deportation of three local Jewish families as they "are against the present [state] order." The Jewish Section logged both reports and, in a handwritten note dated July 27, 1942, its director noted, "The Jews in question, sent to a camp." United States Holocaust Memorial Museum (USHMM) Archive, RG.1998.A.0019, Ustaša Supervisory Office, Jewish Section, Reel 6, No. 3607.

79. On the massacre, see Radivoje Lukić, "Pripreme za ustanak i prve borbe u srezu brčanskom," in *Istočna Bosna u NOB-u 1941–1945: Sjećanja učesnika*, ed. Nisim Albahari et al., vol. 1 (Belgrade: Vojnoizdavački zavod, 1971), 207–8; and Romano, *Jevreji Jugoslavije*, 132–33. According to Aleksandar Stajić and Jakov Papo, approximately 150 native and 200 Austrian Jews were massacred on December 10–11 and 16–17. See Stajić and Papo, "Ubistva i drugi zločini," 244–46.

80. The fate of the Jews of Zavidovići and Olovo in eastern Bosnia illustrates this point. On November 25, 1941, the commander of the Home Guard in Zavidovići, who days earlier had engaged the Partisans in a battle for the town, sent an urgent telegram to his regional commander, noting that in the Olovo operational

zone, "not a single Jew is in a camp." Their immediate deportation was urged. The telegram was forwarded to the Interior Ministry, which tasked the Jewish Section to resolve the issue. On December 10, 1941, the Jewish Section's deputy director, Vilko Kühnel, informed the local Ustaša security police that "all Jews of Olovo district are to be arrested and sent to Jasenovac, and the Jewish women to Đakovo." USHMM Archive, RG.1998.A.0019, Ustaša Supervisory Office, Reel 2, No. 7889.

81. On the deportation of Sarajevo's Jews, see Freidenreich, *Jews of Yugoslavia*, 15–25; Emily Greble, *Sarajevo, 1941–1945: Muslims, Christians, and Jews in Hitler's Europe* (Ithaca: Cornell University Press, 2011), 115–17; Stajić and Papo, "Ubistva i drugi zločini," 235–38. The last large-scale deportation from Sarajevo included five hundred Jewish women and children and occurred on December 22, 1941.

82. USHMM Archive, RG-1998.A.0027, NDH Ministry of Internal Affairs, Reel 1, No. 3801.

83. USHMM Archive, RG-1998.A.0027, NDH Ministry of Internal Affairs, Reel 1, No. 2952.

84. Stajić and Papo, "Ubistva i drugi zločini," 239.

85. These logistical problems may explain why the Jews of many western Bosnian towns—for example, the 400 Jews of Banja Luka and the 141 Jews of Bihać—were not swept up in the arrests and deportations of September–December 1941. They would be arrested and deported in the summer of 1942. See Romano, *Jevreji Jugoslavije*, 243–44.

86. Cited in Lengel-Krizman, "Contribution," 42.

87. A series of Croatian Home Guard reports from May 1942 confirm this assessment. USHMM Archive, RG.1998.A.0019, Ustaša Supervisory Office, Jewish Section, Reel 7, No. 4328.

88. The Ustaša authorities referred to the facility as a "ghetto," and in fact it had the characteristics of other ghettoes in Nazi-occupied Europe: it segregated Jews from the rest of the population; it was temporary; and its inhabitants were subsequently deported to camps. USHMM Archive, RG.1998.A.0019, Ustaša Supervisory Office, Jewish Section, Reel 6, No. 3911.

The local Home Guard command was apparently not satisfied with the decision. In mid-July 1942, the Second Home Guard Corps reported to Zagreb that the Jews of Osijek's environs should be deported "so that their clandestine work can be prevented," and noted that German officials had repeatedly stated "that we have not taken radical measures in this regard." *Zbornik NOR*, V/32, doc. 134, p. 375.

89. Odavić, "Sabirni logor Tenje," 209–11.

90. Lengel-Krizman, "Logori za Židove u NDH," 99.

91. On the deportations between August 1942 and May 1943, see Goldstein and Goldstein, *Holokaust u Zagrebu*, 424–34, 465–76; and Korb, *Im Schatten des Weltkriegs*, 413–23.

92. Korb, *Im Schatten des Weltkriegs*, 413–15.

93. "Ustaški pokret je u Hrvatskoj obračunao s razornim židovstvom," *Hrvatski narod*, May 3, 1942, 6.

94. The Auslandsorganisation was the foreign organization of the Nazi Party. "Dužnostnici NSDAP na izložbi 'Židovi,'" *Hrvatski narod*, May 31, 1942, 2; and Zvonimir Sisački, "Borba Hrvata protiv Židova u prošlosti," *Hrvatski narod*, February 23, 1942, 12.

95. "Hrvatska protužidovska izložba," *Hrvatski narod*, April 14, 1942, 9.

96. S. R. Žrnovački, "Židovi podgrizaju narodni život," *Hrvatski narod*, February 7, 1942, 2.

97. "Protužidovski slikopisi," *Hrvatski narod*, April 30, 1942, 4.

98. "Rekordan posjet izložbe 'Židovi,'" *Hrvatski narod*, May 15, 1942, 5.

99. The authorities encouraged peasant attendance and offered inducements such as reduced train fares to rural travelers who provided an admission ticket to the exhibition. It is likely, however, that most attendees were city dwellers. "Veliko zanimanje seljaka za izložbu 'Židovi,'" *Hrvatski narod*, July 3, 1942, 5; "Preko 30.000 osoba na izložbi 'Židovi' u Osijeku," *Hrvatski narod*, July 21, 1942, 4; and "Izložba 'Židovi' u Sarajevu," *Hrvatski narod*, September 18, 1942, 6.

100. Korb, *Im Schatten des Weltkriegs*, 417–18; and Lengel-Krizman, "Logori za Židove u NDH," 95–96.

101. Korb, *Im Schatten des Weltkriegs*, 419.

102. Browning, *Final Solution and the German Foreign Office*, 124–25.

103. Broucek, *Ein General im Zwielicht*, 148.

104. Korb, *Im Schatten des Weltkriegs*, 422.

105. Kisić Kolanović, *Mladen Lorković*, 190.

106. Browning, *Final Solution and the German Foreign Office*, 114.

107. Browning, *Final Solution and the German Foreign Office*, 115, 119. For the diplomatic back-and-forth between Berlin, Rome, and Zagreb, see Léon Poliakov and Jacques Sabille, *Jews under the Italian Occupation*, foreword by J. Godart (Paris: Edition du Centre, 1955), 131–50.

108. Kisić Kolanović, *Mladen Lorković*, 227–28.

109. Kisić Kolanović, *Mladen Lorković*, 230.

110. As told by Casertano to and noted by the Croatian foreign minister on February 23, 1943. Kisić Kolanović, *Mladen Lorković*, 272–73.

111. In May and July 1943, the Italians transferred three thousand Jews to the island of Rab, which was temporarily liberated by the Partisans following the Italian-Allied armistice. Menachem Shelah, "The Italian Rescue of Yugoslav Jews, 1941–1943," in *The Italian Refuge: Rescue of Jews During the Holocaust*, ed. Ivo Herzer (Washington, DC: Catholic University of America Press, 1989), 214–15.

112. Korb, *Im Schatten des Weltkriegs*, 419–20; and Lengel-Krizman, "Logori za Židove u NDH," 96.

113. Korb, *Im Schatten des Weltkriegs*, 420. This assessment is also provided by Jaša Romano and Lavoslav Kadelburg, who argue that the Nazi authorities did not consider the Ustaša regime "fully capable of enforcing a prompt, effective and thorough policy of genocide." See Romano and Kadelburg, "The Third Reich," 688.

114. See Carsten Dams and Michael Stolle, *Die Gestapo: Herrschaft und Terror im Dritten Reich* (Munich: C. H. Beck, 2008), 168.

115. Hilberg, *Destruction of the European Jews*, vol. 2, 718.

116. Jelić-Butić, *Ustaše i Nezavisna Država Hrvatska*, 180.

117. Wendy Lower, "The History and Future of Holocaust Research," *Tablet*, April 26, 2018, https://www.tabletmag.com/jewish-arts-and-culture/culture-news/260677/history-future-holocaust-research, accessed November 3, 2019. See also Lower, "Decentring Berlin: Europeanization of Holocaust History," *Journal of Modern European History* 16, no. 1 (February 2018): 32–39.

118. Romano, *Jevreji Jugoslavije*, 133.

119. See Jonathan E. Gumz, "Wehrmacht Perceptions of Mass Violence in Croatia, 1941–1942," *Historical Journal* 44, no. 4 (December 2001): 1015–38.

CHAPTER 6. GERMAN COLLECTIVE GUILT IN THE NARRATIVES OF SOUTHEASTERN EUROPEAN HOLOCAUST SURVIVORS

This chapter was submitted as part of the Czech Science Foundation grant project, grant number 16-16009S. The research was also made possible thanks to patient editing by Jacob Maze from Charles University in Prague. Kateřina Králová is particularly indebted to the Leibniz Institute for East and Southeast European Studies and the Graduiertenschule für Ost- und Südosteuropastudien, which enabled her work on this chapter during her fellowship in Regensburg.

1. Tomas Sniegon, *Vanished History: The Holocaust in Czech and Slovak Historical Culture* (New York: Berghahn, 2014), 13–17. See also Klas-Göran Karlsson, "The Uses of History and the Third Wave of Europeanisation," in *A European Memory? Contested Histories and Politics of Remembrance*, ed. Bo Stråth and Malgorzata Pakier (New York: Berghahn, 2010), 38–55.

2. Tony Judt, *Postwar: A History of Europe since 1945* (New York: Penguin, 2006), 803.

3. Pieter Lagrou, "Return to a Vanished World: European Societies and the Remnants of their Jewish Communities, 1945–1947," in *The Jews are Coming Back*, ed. David Bankier (New York: Berghahn, 2005), 13–15.

4. Saul Friedländer, *When Memory Comes* (New York: Farrar, Straus & Giroux, 1979).

5. Carl Jung, *Letters, Vol. 1: 1906–1950* (Princeton, NJ: Princeton University Press, 1973), 368–70. More recent works on the matter include Norbert Frei, *1945 und wir: Das Dritte Reich im Bewusstsein der Deutschen* (Munich:

C. H. Beck, 2005) and Tobias Ebbrecht and Timo Reinfrank, "Deutsche Schuld und die Störenfriede der Erinnerung," in *The Final Insult. Das Diktat gegen die Überlebenden: Deutsche Erinnerungsabwehr und Nichtentschädigung der NS-Sklavenarbeit* (Münster: Unrast, 2003).

6. Most of the interviews related to the Holocaust in the archive were recorded during the 1990s. The majority of the interviewees were born between 1910 and 1940. To facilitate working with such a vast amount of material, researchers are provided with advanced search engines, including a list of 62,000 keywords, which are coded in the interviews themselves. "USC SF Visual History Archive," accessed December 12, 2017, http://vhaonline.usc.edu.

7. Only a minuscule Jewish community of approximately two hundred persons existed in prewar Albania, but there is just one interview available in the VHA, which is why Albania was excluded from our research. On numbers, see "Jewish Population of Europe in 1933: Population Data by Country," United States Holocaust Memorial Museum, "The Holocaust," Holocaust Encyclopedia, accessed January 20, 2014, http://www.ushmm.org/wlc/en/article.php?ModuleId=10005161.

8. "USC SF Visual History Archive," accessed December 21, 2017, http://vhaonline.usc.edu.

9. Qualitative research in the field of oral history typically works with such a limited number of interviews. Despite this, we tried to keep our sample as balanced as possible while selecting representative cases. See David Silverman and Amir Marvasti, *Doing Qualitative Research: A Comprehensive Guide* (Thousand Oaks, CA: SAGE, 2009), 163.

10. David K. Dunaway and Willa K. Baum, eds., *Oral History: An Interdisciplinary Anthology* (Walnut Creek, CA: AltaMira Press, 1996); and Miroslav Vaněk and Pavel Mücke, *Třetí strana trojúhelníku: Teorie a praxe orální historie* (Prague: Fakulta humanitních studií, 2012).

11. See Aleida Assmann, "History, Memory, and the Genre of Testimony," *Poetics Today* 2 (2006): 261–73.

12. This method is further described in Helen Malson, "Fictional(ising) Identity? Ontological Assumptions and Methodological Productions of ('Anorexic') Subjectivities," in *The Uses of Narrative: Explorations in Sociology, Psychology, and Cultural Studies*, ed. Molly Andrews et al. (New Brunswick: Transaction Publishers, 2004), 150–63.

13. Daniel J. Elazar, *The Balkan Jewish Communities: Yugoslavia, Bulgaria, Greece, and Turkey* (Lanham, MD: University Press of America, 1984).

14. Halil İnalcık, "Foundations of Ottoman-Jewish Cooperation," in *Jews, Turks, Ottomans: A Shared History, Fifteenth through the Twentieth Century*, ed. Avidgor Levy (Syracuse: Syracuse University Press, 2002), 3–4; Eveline Brugger et al., *Geschichte der Juden in Österreich: Österreichische Geschichte*, Band 15 (Vienna: Ueberreuter, 2006), 219–29, 407–11, 460–64.

15. Jeffrey K. Olick, *The Politics of Regret: On Collective Memory and Historical Responsibility* (New York: Routledge, 2007), 27–30.

16. Wolfgang Benz, ed., *Dimension des Völkermords: Die Zahl der jüdischen Opfer des Nationalsozialismus* (Munich: R. Oldenbourg Verlag, 1991), 11–12; and Kateřina Králová, "Diverse Perspectives on Jewish Life in Southeast Europe: The Holocaust and Beyond," *South-East European and Black Sea Studies* 17, no. 2 (Summer 2017): 155–63.

17. These minorities were similar to the Jews in that they were very diverse. For the purpose of this study, we will use the term *minorities* as related to the states of citizenship in the interwar period or the term *Germans* as used in the interviews we present.

18. Royal dynasties could be mentioned, as well. Pashanko Dimitroff, *Boris III of Bulgaria, 1894–1943: Toiler, Citizen, King* (Lewes: Book Guild, 1986); Michael Kroner, *Die Hohenzollern als Könige von Rumänien: Lebensbilder von vier Monarchen 1866–2004* (Heilbronn: Johannis Reeg, 2004); and Wolf Seidl, *Bayern in Griechenland: Die Geschichte eines Abenteuers* (Munich: Süddeutscher Verlag, 1970). See also Sorina Paula Bolovan and Ioan Bolovan, *Germanii din Română, Perspective istorice și demografice* (Cluj-Napoca: Fundaţia Culturală Română, 2000); Kirsten Fast and Jan Peter Thorbecke, eds., *Griechen und Deutsche: Bilder vom Anderen* (Stuttgart and Darmstadt: Württembergisches Landesmuseum Stuttgart und Hessisches Landesmuseum Darmstadt, 1982); and Holm Sundhaussen, "Die Deutschen in Jugoslawien," in *Deutsche im Ausland—Fremde in Deutschland: Migration in Geschichte und Gegenwart*, ed. Klaus J. Bade (Munich: Beck, 1992), 56.

19. Mirna Zakić, *Ethnic Germans and National Socialism in Yugoslavia in World War II* (Cambridge: Cambridge University Press, 2017), 36–40.

20. In her testimony, Lili A. uses German toponyms regularly, as she gave her whole interview in German, after having lived in West Germany since 1966.

21. Cf. Sundhaussen, "Die Deutschen in Jugoslawien," 61; and Jiří Kocián, "Deutsche," in *Nationale Minderheiten im sozialistischen Jugoslawien: Brüderlichkeit und Eigenheit*, ed. Kateřina Králová, Jiří Kocián, and Kamil Pikal (Frankfurt: Peter Lang, 2015), 151–66.

22. Lili A., ID 12825, USC Shoah Foundation Visual History Archive, accessed at the Malach Center for Visual History at the Charles University Prague, with support of the LM2015071 LINDAT/Clarin Infrastructure. This applies to all the interviews presented further on.

23. Max G., ID 25547. On German schools in Romania, see Georges Castellan, "The Germans of Rumania," *Journal of Contemporary History* 6, no. 1 (January 1971): 57–58.

24. Izidor D., ID 46806.

25. As she mentions further in her interview, at home they spoke mostly Spanish and French. Ivonne K., ID 41963.

For more on German schools in interwar Thessaloniki, see Devin E. Naar, *Jewish Salonica: Between the Ottoman Empire and Modern Greece* (Standford, CA: Stanford University Press, 2016).

26. Frenty A., ID 47797.

27. The emigration to Palestine was made possible after Spain, as a neutral country, intervened in Berlin for their release. Some Jews possessed Spanish citizenship and were therefore given this opportunity. Haim Avni, "Spanish Nationals in Greece and their Fate during the Holocaust," *Yad Vashem Studies on the European Jewish Catastrophe and Resistance* 8 (1970): 31–68.

28. Elias C., ID 48297.

29. Revekka A., ID 45239.

30. Ivonne K., ID 41963.

31. On wartime famine in Greece, see Mark Mazower, *Inside Hitler's Greece* (Yale: Yale Nota Bene, 2001), 30–52, and especially Violetta Hionidou, *Famine and Death in Occupied Greece, 1941–1944* (Cambridge: Cambridge University Press, 2006). On the Jews in occupied Greece, see Maria Kavala, "Thessaloniki sti Germaniki Katochi (1941–1944): Kinonia, ikonomia, diogmos Evreon" [Thessaloniki under German Occupation (1941–1944): Society, Economy, Expulsion of Jews] (PhD dissertation, Panepistimio Kritis Rethymno, 2009), 178–236.

32. Frenty A., ID 47797.

33. Bellina A., ID 20080.

34. Bellina A., ID 20080.

35. Max G., ID 25547.

36. Max G., ID 25547.

37. Max G., ID 25547.

38. Izidor D., ID 46806.

39. Revekka A., ID 45239.

40. Elias C., ID 48297.

41. Beruria S., ID 33668.

42. Edith F., ID 9502.

43. Helen S., ID 36035.

44. Olick, *Politics of Regret*, 27–30.

45. Tullia Santin, *Der Holocaust in den Zeugnissen griechischer Jüdinnen und Juden* (Berlin: Duncker & Humblot, 2003), 191.

46. Ivonne K., ID 41963.

47. Revekka A., ID 45239.

48. Santin, *Der Holocaust in den Zeugnissen*, 193.

49. Elias C., ID 48297.

50. Ivonne K., ID 41963.

51. Leslie P., ID 52426.

52. Leslie P., ID 52426.

53. Helen S., ID 36035.

54. Mirjam D., ID 20374.

55. Here he reflects on Daniel Golhagen, *Hitler's Willing Executioners: Ordinary Germans and the Holocaust* (New York: Alfred A. Knopf, 1996).

56. Max G., ID 25547.

57. Frenty A., ID 47797.

58. Ivonne K., ID 41963.

59. Vera H., ID 54894.

60. Lili A., ID 12825.

61. Edith F., ID 9502.

62. Lili A., ID 12825.

63. Frenty A., ID 47797.

64. Leslie P., ID 52426.

65. Mimi P., ID 38790.

66. Frenty A., ID 47797. From the context of the interview, it is not clear whether there actually were any Germans present or this was the narrator's assumption.

67. This is similar to Wolfgang Benz's critique of Hannah Arendt. Benz, *Dimension des Völkermords*, 11–12; Hannah Arendt, *Eichmann in Jerusalem: A Report on the Banality of Evil* (New York: Penguin Books, 1964), 181–93.

CHAPTER 7. MULTIPLY ENTANGLED

Research for this article has been supported by the Bundesbeauftragte für Kultur und Medien (BKM). I would like to thank Chris Molnar, Mirna Zakić, Rolf Wörsdörfer, and the anonymous reviewers for their insightful comments, Christoph Rass for introducing me to ancestry.com, and Lars Kravagna (Osnabrück) for his help with formatting. A special note of gratitude is due to Anne Eisert, Ellen Ince, Otmar Krajec, and Margarete Panagiotidis for sharing personal memories and documents with me, without which this story would have been much poorer.

1. Passenger manifesto of SS *Westphalia*, sailing from Hamburg, July 25, 1928, arriving at Halifax, August 5, 1928. Ancestry.com. Canadian Passenger Lists, 1865–1935. This and all subsequent web references were last accessed on February 12, 2018.

2. CM/1, Application for Assistance PCIRO, Ana Klun, May 28, 1949, 3.2.1.3 / 80692106/ ITS Digital Archive, Arolsen Archives.

3. Manifest of Inbound Passengers (Aliens), Class Tourist, from Cherbourg, May 17, 1950, on SS *Queen Mary*, arriving at port New York, May 22, 1950. Ancestry.com. New York, Passenger Lists, 1820–1957.

4. Joachim Hösler, "Gottscheer—Geschichte, Selbstverständnis, Außenwahrnehmung," in *Spurensuche in der Gottschee: Deutschsprachige Siedler in*

Slowenien, ed. Mitja Ferenc and Joachim Hösler (Potsdam: Deutsches Kulturforum Östliches Europa, 2011), 15–16.

5. See, for instance, Hugo Grothe, *Die deutsche Sprachinsel Gottschee in Slowenien: Ein Beitrag zur Deutschtumskunde des europäischen Südostens* (Münster: Aschendorff, 1931).

6. For a concise overview of this history, see also Rolf Wörsdörfer, "Identità germaniche al confine orientale: Il caso della Gottschee/Kocevje," *Giornale di Storia contemporanea* 22, no. 2 (2018): 21–36.

7. Tara Zahra, "'Prisoners of the Postwar': Expellees, Displaced Persons, and Jews in Austria after World War II," *Austrian History Yearbook* 41 (April 2010): 191–215.

8. Verzeichnis der Volks- und Reichsdeutschen Umsiedler, die auf Grund des Abkommens vom 31. August 1941 aus der Provinz Laibach umgesiedelt wurden, http://gottschee.net/Dateien/Dokumente/Web%20Deutsch/Umsiedlungsverzeichnis/start.php. The complete resettlement records are available online. They are searchable and sortable according to different criteria, including surname, place of birth, and place of last residence, allowing for the relatively easy construction of a geographic sample. In this case, the records included all the inhabitants of Lienfeld at the time of resettlement (211 individuals from 47 households), as well as native Lienfelders living elsewhere (44 individuals). All subsequent references in this chapter to the resettler list refer to data obtained through this website.

9. For a systematic overview, see the General Inventory of the ITS archive, https://arolsen-archives.org/en/search-explore/search-online-archive/inventory/.

10. In the ITS archive, CM/1 records are filed under the registration 3.2.1, with 3.2.1.3 containing the files originating in Austria.

11. This information can be extracted from the Central Name Index (0.1) and from passenger lists (3.1.3.2).

12. Ancestry.com is a commercial database providing access to a variety of digitized sources relevant for genealogical research mainly taken from North American and European archives. These records are indexed and searchable by name and other criteria such as date and place of birth. Despite its commercial nature, it is an invaluable and reliable source for the record matching necessary for this kind of historical migration research.

13. For a history and critique of the concept of "linguistic islands," see Heinke M. Kalinke, "Sprachinselforschung," in *Online-Lexikon zur Kultur und Geschichte der Deutschen im östlichen Europa*, ome-lexikon.uni-oldenburg.de/p32772 (Stand 02.07.2015). See also Pieter Judson, "When Is a Diaspora Not a Diaspora? Rethinking Nation-Centered Narratives about Germans in Habsburg East Central Europe," in *The Heimat Abroad: The Boundaries of Germanness*, ed. Krista O'Donnell, Renate Bridenthal, and Nancy Reagin (Ann Arbor: Michigan University Press, 2005), 219–47.

14. Hösler, "Gottscheer," 15.

15. Hösler, "Gottscheer," 15.

16. Die Bevölkerung der im Reichrathe Vertretenen Königreiche und Länder nach Religion, Bildungsgrad, Umgangssprache und nach ihren Gebrechen. 2. Heft der "Ergebnisse der Volkszählung und der mit derselben verbundenen Zählung der häuslichen Nutzthiere vom 31. December 1880," bearbeitet von der K. K. Direction der Administrativen Statistik (Vienna: Kaiserlich-Königliche Hof- und Staatsdruckerei, 1882), http://anno.onb.ac.at/cgi-content/anno-plus?aid=ors&datum=0001&size=45&page=276.

17. Marjan Drnovšek, "Izseljevanje Kočevarjev v Združene Države Amerike," *Dve Domovine* 21 (2005): 15.

18. Hösler, "Gottscheer," 21.

19. Ulf Brunnbauer, "Globalizing Southeastern Europe: The Economic Causes and Consequences of Overseas Emigration up until 1914," *Jahrbuch für Wirtschaftsgeschichte* 55, no. 1 (June 2014): 37.

20. Heinz Fassmann, "Emigration, Immigration and Internal Migration in the Austro-Hungarian Monarchy, 1910," in *Roots of the Transplanted, Vol. 1: Late 19th Century East Central and Southeastern Europe*, ed. Dirk Hoerder and Inge Blank (Boulder, CO: East European Monographs, 1994), 299; and Annemarie Steidl, "Transatlantic Migration from the Late Austrian Empire and Its Relation to Rural-Urban Stage Migration," in *European Mobility: Internal, International, and Transatlantic Moves in the 19th and Early 20th Centuries*, ed. Annemarie Steidl et al. (Göttingen: Vandenhoeck & Ruprecht Unipress, 2009), 218.

21. Fassmann, "Emigration," 259–60.

22. Drnovšek, "Izseljevanje Kočevarjev," 13.

23. Drnovšek, "Izslejevanje Kočevarjev," 20.

24. Arnold Suppan, ed., *Deutsche Geschichte im Osten Europas: Zwischen Adria und Karawanken* (Berlin: Siedler, 1998), 368.

25. Hösler, "Gottscheer," 25.

26. Treaty of Peace with Austria (St. Germain-en-Laye, 10 September 1919), http://www.austlii.edu.au/au/other/dfat/treaties/1920/3.html.

27. Suppan, *Deutsche Geschichte*, 363; and Mitja Ferenc, "Für immer untergegangen? Die Gottscheer im 20. Jahrhundert," in *Spurensuche*, ed. Ferenc and Hösler, 44.

28. Arnold Suppan, *Jugoslawien und Österreich 1918–1938: Bilaterale Außenpolitik im europäischen Umfeld* (Cologne: Böhlau, 1996), 919.

29. On the Nazification of the Slovene Germans, see the classic study by Dušan Biber, *Nacizem in nemci v Jugoslaviji, 1933–1941* (Ljubljana: Cankarjeva založba, 1966). About the more numerous Danube Swabians of the Yugoslav Banat, see Mirna Zakić, *Ethnic Germans and National Socialism in Yugoslavia in World War II* (Cambridge: Cambridge University Press, 2017).

30. Rogers Brubaker, "Homeland Nationalism in Weimar Germany and 'Weimar Russi'," in *Nationalism Reframed: Nationhood and the National Question in the New Europe*, ed. Rogers Brubaker (Cambridge: Cambridge University Press, 2000), 107-47.

31. Valdis O. Lumans, *Himmler's Auxiliaries: The Volksdeutsche Mittelstelle and the German National Minorities of Europe, 1933-1945* (Chapel Hill: University of North Carolina Press, 1993). To be sure, the Nazis did not invent the concept and terminology of *Volksgruppen*. For instance, the association of German minorities in Europe had been known as *Verband der deutschen Volksgruppen in Europa* since 1929. However, the Nazis took the organization and disciplining of these groups to a new level. For a history and critique of the *Volksgruppen* concept, see Samuel Salzborn, *Ethnisierung der Politik: Theorie und Geschichte des Volksgruppenrechts in Europa* (Frankfurt am Main: Campus Verlag, 2005).

32. Hans Hermann Frensing, *Die Umsiedlung der Gottscheer Deutschen: Das Ende einer südostdeutschen Volksgruppe* (Munich: Oldenbourg, 1970), 18f.

33. Wilhelm Lampeter, "Die Gottscheer Volksgruppe 1930-1942," no date (probably mid-February 1942), quoted in Frensing, *Umsiedlung*, 12.

34. Quoted after Frensing, *Umsiedlung*, 71.

35. Frensing, *Umsiedlung*, 71.

36. Frensing, *Umsiedlung*, 72.

37. Rolf Wörsdörfer, "Transnationale Aspekte italienischer und deutscher Besatzungsherrschaft in Slowenien 1941-1945," in *Die "Achse" im Krieg: Politik, Ideologie und Kriegführung 1939-1945*, ed. Lutz Klinkhammer, Amedeo Osti Guerrazzi, and Thomas Schlemmer (Paderborn: Schöningh, 2010), 340-67.

38. Götz Aly, *"Endlösung": Völkerverschiebung und der Mord an den europäischen Juden* (Frankfurt am Main: Fischer, 1995), 36-37.

39. This list of resettlement campaigns and the respective numbers is based on Philipp Ther, *Die Dunkle Seite der Nationalstaaten: "Ethnische Säuberungen" im modernen Europa* (Göttingen: Vandenhoeck & Ruprecht, 2011), 113-17.

40. Frensing, *Umsiedlung*, 24-27.

41. A comprehensive analysis of the racially motivated settlement plans of the Nazis is provided by Isabel Heinemann, *"Rasse, Siedlung, deutsches Blut": Das Rasse- und Siedlungshauptamt der SS und die rassenpolitische Neuordnung Europas* (Göttingen: Wallstein, 2003).

42. According to Götz Aly's classic argument, in the case of the Jews the resettlement-expulsion nexus ultimately resulted in the Holocaust. See Aly, *Endlösung*, 13-21.

43. Frensing, *Umsiedlung*, 48, 54, 59-60; and Wörsdörfer, "Transnationale Aspekte," 359-61.

44. Markus Leniger, *Nationalsozialistische "Volkstumsarbeit" und Umsiedlungspolitik 1939-1945: Von der Minderheitenbetreuung zur Siedlerauslese* (Berlin: Frank & Timme, 2006); Lumans, *Himmler's Auxiliaries*, chapters 7-10;

and Maria Fiebrandt, *Auslese für die Siedlergesellschaft: Die Einbeziehung Volksdeutscher in die NS-Erbgesundheitspolitik im Kontext der Umsiedlungen 1939–1945* (Göttingen: Vandenhoeck & Ruprecht, 2014).

45. Frensing, *Umsiedlung*, 64.
46. Frensing, *Umsiedlung*, 92–93.
47. Frensing, *Umsiedlung*, 92–93.
48. Frensing, *Umsiedlung*, 95–97.
49. Frensing, *Umsiedlung*, 116–17.
50. Hösler, "Gottscheer," 37.
51. Abschlussbericht der EWZ, no date, quoted in Frensing, *Umsiedlung*, 165–72.
52. These documents are all dated October 27, 1941. I thank my aunt Anne Eisert and my cousin Ellen Ince for providing me with copies from their private archive.
53. Timeline established in an email communication with my uncle Otmar Krajec, November 5, 2017. See also Josef Krajec's registration with the miners' insurance (*Knappschaft*) dated May 27, 1943, in List of political, social security and labour employment office records, 2.1.1.1 / 70419135 / ITS Digital Archive, Arolsen Archives.
54. Hösler, "Gottscheer," 36.
55. Email communication with my uncle Otmar Krajec, November 12, 2017.
56. Hösler, "Gottscheer," 36. For a vivid description of the flight, see Edeltraud M. Krauland, *Gottschee: The Resettlement Years* (Cheyenne, WY: E. M. Krauland, 1994), 130–57.
57. The loss of citizenship of disloyal minorities was enabled by Article 16 of the new citizenship law of August 1945. In 1948, the law was amended by Article 35, which specifically stripped Germans residing abroad of their Yugoslav citizenship, thus barring their return. See Hans-Joachim Seeler, *Das Staatsangehörigkeitsrecht von Jugoslawien* (Frankfurt am Main: Metzner, 1956), 51, 135, quoted after Edvin Pezo, *Zwangsmigration in Friedenszeiten? Jugoslawische Migrationspolitik und die Auswanderung von Muslimen in die Türkei, 1918 bis 1966* (Munich: Oldenbourg, 2013), 103n51.
58. Zahra, "'Prisoners of the Postwar.'"
59. Gerard D. Cohen, *In War's Wake: Europe's Displaced Persons in the Postwar Order* (Oxford: Oxford Univeristy Press, 2012), chapter 5.
60. Cohen, *In War's Wake*, 106–8.
61. Cohen, *In War's Wake*, 110.
62. Alexander Freund, *Aufbrüche nach dem Zusammenbruch: Die deutsche Nordamerika-Auswanderung nach dem Zweiten Weltkrieg* (Göttingen: Vandenhoeck & Ruprecht Unipress, 2004), 215, 217. See also Karin Nerger-Focke, *Die deutsche Amerikaauswanderung nach 1945: Rahmenbedingungen und Verlaufsformen* (Stuttgart: Hans-Dieter Heinz, 1995), 124.

63. Constitution of the International Refugee Organization, Annex I, Part II, No. 4, February 16, 1946, https://www.loc.gov/law/help/us-treaties/bevans/m-ust000004-0284.pdf.

64. Emil Brix, *Die Umgangssprachen in Altösterreich zwischen Agitation und Assimilation: Die Sprachenstatistik in den zisleithanischen Volkszählungen 1880 bis 1910* (Vienna: Böhlau, 1982), 27–30, 36–66.

65. Tara Zahra, *Kidnapped Souls: National Indifference and the Battle for Children in the Bohemian Lands, 1900–1948* (Ithaca, NY: Cornell University Press, 2008), 186.

66. On national indifference, see Zahra, *Kidnapped Souls*; Tara Zahra, "Imagined Noncommunities: National Indifference as a Category of Analysis," *Slavic Review* 69, no. 1 (Spring 2010): 93–119. On the switching of nationality by so-called "amphibians," see Chad Bryant, "Either German or Czech: Fixing Nationality in Bohemia and Moravia, 1939–1946," *Slavic Review* 61, no. 4 (Winter 2002): 683–706.

67. For rehabilitation of *Volksliste* members, see Hugo Service, *Germans to Poles: Communism, Nationalism and Ethnic Cleansing after the Second World War* (Cambridge: Cambridge University Press, 2013). For the continuum of switching back and forth between nationalities, see John J. Kulczycki, *Belonging to the Nation: Inclusion and Exclusion in the Polish-German Borderlands, 1939–1951* (Cambridge, MA: Harvard University Press, 2016).

68. About the Germanization of Slovenes in German-occupied Slovenia, see Wörsdörfer, "Transnationale Aspekte," 357–58.

69. For other cases of ethnic Germans attempting that kind of national conversion when faced with IRO eligibility officers, see Cohen, *In War's Wake*, 44–46. About the meaning of DP nationality registrations in IRO forms, see Diane F. Afoumado, "The 'Care and Maintenance in Germany' Collection—A Reflection of DP Self-Identification and Postwar Emigration," in *Displaced Persons: Leben im Transit—Überlebende zwischen Repatriierung, Rehabilitation und Neuanfang*, ed. Rebecca Boehling, Susanne Urban, and René Bienert (Göttingen: Wallstein, 2014) (Freilegungen: Jahrbuch des International Tracing Service, 3), 217–27.

70. Intergovernmental Committee on Refugees, Registration Record, Stefan Poje, June 21, 1947, 3.2.1.3 / 80786568 / ITS Digital Archive, Arolsen Archives.

71. Intergovernmental Committee on Refugees, Registration Record, Elisabeth Poje, June 24, 1947, 3.2.1.3 / 80786569 / ITS Digital Archive, Arolsen Archives.

72. Intergovernmental Committee on Refugees, Registration Record, Rosina Poje, June 23, 1947, 3.2.1.3 / 80786570 / ITS Digital Archive, Arolsen Archives.

73. See for example the CM/1 Applications for Assistance by Karl Kraker, 3.2.1.3 / 80705202; Josef Wolf, 3.2.1.3 / 80883483; Anton Stimitz, 3.2.1.3 / 80841392; Josef Handler, 3.2.1.3 / 80647290; Hilda Schleimer 3.2.1.3 / 80816257, all in ITS Digital Archives, Arolsen Archives.

74. Ben Shephard, *The Long Road Home: The Aftermath of the Second World War* (New York: Anchor Books, 2010), 81–83.

75. About similar processes among other DP groups, see Cohen, *In War's Wake*, 42.

76. Application for Assistance, PCIRO, Stefan Poje, February 23, 1949, 3.2.1.3 / 80786567 / ITS Digital Archives, Arolsen Archives.

77. Application for Assistance, PCIRO, Stefan Poje, February 23, 1949, 3.2.1.3 / 80786567 / ITS Digital Archives, Arolsen Archives.

78. Petition for Review, Stefan Poje, March 1, 1949, 3.2.1.3 / 80786571 / ITS Digital Archives, Arolsen Archives.

79. IRO, Decision of the Review Board, May 26, 1949, 3.2.1.3 / 80786572 / ITS Digital Archives, Arolsen Archives.

80. Application for Assistance PCIRO, Ana Klun, May 28, 1949, 3.2.1.3 / 80692106/ ITS Digital Archive, Arolsen Archives.

81. Application for Assistance PCIRO, Ana Klun, May 28, 1949, 3.2.1.3 / 80692106/ ITS Digital Archive, Arolsen Archives.

82. Margarete Panagiotidis, personal communication; and Otmar Krajec, email communication, November 12, 2017.

83. Email communication with Otmar Krajec, November 12, 2017.

84. I found reference to forty-four individuals named "Klun" in the ITS digital archives, including a Johann (Ivan) Klun from Ribnica, who identified as Slovene (2.2.2.1 / 72991266). Others identified as Croats, Yugoslavs, Italians, and Italians from Venezia-Giulia.

85. Application for Assistance PCIRO, Ana Klun, May 28, 1949 3.2.1.3 / 80692106/ ITS Digital Archive, Arolsen Archives. The "Kulturbund" the document refers to is likely the Steierischer Heimatbund. The Swabian-German Kulturbund—the association of ethnic Germans in Yugoslavia—was dissolved in 1941. I thank Rolf Wörsdörfer for pointing out this detail.

86. Cohen, *In War's Wake*, 39.

87. Bryant, "Either German or Czech."

88. DP registration cards for Janez, Paulina, and Hilda Cerne, June 17, 1949, 3.1.1.1 / 69036090–3, and passenger list of the USAT *General Muir*, 3.1.3.2 / 81665881, all in ITS Digital Archive, Arolsen Archives. The correct spelling of the name in Slovenian would be Černe, with a diacritical mark.

89. Her sponsorship is noted in the passenger list, 3.1.3.2 / 81665881 / ITS Digital Archive, Arolsen Archives.

90. Naturalization record for Julia Plesche, March 28, 1944, Brooklyn, New York, retrieved via www.ancestry.com.

91. Passenger list for the SS *Resolute* sailing from Hamburg to New York on July 11, 1922, retrieved via www.ancestry.com.

92. Application for Assistance, PCIRO, Maria Marn, January 6, 1948, 3.2.1.3 / 80739023 / ITS Digital Archive, Arolsen Archives, and her handwritten letter of June 6, 1949 denying that she was *volksdeutsch* (3.2.1.3 / 80739024).

93. International Refugee Organization, Decision of the Review Board, February 27, 1950, 3.2.1.3 / 80739025 / ITS Digital Archive, Arolsen Archives.

94. Passenger list for KLM flight KL 651 from Amsterdam to Curacao, February 28, 1950. Ancestry.com. New York, Passenger Lists, 1820–1957.

95. Passenger list for KLM flight KL 651 from Amsterdam to Curacao, February 28, 1950. Ancestry.com. New York, Passenger Lists, 1820–1957.

96. Manifest of Inbound Passengers (Aliens), Class DP from Bremerhaven, August 7, 1951 on USNS *General S. D. Sturgis*, arriving at port of New York, August 17, 1951. Ancestry.com. New York, Passenger Lists, 1820–1957. Naturalization record for Maria Marn, May 3, 1955, Brooklyn, New York. Ancestry.com. US Naturalization Records Indexes, 1794–1995.

97. MIFLY 12606 ex Munich/Riem, Germany on December 24, 1956, 3.1.3.2 / 81759601 / ITS Digital Archive, Arolsen Archives.

98. Declaration of Intention, Pauline Schleimer, Brooklyn, March 10, 1925. Ancestry.com. New York, State and Federal Naturalization Records, 1794–1943; Passenger list SS *Resolute*, passengers sailing from Hamburg to New York, October 3, 1922. Ancestry.com. New York, Passenger Lists, 1820–1957.

99. Application for Assistance, PCIRO, Max Schleimer, February 10, 1949, 3.2.1.3 / 80816266 / ITS Digital Archive, Arolsen Archives.

100. Application for Assistance, PCIRO, Josef Handler, December 9, 1948, 3.2.1.3 / 80647290; and Application for Assistance, PCIRO, Hilda Schleimer, December 10, 1948, 3.2.1.3 / 80816255, both in ITS Digital Archive, Arolsen Archives.

101. Pauline Schleimer, Kutztown, Pennsylvania, to IRO Austria, September 15, 1949, 3.2.1.3 / 80816256 / ITS Digital Archive, Arolsen Archives.

102. Manifest of Inbound Passengers (Aliens), Class Tourist from Genoa, March 28, 1950, on *Italia* arriving at port of New York April 12, 1950. Ancestry.com. New York, Passenger Lists, 1820–1957.

103. Manifest of Inbound Passengers (Aliens), Class Tourist from Genoa, May 2, 1950, on *Italia* arriving at port of New York May 15, 1950. Ancestry.com. New York, Passenger Lists, 1820–1957.

104. Pan American Airways flight 88846, June 23, 1950, ex London. Ancestry.com. New York, Passenger Lists, 1820–1957.

105. Passenger list for *General Langfitt*, January 9, 1957, 3.1.3.2 / 81701190 / ITS Digital Archive, Arolsen Archives.

106. According to the inflation calculator of the Official Data Foundation, this would be the equivalent of almost $60,000 in today's terms. "$5,600 in 1950 → 2019 | Inflation Calculator." US Official Inflation Data, Alioth Finance, November 1, 2019, https://www.officialdata.org/us/inflation/1950?amount=5600.

107. Manifest of Inbound Passengers (Aliens), Class Tourist, from Cherbourg, May 17, 1950, on SS *Queen Mary*, arriving at port New York, May 22, 1950. Ancestry.com. New York, Passenger Lists, 1820–1957.

108. Freund, *Aufbrüche*, 218.

109. Freund, *Aufbrüche*, 226.

110. Freund, *Aufbrüche*, 220.

111. History of the Gottscheer Relief Association, http://www.gottscheenewyork.org/relief_history.html.

112. In the historical survey of the postwar period on their homepage, the Gottscheer Relief Association writes that this did happen to some people resettled under the NCWC quota. See History of the Gottscheer Relief Association, http://www.gottscheenewyork.org/relief_history.html.

113. For patterns of immigrant settlement and spatial mobility in the United States, see Alejandro Portes and Rubén G. Rumbaut, *Immigrant America: A Portrait*, 3rd ed. (Berkeley: University of California Press, 2006), 37–66. For a concise discussion of ethnic neighborhoods past and present in New York City, see Nancy Foner, *From Ellis Island to JFK: New York's Two Great Waves of Immigration* (New Haven, CT: Yale University Press, 2000), 36–69.

114. Naturalization record for Anna Scheschareg (Sesarek), née Klun, Brooklyn, New York, January 17, 1956. Ancestry.com. US Naturalization Records Indexes, 1794–1995.

115. Wörsdörfer, "Identità germaniche," 33.

116. Zahra, "'Prisoners of the Postwar,'" 209.

117. For Lampeter's East German university career as an agronomist, see his entry in Professorenkatalog der Universität Leipzig, http://research.uni-leipzig.de/catalogus-professorum-lipsiensium/leipzig/Lampeter_2016.

118. *Gesetz zur Regelung von Fragen der Staatsangehörigkeit vom 22. Februar 1955*, erläutert von Dr. jur. Werner Hoffmann (Stuttgart: Kohlhammer, 1955), 21–30.

119. List compiled by Arbeitsamt München, 2.1.1.1 / 70071208 / ITS Digital Archive, Arolsen Archives. Friedrich still appeared on the resettler list, but he put down Munich as his current residence.

120. Request for Records Check, Johann Stimitz, 6.3.3.1 / 106861540 / ITS Digital Archive, Arolsen Archives.

121. Margarete Panagiotidis, personal communication.

CHAPTER 8. WE HAD TO LEAVE OUR REALLY GOOD DOG

1. With its late thirteenth-century conquest by the Habsburgs, the Gottschee became a feudal domain of the Carinthian-based Counts of Ortenburg. The Gottschee region, a hilly, forested, karstic land with marginal croplands, was largely uninhabited at this time. As part of a larger Habsburg push to populate its southern frontiers, the Ortenburgs colonized the Gottschee in the fourteenth century with agricultural settlers from their holdings in Carinthia and Tyrol, with additional settlers arriving from Thuringia and Franconia. Anja Moric, "Ohranjanje kočevarščine, narečja kočevskih Nemcev, v Sloveniji, Avstriji, Nemčiji, Kanadi in ZDA," *Razprave in gradivo: Revijo za narodnostna vprašanja* 61 (April 2010): 93.

2. Alenka Auersperger, "Še enkrat o selitvi volksdeutscherjev med II. svetovno vojno," *Arhivi* 36, no. 2 (2013): 238.

3. Ana Trbovich, *A Legal Geography of Yugoslavia's Disintegration* (New York: Oxford University Press, 2008), 42n260.

4. Danielle Drozdzewski, Sarah De Nardi, and Emma Waterton, "Geographies of Memory, Place and Identity: Intersections in Remembering War and Conflict," *Geography Compass* 10, no. 11 (2016): 447, 450.

5. Drozdzewski et al., "Geographies of Memory," 449.

6. Ieva Zake, "The Exempt Nation: Memory of Collaboration in Contemporary Latvia," in *Secret Agents and the Memory of Everyday Collaboration in Communist Eastern Europe*, eds. Peter Apor, Sandor Horvath, and James Mark (London: Anthem, 2017), 62

7. As this chapter is concerned with how Gottscheers remember their homeland, the German spelling (Gottschee) will be used throughout. The first time a Gottscheer village or place name appears, it will be accompanied by its Slovene version in brackets. The only exception is Kočevski Rog (Gottscheer Hornwald), which because of its infamy as a postwar site of mass killings by the communist regime by the communist regime retains its better known Slovene appellation. Place names outside the Gottschee use the Slovene spelling.

8. Mitja Ferenc, "The Fate of Gottschee: During and After the War," *The Gottschee Tree* (December 2006), 4.

9. Ferenc, "The Fate of Gottschee," 9.

10. Thomas Bencin, *Gottschee: A History of a German Community in Slovenia from the Fourteenth to the Twentieth Century* (Sonora, CA: The Gottscheer Research and Genealogy Association, 1995), 51.

11. The Yugoslav Kulturbund was established in the city of Novi Sad (Vojvodina region) in 1920, and, as historian Mirna Zakić noted, was to be "an ostensibly nonpolitical organization for cultural and educational activities" of the German minority, but "nonetheless, involved itself in politics." Mirna Zakić, *Ethnic Germans and National Socialism in Yugoslavia in World War II* (Cambridge: Cambridge University Press, 2017), 36.

12. Erich Petschauer, *"Das Jahrhundertbuch": Gottschee and Its People through the Centuries* (New York: Gottscheer Relief Association, 1984), available without corresponding page numbers at http://www.gottschee.net/Dateien/20%20Jhd/Web%20Englisch/Petschauer/20%20cen%2002.htm#); Mitja Ferenc, *Gottschee: The Lost Cultural Heritage of the Gottscheer Germans* (Louisville, CO: Gottscheer Heritage and Genealogy Association, 2001), 78.

13. Auersperger, "Še enkrat o selitvi volksdeutscherje," 238.

14. John Tschinkel, *The Bells Ring No More* (Ljubljana: Modrijan, 2010), 64, 67.

15. Zakić, *Ethnic Germans and National Socialism*, 36.

16. Tschinkel, *Bells*, 68.

17. Janko Jarc, *Partizanski Rog* (Maribor: Založba Obzorja, 1977), 39.

18. John Tschinkel, "The End of the Gottscheer as an Ethnic Group; The Documented Facts" (self-published, 1999), 32. Tschinkel, an American Gottscheer who experienced the war, quotes extensively from Hans Hermann Frensing's 1970 account, which was produced for the South East German Historical Commission (Südostdeutschen Historische Kommission), and is one of the first reliable document-based histories; see Hans Hermann Frensing, *Die Umsiedlung der Gottscheer Deutschen: Das Ende einer südostdeutschen Volksgruppe* (Munich: Oldenbourg, 1970).

19. Auersperger, "Še enkrat o selitvi volksdeutscherje," 244.

20. Matthew Frank, *Making Minorities History: Population Transfer in Twentieth-Century Europe* (Oxford: Oxford University Press, 2017), 120.

21. Tschinkel, "End," 8.

22. Tschinkel, "End," 9.

23. Norman Naimark, *Fires of Hatred: Ethnic Cleansing in Twentieth-Century Europe* (Cambridge, MA: Harvard University Press, 2001), 4.

24. Frensing, *Die Umsiedlung*, quoted in Tschinkel, "End," 10.

25. Auersperger, "Še enkrat o selitvi volksdeutscherje," 241.

26. Auersperger, "Še enkrat o selitvi volksdeutscherje," 241.

27. Frensing, *Die Umsiedlung*, quoted in Tschinkel, "End," 12.

28. Tschinkel, "End," 13.

29. Tschinkel, "End," 12.

30. A copy of Lampeter's list of suspect Gottscheers can be found in Auersperger, "Še enkrat o selitvi volksdeutscherje," 245–49.

31. Frensing, *Die Umsiedlung*, quoted in Tschinkel, "End," 16.

32. Helga Harriman, "Slovenia as an Outpost of the Third Reich," *East European Quarterly* 5, no. 2 (1971): 228.

33. Ferenc, "Fate," 4.

34. Ferenc, "Fate," 8.

35. Ferenc, "Fate," 4; and Harriman, "Slovenia as an Outpost," 229.

36. Tschinkel, *Bells*, 310–11, 328; and Tone Ferenc, "The Austrians and Slovenia," in *Conquering the Past: Austrian Nazism Yesterday and Today*, ed. F. Parkinson (Detroit: Wayne State University Press, 1989): 208.

37. Harriman, "Slovenia as an Outpost," 229.

38. Frensing, *Die Umsiedlung*, quoted in Tschinkel, "End," 21.

39. Auersperger, "Še enkrat o selitvi volksdeutscherje," 244.

40. Christopher Hutton, *Linguistics and the Third Reich: Mother-Tongue Fascism, Race and the Science of Language* (London: Routledge, 1999), 153.

41. Hutton, *Linguistics and the Third Reich*, 153.

42. Harriman, "Slovenia as an Outpost," 229.

43. Tone Ferenc, *Nacistična raznarodovalna politika v Sloveniji v letih 1941–1945* (Maribor: Obzorja, 1968), 667.

44. Ferenc, *Nacistična*, 667.

45. Tschinkel, *Bells*, 328.

46. Harriman, "Slovenia as an Outpost," 229.

47. Ferenc, *Nacistična*, 667.

48. Ferenc, *Nacistična*, 667.

49. Auersperger, "Še enkrat o selitvi volksdeutscherje," 255.

50. See Igor Mekina, "Nemci, ki so bili partizani," *Mladina*, February 27, 2004, http://www.mladina.si/96562/nemci-ki-so-bili-partizani/.

51. Ferenc, "Fate," 10.

52. Ferenc, "Fate," 10.

53. Konrad Mausser, "Resettlement and Resettling," *The Gottschee Tree* (June 2004), 12. See also the testimony of Angela Schauer Janesch, "Sterntal (Strnišče) Concentration Camp," *The Gottschee Tree* (December 2004), 8–10.

54. Ferenc, "Fate," 9.

55. Heinrich Wittine, "The People of the Former Enclave of Gottschee: During the Years 1919–1945," *The Gottschee Tree* (March 2005), 7.

56. Wittine, "People of the Former Enclave," 7.

57. Ferenc, "Fate," 6.

58. Ferenc, "Fate," 16.

59. Dan Stone, "Genocide and Memory," in *The Oxford Handbook of Genocide Studies*, ed. Donald Bloxham and A. Dirk Moses (Oxford: Oxford University Press, 2010), 103.

60. Wulf Kansteiner, "Finding Meaning in Memory: A Methodological Critique of Collective Memory Studies," *History and Theory* 41 (2002): 188.

61. Tony Judt, *Postwar: A History of Europe since 1945* (New York: Penguin, 2006), 269.

62. "Looking Back: 50 Years Ago a Committee Became the Relief Organization," *Gottscheer Relief Association* (Winter 1995/96), 3.

63. Paul Toomey, "Gottscheers Recall Tradition and Pride at Annual Celebration," *Times*, April 29, 1993, 9.

64. Most testimonies and material were collected during a 2015 research trip to the Gottschee Archive housed at St. John's University in the borough of Queens, which was established in 1997 as a partnership between the university and the Gottscheer Relief Association.

65. Janesch, "Sterntal (Strnišče) Concentration Camp," 3.

66. Sophie Sandor and Helmut Tramposch, "Gottscheer Relocation (Umsiedlung) to Brezice (Ranner Dreieck)," *The Gottschee Tree* (September 2006), 3.

67. Tschinkel, "End," 6.

68. Mausser, "Resettlement and Resettling," 6.

69. Max Mische, "Franziska Speaks," *The Gottschee Tree* (December 1995), 7.

70. "Oral Interview of Albert Stiene," interviewed by Irene Tramposch Bigot *The Gottschee Tree* (September 2007), 9.

71. Auersperger, "Še enkrat o selitvi volksdeutscherje," 238.

72. Bencin, *Gottschee*, 34; Albin Petschauer, "Albin Petschauer's Life Story," *The Gottschee Tree* (March 2005), 9; Janesch, "Sterntal (Strnišče) Concentration Camp," 4; and "Memories of Plosch," *The Gottschee Tree* (March 1999), 12.

73. Ted Meditz, "Recollection: A Life History During the 20th Century," *The Gottschee Tree* (December 2001), 4.

74. Wittine, "People of the Former Enclave," 6.

75. Wittine, "People of the Former Enclave," 6.

76. Edeltraud Krauland Kneier, "The Resettlement of 1941: A Journey of No Return," *The Gottschee Tree* (December 1991), 1.

77. Janesch, "Sterntal (Strnišče) Concentration Camp," 6.

78. Tschinkel, *Bells*, 310.

79. Janesch, "Sterntal (Strnišče) Concentration Camp," 4; Mische, "Franziska," 7; "Memories of Plosch," 12; and "Oral Interview of Albert Stiene," 13.

80. Janesch, "Sterntal (Strnišče) Concentration Camp," 4; and Kneier, "Resettlement of 1941," 2.

81. Meditz, "Recollection," 4.

82. Tschinkel, "End," 18.

83. Tschinkel, "End," 18.

84. Janesch, "Sterntal (Strnišče) Concentration Camp," 5.

85. Johanna Schmuck, "Life of Johanna Bukowitz Schmuck," *The Gottschee Tree* (September 1998), 5.

86. Mausser, "Resettlement and Resettling," 6.

87. Bencin, *Gottschee*, 37.

88. Bencin, *Gottschee*, 37.

89. Martha Hutter, "World News that Speaks to Us," *Gottscheer Relief Organization* (Winter 2009/2010), 6.

90. Janesch, "Sterntal (Strnišče) Concentration Camp," 10.

91. Mausser, "Resettlement and Resettling," 17.

92. Michael Shafir, *Between Denial and "Comparative Trivialization": Holocaust Negationism in Post-Communist East Central Europe* (Jerusalem: The Hebrew University, The Vidal Sassoon International Center for the Study of Anti-Semitism, 2002), 60.

93. Max Mische, "An Unexpected Trip to Brežice (Rann) with Mitja Ferenc," *The Gottschee Tree* (March 2001), 15–16.

94. Kneier, "Resettlement of 1941," 2.

95. Karl Brunner, "Gottschee: Act of Reconciliation," *Die Kleine Zeitung*, October 31, 1989, translated for *The Gottschee Tree* (September 1990), 1.

96. Ernst Eppich, "Impressions from a Trip Back Home," *Gottscheer Relief Association* (Winter 1999/2000), 5.

97. Maridi Tscherne, "Women's Camp in Verdreng," *Bakh-Pot*, August 1999, 7.

98. Ferenc, "Fate," 6.

99. Ferenc, "Fate," 6.

100. Ferenc, "Fate," 6.

101. Johann Fink, "Wrong Approach on Bosnia," *The Tablet*, September 1993.

102. Bencin, *Gottschee*, 44.

103. Tschinkel, "End," i.

104. Michelle Mouton, "The *Kinderlandverschickung*: Childhood Memories of War Re-Examined," *German History* 37, no. 2 (2018): 188.

105. Hutter, "World News that Speaks," 6.

106. Quoted in Drozdzewski et al., "Geographies of Memory," 453.

107. Reply of Jim Heimann to AVNOJ Decrees posted by J. Tschinkel, December 29, 2002, http://gottschee.net/forum/messages/10.html.

108. Petschauer, *Das Jahrhundertbuch*; and Auersperger, "Še enkrat o selitvi volksdeutscherje," 240.

109. Vered Vinitzky-Seroussi and Chana Teeger, "Unpacking the Unspoken: Silence in Collective Memory and Forgetting," *Social Forces* 88, no. 3 (March 2010): 1112.

110. Zygmunt Bauman, *Modernity and the Holocaust* (Cambridge: Polity Press, 1989): 18.

111. A. Dirk Moses, "The Canadian Museum for Human Rights: The 'Uniqueness of the Holocaust' and the Question of Genocide," *Journal of Genocide Research* 14, no. 2 (June 2012): 217.

CHAPTER 9. FROM MODEL TO WARNING

This chapter is a reworked and revised version of "Schweigen, Störung und Stimmigkeit: Erinnerungen an die Umsiedlung 'Heim ins Reich' unter den Buchenlanddeutschen," in *Germanisierung im besetzten Ostoberschlesien während des Zweiten Weltkriegs*, ed. Hans-Werner Retterath (Münster: Waxmann, 2018), 273–303. I would like to thank Hans-Werner Retterath for his comments on an earlier version of this chapter and the permission to republish it here. I am also grateful to the editors and anonymous reviewers of the current volume for their careful reading of the text and helpful comments and insights.

1. On this, see Valdis O. Lumans, *Himmler's Auxiliaries: The Volksdeutsche Mittelstelle and the German National Minorities of Europe, 1933–1945* (Chapel Hill: University of North Carolina Press, 1993).

2. Hans Henning Hahn and Eva Hahn, *Die Vertreibung im deutschen Erinnern: Legenden, Mythos, Geschichte* (Paderborn: Schöningh, 2010), esp. 168–209, here 180. "The expulsions" or "flight and expulsion" (*die Vertreibung* or *Flucht und Vertreibung* in German) is used as shorthand to refer to the events that resulted in an estimated 12 million German citizens and members of German

minorities fleeing or being expelled from their ancestral homes and homelands in central and eastern Europe between 1944 and 1952.

3. See, e.g., Flavius Salomon, "Die Umsiedlung 'heim ins Reich' von 1940: Erinnerungen und Lebensberichte Deutscher aus Bessarabien," in *Deutsche und Rumänen in der Erinnerungsliteratur: Memorialistik aus dem 19. und 20. Jahrhundert als Geschichtsquelle*, ed. Krista Zach und Cornelius R. Zach (Munich: IKGS Verlag, 2005), 205–16. Most recently, see Mariana Hausleitner, "*Viel Mischmasch mitgenommen*": *Die Umsiedlungen aus der Bukowina 1940* (Berlin: De Gruyter Oldenbourg, 2018).

4. The expression used was "nichthaltbare Splitter des deutschen Volkstums" (unsustainable splinters of German culture): see Adolf Hitler, "Erlaß des Führers und Reichskanzlers zur Festigung deutschen Volkstums vom 7. Oktober 1939," in *Themenportal Europäische Geschichte*, 2007, www.europa.clio-online.de/quelle/id/artikel-3303, accessed August 27, 2018.

5. Elizabeth Harvey, "Management and Manipulation: Nazi Settlement Planners and Ethnic German Settlers in Occupied Poland," in *Settler Colonialism in the Twentieth Century: Projects, Practices, Legacies*, ed. Caroline Elkins and Susan Pedersen (New York: Routledge, 2005), 95–112, here 99.

6. See, e.g., Hans Richter, *Heimkehrer: Bildberichte von der Umsiedlung der Volksdeutschen aus Bessarabien, Rumänien, aus der Süd-Bukowina und aus Litauen* (Berlin: Eher, 1941); see also the film *Heimkehr* (1941, dir. Gustav Ucicki, screenplay by Gerhard Menzel).

7. Mathias Beer, "Umsiedlung, Vernichtung, Vertreibung: Nationale Purifizierung in Europa während und am Ende des Zweiten Weltkriegs," in *Auf dem Weg zum ethnisch reinen Nationalstaat? Europa in Geschichte und Gegenwart*, ed. Mathias Beer (Tübingen: Attempto Verlag, 2004), 127.

8. Dirk Jachomowski, *Die Umsiedlung der Bessarabien-, Bukowina- und Dobrudschadeutschen: Von der Volksgruppe in Rumänien zur "Siedlungsbrücke" an der Reichsgrenze* (Munich: Oldenbourg, 1984), 81, 105.

9. The American journalist Rosie G. Waldeck, who was in Romania when the resettlements took place, reported on the celebratory mood among resettlers from Bessarabia in the port of Galați. Rosie G. Waldeck, *Athene Palace, Bucharest: Hitler's "New Order" Comes to Romania* (London: Constable, 1943), 239, et seq.

10. On this, see, e.g., Isabel Heinemann, "*Rasse, Siedlung und deutsches Blut*": *Das Rasse- und Siedlungshauptamt der SS und die rassenpolitische Neuordnung Europas* (Göttingen: Wallstein, 2003); Markus Leniger, *Nationalsozialistische "Volkstumsarbeit" und Umsiedlungspolitik 1939–1945: Von der Minderheitenbetreuung zur Siedlerauslese* (Berlin: Frank und Timme, 2006).

11. Harvey, "Management and Manipulation," 95, 108; and Rainer Schulze, "Forgotten Victims or Beneficiaries of Plunder and Genocide? The Mass Resettlement of ethnic Germans 'heim ins Reich,'" *Annali dell'Instituto storico-germano in Trento* XXVII (2001): 533–64.

12. See "Der so genannte Menscheneinsatz als verkannter Menschenmissbrauch," in Hahn and Hahn, *Die Vertreibung*, 173–82.

13. Doris Bergen, "The Volksdeutsche of Eastern Europe and the Collapse of the Nazi Empire 1944–1945," in *The Impact of Nazism: New Perspectives on the Third Reich and Its Legacy*, ed. Alan Steinweis and Daniel Rogers (Lincoln: University of Nebraska Press, 2003), 101–28, here 108.

14. See Wolfgang Benz, "Der Generalplan Ost: Zur Germanisierung des NS-Regimes in den besetzten Ostgebieten 1939–1945," in *Die Vertreibung der Deutschen aus dem Osten: Ursachen, Ereignisse, Folgen*, ed. Wolfgang Benz and Hellmuth Auerbach (Frankfurt am Main: Fischer, 1995), 45–55, here 55.

15. Doris Bergen, "The Nazi Concept of 'Volksdeutsche' and the Exacerbation of Anti-Semitism in Eastern Europe 1939–45," *Journal of Contemporary History* 29, no. 4 (1994): 569–82; see also Doris Bergen, "Tenuousness and Tenacity: The Volksdeutschen of Eastern Europe, World War II, and the Holocaust," in *The Heimat Abroad: The Boundaries of Germanness*, ed. Krista O'Donnel, Renate Bridenthal, and Nancy Reagin (Ann Arbor: University of Michigan Press, 2005), 267–86.

16. After the war, no one was even really held accountable. Hahn and Hahn, *Die Vertreibung*, 180–82.

17. In the interest of conciseness and clarity, I use the compound noun "Bukovina Germans" and, at times, simply "Bukovinians" to refer to self-identifying ethnic Germans from Bukovina. The former is a literal translation of the German *Bukowina Deutsche* or *Buchenlanddeutsche* used widely by members of this group and government authorities after 1945, and the latter a translation of the older and broader notion of *Bukowiner*.

18. For more numbers and on this specific case, see Jachomowski, *Die Umsiedlung*, and Hausleitner, "*Viel Mischmasch mitgenommen.*"

19. Heinemann, "*Rasse, Siedlung und deutsches Blut,*" 246.

20. Jachomowski, *Die Umsiedlung*, 141.

21. Ortfried Kotzian, *Die Umsiedler: Die Deutschen aus West-Wolhynien, Galizien, der Bukowina, Bessarabien, der Dobrudscha und in der Karpatenukraine* (Munich: Langen Müller, 2005), 175.

22. This is based on the research carried out for my doctoral dissertation and the around fifteen oral history interviews I conducted in this context. The latter are analyzed in more detail in Gaëlle Fisher, "Locating Germanness: Bukovina and Bukovinians after the Second World War" (PhD diss., University College London, 2015), 234–60. See also Gaëlle Fisher, *Resettlers and Survivors: Bukovina and the Politics of Belonging in West Germany and Israel, 1945–1989* (New York: Berghahn, 2020).

23. On this, see e.g., Robert Moeller, "Germans as Victims? Thoughts on a Post-Cold War History of World War II's Legacies," *History and Memory* 17, no. 1–2 (Spring-Winter 2005): 147–94; and Constantin Goschler, "'Versöhnung' und

'Viktimisierung': Die Vertriebenen und der deutsche Opferdiskurs," *Zeitschrift für Geschichtswissenschaft* 53, no. 10 (2005): 873–84, here 878.

24. Pertti Ahonen, "The Impact of Distorted Memory: Historical Narratives and Expellee Integration in West Germany, 1945–1970," in *European Encounters: Migrants, Migration and European Societies since 1945*, ed. Rainer Ohliger, Karen Schönwälder, and Triadafilos Triadafilopoulos (Farnham: Ashgate, 2003), 236–54.

25. See, e.g., Charles Maier, *The Unmasterable Past: History, Holocaust, and German National Identity* (Cambridge, MA: Harvard University Press, 1988).

26. Norbert Frei, *1945 und Wir: Das Dritte Reich im Bewußtsein der Deutschen* (Munich: Deutscher Taschenbuch Verlag, 2005).

27. For more on this, see Mary Fulbrook, "History Writing and 'Collective Memory,'" in *Writing the History of Memory*, ed. Stefan Berger and Bill Niven (London: Bloomsbury, 2014), 65–88.

28. An estimate based on the *Landsmannschaft der Buchenlanddeutschen*'s figures from 1952–1953 suggests that there was a total of approximately 69,000 Bukovina Germans, of whom around 8,000 ended up in Austria, another 10,000 in the GDR, some 3,000 of whom were back in Romania, and the rest in the Federal Republic. For more on this, see "Deutsche aus der Bukowina," in *Lexikon der Vertreibungen: Deportation, Zwangsaussiedlung und ethnische Säuberung im Europa des 20. Jahrhunderts*, ed. Detlef Brandes, Holm Sundhaussen, and Stefan Troebst (Wien: Böhlau, 2010), 136–38.

29. For an overview of the situation, see Pertti Ahonen, *People on the Move: Forced Population Movements in Europe in the Second World War and Its Aftermath* (Oxford: Berg, 2008).

30. Only in 1950 were all *Umsiedler* collectively granted German citizenship in West Germany. On other groups of resettlers, see Bastian Filaretow, *Kontinuität und Wandel: Zur Integration der Deutsch-Balten in die Gesellschaft der BRD* (Baden Baden: Nomos Geschichte, 1990), esp. 306–16; and Ute Schmidt, *Die Deutschen aus Bessarabien: Eine Minderheit aus Südosteuropa (1814 bis heute)* (Cologne: Böhlau, 2003), esp. 278–310. On the debates concerning the granting of German citizenship in what was to become West Germany in general, see Andrew Demshuk, "Citizens in Name Only: The National Status of German Expellees, 1945–1953," *Ethnopolitics: Formerly Global Review of Ethnopolitics* 5, no. 4 (2006): 7–9, 383–97.

31. See Rudolf Wagner, "Die vorlandsmannschaftliche Zeit," in *10 Jahre Landsmannschaft der Buchenlanddeutschen 1949–1959: Gründung, Werdegang und Jubiläum*, ed. Hans Prelitsch (Munich: Landsmannschaft der Buchenlanddeutschen, 1959).

32. The use of the word as a general euphemism for all Germans who lost their homeland in the Soviet Zone of Occupation and later the German Democratic Republic is a separate matter. In West Germany, the terminology used

was "refugees" (*Flüchtlinge*) or "expellees" (*Vertriebene*). Later, people leaving the GDR were sometimes also designated as *Umsiedler* (or *Übersiedler*, lit.: migrants from across the border), but this had no real connection to the Nazi term or the case of resettlers.

33. "Das Bundestreffen 1951: Eine Bestandsaufnahme des Buchenlanddeutschtums," *Raimund-Kaindl-Bund* 2 (Munich, 1951).

34. Quotation from the letter of Franz Lang, read out aloud in the opening address, in "Das Bundestreffen 1951," 3 et seq. here, 4.

35. Lang, "Das Bundestreffen 1951," 4.

36. For more on Wagner, see Fisher, *Resettlers and Survivors*, 97–98 and Hausleitner, *"Viel Mischmasch mitgenommen,"* 123–25.

37. "Das Jahr 1940: Ende und Anfang einer historischen Entwicklung des Buchenland-Deutschtums," in "Das Bundestreffen 1951," 7–10.

38. Rudolf Wagner, "Probleme zur Umsiedlung der Deutschen aus der Bukowina," *Südostdeutsche Heimatblätter* 4 (1955): 168–74, here 169–70.

39. Wagner, "Probleme zur Umsiedlung," 172.

40. Wagner, "Probleme zur Umsiedlung," 170.

41. Wagner, "Probleme zur Umsiedlung," 170.

42. Wagner, "Probleme zur Umsiedlung," 170.

43. See Hahn, *Die Vertreibung*, 202–3.

44. Wagner, "Probleme zur Umsiedlung," 172.

45. "Bericht des Dr. Rudolf Wagner aus Gurahumora (Gura Homorului), Județ Câmpulung (Kimpolung) in der Bukowina: Die Umsiedlung der Volksdeutschen aus der Bukowina im Jahre 1940," in *Dokumentation der Vertreibung der Deutschen aus Ost-Mitteleuropa. Bd. III. Das Schicksal der Deutschen in Rumänien*, ed. Bundesministerium für Vertriebene, Flüchtlinge und Kriegsgeschädigte (Theodor Schieder) (Bonn: Bundesministerium für Vertriebene, 1957), 13–17.

46. Hugo Weczerka, "Die Deutschen im Buchenland," *Schriftenreihe der Göttinger Arbeitskreis* 51 (Würzburg: Holzner, 1955), 40.

47. Weczerka, "Die Deutschen im Buchenland," 40.

48. Weczerka, "Die Deutschen im Buchenland," 40–41.

49. See, e.g., Erwin Massier, Josef Talsky, and B. C. Grigorowicz, eds., *Bukowina: Heimat von gestern* (Karlsruhe: self-published, 1956), 285.

50. Sound Archive (Tonarchiv des Instituts für die Volkskunde der Deutschen im östlichen Europa [IVDE]). On this source and Johannes Künzig, see Elisabeth Fendl, "Der karpatendeutsche Bestand im Tonarchiv des Johannes-Künzig-Instituts in Freiburg," *Karpaten-Jahrbuch* 57 (2005): 138–47; Willi Oberkrome, "Regionalismus und historische 'Volkstumsforschung' 1890–1960," in *Südostforschung im Schatten des Dritten Reiches: Institutionen—Inhalte—Personen*, ed. Mathias Beer and Gerhard Seewann (Munich: Oldenbourg, 2004), 39–48.

51. Interview with Jakob K. and Johann G., Karlsruhe 1955, Tonarchiv des IVDE Freiburg, Sig. 0172-1/0001.

52. Jakob K. and Johann G., Karlsruhe, Sig. 0172-1/0001.

53. Josephine S., Owingen 1955, Tonarchiv des IVDE Freiburg, Sig. 0144-1/0008.

54. Interview with Jakob M., Peterstal 1953, Tonarchiv des IVDE Freiburg, Sig. 0014-1/0001. The contrast with the few interviewees who were settled in occupied Alsace-Lorraine is nevertheless striking. They, in contrast, claimed never to have felt at home there. Interview with Peter and Jakob E., Darmstadt Eberstadt 1958, Tonarchiv des IVDE Freiburg, Sig. 0286-2/000; and interview with Johann H., Kaiserslauten 1952, Tonarchiv des IVDE Freiburg, Sig. 0007-1/0023.

55. Interview with Anton S. and his wife Karoline, Schapbach 1955, Tonarchiv des IVDE Freiburg, Sig. 0160-1/0001.

56. Interview with Jakob M., Peterstal 1953, Tonarchiv des IVDE Freiburg, Sig. 0014-1/0001.

57. Harvey, "Management and Manipulation," 108.

58. Markus Krzoska, "Fremd unter den Volksgenossen? Deutschbalten im Reichsgau Wartheland 1939-1945," manuscript of the paper delivered at the 64. Baltischen Historikertreffen in Göttingen on June 18, 2011, 13.

59. Hermann Lübbe, "Der Nationalsozialismus im deutschen Nachkriegsbewußtsein," *Historische Zeitschrift* 236 (1983): 579-99.

60. Bergen, " Volksdeutsche of Eastern Europe," 119.

61. In a survey conducted by the Americans during the occupation period, more than half of the Germans questioned agreed with this statement about National Socialism. Mary Fulbrook, *German National Identity after the Holocaust* (Oxford: Polity Press, 1999), 52.

62. See Hahn and Hahn, *Die Vertreibung*.

63. See Aleida Assmann and Ute Frevert, *Geschichtsvergessenheit—Geschichtsversessenheit: Vom Umgang mit deutschen Vergangenheiten nach 1945* (Stuttgart: Deutsche Verlags-Anstalt, 1999).

64. Rudolf Wagner, "Die Umsiedlung der Deutschen aus der Bukowina," in *Buchenland: Hundertfünfzig Jahre Deutschtum in der Bukowina*, ed. Franz Lang (Munich: Verlag des Südostdeutschen Kulturwerks, 1961), 509-27, here 521.

65. Wagner, "Die Umsiedlung der Deutschen," 510.

66. Wagner, "Die Umsiedlung der Deutschen," 517.

67. Wagner, "Die Umsiedlung der Deutschen," 521.

68. Wagner, "Die Umsiedlung der Deutschen," 522, 525.

69. Wagner, "Die Umsiedlung der Deutschen," 525-26.

70. Johann Christian Dressler, *Illischestie—Chronik der Bukowiner Landgemeinde* (Freilassing: Pannonia Verlag, 1960), 553.

71. Dressler, *Illischestie*, 553.

72. Dressler, *Illischestie*, 553.

73. See Assmann and Frevert, *Geschichtsvergessenheit—Geschichtsversessenheit*, 144.

74. Norbert Gaschler, "Die Umsiedlung der Buchenlanddeutschen im Spätherbst 1940 und ihre Folgen für die Katholiken und ihre Priester aus Bessarabien, der Bukowina und der Dobrudscha" (in two parts), *Analele Bucovinei*, Anul XVII, no. 1 (2010): 301–42, and XVII, no. 2 (2010): 427–36.

75. Gaschler, "Die Umsiedlung der Buchenlanddeutschen," 435–36.

76. Gaschler, "Die Umsiedlung der Buchenlanddeutschen," 340.

77. Josef Neuburger, *An den Hängen der Karpaten: Buchenhain—die Heimat unserer Deutschböhmen* (Kirchberg: self-published, 1986); citations here from the version edited by Irmtraud and Adolf Schaper (Bad Lippspringe: self-published, 2008).

78. Neuburger, *An den Hängen*, 193, 191.

79. Neuburger, *An den Hängen*, 203, 207, 202.

80. Neuburger, *An den Hängen*, 200.

81. Neuburger, *An den Hängen*, 213.

82. Neuburger, *An den Hängen*, 213.

83. Neuburger, *An den Hängen*, 203.

84. Neuburger, *An den Hängen*, 240.

85. Neuburger, *An den Hängen*, 240.

86. Neuburger, *An den Hängen*, 240.

87. See Jachomowski, *Die Umsiedlung*, 207; Sophie Wellisch "The Second World War Resettlement of the Bukovina Germans," *Immigrants and Minorities* 3, no. 1 (1984): 49–68, here 63. As late as 1989, some historians were still describing resettlement as salvation ("eine Rettung"): Ute Schmidt, "Zweifacher Heimatverlust—Integration ohne Revanchismus: Ein Forschungsprojekt über die Bessarabiendeutschen in der Bundesrepublik," *Jahrbuch für ostdeutsche Volkskunde* 32 (1989): 357–84, here 372. An interesting exception is Hans Erich Volkmann, who presented Germanization as the main aim of resettlement. Volkmann, "Zur Ansiedlung der Deutschbalten im 'Warthegau,'" *Zeitschrift für Ostforschung* 30, no. 4 (1981): 527–58, here 527.

88. Irma Bornemann, ed., *Mit Fluchtgepäck die Heimat verlassen . . . 50 Jahre seit der Umsiedlung der Buchenlanddeutschen* (Augsburg: Verlag der Süddeutsche, 1990).

89. William Niven, *Facing the Nazi Past: United Germany and the Legacy of the Third Reich* (London: Routledge, 2002); and Ruth Wittlinger, *German National Identity in the Twenty-First Century: A Different Republic After All?* (Basingstoke: Palgrave Macmillan, 2010).

90. Bill Niven, ed., *Germans as Victims: Remembering the Past in Contemporary Germany* (Basingstoke: Palgrave Macmillan, 2006); Maren Röger, *Flucht,*

Vertreibung und Umsiedlung: Mediale Erinnerungen und Debatten in Deutschland und Polen seit 1989 (Marburg: Herder-Institut, 2011).

91. Götz Aly and Susanne Heim, *Vordenker der Vernichtung: Auschwitz und die deutschen Pläne für eine neue europäische Ordnung* (Hamburg: Hoffmann und Campe, 1991). Later, Aly even argued that resettlement had been a motor for the genocide insofar as the resettlers had been promised the property of the murdered. See Götz Aly, *"Endlösung": Völkerverschiebung und der Mord an den europäischen Juden* (Frankfurt am Main: Fischer, 1995). This thesis is somewhat controversial. On the debate, see Valdis O. Lumans, "A Reassessment of Volksdeutsche and Jews," in *The Impact of Nazism: New Perspectives on the Third Reich and Its Legacy*, ed. Alan Steinweis and Daniel Rogers (Lincoln: University of Nebraska Press, 2003), 81–100.

92. See, e.g., Lumans, *Himmler's Auxiliaries*, which appeared in 1993. This is also the category under which the German Historical Museum has included this event: https://www.dhm.de/lemo/kapitel/der-zweite-weltkrieg/aussenpolitik/umsiedlung-aus-der-bukowina.html (last accessed July 19, 2017).

93. The first part of the book is entitled "Das 'Umsiedlungs'-Phänomen: Grundgedanken zum Verständnis der Gesamtproblematik" (The Phenomenon of Resettlement: Thoughts on Explaining This General Problem). This equated the word "resettlement" with "forced displacement." Beneath this, an unreferenced picture shows people fleeing. Based on their appearance, however, it is presumably a picture from the Yugoslav Wars in the 1990s. Kotzian also directly addressed Aly's claims: Kotzian, *Umsiedler*, 15, 179.

94. Many of these sources have now been deposited in the archive of the Bukovina Institute in Augsburg. See Archiv des Bukowina-Instituts an der Universität Augsburg.

95. See, e.g., the website http://www.bukowinafreunde.de/ (last accessed August 9, 2019).

96. See, e.g., Elfriede Reif, "Umsiedlung und Lagerleben in Wartha/Schlesien," *Kaindl-Archiv* 43 (2000): 119; and Karoline Seeberger, "Noh sin ich zu mein'm Linnebaam gang, un hun for mich gedenkt . . .," *Kaindl-Archiv* 43 (2000): 114–15.

97. Reif, "Umsiedlung und Lagerleben," 121.

98. Interview with the "second generation" Bukovina German and founder of the website Bukowina Freunde Alfred Wanza with Peter Lehner: http://bukowinafreunde.de/Neuer%20Ordner/faq/Gespraech_mit_dem_Peter_Lehner_geboren_in_Czernwitz_mit_Stationen_in_Pommern_%28heute_Polen%29,_Oesterreich,_%20Deutschland_und_der_Schweiz.pdf (last accessed July 19, 2017).

99. Gaby Coldewey, "Von der 'Rumänisierung' zur 'Eindeutschung': Dr. Paula Tiefenthaler erinnert sich an ihre Jugend in der Bukowina und die Umsiedlung der Bukowinadeutschen ins 'Dritte Reich,'" *Spiegelungen* 2, no. 2 (2007): 178–90, here 189.

100. Gaby Coldewey, "Es hat mich belastet, es bewegt mich noch heute": Edith Schütrumpf erinnert sich. Erlebnisse einer Bukowinadeutschen in den Kriegsjahren 1939–1945," *Spiegelungen* 1, no. 2 (2006): 39–53.

101. Berta Vogel, "Zur Umsiedlung aus dem rumänischen Südbuchenland 1940," *Der Südostdeutsche*, nr. 4, April 20, 2014, 4 (written 2003).

102. Regina Schröcker, "Meine Lebensgeschichte und die Umsiedlung," *Der Südostdeutsche*, nr. 3, March 20, 2011, 3f (written 2002).

103. Vogel, "Zur Umsiedlung aus dem rumänischen Südbuchenland 1940."

104. Coldewey, "Es hat mich belastet, es bewegt mich noch heute," 46.

105. See, e.g., the account of E. S. dating from 2002: Akademie der Künste, Literaturarchiv, Walter Kempowski Archiv, nr. 6530. This was also the case of the opening statement of Regina Schröcker's account: Schröcker, "Meine Lebensgeschichte und die Umsiedlung," 3f, as well as the opening statement of Genunea Musculus, *Czernowitz liegt nicht nur in der Bukowina* (Berlin: Osteuropa Zentrum Berlin, 2011), 5.

106. This was the case of Edith Schütrumpf, for example, who explicitly distanced herself from the organization. It is also remarkable that accounts of resettlement from the early 2000s were often only published in the newspaper *Der Südostdeutsche* in the 2010s.

107. On this, see Fisher, "Locating Germanness," 219.

108. As others have shown, it has been difficult for many Germans, even members of later generations, to link knowledge about National Socialism and personal wartime experiences of suffering. See Harald Welzer, Sabine Moller, and Karoline Tschuggnall, *Opa war kein Nazi: Nationalsozialismus und Holocaust im Familiengedächtnis* (Frankfurt am Main: Fischer, 2002).

109. Jeffrey K. Olick, *The Politics of Regret: On Collective Memory and Historical Responsibility* (New York: Routledge, 2007).

110. Emily Kneightly and Michael Pickering, *Mnemonic Imagination: Remembering as Creative Practice* (Basingstoke: Palgrave Macmillan, 2012), 12.

111. Gabriele Rosenthal, *"Als der Krieg kam, hatte ich mit Hitler nichts mehr zu tun": Zur Gegenwärtigkeit des "Dritten Reiches" in Biographien* (Opladen: Leske und Budrich, 1990), 21.

112. Dan Diner, *Beyond the Conceivable: Studies on Germany, Nazism, and the Holocaust* (Berkeley: University of California Press, 2000), 223.

CHAPTER 10. COMMEMORATING THE LOST *HEIMAT*

1. Wolfgang Wippermann, *Der "deutsche Drang nach Osten": Ideologie und Wirklichkeit eines politischen Schlagwortes* (Darmstadt: Wissenschaftliche Buchgesellschaft, 1981). Specifically, Wippermann notes five technological, economic, and social innovations introduced by German "bearers of culture" in the time of the settlement of the East, which provided the basis for these assertions: the iron plow, the city in the legal sense, agricultural and village layouts,

the legal standing of peasants, and general German industriousness (101–2). The emphasis on German cultural and political supremacy more than implies the inferiority of Slavic subjects in the same fields.

2. Fritz Heinz Reimesch, "Die europäische Leistung der Deutschen im Südosten Europas," in *Festschrift zur Ostlandkreuz-Weihe am 1. und 2. Juli 1950, Geislingen an der Steige, Württemberg*, ed. Landesverband der vertriebenen Deutschen in Württemberg, Kreisverband Göppingen (Geislingen: n.p., n.d.), 37–41.

3. Reimisch, "Die europäische Leistung der Deutschen im Südosten Europas," 41.

4. Reimisch, "Die europäische Leistung der Deutschen im Südosten Europas," 41.

5. Reimisch, "Die europäische Leistung der Deutschen im Südosten Europas," 41.

6. Jeffrey Luppes, "To Our Dead: Local Expellee Monuments and the Contestation of German Postwar Memory" (PhD dissertation, University of Michigan, 2010). The monuments in the second cluster feature exculpatory iconography to address the physical suffering of the expellees and purport their collective innocence. They are indicative of the "symbolic politics" pursued by the expellee organizations in the post-*Ostpolitik*, post-Holocaust era. No longer about retrieving lost territory, the expellee organizations erected these monuments in the pursuit of societal acknowledgment of the expellees' supposed innocent suffering. Stephan Scholz's *Vertriebenendenkmäler: Topografie einer deutschen Erinnerungslandschaft* (Paderborn: Ferdinand Schöningh Verlag, 2015) is another general investigation of expellee monuments.

7. For more on the formation and postwar activities of the expellee organizations, see Pertti Ahonen, *After the Expulsion: West Germany and Eastern Europe, 1945–1990* (Oxford: Oxford University Press, 2003); and Matthias Stickler, *Ostdeutsch heißt Gesamtdeutsch: Organisation, Selbstverständnis und heimatpolitische Zielsetzungen der deutschen Vertriebenenverbände 1949–1972* (Düsseldorf: Droste Verlag, 2004).

8. G. C. Paikert, *The Danube Swabians: German Populations in Hungary, Rumania and Yugoslavia and Hitler's Impact on their Patterns* (The Hague: Martinus Nijhoff, 1967), 2.

9. Eve Eckert Koehler, "Foreword," in *The Danube-Swabians in the Pannonian Basin: A New Ethnic Group*, ed. Anton Tafferner, Josef Schmidt, and Josef Volkmar Senz (Milwaukee: Danube Swabian Association, 1982), n.p.

10. Mirna Zakić, *Ethnic Germans and National Socialism in Yugoslavia in World War II* (Cambridge: Cambridge University Press, 2017), 35.

11. The Bundestag passed the *Bundesvertriebenengesetz* (BVFG—Federal Expellee Law) in May 1953.

12. Konrad G. Gündisch, "Die deutsche Siedlung in Südosteuropa: Ein Überblick," in *Die Donauschwaben. Deutsche Siedlung in Südosteuropa:*

Ausstellungskatalog, ed. Innenministerium Baden-Württemberg (Sigmaringen: Jan Thorbecke Verlag, 1987), 11.

13. For harrowing firsthand accounts of flight and expulsion, see Bundesministerium für Vertriebene, Flüchtlinge und Kriegsgeschädigte (ed.)'s colossal, multivolume (and not entirely unproblematic) *Dokumentation der Vertreibung der Deutschen aus Ost-Mitteleuropa* (Munich: Deutscher Taschenbuch Verlag, 1984), particularly volume 2: *Das Schicksal der Deutschen in Ungarn* (Munich: Deutscher Taschenbuch Verlag, 1984 [1956]), volume 3: *Das Schicksal der Deutschen in Rumänien* (Munich: Deutscher Taschenbuch Verlag, 1984 [1957]), and volume 5: *Das Schicksal der Deutschen in Jugoslawien* (Munich: Deutscher Taschenbuch Verlag, 1984 [1961]).

14. For more on the connection of the Danube Swabians to National Socialism, see Paikert, *The Danube Swabians*; Georg Wildmann, "Die Donauschwaben und der Nationalsozialismus," in *Die Donauschwaben in der Zwischenkriegszeit und ihr Verhältnis zum Nationalsozialismus*, ed. Felix Ermacora Institut (Vienna: Felix Ermacora Institut, 2003), 76–161; and Zakić, *Ethnic Germans and National Socialism*.

15. See Stephan Scholz, Bill Niven, and Maren Röger, ed., *Die Erinnerung an Flucht und Vertreibung: Ein Handbuch der Medien und Praktiken* (Paderborn: Verlag Ferdinand Schöningh GmbH, 2015).

16. Paikert, *Danube Swabians*, 299.

17. Méri Frotscher, "A Lost Homeland, a Reinvented Homeland: Diaspora and the 'Culture of Memory' in the Colony of the Danube Swabians of Entre Rios," *German History* 33, no. 3 (2015): 439–61.

18. Katharine Stenger Frey, *The Danube Swabians: A People with Portable Roots* (Belleville, Ontario: Mika Publishing Company, 1982).

19. Raymond Lohne, *German Chicago: The Danube Swabians and the American Aid Societies* (Charleston, SC: Arcadia Publishing, 1999). For more on the commemoration of flight and expulsion in the United States, see Jeffrey Luppes, "Land der unbegrenzten erinnerungspolitischen Möglichkeiten? Die Vertriebenendenkmäler außerhalb von Cleveland und Saint Louis," in *Cultural Landscapes: Transatlantische Perspektiven auf Wirkungen und Auswirkungen deutscher Kultur und Geschichte im östlichen Europa*, ed. Tobias Weger and Andrew Demshuk (Oldenburg: Federal Institute for Culture and History of Germans in Eastern Europe (BKGE), 2015), 247–64.

20. Luppes, "To Our Dead," 5.

21. According to census data, of the approximately 655,000 expellees from southeastern Europe living in the Federal Republic in 1970, 268,000 lived in Baden-Württemberg. Bavaria was home to the second highest number, with 144,000. Markus Leuschner, *Heimat und Schicksal: Eine kurze Chronologie* (Bonn: BdV, 2008).

22. The word *"Patenschaft"* means literally "sponsorship," as of a child by

godparents. Patenschaften in this context were typically established between cities or counties of similar size or with historical, cultural, geographical, and economic ties. They also came about, as in this case, when large numbers of expellees from a particular locale in the eastern provinces congregated in a specific area in the West. However, the relationship entailed much more than a typical partnership between equal sister cities. Writing about this arrangement between cities of North Rhine-Westphalia and the eastern provinces, Alfons Perlick noted that through a Patenschaft, an eastern German city was still "spiritually in existence." Because the German cities of the East were themselves unable to maintain their traditions and culture due to the political situation at that time, West German cities or Länder were to assume that responsibility for them. The total number of such arrangements in West Germany reached approximately 350 by the end of the 1960s. See Alfons Perlick, ed., *Das west-ostdeutsche Patenschaftswerk in Nordrhein-Westfalen* (Düsseldorf: Wegweiserverlag, 1961).

23. Most attribute the beginning of the more widespread readiness to reassess remembrance of the German past to a series of high-profile criminal trials starting with the Einsatzgruppe trial held in Ulm in 1958, at which the mass killing of Jews in Poland and the Soviet Union was comprehensively presented in public for the first time. On this topic, see Detlef Siegfried, "Zwischen Aufarbeitung und Schlußstrich: Der Umgang mit der NS-Vergangenheit in den beiden deutschen Staaten 1958 bis 1969," in *Dynamische Zeiten: Die 60er Jahre in den beiden deutschen Gesellschaften*, ed. Axel Schildt, Detlef Siegfried, and Karl Christian Lammers (Hamburg: Christians, 2000), 79. Prior to the 1960s, discussions of responsibility had facilitated the widespread popularity of the narratives of the past focusing on German victimhood, including those put forward by the expellees. The Nuremberg trials in the fall of 1945 and the successor trials from 1946 to 1949, as well as the Allies' broader efforts to denazify German society, did little to implicate the rest of the populace in the crimes of the Nazis. Indeed, one could argue they had done the opposite. Writing about the Nuremberg trials, Jeffrey Herf notes, "Nuremberg ... represented rejection of the collective guilt of the entire German people and the reaffirmation of the principle of individual political and moral responsibility." See Jeffrey Herf, *Divided Memory: The Nazi Past in the Two Germanys* (Cambridge, MA: Harvard University Press, 1997), 208. In much the same way, the denazification of the rest of the German population as a whole, an enormous bureaucratic undertaking, produced similar results. Alf Lüdtke maintains that the entire project "tended to stimulate the notion that the masses were not responsible, allowing the *Mitläufer* to perceive themselves as much closer to the victims than to the perpetrators." See Alf Lüdtke, "Coming to Terms with the Past: Illusions of Remembering, Ways of Forgetting Nazism in West Germany," *Journal of Modern History* 65, no. 3 (September 1993): 549. In other words, rejection of collective guilt opened up a space rapidly filled by German-centered memory, such as the commemoration

of flight and expulsion. Overall, as Robert G. Moeller argues, the move away from any suggestion of German culpability to German victimization had the purpose of "ma[king] it possible to talk about the end of the Third Reich without assessing responsibility for its origins, to tell an abbreviated story of National Socialism in which all Germans were ultimately victims of a war that Hitler started but everyone lost." See Robert G. Moeller, "War Stories: The Search for a Usable Past in the Federal Republic of Germany," *American Historical Review* 101, no. 4 (October 1996): 1013. Moeller is also the author of *War Stories: The Search for a Usable Past in the Federal Republic of Germany* (Berkeley: University of California Press, 2001). In this important book, Moeller responds to the notion that Germans were unable to mourn the recent past, and more broadly, to the belief that Germans avoided any recollection of Nazi rule during the 1940s and 1950s. Moeller asserts that German remembrance then focused exclusively on German suffering in an exaggerated way.

24. In the original German: "Von Ulm aus zogen deutsche Siedler im 18. Jahrhundert auf der Donau nach dem Südosten Europas. ihre Nachfahren, vom Schicksal nach dem Zweiten Weltkrieg vertrieben, kehrten in das Land ihrer Väter zurück."

25. In the original German: "Einige tausend überlebende Rückkehrer wanderten aus Not und Verzweiflung in andere europäische länder und nach Übersee aus. So zerstreuten sich die Donauschwaben über die ganze Welt und wurden überall geachtete Bürger. Auch ihrer sei in ehren gedacht."

26. In the original German: "Donauschwaben: Den Toten der Heimat, des Krieges und der Vertreibung."

27. Of course, this idea of a territory tied together by its Germans owes a lot to Nazi perceptions.

28. The three words in German are: *Aussiedlung, Ansiedlung,* and *Rückkehr.*

29. In the original German: "Eine halbe Million Deutsche fanden im Banat fast 300 Jahre lang Heimat."

30. The rivers Mureş, Tisa/Tisza, and the Danube comprise respectively the northern, western, and southern flanks; the Carpathian Mountains, also displayed, constitute the eastern edge.

31. The Germans of the Serbian Banat were also not expelled, but many fled in 1944 or left in 1948.

32. The Batschka region straddles the territory on the Hungarian-Serbian border.

33. In the original German: "Billed wurde 1765 unter Kaiserin Maria Theresia von deutschen Kolonisten gegründet. Nach schwerem Anfang wuchs und entwickelte sich die Gemeinde zu einem blühenden Schwabendorf. Unter völkischem und politischem Druck kehrten die Deutschen nach 200 Jahren in ihr Mutterland zurück." The inscription on the left is accompanied by an engraved image of the war memorial erected after the First World War in Billed. The text

reads: "We commemorate in awe, gratitude, and love our dead, the fallen of both world wars, the victims of flight, of deportation to Russia, the deportation to Bărăgan, all our dead in the Heimat, and our deceased countrymen in all the world," or in the original German: "Wir gedenken in Ehrfurcht, Dankbarkeit und Liebe unserer Toten, der Gefallenen der beiden Weltkriege, der Opfer der Flucht, der Rußlanddeportation, der Baraganverschleppung, aller unserer Toten in der Heimat und der verstorbenen Landsleute in aller Welt."

34. The full text of the speech, from which this information and the quotations were drawn, was compiled in a *Festschrift* produced on the occasion of the monument's dedication in 1987. I thank Werner Gilde of the *Billeder Heimatgemeinschaft* for providing me with this unpublished text.

35. With the exception of the Communist Party, all political parties in West Germany at least publicly advocated revisiting Germany's postwar border question.

36. On this point, see Eugen Lemberg, "Der Wandel des politischen Denkens," in *Die Vertriebenen in Westdeutschland: Ihre Eingliederung und Ihr Einfluss auf Gesellschaft, Wirtschaft, Politik und Geistesleben*, vol. 3, ed. E. Lemberg and F. Edding (Kiel: Ferdinand Hirt, 1959), 435–74, esp. 440f.

37. For scores of examples, see Luppes, "To Our Dead," and Scholz, *Vertriebenendenkmäler*. This is not to say that southeastern European Germans are not included in monuments that make territorial demands. For example, with the inscription "WIR FORDERN UNSERE HEIMAT (We demand our Heimat), the monument in Schelklingen, Baden-Württemberg (erected in 1955), includes the names of the former eastern provinces of the German Reich as well as the regions in the Southeast.

38. This includes of course the *Aussiedler* and *Spätaussiedler* from the Balkans.

39. For an account of the difficulties of one Danube Swabian in integrating into West German society, see Rosemarie Bovier's memoir *Heimat ist das, wovon die anderen reden: Kindheitserinnerungen einer Vertriebenen der zweiten Generation* (Göttingen: Wallstein Verlag, 2014). For many other examples of the discrimination faced by expellees, see Andreas Kossert, *Kalte Heimat: Die Geschichte der deutschen Vertriebenen nach 1945* (Munich: Siedler, 2008); Albrecht Lehmann, *Im fremden ungewollt zuhaus: Flüchtlinge und Vertriebene in Westdeutschland, 1945–1990* (Munich: Verlag C. H. Beck, 1991); and Ulrich Völklein, *"Mitleid war von niemand zu erwarten": Das Schicksal der deutschen Vertriebenen* (Munich: Droemer, 2005). Indeed, while conducting research in Baden-Württemberg, I found that some expellees were unable to contain their dissatisfaction over the internecine squabbling in pursuit of their common goals. In particular, the lack of élan on the part of southeastern European Germans and Germans from Russia in mobilizing their numerically stronger organizations has been the source of much consternation on the part of the other groups.

CHAPTER 11. CROATIAN ÉMIGRÉS, POLITICAL VIOLENCE, AND COMING TO TERMS WITH THE PAST IN 1960S WEST GERMANY

This chapter is a shortened and substantially revised version of chapter two of my book, *Memory, Politics, and Yugoslav Migrations to Postwar Germany* (Bloomington: Indiana University Press, 2018). It appears with permission of Indiana University Press.

1. Eighteen of the Croats were arrested shortly after the attack, while eight more were apprehended within days. This description of the attack is drawn from the following press reports: "Explosionen und Schüsse im Diplomatenviertel: Junge Kroaten verüben Bombenattentat auf die jugoslawische Handelsmission in Bad Godesberg," *Süddeutsche Zeitung* (hereafter *SZ*), November 30, 1962; "Bombenanschlag auf die jugoslawische Mission in Bad Godesberg," *Frankfurter Allgemeine Zeitung* (hereafter *FAZ*), November 30, 1962, 1; and "Kroatische Attentäter unter Anklage," *FAZ*, August 16, 1963, 5–6. See also Alexander Clarkson, *Fragmented Fatherland: Immigration and Cold War Conflict in the Federal Republic of Germany, 1945–1980* (New York: Berghahn, 2013), 66–67.

2. Other recent works that adopt this insight include Andrew Demshuk, *The Lost German East: Forced Migration and the Politics of Memory, 1945–1970* (New York: Cambridge University Press, 2012); Anna Holian, *Between National Socialism and Soviet Communism: Displaced Persons in Postwar Germany* (Ann Arbor: University of Michigan Press, 2011); Cornelia Wilhelm, ed., *Migration, Memory, and Diversity: Germany from 1945 to the Present* (New York: Berghahn, 2017); and Michael Meng, "Silences about Sarrazin's Racism in Contemporary Germany," *Journal of Modern History* 87, no. 1 (2015): 102–35. For an introduction to the relationship between memory and migration, see Irial Glynn and J. Olaf Kleist, "The Memory and Migration Nexus: An Overview," in *History, Memory, and Migration: Perceptions of the Past and the Politics of Incorporation*, ed. Irial Glynn and J. Olaf Kleist (New York: Palgrave Macmillan, 2012), 3–29.

3. Jozo Tomasevich, *War and Revolution in Yugoslavia, 1941–1945: Occupation and Collaboration* (Stanford, CA: Stanford University Press, 2001), 755–56.

4. On the various groups fleeing toward the Austrian border, see Florian Thomas Rulitz, *The Tragedy of Bleiburg and Viktring, 1945*, trans. Andreas Niedermayer (DeKalb: Northern Illinois University Press, 2016), 21–23.

5. Arnold Suppan, *Hitler—Beneš—Tito: Konflikt, Krieg und Völkermord in Ostmittel- und Südosteuropa* (Wien: Verlag der Österreichischen Akademie der Wissenschaften, ÖAW, 2014), 1206, 1351–53.

6. The number of people killed at Bleiburg has been the source of continual debate, with numbers varying dramatically. See Tomasevich, *War and Revolution in Yugoslavia*, 760–65.

7. Gerald Steinacher, *Nazis on the Run: How Hitler's Henchmen Fled Justice* (Oxford: Oxford University Press, 2011), 129–36.

8. Clarkson, *Fragmented Fatherland*, 59. For an overview of the Croatian émigré community in Germany and its relationship to Pavelić and the Ustaša movement, see Büro für heimatvertriebene Ausländer to AA, Betr.: "Die kroatische politische Emigration in Westdeutschland," September 18, 1959, Politisches Archiv des Auswärtigen Amts (hereafter PA AA), B 12, 561, 1–11.

9. On the murder of Serbs, Jews, and Roma in the NDH, see Alexander Korb, *Im Schatten des Weltkriegs: Massengewalt der Ustaša gegen Serben, Juden und Roma in Kroatien 1941–1945* (Hamburg: Hamburger Edition, 2013).

10. Krunoslav Draganović, "The Biological Extermination of Croats in Tito's Yugoslavia," in *The Croatian Nation in its Struggle for Freedom and Independence: A Symposium by Seventeen Croatian Writers*, ed. Antun F. Bonifačić and Clement S. Mihanovich (Chicago: "Croatia" Cultural Publishing Center, 1955), 296, 302. On the elaboration of the Bleiburg myth during the Cold War and beyond, see Pål Kolsto, "Bleiburg: The Creation of a National Martyrology," *Europe-Asia Studies* 62, no. 7 (September 2010): 1153–74; and the *Croatian Political Science Review* 55, no. 2 (2018), which is dedicated to the memory of Bleiburg.

11. Robert G. Moeller, "Germans as Victims? Thoughts on a Post-Cold War History of World War II's Legacies," *History and Memory* 17, no. 1/2 (2005): 151.

12. Robert G. Moeller, *War Stories: The Search for a Useable Past in the Federal Republic of Germany* (Berkeley: University of California Press, 2001); Neil Gregor, *Haunted City: Nuremberg and the Nazi Past* (New Haven, CT: Yale University Press, 2008); Frank Biess, *Homecoming: Returning POWs and the Legacies of Defeat in Postwar Germany* (Princeton, NJ: Princeton University Press, 2006); and Gilad Margalit, *Guilt, Suffering, and Memory: Germany Remembers its Dead of World War II*, trans. Haim Watzman (Bloomington: Indiana University Press, 2010).

13. For more on the Croatian émigré community and its support among West Germans during the 1950s and early 1960s, see Christopher A. Molnar, *Memory, Politics, and Yugoslav Migrations to Postwar Germany* (Bloomington: Indiana University Press, 2018), chapter 1; and Clarkson, *Fragmented Fatherland*, 58–65.

14. See, for example, "Kroaten," Anlage 1, 1952, Bundesarchiv Koblenz (hereafter BAK), B 206 / 1083, 6–7, 9; Hundhammer to Ministerpräsidenten Dr. Ehard; Betrifft: Kroatisches Nationalkomitee, April 17, 1953, Bayerisches Hauptstaatsarchiv (hereafter BHStA), StK / 17067; and Cramer to AA, von Mirbach, "Die jugoslawische Emigration von 1914 bis zur Gegenwart," June 20, 1956, PA AA, B 85 / 562, 74, 76, 77, 81.

15. On the early Federal Republic's unwillingness to probe deeply into Germans' association with National Socialism, see Norbert Frei, *Adenauer's Germany and the Nazi Past: The Politics of Amnesty and Integration*, trans. Joel Golb (New York: Columbia University Press, 2002).

16. On the geopolitical considerations that led radical Croatian émigrés in West Germany and elsewhere to turn to political violence, see Mate Nikola Tokić, "The End of 'Historical-Ideological Bedazzlement': Cold War Politics and Émigré Separatist Violence, 1950–1980," *Social Science History* 36, no. 3 (2012): 421–45.

17. The divisions both before and after the Mehlem attack are visible throughout the following report: Mende to the AA, Krafft von Delmensinge, Betr.: "Übersicht über die Organisationen der Emigranten aus Jugoslawien," April 9, 1963, PA AA, B 42 / 99.

18. Studiengruppe Südost report: Aus der kroatischen Emigration in der Bundesrepublik, Ergänzung zu Bericht 6/63, March 27, 1963, PA AA, B 42 / 99, 1–3. Of the major émigré groups in the FRG, only the United Croats of Germany (Ujedinjeni Hrvati Njemačke, UHNj) did not take part in the meeting in Cologne, and this was because the Mehlem attack had opened a major rift between the old and new guard in the UHNj.

19. Mende to AA, Betr.: Gründung eines kroatischen Verteidigungskomitees, April 23, 1963, PA AA, B 42 / 99, 1.

20. Berislav Gjuro Deželić, *Wen trifft die Schuld für das Attentat von Mehlem?* (Münster: Mlada Hrvatska), 2, in Staatsarchiv München (hereafter StAM), Pol. Dir. / 9660. The booklet is undated, but the Munich police obtained a copy in August 1963, which suggests that it was also published in that year. On Deželić's political affiliations, see Baumer to the Bundeskriminalamt SG Bad Godesberg, Betr.: Kriminalpolizeiliche Erkenntnisse über das Verhalten jugoslawischer Emigranten und Gastarbeiter in der BRD, hier: Anschlag am 29.11.62 auf die Königlich Schwedische Botschaft—Jugosl. Abt.—in Bad Godesberg-Mehlem, August 7, 1963, StAM, Pol. Dir. / 9660.

21. Deželić, *Wen trifft die Schuld*, 2–3, StAM, Pol. Dir. / 9660.

22. Deželić, *Wen trifft die Schuld*, 4.

23. Stjepan Hefer, *Freiheit und Selbstbestimmungsrecht auch für Kroatien* (Buenos Aires: Informationsdienst der Kroatischen Befreiungsbewegung, 1964), 42, in PA AA, B 42 / 101.

24. Hefer, *Freiheit*, 37–40.

25. Hefer, *Freiheit*, 42.

26. Aufzeichnung, with a copy of the following flyer: "Bomben fielen am 29. November 1962 in Mehlem," March 13, 1964, PA AA, B 42 / 101.

27. Hefer, *Freiheit*, 41.

28. Deželić, *Wen trifft die Schuld*, 3.

29. Mirna Zakić, *Ethnic Germans and National Socialism in Yugoslavia in World War II* (Cambridge: Cambridge University Press, 2017). For a brief summary of the fate of the Donauschwaben in Yugoslavia, see Suppan, *Hitler—Beneš—Tito*, 1475–80.

30. For an example of this strategy during the 1950s, see Studiengruppe Südost report to AA, Aus der kroatischen Emigration, Mai-Juni 1956, July 10, 1956, PA AA, B 12 / 561: 2.

31. Berislav Gjuro Deželić, *An Widerständen wächst ein Volk: Der Freiheitskampf des kroatischen Volkes von 1918 bis 1963* (Krefeld: Draga, 1964), 5.

32. Deželić, *Wen trifft die Schuld*, 2.

33. Hefer, *Freiheit*, 33, 38–39; and Aufzeichnung, with a copy of the following flyer: "Bomben fielen am 29. November 1962 in Mehlem," March 13, 1964, PA AA, B 42 / 101.

34. Branimir Jelić, *Ein Überblick der geschichtlichen Entwicklung Kroatiens bis zum heutigen Tage*, 2nd ed. (Berlin: self-published, 1964), 30, in BHStA, StK / 17067. Jelić's claim was based on a February 1963 interview of Ivan Boras, another Croatian émigré, in the right-radical *Deutsche National-Zeitung*. On this, see Manfred Kittel, "Eine Zentralstelle zur Verfolgung von Vertreibungsverbrechen? Rückseiten der Verjährungsdebatte in den Jahren 1964 bis 1966," *Vierteljahrshefte für Zeitgeschichte* 54, no. 2 (2006): 181–82.

35. "Tito mit Eichmann verglichen," *FAZ*, April 3, 1964, 7.

36. Presse- und Informationsamt der Bundesregierung, Vermerk, Betr.: Kroatische Emigrantenzeitung Der Kroatische Staat übt Kritik an deutschen Behörden im Zusammenhang mit dem Prozeß gegen die kroatische Emigranten, June 19, 1964, PA AA, B 42 / 101, 7.

37. Clarkson, *Fragmented Fatherland*, 69.

38. Anton Berger, "Chronik: Jugoslawien, Januar-Juni 1964," *Osteuropa* 15, no. 9 (September 1965): 626. The main defendant, Franjo Perčić, was sentenced to fifteen years in prison, the former Catholic priest Rafael Medić-Skoko was sentenced to four and a half years in prison, and seventeen others were sentenced to time served prior to the trial.

39. "Die Hintergründe des Bad Godesberger Bomben Attentats," *Deutsche Soldaten-Zeitung*, December 7, 1962, quoted in Kaja Shonick, "Émigrés, Guest Workers, and Refugees: Yugoslav Migrants in the Federal Republic of Germany, 1945-1995" (PhD dissertation, University of Washington, 2008), 76.

40. "Wir können nicht vergessen . . .," *Die Zeit*, March 20, 1964.

41. Hölzl to the Ministries of Interior of the West German states, Betr.: Überwachung radikaler Emigrantengruppen durch die Verfassungsschutzämter, April 9, 1963, BHStA, MInn / 97595, 3–4.

42. Die Ostemigranten in der Bundesrepublik, March 11, 1963, BHStA, MInn / 97575, 2–3, and Nühlen to the Landesämter für Verfassungsschutz, Betr.: Erkenntnisse über Organisationen von Ostemigranten in der Bundesrepublik, October 20, 1964, BHStA, MInn / 97575.

43. Annemarie H. Sammartino, *The Impossible Border: Germany and the East, 1914–1922* (Ithaca: Cornell University Press, 2010), 171–85.

44. Sammartino, *Impossible Border*, 187–93, quote on p. 187.

45. See Moeller, *War Stories*; Gregor, *Haunted City*; and Margalit, *Guilt, Suffering, and Memory*.

46. For a brief summary, see Wulf Kansteiner, "Losing the War, Winning the Memory Battle: The Legacy of Nazism, World War II, and the Holocaust in the Federal Republic of Germany," in *The Politics of Memory in Postwar Europe*, ed. Richard Ned Lebow, Wulf Kansteiner, and Claudio Fogu (Durham, NC: Duke University Press, 2006), 112–20.

47. Devin O. Pendas, *The Frankfurt Auschwitz Trial, 1963–1965: Genocide, History, and the Limits of the Law* (Cambridge: Cambridge University Press, 2006), 251.

48. Kansteiner, "Losing the War," 115–16.

49. Moeller, *War Stories*, 174–80.

50. Ladislaus Hory and Martin Broszat, *Der kroatische Ustascha-Staat: 1941–1945* (Stuttgart: Deutsche Verlags-Anstalt, 1964), 22, 26, 27, 27n40.

51. See for example, Willi Kinnigkeit, "Die meisten distanzieren sich vom Terror," *SZ*, December 13, 1962; "Kroatische Attentäter unter Anklage," *FAZ*, August 16, 1963; and "Verbrecher aus verlorener Ehre?," *Die Zeit*, April 12, 1963.

52. "Kroaten: Bombe und Kreuz," *Der Spiegel*, May 1, 1963, 38.

53. "Kroaten: Bombe und Kreuz," *Der Spiegel*, May 1, 1963, 38–40.

54. *Panorama* broadcasts from December 16, 1962 and April 8, 1963; https://daserste.ndr.de/panorama/archiv/1962/panorama2117.html and https://daserste.ndr.de/panorama/archiv/1963/panorama3241.html, accessed on April 3, 2018.

55. Deutscher Bundestag, Plenarprotokoll, 04/81, June 26, 1963, 3896.

56. "Von Patrioten erwarte ich Mut zur Wahrheit: Bonner Prozeß gegen Exil-Kroaten eröffnet; Das Attentat von Mehlem," *FAZ*, March 13, 1964, 8; and Nina Grunenberg, "'Wir können nicht vergessen . . .,' Prozeß gegen 26 Kroaten; Geheimbündelei im Exil," *Die Zeit*, March 20, 1964.

57. "Von Patrioten erwarte ich Mut zur Wahrheit," *FAZ*, March 13, 1964, 8.

58. Grunenberg, "Wir können nicht vergessen . . .," *Die Zeit*, March 20, 1964.

59. "Exil-Kroaten: Einig durch Dynamit," *Der Spiegel*, April 29, 1964, 52.

60. Brand to AA; Betreff: Sachbericht des Bayer. Landesamts für Verfassungsschutz über "Die nationalistischen Organisationen der Ostemigranten, III. Teil, Jugoslawische Emigration," March 28, 1963, PA AA, B 42 / 99, 1.

61. Presse- und Informationsamt der Bundesregierung, Vermerk, Betr.: Kroatische Emigrantenzeitung Der Kroatische Staat übt Kritik an deutschen Behörden im Zussamenhang mit dem Prozeß gegen die kroatische Emigranten, June 19, 1964, PA AA, B 42 / 101, 2, 3, 4; and Nina Grunenberg, "Wir können nicht vergessen . . .," *Die Zeit*, March 20, 1964.

62. Clarkson, *Fragmented Fatherland*, 75. West German intelligence estimates suggest that between 1962 and 1969, Croatian émigrés carried out about

forty acts of political violence in the Federal Republic against supporters, representatives, and institutions of the Yugoslav state. See also Mate Nikola Tokić, "Landscapes of Conflict: Unity and Disunity in post-Second World War Croatian Émigré Separatism," *European Review of History* 16, no. 5 (October 2009): 739–53.

63. Christopher R. Browning, *Ordinary Men: Reserve Police Battalion 101 and the Final Solution in Poland* (New York: HarperCollins, 1992), xvii.

64. Browning, *Ordinary Men*, 155–58.

65. Browning, *Ordinary Men*, 155.

66. Caroline Sharples, *West Germans and the Nazi Legacy* (London: Routledge, 2012), 4, 7, 135.

67. Sharples, *West Germans*, 135.

CHAPTER 12. PHOTOGRAPHIC (RE)MEMORY

1. Jacques Derrida, *Archive Fever: A Freudian Impression* (Chicago: University of Chicago, 1996), 36.

2. James Young, *Writing and Rewriting the Holocaust: Narrative and the Consequences of Interpretation* (Bloomington: Indiana University Press, 1990), 335.

3. Gerd Gemünden, "Nostalgia for the Nation: Intellectuals and National Identity in Unified Germany," in *Acts of Memory: Cultural Recall in the Present*, ed. Mieke Bal, Jonathan Crewe, and Leo Spitzer (Hannover, NH: University Press of New England, 1999), 131.

4. Roland Barthes, *Camera Lucida: Reflections on Photography* (New York: Hill and Wang, 2010), 82.

5. Ernst Jünger, *On Pain* (New York: Telos, 2008), 40.

6. Marianne Hirsch, *Family Frames: Photography, Narrative, and Postmemory* (Cambridge, MA: Harvard University Press, 1997), 7–15.

7. Alison Landsberg, *Prosthetic Memory: The Transformation of American Remembrance in the Age of Mass Culture* (New York: Columbia University Press, 2004), 120–21.

8. The widely broadcast images and video footage of 9/11 are an example of this type of embodied memory, where many people were not physically present to experience and endure the horrors of the events, but most still remember 9/11 vividly because of the media exposure. See Marita Sturken, *Tourists of History: Memory, Kitsch, and Consumerism from Oklahoma City to Ground Zero* (Durham, NC: Duke University Press, 2007), 165–98.

9. Although in her theorization of prosthetic memory Landsberg does address memory transference from the perspective of the *Nachgeborenen*, or the generation born after World War II, she does not consider other sensory experiences outside of the visual realm that perform equally important work in mediating memory, including the awareness of spaces and audio-visual memory transference.

10. Elements of Titoism are characterized by policies and practices based on the principle that in each country, the means of attaining ultimate communist goals must be dictated by the conditions of that particular country, rather than by a pattern set in another country. It is distinct from Joseph Stalin's Socialism in One Country theory, as Tito advocated cooperation between nations through the Non-Aligned Movement, while at the same time pursuing socialism in whatever ways best suited particular nations. As a result, Tito was welcomed by Western powers as an ally. However, the Soviets and their satellite states often accused Yugoslavia of Trotskyism and fascism, charges loosely based on Tito's concept *samoupravljanje* (self-management). Due to Tito's political stance, Yugoslavia was excluded from the Communist Information Bureau (Cominform) in 1948. See Robert Bideleux and Ian Jeffries, *The Balkans: A Post-Communist History* (New York: Routledge, 2007), 340–49.

11. The fact that Tito was relatively well-liked among the Western countries and that he received American funds for economic development not only speaks to his position against the Soviet Union, but also to his forward thinking and cosmopolitan hopes for a prosperous Yugoslavian economy and growth.

12. There have been many forensic efforts throughout the decades after the war in an attempt to dig up mass graves and come up with an accurate estimate of victim numbers. The United States Holocaust Memorial Museum (USHMM) in Washington, DC, presently estimates that the Ustaša regime murdered between 77,000 and 99,000 people in Jasenovac between 1941 and 1945. The official memorial site quotes a similar number, ranging from 80,000 to 100,000.

13. From here on, I will use Ustašas, the plural of the Croatian word and name of the political regime.

14. According to the United States Holocaust Memorial Museum the death tolls are 15,000–20,000 Yugoslavian Jews, 12,000 Bosnian Muslims, and 50,000 Serbs.

15. The German term *Wiedergutmachung* literally means "to make good again" but refers more generally to postwar reparations.

16. *Lebensraum* refers more broadly to the politics and policies of settler colonialism during the Third Reich.

17. For example, in Nusret Sivac's memoir *Kolika je u Prijedoru čaršija: Zapisi za nezaborav* (*How Big Is the City of Prijedor: Recollections to Ward of Forgetting*, Sarajevo: BONIK, 1995), the phrase "Willkommen in Omarska" (Welcome to Omarska) comes up repeatedly as something that prisoners heard from guards upon their arrival. The phrase was utilized as a way to intimidate the victims by drawing a direct parallel between the extermination camps during the Holocaust and the camp at Omarska.

18. As Barbie Zelizer notes in her influential book *Remembering to Forget*, the images taken by professional journalists (e.g., Margaret Bourke-White) and amateur photographers (e.g., soldiers and guards) alike were largely shaped into a

recognizable "Holocaust format" by British and American newspapers and magazines, once they made it over to the editors abroad. The initial flood of images was so overwhelming that a plethora of photos were published, often without any captions or even accompanied by entirely incorrect captions and descriptions. The interest was not in accuracy, but rather the "novelty" and element of validating facticity that these photographs possessed. Later the photographs were edited more heavily and took on the iconic format that has become the expected aesthetic for genocide photographs. Thus, the photographic formats were influenced by the media and not individual photographers per se, although certain professional photographers, such as Margaret Bourke-White, had a heavy editorial hand when it came to the construction of the quintessential Holocaust format. What is vital here is that the Holocaust was the first atrocity to be documented in such a way (in part due to the available technology). Thus, it is the Holocaust that set the aesthetic tone for future genocides (e.g., Bosnia).

19. Barbie Zelizer, *Remembering to Forget: Holocaust Memory through the Camera's Eye* (Chicago: University of Chicago Press, 1998), 89.

20. Zelizer, *Remembering*, 87.

21. Zelizer, *Remembering*, 92.

22. Zelizer, *Remembering*, 92.

23. Swanee Hunt, *This Was Not Our War: Bosnian Women Reclaiming the Peace* (Durham, NC: Duke University Press, 2004), 9–13.

24. Noel Malcom, *Bosnia: A Short History* (New York: New York University Press, 1996), 242–45.

25. The ITN crew was a television crew that set out to capture footage of the camp conditions. Therefore the entire interaction between the crew and the inmates is captured on camera and can be viewed still to this day through the ITN website and on countless other online sites and sources, such as YouTube.

26. The staging of atrocity photos is not unique to Bosnia. Many recognizable Holocaust photos, such as the ones in *Life* magazine shot by Margaret Bourke-White and the now iconic Buchenwald photo, were also staged.

27. Manjača was regarded as a transit camp, and prisoners were often brought there from Omarska and other neighboring camps and then held for a few days or weeks before being transported again to another camp.

28. J.F.O. McAllister, "Atrocity and Outrage," *Time*, August 17, 1992, http://content.time.com/time/magazine/article/0,9171,976238,00.html, accessed May 10, 2010.

29. Susan Sontag, *Regarding the Pain of Others* (New York: Farrar, Straus & Giroux, 2003), 99–103.

30. Michael Rothberg, *Multidirectional Memory: Remembering the Holocaust in the Age of Decolonization* (Stanford, CA: Stanford University Press, 2009), 1–7.

31. Bideleux and Jeffries, *Balkans*, 356–59.

32. The Federal Statistical Office of Germany elaborates that in the 1950s and 1960s, in response to a combination of high economic growth and internal labor shortages, West Germany signed a series of bilateral recruitment agreements, first with Italy (1955), then with Spain (1960), Greece (1960), Turkey (1961), Portugal (1964), and finally with Yugoslavia (1968). The influx of Bosnian refugees and immigrants was primarily established during Tito's Yugoslavia, when Bosnians were allowed to go to Germany as guest workers, often working construction and manual-labor jobs.

CHAPTER 13. THE POLITICS OF SCREEN MEMORY IN NICOL LJUBIĆ'S *STILLNESS OF THE SEA*

1. The definitions of the terms "ethnic cleansing" and "genocide" are contested, and many argue that what has been labeled ethnic cleansing in the former Yugoslavia is simply a weak euphemism for genocide. Emphasizing the distinctions between these terms is not within the purview of this chapter. See Donald Bloxham and A. Dirk Moses, eds., *The Oxford Handbook of Genocide Studies* (Oxford: Oxford University Press, 2010); George J. Andreopoulos, ed., *Genocide: Conceptual and Historical Dimensions* (Philadelphia: University of Pennsylvania Press, 1994); and Kurt Jonassohn and Karin Solveig Bjornson, *Genocide and Gross Human Rights Violations in Comparative Perspective* (New Brunswick, NJ: Transaction Publishers, 1998).

2. Christopher A. Molnar and Mirna Zakić, "Introduction: German-Balkan Entangled Histories in the Twentieth Century," in *German-Balkan Entangled Histories in the Twentieth Century*, ed. Molnar and Zakić (Pittsburgh, PA: Pittsburgh University Press, 2020), 21.

3. Nicol Ljubić, *Meeresstille: Roman* (Hamburg: Hoffmann und Campe, 2010).

4. Nicol Ljubić, *Stillness of the Sea*, trans. Anna Paterson (Glasgow: Vagabond Voices, 2011).

5. Richard Ned Lebow, "The Memory of Politics in Postwar Europe" in *The Politics of Memory in Postwar Europe*, ed. Richard Ned Lebow, Wulf Kansteiner, and Claudio Fogu (Durham, NC: Duke University Press, 2006), 27.

6. For discussions of the prominence of World War II in literature and film in the 1990s, refer to Anne Fuchs, *Phantoms of War in Contemporary German Literature, Films and Discourse: The Politics of Memory* (Basingstoke: Palgrave Macmillan, 2008); Meike Herrmann, *Vergangenwart: Erzählen vom Nationalsozialismus in der deutschen Literatur seit den neunziger Jahren* (Würzburg: Königshausen & Neumann, 2010); and Heidi M. Schlipphacke, *Nostalgia after Nazism: History, Home, and Affect in German and Austrian Literature and Film* (Lewisburg: Bucknell University Press, 2010).

7. For multiple perspectives on the memory boom, refer to sociologists Daniel Levy and Natan Sznaider, *The Holocaust and Memory in the Global Age*,

trans. Assenka Oksiloff (Philadelphia: Temple University Press, 2006); historical sociologist John Torpey, ed., *Politics and the Past: On Repairing Historical Injustices* (Lanham, MD: Rowman & Littlefield, 2003); Andreas Huyssen, *Present Pasts: Urban Palimpsests and the Politics of Memory* (Stanford, CA: Stanford University Press, 2003); political scientist Wolfgang Bergem, ed., *Die NS-Diktatur im deutschen Erinnerungsdiskurs* (Opladen: Leske + Budrich, 2003); Richard Ned Lebow, Wulf Kansteiner, and Claudio Fogu, eds., *The Politics of Memory in Postwar Europe* (Durham: Duke University Press, 2006); political scientists Eric Langenbacher and Yossi Shain, eds., *Power and the Past: Collective Memory and International Relations* (Washington, DC: Georgetown University Press, 2010); and Aleida Assmann and Sebastian Conrad, eds., *Memory in a Global Age: Discourses, Practices and Trajectories* (Houndsmills: Palgrave Macmillan, 2010).

8. See, for example, Helena Gonçalves da Silva et al., eds., *Conflict, Memory Transfers and the Reshaping of Europe* (Newcastle: Cambridge Scholars, 2010).

9. Levy and Sznaider, *Holocaust*, 2.

10. Levy and Sznaider, *Holocaust*, 3.

11. See Benjamin R. Barber, *Jihad vs. McWorld* (New York: Ballantine Books, 1996); and Thomas L. Friedman, *The Lexus and the Olive Tree* (New York: Farrar, Straus & Giroux, 1999). For an overview of the debate surrounding globalization and cultural homogenization, refer to the introduction of Bernd Wagner, ed., *Kulturelle Globalisierung: Zwischen Weltkultur und kultureller Fragmentierung* (Essen: Klartext Verlag, 2001).

12. Levy and Sznaider, *Holocaust*, 11–12.

13. See Elena Messner, "'Literarische Interventionen' deutschsprachiger Autoren und Autorinnen im Kontext der Jugoslawienkriege der 1990er," in *Kriegsdiskurse in Literatur und Medien nach 1989*, ed. Carsten Gansel and Heinrich Kaulen (Göttingen: V & R Unipress, 2011), 107–18. For a detailed conceptualization of balkanization, see Maria Nikolaeva Todorova, *Imagining the Balkans*, updated ed. (Oxford: Oxford University Press, 2009).

14. For example, Boris Previsic claims, "Der Balkanraum ... figuriert in der deutschen Literatur größtenteils als Projektionsraum, der sich durchwegs auch auf eine historisch begründete Folie bezieht." ("Eine Frage der Perspektive: Der Balkankrieg in der deutschen Literatur," in *Literatur der Jahrtausendwende: Themen, Schreibverfahren und Buchmarkt um 2000*, ed. Evi Zemanek and Susanne Krones [Bielefeld: Transcript, 2008] 96). However, Previsic identifies a change in this trend in Saša Stanišić's semiautobiographical novel, *Wie der Soldat das Grammofon repariert* (2006), which tells the story of a young Yugoslavian refugee's migration to Essen and emphasizes the importance of narrating events, especially those about war. In addition, much like in *Stillness of the Sea*, Stanišić's novel presents the harsh reality of living in Germany as an immigrant or refugee. Furthermore, *Wie der Soldat das Grammofon repariert* does not simply project German concerns onto the former Yugoslavia, but creates

dialogue between these cultures. For analyses of *Wie der Soldat das Grammofon repariert*, refer to Matteo Galli, "Wirklichkeit abbilden heißt vor ihr kapitulieren: Sasa Stanisic," in *Eine Sprache—viele Horizonte . . . Die Osterweiterung der deutschsprachigen Literatur: Porträts einer neuen europäischen Generation*, ed. Michaela Bürger-Koftis (Wien: Praesens, 2008), 53–63; and Helena Gonçalves da Silva, "Trauma and Displacement as a Place of Identity in Sasa Stanisic's Novel *How the Soldier Repairs the Gramophone*," in *Conflict, Memory Transfers and the Reshaping of Europe*, ed. Helena Gonçalves da Silva et al. (Newcastle: Cambridge Scholars, 2010), 68–81.

15. Sigmund Freud, *Zur Psychopathologie des Alltagslebens: Über Vergessen, Versprechen, Vergreifen, Aberglaube und Irrtum* (Leipzig: Internationaler Psychoanalytischer Verlag, 1922).

16. Miriam Bratu Hansen, "'Schindler's List' is not 'Shoah': The Second Commandment, Popular Modernism, and Public Memory," *Critical Inquiry* 22, no. 2 (1996): 292–312; and Huyssen, *Present Pasts*.

17. In a similar vein, though she does not refer specifically to screen memory, Elena Messner asks in "'Literarische Interventionen' deutschsprachiger Autoren und Autorinnen im Kontext der Jugoslawienkriege der 1990er," "Ist der Jugoslawienkrieg also tatsächlich nur ein Stellvertreterkonflikt für das je eigene politische und geschichtliche Selbstverständnis?" (116).

18. Michael Rothberg, *Multidirectional Memory: Remembering the Holocaust in the Age of Decolonization* (Stanford, CA: Stanford University Press, 2009), 12.

19. Rothberg, *Multidirectional Memory*, 13.

20. Rothberg, *Multidirectional Memory*, 14.

21. Prior to *Stillness of the Sea*, Ljubić published *Mathildes Himmel: Roman* (Frankfurt am Main: Eichborn, 2002); *Genosse Nachwuchs: Wie ich die Welt verändern wollte* (Munich: Deutsche Verlags-Anstalt, 2004); and *Heimatroman oder Wie mein Vater ein Deutscher wurde* (Munich: Deutsche Verlags-Anstalt, 2006). While *Stillness of the Sea* is his first literary work to grapple with recent wars and ethnic cleansing, it continues a literary discussion of several themes central to his earlier semiautobiographical *Heimatroman*, including nationality, belonging, memory, family history, identity, and (im)migration. Since the publication of *Stillness*, Ljubić has written the following works: *Als wäre es Liebe: Roman* (Hamburg: Hoffmann und Campe, 2012); *Schluss mit der Deutschenfeindlichkeit! Geschichten aus der Heimat* (Hamburg: Hoffmann und Campe, 2012); and *Ein Mensch brennt: Roman* (Munich: Deutscher Taschebuch Verlag, 2017).

22. See Molnar and Zakić's discussion of the West German labor recruitment program in the introduction to this volume.

23. Such a scholarship program actually exists: the Berlin-Stipendien of the Stiftung EVZ (Erinnerung, Verantwortung und Zukunft).

24. See Irmgard Ackermann, "Die Osterweiterung in der deutschsprachigen 'Migrantenliteratur' vor und nach der Wende," in *Eine Sprache—Viele Horizonte*

... *Die Osterweiterung der deutschsprachigen Literatur: Porträts einer neuen europäischen Generation*, ed. Michaela Bürger-Koftis (Vienna: Praesens, 2008), 13–22; Brigid Haines, "The Eastern Turn in Contemporary German, Swiss and Austrian Literature," *Debatte* 16, no. 2 (2008): 135–49; and Brigid Haines and Anca Luca Holden, eds., *The Eastern European Turn in Contemporary German-Language Literature*, spec. issue of *German Life & Letters* 68, no. 2 (2015): 145–333.

25. For a review of Austrian literature that represents the collapse of the former Yugoslavia and its legacy, see Anna Zimmer, "Putting the Past and Present on Trial: Migration and Memory in Ludwig Laher's Documentary Novel, *Verfahren*," *The Eastern European Turn in Contemporary German-Language Literature*, spec. issue of *German Life & Letters* 68, no. 2 (2015): 190–210.

26. Terézia Mora, *Alle Tage: Roman* (Munich: Luchterhand, 2004).

27. Terézia Mora, *Day In Day Out*, trans. Michael Henry Heim (New York: Harper Perennial, 2007).

28. Melinda Nadj Abonji, *Tauben fliegen auf: Roman* (Salzburg: Jung und Jung, 2010).

29. Melinda Nadj Abonji, *Fly Away, Pigeon*, trans. Tess Lewis (London: Seagull Books, 2014).

30. Juli Zeh, *Die Stille ist ein Geräusch: Eine Fahrt durch Bosnien* (Frankfurt am Main: Schöffling, 2002).

31. A comparative analysis of these two artworks and their portrayal of war tribunals could prove productive in further examining the literary depiction of international law.

32. Zafer Şenocak, *Gefährliche Verwandtschaft: Roman* (Munich: Babel-Verlag, 1998).

33. Zafer Şenocak, *Perilous Kinship*, trans. Tom Cheesman (Swansea: Hafan Books, 2009).

34. Leslie A. Adelson, *The Turkish Turn in Contemporary German Literature: Toward a New Critical Grammar of Migration* (New York: Palgrave Macmillan, 2005), 86.

35. For additional analyses of *Gefährliche Verwandtschaft*, refer to Monika Shafi, "Joint Ventures: Identity Politics and Travel in Novels by Emine Sevgi Özdamar and Zafer Şenocak," *Comparative Literature Studies* 40, no. 2 (2003): 193–214; Margaret Littler, "Guilt, Victimhood, and Identity in Zafer Şenocak's 'Gefährliche Verwandtschaft,'" *German Quarterly* 78, no. 3 (2005): 357–73; Friederike Eigler, *Gedächtnis und Geschichte in Generationsromanen seit der Wende* (Berlin: Erich Schmidt Verlag, 2005); and Tom Cheesman, *Novels of Turkish German Settlement: Cosmopolite Fictions* (Rochester: Camden House, 2007).

36. For more on *Väterliteratur*, see Ernestine Schlant, *The Language of Silence: West German Literature and the Holocaust* (New York: Routledge, 1999); and Erin Heather McGlothlin, *Second-Generation Holocaust Literature: Legacies*

of Survival and Perpetration (Rochester, NY: Camden House, 2006). In addition, *Stillness of the Sea*'s focus on father figures is shared by Marica Bodrožić, *Das Gedächtnis der Libellen: Roman* (München: Luchterhand, 2010), which tells the story of a young woman from Croatia who lives happily in Germany and travels freely in Europe, but must come to terms with the dark deeds of her father in Croatia in the 1990s.

37. Ljubić, *Stillness*, 142.

38. Ljubić, *Stillness*, 73.

39. Speaking of the guilt of the Serbs, a history professor in Robert's university department explains, "'Well, it's tragic,' the professor said, 'but it's a historical fact that Serbia is, it seems, the only country that hasn't faced up to the need for national catharsis. By now, it has been left alone with its guilt complex, isolated from the rest of the world, for almost twenty years. The end of the war didn't offer a new beginning for the Serbs: the same old war leader still held office and, even after his fall, they had only a brief glimpse of hope before [Prime Minister Zoran] Đinđić was shot. Try to imagine what it all meant for the young in Serbia. They suffer to this day. In their generation, they're the only ones who aren't allowed to travel freely in Europe, because Europe rejects their country.'" Ljubić, *Stillness*, 106. I return to a discussion of discrimination against Serbs later in the chapter.

40. For an analysis of Šimić's prosecution and the ICTY in *Stillness of the Sea*, refer to Jill S. Smith, "The Tribunal on Trial: Europe and the Arbitration of War," *Telos: Critical Theory of the Contemporary*, October 13, 2014, http://www.telospress.com/the-tribunal-on-trial-europe-and-the-arbitration-of-war-\crimes/. Smith argues, "What Ljubić's novel goes on to do is to call the prosecutor's tactics into question by drawing a more complex portrait of Šimić and his family.... It [the court] has investigated the individual guilt or innocence of the defendant rather than the systematic persecution of Bosnian Muslims" (n.p.). Smith recognizes the legacy of Hannah Arendt's 1963 work *Eichmann in Jerusalem: A Report on the Banality of Evil* in the novel, but asserts that Ljubić's critique is not as convincing as Arendt's.

41. Ljubić, *Stillness*, 126–27.

42. For more information on Koljević, refer to Gabriel Partos, "Obituary: Nikola Koljevic," *The Independent*, February 4, 1997; Tim Judah, *The Serbs: History, Myth, and the Destruction of Yugoslavia* (New Haven, CT: Yale University Press, 2009); and Matthew Battles, *Library: An Unquiet History* (New York: W. W. Norton, 2003).

43. Ljubić, *Stillness*, 71–72.

44. Narrative as a means to work through the past and overcome trauma is not the focus of my analysis. However, *Stillness of the Sea* could certainly be analyzed from a trauma studies perspective. Analyses of memory often prominently figure the role of trauma. See, for example, Cathy Caruth, *Unclaimed Experience:*

Trauma, Narrative, and History (Baltimore: Johns Hopkins University Press, 1996); Dominick LaCapra, *Representing the Holocaust: History, Theory, Trauma* (Ithaca: Cornell University Press, 1994); Kalí Tal, *Worlds of Hurt: Reading the Literatures of Trauma* (Cambridge: Cambridge University Press, 1996); Nigel C. Hunt, *Memory, War, and Trauma* (Cambridge: Cambridge University Press, 2010); and Shoshana Felman and Dori Laub, *Testimony: Crises of Witnessing in Literature, Psychoanalysis, and History* (New York: Routledge, 1991).

45. Ljubić, *Stillness*, 72.

46. Ljubić, *Stillness*, 102.

47. Ljubić, *Stillness*, 106.

48. Ljubić, *Stillness*, 74.

49. Hans Kundnani, "Perpetrators and Victims: Germany's 1968 Generation and Collective Memory," *German Life & Letters* 64, no. 2 (April 2011): 281.

50. In contrast, a second screen memory, namely the collective memory of Germans as victims of the World War II air war during the debate about the Iraq War in 2002–2003, was utilized to support Gerhard Schröder's protest of the US-led bombing campaign in Iraq (Kundnani, 272). This screen memory plays an important role in Thomas Lehr, *September. Fata Morgana: Roman* (Munich: Hanser, 2010). For an analysis of this novel, see Anna Zimmer, "Abschied von typischen 9/11 (Satz-)Zeichen: Multidirektionale Erinnerungen aus New York und Bagdad in Thomas Lehrs *September. Fata Morgana*," in *Abschied von 9/11?—Distanznahmen zur Katastrophe*, ed. Stephan Packard and Ursula Hennigfeld (Berlin: Frank & Timme, 2013), 87–107.

51. Ljubić, *Stillness*, 157–58.

52. Ljubić, *Meeresstille*, 162.

53. The German journalist Thomas Deichmann called the authenticity of these photos into question in 1997, which Ana discusses briefly without referencing Deichmann specifically (Ljubić, *Stillness*, 158). For a discussion of the media controversy that ensued following Deichmann's claims, refer to Herbert N. Foerstel, *From Watergate to Monicagate: Ten Controversies in Modern Journalism and Media* (Westport, CT: Greenwood Press, 2001); and David Campbell, "Atrocity, Memory, Photography: Imaging the Concentration Camps of Bosnia—the Case of ITN versus *Living Marxism*, Parts 1 and 2," *Journal of Human Rights* 1, no. 1–2 (2002): 1–33 and 143–72.

54. Ljubić, *Stillness*, 158.

55. Philip Hammond, "Humanizing War: The Balkans and Beyond," in *Reporting War: Journalism in Wartime*, ed. Stuart Allan and Barbie Zelizer (London: Routledge, 2004), 175.

56. Hammond, "Humanizing War," 175. For a discussion of the capacity of the international press to validate political action and the power of printed images, refer to Barbie Zelizer, "When War is Reduced to a Photograph," in *Reporting War: Journalism in Wartime*, ed. Stuart Allan and Barbie Zelizer (London:

Routledge, 2004), 115–35. Zelizer compares images of the 1990s from Africa and those from the Balkans, which resembled Holocaust-era photographs: "While conflicts in both Africa and Asia generated little world interest because in one view the 'bone-thin men behind barbed wire in the Balkans, on the doorstep of the West, resonate[d] more deeply . . . than the many horrors of Asia and Africa' . . ., pictures nonetheless appeared" (120).

57. Ljubić, *Stillness*, 102.
58. Hammond, "Humanizing War," 182.
59. Ljubić, *Stillness*, 71.
60. Ljubić, *Stillness*, 158.
61. Ljubić, *Stillness*, 170.
62. Ljubić, *Stillness*, 57.
63. Ljubić, *Stillness*, 165–66.
64. Ljubić, *Stillness*, 182. Here, the English translation lacks a few important details present in the original German: "'Das ist nicht deine Erinnerung. Du warst weit weg. Du hattest dein Leben und deine Sorgen'" (Ljubić, *Meeresstille*, 188). Not only is the tense different, but the original German also underscores the distance between Robert and the war. I offer an alternative translation: "'That's not your memory. You were far away. You had your life and your worries.'"
65. Some of this confusion may be due to the dichotomous relationship of victims and perpetrators. See Michael Rothberg, "Trauma Theory, Implicated Subjects, and the Question of Israel/Palestine," *Profession*, May 2, 2014, https://profession.mla.hcommons.org/2014/05/02/trauma-theory-implicated-subjects-and-the-question-of-israelpalestine/. Rothberg's theory of implicated subjects may offer a third category that aptly describes Robert and many Germans: "Neither simply perpetrators nor victims, though potentially either or both at other moments, implicated subjects are participants in and beneficiaries of a system that generates dispersed and uneven experiences of trauma and well-being simultaneously." He continues, "The concept of implication asks us to think how we are enmeshed in histories and actualities beyond our apparent and immediate reach, how we help produce history though impersonal participation rather than direct perpetration. It shifts attention to the other side of precariousness: to complicity and privilege" (n.p.). Robert seems to deeply feel his enmeshment in the history of the former Yugoslavia, but does not directly acknowledge his possible complicity nor his privilege.
66. Ljubić, *Stillness*, 124.
67. Rothberg, *Multidirectional*, 28.
68. Ljubić, *Stillness*, 104.
69. Ljubić, *Stillness*, 104–5.
70. Smith's assessment of the end of the novel in "Tribunal on Trial" is more critical than my own: "If, however, as the novel leads us to believe, every culture or every nation has its share of victims and perpetrators, and if violence is simply

a part of the human story, where is the space for intervention and for the prevention of violence" (n.p).

71. See Lyn Marven and Stuart Taberner, eds., *Emerging German-Language Novelists of the Twenty-First Century* (Rochester: Camden House, 2011).

CONTRIBUTORS

Amila Becirbegovic is assistant professor of German and ethnic humanities at California State University, Fresno. She received her PhD in German literature and critical theory from the University of California at Davis. She is interested in twentieth-century visual culture, with a specific focus on atrocity and genocide representations and cultural (re)memory. Her work has been published in *Humanities* and *Nationalities Papers*.

Mark Biondich has been an adjunct research professor at Carleton University's Institute of European, Russian and Eurasian Studies, in Ottawa, Canada, since 2008. He holds a PhD from the University of Toronto. He teaches courses on modern southeastern European history and the post-Communist transitions, and has published numerous scholarly articles and two books, most recently *The Balkans: Revolution, War, and Political Violence since 1878* (Oxford University Press, 2011).

Gaëlle Fisher earned her PhD in history from University College London. Since January 2017, she has been a postdoctoral researcher at the Center for Holocaust Studies of the Institute for Contemporary History in Munich. Her first book, *Resettlers and Survivors: Bukovina and the Politics of Belonging in West Germany and Israel, 1945–1989*, appeared with Berghahn Books in 2020. She has also published articles in *German History*, *East European Politics and Societies*, and the *Leo Baeck Institute Year Book*.

David Hamlin is professor of history and department chair at Fordham University and holds a PhD from Brown University. He is the author of *The German Empire in the East: Germans and Romania in an Era of Globalization and Total War* (Cambridge University Press, 2017) and *Work and Play: The Production and Consumption of Toys in Germany, 1880–1914* (University of Michigan Press, 2007). He is currently working on a project exploring how visions of the postwar economic order shaped war aims in World War I.

Jiří Kocián is a PhD candidate at the Institute of International Studies, Charles University, Prague, and the coordinator of the Malach Center for Visual History at the Institute of Formal and Applied Linguistics at Charles University. He is the coeditor or coauthor of several volumes about Jewish minorities in southeastern Europe, oral history, memory and identity, and (post-)Communist social transformation.

Kateřina Králová is associate professor at the Institute of International Studies at Charles University, Prague, from which she also holds a PhD. She is the author of *Das Vermächtnis der Besatzung: Deutsch-griechische Beziehungen seit 1940* (Böhlau, 2016), which was also published in Czech and Greek. Her second book project about Holocaust survivors in postwar Greece is currently under review.

Gregor Kranjc is associate professor of history at Brock University and holds a PhD from the University of Toronto. In 2007–2008, he served as senior historian with the War Crimes and Crimes against Humanity section of the Canadian Department of Justice in Ottawa, researching alleged war crimes committed during the breakup of Yugoslavia. He is the author of *To Walk with the Devil: Slovene Collaboration and Axis Occupation, 1941–1945* (University of Toronto Press, 2013).

Jeffrey Luppes is associate professor of German at Indiana University, South Bend, and holds a PhD from the University of Michigan. His work has appeared in *German Politics and Society* and *Seminar: A Journal of Germanic Studies*. His current research project examines the representation and commemoration of flight and expulsion of Germans in Austria.

Christopher A. Molnar is associate professor of history at the University of Michigan, Flint, and holds a PhD from Indiana University. His book, *Memory, Politics, and Yugoslav Migrations to Postwar Germany*, was published by Indiana University Press in 2018. He is currently working on a book project examining migration and neo-Nazi violence in the years immediately following German reunification.

Jannis Panagiotidis is scientific director at the Research Center for the History of Transformations (RECET) at the University of Vienna. He obtained his PhD at the European University Institute in Florence, Italy, and is the author of *The Unchosen Ones: Diaspora, Nation, and Migration in Israel and Germany* (Indiana University Press, 2019).

Christian Promitzer is senior research fellow at the Institute for History at the University of Graz, from which he also holds a PhD. He is the author of numerous articles and coeditor of several volumes dealing with Austria's historical entanglements with the South Slavs, civil society, post-Communist historiography, hidden minorities in southeastern Europe, and the history of epidemic diseases and their prevention in the Balkans.

Bernd Robionek obtained his PhD from Humboldt University in Berlin. He is the author of *Ethnische Ökonomie im politischen Spannungsfeld: Das deutsche Genossenschaftswesen in der Vojvodina (1922–41)* (Verlag Dr. Kovač, 2019). His current research focuses on Yugoslav state security services and anti-Yugoslav political emigration before and after World War II.

Mirna Zakić is associate professor of German history at Ohio University. She holds a PhD from the University of Maryland. Her book *Ethnic Germans and National Socialism in Yugoslavia in World War II* was published by Cambridge University Press in 2017. Her work has also appeared in the *Journal of Contemporary History* and *Holocaust and Genocide Studies*.

Anna E. Zimmer is assistant professor in the Department of Languages, Literatures, and International Studies at Northern Michigan University. She holds a PhD from Georgetown University and researches and writes about twentieth- and twenty-first-century Germanophone literature, memory, and migration studies. Her current research project focuses on European representations of recent refugees in diverse media, from popular crime fiction to avant-garde film.

INDEX

Note: Page numbers in *italics* refer to figures.

A-cases, 98, 145, 185, 187, 191
AA. *See* Auswärtiges Amt (German Foreign Office)
Abel, Wolfgang, 74
Abonji, Melinda Nadj, 255
Abromeit, Franz, 109, 110, 111, 112
Ackermann, Irmgard, 255
Adelson, Leslie, 256
Agraria, 46, 47, 55, 59
Agricultural Central Credit Bank (Landwirtschaftliche Zentral-Darlehenskasse, LZDK), 47, 48, 53, 59; Avis and, 50, 56, 58, 60
agriculture, 17, 34, 45, 48, 160, 165, 215
Ahnenauswandererdenkmal (Ancestral Emigrant Monument), 207, 208, 214
Ahonen, Pertti, 184
Albanians, 69, 71, 73
Alić, Fikret, 244
Alsace-Lorraine, 183, 205, 331n54
Alternative for Germany (party), rise of, 17
Altreich, 137, 144, 145, 150, 156, 183, 192, 193
Aly, Götz, 196, 333n91, 333n93
Anschluss, Gottscheers and, 161
Anthropological Institute, 63, 76

anthropology, 64, 69–71, 232; racial, 62, 66, 70–71, 71–73, 74–76
anti-communism, 14, 148, 176, 177, 184, 195, 198, 217–18, 228, 230; Nazi, 22; postwar, 190; transformation of, 93
anti-Jewish policy, 20, 95, 96, 98, 100, 104, 110, 118, 128
anti-Semitism, 20, 55–59, 96, 100, 110, 128, 129, 224, 225
Antonescu, Ion, 12, 121
Arendt, Hannah, 313n67, 352n40
Arko, Hans, 142, 161
Arolsen Archives, 139
Art Pavilion (Zagreb), 109
Artuković, Andrija, 109
assimilation, 66, 150, 191; Gottscheer, 178–79; Slovene, 160, 161
Auersperger, Alenka, 161
Auschwitz-Birkenau, 12, 16, 96, 101, 103, 108, 124, 126, 175, 194, 199, 225, 246, 247; atonement for, 258–64; deportations to, 109–12; experience of, 120
Auslandsorganisation, 110, 308n94
Aussiedler, 87, 339n38
Austro-Hungarian Empire, 80, 138, 141, 204; defeat of, 3, 10, 22; German alliance with, 31; influence

361

of, 117; Romania and, 31–32, 41; Russia and, 32

Auswärtiges Amt (AA) (German Foreign Office), 41, 51, 55, 56

Avis, 18, 49–50, 54, 57, 60; AA and, 55; birth of, 46–48; cooperative system and, 46; economic factors and, 48; egg sales by, 47, 49, 288n91; LZDK and, 50, 56, 58, 60; political engagement by, 59; quota for, 52, 53; special treatment for, 51–52; trade relations and, 60

Awender, Johann, 57

Bačka/Bácska, 19, 49, 52, 56, 57, 79, 87, 211, 280n6

Baden-Württemberg, 144, 202, 206, 207, 208, 209, 212, 213, 336n21, 339n39

Balkan Wars, 31, 32, 119

Balkans, 5, 85, 119, 207, 214; anthropological examinations of, 69–71; crisis in, 3; ethnography of, 63; German influence in, 11, 30, 61, 62, 64, 66, 77, 202, 203, 215, 267n8, 268n12; racial anthropology on, 74–76; remembering, 254–55; reordering of, 7, 17; sovereignty of, 43

Ballin, Albert, 35

Banat, 49, 51, 52, 53, 56, 57, 59–60, 79, 85, 210, 212, 280n6, 338n31; history of, 83; Romanian, 82; Serbian, 12, 19, 80, 82

Banat Germans, 12, 19, 63, 80, 81, 82, 83, 86, 88, 89, 91, 93, 209, 212; conscription of, 90

Banater Beobachter, 89

Banja Luka, 106, 244, 307n85

Bărăgan Plain, 205, 213, 339n33

Baraković, Ivica, 101–2, 109

Barić, Ante, 103

Barthes, Roland, 232

Bauman, Zygmunt, 179

Baur, Erwin, 63

Becirbegovic, Amila, 24, 25, 260

Beck, Ulrich, 252

Beisner, Wilhelm, 305n65

Belgrade, 46, 49, 50, 54, 59, 82, 85, 171, 240; Jews in, 128

Benz, Wolfgang, 313n67

Bergen, Doris, 181, 190

Bergen-Belsen, 120, 129

Berlin Society for Anthropology, Ethnology, and Prehistory, 70

Berlin Wall, 216, 248, 250

Bern International Convention, 42

Bessarabia, 67, 143, 171, 202, 327n9

Bideleux, Robert, 248

Biondich, Mark, 20

Bismarck, Otto von, 9, 31, 32, 126; Balkans and, 3–4, 267nn2–3

Bleiburg, 217, 218, 221, 340n6, 341n10

Bodrožić, Marica, 352n36

Bolsheviks, 19, 35, 104, 107, 224

Bonn, 24, 227, 228; attack in, 216, 217, 219, 230

Boras, Ivan, 343n34

Bosnia, 4, 65, 106, 107, 248; atrocities in, 231; concentration camps in, 241; German relations with, 232; Jews in, 20; war crimes in, 26

Bosnia and Herzegovina, 231, 235, 255; rebellion in, 3, 24; refugees from, 15; war in, 259

Bosnian Muslims, 98, 113, 235, 238, 239, 240, 242, 248, 249, 261; death toll of, 346n14; SS recruitment of, 302n16

Bosnian War, 231, 247, 248, 249

Bosnians, 240, 249, 262; ethnic cleansing and, 16; return of, 15; Serbs and, 24, 244

INDEX 363

Bourke-White, Margaret, 346n18, 347n18, 347n26; photo by, *243*
Bovier, Rosemarie, 339n39
Brandt, Willy, 15
Brătianu, Ion I. C., 31
Brčko, 107
Broszat, Martin, 225
Browning, Christopher, 229
Brücker, Christian, 83, 85, 86, 87
Bryant, Chad, 151
Buchenhain/Pojana Mikuli, 194, 195
Buchenwald, 241, 242, *243*, 245
Budak, Mile, 99
Budapest, 118, 128, 209
Bukovina, 9, 22–23, 143, 185, 194, 201, 328n17; departure from, 189; memories of, 199; resettlement in, 193; Romania and, 182, 190; social relations in, 189
Bukovina Germans (Bukovinians), 182–84, 186, 187, 189, 193, 194, 198, 199, 201, 328n17; communism and, 195; depiction of, 184, 193, 195; diversity of, 23; experiences of, 200; fate of, 192; Germany and, 187–88; Holocaust and, 198–99; kinship/subordination and, 186; memories of, 199; National Socialism and, 200; Poles and, 189; resettlement of, 183–84, 184–90, 191, 192–93, 195–98, 200
Bukovina-Institute, 196, 333n94
Bukowina Freunde, 333n98
Bulgaria, 11, 12, 67, 78, 119, 123, 171; Central Powers and, 9; Cold War and, 13; Romania and, 31, 36
Bulgarians, 9, 61, 67, 69, 70
Bundestag, 130, 208, 226
Burleigh, Michael, 6

Caprivi, Leo von, 31
Care and Maintenance (CM/1) files, 139, 152
Carinthia, 138, 146, 153, 155, 321n1
Carol I, King of Romania, 31
Carpathians, 67, 94, 202, 338n30
Casertano, Raffaele, 111, 308n110
Cathedral Church of Timişoara, 211
Catholic Church, 12, 65, 176, 218, 222, 228, 230
Central Europe. *See* Mitteleuropa
Central European Oil Company, 37, 41, 44
Central Powers, 9, 44, 71; Romania and, 31, 32, 35, 39, 40
Cerne, Janez, 151, 152
Cerne née Jonke, Paulina, 151, 152
Certeau, Michel de, 178
Četniks, 106, 167, 217
citizenship, 102, 185, 197, 205; American, 22; Austrian, 155; for the East, 193; German, 145, 155–56, 329n30; minorities and, 311n17; Yugoslav, 146, 317n57
citizenship laws, 100, 102, 104, 317n57
Clinton, Bill, 261
Clodius, Carl, 55, 56
CM/1. *See* Care and Maintenance files
Cold War, 94, 182, 184, 201; Croatian émigrés and, 217–19; emergence of, 5, 13–14; end of, 6, 14, 15, 23, 250, 252; experience of, 7, 13, 237; migration and, 14; resettlement and, 190–95
collaborators, 12, 21, 47, 167, 174, 229
collective guilt, 20, 114, 124, 125, 130, 176, 184, 337n23; concept of, 120, 131, 184; narrative of, 115, 118, 122, 127, 131, 133; transfer of, 126
colonization, 4, 66, 82, 86, 88, 92, 93; endorsement of, 81; German, 90, 91; memory of, 161; settler, 61, 181

communism, 14, 106, 148, 158, 179, 194, 201, 221; eastern European, 21; international, 100; spread of, 182
Communist Information Bureau (Cominform), 346n10
community: conceptions of, 182; ethnic German, 158, 183; of experience/identification, 184; migrant, 155, 157
concentration camps, 121, 125, 131, 170, 174, 199, 222, 237–38, 241, 246, 261; building, 242; Croatian, 104–9; liberation of, 233; mass death in, 14; Nazi, 24, 226; Serb-run, 242
Congress of Berlin, 3
cooperatives, 46; agricultural, 48; economic, 18, 48; ethnic German, 48, 57, 281n9; German-Jewish, 58
crimes, 218, 256; fascist/communist, 178–75, 179; mass, 65, 78; Nazi, 21, 25, 93, 179, 191, 222, 225, 228, 229, 251, 337n23; Serbian, 26; war, 14, 25, 26, 225, 229, 247
Croatia, 12–13, 65, 143, 150, 220, 221; Holocaust in, 100–101; independence of, 97, 235, 239; Jews in, 20, 110, 111; memory of, 239; recognition of, 15; Serb minority in, 99; spheres of interest in, 96, 97
Croatian Archeological Society, 73
Croatian Crusaders Brotherhood, 224
Croatian émigrés, 24, 224, 225, 227–28; attitudes toward, 223; condemnation of, 228; defense strategy of, 219; fascism and, 226, 230; German sympathy and, 223; media and, 227, 228; Mehlem attack and, 220, 221; political violence and, 223; settlement of, 217–19; wartime pasts of, 227, 229

Croatian Foreign Ministry, 227, 304n50
Croatian Home Guard, 101, 106, 107, 108, 109, 167, 306n72, 306n80, 307n87, 307n88
Croatian Liberation Movement, 220
Croatian Parliament, 103, 109
Croatian Peasant Party, 220
Croatian State Information and Propaganda Office, 109, 110
Croatian State Radio, 104
Croatian State Railways, 110
Croats, 21, 24, 61, 63, 65, 68, 69, 105, 113, 211, 218, 221, 224, 229–30; anti-fascist, 238; Catholic, 235, 239, 249; depiction of, 217, 223; Serbs and, 78; South Slavs and, 76
Crvenković, Filip, 111
culture, 94, 124, 129, 156, 160, 207, 210, 211, 214, 215, 234, 251; bearers of, 204; change of, 254; Croatian, 219–20; German, 23–24, 117, 119, 120, 327n4, 334n1; Gottscheer, 163, 164, 169; high, 122, 161; memory, 14, 184, 206; theory, 203, 209; Western, 208
Cvijić, Jovan, 71

Dąbie, 73
Dachau, 125, 127
Daily Mail, 244
Đakovo, 104, 105, 108, 307n80
Dandl, Otto Ritter von, 40
Danica, 104, 305n67
Danube Commission, 42, 44
Danube River, 41, 62, 83, 84, 85, 87, 89, 91, 204, 208, 209, 211, 215; German settlements on, 23, 202, 205, 207; shipping on, 42, 43
Darré, Walther, 76
Dayton Peace Agreement, 15, 248

INDEX

"Decree on the Protection of National and Aryan Culture of the Croat Nation," 102
Dehn, Paul, 4
Deichmann, Thomas, 353n53
Deniker, Joseph, 71
Department for the Protection of the People (Odeljenje za zaštitu naroda, OZNA), 166
deportations, 12, 78, 95, 100, 104–9, 109–12, 113, 164, 169, 170
Der Angriff, 57
Der Landwirt, 52
Der Spiegel, 226, 227, 244
Der Südostdeutsche, 197, 334n106
Derrida, Jacques, 231
Deutsche Arbeitsfront (German Labor Front), 57
Deutsche Bank, 32, 36
Deutsche Gesellschaft für Rassenhygiene (German Society for Racial Hygiene), 76
Deutsche Soldaten-Zeitung, 223
Deutsche Stiftung (German Foundation), 46
Deutscher Schutzband für Grenz- und Auslandsdeutschtum (German Defense League for German Affairs in Border and Foreign Regions), 63
"Deutschlandlied" ("Song of Germany"), 94
Deželić, Berislav, 220, 221, 222
Die Zeit, 223
Đinđić, Zoran, 352n39
Diplich, Hans, 85, 89
Directorate for Public Order and Security (Ravnateljstvo za javni red i sigurnost, RAVSIGUR), 102, 107
Directorate of the Ustaša Police (Ravnateljstvo Ustaškog redarstva, RUR), 102

Disconto Gesellschaft, 32, 33, 36
displaced persons (DPs), 185, 318n69, 319n75; camps, 166, 168; Gottscheer, 146, 147, 168; Slovenian, 150–51
District Captaincy (Bezirkshauptmannschaft) of Gottschee, 140
Division for Cultural Policy (NSDAP), 74
Dobruja, ethnic Germans in, 67, 143
Dokumentation der Vertreibung, 187
Donauschwaben, 23, 87, 203, 208, 209, 212, 213, 214, 215, 221, 222; historic overview of, 204–6; monuments of, 206–7
Donauschwabenufer (Banks of the Danube Swabians), 208, 213
Dostoyevsky, Fyodor, 235
DP Act (1948), 146–47
DP Act (1950), 155
DPs. *See* displaced persons
Drang nach Osten (Drive to the East), 177, 202
Duisberg, Carl, 35

East, Germany and, 5–8, 103–4
East Prussia, 203, 206, 214
Eastern Bloc, 5, 13, 114
"Eastern Turn," 255–58
economic activity, 6, 10, 33, 36, 65, 232, 348n32; Central European, 43–44; German, 215; reshaping, 41–42; Romanian, 43–44; Yugoslav, 346n11
economic crash (2008), 16
economic war, 30, 34, 37
education, 67, 118, 160, 169, 200, 322n11; nazification of, 81
egg production/sales, 47, 49, 50, 51, 55, 56, 288n91, 289n108; monopoly on, 54
Eichmann, Adolf, 14, 222, 225

Eickstedt, Egon von, 63, 71, 74, 75, 76
Einsatzgruppen, 112; trial, 207, 337n23
Einwandererzentralstelle (EWZ), 144, 150
emigration, 87, 154; networks and, 151–56; overseas, 154 (table)
Emona (real estate company), 164
Entente Powers, 9, 33, 34, 37, 40, 349
Entnordung, 67, 68, 75
Eppich, Josef, 142, 145
Erhard, Ludwig, 208
Erneuerer, 55, 60
ethnic cleansing, 16, 66, 99, 162, 163, 172, 176, 179, 238, 239, 250, 258, 265
ethnic Germans (*Volksdeutsche*), 5, 18, 21, 22–23, 24, 52, 55, 57, 59, 60, 80, 81, 83, 98, 113, 118, 148, 149, 154, 156, 164, 177, 181, 182, 183, 185: cooperative union of, 46; depiction of, 91; development of, 89; Eugene of Savoy and, 82; expulsion of, 6, 92, 168; Gottscheers and, 147; legacy of, 23; martial heritage of, 85–86; movement of, 14, 47, 180; resettlement and, 196, 198; Serbian Banat and, 12; treatment of, 93, 166; Volhynian, 143, 158
ethnic groups, 61, 65, 86, 151; depiction of, 18–19, 232; displacement of, 21
ethnicity, 57, 88, 118, 187, 189, 190; conceptions of, 182; German, 24, 52, 166
Eugene of Savoy, Prince, 19, 92–93; achievements of, 89; Balkan conquest of, 79, 80, 83; Central Europe and, 90; colonization and, 82; empire and, 88; Hitler and, 19, 86–92; legacy of, 82, 83–84, 94;

narratives about, 85; propaganda about, 81, 83; *Reichsidee* and, 84
European Economic Community, 15
European Union, 15, 16
EWZ. *See* Einwandererzentralstelle
Expanded Program to Send Children to the Countryside (Erweiterte Kinderlandverschickung, EKLV), 177
expellees, 14, 185, 187, 204, 214, 230; German, 228; Gottschee, 22; societal acknowledgment of, 335n6
expulsion, 14, 82, 139, 159, 167, 181, 187, 192, 195, 196–97; mass, 92; postwar, 174–79; resettlement and, 316n42; trauma of, 168
extermination camps, 64, 77, 125, 175, 222, 238, 346n17
"Extraordinary Legal Decree Command" (NDH), 104

fascism, 124, 130, 176, 217, 235; Croatian, 223–30
Fascist Italy, influence of, 20, 96–97
Federal Republic of Germany, 180, 215, 219, 251; anti-communism in, 187; Bukovina Germans and, 189, 191, 193, 329n28; Cold War and, 13–14; Croats and, 226; Danube Swabians and, 23; expellee monuments in, 206; migration and, 217; resettlement in, 184–90
Federal Statistical Office, 248, 348n32
Ferenc, Mitja, 166, 175, 176
Fertik, Ted, 33
Final Solution, 90, 95, 109, 112, 113, 196
"first expellees" argument, 196
Fischer, Eugen, 63, 74, 75
Fischer, Fritz, 29, 32–33, 44
Fischer, Joschka, 16, 17, 259
Fisher, Gaëlle, 22–23
folktales, ethnic German, 82, 298n20

foreign exchange, 38, 41, 57
foreign policy, 16, 33, 252, 258, 260; German, 32–33, 45, 196
Francetić, Jure, 107–8
Frankfurter Allgemeine Zeitung, 227
Frantner, Josef, 58
Frederick II, 90
French Foreign Ministry, Little Entente and, 53
Frenkel, Samuel, 57
Frensing, Hans Hermann, 163, 323n18
Freud, Sigmund, 253–54
Friedländer, Saul, 114
Frković, Mate, 226
Fütterer, Karl, 54–55, 55–56

Garner, Margaret, 234
Gaschler, Norbert, 192–93
Gastrecht, 224, 225
Gemünden, Gerd, 232
General Muir (ship), 151
Generalgouvernement, 101, 183
Generalplan Ost, 66
genocide, 16, 96, 113, 181, 182, 200, 221, 222, 229, 232, 234, 251; Armenian, 256; Bosnian, 239–40, 242, 347n18; contemporary, 249; future, 231; (re)memory of, 240–42, 244–48; Rwandan, 250, 261, 262; as shared cultural memory, 233
German Empire: borders of, 81–86; East and, 6; oil interests of, 36; territorial claims of, 202
German Foreign Ministry, 12, 37, 90, 98, 111; Croatian government and, 99; spheres of influence and, 301n6
German Historical Museum, 333n92
German literature, "Eastern Turn" in, 255–58

German Reich, 89, 144, 212, 213, 214, 215; Gottscheers and, 142
German Resettlement Company (Deutsche Umsiedlungs Treuhandgesellschaft, DUT), 164
German Settlement Association (Deutsche Ansiedlungsgesellschaft, DAG), 172–73
German Volk, 19, 23, 80, 81, 88, 90, 203; Gottscheers and, 145
Germanization, 75, 164, 165, 183, 187, 190, 191, 201
Germanness, 85, 88, 183, 208, 210, 215, 253
Germans: Baltic, 158, 183; Bessarabian, 183, 207; Danube, 89; depiction of, 8, 223; empathy for, 124; Hungarian, 206, 207; Jews and, 70, 117–20; Reich, 90, 170, 183; Slovene, 315n29; Zipser, 204. *See also* Banat Germans; Bukovina Germans; ethnic Germans
Gerstenmaier, Eugen, 208
Gesemann, Gerhard, 62, 67, 76
Gestapo, 100
Gliebe, Father Joseph, 163, 164
global markets, 33–34, 35
Golden Dawn, 130
Goldstein, Ivo, 100–101, 303n30
Gospić, 104, 105, 303n30
Gottschee, 21, 142, 149, 160–68, 321n1, 322n7; annexation of, 162; migration and, 139–41; population of, 141, 145
Gottschee (town), 160–61, 166, 178; architecture of, 176; occupation of, 162, 169; population of, 167; surface area of, 167–68
Gottschee Archive, 324n64
Gottschee Tree, 177
Gottscheer Landsmannschaft (Homeland Association), 176, 179, 188, 192–93

Gottscheer Relief Association, 155, 321n112, 324n64
Gottscheer Relief Organization, 168
Gottscheer Zeitung, 163, 170
Gottscheers: American, 141, 159, 168, 169, 175, 177; Anschluss and, 161; assimilation of, 150, 178–79; deportation of, 164, 169, 170; diaspora of, 159, 160, 177, 178; economic skills of, 164; entanglement of, 141–43, 150–51; ethnic cleansing and, 176; ethnic Germans and, 147; experience of, 159, 160, 171; expulsion of, 139, 159, 167, 168, 174–79; homeland of, 158, 322n7; memory of, 159, 173; migration of, 155, 156, 160; Nazi occupation and, 174; Nazified leadership of, 144, 158, 160, 161, 177; NCWC and, 155; Partisans and, 174; resettlement and, 138, 139, 147, 151, 156, 160, 162, 163–64, 166–70, 172, 173; Slovenes and, 146–51, 161, 163, 164, 165, 168, 169, 171–76, 179; Slovenia and, 159, 160, 179; victimhood and, 159, 176, 178
Gould, Eliga, 8
Greater German Reich, 64, 86, 90, 94, 110, 137, 143
Greece: Cold War and, 13; communication lines, with, 301n5; Eastern Bloc and, 5; financial decline of, 16; German occupation of, 11–12, 121
Greek Orthodox Church, 70
Greek Parliament, 130
Greifelt, Ulrich, 90
Gross, Stephen, 10
Grosslaschitz (Velike Lašče), 140
Grossraumwirtschaft, 44
guest workers, 15, 254, 348n32

Gündisch, Konrad, 205
Günther, Hans F. K., 71, 73, 74
Gypsies. *See* Roma

Haberlandt, Arthur, 72
Habsburg Empire, 80, 83, 86, 93, 138, 161; Balkans and, 8; Bukovina Germans and, 182; fortification of, 84; Gottscheers and, 140, 141; victory for, 79
Habsburg Military Border, 79, 86, 88
Habsburgs, 32, 73, 79, 80, 82, 85, 87, 88, 94, 99, 140, 147; dominance of, 9; Romanians and, 33; sovereignty of, 41
Hague, The, 249, 254, 257, 258, 261, 263
Hahn, Eva, 180
Hahn, Hans Henning, 180
Haines, Brigid, 255
Hallstein Doctrine, 13
Hamlin, David, 17, 18
Hammond, Philip, 261, 262
Handke, Peter, 26
Handler, Helene, 153
Handler, Josef, 153
Handler, Klara, 153
Hansen, Miriam, 253
Harlan, Veit, 110
Harriman, Helga, 165
Hartman & Conen, 57, 58, 288n104, 288n108
Harvey, Elizabeth, 181, 190
Hefer, Stjepan, 108, 220, 221
Hegel, Georg Wilhelm Friedrich, 251
Heim, Susanne, 196
Heim ins Reich (Home to the Reich) program, 14, 22–23, 137, 143, 158, 170, 179, 180
Heimat, 80, 87, 92, 142, 186, 187, 204, 208–9, 210, 211, 213, 214, 215; loss of, 181, 203

Heinrich VII, Prince Reuss, 31
Helfferich, Karl, 35, 39, 40, 43
Helm, Hans, 98, 110, 112
Herf, Jeffrey, 337n23
Hertling, Georg von, 42
Hesch, Michael, 74, 75
Himmler, Heinrich, 90, 162, 165
Hippler, Fritz, 110
Hirsch, Marianne, 233, 242, 246
history: Banat German, 89; cultural, 83; economic, 45; ethnicizing/nationalizing, 139–40; folk, 63; German-Balkan, 5, 7, 8, 15; imperial, 126; oral, 116, 159, 310n9; racial, 76
Hitler, Adolf, 11, 64, 81, 83, 94, 101, 110, 118, 126, 222; Croatia and, 96, 226; ethnic Germans and, 89; Eugene of Savoy and, 19, 86–92; Gottscheers and, 142, 143, 161, 162, 163, 165, 169, 170; Kingdom of Yugoslavia and, 68; Pavelić and, 12–13, 99, 111, 226; Tito and, 235, 237, 239; Yugoslavia and, 77–78
Hochkultur, Austro-German, 161
Hölderlin, Friedrich, 251
Holocaust, 7, 25, 64, 74, 96, 118, 175, 196, 222, 225, 229, 231, 241, 249, 256, 265; Bukovina Germans and, 198–99; commemoration of, 114; comparisons to, 242; cosmopolitanization of, 252–53; in Croatia, 100–101; ethnic cleansing and, 250; experience of, 126; German understanding of, 129, 130; history of, 112, 180, 184, 228; imagery of, 198, 231, 233, 260, 261; memory of, 16, 25, 120–25, 133, 198, 199, 231, 232, 235–40, 253, 261; NDH and, 20, 95, 112, 112–13, 300n2; (re)memory of, 233, 240–42, 244–48; responsibility for, 19–20,
120, 251; survivors of, 114, 115, 116, 124, 125, 128, 130, 131, 185
Holy Roman Empire, 83, 296n10
homosexuals, crimes against, 218
Horstenau, Edmund Glaise von, 98
human rights, 24, 261, 265
Human Rights Watch, 244
humanitarianism, 258–64
Hungarians, 36, 75, 205, 207, 211, 255
Hunt, Swanee, 242
Huyssen, Andreas, 253

ICTY. *See* International Crime Tribunal for the Former Yugoslavia
identity, 21, 24, 201, 265; dictating, 262; ethnic, 156; formation, 180; German, 22, 139, 164, 260; Gottscheer, 22, 159, 179; group, 183; individual, 22, 25; national, 17, 22, 25, 94, 156, 232, 251–53, 254, 262; Slovenian, 139
ideology: Nazi, 19, 62, 80, 94, 131, 142, 161; political, 213; racial, 232; völkisch, 76
imagery, 211; Bosnian, 246, 247; Holocaust, 198, 222, 231, 233, 260, 261
immigration, 154–55, 264; ethnic German, 146–47, 154; Greek, 15; restrictions on, 141; Serbian, 25
Imperial Economics Office, 34, 35
Imperial War Council, 79
Independent State of Croatia. *See* Nezavisna Država Hrvatska
Independent Television News (ITN), 240, 241, 242, 243, 244, 347n25
Ingrao, Charles W., 79
Institut für Grenz- and Auslandstudien (Institute for Border and Foreign Studies), 63
Institut für Rassen- und Völkerkunde (Institute for Racial Science and Ethnology), 74

Institute of Contemporary History (Munich), 225
Intergovernmental Committee on Refugees, 148
Interior Ministry (NDH), 107–8, 307n80
International Committee for European Migration (ICEM), 155
International Crime Tribunal for the Former Yugoslavia (ICTY), 245, 246, 255, 265, 352n40
International Military Tribunal (Nuremberg), 229
International Refugee Organization (IRO), 139, 146, 147, 148, 150, 151, 152, 153, 155, 156
International Tracing Service (ITS), 139, 314nn9–10, 319n84
Italia (ship), 153
Italian Foreign Ministry, demarcation line and, 301n6
Italian military, 77, 96, 97, 111, 123
ITN. *See* Independent Television News
ITS. *See* International Tracing Service

Jadovno, 101, 104, 105, 303n30
Janko, Josef "Sepp," 83, 85–86, 87, 93; on colonization, 88, 89; German Empire and, 297n27
Jasenovac camp system, 105, 111, 112, 226, 237–38, 239; Camp V of, 101; deportation to, 107, 305n64; memorial at, *238*
Jeffries, Ian, 248
Jelić, Branimir, 222, 225, 343n34
Jewish businesses, 50, 51, 57–58, 59
Jewish community, 100, 105, 109, 131, 301n3
Jewish property, 81, 103, 194, 304n50
Jewish question, 101, 102, 106, 109, 110, 112, 113

Jewish Section (*Židovski odsjek*), 101–2, 103, 107, 108, 109, 110
Jews, 5, 19, 20, 21, 46, 65, 72, 70, 77, 78, 81, 116, 122, 123, 124, 126; Balkan, 120; Banat, 12, 90; Bosnian, 108; characterization of, 100; communists and, 106; Croatian, 100, 101, 102, 103, 105, 109, 226; deportation of, 12, 100, 102, 104–9, 110; economic influence against, 10; experiences of, 115, 120; expulsion of, 111, 181, 187; German, 57, 58; Greek, 12, 64, 120; Macedonian, 64; murder of, 12, 65, 100, 101, 104–9, 199, 218, 226, 227, 229, 337n23; Partisans and, 111, 112; persecution of, 12, 96, 103–4, 107, 113, 114, 115, 121, 127, 131, 198, 199; population, 108, 113, 116; resettlement and, 101, 187; Serbian, 12, 238, 240; Spanish, 312n27; Thessalonian, 77; Thracian, 64; victimization of, 23, 127, 131, 218, 239; Yugoslav, 57, 64, 120, 238, 249
Jews, The (exhibition), 109
Joint Committee for the Defense of the Croatian Patriots, 219
Joseph II, Emperor, 88, 298n40
Judt, Tony, 114
Jung, Carl Gustav, 114
Jünger, Ernst, 233

Kadelburg, Lavoslav, 309n113
Kaiser-Wilhelm-Institut für Anthropologie, menschliche Erblehre und Eugenik (Kaiser Wilhelm Institute for Anthropology, Human Heredity, and Eugenics), 69, 74
Kalvarienberg, 212, 213
Kammerhofer, Konstantin, 98
Kansteiner, Wulf, 168

INDEX 371

Karadžić, Radovan, 257, 258, 263
Karlsruhe, 212–15
Kasche, Siegfried, 98, 111, 112
Keraterm, 242
Kerestinec, 104
Kiderlen-Wächter, Alfred von, 32
Kingdom of Serbs, Croats, and Slovenes, 137, 141
Kingdom of Yugoslavia, 18, 20, 61, 68, 137; destruction of, 22, 62, 78
Klun, Alois, 137, 141
Klun, Anna (Ana), 137, 145, 149–50, 151, 154, 155
Klun, Frieda, 137, 138, 145, 150
Klun, Johann (Ivan), 319n84
Kneightly, Emily, 200
Kočevski Rog (Gottscheer Hornwald), 166, 167, 176, 322n7
Koch, Erich, 208
Kocián, Jiří, 20, 21
Koerner, Paul von, 37
Korb, Alexander, 101
Košak, Vladimir, 103, 110, 304n49
Kosovo War, 5, 16, 273n58
Kotsonis, Yanni, 60
Kotzian, Ortfried, 196, 333n93
Kraft, Stephan (Stefan), 47, 51, 55, 59, 60
Kraitschek, Gustav, 71
Krajec, Josef (Jože), 137, 145, 151, 317n53
Krajec, Otmar, 317n53
Králov, Kateřina, 20, 21
Kresse, Franz, 156
Kresse, Friedrich, 156
Krier, Peter, 212–13
Krokodil, 235, 236, 237; caricature from, *236*
Kruščica, 104, 105, 107
Krzoska, Markus, 190
Kühlmann, Richard, 29, 44
Kühnel, Vilko, 101–2, 107, 111, 307n80

Kulturbund, 46, 48, 118, 150, 154, 160, 170; ethnic Germans and, 281n13; Gottschee, 161; Yugoslav, 322n11
Kulturträger, 23, 202, 203, 212
Kundnani, Hans, 259–60
Künzig, Johannes, 188, 189, 190
Küppers, Gustav Adolf, 62, 63, 64, 66, 76, 77, 78; anthropological examinations and, 69–70
Kvaternik, Eugen "Dido," 101, 102, 107, 305n65
Kvaternik, Slavko, 96, 101

labor recruitment, 15, 273n52, 350n22
Lagarde, Paul, 4
Laković, Saveta, 53
Lampeter, Wilhelm (Willi), 142, 155, 160, 161, 178; Gottscheers and, 323n30; Kulturbund and, 170; Rann Triangle and, 165; removal of, 162; resettlement and, 163–64
Landesämter für Verfassungsschutz (State Offices for the Protection of the Constitution), 223–24
Landsberg, Alison, 234, 345n9
Landsmannschaft (Homeland Society of Banat Danube Swabians), 207, 211
Landsmannschaft der Buchenlanddeutschen (Homeland Society of Bukovina Germans), 186, 192, 195, 197, 199, 329n28
language: Croatian, 219; German, 10, 85, 91, 94, 117, 118, 119, 120, 124, 131, 148, 220, 221, 254, 255; Gottscheer, 165, 169; Slavic, 65, 68; Slovenian, 148, 149, 150, 151
Lebensraum, 61, 75, 239, 346n16
Lebow, Richard Ned, 251
Lebzelter, Viktor, 72, 73, 77
"Legal Decree Regarding the Sending of Suspect and Dangerous Persons

to Forced Labor in Collection and Labor Camps" (NDH), 305n65
Leipziger Vierteljarhsschrift für Südosgteuropa (Quarterly for Southeast Europe), 74
Lendl, Egon, 76
Lengel-Krizman, Narcisa, 303n36
Lenz, Fritz, 63
Levi, Moric, 305n66
Levy, Daniel, 252, 273n58
Lienfeld/Livold, 137, 138, 140, 145, 149, 150, 152, 153; emigration from, 154 (table)
Lienfelders, 138, 148, 151, 154, 155, 156
Little Entente, 53, 59
livestock, 4, 47, 52, 57, 160, 164
Ljubić, Nicol, 25, 250–51, 256, 261, 263, 264, 265; Balkans/Berlin and, 254–55; memory and, 250, 252
Ljubljana (Laibach), 160, 162, 171, 176; assimilation in, 179
Loborgrad, 104, 105, 108, 110
Lorković, Mladen, 102, 111
Lower Sava, 144, 162, 164, 171, 172, 174, 175
Lower Styria, 137, 153, 171; Gottscheers in, 138, 145; resettlement to, 143–46, 148; Slovenes in, 147
Lower, Wendy, 112
Ludendorff, Erich, 43
Lüdtke, Alf, 337n23
Luppes, Jeffrey, 23
Luschan, Felix von, 71
LZDK. *See* Agricultural Central Credit Bank

Macedonia, 4, 12, 63, 64, 235
Malcolm, Noel, 242
Maleš, Branimir, 75
Manjača, 242, 244, *245, 246*

Mannschaft (Gottschee), 142, 161
Marburg (Maribor), 162, 173, 220
Marghiloman, Alexandru, 29
Maria Theresa, Empress, 88, 212, 338n33
Marn, Albert, 152
Marn, Heinrich, 152
Marn, Heinrich, Jr., 152
Marn, Josef, 152
Marn née Tscherne, Maria, 152
Marshall, Penny, 243
mass murder, 65, 104–9, 229, 322n7
media, 227, 234, 247; outlets, 248; representation, 21, 250; visual, 232; West German, 228
Medić-Skoko, Rafael, 222–23, 343n38
Mehlem attack, 216, 217, 219–29, 342nn17–18
memory, 7, 8, 25, 80, 116, 129, 180, 201, 225, 249, 254; boom, 198, 251–53; Bosnian, 231, 242; collective, 22, 117, 159, 168, 178, 179, 241, 250, 252, 253, 260; community, 125, 131, 133; cosmopolitan, 252; cultural, 233, 247; distorted, 184; entangled, 232, 235–40, 247; German, 22, 24, 88, 184, 262, 337n23; Gottscheer, 159; historical, 19, 251; Holocaust, 16, 25, 120–25, 133, 198, 199, 231, 232, 235–40, 261; hyper-mediated, 247; individual, 21, 117; migration and, 14; narratives of, 168–69, 179; national, 252; photography and, 233–35; prosthetic, 233, 234, 345n9; public, 230; recycling, 233; repressed, 253, 265; screen, 253–54, 264, 265; shared, 169; transference, 233, 247, 345n9; wartime, 7, 25, 120–25, 232, 235–40, 254, 262
Mengele, Josef, 74

INDEX 373

Mercy, Count Claude Florimond de, 79, 86, 93
Mešić, Ademaga, 102
Messner, Elena, 350n17
Metajna, 104
Michael I, King, 121, 123
Michitsch, Victor, 176
migration, 8, 66, 80, 157, 217; ex-Yugoslavian, 248; Gottschee and, 139–41; Jewish, 247; memory and, 14, 248–49; resettlement and, 197; Turkish, 247, 256; wave of, 14–15
Milković, Josip, 104
Milošević, Slobodan, 26, 239, 240, 258
Ministry of Human Rights and Refugees (Bosnia), 248
Ministry of National Economy (NDH), 103
Ministry of the Interior (FRG), Mehlem attack and, 224
minorities: citizenship and, 311n17; ethnic, 11, 12, 143; German, 21, 45, 53–55, 63, 138, 139, 143–44, 156; Hungarian, 255; Jews and, 311n17; religious, 11, 12
Mische, Max, 175
Mit Fluchtgepäck die Heimat verlassen…50 Jahre seit der Umsiedlung der Buchenlanddeutschen, 195
Mitteleuropa, 4, 9, 10, 270n26; petroleum for, 38
Moeller, Robert G., 218, 338n23
Molnar, Christopher A., 24, 30, 99–100, 250
Molotov, Vyacheslav, 192
Molotov-Ribbentrop agreement, 181
Montenegrins, 69, 71, 76
Montenegro, 52, 67, 72, 235; war declaration by, 3
monuments, 209, 212, 242, 335n6, 339n37; Danube Swabian, 206–7; expellee, 206–7, 335n6

Mora, Terézia, 255
Morrison, Toni, 234
Mouton, Michelle, 177
Mrakovica memorial, 242
Mühlmann, Wilhelm Emil, 62, 64, 66, 67, 68, 76, 77, 78; anthropological examinations and, 69–70; racial science and, 63, 69
Müller, Gebhard, 208
Müller-Guttenbrunn, Adam, 82
Murat, Vladimir, 222
Museum für Völkerkunde (Museum of Ethnology), 69
Museum of Natural History (Vienna), 72
Muslims, 3, 70, 84, 256, 258, 264; murder of, 255. *See also* Bosnian Muslims
Mussolini, Benito, 11, 64, 111, 169

Nabokov, Vladimir, 224
Naimark, Norman, 162, 163
narratives, 116, 159, 177, 199, 244; collective guilt, 115, 122, 127, 131, 133, 200; Gottscheer, 168–69, 179; memory, 168–69, 179; postwar, 93; victim-perpetrator, 131, 133
National Catholic Welfare Council (NCWC), 155, 321n112
National Socialism, 21, 75, 86, 118, 128, 143, 170, 182, 201, 205, 206, 241, 251; commitment to, 131, 197; defending, 23; end of, 76; ethnic German development and, 89; Gottscheers and, 142; legacy of, 22, 89, 94, 257, 264; memory of, 24, 180, 184; resettlement and, 187, 190, 191, 193, 196, 197, 198; rise of, 17, 120; victims of, 125, 255
National Theater (Belgrade), 82

nationalism: Croatian, 228; German, 25, 82, 94, 162; Pan-German, 4; Serb, 106; Yugoslav, 25

Nationalsozialistische Deutsche Arbeiterpartei (NSDAP), 55, 63, 72, 74, 110

NATO, 250, 261; bombing by, 5, 16, 251, 259, 265

Naumann, Friedrich, 9, 270n26

Nazi New Order, 81, 84, 181

Nazis, 17, 75, 84–85, 88, 127, 129, 158, 192, 203, 227, 228, 232, 237, 242; agriculture and, 45; atrocities of, 24; collaboration with, 222; Croatia and, 239; distribution of power by, 112; ethnic cleansing and, 238; Gottscheers and, 156; Jewish businesses and, 50; resettlement by, 184–85; rule by, 80–81, 82; scientific research by, 19; *Volksgruppen* and, 316n31

NCWC. *See* National Catholic Welfare Council

NDH. *See* Nezavisna Država Hrvatska

neo-Nazism, 130, 131, 265

networks, 33, 41, 44, 104, 138, 157, 264; emigration and, 151–56; memorial, 265; migrant, 139; trade, 45; transnational, 30; transportation, 10, 43

Neuburger, Josef, 194, 195, 198

Nezavisna Država Hrvatska (NDH), 65, 76, 78, 102, 109, 110, 111, 117, 144, 217, 218, 228; creation of, 11, 95, 103, 124, 226; criticism of, 99; ethnic/religious minorities and, 12; Final Solution and, 113; German economic policy in, 302n12; German occupation and, 97–100; Gottscheers and, 162; Holocaust and, 20, 95, 112–13, 300n2; Italo-German occupation regimes and, 96–97; Jews and, 20, 101, 103, 112–13; mass murder and, 107; resources for, 98; security situation for, 99; sovereignty of, 96, 100; Third Reich and, 68; Ustašas and, 12

Non-Aligned Movement, 346n10

Non-Ferrous Metal Industry Act, 34

North-Rhine-Westphalia, 206, 337n22

Novi Sad/Neusatz, 46, 49, 52, 55, 58, 60, 87, 88, 118, 127

NSDAP. *See* Nationalsozialistische Deutsche Arbeiterpartei

O-cases, 183, 185, 187, 191, 193, 198

Oberste Heeresleitung (OHL), 41

OF. *See* Slovene Liberation Front (Osvobodilna fronta)

Office for the Protection of the Constitution (FRG), 224, 227

Office for the Renewal of the Economy (NDH), 103

Office of Nationalized Property (NDH), 103

Office of the Reichskommissariat for the Strengthening of Germandom (RKFDV), 90, 162

Office of the State Prosecutor (FRG), 228

Official Data Foundation, 320n106

Omarska, 241, 242, 246, 249, 346n17, 347n27

Organisation Todt, 111, 124

Osijek, 105, 106, 110, 117, 118, 306n69, 307n88; Jews in, 97, 103, 108, 109

Osttagung deutscher Wissenschaftler (Conference of German Scholars on the East), 66

Ottoman Empire, 70, 79, 239, 240; Balkan history and, 8; influence of, 117; war on, 3

Ottomans, 3, 79, 80, 84–85, 86, 93, 205; expulsion of, 82

Pag island, 101, 104, 105
Paikert, G. C., 204, 206
Panagiotidis, Jannis, 21, 22
Pančevo/Pantschowa, ethnic Germans and, 88
Panorama (news program), 226, 227, 228
Partisans, 96, 106, 107, 119, 146, 149, 159, 166, 175, 179, 189, 217–18, 221, 238, 239; attacks by, 167, 171, 173; Gottscheers and, 174; Jews and, 111, 112; resistance by, 160
Party of the Germans (Partei der Deutschen), 46–47, 48
past, 6, 201, 227; confronting, 25, 200, 232, 251; exporting, 264–65; Nazi, 217, 225, 230, 232, 234, 237, 251; repressing, 253–54; visualization of, 233–35
Patenschaft, 206, 207, 336–37, 337n22
Pavelić, Ante, 100, 101, 102, 110, 217, 219, 220, 302n24, 304n49, 341n8; Hitler and, 12–13, 99, 111, 226, 302n11; Italy and, 96; Jews and, 104; legacy of, 227; NDH and, 218; press statement by, 303n36; rise of, 226; Ustaša movement and, 95
peasant (*Bauer*), 86, 87, 143
peasant-soldier (*Bauer-Soldat, Wehrbauer*), 86
Pendas, Devin, 225
Perčić, Franjo, 343n38
Perić, Leon, 305n6
Perlick, Alfons, 337n22
petroleum, 40; exporting, 37, 43; German, 36, 37; question, 39; Romanian, 10, 17, 29, 36, 37–38, 41
Petrovaradin/Peterwardein, 87–88

Petrovgrad, 49, 56
Pfizer, Theodor, 207–8
Phelps, Arthur, 92
photography: atrocity, 241, 245–46; liberation, 245; memory and, 233–35; racial, 65–69
Pianist, The, 199
Pickering, Michael, 200
Pöch, Rudolf, 71, 72–73
Poiana Micului, 194, 199
Poje, Elisabeth, 148
Poje, Rosina (Rozina), 148
Poje, Stefan, 148–49
Poland: ethnic Germans in, 143; German occupation of, 7; Russian, 41
Poles, 198, 229; Bukovinians and, 189; criticism of, 190; expulsion of, 181, 187; murder of, 181; resettlement and, 187
politics, 14, 90, 130, 157, 186, 200, 203, 211, 251; contemporary, 250; diaspora, 140; European, 16; German minority, 53–55, 59; identity, 232; memory, 249; nationality, 82; of regret, 199; Romanian, 37
Pontus agency, 51, 58
Popov, Metodi, 75
Popović, Daka, 52, 223
Popović, Momčilo, 222
Potsdam Agreement, 146
poultry, 48, 56, 57, 58, 59, 60
Predić, Uroš, 240
prejudices, 19, 99, 123, 128, 264
Previsic, Boris, 349n14
Prijedor, 240, 242, 244
"Prinz Eugen" Waffen-SS division, 81, 82, 90, 91, 92, 93, 113
prisoners of war, 71–72, 73, 222, 225
Promitzer, Christian, 18, 19
propaganda, 92, 181; Banat German, 81, 86; Croatian, 220; ethnic German, 82, 83, 91; Nazi, 80, 188, 194;

political, 235, 237; Soviet, 236, 237; Ustaša, 100

Queen Mary (ship), 154
Queens, Gottscheers in, 152, 155, 168. *See* Ridgewood

Race and Settlement Main Office (SS), 75
race laws, 100, 104
racial doctrine, 61–62, 64, 75, 76
racial hierarchy, 172, 179
racial hygiene, 63, 66, 74
racial science (*Rassenkunde*), 18, 62, 63, 68, 70, 75, 76–78
racial theory, 61, 69, 73, 74
racial types, 69, 70, 72, 73, 75
racism, 86, 126, 128, 182, 189
Radio Belgrade, 91
Radio Television of Serbia (RTS), 240
Rakić, Žarko, 53
Rann (Brežice) Triangle, 137, 144–45, 149, 150, 160, 162, 163, 164, 166, 168, 169, 175, 179; conditions in, 165; life in, 170–74
RAVSIGUR. *See* Directorate for Public Order and Security (Ravnateljstvo za javni red i sigurnost)
raw materials, 30, 34, 38, 40, 41, 100
Reche, Otto, 71, 73, 74, 75
Red Cross, 167, 175, 244
Refugee Relief Act (RRA), 155
refugees, 15, 16, 178; Austrian, 107; Bosnian, 5, 247, 248, 348n32; ex-Yugoslavian, 248; foreign, 185; Gottscheer, 146; Jewish, 301n3; Yugoslavian, 235, 249
Reich Ministry of Agriculture, 51
Reich Security Main Office (RSHA), 98, 101; deportations and, 109–12
Reichel, Heinrich, 66
Reichsbank, 38, 39, 40

Reichsbauernführer, 76
Reichsdeutsche, 81, 183
Reichsidee (imperial idea), 84
Reichskomitee für öffenlichen Gesundheitsdienst (Reich Committee for Public Health Service), 76
Reichsnährstand, 55
Reichstag, 3, 162
Reimesch, Fritz Heinz, 202, 203
Reserve Police Battalion 101, 228–29
resettlement, 80, 145, 153, 156, 162, 163–64, 172, 180; Bukovina-German, 182–84; Cold War and, 190–95; Croato-German, 99; experience of, 170, 182, 187, 188, 191, 197; Final Solution and, 196; Germanization and, 201; history of, 183, 197; justifying, 184–90; narratives of, 199–200; Nazi, 138, 151, 181; occupation and, 169–70; policy of, 157, 187, 188; remembering, 195–201; trauma of, 168; voluntary, 181, 183, 186–87
resettlement camps, 183, 189, 198
Resettlement Commission (Nazi), 173, 186
Resettler Identity Cards (*Umsiedlerkarten*), 197
resettlers (*Umsiedler*), 14, 181, 183, 185, 198; disappointment of, 189, 190
resistance, 11, 65, 92, 93, 95, 113, 129, 170, 193, 206; Bosnian Muslim, 238; Partisan, 160, 166, 239, 242; Serbian, 77, 97, 106
Resolute (ship), 319n91, 320n98
Rhineland-Palatinate, 205, 207, 213
Ribbentrop, Joachim von, 111
Ribnica, 140, 149, 150, 319n84
Ridgewood neighborhood, Gottscheers in, 152, 155, 168, 169

RKFDV. *See* Office of the Reichskommissariat for the Strengthening of Germandom
Roatta, Mario, 111
Robert Bosch Foundation, 254
Robionek, Bernd, 18
Rolleder, Anton, 72
Roma, 5, 61, 73, 74, 78, 81, 165, 238, 249; murder of, 12, 218, 227
Romania, 6, 11, 12, 18, 74; Austria-Hungary and, 31–32, 41; Bukovina and, 182, 190; Bulgaria and, 31, 36; Central Powers and, 31, 32, 35, 39, 40; Entente and, 9; ethnic Germans in, 14, 143, 164, 191, 205, 206; German relations with, 17, 30–31, 32, 33, 41; Jewish policies in, 121; Serbia and, 80; surrender of, 10
Romanian Army, 35
Romanians, 29, 69, 75, 79, 211
Romano, Jaša, 309n113
Rome Accords, 96, 301n6
Rosenthal, Gabriele, 200
Rothberg, Michael, 247, 253–54, 354n65
Royal Navy, 34, 41
Royal Yugoslav Army, 160
RSHA. *See* Reich Security Main Office
Rudolfsgnad, 205, 211–12
Russia: Austria-Hungary and, 32; collapse of, 29; expansionism of, 31; German occupation of, 7
Russian-Ottoman war, 70
Russian Revolution, 9–10
Russo-Turkish War, 3

S-cases, 183, 187, 198
SA. *See* Sturmabteilung
Sachsenhausen, 305n65
Said, Edward, 7
Salzburg, 76, 99, 140
Sammartino, Annemarie, 224
Santin, Tullia, 126
Sarajevo, 97, 105, 110, 263; arrests in, 107; confinement in, 105; deportation from, 307n81; Jews in, 97, 103, 108
Sava River, 62, 144, 237
Sava-Sotla region. *See* Lower Sava
Saxons, Transylvanian, 74, 75, 202, 204
Sazonov, Sergei, 31
Schager née Jonke, Lina, 152
Schelling, Friedrich Wilhelm Joseph, 251
Scheschareg, Max, 137
Schindler's List, 122, 199
Schleimer, Hilda, 153, 154
Schleimer, Max, Jr., 153
Schleimer, Max, Sr., 153
Schleimer, Pauline, 153
Schleimer, Theresia, 153
Schleimer née Preiditsch, Helena, 153
Schleimer née Rankel, Maria, 153
Schmid, Hans-Christian, 255
Schröcker, Regina, 199, 334n105
Schröder, Gerhard, 261, 353n49
Schütrumpf, Edith, 199, 334n106
Schwidetzky, Ilse, 75, 76
Security Service (Sicherheitsdienst, SD), 305n65
segregation, 100, 101–3, 307n88
Self-Help Organization of German Resettlers from Bukovina (*Hilfskommittee*), 185
Şenocak, Zafer, 256
Serbia, 73, 235, 239, 249, 262; NATO bombing of, 5, 16, 251, 259, 264; Romania and, 80; war declaration by, 3
Serbian Orthodox Christianity, 12, 65
Serbs, 5, 49, 65, 68, 69, 71, 79, 81, 82,

105, 211, 217, 240, 256, 258, 261, 262, 264; Bosnians and, 24, 244, 253; Croats and, 78; ethnic, 20, 238; extremist, 242; murder of, 106, 218, 226, 227, 239; Orthodox, 235, 239, 249; persecution of, 96; resistance by, 97; treatment of, 77

Shafir, Michael, 175

Shakespeare, William, 257

Siebold, Max, 48, 56, 60

Siege of Belgrade, 79, 82

Siege of Vienna, 79

Sieger, Robert, 204

Silesia, 63, 144, 188, 203, 206, 214

Siroče na majčinom grobu (Predić), 240

Sivac, Nusret, 346n17

Slana, 104

Škerlj, Božo, 75

Slavonski Brod, 127

Slavs, 19, 46, 53, 61, 67, 68, 202; colonization by, 52; struggle with, 177; violence against, 23

Slovakia, 204

Slovaks, 61, 63, 77

Slovene Catholic Church, 176

Slovene Liberation Front (Osvobodilna fronta, OF), 166

Slovenes, 21, 22, 68, 137, 144, 156, 158, 160, 170, 217; collaboration against, 176; ethnic cleansing of, 159, 172, 179; expulsion of, 164, 165, 171–72, 173; Gottscheers and, 146–51, 161, 163, 164, 165, 168, 169, 171–76, 179; passing for, 146–51; population of, 144; resettlement and, 99; victimhood and, 176

Slovenia, 21, 99, 143, 144, 149, 160, 166, 173, 175; execution sites in, 174; expulsion from, 159; German minorities in, 63, 141, 147; Gottscheers and, 159; independence of, 158, 176, 235, 239; Nazi oppression of, 169; occupation of, 162; recognition of, 15; trisection of, 162

Slovenianness, 150, 151, 179

Social Democrats, 15, 226

Socialism in One Country theory, 346n10

"Song of Prince Eugene," 82, 91–92

"Song of the Banat Germans," 82

Sontag, Susan, 247

Šosberger, Oskar, 57

South Slavs, 68, 73, 75, 76, 217

South Tyrol, 143, 164, 171; ethnic Germans in, 164

Southeastern Europe, 75, 212; anthropological examinations of, 69–70; German domination of, 5–8, 13; methodology/testimonies from, 116–17; nations/races of, 63–65; *völkisch* view of, 63–65

Soviet Union, 122, 191, 205, 213, 236; campaign against, 77; ethnic Germans in, 14; German invasion of, 7, 103–4, 105; invasion by, 182; as regional hegemon, 13

Spanish Civil War, 118

Srbik, Heinrich von, 84

SS, 18, 64, 75, 97, 109, 110, 112, 123, 171, 186, 196, 198, 235; Croatian, 98, 238; recruitment by, 302n16

St-Fälle, 145

Stalin, Joseph, 235, 237, 346n10

Stalingrad, 12, 64, 122

Stanišić, Saša, 26, 231, 349n14

Stara Gradiška prison, 101

State Directorate for Economic Renewal (NDH), 103

State Directorate for Renewal (NDH), 103

State Treasury (NDH), 103

INDEX

Steierischer Heimatbund, 147, 319n85
Stein, Freiherr Hans Karl von, 35
Stepinac, Alojzije, 226
stereotypes, 19, 131, 181, 254; cultural, 110, 120; ideology and, 232
Sterntal (Strnišče), 166, 174, 175
Stiene, Albert, 170
Stillness of the Sea (*Meeresstille*, Ljubić), 25, 251, 252, 257, 262, 263; characters of, 253; Eastern Turn and, 255; memories/histories and, 256; prize for, 254; tension in, 264; translation of, 250
Stimitz, Johann, 156
Stimitz, Maria, 156
Stone, Dan, 168
Stone Flower Memorial, 238–39, *238*
Sturm (film), 255
Sturmabteilung (Storm Detachment, SA), 63, 161
Stuttgart, 153, 160, 207, 213
Styria (Štajerska), 22, 146, 153, 155, 160, 162, 166
Subdivision of Eugenics and Racial Policy (Vienna), 72
Süddeutsche Zeitung, 227
Südosteuropa-Institut (Institute on Southeast Europe), 74
Šuštar, Alojzij, 176
Swabian Museum, 207
Swabians, 46, 48, 56–57, 59; Banat, 210, 296n10; Danube, 23, 87, 203, 204–6, 206–7, 208, 209, 212, 213, 214, 215, 221, 222; economic interests of, 49; poultry and, 58, 60
Sznaider, Natan, 252, 273n58

Tag der Donauschwaben (Day of the Danube Swabians), 207
taxation, 34, 37, 38, 40
Teeger, Chana, 179
Tenje, Jews in, 108, 109, 110

Teutonic Knights, 6
Thessaly, 4, 119, 130
Third Gendarmerie Battalion (NDH), 106
Third Reich, 5, 15, 18, 55, 64, 65, 69, 78, 81, 82, 96; Banat Germans and, 19; Croatia and, 302n11; defeat of, 92; East and, 6; economic planning in, 44, 62; German dominance and, 4; German understanding of, 129; influence of, 76; Jewish policy and, 113; memory of, 225, 230, 232; migration and, 14; NDH and, 68; racial/spatial planning and, 77; self-destruction of, 174; shadow of, 21; trade with, 45; Ustašas and, 112, 229
Thrace, 4, 9, 12, 64, 67, 68
Thuringia, 138, 144, 145, 321n1
Timişoara/Temeschburg, 60, 85, 211
Tito, Josip Broz, 14, 15, 167, 174, 176, 177, 205, 217, 219, 220, 221; caricature of, 232, 236, *236*, 237; Croats and, 222; Danube Swabians and, 222; death of, 235; economic development and, 346n11; Gottscheers and, 159; Hitler and, 235, 237, 239; memorials and, 239; Partisans and, 221; Stalin and, 235, 237
Todorova, Maria, 7, 8
Tooze, Adam, 33
tourism, 6, 128, 159, 168
trade, 8; agreements, 50–51, 53–55; international, 45; reciprocal, 54; regulations, 50–51; Yugoslav-German, 55, 58
transnationalism, memory boom and, 251–53
Transylvania, 9, 32, 67, 74, 117, 204; German minorities in, 63
Treaty of Brest-Litovsk, 10, 29

Treaty of Bucharest (1913), 31–32
Treaty of Bucharest (1918), 10, 17, 29–30, 35–44; petroleum and, 37–38; prewar policies and, 44; Romania and, 39
Treaty of Paris, 42
Treaty of Saint-Germain, 141
Treblinka, 12
Tripartite Pact, 11, 68, 171
Trnopolje, *243*; concentration camp at, 240, 241, 242, 244, 249, 260–61
Trotskyism, 235, 346n10
Tscherne, Heinrich, 152
Tscherne, Johann, 151, 152
Tscherne, Pauli, 151
Tscherne-Jonke family, 152, 153
Tschinkel, John, 171, 172, 178, 323n18; on emigration issue, 169; Gottscheers and, 177
Turkish Wars, 203
Turks, 70, 83, 84–85, 256

Ulm, 207–12, 213, 214
Ulmer Schachtel, 209, 210
United Croats of Germany, 342n18
United States Holocaust Memorial Museum (USHMM), 249, 346n12, 346n14
Upper Silesia, 153, 183, 189
Urheimat, 206, 208, 209, 215
USC Shoah Foundation, 20; Visual History Archive (VHA), 115, 116, 117, 310n7
Ustašas, 24, 65, 95, 97, 101, 102–3, 107, 108, 167, 218, 219, 222, 226, 228, 239; anti-Jewish policies and, 96; atrocities by, 227; camps, 103, 105, 112, 238, 305n65; death squad, 104; deportation and, 105; forced labor and, 118; ideological principle of, 20; Jews and, 101, 113; massacres by, 106; militia, 96, 99,
104; NDH and, 12; regime, 11, 12, 305n65, 307n88; Serbs and, 98, 239; South Slavs and, 76; Third Reich and, 112, 229; violence of, 113
Ustaša police, 98, 105, 109, 110, 111, 307n80
Ustaša Police Directorate, 105

Väterliteratur, 256, 257
Večernje Novosti, 240
Velika Kikinda, 49, 57
Veliki Bečkerek, 49, 56
Veliko Mraševo, 172
*Vergangenheitsbew*ältigung, 200, 217, 251
Verschuer, Otmar Freiherr von, 74
VHA. *See* USC Shoah Foundation Visual History
victimhood, 14, 127, 182, 190, 191, 196, 200, 230, 239; German, 337n23; Gottscheer, 159, 176, 178
Vinitzky-Seroussi, Vered, 179
violence, 23, 100, 114, 133, 200, 242, 257, 262; communist, 176; criminal, 92; denunciation of, 224; memory of, 131; political, 24, 219, 223, 230, 345n62; wartime, 125
Virchow, Rudolf, 70
Višegrad, 255, 259, 263
Vogel, Berta, 199
Vojvoda Stepa, 52–53
Vojvodina, 46, 47, 49, 52, 56, 59, 270n6, 322n11
Volk und Rasse, 76
Volk und Reich (publishing house), 63
Völkertafel (Tableau of Nationalities), 70
Volksbund für das Deutschtum im Ausland (National Union for Germandom Abroad, VDA), 55
Volksdeutsche. *See* ethnic Germans
Volksdeutsche Mannschaft, 161

Volksdeutsche Mittelstelle, 161
Volksdeutsche Stunde, 91
Volksgruppen, 55; Gottscheer, 142, 143, 144, 145
Volkskörper, 75, 143–44
Volksliste, 147, 318n67
Volkstum im Südosten, 76
Volner, Žiga, 109
von Caprivi, Leo, 274n6
von Loesch, Karl Christian, 62, 63, 64, 65, 76, 77, 78; anthropological examinations and, 69–70

Waffen-SS, 81, 82, 90, 91, 92, 93, 113
Wagner, Rudolf, 186, 187, 191, 192, 196
Waldeck, Rosie G., 327n9
Waldow, Wilhelm von, 36
Wallenberg, Raoul, 128
Wannsee Conference, 101, 109
War Food Office (Germany), 36
Warsaw Pact, break from, 268n11
Waschneck, Erich, 110
Weczerka, Hugo, 187, 188
Wehenkel, Günter, 280n8
Wehrmacht, 64, 77, 96, 98, 100, 113, 124, 251; NDH and, 97
Weimar Republic, 18, 142, 224
Weninger, Josef, 71, 72
West Germans, 216–17; expellees and, 230; National Socialism and, 201
West Germany. *See* Federal Republic of Germany
Westphalia (ship), 313n1
Wilhelm II, Kaiser, 4, 31, 94
Williams, Ian, 243
Wippermann, Wolfgang, 202, 334n1
Wolff, Larry, 7
World War I, 1, 8, 9, 11, 15, 17, 18, 29–30, 52, 54, 62, 72, 73, 77; emigration following, 140–41;
Gottscheers and, 141–43; Romania and, 32, 33–35
World War II, 11, 13, 16, 45, 64, 90, 96, 116, 117, 119, 124, 125; displacement during, 21; end of, 7, 76, 250; expulsions and, 187, 196–97; history of, 180; legacy of, 258–64; memory of, 7, 25, 114–15, 120–25, 130, 235–40, 241, 254; migration and, 14; outbreak of, 17; political/cultural representations following, 236–37; return of Germans following, 208, 209
Wörsdörfer, Rolf, 319n85
Wülker, Heinz, 76

Yugoslav Ministry of Agriculture, 53
Yugoslav Trade Ministry, 52, 53, 54
Yugoslav Trade Mission (Bonn), 24, 216, 217, 219, 220, 222; Croatian émigrés and, 228
Yugoslav Wars, 6, 239, 248, 333n93
Yugoslavia: breakup of, 250; Eastern Bloc and, 5; ethnic Germans in, 206, 281n10; intervention in, 95, 251

Zagreb, 96, 98, 99, 100, 101, 102, 104, 109, 111, 112, 113, 123; anti-Jewish measures in, 106; arrests in, 105, 107; Jews in, 97, 103, 110
Zagreb Assembly, 104
Zahra, Tara, 146
Zakić, Mirna, 19, 30, 100, 161, 204, 250, 322n11
Zeh, Juli, 255
Zeitschrift für Rassenkunde, 75
Zelizer, Barbie, 241, 346n18, 354n56
Židovi (film), 110
Žilitj, Svetozar, 53
Zimmer, Anna E., 6, 25

www.ingramcontent.com/pod-product-compliance
Lightning Source LLC
Chambersburg PA
CBHW030527010526
44110CB00048B/662